ARTHUR J MARDER was a meticulous researcher, teacher and writer who, born in 1910, was to become perhaps the most distinguished historian of the modern Royal Navy. He held a number of teaching posts in American universities and was to receive countless honours, as well as publish some fifteen major works on British naval history. He died in 1980.

BARRY GOUGH, the distinguished Canadian maritime and naval historian, is the author of *Historical Dreadnoughts: Arthur Marder, Stephen Roskill and the Battles for Naval History*, recently published by Seaforth Publishing.

ADMIRAL OF THE FLEET SIR JOHN FISHER
First Sea Lord, 21 October 1904–25 January 1910

[*photograph by Beresford, London, in National Portrait Gallery*

FROM THE
DREADNOUGHT
TO
SCAPA FLOW

The Royal Navy in the Fisher Era 1904–1919

VOLUME I
THE ROAD TO WAR 1904–1914

ARTHUR J MARDER
INTRODUCTION BY BARRY GOUGH

Naval Institute Press
Annapolis

Copyright © Arthur J Marder 1961
Introduction copyright @ Barry Gough 2013

First published in Great Britain in 2013 by
Seaforth Publishing,
Pen & Sword Books Ltd,
47 Church Street,
Barnsley S70 2AS

www.seaforthpublishing.com

Published and distributed in the
United States of America and Canada by the
Naval Institute Press,
291 Wood Road, Annapolis,
Maryland 21402-5034

www.nip.org

British Library Cataloguing in Publication Data
A catalogue record for this book is available from the British Library

Library of Congress Control Number: 2013937405

(UK) ISBN 978 1 84832 162 5
(US) ISBN 978 1 59114 259 1

Printed and bound by CPI Group (UK) Ltd, Croydon, CRO 4YY

To Jan

Teacher, tender comrade, wife . . .

Introduction

IN 1961, Volume I of a work of naval history and indeed international affairs appeared that was to change the way that the Royal Navy's experience in the run-up to the First World War was viewed by the reading public. In its depth of research, thoroughness of analysis and clarity of exposition, that volume set a new standard in naval history and attracted widespread attention in and out of the Royal Navy. It became a matter of curiosity, even amazement, that the author was an American based in far-off Honolulu. But truth to tell, that author, Arthur Jacob Marder, was already a well-known force among those writing modern history. Not only had he written the stellar *The Anatomy of British Sea Power: a History of British Naval Policy in the Pre-Dreadnought Era* – all about the years 1880–1905 and published precisely at Britain's most perilous moment, 1940 – he had also edited the private, even secret, journal of the admiral and historian Sir Herbert Richmond, one of the brightest, if iconoclastic, scholars and naval thinkers of his time. To this growing corpus of solid work Marder had contributed a three-volume compendium *Fear God and Dread Nought*, a combined biography and edition of letters of 'Jacky' Fisher (as well as various smaller studies in Japanese naval history and biographical accounts of Winston Churchill as First Lord of the Admiralty, 1911–15, and Fisher). Marder had advanced through time from one appreciably difficult subject to another, always keeping the Royal Navy squarely in his sights. Thus when the initial volume of *From the Dreadnought to Scapa Flow* appeared it was the continuation of a long arc that began in a much earlier time and place, indeed to his undergraduate student days at Harvard.

Even until his death from cancer on Christmas Day 1980, and indeed down to our own times, it is still interesting to think that an American should have been the champion of the Royal Navy's history in some of its darkest hours. It was his immense skills as a researcher and brilliance as a writer – the essential combined capacities of an historian – that made for such compelling contributions to historical literature. He was gifted with inquisitiveness to a degree that was matched by his tenacity in uncovering secrets and tracking down motivations. And given the essential requirements of the reading public of that age – that good history have broad appeal – Marder's talents were given free rein. To this day his *magnum opus* is read with wide appreciation and much benefit, for it was the first time that a comprehensive account was given of the trials and tribulations of Great Britain fighting for its life at the centre of a maritime war waged on near and distant seas, the outcome of which was by no means certain for the statesmen and sailors who were holding the trident of Neptune.

Not only did readers then as now wonder why it was that some of the greatest writers of English naval affairs were American, it was still a matter of puzzle (though quite a matter of chance) that their surnames all ended in 'M' – Alfred Thayer Mahan, who had in his *Influence of Sea Power upon History* books and his biography of Lord Nelson explained to the world the role of British mastery of the seas, Garrett Mattingly, who had written that undeniable favourite *The Armada*, which is still in print, and now Marder, doyen of the mid-twentieth century's naval historians, the most thorough researcher and the most vital of writers. Modesty was a personal characteristic that Marder exhibited. He was fond of pointing out that chance often knocked at his door, directing his affairs in ways that he was to find unexpected though, in the end, congenial.

He was born in Boston on 8 March 1910, the oldest of five children born to Russian Jewish immigrants Maxwell and Ida Marder. Hard work and dedication, plus undoubted intellectual capacities, drove him to top place in his high school, Boston English, and then admission to Harvard, perhaps despite the quota system that limited Jewish entry. He had the benefit of an outstanding undergraduate education, including sitting at the feet of William Langer, the highly regarded professor of international affairs and imperialism. Marder loved to tell the story of how, when running down the broad stairs of the Widener Library of Harvard to keep a lunch date, he ran headlong into the august Langer, who gathered his professorial composure to ask the youngster what his graduating thesis was to be. Marder blurted out in reply something about German generals in the late war. Langer dissuaded him. He pointed out that Lord Haldane's failed mission to Berlin at a critical time in Anglo-German naval rivalry was a subject in which documents had recently become available in print. Marder took up Langer's recommendation, and he never left naval subjects thereafter – right down to his last book, published posthumously in two volumes,

Old Friends, New Enemies, all about the Royal Navy and the Imperial Japanese Navy. A second event that had chance as a feature was finally getting to see in the late 1930s hitherto unavailable Admiralty papers, held in the Admiralty Archives, a story I have told at length in *Historical Dreadnoughts: Arthur Marder, Stephen Roskill and Battles for Naval History* (Seaforth, 2010). Marder's persistence, coupled with an agreeable change of circumstances, allowed him to get access to Admiralty papers and to use them in his work, provided they were not cited directly, thereby protecting confidentiality and the names of living persons and their families. Reputations and privacy had to be protected, and the Official Secrets Act was not the only requirement that those in authority exercised. The third beneficial chance came when a senior admiral intervened, having heard that Marder had been given access to privileged documents that he needed to complete his work for *From the Dreadnought to Scapa Flow*: he knew the man in Whitehall to speak to and this he did, to Marder's undying gratitude. Getting access to the documents was the first challenge; using them in his texts was the second. Readers of this book must remember that Marder always lived under the watch of censors including those at the Admiralty, the War Office, and sometimes the Air Ministry plus the Cabinet, and that from the beginning to the end of his work on the Royal Navy his work had to be passed through official hands for the necessary clearance. Publishers required this, too, and they often guided Marder through the difficult minefields, giving reassurance and calling for patience and restraint.

In 1944, after many unsuccessful attempts to obtain permanent employment as a working historian and as a university teacher (always his lifetime ambition from about the age of 13), Marder was appointed Associate Professor at the University of Hawaii. He had previously worked in Colonel William Donovan's office of Coordinator of Information (later part of Central Intelligence Agency) in Washington, DC, taken an intensive course in Japanese, and become an instructor in university-level preparation for Army officer trainees. Attempts to join the United States Navy, the Royal Navy and the Royal Canadian Navy so that he could do his part in what he regarded as 'Marder's war' failed him. He had earlier watched Hitler's rapid rise to power from afar, and then he saw Italy and Japan join in the war against Great Britain that, with the British Empire, stood alone until Pearl Harbor. A sound basis in French, German and Russian history, particularly diplomatic aspects, gave him a broad knowledge. His reading in East Asian as well as Mediterranean history was extensive.

In the testing circumstances of those times, the old order was collapsing quickly around Marder. Privately he must have fought the isolationist tendencies that existed in American public opinion.

The study of British history and the years spent in Britain on research infused an anglophilia in Marder, one that he did not shy away from though he was as critical as was possible in treating the foibles and shortcomings of his historical subjects. He was fond of British admirals. He found in admirals' wives sources of support and ways of networking that he had not previously imagined. Some of them wore more gold braid than their husbands; they often made contacts and documents available to Marder that speeded his inquiries. He found the companionship of admirals entirely agreeable, and he liked to say that it was a good thing that Langer had dissuaded him from studying German generals, whom Marder thought a most uncongenial bunch and who were, in any event, not very good at making war. Marder necessarily built up a vast network of correspondents, many of them officers in the Royal Navy. He would draw up a list of questions, some general, some specific, and his correspondent would reply. Some very full replies are to be found in his papers at the University of California, Irvine. Added to those files are letters sent in appreciation or comment about his books. At the same time he was active in the historical profession in the United States, more particularly the American Historical Association, and this, too, gave him a broad scholarly network in his own country. British naval history was not a common subject to study in American academe. Naval history was not a normal course in History at American universities. Hence Marder was regarded as a specialist in his chosen field. He never taught naval history as such. His burning passion was to teach undergraduates about historical method – selection of documents, the study of historiography, the roles of chance and fate, the role of psychoanalysis and personality study, the interplay of character and circumstance, counteracting bias, and the illusions of scientific history. Narrative history was to Marder the essential thing, and to be able to tell a good story that was based on as full a basis of historical detail as possible was his aim.

* * *

Those who read his *From the Dreadnought to Scapa Flow* today and in the future will be amazed at the long arc of narrative that takes the story from 1904 to 1919. Marder had enough sense of European literature to realise that he was writing dispassionately about triumph and tragedy, and in the end, when he brought his narrative to a close with the internment of the German High Seas Fleet, the battle that the diplomats were waging in Paris regarding the surrendered enemy naval assets, the scuttling of the German ships at Scapa Flow, and, with a view to the future, the disputation exhibited by British and American statesmen and admirals about who would dominate the naval affairs of the future, we sense that he was pointing the way to a new and even darker world.

That world was, of course, the one he inhabited. But there is yet one other feature of Marder's work that needs mention here by way of preface or introduction: Marder got behind the scenes in British naval thinking for the first time. This, to him, was the war behind the war. He was interested in personal motivation. He was interested in policy formation, essential to the ascribing of success or, conversely, failure. The interplay of the First Lord of the Admiralty, the political head of the Service with a seat in Cabinet, and the First Sea Lord, the professional head of the Service and in effect the chief naval officer, fascinated him. His study of Fisher had sharpened his interest, and beginning with the first and continuing right through the five volumes we see this interaction at work. We sense the shifts of positions as circumstances change. We see that some personalities cannot work with their opposites. We follow the demands by press and Parliament for changes of command. Throughout we see how Marder had mastered the personnel files, how he made firm judgements of his subjects, and how he never shied away from playing the role of an all-seeing judge, one with temperate positions, one who makes sober judgements. That having been said, a charge might be made against Marder for being soft on Jacky Fisher. Marder subtitled the book *The Royal Navy in the Fisher Era*, that era beginning in 1904, when Fisher came to the Admiralty for the first time as First Sea Lord, and ending in Fisher's fading days. Marder's attraction to Fisher was fuelled by his own reforming zeal and his impatience with old ways. Marder did not shy away from discussing Fisher's faults (which were many), nor did he ignore the quarrels in the Service that arose from these, but he was prepared to see in Fisher the man who prepared the Navy for its great struggle, a struggle carried through against all perils and astounding difficulties ashore and afloat to victory. The command of the sea had never been lost. Great Britain and the British Empire remained intact.

At the beginning of his first of five volumes Marder introduces the opening scene of this long saga with Fisher's arrival at the Admiralty. The era was already fraught with concerns about Germany's increasing naval power. The Fisher revolution begins, aided and even nurtured by First Lord of the Admiralty Earl Selborne's naval reforms, many of which are impossible to implement because of the class-consciousness of the Senior Service at that time. Engineers and Lower Deck presented intractable problems that Fisher could not solve. Fisher's reforms also require the scrapping of smaller and slower warships on distant stations, the reorganisation of fleet units, and the redistribution of the fleet, meaning essentially the gathering of units for a potential action in the North Sea. Onto this scene comes the revolutionary all-big-gun, fast and heavily armoured battleship *Dreadnought*, itself enough to stir up all sorts of difficulties even without Fisher's fight with Admiral Charles Beresford, which Fisher does not win to his satisfaction, the Prime Minister, Asquith, already having seen in the First Sea Lord a difficult and divisive force. Thus having given a summary of the British naval scene in the first decade of the century, Marder turned to the Germans and their naval challenge. We follow with interest the role of Tirpitz, we see the calculations about British naval supremacy on paper, and we examine first German naval attempts to get a place in the sun in Morocco. Fisher retires in 1910 and is made a peer, and the Admiralty settles in under less firm hands.

Already the battle lines have been drawn, for Marder has portrayed the darkening horizon as British statesmen fail to placate the Germans by negotiations and missions. He explains Parliamentary response to public agitation by the voting for more dreadnoughts so as to insure British naval supremacy. Fisher's sternly defended Two Power Standard has now long since vanished. Winston Churchill arrives as First Lord of the Admiralty in 1911, soon to become the champion of the superdreadnoughts, and so carries through the 1913 naval estimates with thoroughness and decision. This adroit piece of statecraft made him the doyen of the Navy in later years for it gave the Navy some of its biggest ships, many of which saw service in the subsequent war. Right to the end of this first volume we are treated to an explanation and examination of such vital topics (each of which alone could deserve an historical monograph) as: the problems of the Mediterranean (France, Italy and Turkey), the Committee of Imperial Defence's work and gallant attempts at inter-service cooperation and planning, the prevailing strategies and tactics of the era, defensive and offensive strategies in fleet actions, commerce warfare, and combined operations. The development of tactical thought exposes the weakness in British thinking as the war looms ever closer. And finally, the grand examination of British and German fleets, men and material, on the eve of the First World War – the paucity of top-notch admirals, the over-reliance on great guns at sea, naval deficiencies in bases in the North Sea, and the role of naval rivalry in the coming of the Anglo-German war. All of these and much more Marder had considered as well as explained. The appendix lists British and German dreadnoughts and battlecruisers as of August 1914. For the first time a portrait had been given of the Royal Navy, its men and materiel, its preoccupations and expectations and its challenges and responses in the lead up to the eve of the First World War. The high praise rightly granted it by press and readers of the era was coupled with the hope that the next volume, expected to be the second and last of the work, would soon appear.

Before closing, the story of the trials and tragedies of this volume and its successors needs to be told, if by way of reminder of how dreadful accidents can beset a working writer. Marder had intended a longer volume than the one that is reprinted here (note the preface is dated June 1960). On 12 May, at the University of Hawaii, Marder had finished his term's teaching. He had marked the final examinations and placed them in two boxes in his university office so that janitors, according to instructions he gave the senior janitor (who subsequently was off work the next week), could clear them away and incinerate them. Through one foul-up or another, the duty janitor disposed of two boxes of Marder's research notes, his raw materials for the June 1915 to June 1919 chapters. It was a tragedy in the literary line such as Thomas Carlyle had faced with the manuscript of his *French Revolution* or T E Lawrence with his text about Arabia.

Heartbroken, Marder thought about abandoning the rest of the project. He rewrote his preface into the one that is included in this reprint. His publisher, Oxford University Press, agreed to make the work into more than one volume, imagining that two would suffice to bring the story to the close of the war. From Marder's point of view, in the end, and for subsequent topics of the longer work, he was obliged to redo much of his research. He faced difficulties in getting satisfactory damages from his university and a court action ensued. The university admitted that it had a vested interest in Marder's research project, and release time was granted so that distant travel could be undertaken by him, and copying expenses allowed for and covered. Difficulties ensued, however. Painstaking work in British periodicals and newspapers could not be replicated as thoroughly as he hoped. Some of the manuscript materials could not be retraced. His naval friends in England, notably Vice Admiral Sir Peter Gretton, himself an historian of note, gave appreciative and indeed heroic support, believing as they did that Marder was the only working scholar who could write a balanced and unbiased history of the Royal Navy in the First World War, the matter of Jutland being that of greatest lack of clarity and explanation. Captain John Creswell, a noted authority on tactics and sea warfare, came forward to offer all sorts of advice that a sailor might know and a land-based author would not. Captain Stephen Roskill, author of the Cabinet Office official history *The War at Sea*, gave Marder much help, though he was hard-pressed to get his own books completed and cleared for release. But more urgently, for its part, the Admiralty made sure that they eased Marder's research work on his early return to London (and assisting in microfilming and copying). Speed was of the essence, for playing catch-up was now of vital concern if Marder and his publisher were to keep to their intended fast pace. This behind the scenes story of this first volume of *From the Dreadnought to Scapa Flow* is one for the ages, and with generous spirit in the preface to the second volume he paid tribute to the three janitors of the University of Hawaii who had inadvertently proved a boon to the project. That was the measure of the man. Happy warrior that he was in the history line he had moved from one field of battle to another.

When the first volume of *From the Dreadnought to Scapa Flow* appeared to such acclaim and satisfaction, its successor was eagerly awaited. That not one but four additional volumes were to appear before the whole reached completion is a story for other times and other places in this reprint series. Marder undoubtedly was wildly optimistic in thinking that the whole epic, warts and all, could be completed in a comprehensive compass of a volume or two. The story is also told in *Historical Dreadnoughts*. His indulgent publisher, realising that their prize historian was writing great history, gave him all the freedom of movement and the space he needed. What other historian had this privilege? History nowadays is not written on such a noble scale, and more's the pity, for the remarkably thorough coverage of such a vast subject is Marder's gift to the annals of civilisation. No historian of our own times would attempt such a thing, for tastes and requirements have changed and contemporary naval historians have moved on to other topics and concerns (and rightly so). Marder is not imperishable, but he left to the corpus of historical literature a work for the ages, now happily reprinted for the very first time.

BARRY GOUGH,
Victoria, BC, Canada

Preface

In 1940 there was published my *Anatomy of British Sea Power: a History of British Naval Policy in the Pre-Dreadnought Era, 1880–1905*. Its sequel has been long delayed because of the war and the unavailability of certain crucial source material. It is, like its predecessor, based on a mass of unpublished material, virtually all published works of any value to the subject, Parliamentary papers, *Hansard's Parliamentary Debates*, the leading newspapers, periodicals, and professional journals, and correspondence and interviews with officers and civilians having first-hand knowledge of the subject. Owing to a dreadful accident reminiscent of what happened to the manuscript of Carlyle's *French Revolution*, most of my material for the 1915–19 years was destroyed in May 1959. I am re-doing the lost work and hope to complete the volume on the naval aspects of the war and its immediate aftermath before too long. Meanwhile, there seems little point in withholding publication of the completed portion of the manuscript.

Although I have in the present volume been concerned with many facets of the history of the Royal Navy during the pre-war decade, I have kept my eyes fixed on Ariadne's thread—the *British* aspects of the Anglo-German naval rivalry. Its terminal points are indicated by the revolutionary battleship type, the dreadnought, whose introduction ushered in the most intensive phase of the rivalry, and Scapa Flow, the wartime base of the Grand Fleet and the site of the climactic scuttling of the Kaiser's Fleet on 21 June 1919. The same years mark the 'Fisher Era' in the Royal Navy. From October 1904 to January 1910 the redoubtable 'Jacky' Fisher dominated the Navy as it has never been dominated by a single individual. Thereafter, until his restoration in October 1914, he exerted a powerful influence on naval policy behind the scenes. Mounting wartime differences with Churchill, the First Lord, resulted in his abdication, for such it was, in May 1915. He was never again prominent in the war councils of the nation, but the Admiralty (Sea Lords and Naval Staff) and the Navy were run for the balance of the war and for better or worse by his disciples and former assistants, Jellicoe, Jackson, Wemyss, Oliver, *et al.* The entire period was also one in which *matériel* considerations bulked somewhat larger than the more 'sublime' aspects of naval warfare, strategy and tactics. Fisher was the father of the *matériel* school. It is, then, hardly a misnomer to call the 1904–19 period the Fisher Era in the Royal Navy.

The dictum of Sir Charles Firth that 'the art of telling a story is [an] essential qualification for writing history' has guided my efforts, however unsuccessfully. One way I have attempted to achieve this result has been to eliminate the impedimenta of scholarship like the meticulous acknowledgment for every word that has been borrowed. Another way has been to stress the people who made the naval history of the period. A point that strikes the historian forcibly is the amount that personality affects history. I have also attempted to go beyond a mere description of events. A knowledge of the motivations of individuals and groups is both interesting and essential; likewise the relating of public opinion, both professional and lay, to the formation of naval policy, since naval policy was never formed in a vacuum. For purposes of this study it is an academic point whether newspapers, periodicals, and organizations voice public opinion or make it—whether they lead or follow. The important fact is that the makers of British naval policy were influenced by public opinion as reflected, accurately or not, in Parliament, newspapers, periodicals, and the activities of organizations.

The preparation of this volume and of the one to follow has put me under an immense debt of gratitude to a myriad of people and institutions who have given most graciously of financial aid, time, and material. I must begin with the John Simon Guggenheim Memorial Foundation (with an affectionate bow towards that great friend of scholars, Dr. Henry Allen Moe, the Secretary-General), the American Philosophical Society, and the Social Science Research Council, which admirable organizations made possible extended periods of research in England. The University of Hawaii lightened my labours considerably through granting me reductions in teaching load, a semester of freedom from all regular duties, secretarial assistance, and funds for the purchase of photographed material. My warmest thanks go to President Laurence H. Snyder, Provost Willard Wilson, and Dean Robert W. Hiatt for making all this possible.

I am profoundly grateful to the following individuals, libraries, and government departments for the use of invaluable unpublished

material: Her Majesty Queen Elizabeth II, Sir Owen Mors-
head, one-time Librarian at Windsor Castle, and his able
successor, Mr. R. C. Mackworth-Young: the *Royal Archives* at
Windsor Castle; the Lords Commissioners of the Admiralty
(among whom I simply must single out the First Lord of the
Admiralty, the sixth Baron Carrington, his immediate predecessor,
the tenth Earl of Selkirk, and Sir John Lang, the Secretary): the
Admiralty Record Office archives, the *German Ministry of Marine archives,*
the (Rear-Admiral Roger M.) *Bellairs Papers,* the (Admiral of the
Fleet Sir Henry) *Jackson Papers,* and the Naval Staff monographs
on the First World War and miscellaneous papers of interest in the
Admiralty Library and the Historical Section; the Public Record
Office: the *War Office archives* (used only for General Staff war
plans); the Trustees of the British Museum: the *Balfour, Campbell-
Bannerman,* and *Jellicoe Papers*; the Dowager Countess Jellicoe:
some important *Jellicoe Papers* apparently not included with the
main collection at the British Museum; the National Archives and
Records Service, Washington, D.C.: *United States Navy Department
Records*; the National Maritime Museum at Greenwich: the papers
of Sir W. *Graham Greene* (Secretary of the Admiralty, 1911–17)
and of various admirals of importance in the Fisher Era—May,
Richmond, Madden, Milne, Howard Kelly, but particularly the
(Sir Alexander) *Duff,* (Sir Sydney) *Fremantle,* and (Sir Frederick)
Hamilton Papers; Lady Duff: supplementary material pertaining
to her husband's career during the war; Balliol College, Oxford:
the *Asquith Papers* at the Bodleian; the second Earl Beatty: the
Beatty Papers; Lady Carson and the Hon. Edward Carson: the
Carson Papers; Commander T. C. Crease: the *Crease Papers* (Cap-
tain Thomas E. Crease was Fisher's Naval Assistant); the third
Viscount Esher and the Hon. Lionel Brett: the *Esher Papers* (the
second Viscount Esher); the late Nina, Dowager Duchess of
Hamilton, the late first Viscount Lambert, and the fourteenth
Duke of Hamilton: the *Fisher Papers* at Lennoxlove; the second
and third Barons Fisher: the *Fisher Papers* at Kilverstone Hall; the
eighth Marquess of Lansdowne: the *Lansdowne Papers* (the fifth
Marquess of Lansdowne); Mr. David McKenna: the *McKenna
Papers*; Admiral of the Fleet Sir Henry Oliver and Vice-Admiral
R. D. Oliver: the *Oliver Papers* (recollections of the former); Mrs.
Margaret Staveley and Lieutenant-Commander W. D. M.
Staveley: the *Sturdee Papers*; Vice-Admiral Sir St. John Tyrwhitt,

second Baronet: the *Tyrwhitt Papers*; the Hon. Mrs. F. Cunnack: the *Wester Wemyss Papers*. Certain of these private collections, notably the Jellicoe, Beatty, Asquith and Lennoxlove MSS., have copies of some of the Admiralty material, including Cabinet papers like the C.I.D. minutes and papers. I have made no attempt to indicate duplication of material in the unpublished sources.

The manuscript profited greatly from a constructive reading by Sir John Lang, Rear-Admiral P. W. Gretton, of the Imperial Defence College, Lieutenant-Commander P. K. Kemp, the Admiralty Librarian and Head of the Historical Section (who was helpful in many other ways), and Commander M. G. Saunders, of the Historical Section. Admiral the Hon. Sir Reginald Plunkett-Ernle-Erle-Drax, Rear-Admiral W. S. Chalmers, and Captain S. W. Roskill, the Official Naval Historian, furnished valuable critiques of the last three chapters. Admiral Drax also provided some useful papers. These gentlemen must not be held responsible for any errors of fact or interpretation in this volume. They are all my own!

Of aid to the project in various ways were the third Earl of Balfour, the first Baron Hankey, Admirals of the Fleet Viscount Cunningham of Hyndhope, Lord Chatfield, Sir Charles Forbes, and the late Sir Osmond de B. Brock, Admirals Sir William James, Sir Barry Domvile, H. M. Edwards, and J. H. Godfrey, the late Admirals Sir Reginald Bacon, Sir Frederic Dreyer, and Sir Sydney Fremantle, Vice-Admirals Sir Geoffrey Barnard and K. G. B. Dewar, Rear-Admiral H. G. Thursfield, Lieutenant-Commander Peter Troubridge, Mr. C. V. Hill, Deputy Librarian of the Admiralty, Mr. H. R. Aldridge, Deputy Keeper of Manuscripts at the British Museum, Mr. D. H. Turner, of the Museum's Department of Manuscripts, Miss Katherine Lindsay-Mac-Dougall, formerly Custodian of Manuscripts at the National Maritime Museum, Lieutenant-Commander D. W. Waters, Mr. G. P. B. Naish, and Miss S. L. Fisher, of the National Maritime Museum, the late Sir W. Graham Greene, Professor Michael A. Lewis, late of the Royal Naval College, Miss Enid Price Hill, of the Royal Archives, Professor Robin D. S. Higham, of the University of North Carolina, Mr. Peter M. Stanford, Mr. Everett T. Moore, Head of the Reference Library at the University of California, Los Angeles, and his staff, Mr. Henry J. Dubester,

Chief of the Reference and Bibliography Division, Library of Congress, and his staff, Mr. A. P. Young and Miss V. S. Heath, of the Admiralty Library, Professor Jacob Adler, Miss Joyce Wright, and Mrs. Judith Tokunaga (the perfect secretary), of the University of Hawaii, Mrs. Maria Hormann, formerly of the University of Hawaii, Miss M. B. Johnston, Curator of the Fisher Papers at Lennoxlove, Commander F. Barley and Mr. W. Pfeiffer, of the Historical Section, Admiralty, Mr. Guy H. Cholmeley, Mr. Vincent Quinn, Deputy Librarian of Balliol, Mr. H. H. Elmers, one-time Head of the Admiralty Record Office, Mr. P. D. Nairne, Principal Private Secretary to the First Lord of the Admiralty, Mr. F. H. Wilkinson, Departmental Records Officer at the Admiralty, Mr. A. E. Culley, of the Admiralty's Accommodations Section, Mr. A. Victor Hull, of the Department of Printed Books at the British Museum, Messrs. A. W. Mabbs, R. L. Anslow, and Peter Fellows, of the Public Record Office, Lady Allardyce, Mr. John R. B. Brett-Smith, President of the Oxford University Press, New York—and finally and indispensably, Mr. Geoffrey Cumberlege, one-time Publisher of the Oxford University Press, London, his worthy successor, Mr. John Brown, and his staff at Amen House, whose encouragement and extraordinary patience have been more than I have deserved.

I wish to thank the following publishers for their kind permission to quote from the copyrighted material indicated: George Allen & Unwin Ltd., from Michael Lewis's *The Navy of Britain*; Odhams Press Ltd. and Charles Scribner's Sons, from Sir Winston Churchill's *The World Crisis*, Vol. i; John Murray, from Lord Hardinge of Penshurst's *Old Diplomacy* and Admiral Sir Percy Scott's *Fifty Years in the Royal Navy*; the Clarendon Press, Oxford, from E. L. Woodward's *Great Britain and the German Navy*; Victor Gollancz, Ltd., from Vice-Admiral K. G. B. Dewar's *The Navy from Within*; H.M. Stationery Office, from *British Documents on the Origins of the War, 1898–1914*, edited by G. P. Gooch and Harold Temperley; The Times Publishing Company, Limited, from leaders in *The Times* of 8 July 1908 and 18 March 1914; *The Twentieth Century*, from Admiral Sir Herbert Richmond's article, 'The Service Mind', in *The Nineteenth Century and After*, January 1933.

In conclusion, a few explanatory notes are in order. It has, unfortunately, not been possible to indicate the source of some of the documents cited in footnotes. . . . The term 'navalist' is a coinage. It refers to those people, civilians and officers, who actively supported a big-navy policy. 'Navalism' is the big-navy movement. . . . I have made use of the many pertinent articles in the *Naval Review* (see below, p. 403), but, in accordance with the policy of this splendid journal, without citing it by name. . . . The volume on the war will include a full bibliography of the sources used for both volumes. . . . It may be helpful to note certain abbreviations used in the text which may not be intelligible to the uninitiated:*

C.I.D.	:	Committee of Imperial Defence
C.O.S.	:	Chief of the Admiralty War Staff†
D.N.C.	:	Director of Naval Construction
D.N.I.	:	Director of Naval Intelligence
D.N.O.	:	Director of Naval Ordnance
N.I.D.	:	Naval Intelligence Department

Honolulu, Hawaii   ARTHUR J. MARDER
June 1960

*I would not want any reader to make the kind of mistake related by Lady Murray in her biography of her husband, the one-time Secretary of the Admiralty, Sir Oswyn Murray: 'To save time initials were used for the Heads of Departments, D.N.I. for instance being used for the Director of Naval Intelligence, and these initials could be confusing for a new-comer. On one occasion a request for stationery was given to a girl to type and address. The mystic letters K. of S. & P. presented no difficulty to her, and she addressed the request to "the King of Spain and Portugal". This potentate not being known in the Admiralty, the error was quickly discovered, and the Keeper of Stationery and Printing duly delivered the goods.'

†'C.O.S.' is used nowadays for the Chiefs of Staff Committee set up in 1923.

Contents

CONTENTS

xiv

CONTENTS

List of Illustrations

PLATES

xxi

Map

Fisher's Years of Power, 1904–1910

I

Prologue

What shall we do to be saved in this world? There is no other answer but this, Look to your moat. The first article of an Englishman's political creed must be that he believeth in the sea.   MARQUESS OF HALIFAX, 1694.

Were you to run your business on the same lines as the army and navy are run, you would be bankrupt in three months.
            REAR-ADMIRAL LORD CHARLES BERESFORD, 1898.

1. THE SPIRIT OF THE AGE

IN THE latter part of the nineteenth century and the early twentieth century war was not generally regarded in the western world with dread and as a confession that civilization had failed. The pacifists were beginning to emerge and there was much public discussion of the horrors and injustice of war. But this was not the prevalent feeling. A hundred years without a major war had made many people inclined to forget the horrors of war. Moreover, to the pre-1914 generation war was the law of the civilized world as much as of the uncivilized. Clashes between nations were certain to take place periodically. Universal peace was a mere will-o'-the-wisp. Not only were wars inevitable, but it was desirable that this should be so. 'War represents motion and life, whereas a too prolonged peace heralds in stagnation, decay, and death . . . it has only been by war that from these humble beginnings it has been possible by evolution and natural selection to develop so comparatively perfect a creature as man.'[1] Again, it was held that the relentless extermination of 'inferior individuals and nations' was a natural means of improvement of the race. 'War remains the means by which, as between nations or races, the universal law that the higher shall supersede the lower continues to work.'[2] These quotations could be multiplied *ad infinitum*.

The state of international relations in the last pre-war decades made war seem likely. Aggressive imperialism—the mania for

[1] Lieutenant-General Sir Reginald C. Hart, 'A Vindication of War', *Nineteenth Century*, Aug. 1911.
[2] Harold F. Wyatt, 'God's Test by War', *ibid.*, Apr. 1911.

annexing or otherwise controlling territory—was piling up the fuel for Armageddon. Contributing their share were the violent press campaigns and the hectic armament races, the latter intensified by the unending contest in military development between the menace and the antidote.

In such a tinderbox age it was believed that no government and no people would respect vacillation or weakness. The 'big stick' was the most eloquent argument of diplomacy and the best guarantee of national security. For Britain the Navy was the big stick that really mattered. The British faith in this weapon was tremendously fortified by *The Influence of Sea Power upon History, 1660–1783*, published in 1890 by an unknown American naval captain, Alfred Thayer Mahan. A companion volume, *The Influence of Sea Power upon the French Revolution and the Empire*, appeared in 1892. These works effected a revolution in the study of naval history 'similar in kind to that effected by Copernicus in the domain of astronomy.' Mahan's main purpose was to wake his countrymen up to the supreme importance of sea power. The books attracted world attention and were especially influential in England, where eyes were only half-opened to the meaning of the command of the sea. Mahan did not discover anything new; but whereas historians had treated naval history for the most part as a series of external episodes, subsidiary and subordinate to contemporary military enterprises, Mahan showed, almost for the first time, what sea power really was and what its influence had been in history. He proved by a wealth of concrete example that sea power was silent and far-reaching in its operations, affecting the national well-being in peace and the national strength for war in many directions. He reminded the British of their special stake in naval supremacy.

'There are two ways in which England may be afflicted. The one by invasion . . . the other by impeachment of our Trades . . .' In these words of Sir Walter Raleigh we have the *raison d'être* of British sea power throughout the ages. Trade protection and security from invasion both depended on sea power. The former became a pressing matter in the late nineteenth century, when most of British foodstuffs and the industrial raw materials needed for industry were coming from abroad. Deprived of her trade, Britain could not possibly have maintained her industries, fed her rapidly growing population, or equipped her armies.

4

The humanitarian and beneficent influence exercised by the Royal Navy was commonly introduced to buttress Britain's claims to naval supremacy. British sea power, it was pointed out, had been used as the servant of mankind by destroying the slave trade and piracy and by safeguarding law and order throughout the world. Also, as *The Observer* put it (18 July 1909), 'Without the supremacy of the British Navy the best security for the world's peace and advancement would be gone. Nothing would be so likely as the passing of sea-power from our hands to bring about another of those long ages of conflict and returning barbarism which have thrown back civilisation before and wasted nations.'

As Lord Palmerston used to say, England had no eternal friendships and no eternal enmities, but only 'eternal interests'. These were three in number and closely related—broad concerns of British policy for three hundred years: (1) the maintenance of a stronger navy than that possessed by any likely combination of powers—that is to say, no power or combination of powers should deprive Britain of control of the seas, particularly the seas which wash the British Isles; (2) the independence of the Low Countries —no hostile power should control the European shores of the English Channel; (3) the maintenance of the balance of power in Europe—no single power should dominate the continent of Europe.

At the turn of the century these vital interests, these means of securing Great Britain and the British Empire, began to be seriously threatened for the first time since Napoleon's heyday. The German Navy Laws of 1898 and 1900 heralded the advent of a potentially formidable naval competitor—a navy that was to be so powerful that, to use the official formula (1900), 'if the strongest naval power engaged it, it would endanger its own supremacy'. Ominous was the fact that this coincided with a growing deep and widespread distrust of German aims in England. The villain here was the German government's adoption of a *Weltpolitik* which made friction with the leading colonial power inevitable. The Kruger Telegram (1896) first revealed to the British the hostile character of official German policy. Deeply resented was the German government's policy of profiting from Britain's predicament in South Africa. The agreements providing for the eventual partition of the Portuguese colonies (1898) and partitioning Samoa (1899) were among the concessions and

5

compromises wrested from Britain. The British regarded these agreements as blackmail. The virulence of German Anglophobia during the South African War removed any doubts about the essential unfriendliness of German public opinion. And all the while, poisoning relations, was the programme of the Pan-German movement, which envisaged German control of the Low Countries and much else in Europe. These ambitions would not have been taken too seriously in England but for one factor: the Pan-Germans were never officially and whole-heartedly disavowed by the German government.

At the turn of the century, Britain stood in not-so-splendid isolation. France and Russia, allies since 1894, appeared incurably hostile; relations with the United States had been strained by the Venezuelan boundary dispute, but were improving; Germany, rejecting British overtures in 1898 and 1899 for a rapprochement, was dead set on using Britain's ticklish world position to wrest advantages for herself; Austria and Italy were friendly, but as Germany's allies could not be relied on.

The spirit of the age, the state of Anglo-German relations, and Britain's isolation pointed up the pressing need for a powerful and efficient Fleet. There was some question whether the Royal Navy could meet these specifications.

2. THE ROYAL NAVY AT THE TURN OF THE CENTURY

The Key to an understanding of the 'Fisher Era' proper (1904–1910) lies in a consideration of the naval milieu at the turn of the century and in the work of Admiral Sir John Fisher in the years 1899–1904. The great Jubilee naval review of 1897 had instilled in Englishmen a spirit of bursting pride and confidence in their Navy, and a year later the Fashoda crisis confirmed the English in the belief that theirs was just about the finest fleet that had ever sailed the seas. Pride in the Navy, the saviour of peace with honour, overflowed into unlimited confidence. 'Of really powerful, formidable navies,' puffed one British service periodical, 'there does not exist at the present moment one in the world except our own.' In reality, the British Navy at the end of the nineteenth century had run in a rut for nearly a century. Though numerically a very imposing force, it was in certain respects a drowsy, inefficient, moth-eaten organism.

6

The Navy scares of 1884 and 1888, in exposing the backward state of the Navy, had stimulated reforms, particularly during the régime as First Sea Lord of that silent, stubborn, brilliant administrator, Admiral Sir Frederick Richards (1893–9). The huge shipbuilding programmes of 1894 and after had given the Navy numerical superiority over the Franco-Russian Alliance. Gone were the hodge-podge battleship designs of the 1880's. The 'Royal Sovereigns' and their successors, the creations of Sir William White, the Director of Naval Construction (1885–1902), were the envy of the Continent. Notable advances in the nineties were a vast programme of naval works and a scheme for manning the Fleet. The Naval Intelligence Department was developed into a very useful tool. Annual partial mobilizations of the Navy were started in 1888. This, too, was an era of magnificent seamanship. Yes, much had been accomplished since 1884, but much more remained to be done before the Navy was a thoroughly efficient, battle-ready force.

Successive naval administrations had shrunk from the changes which science and its application to warfare had rendered inevitable. Officers and men were still being trained in the elements of sail seamanship, though sails had all but disappeared by the 1890's, and the steam engine, hydraulics, and electricity were supreme.

The higher training of officers was neglected. The officers had a scanty knowledge of the tactics and strategy of the new era, although the introduction of the iron-clad warship, the steam engine, long-range ordnance, the torpedo, the submarine, mine, wireless, and high-explosive shell had profoundly modified the tactics of the sailing-ship era and the application of the principles of strategy. There was no staff or war college for the study of these subjects, nor was there much encouragement for young officers to learn the principles of strategy and tactics by reading naval history.

Lord Charles Beresford, the probable Commander-in-Chief in a naval war of the near future, was reported to have stated in 1902 that 'he was now 56 years old, with one foot in the grave, and he had only tactically handled three ships for five hours in his life, and that was a great deal more than some of his brother admirals'. Recalls one admiral: 'Fleet drills took the form of quadrille-like movements carried out at equal speed in accordance with geometrical diagrams in the signal book. These corybantic exercises, which entirely ignored all questions of gun and torpedo fire, laid tremendous stress on accuracy and precision of movement.'[3] Apparently these drills and evolutions were devised less for their war value than for their competitive value, with ship pitted against ship.

Naval strategy was equally neglected. Owing to the First Sea Lord having neither the time nor the organization for the purpose, detailed war plans were lacking in the 1890's. During the Mediterranean tension in the middle of 1893, the British Commander-in-Chief more than once complained that he had not been given any war plans. The first reasonably detailed plan of war in the event of conflict with France and Russia was drawn up only in the midst of the Fashoda crisis of 1898. Complete plans began to be developed only after this time.

When Fisher joined the Board of Admiralty as Second Sea Lord in 1902, he remarked that the ideas of warfare of his colleagues were of the bow-and-arrow epoch. In fact, it was still the 'spit and polish' era. As in the opening scene of *H.M.S. Pinafore*, the sailors in 1900 were still polishing the brasswork. The pride of the naval profession was to a considerable extent centred in the smartness of the men-of-war. Therein lay the road to promotion.

The torpedo was generally regarded as unworthy of serious attention, and even gunnery was not taken too seriously. Admiral of the Fleet Sir Reginald Tyrwhitt has written of his midshipman days in the Mediterranean Fleet in the late 1880's: 'Gunnery was merely a necessary evil. Target practice *had* to be carried out once in each quarter of the year . . . no one except the Gunnery Lieutenant took much interest in the results. Polo and pony-racing and amusements were more important than gun drill, not that midshipmen took any part in the polo or racing, but we were all very proud of the exploits of our Senior Officers.'[4] Indeed, as late as the nineties, gunnery practice was considered a nuisance, and instances of ammunition being thrown overboard were not uncommon. Gunnery practice was limited to 2,000 yards, little greater than the range in Nelson's time, because no system of controlling fire at long range had been evolved. Since it dirtied the paint-work of a ship, it was hurried through as quickly as possible. One admiral used to judge the efficiency of a ship, after an in-

[3] Vice-Admiral K. G. B. Dewar, *The Navy from Within* (London, 1939), pp. 25–6.
[4] Tyrwhitt's uncompleted, unpublished memoirs; Tyrwhitt MSS.

spection tour, by the condition of his white kid gloves after he had concluded his visit! When flagships were engaged in shooting drills, admirals often remained on shore to escape the din. It is not, therefore, surprising that the annual prize-firing resulted in only a small percentage of hits. In 1902, British warships missed the target more than twice out of three rounds.

The faulty, obsolete system of education, with its stress on outmoded subjects and discouragement of independent thought, produced few admirals of conspicuous ability. Fisher was constantly occupied with the problem of the paucity of 'first-class intellects' among the senior officers.

As regards the seamen, lower-deck life was uncomfortable, to put it mildly. The Navy fare was still 'hard tack', hard labour, harsh discipline, and poor pay. Discipline was based on the St. Vincent principle that it must rest on fear and that fear was to be instilled by severe punishment. Navy victualling was a disgrace. Giving the seaman a knife and fork with which to eat his dinner, instead of using his fingers, was regarded as somehow subversive of discipline and pandering to undue luxury. By the first years of the twentieth century the issue of hard biscuits, the unappetizing and coarsely-prepared meals served to the sailor, and the absence of table cutlery were legitimate subjects of public comment. Nevertheless, considering the conditions under which they lived, the morale of the seamen was surprisingly high.

Mahan, the English naval Mohammed, held, with universal approval, that one of the important elements of naval power consisted in the concentration of strength. There was little concentration in 1900, British sea power being scattered over the whole world. The newest and most powerful ships, it is true, were stationed in the Mediterranean and in home waters; but, generally speaking, outside European waters there was an odd assortment of ships ('bug traps') able neither to fight nor to run away. Furthermore, for nearly two-thirds of the year, while the Channel Squadron (renamed Channel Fleet in 1903) cruised in Irish and Spanish waters, there was no organized naval force in home waters. During these long absences of the Channel Squadron British waters were left denuded of a regular fleet, since the Reserve Squadron (renamed Home Squadron, then Fleet, in 1902–3) was in a chaotic state. It consisted of nine older battleships. Manned with but two-thirds of their complements, they were strung round the coast of the United Kingdom, safely secured and swinging round buoys in harbour. Once a year, for ten or twelve days, these ageing tubs took on increased complements for a little cruising. Fred T. Jane, the naval expert, justly called the Reserve Squadron 'an absolute disgrace to a naval Power'. This was proven in the 1901 home manœuvres, when a far smaller squadron administered a crushing defeat to it. There were, in addition, the entirely unmanned ships of the Fleet Reserve and the Dockyard Reserve.

Such, in brief, was the state of the Fleet in 1900. In its peace-time functions—suppressing native risings, rescuing slaves and ships in distress, exterminating pirates, trapping smugglers, aiding the victims of earthquakes and other disasters, charting the seas, and 'showing the flag'—the Navy was efficient. What was so desperately wrong was that it had its priorities so upside down. Spit and polish and seamanship were more important than preparation for war. Beresford could well complain that 'the Fleet is not ready to fight, or nearly ready to fight . . . our want of preparation in many ways is WORSE than the Army before South Africa exposed necessities that were wanting.'[5]

Fundamentally, the backward state of the Navy stemmed from the fact that it had for nearly a century enjoyed a peace routine and that Britain's title of Mistress of the Seas had not been seriously challenged. For the heirs of Nelson warlike ventures were disappointingly few. The last time the Navy had fired a shot in anger against a great power was off the Crimean coast in 1855–6. Except for times of diplomatic crisis and other extra-ordinary occasions, naval life had indeed become one long holiday, as the autobiographies of nineteenth-century admirals abundantly illustrate. Moreover, serious naval rivals had been lacking. The French Navy, the Royal Navy's leading competitor in the nine-teenth century, was much below it in *matériel* strength and personnel. The Russian Navy, Europe's third-ranking fleet at the end of the century, was notoriously inefficient, and its strongest units were locked up in the Black Sea. The fact that no nation apparently wished seriously to challenge British naval supremacy bred a fatal lethargy and a 'Two skinny Frenchmen and one Portugee, one jolly Englishman could lick all three' frame of mind.

The innate conservatism of the Navy is the second great factor

[5] Beresford to Balfour, 8 Apr. 1900; Balfour MSS.

PLATE I

2. THE EARL OF CAWDOR
First Lord, February–December 1905
[From a drawing by Frank Dicksee, R.A.]

1. THE EARL OF SELBORNE
First Lord, October 1900–February 1905
[Radio Times Hulton Picture Library]

PLATE II

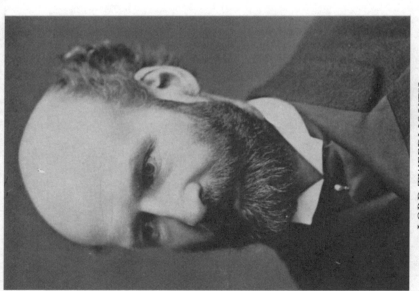

1. LORD TWEEDMOUTH
First Lord, December 1905–April 1908
[Radio Times Hulton Picture Library]

2. THE RT. HON. REGINALD McKENNA
First Lord, April 1908–October 1911
[photograph at the Admiralty]

explaining the condition of the service, and is to some extent a derivative of the first. Declared *The Times* (20 April 1906), 'The Navy is a very conservative service, tenacious of tradition, deeply and rightly imbued with the sentiment of its glorious past, and very suspicious of any innovations which seem to ignore that tradition.' No less a personage than Sir Frederick Richards could object in 1900 to the abolition of the system of masted-ship training. 'You have got an established system and a time-honoured one, so why alter it?' The Admiralty and senior officers generally were not receptive to new ideas and looked upon the ideas of junior officers with impatience. On one occasion a sea lord wrote across a practical suggestion by a lieutenant, 'On what authority does this *lieutenant* put forward such a proposal?' The Lieutenant, by the way, became Admiral of the Fleet Sir Doveton Sturdee, Bt. The ablest minds in the Navy lived in the day before yesterday. Officers, even when awake to the weakness of existing arrangements, did not trouble to challenge them, for capacity to think and an independent and critical mind were apt to be handicaps.

3. THE PROTO-NAVAL RENAISSANCE, 1899–1904

The Navy went right on living on its old tradition and enjoying its state of quiescence until the close of the century. The rise of potent American and Japanese fleets in the last years of the nineteenth and first years of the new century scarcely ruffled British calm, even if they were undermining Britain's strategic dominance in non-European waters. These were the fleets of friendly powers, with whom Britain had no serious points of conflict. A far more ominous threat was Germany, an unfriendly and aggressive European power which was seeking to add naval to military supremacy. Her Navy was one to be respected and feared. The dead weight of tradition which hampered the Royal Navy was never felt in the Emperor William's new Fleet, which had no heroic past and outworn traditions behind it to obscure modern realities in a sentimental haze. Young, alert, and ambitious, the German Navy placed a premium on initiative and new ideas. Its potential size and its concentration in home waters, and especially its high quality and readiness for battle, impressed professional observers in Britain. With the passage of the German Navy Acts of 1898 and 1900 there began the awakening of the Royal Navy. An influence in the same direction was the South African War. The Army's bitter experiences gave Britain a terrific psychological jolt. It was realized by every thinker in the service that a naval war might find the Fleet as unprepared as the Army had been.

Beginning in 1899–1900, a little band of ardent reformers with no reverence for the past, younger officers with ideas, vision and energy, began to crystallize around Admiral Sir John Fisher, Commander-in-Chief of the Mediterranean Fleet, 1899–1902. In season and out of season they worked to sweep out the cobwebs—to awaken the naval profession and the country to what was meant by efficient naval administration and naval preparedness for war. Indeed, 'the efficiency of the Fleet and its instant readiness for war' became the virtual slogan of the Fisherites. Their system was set on foot in the Mediterranean, where the administrative and organizing genius of Fisher, supported and stimulated by a galaxy of fine younger minds, vastly improved the efficiency of the Fleet in less than three years.

There was no wasting of time by officers and men over sail-drill and other obsolete things. Fisher encouraged the officers to study the problems of modern warfare by offering cups for essays on battle formations and strategical dispositions, by inviting officers to formulate their opinions on cruising and battle formations (contrary to the tradition that the admiral alone, or with the flag captain, worked out the fleet's operations), and by giving witty, inspiring lectures on the principles of war. He carried out long-distance, high-speed steaming trials over the protests of engineer officers and despite the misgivings of the First Lord. As Beresford wrote in his *Memoirs*: 'From a 12-knot Fleet with numerous break-downs, he made a 15-knot Fleet without breakdowns.' The Admiral realized a pet ambition in 1901: joint operations between the Mediterranean and Channel Fleets, which would act together in war. No great tactician himself, he started tactical and strategi-cal exercises based on the probabilities of war in place of the traditional routine cruises and steam tactics. He insisted on the need for constant gunnery practice and introduced long-range target practice. It was begun in the battleship *Caesar* (1899) at 6,000 yards. He encouraged the competitive spirit in gunnery by instituting the Challenge Cup for heavy-gun shooting. As a result of such methods naval gunnery advanced by leaps and bounds. It must, however, be noted that Fisher was building on foundations laid by Captain Percy Scott since 1897, of which more elsewhere. In addition, many of Fisher's future reforms, such as the concentration of the Fleet, the reform of naval education, and the wholesale introduction of oil fuel, were germinating.

The naval revolution began in earnest during Fisher's tenure as Second Sea Lord (June 1902–August 1903) with the significant personnel reforms announced in December 1902—the 'Selborne Scheme', which we will examine in Chapter III. On 31 August 1903 Fisher hoisted his flag as Commander-in-Chief at Portsmouth, a post which would enable him to superintend the establishment of the new college at Osborne, while affording time for maturing fresh schemes of naval reform. It was at Portsmouth that the ideas of a dreadnought (conceived in the Mediterranean period) and of a battle cruiser took concrete form.[6] At Portsmouth, too, he worked out the substance of the nucleus-crew reform, and became aware of the tremendous potentialities of the submarine.

The Fisher system was introduced, bag and baggage, when the Admiral became First Sea Lord on 21 October 1904—Trafalgar Day, the day of his patron saint. Although some Englishmen have never been quite sure of it, the verdict of history is that in Fisher the Navy and the nation had found their man—a strong man ready to face the tremendous responsibility and personal risk of carrying out a constructive revolution in a service rendered by the very pride of its traditions one of the most conservative in the world.

---

[6] In the 1903 Jane's *Fighting Ships* there appeared an article by Colonel Cuniberti, the Italian naval constructor, on 'An Ideal Warship for the British Navy'. His design foreshadowed the main features of the dreadnought type: the all-big-gun armament and a speed superior to that of all battleships afloat. It is very likely that Fisher read this article, which was widely commented on in the service press, and that it strongly influenced his thinking.

II

Fisher as First Sea Lord

I have known personally a dozen men who have been in my time among
the most remarkable and famous men in the world. Lord Fisher was the most
fascinating of them all and the least like any other man.

J. L. GARVIN in an unpublished letter of ca. 1928.

He was a mixture of Machiavelli and a child, which must have been
extraordinarily baffling to politicians and men of the world.

ESTHER MEYNELL, A Woman Talking.

I. THE MAN

WHEN he returned to Whitehall in 1904, Fisher was a
man of 63, 'but still the youngest man of the Navy in
brain and heart and energy'. He was 'of medium height
and square of build, with very round, wide-open [light grey] eyes,
which fixed the gaze and compelled attention. His general expression was slightly supercilious, which, however, was constantly
changing during conversation to a flickering smile, for an under-
current of humour always pervaded his general talk.' His was an
intensely pugnacious face. 'The full eye, with its curiously small
pupil, the wide, full-lipped mouth, drooping mercilessly at the
corners, the jaw jutting out a good-humoured challenge to the
world, all proclaim a man who neither asks nor gives quarter.'[1]
His hair was grey-white, with a wiry tuft that fell across the upper
reaches of his forehead. To complete the picture, there was something about his face that suggested the East. His enemies caused
rumours to be spread that he was a Malay, the son of a Cingalese
princess, the inference being that this was the origin of his 'Orien-
tal' cunning and duplicity! And not only his domestic enemies.
Captain Widenmann, the German Naval Attaché in London
(1907–12), referred to him in his reports as the 'unscrupulous (or
cunning) half-Asiatic'. Fisher was alternately amused and annoyed by the persistence of this legend.

---

[1] Admiral Sir Reginald H. S. Bacon, The Life of Lord Fisher of Kilverstone (London,
1929, 2 vols.), i. 246–7; A. G. Gardiner, Pillars of Society (London, 1913), p. 348.

In effect, if not in fact, he was the Board of Admiralty between 21 October 1904 and 25 January 1910. He was at the same time one of the most interesting personalities of the twentieth century. He owed nothing to influence, wealth, or social position, but everything to sheer ability, character, and perseverance. As he said, 'I entered the Navy penniless, friendless and forlorn. I have had to fight like hell, and fighting like hell has made me what I am.' He was idolized by the man in the street for his rise to the top of his profession through ability, as well as for his personification of the typical sea-dog. He was noted for his sense of humour, story-telling ability, sparkling wit, gaiety, charm, and boyish enthusiasm. He was one of the great conversationalists of his time. 'His talk was racy, original, full of mother wit, and irradiated by a humour which was bracing and pungent as the salt of the sea itself.' He kept the heart of a child, and this was no doubt the secret of his amazing vitality and freshness. 'His spirits were unquenchable: when we asked him to dinner, it was as likely as not that he would come into the room dancing a hornpipe, and there seemed to be no company in which he was not absolutely at home. In all this he was absolutely unaffected and simple, without a trace of pose or affectation.'[2]

In his official capacity Fisher could be arrogant, stern, unrelenting, and, when serious mistakes were made, even cruel. 'None of us on his staff could be certain we would still have the job next day,' Admiral of the Fleet Sir Henry Oliver recalls. And yet he could be tender-hearted, affectionate, and rather sentimental. He was very appreciative of anything done for him, and he never failed to respond to the smallest sign of affection, admiration, or gratitude. His 'cruel mouth' needed little provocation to smile, a smile that completely altered his expression. Children, those wise critics, loved him. He was enchanting to them, whether playing with them or letting them try on his admiral's coat blazing with stars.

At bottom he was a humble human being, with a humility born of deep religious conviction. 'He had a firm belief in Divine intervention in the affairs of this life; if he had doubts about justice in this world, he had none about matters being evened out in the next!' The early service saw him, when at the Admiralty, in almost daily attendance at Westminster Abbey or St. Paul's.

[2] J. A. Spender, *Life, Journalism and Politics* (London, 1927, 2 vols.), ii. 67.

Three sermons a day were not unusual for him. The Dean of Westminster, hearing that the Admiral had been to four sermons in one day, warned him against contracting 'spiritual indigestion'! But even more than attending services, he loved to sit in a church and meditate.

His knowledge of the Bible was extraordinary, and he could quote Scripture like a Puritan divine. 'Often he felled an opponent to earth with a text' or capped an argument with an apt quotation from the Old or the New Testament. When the Battle of Tsushima was fought, the Prime Minister, Balfour, was in Scotland. Fisher wanted to let him know that the Japanese had won, Admiral Togo concentrating on, and putting out of action, the Russian flagship. Instead of entering into a long explanation, the First Sea Lord merely announced the fact of the victory, adding, 'See 1 Kings 22 . 31.' Reference to the Bible revealed Togo's tactics: 'The King of Syria commanded his thirty and two captains that had rule of his chariots, saying, "Fight neither with small nor great save only with the King of Israel."' While declaring that the teachings of history had no value, that 'history is a record of exploded ideas', he never failed to use Biblical history to point an argument or clinch a conclusion. Nor did he hesitate to use naval history either *when it would help his cause*!

Fisher had neither knowledge of nor, excepting inter-ship football and cricket matches, interest in sports and games. He drank and smoked in moderation and for long periods did without them. A walk up and down a ship or garden, conversation with old friends, an insatiable reading of newspapers after dinner, a novel between dinner and bedtime, and, above all, sermons and dancing —these were virtually his only relaxations. Outside sermons, dancing, and his family, the Navy was his only love, his whole life.

Few men have worked harder at their calling. So long as age permitted, his vigour was remarkable, and he was able to do what would have exhausted most men. He retired very early, at 9.30 p.m., and was up, ready for work, at 5 or 5.30 a.m., though very often as early as 4 a.m. Much of the day's work was done in these morning hours before breakfast. At the Admiralty he was an indefatigable worker, with Sunday morning work not unusual. His private secretary when he was Second Sea Lord 'never met anyone who could dispose of papers at the rate he could. . . . His energy for a man of over 60 was wonderful. A medical man told him he had such wonderful vitality that he "ought to have been twins." He was very fond of repeating this and one day he got the reply from a favourite commander, "What a mercy you were not! Just think of two of *you* in the Navy!" The idea made him chuckle.'[3]

In addition to fabulous energy, Fisher was gifted with two other great assets of the born administrator: an exceptional memory and the 'pertinacity of a debt collector' in the pursuit of a goal. One facet of his pertinacity was his favourite saying, 'Reiteration is the secret of conviction.' But pertinacity never hardened into dogmatism. 'A silly ass at the War Office wrote a paper to prove me inconsistent. Inconsistency is the bugbear of fools. I wouldn't give a d—— for a fellow who couldn't change his mind with a change of conditions! Ain't I to wear a waterproof because I didn't when the sun was shining?'[4]

Then there were his unparalleled powers of persuasion, a product of his knowledge, sincerity, and forcefulness in speech and writing. The heads of the big shipbuilding, engineering, and ordnance firms, professors, and many other great and clever men always seemed anxious, ready, and willing to carry out his views, and with dispatch. No person in his day could get big things done quicker than could Fisher. In 1927 Lord Hankey rated Fisher and Beatty as the only two First Sea Lords of the twentieth century who 'could really talk on even terms to the highest Cabinet Ministers and stand up to them in argument'.[5] Yet Fisher was not always successful in arguing a point verbally with the great politicians. This has a partial explanation in his inability sometimes to state a case clearly, but even more so in his bitter contempt of the general run of politicians, high and low—less for their want of brains than for their lack of character, especially moral courage, as evidenced, for example, by their wavering from one side to the other in his quarrel with Beresford. He once likened Cabinet Ministers to 'frightened rabbits'. In his later years, he would say that the politicians had deepened his faith in Providence. How otherwise could one explain Britain's continued existence as a

[3] Sir Charles Walker, 'Some Recollections of Jacky Fisher'; Kilverstone MSS.
[4] Fisher to Balfour, 11 Apr. 1910; Balfour MSS.
[5] Hankey to Beatty, 30 Apr. 1927; Rear-Admiral W. S. Chalmers, *The Life and Letters of David, Earl Beatty* (London, 1951), pp. 381–2.

nation and the fact that the British Empire was never stronger and more feared?

Once a decision was reached, Fisher did not trouble himself with the details. He left these to the officials in the Admiralty in whom he had confidence. A few months before he became First Sea Lord, he told Lord Knollys, the King's Private Secretary, that 'If ever I go to the Admiralty . . . and you should happen to call in there, you would find me walking up and down with my hands in my pockets thinking of schemes for worrying all our different Fleets to make them more ready for battle! And I should say to my satellites and understrappers at the Admiralty "that I wasn't going to keep dogs and bark myself also," so if they sent me on papers *I should get another dog!*'[6]

He had a horror of paper controversies. His 'simple but drastic method' of ending such controversies is illustrated in this delightful story:

Fisher got tired of a perennial discussion with the War Office over Highlanders' spats. A vast file of papers about it came round two or three times a year and had done so for years. A Highland Regiment had arrived in Malta from the east and been put in quarantine. To avoid delaying the ship they had been camped on Comino Island. They had been landed on the beach by the Navy and the spats had got wet and discoloured. The War Office said the Admiralty should pay for them and the Admiralty had always refused. Fisher threw the whole file of papers on the fire and told me that when the Registry asked for them I was to say that he had taken the papers to his house. He knew no one dared to ask him for them. There was also a long standing quarrel about payment for repair and painting of Horse boats and Fisher settled this in this way.[7]

He rarely used the telephone in his work, preferring to transact business in person; nor did he do much dictating. Although his minutes and letters were typed for official purposes, most of his correspondence was in his own writing, which remained clear and bold up to the end of his life. A vigorous, exuberant writer, he had a genius for coining telling phrases and using apt illustrations drawn from his vast stock of anecdotes and Biblical lore. The lurid

---

[6] Fisher to Knollys, 22 Apr. 1904; Windsor MSS.

[7] Admiral Sir William James, *A Great Seaman: the Life of Admiral of the Fleet Sir Henry F. Oliver* (London, 1956), p. 116, quoting from Admiral Oliver's unpublished reflections.

imagery and ferocious invective of much of his correspondence (his enemies were all 'skunks', 'pimps', 'sneaks', or worse, often with a harsh modifying adjective like 'pestilent' or 'damnable') give the impression of a man writing at breakneck speed with a pen dipped in molten lava. The expressions with which he closed his letters to intimates, such as 'Yours till Hell freezes' and 'Yours till charcoal sprouts', were characteristic. He 'spoke, wrote, and thought in large type and italics; when writing he underlined his argument with two, three, or even four strokes with a broad-nibbed pen, and when talking, with blows of his fist on the palm of the other hand. "I wish you would stop shaking your fist in my face," said King Edward when being subjected to some of Fisher's forcible arguments; and every one of his many listeners might have made the same remark.'[8]

2. HIS FIRST LORDS

The Board of Admiralty was the supreme naval authority, wielding the powers of the King and of His Majesty's government. The pivot and centre of the whole was the First Lord of the Admiralty. It is the British tradition, well established by the 1870's, that the First Lord is responsible to the Cabinet, and ultimately to Parliament, for all decisions and actions of the Board or of its individual members. That being so, all Board members must be responsible to the First Lord, and this responsibility is *total*. There can be no nonsense about 'rendering unto the civilians the things that are civilian and unto the brass the things that are brass'. Even Fisher, strong man that he was, never failed to seek the First Lord's full approval and support for a decision or policy of any importance at all.

It was not unusual in the eighteenth century for a high-ranking officer to hold the office of First Lord. Anson, Hawke, St. Vincent, and Barham are examples. But since Barham in the early nineteenth century the First Lord has invariably been a civilian, although two *retired* naval officers have served as First Lord: the fourth Duke of Northumberland, in 1852–3, and Sir Bolton Eyres (afterwards first Viscount) Monsell, in 1931–6. This tradition was so strong by 1914 that it was a powerful factor in depriving Fisher of the post in 1915–17.

[8] Bacon, *Fisher*, i. 236.

The other 'Lords Commissioners of the Admiralty' consisted of the four sea lords—all naval officers—and two civil lords and two chief secretaries. There had been doubt for many years as to the exact position and responsibilities of the First Sea Lord, and, indeed, of the other Board members. The distribution of business was chaotic, with everyone having a finger in everyone else's pie. Fisher had this chaos ended on 20 October 1904. The new definition of duties made it quite clear that the First Sea Lord was responsible for the 'fighting and sea-going efficiency of the Fleet', and that he was the chief professional adviser of the First Lord. The Second Sea Lord was responsible for the manning and training of the Fleet; the Third Sea Lord (the Controller), for design of ships and, later, aeroplanes and airships; the Fourth Sea Lord, for the transport service and naval stores; the Civil Lord, for works, buildings, and Greenwich Hospital. An Additional Civil Lord was created in 1912 (until 1917) for handling contracts and dockyard business. Finally, there were the Parliamentary and Financial Secretary, who had to be an M.P., and the Permanent Secretary,[9] the only civil servant on the Board. The former looked after financial matters, such as the navy estimates. (The post was abolished in October 1959, the Civil Lord taking over the work.) The latter was concerned with general office organization and correspondence and served as an expert on procedure and precedent. The Parliamentary and Permanent Secretaries were only *de facto* members of the Board, not becoming *de jure* members until 1929 and 1940, respectively.

Until Lord Spencer's Board (1892–5) it was customary for the entire Board to resign when a general election took place. Since that time, only the three political appointees, the First Lord, the Civil Lord, and the Parliamentary Secretary, have resigned on such occasions. (Strictly speaking, they place their posts at the disposal of the Prime Minister, who either reappoints them or appoints others in their stead.) The sea lords, except for the First Sea Lord, normally held their appointments for not more than three years, then returned to sea.

By all pragmatic tests the British system of naval administration has worked. It has worked because the above-mentioned principles

---

[9] Although the style used in the twentieth century is 'Permanent Secretary', I much prefer 'Secretary', because it has, as Sir John Lang says, 'the flavour of Pepysian tradition about it.' And so 'Secretary' it will be hereafter in these pages.

have worked; and these have worked because the First Lords generally have been able men, skilful parliamentarians, and possessed of the common sense to listen to professional advice and of the skill in human relations needed to get along with the admirals. Take the modern First Lords through World War I (1885–1919): Hamilton, Spencer, Goschen, Selborne, Cawdor, Tweedmouth, McKenna, Churchill, Balfour, Carson, and Geddes.

There was only one really weak First Lord among them (and that in part due to poor health): Tweedmouth. The others ranged from reasonably able to very able, with more of them leaning towards the second than the first. As regards the First Lord's relations with his professional advisers, the crux of this is, of course, the First Lord's relations with the First Sea Lord. Ordinarily—and it is my impression, consciously—the British have tried to choose First Lords and First Sea Lords who would be temperamentally compatible and who would complement and supplement each other. This would explain the great success of the McKenna–Fisher combination (1908–10). But when this principle was disregarded or not taken fully into account, as, unfortunately, more than once in World War I, the results were bad. Two instances: Churchill–Fisher (1914–15) and Balfour–Jackson (1915–16), First Lords and First Sea Lords who were *too much alike*. In the case of Churchill–Fisher it made for a basic incompatibility in their official relations (though they loved each other as persons!); in the case of Balfour–Jackson, while their official relations were good, they were not successful as a team because they did not supplement each other. Thus, *both* lacked drive, energy, and the aggressive instinct so important in war.

As for the First Lords with whom Fisher worked (1904–10), the second Earl of Selborne (November 1900–March 1905) was an active and able one who, because his mind was receptive to new ideas and because he believed in Fisher's genius, was content to let him have a free rein. He supported him to the hilt and shared in the credit for the achievements of the 1904–5 revolution. Selborne resigned in March 1905 and went to South Africa as High Commissioner. Fisher paid him this tribute in his *Memories*: '. . . never did any First Lord hold more warmly the hand of his principal adviser than Lord Selborne held mine.' The appraisal of the German Naval Attaché was not so kind. Selborne 'is easily influenced by men whom he has recognized as efficient . . . he is entirely subservient to the influence of Sir John Fisher and subscribes blindly to his proposals.'[10]

The third Earl Cawdor (First Lord, March–December 1905) was a small, mild-mannered gentleman, shrewd and industrious, who had made a good reputation as a sound and alert businessman. Fisher was 'overjoyed' about his appointment. But Cawdor did not hold office long enough to do full justice to his abilities and to learn his new job, his first ministerial appointment. Moreover, he was in bad health during his term of office. Like Selborne, he co-operated fully with his chief professional adviser.

On the fall of the Conservative Government, the second Baron Tweedmouth succeeded Cawdor as First Lord (December 1905–April 1908), 'a position for which he is about as qualified as for the Office of Astronomer Royal,' opined the *National Review* (November 1907). He was a pleasant, colourless man of barely average abilities. Baffled and torn between the Fisherites and the anti-Fisherites, he never knew which way to turn. He had neither the strength of will nor the other talents which make an able administrator. Knowing little about things naval, he had no opinions of his own and rarely interfered with the sea lords. He lost prestige when it was disclosed that he was the owner of half the ordinary shares in Meux and Co., the firm which had received the contract for supplying beer to the Navy. The financial difficulties of his last years and the first symptoms of a brain ailment were, no doubt, extenuating factors in explanation of his undistinguished tenure as First Lord.

Upon Asquith's accession as Prime Minister, April 1908, in succession to Campbell-Bannerman, there was some reconstruction of the Government. Tweedmouth exchanged the Admiralty for the less exacting post of Lord President of the Council. The transfer was deplored by few. His successor, Reginald McKenna, was the most important of Fisher's pre-war First Lords (April 1908–October 1911). He was not yet 45—a man of fine athletic figure, slim and erect, who had been a Cambridge rowing blue. His work as President of the Board of Education, 1907–8, had merited his promotion to the Admiralty. The assets of a first-class administrator were his: a remarkably keen, orderly, and clear

[10] Captain von Coerper to Tirpitz, 25 Jan. 1905; German Ministry of Marine MSS.

mind, cool, mathematical judgment, great courage and industry (he dealt with his official papers immediately they arrived), a wide knowledge of Parliamentary procedure, and the barrister's gift of stating his case lucidly and logically and driving home his points. (He had practised at the Bar before entering the House of Commons.) But with all his brilliant abilities and his geniality and charm, McKenna was an unpopular First Lord and a failure as a politician. His 'donnish', 'superior' manner in the House of Commons, his curtness in the course of question and answer across the floor of the House, repelled many. 'His manner was precise, attorney-like and irritating.' His popularity was not enhanced in the economy wing of the Liberal Party by the common belief that he, who as Financial Secretary to the Treasury (1905) had been known as a strict economist and who was expected to keep the navy estimates down, had allegedly become the tool of the admirals and of their combative representative on the Board, Fisher. Whereas Fisher's relations with Selborne, Cawdor, and Tweedmouth had been purely formal, if pleasant, the old sea-dog got along famously with McKenna. They made an invincible team, working together closely, loyally, and cordially, and becoming affectionate friends. McKenna identified himself with a high standard of naval sufficiency and efficiency, and by 1911 he had won for himself the goodwill, respect, and confidence, if not quite the affection, of the Navy. But to the end he did not possess the full support of the House. Incidentally, Churchill, not McKenna, had been Fisher's first choice as successor to Tweedmouth, and Churchill afterwards felt that he could have had the Admiralty had he pressed for it.

3. GUIDING PURPOSES

Economy and efficiency were the motives underlying Fisher's great reforms. The former subject calls for elaboration, since it has always been overlooked by the critics in appraising the reforms. Between the Naval Defence Act (1889) and 1904 the navy estimates had approximately trebled under both Liberal and Conservative Governments. They had increased from £27,522,000 in 1900 to £36,889,000 in 1904, although there had been no corresponding increase on the part of other naval powers. In the navy debates of 1903 and 1904 grave protests were heard not merely from the Liberal benches, but from those on the ministerial side of the House. *The Times* (25 February 1904) referred to the increase in the estimates as 'a grievous and growing burden', and its Naval Correspondent, J. R. Thursfield, a big-navy enthusiast and a good friend of Fisher, wrote him that they could not 'go on spending money indefinitely; and what I fear day and night is that unless retrenchment comes from within there will come upon us an irresistible wave of reaction and reduction which will do infinite mischief. . . . I don't know how you feel about this matter, but it haunts me like a nightmare.'[11]

Fisher could not fail to be influenced by the uneasiness with which the country viewed the relentless growth of naval and military expenditure. Economies there must be. Like Napoleon, he was that very rare bird, the fighting man who considers the taxpayer. He denied that 'fighting efficiency is inalienably associated with big Estimates! The exact opposite is the real truth! Lavish naval expenditure, like human high-living, leads to the development of latent parasitical bacilli which prey on and diminish the vitality of the belligerent force whether in the human body or in the fighting ship! . . . Parasites in the shape of non-fighting ships, non-combatant personnel, and unproductive shore expenditure must be extirpated like cancer—cut clean out!'[12] A Navy Estimates Committee (the First Sea Lord as chairman, the Parliamentary Secretary, the [Permanent] Secretary, and the Accountant-General) was set up by the First Lord in November 1904 to scrutinize the votes in the estimates each year, 'in order to see what economies, if any, can be effected consistent with the fighting efficiency of the Fleet and its instant readiness for war.' The heads of departments at the Admiralty had to show how each item of expenditure would contribute to the fighting efficiency of the Fleet, or the item was eliminated. Reductions in the estimates were made possible through the scrapping of obsolescent ships and the consequent savings on repairs and maintenance, and through the reorganization on business lines of all the dockyards.

The 'Frankenstein growth of parasitic dockyard expenditure' especially appalled Fisher. Drastic dockyard reforms included the discharge of 6,000 redundant workmen, the reduction of seven 'useless' foreign dockyards to a cadre, a simplification of stocks,

---

[11] 20 June 1904; Lennoxlove MSS.
[12] Letter of June 1907; *ibid.*

and the reduction of enormous reserves of unimportant stores which could be replaced at any time. Horrible things that were done under the heading of 'stores' included the purchase of an 'amazing array of tumblers'. 'The surgeon had his own particular pattern of tumbler, and the purser his, and they had to be stored in enormous quantities so that neither the surgeon nor the purser should run the horrid risk of being short of his own particular tumbler. Everyone was aghast when I suggested that the purser and the surgeon might use the same kind of tumbler!'[13]

The reductions actually effected in the estimates were as follows:

	£
In 1905–6	3,500,000
,, 1906–7	1,520,000
,, 1907–8	450,000

The 1907–8 reduction was not more substantial because of a Treasury decision not to provide by loan for the completion of the works scheduled in the Naval Works Act of 1905—a decision which entailed extra provision of over a million pounds in the estimates. Thereafter, certain automatic increases in the votes and above all the intensification of the Anglo-German naval rivalry ended the downward trend of the estimates. When Fisher went to the Admiralty, the estimates, in 1904–5, were £36,889,500. The lowest point reached was in 1907–8: £31,419,500. In 1909–10 the estimates were £35,142,700, and in 1914–15, £51,550,000.

Fisher was all the more anxious to effect certain economies, because, in his view, they increased the war readiness of the Fleet. Thus: 'There is only so much money available for the Navy—if you put it into chairs that can't fight, you take it away from ships and men who can. Fancy 10,000 chairs being kept in stock, as a typical illustration of misapplied money!'[14]

The war readiness of the Fleet was absolutely essential in view of the rapidly developing German naval challenge and his belief that 'the German Empire is the one Power in political organization and in fighting efficiency, where one man (the Kaiser) can press the button and be confident of hurling the whole force of the empire instantly, irresistibly, and without warning on its

[13] Esther Meynell, *A Woman Talking* (London, 1940), pp. 70–1.
[14] Fisher's memorandum, 'Notes Prepared for the First Lord', July 1906; Lennoxlove MSS.

enemy.'[15] It was his settled conviction that the Germans would bide their time until they could catch the British Navy unprepared, since they could not hope to match it in numbers. At the selected moment and without warning they would make war on England and attempt to wrest from her the mastery of the seas. He worked and planned for a sufficient and efficient Navy with that conflict always in view. The 'selected moment' he believed would be on a week-end, probably on a week-end with a Bank Holiday. This view was a great nuisance to his staff at Whitehall, who rarely could get a week-end off. When they did get the time off, the concession was hedged round by all sorts of arrangements about communications and instant return. War with Germany did come on a week-end with a Bank Holiday!

Fisher did not confine his preparations to the naval sphere. Never one to stick to his last, he was full of ideas on foreign policy that were not without effect. The Admiral had a shrewd, realistic political sense. He was one of the architects of the Triple Entente; but he went further. Regarding war with Germany as inevitable, he always maintained that Britain needed above all a *quadruple* alliance, with France, Russia, and Turkey as the other partners. For a naval war, he held that Britain needed especially the alliance of Russia and Turkey—Russia for the naval diversion she could create in the Baltic, and Turkey so that communications with Russia via the Black Sea would remain open, and because of the influence of Turkey on Islam. 'We are the greatest Mohammedan power on earth.' As early as October 1904, at a time when it was very unpopular to do so, we find the new First Sea Lord urging the conclusion of an alliance with Russia. His Turkish policy goes back at least to the time of his Mediterranean command. The stupidity of the official policy of alienating Turkey was a favourite theme. He was opposed to the Japanese Alliance, 'the very worst thing that England ever did for herself', and he always worked for close Anglo-American co-operation. Above and beyond all else was Fisher's violent hostility to Germany. He shared the Teutophobia of friends and associates like the journalist Arnold White, the Portuguese Ambassador Soveral, and Lord Esher.

The five major reforms, in the order in which they will be considered, were (1) the new scheme of education for young

[15] Fisher to King Edward, late 1906; Sir Sidney Lee, *King Edward VII: a Biography* (London, 1925–7, 2 vols.), ii. 333.

PLATE III

THE RT. HON. WINSTON CHURCHILL
First Lord, October 1911–May 1915

[photograph by Dinham, London

PLATE IV

2. THE RT. HON. WINSTON CHURCHILL
Caricature by 'Nibs'
[from *Vanity Fair*, 2 March 1911

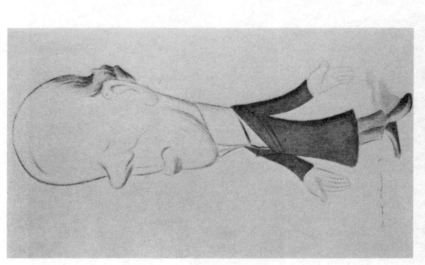

1. THE RT. HON. REGINALD McKENNA
Caricature by Max Beerbohm, 1913
[from *Fifty Caricatures* (*Heinemann*)

officers (with various subsidiary personnel reforms); (2) the introduction of the nucleus-crew system; (3) the scrapping of obsolete
warships; (4) the redistribution of the fleets in accordance with
modern requirements; (5) the introduction of the all-big-gun type
of battleship and cruiser. The first was announced on Christmas
Day, 1902, when Fisher was Second Sea Lord, and went into effect
during his time at Portsmouth and during his first year as First
Sea Lord. The next three were announced, and the fifth foreshadowed, in an Admiralty memorandum and circular letter to
the Commanders-in-Chief, dated 6 December 1904 and published
on 12 December.

III

The Fisher Revolution

It was largely due to his genius, his labours, and his driving power that, on the outbreak of war, the Royal Navy was so much more efficient than it would have been without him. It is recorded that Napoleon was fond of saying, 'Ask me for anything except time.' Fisher gained for us time—priceless time—the equivalent of, say, five years.

ADMIRAL SIR FREDERIC DREYER, *The Sea Heritage*.

His great claim to fame is that he succeeded in making us *think*. Before he asserted himself, the spirit and discipline of the Navy were excellent, but we were in a groove in which merit was decided and rewards given for smartness in drills, in appearance of ships, and in handling them in close order. Fisher got us out of that groove and made us realize that the object of our existence was fighting, and that our training, our habits, our exercises, and our thoughts must always have that in view.

ADMIRAL SIR SYDNEY FREMANTLE to the author in 1946.

1. PERSONNEL REFORMS

FISHER has often been reproached for excessive preoccupation with the *matériel* as distinct from the personnel of the Navy. Actually, to Fisher the man was always more important than the machine, since he knew it was not ships but the human element that won battles. He continually insisted that the officers and men —their skill, resource, and readiness to respond to any emergency —were the elements in sea power which were of paramount importance. He practised what he preached.

The naval revolution began with significant personnel reforms, the most important being the 'Selborne Scheme' of 1902, which was launched in 1903–5. The crux of the scheme was the system of common entry and training for all executive officers. Instead of there being executives, engineers, and marines—all entered separately and trained separately—there was to be a common entry and training of officers at the newly established Royal Naval Colleges of Osborne and Dartmouth (two years at each), and in the following four to five years as cadets, midshipmen, and sub-lieutenants in a training ship and in a ship of the Fleet. At about 22, their common training over, the young officers, now lieutenants, were to complete their training by specializing in one of the three 'lines' : those who wished to join the executive branch—either as general service officers or as specialists in gunnery, torpedoes, or navigation—and those who wished to specialize in engineering or join the Royal Marines. No lieutenant could specialize in more than one branch. On attaining the relative rank of commander the officer would in most cases drop his specialty, but some of the engineering and marine lieutenants would continue to perform specialist duties as commanders; and some, again, of these would remain specialists in their respective branches in the senior ranks of the service. Those who desired to do so would necessarily forgo the chance of obtaining command of ships or squadrons, but would be eligible to fill high offices in the Admiralty and in the dockyards, or in the Corps of Marines.

Under the old system of training, the engineer officer, marine officer, and executive officer underwent entirely different courses of instruction with results inimical to the *esprit de corps* of the Fleet. In particular, a wall had been erected between the engineers and the executives on account of the comparative lack of education, polish, and family background of the engineer, a differentiation accentuated on shipboard by difference in status. Thus, the engineer officer could not command a ship. The snobbishness and arrogance of the 'Executive N.O.s' towards their fellow-naval officers who were not executive—the 'pusser' (purser, paymaster) and the 'schoolie' (naval instructor = instructor officer) as well as the 'plumber' or 'greaser' (engineer)—had its historical origin in the fact that up to about 1843 the only 'commissioned' officer was the 'executive' officer.

For years the engineers had carried on a powerful agitation, supported by the technical press, for executive rank and equal treatment with executive officers, including similar uniform. Fisher proposed to wipe out the wall of partition between engineers and executives by recruiting the two from exactly the same class and educating them together at the beginning. The engineer officer would have sufficient navigational training to take command of a ship *if necessary*, and *if necessary* the deck officer could help in the engine-room. That is, officers of the executive and engineering branches would, to a degree, become interchangeable. But there were still differences in titles and uniforms.

The Royal Marines were brought under the same system

because, limited by their infantry training, they performed no naval duties on board ship (except for a few engaged in intelligence work) and were actually employed a maximum of six to twelve hours a week on duty connected with the Corps. The Admiralty regarded this as a great waste. Moreover, the officers of the Marine Corps considered themselves military officers rather than naval officers. In future they were to be trained from the start like any other naval officer, so that they would do useful work on board ship and feel more a part of the Navy.

The creation of a uniform corps of officers in the interests of unity and harmony was, then, one basic reason for the common entry and training. The other, and still more important one, was the mechanization of the Navy—the recognition that since a modern warship was a mass of intricate machinery, it was essential that all officers should know at least a little about engines. Accordingly, a thorough course in engineering, theoretical and practical (about one-third of the time), was included in the course of study at the colleges and in the training period at sea.

Beresford, before his mind had been clouded by his great feud with Fisher, could write him: 'In 20 years' time Naval Officers will wonder how a steam navy could possibly have been run and administered by an executive who knew nothing whatever about steam or mechanical appliances, although every evolution, action, and duty could only be carried out by the aid of machines and skilled mechanics.'[1] And so keen a critic of Admiralty policy as Admiral Custance remarked in 1906 that the modern officer should have as intimate a knowledge of his ship as had his predecessor, and 'if he controls and manages the motive mechanism, he will do no more than did the seamen of the Elizabethan age.' But serious opposition there was, as we shall see.

It is perfectly clear that the selection of the commissioned officers was confined to the sons of well-to-do parents, whether of the middle class, the gentry, or the aristocracy. This irked Fisher, who was a democrat, and perhaps even a socialist at heart. As early as 1902 he was insisting that 'brains, character, and manners are not the exclusive endowment of those whose parents can afford to spend £1,000 on their education. . . . Let every fit boy have his chance, irrespective of the depth of his parents' purse.'[2] He

[1] Letter of Apr. 1903; Lennoxlove MSS.
[2] Fisher, *Records* (London, 1919), pp. 160–1.

estimated that the cost of naval training excluded from the service altogether the son of any parent whose income was under £700 a year. There were not more than 300,000 persons with such an income. 'Reckoning five people to a family, it follows that there are not more than 1,500,000 people in all from whom officers for the Navy can be taken—and of these, half, or more than half, are women or children. The remainder of the population is 41,500,000, and of these no single one can ever hope to become an officer in the Navy! Surely we are drawing our Nelsons from too narrow a class.'[3]

This state of affairs suited naval officers as a whole, who were reluctant to throw open their ranks to all aspirants, regardless of their origins. This was due in part to a desire to maintain class privilege. The leading service publication, the *Naval and Military Record*, was frank about it (22 June 1910): 'We should view with grave apprehension any attempt to officer the fleet at all largely with men of humble birth.' The argument was that a naval officer must be a gentleman, and that a gentleman was born and not made, and, as a rule, he could be born only of gentle parents. As important was the fear of lowering the standard, which, it was maintained, was set not by intellectual ability alone but even more by the extent to which personality and character had been fostered.

Such talk annoyed Fisher. He was well in advance of the class prejudices of the officers' corps when he declared that 'this democratic country won't stand 99 per cent *at least* of her Naval Officers being drawn from the "Upper Ten". It's amazing to me that any-one should persuade himself that an aristocrat Service can be maintained in a democratic state. The true democratic principle is Napoleon's: "*La carrière ouverte aux talents!*" '[4] But Fisher's main tack was 'the far higher ground of efficiency': military genius was probably no exclusive monopoly of the well-to-do classes; Nelson himself would have been unable under existing conditions to enter the Navy; and the wider they spread the net, the more likely they were to catch Nelsons in it.

He wanted to see all fees abolished at the Osborne and Dart-

[3] Fisher's memorandum, 'State Education in the Navy', Mar. 1906; Lennoxlove MSS. *The Times* of 27 Oct. 1911 reproduced some of the material in a leader.

[4] Fisher to Esher, 5 Aug. 1910; Arthur J. Marder, *Fear God and Dread Nought: the Correspondence of Admiral of the Fleet Lord Fisher of Kilverstone* (London, 1952–9, 3 vols.), ii. 334. (Hereafter cited by title only.)

mouth Naval Colleges, so that with full State-paid education (the State was then paying two-thirds) entry to the commissioned ranks of the Navy would be thrown open as widely as possible. The Admiral all along stressed that the State should undertake the expense of educating *all* cadets, since if only the poor were helped, 'mischievous class distinctions' would inevitably arise among the cadets. His campaign finally bore some fruit. In 1913, when Churchill was First Lord, annual fees were reduced nearly 50 per cent (from £75 to £40) for one-quarter of the entrants in any year. This one-quarter was to be divided into, not more than 10 per cent, the sons of officers, and the remaining 15 per cent, the sons of other needy parents. However incomplete, the reduction was a step in the right direction. In 1947, at last, the principle of free education for all naval cadets was introduced.

The higher training of officers, long neglected, was given a fillip during Fisher's tenure at Whitehall. While in the Mediterranean, he was instrumental in the early development of a full-fledged naval war college, although his exact role is not clear. Hitherto there had been nothing like it. At the Royal Naval College, moved from Portsmouth to Greenwich in 1873, the courses 'had no relation either to the processes of fighting or the principles of war'. They were never intended for any such purpose, being strictly technical courses for the training of sub-lieutenants, naval constructors, etc. There had also been a few tentative, half-fledged experiments in 'teaching war', held at the principal ports. They consisted of mere series of lectures at which attendance was voluntary, and for attending which officers did not even receive full pay. But the 'War Course', started in late 1900 for commanders and captains, was the real thing, entirely distinct on the one hand from the Royal Naval College (though held in the same range of buildings), and, on the other, sharply contrasted with the voluntary, half-pay affairs held at the ports. The Course was originally eight months. It was divided in 1903 into two courses of four months each to enable more officers to attend. The basic syllabus included naval history, strategy, tactics, and international law. The Course was, from the first, 'compulsory'—that is, it was an 'appointment', like any other appointment carrying full pay. It is this Course, transferred from Greenwich to Portsmouth (1906–14), then back to Greenwich (1920–39, 1947–), ·disappearing temporarily for the duration of the two world wars, which survives to this day under the name (since 1920) of 'Senior Officers' War Course'. Today it is often spoken of as the 'War College' or the 'Naval War College'. In Fisher's day it was called the 'War Course College' (1900–7) and 'Royal Naval War College' (1907–1914). In 1908 Fisher expanded its functions to include the investigation of problems sent down to it from N.I.D.

Together with the modernization of the education of officers and cadets, Fisher effected a minor revolution in the policy of promotions. As C.-in-C. in the Mediterranean he had bombarded Selborne with urgent pleas for younger captains and especially younger admirals. 'The increasing average age of our Admirals is appalling! In a few years you'll see them all going about with gouty shoes and hot-water bottles!'[5] Results were forthcoming. The question of promotion was considered by a committee under Lord Goschen. It formulated proposals which were the basis of the order-in-council of 8 December 1903. This order was principally intended to bring capable officers while still young into commands and flag rank, without disturbing the custom of promoting captains to be admirals according to length of service. It endeavoured to obtain this object by lowering the age limits by three to five years and by pensioning officers two to three years earlier when not employed. The youngest captains were now 36 to 37; rear-admirals, from 41; and vice-admirals, from 52.

Under Fisher the officers and men of the Royal Naval Reserve (recruited from merchant seamen and fishermen) were no longer trained on board harbour hulks or at shore batteries armed with obsolete guns, but on board modern sea-going ships, and with the weapons they would actually use in war. This made for a more efficient Reserve. However, the importance of the Naval Reserve was diminished with the development of another reserve, the Royal Fleet Reserve. This consisted of active service ratings, trained men who otherwise would be lost on leaving the Navy. For completeness sake, it should be mentioned that a third type of Reserve was founded in 1903—the Royal Naval Volunteer Reserve, composed principally of amateur sea enthusiasts, coastwise sailors, and yachtsmen. The training of the crew was in the same period adjusted to modern conditions. Rigged training ships

[5] Fisher to Captain Wilmot H. Fawkes (Private Secretary to the First Lord), 18 Feb. 1901; *Fear God and Dread Nought*, i. 353.

disappeared and boys were trained on land, on board ships with nucleus crews, and on sea-going armoured cruisers.

Then there was the gunnery revolution fathered by Captain Percy Scott, who, first in the Mediterranean (1899), and then in Chinese waters (1900), demonstrated the possibility of accurate gunfire. Scott achieved surprising results, not only increasing the accuracy of aim, but the rapidity of fire. He was making 80 per cent of hits at a time when about 30 per cent was the Fleet average. There was nothing mysterious about Scott's system. His three principal inventions—the dotter, the deflection teacher, and the loading tray ('loader')—were essentially methods of loading the guns quickly and aligning their sights rapidly through the roll of a ship.

The initiative towards gunnery efficiency came from the Fleet, seized the public imagination, and at last had its influence on Admiralty policy. By 1902 gunnery was no longer a secondary thing. In 1903 Scott was appointed to the command of H.M.S. *Excellent,* the gunnery school at Whale Island. With Fisher's support he introduced a new system of training, the principle underlying which was that the men should be trained by repeatedly doing the thing, and not by reading out of the gunnery manual and drill book how it was to be done.

The gunnery renaissance received fresh impetus when Fisher took the helm at the Admiralty, with Jellicoe as his very able Director of Naval Ordnance (1905–7). Both were determined to perfect the gunnery of the Fleet. Of great help was the institution in 1905, directly under the First Sea Lord, of the office of Inspector of Target Practice. It was first held by Percy Scott (1905–7), then a rear-admiral. It was his duty to observe and analyse ships' firings, to advise on how the shooting could be improved, and in general to act as a guide to the development of all aspects of gunnery. This short, thick-set person (known as 'the pocket Hercules' in his younger days), with little eyes and an 'Imperial beard and straggly dark moustache making him look far more like the traditional Frenchman than a British naval officer', had a truly extraordinary ability in gunnery matters. Unfortunately, he was not an easy person to work with. He 'had a cocksure manner which brooked no argument'. He was 'rather like the Old Testament seers, who rubbed those in authority the wrong way. . . . Percy Scott did not know how to gild the pill; so he met with more opposition than would have fallen to his lot had he been more diplomatic.'[6] One of the most outspoken of twentieth-century admirals, Admiral Sir Frederic Dreyer, termed Scott 'the most outspoken man I have ever met'. Coerper, the German Naval Attaché, described him as 'an incredible "windbag" and publicity hound'. But Fisher, fully appreciating Scott's inventive genius, energy, and ability to get results, backed him up against opposition. As he used to say: 'I don't care if he drinks, gambles, and womanizes; *he hits the target!*' This was one of Fisher's wisest appointments, since Scott practically doubled the efficiency of fleet gunnery in two years.

Stress at first was on the great annual Gunlayers' Test, when the individual gunlayers fired their guns at short range at a small object, being allowed so many minutes according to the size of the gun. This was a means of testing periodically the skill and accuracy of the gunlayers, which was, said Jellicoe, 'the first essential in long-range firing. . . . If the gun fails to hit, it is no one's fault but the gunlayers'.' Fisher instituted battle practice in the autumn of 1905. The former practices were carried out at a 2,000-yard range; battle practice, at from 5,000 to 7,000 yards, at a fixed 90-foot by 30-foot target, the speed of the ships while firing being 15 knots. Beginning in November 1907, the target was towed, which brought gunnery closer to actual battle conditions. Battle practice was regarded as a test of the fighting efficiency of the ship as a whole, officers and men included.

For eight years there had been an excess of misses over hits. Thus, in 1902 the Fleet made 2,074 more misses than hits; in 1903, 1,032; in 1904, 1,916. 1905 was the first year in the annals of the Royal Navy when the number of hits exceeded the number of misses: 1,017 more, and in 1906, 3,405 more. By 1908 most ships were making much better shooting at 6,000 and 7,000 yards than they had done at 2,000 yards a few years earlier. In 1898, sixty-nine shots out of every hundred fired missed the target; in 1907, twenty-one shots. The value of the British Fleet as a quick and accurate hitting machine was two and a half times what it had been ten years previously.

Fisher was always keenly interested in the welfare of the Lower Deck. Accordingly, with the better war training for the men he

[6] Admiral of the Fleet Lord Chatfield, *The Navy and Defence* (London, 1942), p. 33; Admiral Sir Reginald Bacon, *From 1900 Onward* (London, 1940), p. 155.

made a good start towards removing the long-standing grievances of the Lower Deck with regard to food, quarters, discipline, and professional prospects. The scale of rations was revised upwards. Bakeries were installed in every ship so as to banish 'hard tack' from the Navy, and the seamen were provided with a knife and fork! The ventilation, heating, and sanitary arrangements were modernized. The pay and prospects of the Lower Deck were improved. As regards discipline, after 1905 punishments became fewer and less brutal. This led to better relations between the officers and men. Among the numerous personnel reforms classified by Admiral Bacon as 'minor' were commissions for warrant officers, improvements in the position of the petty officers and increased pensions to chief petty officers, and the establishment of a school of navigation and a school for boy artificers. 'What has passed unobserved is what I am most happy about during my years at the Admiralty in what has been done for the Lower Deck, and I was looking forward to still more!' So Fisher wrote the Editor of the organ of the Lower Deck, *The Fleet*.[7] It was no accident that the Admiral was known to every sailor by the democratic nickname of 'Jacky'. Complaints continued, but Fisher's concern with the welfare of the men, carried on by Churchill in the last pre-war years, resulted in a higher morale which was to bear handsome dividends in 1914–18.

2. THE NUCLEUS-CREW SYSTEM

The nucleus-crew, scrapping, and redistribution reforms were closely interdependent, as will be seen. Each was part of a whole, Fisher maintained. It was a case of 'the house that Jack built', and 'So we must have no tinkering! No pandering to sentiment! No regard for susceptibilities! No pity for any one! We must be ruthless, relentless, and remorseless! And we must therefore have The Scheme! The Whole Scheme!! and Nothing but The Scheme!!!!'[8] Fisher's nucleus-crew system was the high-water mark of all the reserve systems which had been tried in the world's fleets. He deemed it 'the greatest improvement of modern times'.

[7] Fisher to Lionel Yexley, 1 June 1909; *Fear God and Dread Nought*, ii. 22.

[8] Arthur J. Marder, *The Anatomy of British Sea Power: a History of British Naval Policy in the Pre-Dreadnought Era, 1880–1905* (New York, 1940), p. 488. (Hereafter cited by title only.) The title of the English edition (London, 1941) is *British Naval Policy, 1880–1905*.

Its principle was to make the fighting ships in reserve as nearly efficient as possible to the fleet in commission. Under the old system warships were either fully manned and in commission or else in reserve, distributed between the Fleet Reserve and the Dockyard Reserve. The Fleet Reserve consisted of ships ready for mobilization or immediate commissioning, but not immediately required, and ships undergoing minor repairs or alterations. The Dockyard Reserve had obsolete ships partially dismantled and not likely to be brought forward for commission except in the last emergency, and ships undergoing heavy repairs. These latter, when completed, would either pass into the Fleet Reserve or, if required, would be recommissioned for service in the sea-going fleet. The Dockyard Reserve was, then, composed of ships which could not be made immediately available for service.

Each ship of the Fleet Reserve was looked after by a handful of men, known as a care and maintenance party, drawn promiscuously from the naval depots. (The Dockyard Reserve ships had no care and maintenance parties on board; they were looked after by the dockyard itself.) Upon mobilization for manœuvres the Fleet Reserve ships were, literally, at sea, for they were manned *ad hoc* partly by Royal Naval Reserve men, and in any case by complements totally unfamiliar with their ship. They did their best and often worked wonders; but the value of these reserve ships in war was problematical, as proved by their frequent breakdowns in manœuvres and by the results of firing practice. The root of the evil lay in the fact that during the great naval expansion since 1889 there had never been a surplus of personnel sufficient to keep the reserve ships in good condition and to ensure the efficiency of their crews. The large additions to the personnel had been swallowed up by the increase in the number and size of the ships afloat.

Yet something had to be done, as it was obvious to Fisher how little the country would be able to count on the full paper strength of the Fleet in the event of a sudden outbreak of war. Under the Fisher reform the Fleet Reserve was entirely reorganized. It was now the 'Reserve Fleet', and its warships were provided with nucleus crews, that is, manned with two-fifths of their normal complements, including all the specialists in the ship's company and all the officers really essential to the fighting efficiency of the ship. The nucleus crew lived on board, and by means of drills

37

and practice cruises became thoroughly acquainted with the ship and her idiosyncrasies. When mobilization was ordered, or if hostilities broke out, the crews could be completed quickly from the shore barracks and instructional establishments at Portsmouth, Devonport, and Chatham. The nucleus-crew ships were organized into three homogeneous reserve divisions, each based on one of the home ports, Devonport, Sheerness, and Portsmouth. The ships of the Reserve Fleet went to sea for regular quarterly cruises of from ten to fourteen days' duration, carrying out tactics and gunnery exercises. In addition these vessels were completed to full complements for, and took part in, the annual manœuvres. The percentage of breakdowns and cripples was reduced to a negligible quantity. In brief, the Reserve Fleet could at short notice reinforce the active fleet in home waters and give a good account of itself.

There were weak points in the system—for example, in selecting the ratings for nucleus crews it was found difficult to provide a sufficiency of certain classes—but experience showed that Balfour was not exaggerating when he affirmed in 1906 that 'this new Reserve scheme has augmented the fighting power of the British fleet not once or twice, but threefold'. Fisher rightly called the nucleus-crew system 'the keystone of our preparedness for war', since it rendered the whole sea-going fleet as 'instantly ready for war' as was compatible with peace conditions and a peace establishment.

This was all-important in his view. '*Suddenness* is now the characteristic feature of sea fighting! . . . *Readiness for sudden action* has to be the keynote of all we do.' There was, however, at the start no personnel surplus for the new system. That was provided by the complements of the scrapped ships, which leads us to the next of the great reforms.

3. SCRAPPING OF OBSOLETE MEN-OF-WAR

The only economical way to provide the personnel for the nucleus-crew system, Fisher reasoned, was to reduce the sea-going fleet by scrapping ships of comparatively small fighting value. There was another justification for the weeding policy. In Fisher's words: 'The first duty of the Navy is to be instantly ready to strike the enemy, and this can only be accomplished by concentrating our strength into ships of undoubted fighting value, ruthlessly discarding those that have become obsolete.'[9]

Scattered over every ocean and sea on the planet were a large number of isolated, obsolete little gunboats, sloops, and second- and third-class cruisers, employed in police duties of no great importance or in 'showing the flag'. The system was a survival of the days before steam, the telegraph, and wireless, when it took a long time to summon naval assistance in any emergency. This arrangement pleased the Foreign Office and the consuls' daughters, who needed tennis and waltzing partners, and was useful for police duties and relief of distress after an earthquake; but it was useless for war purposes. These ships could fight no modern warship larger than themselves, even when they could fight at all, and their speed was insufficient to enable them to run away. Their officers and crews rusted for lack of training with modern weapons, and rarely could the officers gain any experience of fleet evolutions and other combined exercises during the whole of the commission.

On Fisher's initiative this antiquated and pernicious system of locking up fighting complements in ships that could not fight was at last discarded. Due provision was made for such police purposes as were still deemed necessary: a few gunboats were retained for river service in China and on the west coast of Africa. The other ships were recalled and paid off. Such of them as were not adaptable for some of the auxiliary purposes of war were either broken up or sold out of the service. The great advantage of this bold stroke was that it provided the personnel for the nucleus-crew system.

The policy of scrapping did not end here. It had long been the practice to keep in the Dockyard Reserve, but still on the active list of the Navy, a sizeable number of interesting but more or less useful survivals of a period of rapid constructive evolution—ships with muzzle-loading guns, wooden ships with masts and yards, ships whose armour plate was as vulnerable to modern ordnance as though they had been built of wood. Keeping this 'miser's hoard of useless junk' in any sort of effective repair involved a considerable charge on the annual navy estimates. Fisher would have removed from the effective list all battleships older than the two 'Niles' (launched in 1887–8) and all cruisers below the 23 to 24-

[9] *The Anatomy of British Sea Power*, p. 489.

knot armoured cruisers in construction since 1900. But in the end his extreme proposals were somewhat watered down by a special committee that thoroughly investigated the whole matter. Even then the scrapping policy was ruthless and thorough: 154 ships in all were struck off the effective list 'with one courageous stroke of the pen', as Balfour later described it, or, as Fisher expressed it, by a measure that was 'Napoleonic in its audacity and Cromwellian in its thoroughness'. Ninety of these ships, the 'sheep', were condemned as totally useless and were earmarked for sale. The rest were retained as a Material Reserve. These were the thirty-seven 'llamas', told off for subsidiary purposes of war, such as mine-laying, and twenty-seven 'goats', which were to retain their armaments, but were not to have any money spent on them for maintenance and repair. The llamas and goats were laid up at the three home ports without crews. The special committee which investigated this problem recommended an annual review of the effective list.

Subsidiary advantages of this reform were that it cleared the naval harbours, where many of these ships had occupied valuable berthing space, adding to the ever-growing congestion, and it stopped unproductive expenditure on repairs and upkeep, so effecting an immediate annual saving calculated by Fisher at £845,000 on repairs alone.

4. REDISTRIBUTION OF THE FLEET

The redistribution of the Fleet to meet strategical ('and not sentimental') requirements was the crowning stroke of all. The distribution had been determined in the sailing-ship era, when sea voyages were long and when squadrons to protect trade had to be distributed widely. There were nine squadrons or fleets in 1904. The advent of steam and cable communications, later the wireless, lessened the need for many isolated foreign squadrons. The entire distribution system was rendered wholly obsolete by the Japanese Alliance (1902) and the French Entente (1904), and by the fact that, since 1901–2, the Admiralty had looked upon the German Navy as *the* potential opponent of the Royal Navy. Fisher was one of the earliest to realize the German menace. He was now responsible for concentrating the major portion of the Fleet in home waters.

To make possible this concentration and to increase the efficiency of the foreign squadrons, the latter also were reorganized. 'Five strategic keys lock up the world!' Fisher believed. They were Singapore, the Cape, Alexandria, Gibraltar, and Dover. All belonged to England, 'another proof that we belong to the ten lost tribes of Israel!' Five great fleets were organized to hold these keys, and so organized as to be capable of rapid concentration. Specifically, the squadrons in the Pacific, South Atlantic, and North America stations were withdrawn. The Cape Squadron was to take over the two latter stations and the West Coast of Africa. The Eastern Fleet for war, with its strategical centre at Singapore, was to control completely the ocean east of Suez. It was to consist of the amalgamated squadrons on the Australia, China, and East Indies stations. In peacetime these constituent squadrons were to be separate commands. At the end of their annual manœuvres they were to rendezvous at Singapore for combined fleet exercises. All small vessels with the Cape of Good Hope and Far Eastern Fleets were ruthlessly reduced.

The next step was to concentrate the cream of the Fleet where it belonged—in home waters. In 1904 nearly all the most modern ships were stationed in the Mediterranean (twelve battleships). The Channel Fleet got the next best of them (eight battleships)— and that fleet was, remember, not always in the Channel—and the residue, the Home Fleet, eight battleships of earlier types, was considered ample for the direct defence of home waters. The principal precaution for safeguarding the British Isles from attack was a regulation that the Home and Channel squadrons should not both be absent from British waters at the same time. That was the general situation, and its inherent defects were disclosed when the Dogger Bank crisis (October 1904) compelled the instant recall of four battleships of the Channel Fleet, which happened at the moment to be at Gibraltar, and their temporary attachment to the Home Command. Moreover, it became clear towards the end of 1904 that the existing dispositions needed change. Starting from that date, Admiralty policy was, 'slowly and steadily', to concentrate strength in home waters. The Admiralty later maintained, in the great controversy with Beresford, that they had always kept in view the ultimate creation of a great Home Fleet under a single commander-in-chief, such as was evolved by 1909. 'Such a fleet could not have been created in 1904 without unduly straining the international political situation, and it was necessary to proceed with the utmost caution owing to the sensitive state of public opinion in Great Britain and Germany. The Admiralty claimed that they have arrived at the result aimed at comparatively unobtrusively, and without causing political complications, while the safety of the country has always been fully assured.'[10]

The first stage in the redistribution was Fisher's establishment at the end of 1904 of two large fleets in home waters. The Home Fleet, now renamed the Channel Fleet, was made considerably more powerful. It was raised in strength from eight to twelve battleships by the addition of four battleships withdrawn from the Mediterranean. Their number was further increased to seventeen (reduced to sixteen by the loss of the *Montagu*) in the summer of 1905 by the inclusion of five battleships withdrawn from China. With its strategical centre at Dover, the Channel Fleet cruised between the coast of Ireland and Gibraltar. The old Channel Fleet, renamed the Atlantic Fleet, retained its eight battleships, only now they consisted of ships of the latest class. This fleet, with its permanent base at Gibraltar, was available for the reinforcement of either the Mediterranean Fleet or the Channel Fleet. The Atlantic and Mediterranean Fleets were to carry out combined manœuvres twice a year, the Atlantic and Channel Fleets, once a year. To each of the three European fleets was attached a squadron of armoured cruisers. The old North America and West Indies Squadron was transformed into the 4th Cruiser (or Particular Service) Squadron. It was employed as a training squadron in peacetime, based on Devonport, though as a sop to the colonists in the West Indies, it would annually show the flag in the West Indies and off the coast of South America. In time of war it would join either the Mediterranean or Channel Fleet. In essence, the new distribution scheme meant that three-quarters of Britain's battleships would be readily available against Germany. It was still necessary to keep a strong squadron in the Mediterranean in view of the uncertain attitude of France and Russia during the Russo-Japanese War; but a concentration in home waters was in process of being made. England, instead of looking, as she had

[10] Summary of the Admiralty position in the unpublished 'Report and Proceedings of a Sub-Committee of the Committee of Imperial Defence Appointed to Inquire into Certain Questions of Naval Policy Raised by Lord Charles Beresford', 12 Aug. 1909; Lennoxlove MSS.

looked in the wars of the eighteenth century, to the south and west, now began to look to the east and north. Fisher also saw the great strategic advantages of the fleets exercising where they were likely to fight. He was fond of quoting Nelson's '*The battle ground should be the drill ground.*'

5. THE *DREADNOUGHT* AND THE *INVINCIBLE*

It was in the realm of *matériel* that Fisher's genius was most at home, and here his proudest day was at Portsmouth dockyard on 10 February 1906. The crowds were enormous and their enthusiasm knew no bounds, for the occasion appealed to the popular imagination: the launching by King Edward VII, in an impressive and beautiful ceremony, of the largest, fastest, most powerful battleship in the world. For weeks before the launching the event had been eagerly canvassed in the newspapers. Rumour was busy with regard to the new leviathan. Her size, armament, speed, and supposed secrets of construction attracted and held popular interest. Enthusiasts prophesied, and the public dimly felt, that the latest battleship would mark the beginning of a new epoch in naval history.

The novel features of the *Dreadnought* were: (1) 21 knots speed, 2 knots faster than any battleship building or afloat. (2) A main battery of ten 12-inch guns. This was a great advance from the four 12-inch and the four 9·2-inch guns which constituted the primary armament of the 'King Edwards', the last pre-dreadnought battleship class but one, or even the four 12-inch and ten 9·2-inch guns mounted in the 'Lord Nelsons', Britain's last pre-dreadnought class. The weight of a broadside from the two calibres of gun was: 'King Edwards', 4,160 lb.; 'Lord Nelsons', 5,300 lb.; the *Dreadnought*, 6,800 lb. From the time of the *Dreadnought* to the present day, every capital ship built by every navy has mounted a primary armament of eight to twelve large guns of a single calibre. (3) The absence of secondary armament. There was a special armament of light quick-firing guns (twenty-seven 12-pounders) to repel torpedo attack. (4) The *Dreadnought* was the first turbine-engined big ship in any navy. In Admiral Bacon's judgment, 'No greater single step towards efficiency in war was ever made than the introduction of the turbine. Previous to its adoption every day's steaming at high speed meant several days' overhaul of machinery in harbour. All this was changed as if by magic . . .'[11]

The keel-plate of H.M.S. *Dreadnought* was laid on 2 October 1905, the ship went to sea for trials on 3 October 1906, and was completed in December 1906. (This remarkable building time was made possible by the appropriation of the 12-inch guns and spares ordered for the two 'Lord Nelsons'.) The ship was of illustrious descent. The first of her six predecessors was one of those gallant little vessels which had fought off the Invincible Armada in 1588. No. 5 had fought with Nelson at Trafalgar. Fisher called the dreadnoughts 'Old Testament ships', and the battle cruisers (of which more in a moment), 'the real gems' and 'New Testament ships', because 'they fulfilled the promise of the "Old Testament" ships'.

The Committee on Designs had also reported on the design for the *Invincible*, a new and larger type of armoured cruiser, of which three were included in the 1905–6 programme. The *Invincible* displaced 17,200 tons, was designed for 25 knots, and had an all-big-gun armament. There was nothing between the eight 12-inch guns and the anti-torpedo-craft guns (sixteen 4-inch). With the speed and armament, the main desiderata, fixed, only a medium armour protection was possible—that of the 'Minotaur' class of armoured cruisers.

The *raison d'être* of the battle cruiser was threefold: to have armoured ships (1) to act as super-scouting cruisers, ships fast and powerful enough to push home a reconnaissance in the face of an enemy's big armoured cruisers; (2) fast enough to hunt down and destroy the fastest armed merchant raiders, especially the 23-knot German transatlantic liners, which were known to be carrying guns for commerce destruction in war; (3) to act as a fast wing reinforcing the van or rear of a battle fleet in a general action. The genesis of the type was sound, as the existing armoured cruisers could not fulfil any of these tasks. It is unfortunate that Admiralty statistics often included battle cruisers under dreadnoughts and that the ships came to be called, from 1912, battle cruisers (at first they were known as large armoured cruisers or 'fast battleships', and, in 1911, as 'battleship-cruisers'), for they were not intended to stand up to battleships (certainly not dreadnoughts) not already engaged

[11] Unsigned 'Obituary Notice. Admiral of the Fleet the Right Hon. Lord Fisher of Kilverstone', *Transactions of the Institution of Naval Architects*, Vol. 62 (1920).

with other battleships. Their third function was the least important and tended to obscure their primary duty, which was to find the enemy's battle fleet and report its position, course, speed, and movements.

The principle of the battle cruiser was not new. The fast armoured cruisers of the pre-dreadnought era differed from the pre-dreadnought battleships of that date in much the same way as the battle cruisers differed from dreadnoughts, that is, they were faster but less powerful. And just as Togo, in the Russo-Japanese War, counted his squadron of armoured cruisers as 'capital ships' and put them into the line of battle, but manœuvred them more or less independently of his heavy ships to take advantage of their higher speed, so the Royal Navy planned to use its battle cruisers.

The term 'capital ships' for dreadnoughts and battle cruisers collectively was introduced tentatively by the Admiralty in the 1909 navy scare and caught on by 1912. The term dates back to the reign of Charles II and referred to ships capable of lying in the line of battle.

To Fisher the Navy owed the beginning of the substitution of oil fuel for coal, and the introduction and improvement of the submarine. As far back as 1886 Fisher had a reputation in naval and governmental circles as the 'Oil Maniac'. As First Sea Lord he did everything possible to ensure the supply of oil for the Navy, and to develop new sources of supply. He pioneered the use of oil fuel in the Navy. Fisher was among the few British naval officers prior to World War I to foresee the offensive possibilities of the submarine. As early as 1902, only two years after Britain had begun to build submarines, he was convinced that this new craft would revolutionize naval warfare. He therefore did all he could to build up a strong submarine fleet, even after he left office in 1910.

Despite Fisher's confidence and the support of many eminent politicians and high-ranking officers, some of the reforms gave rise to bitter controversy in the service. Only the nucleus-crew system was generally well received.

IV

Dissension in the Navy: The Major Reforms

The drastic change in naval training inaugurated on Christmas Day, 1902, followed by relentless reforms carried out since October 21st, 1904, have naturally led to intense feeling being manifested, for no Department of the Navy has been left untouched, from the *Dreadnought* revolution down to the introduction of baking of bread in the Fleet instead of the issue of hard biscuit.

FISHER in a memorandum of 1907.

I hold no brief for Jack Fisher, but as I told them, what did his predecessors in office do? Absolutely nothing in view of reforms everywhere required. . . . The dead set made at Fisher is simply disgraceful . . . 'Jacky' has made mistakes (who hasn't?), but as I wrote some time ago to the *Spectator*, he has been the ruling spirit of the most progressive Board of Admiralty I have seen in my 60 years' experience.

ADMIRAL SIR JOHN HOPKINS to Lord Esher, 7 February 1908.

1. THE SELBORNE SCHEME

THE OPPOSITION to the Selborne Scheme of 1902 became especially noisy after 1905, when the new arrangements were in full working order. Admiral of the Fleet Sir Frederick Richards emerged from retirement in November 1907 to express a definite opinion that the new scheme was a 'hazardous experiment', and that an inquiry into its scope and its effect was highly desirable. Among the other vehement critics of the 'great naval blunder' were, to use Fisher's expression, 'pre-historic Admirals' like C. C. Penrose FitzGerald and the one-time ineffectual First Sea Lord (1888–91) Sir Vesey Hamilton, supported by politicians like the former First Lord (1895–1900), Lord Goschen.

Some of the criticism was based on a misapprehension of what the Admiralty policy really was. Critics spoke as though 'interchangeability' were intended to make one and the same officer qualify for service as an expert in many different capacities, as if he were to be, say, an engineer for one commission, a navigator for another, a gunnery lieutenant for a third, a marine for a fourth.

46

Now, in the United States they did this or something very like this; they had real interchangeability. And the critics seemed to have assumed that the English scheme embodied the same idea. For example, Admiral FitzGerald, in a letter to the *Daily Graphic* (10 March 1906), spoke of 'the curious composite officer now being manufactured at Osborne and Dartmouth to perform alternately the duties of a seaman, a marine, and an engineer.' This was typical of much that passed for criticism with people who had not informed themselves as to the real nature of the Admiralty scheme. To repeat what has already been stated, it was only to the age of about 22, when officers attained the rank of lieutenant, that they were to have a common training. After that their paths diverged; specialization began. Each officer would have special knowledge in one particular branch of the service, but all officers would have a general knowledge of the different branches and be able, in case of need, to fulfil the duties in another branch.

There were objections of a snobbish nature, as the executive officers continued to look upon the engineers as their social inferiors, and pictured engineering as a dirty occupation fit only for the 'greasers' and the 'chauffeur admirals', as the engineers were called. Admiral Bacon later claimed that 'three-quarters of the opposition met with by Fisher in introducing his reforms was due to a fear on the part of "Society", and naval officers, that their sons might, under the new scheme of education, be forced to become engineers.'[1] Rosslyn E. Wemyss, Captain of R.N. College, Osborne, observed in 1905 'a tendency on the part of the parents of some of the cadets at Osborne to hope at least that their sons might never become Lieutenants (E), with no chance of commanding ships or fleets, and I have a suspicion that, for this reason, they have in some cases even discouraged their sons in their engineering studies.'[2] In view of this prejudice against the engineering branch, it was natural that an insufficient number volunteered for it. In 1906 Fisher proposed to complete the reform by giving the engineer officers executive ranks and uniforms. He was stopped by the adamant opposition among a great many executive officers. They were dead against the change and preferred to keep the existing distinctions, humiliating though they were to the engineer officers. But the demand of the latter for

[1] Bacon, *Fisher*, i. 199.
[2] Wemyss to Fisher, n.d.; Lennoxlove MSS.

executive rank and status mounted. In 1915, when he was back at the Admiralty, Fisher put through this reform.

Although Selborne had written that 'every endeavour will be made to provide those who enter the Engineering branch with opportunities equal to those of the executive branch, including the same opportunity of rising to flag-rank', this was not realized. There were far fewer Engineering flag officers in the Navy List than Executive flag officers. And from the very nature of the case, the 'plums' of the profession went to those officers who had chosen the executive branch—to those who had been trained to command complete ships, and whole fleets, rather than a single, however vital, *part* of ships and fleets. Moreover, there was still a yawning gap between the 'sacred priesthood of Executive N.O.s' and the 'lesser breeds'. In the opinion of a distinguished civilian long associated with the breed 'Naval Officer': 'Even when I first knew them [1913], the gulf fixed between "Executive" and "Engineer" was *vast*, and had to be seen to be believed.'[3]

There were other, lesser, criticisms of the new scheme, such as the too early age of entry—that it was impossible to discover in a boy of $12\frac{1}{2}$ to 13 (to which the age of entry had been lowered from 14 to $15\frac{1}{2}$) the qualities which make a good officer. Yet the early entry was, for Fisher, one of the most important features of the reform. 'The whole secret is to catch them very young and mould them while they are then so plastic and receptive.'

Among the more thoughtful critics—men like Sir George Clarke, Secretary of the Committee of Imperial Defence, Admiral W. H. Henderson, and Sir Rowland Blennerhassett—the reform was opposed chiefly on one or more of these interrelated grounds: (1) There was great danger that concentration on engineering would inevitably tend to displace the study of tactics and strategy; (2) proficiency in any one of the three branches demanded the whole time and talents of the aspirant; (3) the duties of a deck officer and an engineer were totally distinct and different, and the increasing complication in engines and boilers called for the

---

[3] Letters to the writer, 24 Nov., 5 Dec. 1959. This expert makes the interesting point that the substitution of a school for a training ship was making for a gradual narrowing of the gap. 'Although Osborne and Dartmouth were, superficially, controlled by executive naval officers, the "civilian" influence of university-trained masters was from the first very considerable, and grew in the end to be almost paramount. Perhaps even more important, they were constantly, if invisibly, influencing the executive naval officer staff, too.'

undivided attention and further and deeper specialization of a special class of engineer officer.

Despite modifications, the system justified the faith of its warmest advocates. An American naval officer reported, after a visit of a United States fleet to English waters in 1910, that the British officers considered the Selborne Scheme an improvement.[4] The experience of the U.S. Navy, where common training, introduced in 1899, had proved a great success, confirmed Fisher in its wisdom. 'There can be no doubt,' the British Naval Attaché in the United States reported (April 1908), 'of the versatility of the officers of the modern school . . . It appears that there is a happy medium of efficiency . . . Opinions have been asked of all classes of naval officers . . . all are united in the opinion that any alteration of the general principle of amalgamation would be a regrettable and dangerous set-back.'[5]

Fisher had flamboyantly declared in March 1906: 'Nothing can stop this scheme. Prejudice cannot stop it. Parliament cannot stop it. Satan cannot stop it. Not even the Treasury can stop it. They might as well try to stop an avalanche.'[6] However, in one particular the original scheme had to be altered as early as 1906. It quickly proved impracticable to give young marine officers the same education as other officers. The marine officers did not believe the common training would provide adequately for the training of their young men in the very highly specialized functions expected of the Corps; they would really be, not soldiers, but inferior naval officers. Also the officers of the Corps strenuously opposed the reform because it tended to weaken the connexion of the Royal Marines with the Army. So far as the marines were concerned, the scheme was now abandoned. Marine officers continued to be entered separately.

The only other important change down to the war came in Churchill's time and on his initiative. In August 1912 the age of entry to Osborne was raised to $13\frac{1}{2}$, so as to correspond with the age at which boys finished their preparatory school work. And in March 1913 a supplementary scheme of entry was started to cope with the threatened shortage of officers. This had become a serious

[4] U.S. Navy Department MSS.

[5] N.I.D. Report No. 871, Apr. 1909; *Reports on Foreign Naval Affairs, 1908–9* (Admiralty Library).

[6] Quoted in Rollo Appleyard to Fisher, 7 Nov. 1908; Lennoxlove MSS.

problem with the great dreadnought programmes from 1909 and the expansion of the submarine service, the fleet air service, and the Dominion navies. It took some nine years to produce a lieutenant under the Osborne-Dartmouth system. To remedy the shortage quickly a special entry for public school boys was introduced. A number of the finished products of the public schools between $17\frac{1}{2}$ and $18\frac{1}{2}$ were admitted as cadets annually by a competitive examination and subjected to an intensive eighteen months' naval training, partly on board a cruiser and partly on shore at Devonport, then sent to the Fleet as midshipmen. That is, under this scheme, the cadet received his general education before entering the service, and an officer was turned out in a little less than half the time. As Churchill remarked on this reform, a church would miss some of its best elements if it made no provision for the baptism of those who were of riper years.

Other portions of the scheme were dropped or altered after World War I, particularly as regards engineering officers. The fundamental cause was the increasing demand for specialization as warfare year by year became an ever more complex business. Executive officers found that the time spent on the midshipman's training in engineering did not leave enough time to bring him up to the necessary standard as a seaman and deck officer. Engineer officers reported that it was impossible to make an efficient engineer officer in anything short of the whole of the young officer's time. Again, not enough of the common-entry officers were choosing engineering.

The only thing to be done then was to amend the whole 'Common Entry' system. It was not abolished. A 'Common Entrant' who wanted to choose Engineering could still—can still—do so: but another, and purely 'Engineer', entry had to be added in order to make up for the insufficient numbers who did. With the whole 'pool' idea thus nullified, and with the final realization that the Engineer could not also 'command', there was no longer much point in the original Selborne attempt to coalesce the Executive and the Engineer officers. In 1925, therefore, the latter were brought out of the 'executive' list, where they had been since 1903, and formed into a list of their own. They were still to be called 'Commander (E), Lieutenant (E)', etc., but they reshipped the [pre-1902 distinctive] purple ring and became once more a separate department.[7]

[7] Michael Lewis, *The Navy of Britain : a Historical Portrait* (London, 1948), pp. 198–9.

Osborne College, where living conditions in the unsubstantial bungalows had drawn the attack of parents, was abolished in 1921. Thereafter, all cadets were entered direct to the new Dartmouth for three and three-quarter years. In 1947 the age of entry was raised to 16 and the length of the course halved. Fisher would not have been overjoyed to see the hallowed 'catch-them-young' principle discarded. In 1955–6 further changes raised the age of entry to 17½ (the age at which most of the potential officers finish their schooling) and *reverted to Fisher's original scheme of common early training*, except that the Royal Marine entry is still a separate method of entry, with no initial training at Dartmouth. As of 1 January 1957 the existing division of the list of naval officers into separate Executive, Engineer, Supply and Secretariat, and Electrical Branches was abolished. In place of these four branches, a single General List of officers was formed. 'We have decided that every cadet shall in future enter the Navy as "an officer"— which is his prime function, and that his early training [at Dartmouth] shall be, to the greatest possible extent, common whether he is eventually to become a Seaman [a term now describing the old Executive Officer], an Engineer or a Supply Specialist. Whether common entry shall in due course apply to the Electrical specialist has not yet been settled.'[8] Under the new scheme all General List officers are eligible for command of shore establishments and will fill many appointments ashore previously open only to the Seaman, although only Seamen officers are appointed to command ships. Preceding this reform, in 1955, the differences in titles and uniforms for the non-Executive officers were finally abolished.[9]

Thus the wheel has turned very nearly a full circle. Furthermore, the fundamental principle still obtains: the fighting man, whether bluejacket or officer, must be well versed in all the mechanical appliances with which a modern navy is equipped. Admiral of the Fleet Lord Chatfield some years ago rated the 1902 scheme as among the five 'most successful' of Fisher's reforms, and the late Admiral Sir Sydney Fremantle thought it was his 'most

[8] Admiralty Fleet Order, 1/56; Admiralty MSS. It has since been decided to make these principles applicable to Electrical officers also.

[9] The correspondent quoted above (p. 48) doubts whether 'even now the gulf is *quite* dead, though I do believe that, when the present younger generation becomes the older one, it *will* be dead—quite dead.'

successful reform'.[10] The Admiral might not have agreed at that time, as in later life he asserted that the 1902 scheme had been 'spoiled by the schoolmasters'. But he would have more reason to smile today!

2. THE SCRAPPING POLICY

The scrapping policy was assailed by a large section of the press and the service. Four arguments were used. First, that it denuded distant stations of police forces and lowered British prestige through the disappearance of the flag. Second, and this was the crucial point, that the scrapping policy deprived the Fleet of ships which would have been very useful in the multifarious tasks of trade protection in war. In the words of Richards, it was a case of 'covering the heart and leaving the arteries [trade routes] . . . to take care of themselves on the outbreak of war.'[11] 'The trade routes have been left to Providence,' Beresford claimed in a speech of 30 June 1909. He forgot that in 1902 he himself had urged that the Admiralty should recall 'vessels that could neither fight nor run away'—'useless ships' then 'showing the flag'. Third, and closely related, it was charged that the Board was neglecting the construction of small cruisers to replace the scrapped cruisers. (Excepting a very few that were built earlier, unarmoured or 'protected' cruisers were built only from 1908, and then in modest numbers to replace the obsolescent vessels of their class.) The Navy would presently be reduced to the same condition as was Nelson prior to the Nile; when the next war came, want of cruisers would be found written in the hearts of British admirals. To send large armoured cruisers to run down commerce destroyers was, it was said, absurd; moreover, they would probably be wanted for other purposes. Fourth, historical arguments were trotted out to support the contention that large numbers of small ships were essential to the conduct of the varied operations of naval war.

The Hague Conference of 1907 and the Declaration of London of 1909 emphasized the need for cruisers for commerce protection. The Conference agreed that merchant ships might be transformed

[10] Lord Chatfield's letter of 14 Mar. 1946 and Admiral Fremantle's of 8 Mar. 1946 to the writer.

[11] Richards to Beresford, 29 June 1909, quoted by the latter in his speech to the London Chamber of Commerce, 30 June 1909.

into warships when and where they pleased by the simple process of writing on a piece of paper, hoisting the pennant, and getting the guns out of the hold and into position. The salient point in the Declaration of London was that foodstuffs carried in neutral bottoms might now be declared contraband of war.

Other events played into the hands of Fisher's critics. The terms 'disgrace', 'scandal', and 'national humiliation' were freely used when an earthquake which overwhelmed Kingston, Jamaica, in January 1907 found no British man-of-war in the harbour; United States warships were the first to reach the scene. This situation was attributed to the fact that the patrol of the whole of the Caribbean Sea and the entire interests of Britain's West Indian possessions had been left in charge of a couple of cruisers. Much, too, was made of the absence of British warships from Chile during the earthquakes of August–September 1906, from Cuba during the revolution of February 1906, and from the British protectorate of Zanzibar during a mutiny in September 1906 of the Government police and palace guards.

The Foreign Office felt that the interests of British foreign policy were threatened through the jeopardizing of the lives and property of British subjects partly owing to the reduction of naval police units in distant seas. There were 'important British interests in distant seas where the opportune presence of a British ship of war may avert a disaster which can only be remedied later at much inconvenience and considerable sacrifice.' The Foreign Office proposed an increase in numbers of police units in various parts of the world. The risk of the probable loss of such isolated units at the beginning of a war should be 'faced for the sake of the world-wide interests of the Empire'.[12] The Colonial Office, bitter over the Jamaica incident, supported the Foreign Office. Lord Esher, a member of the Committee of Imperial Defence, thought the Foreign Office position was reasonable. He observed that 'the practical needs of this scattered Empire, especially from the point of view—sentimental, if you please—of Palmerston's "Civis Romanus", have been somewhat overlooked.'[13] The Prince of Wales also thought that Fisher's policy neglected the 'policing of the seas'.

[12] Hardinge (Permanent Under-Secretary of State for Foreign Affairs) to the Admiralty, 14 Mar. 1907; Windsor MSS.
[13] Esher to Knollys, 24 Jan. 1907; *ibid.*

What was the Admiralty's case? Fisher did make due provision for such police purposes as were still necessary: four powerful armoured-cruiser squadrons were employed to show the flag in imposing force whenever it was deemed advisable. The Jamaica earthquake and other disturbances were most regrettable, but they could not be allowed to influence the disposition of British squadrons, since squadrons were not primarily intended to afford relief in such cases. Nor, indeed, could the Admiralty be expected to foresee in what part of the world the next earthquake or other disturbance would take place that required the presence of British warships.

Fisher's reaction to the Foreign Office request of March 1907 was a scathing Admiralty memorandum charging the Foreign Office with inability 'to substantiate a single case of failure on the part of the Admiralty to meet real requirements. . . . It appears necessary to repeat, as the Foreign Office pays no attention to this point, that visits of powerful ships and squadrons have largely taken the place of desultory cruising by small and isolated vessels, and that, so far from injuring, this has greatly enhanced the prestige of British naval power.' The whole matter was put before the Prime Minister, Sir Henry Campbell-Bannerman, with the statement that if the demands of the other departments, which the Admiralty considered unnecessary, were complied with, it would result in an inevitable rise in the navy estimates. The Admiralty emerged with a vote of confidence.

As regards the second and third charges, revolving about the problems of trade protection, Fisher drew the conclusion, from the avowed policy of the French and the war practice of the Russians, that the attack on trade, if undertaken on a grand scale at all, would be carried out by powerful cruiser squadrons. Small ships, therefore, would be ineffective for commerce protection. The Admiralty was developing the large cruiser, so that, after a sufficient number had been assigned to mask those of the enemy, the remainder would be available to destroy any small ships which might be foolish enough to wander about British trade routes.

The critics found their justification in World War I, when from beginning to end England never had a sufficiency of cruisers and small-craft escorts for trade protection. There is an extenuating factor, however. It was the ruthless submarine warfare on commerce which led to the critical situation of 1916–17. Not until the very eve of the war was it realized, by Fisher and only a few others, none in a responsible position, that the submarine might be used against British shipping.

What of the fourth charge? Fisher denied Sir William White's claim that unarmoured or protected cruisers, a class especially hard hit by the scrapping policy, had proved of the greatest value in the Russo-Japanese War. Britain's protected cruisers, he asserted, were useless as scouts or for raiding an enemy's commerce. A single fast armoured cruiser would lap them all up 'like an armadillo let loose on an ant-hill'. Or, as expressed by the D.N.I., 'Their lack of commanding speed and of armour, and consequently of fighting stamina, inexorably consigns them to tactics of evasion and a fugitive role whenever menaced by hostile armoured cruisers. . . . The decisive factor upon which the fate of the ants will thenceforth hang will not be the efficacy of their bite but the speed of their legs.' The idea of building faster, and therefore larger, unarmoured cruisers for general cruiser work in great numbers had to be ruled out. It was too expensive and, anyhow, these 'naval white elephants' would have to run on sighting a hostile armoured cruiser. 'Even if the public purse were bottomless, such a policy would surely be questionable, for the armoured cruiser, costing little more, would be an infinitely better investment. . . . So long as our naval rivals continued to build armoured cruisers, while they refrain from laying the keels of large unarmoured ones, we must logically follow suit.' Britain would employ *armoured* cruisers for scouting, reconnaissance work, and cruiser work in general in blue water, and in this class she had a sufficient preponderance to meet all reasonably probable contingencies.[14] This remained the essence of the Admiralty's position in the Fisher period.

Fisher also concerned himself with the criticism that, in weeding out the small ships of no great power, the whole scheme concentrated attention too exclusively on the fleet as an engine of fighting at sea, and ignored its enormous possibilities for influencing operations ashore—that is, its ability to act against military forces, capturing seaport towns, etc. Fisher did not see how war vessels could influence land operations except by forbidding the enemy free maritime transport of troops or *matériel*. This could be done

[14] Memorandum of Captain Charles L. Ottley, 'The Strategic Aspects of Our Building Programme, 1907', 7 Jan. 1907; Admiralty MSS.

better by using fast powerful ships than weak slow ones, even if greater numbers of the latter were available. Under no condition was it intended to use warships to attack forts or take towns. Here again history proved the critics right, for in the war warships did bombard forts and take towns. Indeed, when the war came, Fisher embarked on a programme of auxiliary construction that slowed down work on battleships. He was ready to cut capital-ship superiority, in dreadnoughts anyway, to gain the 'subsidiary' ends.

3. THE DREADNOUGHT CONTROVERSY

As regards the *Dreadnought*, the battle of the pens began on the day she was launched. In 1908 Fisher spoke of the 'unanimous naval feeling against the *Dreadnought* when it first appeared'. His critics derided the dreadnought policy on technical grounds, and also on the ground that it rendered all existing battleships obsolete, so sweeping away Britain's overwhelming preponderance in pre-dreadnoughts (about three to one over Germany) and giving the Germans a level, or nearly level, start in the competition for naval supremacy. 'The whole British fleet,' Richards wrote Beresford in 1909, 'was . . . morally scrapped and labelled obsolete at the moment when it was at the zenith of its efficiency, and equal not to two but practically to all the navies of the world combined.' The *Manchester Guardian*, usually one of Fisher's supporters, termed the *Dreadnought* his one great mistake (27 January 1910). 'Its effect has been to eat up the economies of Navy reforms and to bring about a period of greater strain in the rivalry of international arms. It was a departure from our traditional policy in construction, which, as befitted a Power which had acquired so great a lead, was one of conservatism. It destroyed much of the advantage that had been secured by past expenditure, and enabled other nations to get on more even terms.' Much the same criticism was made by other Liberal organs and by Liberal Party politicians. The Radical wing of the party deplored the dreadnought type (this 'piece of wanton and profligate ostentation', Lloyd George called it), because, by intensifying the naval competition with Germany, it substantially reduced the sums of money that could be devoted to an expansion of the social services. In 1905, Sir George Clarke secretly begged the new Prime Minister, Campbell-Bannerman, to appoint a committee to reconsider the dreadnought policy. As

Clarke and so many others pointed out, it should be an axiom of British policy never to lead in ship construction, but always to follow with something better, taking advantage of greater speed in shipbuilding.

Fisher never denied that the introduction of the *Dreadnought* was tantamount to starting *de novo*, since the vessel, in his opinion, was equal to any two and a half battleships then existing. But he was certain that the all-big-gun battleship was inevitable, on both technical grounds and on intelligence of what other powers were planning, and this leads us to the heart of our story.

Every indication in 1904–5 pointed to the dreadnought as the battleship of the immediate future. The Russians, Germans, and Japanese were known to be giving the matter serious attention. The report of Fisher's Committee on Designs stated on the authority of 'secret information in the possession of the Admiralty, that a uniform armament of 12-inch guns for the future Russian and Japanese battleships has been decided upon as the outcome of the experience of these two countries in the war between them'. Fisher felt, too, that it was only a question of time before the Germans took the leap. His instinct was correct. Thus, the Emperor noted on a report of 8 December 1904 from the German Naval Attaché in London that Vickers had plans of a battleship armed with ten or twelve 10-inch guns: 'In my opinion this is the armament of the future.'[15] And Fisher knew, as early as the spring of 1904, that the United States was planning to build dreadnoughts.[16] Indeed, two (the *Michigan* and *South Carolina*) were authorized by Congress early in 1905, though not completed until 1909. This being the general situation, it was, in the Admiral's view, imperative for Britain to get the jump, particularly as the Germans were building warships in about the same time as the English.

He knew that the all-big-gun battleship was inevitable because of technological, strategical, and tactical considerations—above all, the development of long-range firing. 'It was,' as Bacon has asserted, 'the advent of long-range shooting, and not the *Dreadnought* herself, which made all existing ships obsolete.' Specifically, the dreadnought type had its origin in these considerations:

[15] Fritz Uplegger, *Die Englische Flottenpolitik vor dem Weltkrieg, 1904–1909* (Stuttgart, 1930), p. 39.
[16] See *The Anatomy of British Sea Power*, pp. 540–3.

(1) The menace of the torpedo to the battle fleet, with its increasing range and accuracy, made imperative longer ranges in action.

(2) A longer battle range was desirable because (a) when coupled with speed, it enabled the battle fleet to choose its range. (b) The Navy had to adopt the longest battle range then feasible, otherwise an enemy skilled in long-range shooting could disable the British ships before they were able to inflict much damage. (c) Gunnery skill could be used to best advantage. Close ranges levelled individuality of marksmanship and were therefore to the advantage of the least-trained gun's crews.

(3) Long-range hitting had become practicable since 1900 with the introduction of satisfactory range-finding instruments.

(4) Individual shells never travel quite equal distances, owing to slight differences in gun borings or in the quality or quantity of the powder. Isolated shots at, say, 5,000 yards, consequently were of little help to the observer. The only known method of ensuring accuracy in long-range firing was (thanks to Percy Scott's work as Captain of H.M.S. *Excellent*) the spotting system of fire control. This meant firing salvoes instead of single rounds, a large group of splashes being easy to observe. When these splashes straddled the target, the exact range had been obtained.

(5) With regard to spotting, Admiral Bacon has explained, 'at long ranges, the differences in "time of flight" and "fall of shot" of two or more patterns of projectiles led to confusion.' Only by firing salvoes with several big guns of the same calibre could there be one kind of splash to show where the shots were falling. This pointed to a uniform heavy-gun armament of eight or more guns.

(6) There would be no closing to a range close enough to allow 6-inch guns (the standard secondary armament) to be used with effect. Therefore, it would be better to use all the available gun weight for the heaviest guns. The 'heaviest gun' was the 12-inch, but Fisher at first was undecided between a main armament of sixteen 10-inch or eight 12-inch guns. The 10-inch was nearly as powerful as the 12-inch, and a battleship could mount more of them. In the end, apparently in October 1904, Fisher favoured the 12-inch armament. The control of fire was thought to be much more efficient in this design with the smaller number of turrets; and the Russo-Japanese War, in the words of Lord Selborne,

'proves the resisting power of ships is greater than was supposed, and that only the hardest knocks count.'[17]

(7) The enormous destructive power of one 12-inch gun, as against a quantity of 6-inch shells. The smashing effect of 12-inch shell on thick armour plate lent it a special power beyond the cumulative effect of smaller shell.

(8) The 12-inch gun was also the most accurate at long ranges: at such ranges the larger the calibre, in guns of an equally advanced pattern, the greater was the probability of hitting, due to the flatter trajectory of the projectile.

(9) Higher speed was a tactical asset in modern warfare. 'Speed is armour' was a favourite Fisher slogan. The fast ship could choose the range and bring her full battery to bear on her enemy, whereas her slow enemy could fight only part of her battery. The *Dreadnought* marked the consummation of a tactical idea which reached maturity when Sir Arthur Wilson, the outstanding tactician of the day, employed it in the 1901 manœuvres, and was proved sound beyond doubt by Togo at Tsushima. It consisted of broadside firing in line-ahead, making use of superior speed and manœuvring capacity to concentrate on a part of the enemy's line. It was Fisher's belief that the Japanese naval successes in the Russian War 'were greatly assisted by, if indeed not solely due' to, greater speed.[18]

The essentials of the *Dreadnought* design were firmly fixed in Fisher's mind by October 1904, and the final design was drawn up in March 1905, following the report of the advisory Committee on Designs. That is, the big decision had been reached before all the naval lessons of the war in the Far East were known in Whitehall. But the Naval Attachés' reports were decisive in converting the Board and, afterwards, in confirming it in the wisdom of the new design. Practically all the engagements by the rival fleets were at long ranges, at which guns of high calibre had been more effective than medium-sized weapons capable of higher rates of

[17] *Naval Necessities*, i. 41–5, 98. *Naval Necessities* are three privately printed volumes containing papers written or collected by Fisher as C.-in-C. at Portsmouth and as First Sea Lord, bearing on the reforms which he introduced or contemplated, 1904–6. Fisher's *Records*, pp. 127–55, gives extensive sections, and Bacon's *Fisher*, i. 284–304, is based on *Naval Necessities*. The last two chapters of the writer's *The Anatomy of British Sea Power* have made full use of the original volumes (now in the Admiralty Library), which have the First Lord's minutes.

[18] *Ibid.*, iii. 236.

fire. The first important dispatch from the Naval Attaché in Japan was dated 28 February 1904 and was read by the Board in late May–early June. What stood out clearly in Captain Troubridge's mind was the immense importance of long-range firing in the actions off Port Arthur and Chemulpo in February. The Admiralty was greatly impressed by the eye-witness report of the new Attaché, Captain Pakenham, on the action of 10 August 1904 in the Gulf of Pechili. (It was studied by the Board in mid-October.) It appeared from this report that the fire effect of the Japanese 12-inch guns was so superior to that of their 10-inch guns that shots from the latter passed unnoticed, 'while, for all the respect they instil, 8-inch or 6-inch guns might just as well be "pea-shooters" . . .' In a dispatch of 1 January 1905 (received at the Admiralty 28 February), the Attaché asserted that the whole conduct and fate of the naval operations in the war had revolved about the 12-inch gun. 'Medium artillery has had its day . . .' Pakenham's report on Tsushima further proved the superiority of long-range firing and heavy guns. It arrived just before the *Dreadnought* was laid down.[19]

There were weighty technical objections to the *Dreadnought* and her successors. The lead was taken by able officers of large experience like Admirals Sir Cyprian Bridge and Reginald Custance, and Admiral of the Fleet Sir Gerard Noel. They received support from the hard-hitting writings of Mahan and Sir William White.[20] The principal technical objections were these, although not all the critics accepted them all:

(1) The *Dreadnought* sacrificed armament to gain speed. Following their powerful ally Mahan, the critics held that speed was of secondary importance to fighting power. Superior speed might not always be of strategical value, and it was an overrated tactical asset. A writer in *Blackwood's Magazine* summed up the argument in these words: 'Battles are the supreme test of the capital ship. They are decided by superior tactics and fighting power. Superior speed confers little, if any, tactical advantage. Fighting power depends upon its *offensive* rather than on its defensive form—upon

---

[19] For the Attachés' reports, see *The Anatomy of British Sea Power*, pp. 530–2.

[20] Mahan's 'Reflections, Historic and Other, Suggested by the Battle of the Japan Sea', *United States Naval Institute Proceedings*, June 1906, was almost the Bible of the anti-dreadnought forces in both countries, although White's 'The Cult of the Monster Warship', *Nineteenth Century*, June 1908, was perhaps the best all-round critique of the dreadnought policy.

weapons rather than on protection. Speed is not a weapon, and does not give protection, except in running away. The aim should therefore be to endow a fleet not with superior speed or protection, but with superior offensive power—*i.e.*, gun power.'[21]

Fisher and those around him saw the matter in a different light. Mahan's authority was brushed aside: however eminent a naval historian, he had no special competence as an authority on tactics or modern construction. The strategic advantages of superior speed were declared to be obvious. It enabled the fleet possessing it to concentrate at any desired spot as quickly as possible, or to overhaul a fleeing squadron. The tactical advantages of superior speed were equally apparent. 'It enables you to force or to decline an action, once in touch with the enemy. It gives you the choice of range at which the action is to be fought, and the power of maintaining that range. With superior speed you can envelop the enemy's line, and you can keep out of range of his torpedoes.'[22] Nor had the speed of the *Dreadnought* been obtained at the expense of offensive qualities. There could be no argument over the superiority of her armament to that of any other vessels afloat. This was the Admiralty position. To the argument of the critics that high speed was the weapon of the weaker fleet, the only advantage conferred being the ability to refuse an action by running away, Fisher cited, in a 1906 paper for the use of the Board, two 'convincing' cases from the Russo-Japanese War showing the fallacy of the argument and how the Japanese successes were greatly assisted by, if not solely due to, a command of speed. One of the cases was the Battle of Tsushima in May 1905. At the start of the battle, Togo held a commanding position and was able to concentrate fire on the head of the Russian line. 'Had they not possessed superior speed, the Japanese would rapidly have lost this advantage, as the Russians turned away to starboard and compelled the Japanese to move along a circle of larger radius; their greater speed enabled the Japanese to maintain their advantage and so continue the concentration of fire on the Russian van until so much damage had been inflicted that the Russians lost all order and were crushed.'

It is worth pointing out, as Fisher often did in Admiralty papers,

[21] 'Lessons from the Battle of Tsu Sima', Feb. 1906.
[22] Admiralty memorandum, 'The Modern Battleship', Oct. 1906; Lennoxlove MSS.

that the desire for superior speed was no new thing, as was implied by many of the opponents of the dreadnought type. The question of speed had always been a prime consideration in England's wars with the great defensive sea powers. The speed of Britisn battleships had steadily risen in the iron-clad era, owing to the desire to keep ahead of foreign nations. The speed of British, French, and German pre-dreadnoughts had increased in twenty years by approximately $2\frac{1}{2}$, 3, and 4 knots, respectively (to about 18 knots). The speed given to British dreadnoughts was therefore only a continuation of long-established policy. If the value of superior speed could be shown, the 21 knots of the early British dreadnoughts, which did not give much margin over what might be achieved in foreign battleships, could not be described as excessive.

(2) Protection was sacrificed in order to increase speed and gun power—a criticism heard more often during and after World War I in the light of combat experience. The Admiralty could, in rebuttal, point to the fact that the *Dreadnought* was as heavily armoured as any British pre-dreadnoughts, excepting only the two 'Lord Nelsons'. All her vitals were believed to be amply protected. In addition, there had been provided a system of underwater armour protection against the effects of a mine or torpedo explosion. The *Dreadnought* was the first vessel to be so protected. Still, it is a fact that the dreadnoughts sacrificed something in the way of protection. 'Hitting is the thing, not armour,' asserted Fisher. It is only fair, however, to point out that in the pre-war years critics generally emulated Fisher in underestimating the importance of protection in capital ships. Custance, for instance, suggested that an insane craze for protection had more or less spoiled every battleship design for more than fifty years. In effect, Custance agreed with Farragut, who had said, 'The best possible protection is that of the fire of one's own guns.'

(3) A greater number of smaller battleships was preferable to a fleet of dreadnoughts. Britain was forcing the game against herself, it was charged; the larger the battleships, the fewer that could be built, so making difficult the provision of the number of ships required for the protection of the Empire; and the loss of single vessels, through accident or in action, would make a dangerous difference to the strength of the Fleet. In short, as Sir William White put it, the Admiralty was placing all its 'naval eggs into one

or two vast, costly, majestic, but vulnerable baskets.' Moreover, it was commonly alleged that a large number of somewhat smaller ships could deliver the more deadly and searching fire while presenting the lesser target. Custance was the principal proponent of a greater number of smaller battleships. Again, it was urged that larger ships meant heavy expenditure in dry docks, basins, and harbours.

The Admiralty retort was that if the number of battleships were doubled, the chances of accidental loss would also be doubled, and that the more powerful the ship in comparison to her opponents, the less likely was she to be sunk or captured in action. Also,

> Such an armament as the Dreadnought carries could not be mounted in a smaller ship, so as to obtain even a moderate coefficient of all-round fire value. The length of modern artillery, the tremendous blast, and the necessity for mutual non-interference are all factors which must be taken into consideration, and a modern barbette cannot be placed just anywhere it happens to fit in. A smaller ship than the *Dreadnought* must have fewer guns, and any economy in building a larger number of hulls to carry the same number of heavy guns into battle is problematical. . . . Another overwhelming argument against mounting the same number of guns in a larger number of smaller ships is that your line of battle is thus unduly prolonged. The tactical difficulties of the admiral are thereby greatly multiplied . . .[23]

We might add that the movement towards greater size had been in progress everywhere for a quarter of a century, and it was practically impossible to reverse the process. The whole spirit of the naval constructor, like that of all scientists, was to produce something better. During White's tenure as D.N.C. (1885–1902) displacement of British first-class battleships had risen by more than 54 per cent (10,000-plus tons to over 16,000 tons). Before the 17,900-ton *Dreadnought* (an increase of 1,500 tons over her immediate predecessors) was laid down, the Japanese had begun to build a ship of 19,000 tons.

More to the point was this Admiralty argument: 'For the increase of 1,500 tons of displacement over the "Lord Nelson" class we have obtained a much more powerful armament, a nearly equal main protection, a vastly superior secondary protection, and a greatly increased sea-keeping power. . . . It appears certain, therefore, that the fullest use has been made of the additional

[23] Admiralty memorandum, 'The Modern Battleship', Oct. 1906.

displacement. [And] this displacement admits of the great advantage of three knots extra speed . . .'[24]

And here is the gem-like retort to the dry-dock argument: 'Apart from the fact that this applies with far greater force to all foreign nations than to ourselves, it should be clearly borne in mind that the docks and harbours exist for our ships, not the ships for the docks. If the necessity for larger ships be shown, the other expenditure which they entail must be faced, for otherwise, if we continue to build ships only because they will go into the existing docks, we shall not require any docks at all—in the day of action our ships will all go to the bottom !'[25]

(4) The technical criticism heard most often was that there was no justification for the elimination of secondary armaments; a proportion of 6-inch guns and rapid-firing guns of small calibre should be retained. A few of the critics of the dreadnought armament—they included Tweedmouth—preferred the 9·2-inch gun for the secondary armament, as in the 'Lord Nelsons'. But most of them favoured the 6-inch gun. Much was made of the claim that Tsushima had been won by the Japanese with the rapid hitting of their 6-inch guns rather than with their heavy guns, and that their wartime experience had led the Russian and Japanese naval authorities to continue the use of secondary armaments. Japan's new battleships, laid down in May 1905, carried mixed armaments of heavy, medium, and light guns; her next battleships, laid down in 1909, carried a uniform armament of big guns, but still mounted a secondary battery of 6-inch weapons. At Tsushima the Japanese had closed to short range to force a quick decision. 'It was the endless stream of six-inch shell that demoralized the Russians at Tsushima—the 12-inch finished them.'[26] It was argued that the 6-inch gun was more accurate than the 12-inch, even at long ranges, and made a greater percentage of hits to rounds fired. Volume of fire—that is to say, a great number of effective blows from projectiles of less size and power—was, on the whole, more likely to secure victory than the more impressive but less numerous impacts and explosions of projectiles from a few

[24] Admiralty memorandum, 'Admiralty Policy in Battleship Design', late 1906; Lennoxlove MSS.

[25] Admiralty memorandum, 'The Modern Battleship', Oct. 1906. This section was probably written by Fisher himself.

[26] Admiral Sir Hedworth Lambton (C.-in-C., China) to McKenna, 24 July 1908; McKenna MSS.

heavy guns. Moreover, the decisive range was likely to be much less than assumed by the advocates of very heavy guns. Thus, if the struggle came in the North Sea, there was little prospect of clear weather nine days out of ten, hence the impossibility of making effective hits at extremely long ranges. (This was a point on which Balfour always felt anxious.) And was it wise to concentrate attention on armour perforation, as was done by the advocates of big-gun armaments? Every modern warship, including the dreadnought type, was highly vulnerable over large areas of the sides, and many vital parts of the armament lay open to effective attack by 6-inch guns. Also, a certain number of rapid-firing guns of very small calibre would be useful auxiliaries in repelling torpedo attacks. The Royal Navy alone had eliminated this type of armament. For example, the contemporary German dreadnoughts and battle cruisers mounted 5·9-inch guns.

The Admiralty disposed of the Tsushima argument in this fashion. Against the poorly trained and demoralized Russians the Japanese had been able to close in and pour in shell after shell with little interference. They thereby acquired a false impression of the real possibilities of short-range action against a formidable enemy. Even more importantly, 'in quoting the Battle of Tsushima, it should be remembered that neither fleet possessed any knowledge of long-range hitting. Control of fire, which alone makes long-range hitting possible, was not adopted by the Japanese until two years after the war [after Japanese observers had attended the British battle practice of 1906]. Hence the range at Tsushima and the gunnery deductions drawn are unreliable.'[27]

As regards the larger matters raised under (4), above, it was, as Admiral Bacon remarked later, a tragic fact about the situation that the country could not be told the whole truth. To the Board it was 'obviously undesirable' to make public in any detail the motives which underlay its building policy. To do so would give foreign rivals the whole of the benefit of the British experience. Thus, it was felt inadvisable to publish the most telling arguments in support of the *Dreadnought* design (and the battle cruiser *Invincible*), since it was based on the results of the long-range battle practice carried out by the Fleet and on the conclusions drawn from the Japanese fleet actions, which the Admiralty was bound

[27] Fisher's commentary on Sir George Clarke's memorandum of Sept. 1907 on 'The Effectiveness of Naval Fire'; Lennoxlove MSS.

to treat very confidentiälly. The results, never made public, obtained by the Fleet in 1905 were significant. At a range of a little under 6,000 yards, in ten minutes (1) compared with two 6-inch guns, two 12-inch guns scored hits with five times the weight of projectiles, 3·3 more than two 9·2-inch guns; (2) the percentage of hits to rounds fired showed the greater accuracy of the heavy gun: 12-inch, 37 per cent, 9·2-inch, 25 per cent, 6-inch, 15 per cent; (3) the comparative effect of shell bursting inside a ship was all in favour of the 12-inch gun, 70 to 1.[28] Besides, it was believed that the original advantage of the secondary battery of 6-inch guns, viz., to penetrate the unarmoured ends or weakly protected gun positions, fell to the ground in the modern ship, where the waterline, guns, and men were so well protected.

The record of the *Dreadnought* in battle practice confirmed the value of an all-big-gun armament. At a range of 8,000 yards in the 1907 battle practice, her first, the ship scored 25 hits in 40 rounds, which placed her as the third ship in the Fleet. But 'the real test of fighting capacity is weight of shell thrown in on the enemy', and here the *Dreadnought* showed 21,250 pounds of shell thrown in eight minutes, which was 75 per cent more weight of shell thrown on to the target than any other battleship.[29] The Battle Practice Return of 1909 showed that the all-12-inch ships got in practically every instance a larger total number of hits than did the mixed armament ships. In reporting these facts to McKenna, Fisher added: 'If the "shower of hits" from the small calibre guns does not materialize in peace, it is not likely that it will be there under war conditions!'[30]

One important concession was made to the critics. So long as a torpedo craft had to come within a range of a few thousand feet of her prey before she could hope to discharge her torpedo with any reasonable prospect of success, it might be safe to rely on 12-pounders to stop her in time. But when the range of the torpedo rapidly grew to 7,000 yards, and destroyers became larger, it

[28] D.N.O. (Jellicoe) memorandum, 24 May 1906; Admiralty MSS. His successor's Assistant, Commander F. C. Dreyer, changed the 12-inch : 9.2-inch figure to nearly 5 to 1; Dreyer's memorandum, 'The One Calibre Big Gun Armament for Ships', Feb. 1908, quoted in Peter M. Stanford, *Corbett's Work with Fisher at the Admiralty, 1904–1910* (unpublished).
[29] 'Report by Director of Naval Ordnance [Bacon] on Battle Practice', 19 Dec. 1907; Lennoxlove MSS.
[30] Fisher to McKenna, 20 Oct. 1909; McKenna MSS.

manifestly became necessary to employ a much heavier armament to stop these craft in time. It was known also that German tactics called for attacking an enemy fleet with flotillas. This would force the Fleet to use its big guns to repel the flotilla attacks, and this would relieve pressure on the German capital ships. Hence all dreadnoughts built subsequently to the original *Dreadnought* were furnished with an anti-torpedo armament of 4-inch guns. Finally, after some thirty dreadnoughts had been built, the Admiralty came back to the 6-inch battery in the 'Iron Duke' class (1911–12 programme). This was after Fisher had left Whitehall and was done over his vehement objections to this 'retrogression'.

Two myths should be dispelled. One is that the *Dreadnought* was designed to act as a deterrent to Germany's naval ambitions by forcing Germany to widen and deepen the Kiel Canal before a ship of the displacement of a dreadnought could pass through its locks.[31] This had the double advantage to England of being a great expense to Germany and of ensuring that years would pass (the summer of 1914) before Germany's dreadnought fleet could be effective—that is, before dreadnoughts could be passed through the Canal to and from the Baltic. Fisher did see these advantages later; he exulted that Germany had been 'paralysed' by the *Dreadnought*, by which he meant that the *Dreadnought* had suspended German (indeed, all foreign) battleship construction for a year and a half and had converted the Kiel Canal into a useless ditch. But there is not a scrap of evidence that this was a factor in the actual designing of the *Dreadnought*. The considerations throughout were purely technological and strategical, fortified by the lessons of the Russo-Japanese War and by the knowledge that other powers were contemplating the introduction of the type.

The other myth is that the *Dreadnought* was entirely the product of Fisher's megalomania and that he imposed it on his colleagues on the Board. The fact is that on technological questions, whatever his leanings might be, Fisher kept an open mind and sought assistance. Thus, in working out the fundamental ideas of the *Dreadnought* at Portsmouth, 1903–4 (when he was Commander-in-Chief there), he had the assistance of the best technical advice: William H. Gard, the Chief Constructor at Portsmouth dockyard, Alexander Gracie, Managing Director of the Fairfield Shipbuilding

[31] See, e.g., Grand-Admiral Alfred von Tirpitz, *My Memoirs* (London, 1919, 2 vols.), i. 201.

and Engineering Company, and various naval officers. The sketch design was ready when Fisher returned to the Admiralty. The only problem seemed to be that of the details of the design. He had the First Lord appoint (22 December 1904) an advisory Committee on Designs, composed of seven civilian experts and seven naval officers, under Fisher's chairmanship, to assist the Admiralty in the selection of the final design. This procedure had two objects: to cut the ground from under the feet of the anticipated opposition, and to get advice on certain questions. To be sure, Bacon, Naval Assistant to Fisher and a member of the Committee, has written that the Committee decided, with one modification, on 'the main design, which it was intended that they should adopt.'[32] But the Committee was a good deal more than a blind. It was given access to official sources of information and, as was common knowledge, consulted with the two principal commanders afloat, Admirals Sir Arthur Wilson and Lord Charles Beresford, then commanding the Home and Channel Fleets, respectively.

The Committee sat between 3 January and 22 February 1905, and reported to the Admiralty in March. Several alternative designs were placed before the Committee, differing mainly in the distribution of the big guns. In the end it decided on a uniform armament of ten 12-inch guns mounted in pairs, so disposed that six could be fired ahead or astern and eight on either broadside. (Since the pre-*Dreadnought* battleships could fire but two 12-inch guns ahead and four on a broadside, the *Dreadnought* was equal to three battleships in firing ahead and to two in broadside firing. In this fact was contained the most revolutionary aspect of the design.) But the important thing is that the design of the *Dreadnought* represented, in the words of Professor J. H. Biles, a member of the Committee, 'the deliberate judgment of the Board of Admiralty, the technical skill of the Present Director of Naval Construction [Philip Watts], and the unanimous advice of the representative Committee on Designs.'[33] Sir William White's public statement in 1889, when the design of the 'Royal Sovereigns' had provoked heated controversy, might well have been repeated by Watts or a Board spokesman: 'The matter, therefore, resolves itself into one of relative authority and experimental information.

[32] Bacon, *From 1900 Onward*, p. 95.
[33] Biles's letter in *The Times*, 23 July 1908.

Under these circumstances, the naval service and the country will probably prefer to accept the conclusions of a responsible and well-informed body like the Board of Admiralty rather than those of any individual.'

In deliberately nullifying Britain's advantage at the height of her battleship predominance by commencing the construction of all-big-gun battleships, Fisher ushered in a new era in naval competition by giving the Germans a chance to start nearly from scratch. Was the dreadnought policy Fisher's greatest blunder, or was it a stroke of genius? The writer feels that it was the latter, an opinion shared by Admiral Sir William James and the late Admiral of the Fleet Sir Osmond de B. Brock and Admiral Sir Frederic Dreyer[34] among many other distinguished officers of recent times. The dreadnought type was on the naval horizon in 1904–5, and therefore it was, as Fisher realized, imperative to gain for England the advantage of leading the way. The strongest justification for his policy is the fact that the dreadnought type was accepted by all the great naval powers. That is, the sincerest flattery was paid to the Admiralty by the imitation of the world. *The Observer* dryly remarked (21 June 1908): 'When Sir William White suggests that both the United States and Germany are foolish and deluded powers slavishly copying the errors of a blind Board in Whitehall, he surely takes up the position of the dissenting juryman who had never met eleven such obstinate fellows in his life.'

The technical criticisms of the battle cruiser followed the same general lines as in the case of the dreadnought. There was also some doubt that the battle cruiser had any likely belligerent utility. Thus, as regards her scouting function, an inferior vessel could do the job equally well, for the enemy could drive off any observing craft it was determined to get rid of. If necessary, he would use battleships of superior force to drive off a battle cruiser. There were criticisms in World War I and afterwards that Fisher's designs, especially the battle cruiser, failed to meet the test of battle. It must be realized, in the first place, that he had no active part in the preparation of the later pre-war ship designs. He was responsible for the conception of the dreadnought and battle

[34] James, *The Sky Was Always Blue* (London, 1951), pp. 53–5; Admiral Brock's letter to the writer, 13 Mar. 1946; Admiral Sir Frederic Dreyer, *The Sea Heritage: a Study of Maritime Warfare* (London, 1955), pp. 37–8.

cruiser types and shared in the preparation of the first designs. Thereafter, the evolution of the designs of the big ships as well as of the smaller craft was primarily the work of the Third Sea Lord (Controller) and his department. The British dreadnoughts, though lacking the solid protection given German dreadnoughts by Tirpitz, met the test of battle at Jutland, their only major test in World War I. And despite criticism that the battle cruisers did not fare well because armour had been sacrificed to speed, they proved their worth at the Falklands and elsewhere. But for the defective magazine arrangements and the role played by the British battle cruisers at Jutland, two units would not have been lost. In the opening encounter preliminary to the battle-fleet action, they were not used as scouts for the Battle Fleet, which was their primary duty. Instead they concentrated on long-range action with the German battle cruisers, something for which Fisher, at least, had never intended them. Whether Beatty was justified in so using them is another matter and will be considered in the wartime volume.

As this chapter has shown. Fisher met with resistance to his major reforms from the very start. During the first two years the opposition did not ruffle him too much. While at times he could be maddened to the point where, as on 12 May 1905, he 'wished to God I could bite them! I will if I get a chance!', his usual mood was expressed by the hope (28 May 1905) that 'attacks "fizzle" out if let alone', and by his reference in a July 1906 memorandum to the 'insignificant agitation' over the reforms. The German Naval Attaché reported that even 'his opponents recognize his efficiency and think of him as the right man in his place'.[35]

The turning-point came in the summer and autumn of 1906. It began with the announcement on 27 July 1906 of a reduced building programme. The agitation over this was a mere zephyr compared to the storm that burst at the end of October.

[35] Coerper to Tirpitz, 25 Jan. 1905; German Ministry of Marine MSS.

V

Dissension in the Navy: The Fisher–Beresford Feud

The first duty to the Service we owe is obedience, and it would not be correct for an officer on full pay to go cruising about the country finding fault with those in authority.

BERESFORD at the London Chamber of Commerce, 20 July 1893.

We must remember that all reforms are opposed, generally by those who are too old, or whose brains are not receptive enough to perceive that 1903 may require different administrations and systems to 1803. . . . A reformer's life is only to be compared to that of an early Christian, and both, perhaps, receive the honour and respect due to them a trifle late.

BERESFORD to Fisher, April 1903.

The quarrel was caused by the clash of two strong wills, two dominant personalities, both working, though in different directions, for what they considered was best for the Navy and the country.

TAPRELL DORLING, *Men o' War.*

I. THE NEW HOME FLEET

IN OCTOBER 1906 the Admiralty issued a memorandum that marked the evolution of a new Home Fleet. It was a logical development of the policy of concentration at home which had been initiated in December 1904. '. . . our only potential foe now being Germany, the common-sense conclusion is that the outlying Fleets no longer require to be maintained at the strength which was admittedly necessary a year ago when France and Russia were our most probable opponents . . .'[1] As matters then stood, the effective reserve vessels were in three independent divisions under the three Commanders-in-Chief of the home ports, who had only a peace supervision over them. Responsibility for them in war belonged to the C.-in-C., Channel. Now, in the autumn of 1906, when the Admiralty was confident that the nucleus-crew system had successfully passed out of the experimental stage, it was decided to combine the three divisions into one fleet, the Home

[1] Admiralty memorandum, 'The Home Fleet', Dec. 1906; Admiralty MSS.

Fleet, under the orders of a single commander-in-chief. He would periodically train and exercise the divisions as a fleet, though they remained attached to their respective ports. The object was to increase the efficiency of the nucleus-crew divisions, since in the absence of the Channel Fleet on its periodical cruises the first brunt of any surprise attack might have to be borne by this new fleet. To enable its commander-in-chief to act effectively in such a crisis, he was given a fully manned division, the Nore Division, based on Sheerness, with six of the thirteen battleships composing the Home Fleet. It was to be sent to sea frequently and was to be ready for instant action at all times. It was formed by withdrawing two battleships from each of the three main sea-going fleets (Channel, Atlantic, Mediterranean). The other two divisions of the new Home Fleet, stationed at Devonport and Portsmouth, represented in a more efficient form the corresponding divisions of the former Fleet Reserve. With at least three-fifths (instead of the former two-fifths) complements it was hoped that every ship would be able to carry out practically all the exercises expected from fully manned ships, and this hope was fulfilled. Actually, these nucleus-crew ships would need no more than a few hours to enable them to put to sea in an equal state of efficiency with the Nore Division. The Atlantic and Home Fleets would come under the orders of the C.-in-C., Channel Fleet, periodically for combined manœuvres and exercises. The general situation was this: the Channel Fleet, strongest of British fleets, had its base at Portland, with two fighting wings thrown out, as it were, to cover the exposed flanks, one at the Nore and the other (Atlantic Fleet) at Berehaven.

The din of protest in the Conservative press and among Conservative politicians was ear-shattering. The Government and Sea Lords had 'betrayed' the nation; the Government was 'sacrificing the security of the Empire to the exigencies of party politics'. It was suggested by many of the critics that the sole purpose of the organization of the Home Fleet was to effect a saving in money. Even so good a friend of the Admiral's as the King's Secretary, Lord Knollys, thought he was going too far. 'He is as clever as a monkey and has persuaded the King that his nucleus [-crew] Fleet will be as efficient in every way as if it were afloat! To my mind this contention is contrary to common sense . . .'[2]

[2] Knollys to Esher, 23 Oct. 1906; Esher MSS.

The specific criticism was of the Admiralty substitution of the ideal of a 'practically ready' fleet—that is, an 'unready fleet', in the view of the critics—for that of a fleet instantly ready for war, because (1) the Home Fleet was not under the immediate and direct command of the Channel C.-in-C., though it would be so in war; (2) the new organization violated one of the first principles of war—that of the concentration of strength in the vital area; (3) a large proportion of the Home Fleet vessels had only nucleus crews on board; (4) the Home Fleet was not being trained to act as a fleet either by itself or with the Channel Fleet; (5) to form the Home Fleet, the main British fleet, the Channel Fleet, had been greatly weakened. The German Fleet, an 'instantly ready fleet', was declared to be in a position to overcome the Nore Division, in case of a sudden declaration of hostilities followed by immediate action, before the Channel Fleet could arrive upon the scene.

The proposal made by many of the critics to undo the damage was the combination of the Channel and Home Fleets. The former lacked torpedo craft and was ill-supplied with cruisers; the latter was too weak in battleships to practise tactics on the scale required in modern war. Moreover, both fleets should be trained continuously together. Again, the principle of concentration would be complied with and the training of the fleet for war would be immensely improved.

The opposition had powerful support in the Foreign Office, which viewed the Fleet redistribution with alarm, even after receiving Fisher's prints on the subject.

It is perfectly childish to expect sane people to believe that ships with nucleus crews lying in home ports can be regarded as efficient items in a fleet, and he [Fisher] has failed to prove that the reductions in our fleets in commission have not reduced our fighting strength. Also it can hardly be denied that the ships available for police duties abroad will be considerably reduced and British interests and policy will suffer for the sake of concentration in the Channel against a possible attack by Germany which even Fisher regards as a very remote eventuality. The only explanation of the scheme is economy and Fisher's desire to truckle to the Liberal party.[3]

Fisher was not without his defenders against what they deemed the absurd and ignorant attacks upon the Home Fleet. His

[3] Hardinge to Knollys, 23 Oct. 1906; Windsor MSS.

supporters believed the Admiralty was practising economy with efficiency, and that the two principles were good bedfellows. But the crucial point in the Admiralty case could not be made public. The underlying idea was to concentrate the strength of the Navy in home waters, and to go about it 'unostentatiously and by slow degrees, for fear of exciting the attention of the German Admiralty.'[4] Fisher deliberately had the dreadnoughts, as completed, quietly sent to the Nore, saying they could not manœuvre with the older ships. In this way, quietly and (it was hoped) without arousing German susceptibilities, a powerful fleet of the best and fastest ships was concentrated in the North Sea—that is, on the probable battleground. Had Fisher been open about it and attached the recalled ships and the dreadnoughts as completed to the Channel Fleet, which was recognized as Britain's first fighting line in home waters, and transferred that Fleet from its base at Portland to the North Sea, the Germans would undoubtedly have interpreted it as a menace and increased their naval strength. This, at any rate, was the reasoning of the Admiralty. There was also this consideration:

Our only probable enemy is Germany. Germany keeps her *whole* Fleet always concentrated within a few hours of England. We must therefore keep a Fleet twice as powerful concentrated within a few hours of Germany. If we kept the Channel and Atlantic Fleets *always* in the English Channel (say in the vicinity of the Nore), this would meet the case, but this is neither feasible nor expedient, and if, when relations with foreign powers are strained, the Admiralty attempt to take the proper fighting precautions and move our Channel and Atlantic Fleets to their proper fighting position, then *at once* the Foreign Office and the Government veto it, and say such a step will precipitate war![5]

The Admiralty was in this instance happy to use the authority of Mahan, who had expressed the opinion that it was not practicable to keep a large navy fully manned in peace—manned to the requirements of war. 'The place of a reserve in a system of preparation for war must be admitted because inevitable.' This salient truth was recognized in all the fleets of the world, and the Home Fleet was the Admiralty's solution of the problem of

[4] Fisher, *Memories* (London, 1919), p. 246. The point was made at the time in such unpublished Admiralty memoranda as 'The Size and Distribution of the Fleets in Commission', n.d. (probably Oct. 1906); Lennoxlove MSS.
[5] Fisher to the Prince of Wales, 23 Oct. 1906; *Fear God and Dread Nought*, ii. 103.

organizing a portion of the Navy in time of peace so as to enable it to take its place in the fighting line with the shortest delay possible. There was also an economic motive: fully to man all the vessels in the reserve would add £4,000,000 annually to the navy estimates. 'But we are already far more than strong enough as it is—why add another four millions to the Navy Estimates to keep the British Navy on a permanent war footing during a period of profound peace?'[6]

Fisher had, in the initial stage of the new redistribution, no intention that the Nore Division should oppose the whole German Fleet in any case. It was to act as an immediate reinforcement to the Channel Fleet in case of war. However, the Channel and Atlantic Fleets, which had an 'overwhelming superiority' over the German Fleet (the Channel Fleet of itself was a match for the German Fleet), were absent on many occasions, cruising or carrying out tactical operations in conjunction. During these times no fully manned ships had been present in home waters. But now the Nore Division would take the first brunt of a sudden attack, in conjunction with the nucleus-crew divisions of the Home Fleet. Actually, it was expected that the Nore Division would 'act as a deterrent to any such schemes as a sudden *coup de main* in the absence of the other squadrons . . .'[7]

Utterly ignored by the critics were the repeated statements of the Admiralty, in 1906–7, that the development of the Home Fleet must be a gradual one, that seen in 1907 it was in an embryonic stage. Its full development would not be reached until 1908–9. The Admiralty declined to indicate the nature of this further development, although later, in the 1909 inquiry, it asserted that it had always been intended that the Home Fleet should ultimately become the great fleet in home waters, absorbing the Channel Fleet. The Nore Division provided the means of doing this without attracting attention. The Home Fleet inspection on 3 August 1907 by the King, and the strategic exercise which immediately followed the dispersion of the fleet from its anchorage at Cowes, demonstrated its efficiency and appears to have allayed some of the public anxiety. In the summer of 1908 the 'Invincible' class

---

[6] Admiralty memorandum, 'The Home Fleet and Admiralty Reforms,' Jan. 1907; Lennoxlove MSS.

[7] Admiralty memorandum, 'Genesis of the Home Fleet', Feb. 1907; Admiralty MSS.

and other powerful capital ships were added to the Home Fleet. This made the Nore Division superior in itself to the whole German Fleet and fully capable of dealing with it, should the Channel and Atlantic Fleets be absent from home waters. This had been the Admiralty intention from the beginning.

The next stage in the reorganization of the fleets in home waters occurred in March 1909, subsequent to Beresford's hauling down his flag. The whole of the naval forces in home waters, excepting the Atlantic Fleet, were united in the Home Fleet and placed under the command of a single flag officer. The former Nore Division became the 1st Division of the Home Fleet; the old Channel Fleet, the 2nd Division; the nucleus-crew vessels, the 3rd Division; and the 'special reserve ships' (reduced nucleus crews), the 4th Division. As for the Atlantic Fleet, to make it more readily available to fulfil its principal function as an additional fully manned division of the main fleet in home waters, its principal anchorage was made the newly completed harbour at Dover. It worked with the Home Fleet at the request of the Home Fleet C.-in-C. The Admiralty still deemed it advisable, however, especially in view of the possible strengthening of the Austrian Fleet, to retain the Atlantic Fleet as an independent force under its own C.-in-C. It could be detached if necessary for service in the Mediterranean without any dislocation of organization and without creating international trouble. If the Atlantic Fleet were a division of the Home Fleet, its dispatch to the Mediterranean would be regarded as a serious movement of British warships. The force for the defence of home waters in the spring of 1909 consisted, then, of the Home Fleet (sixteen fully commissioned and eight nucleus-crew battleships, ten fully commissioned and ten nucleus-crew armoured cruisers, three of which were battle cruisers) and the Atlantic Fleet (six battleships, four armoured cruisers).

2. FISHER'S 'PERSONAL RULE' AND METHODS

From the start, in 1906, the malcontents seized the opportunity to attempt to discredit anew the whole policy of the Admiralty, from the new training scheme down to the dreadnought, and with such new charges as the alleged defects and unreadiness of a great number of ships of the Fleet, the inferiority to Germany in destroyers, the reduction in personnel, and the neglect to provide docking accommodations for the dreadnoughts on the east coast. With the rights and wrongs of these comparatively minor charges we cannot enter here. The 'Syndicate of Discontent' or 'Adullamites' (Fisher's pet terms) were led, in the press, by (1) most of the Conservative organs, including *Blackwood's Magazine*, the *National Review, Daily Express, Daily Mail, Globe, Morning Post, Spectator*, and *Standard*; (2) naval journalists like H. W. Wilson of the *Daily Mail* and L. Cope Cornford, Spenser Wilkinson, Military Correspondent of the *Morning Post*, and Repington, *The Times* Military Correspondent; (3) a number of senior officers, ranging from 'prehistoric fossils' of the retired Admirals C. C. Penrose FitzGerald and Sir Vesey Hamilton species to able admirals on the active list, including Lambton, Noel, Custance, and Beresford, also Sir George Clarke and respected retired admirals and high Admiralty officials like Richards, Sir Edmund Fremantle, and Sir William White; (4) in Fisher's words, 'all the armies of "blue blood" and "society",' headed by Lady Londonderry, wife of the sixth Marquess of Londonderry. Now, excepting a few, the critics did not damn all Fisher's innovations. They differed among themselves as to the merits of the reforms and innovations. 'One complains of the new scheme of naval education, but approves the distribution of the fleet and the present types of the ships. Another likes Osborne but hates dreadnoughts. A third likes both Osborne and dreadnoughts but wants a fleet double the size and reviles the policy of scrapping old vessels.'[8] But in general the critics profoundly distrusted Fisher and his works.[9]

On Fisher's side were ranged, in addition to King Edward and close and influential friends: (1) the Liberal press, which had serious reservations only about the dreadnought and the consequent intensification of the competition in naval armaments. Some of the ablest Liberal editors of modern times were in Fisher's camp, among them W. T. Stead, of the *Review of Reviews*, J. A. Spender, of the *Westminster Gazette*, and A. G. Gardiner, of the

---

[8] McKenna to Asquith, n.d. (mid-Apr. 1909); McKenna MSS.

[9] These are some of the more effective statements of the case for the opposition: articles by 'Civis' in the *Spectator*, 17, 24 Nov., 1, 8, 15, 22 Dec. 1906, 5 Jan. 1907, which were published as a little book early in 1907: *The State of the Navy in 1907*; 'Barfleur' (Custance), *Naval Policy* (London, 1907); 'Admiralty Administration and Naval Policy', *Edinburgh Review*, Jan. 1907; 'Dreadnought', 'Navy and Empire', *National Review*, July 1909; 'A Critic', 'The Case against the Admiralty', *The Times*, 2, 5, 24 Apr., 3 May, 5 June 1909.

Daily News; (2) naval journalists like John Leyland, Archibald Hurd, Gerard Fiennes, and Arnold White, and the outstanding naval historian Julian Corbett; (3) certain Conservative journals, notably *The Times, Daily Telegraph,* and *The Observer,* whose brilliant editor from 1908, J. L. Garvin, a sort of journalistic Fisher, was a particularly staunch Fisherite; (4) the two leading service journals, the *Army and Navy Gazette* and the *Naval and Military Record*; (5) a large segment of the naval profession itself, including such senior officers of repute as George King-Hall and Sir John Hopkins, although more especially the younger officers.[10] The German Naval Attaché estimated that 'in the navy corps he has as many followers as Lord Charles Beresford, although the latter likes to create the impression through the press that he is the favourite.'[11]

Much of the antagonism towards Fisher was involved in the very nature of the work which he had set himself to accomplish. A frightened service found itself being hustled out of the lethargy of a prolonged peace routine into a strenuous preparation for war which flouted practically all the accepted doctrines of the Navy. Little wonder that it gave vent to a cry of agony. It was also natural, as in St. Vincent's day, that every conservative influence should rise against Fisher. Valuing tradition and custom at too high a price, many naval officers, the majority of them on the retired list, seemed constitutionally opposed to change. What was good enough for their grandfathers was good enough for them, and any variation meant that the Navy was going to the dogs. It is a fact that no reform has ever been introduced into the Navy without opposition, both from within and from without. The degree of opposition has varied in proportion to the magnitude of the reform. There had been, for example, in the preceding generation a heated controversy over the abolition of masts and yards which had sharply divided the service.

[10] The best defences of Fisher's work as First Sea Lord include: Corbett, 'Recent Attacks on the Admiralty', *Nineteenth Century,* Feb. 1907 (Fisher's own favourite—it was 'unparalleled and immortal'); Arnold White, 'The First Sea Lord', *Daily Chronicle,* 22 Apr. 1909; Hurd, 'Progress or Reaction in the Navy', *Fortnightly Review,* Apr. 1906; J. R. Thursfield, 'The State of the Navy', *The Times,* 22, 24, 26, 30 Jan., 4, 7, 9, 12 Feb. 1907; and 'A Defence of the Admiralty, by a Correspondent', *The Times,* 12, 17 Apr., 15 May 1909.
[11] Widenmann to Admiral Georg von Müller (the Chief of the Naval Cabinet, which department operated directly under the Emperor and dealt with appointments, promotions, etc.), 8 Oct. 1907; German Ministry of Marine MSS.

However, the unrest and discontent were due as much to Fisher's alleged personal rule and to the methods he used to carry out his reforms. The former has to do with (1) Fisher's 'departure' from the traditional system of Board control, whereby the First Sea Lord had only been *primus inter pares* on the Board, to the existing 'one-man show' initiated by the redistribution of business on 20 October 1904. This redefinition of Board functions made the First Sea Lord solely responsible for 'preparation for war' and for the 'fighting and sea-going efficiency of the Fleet'. (2) The claim that the innovations had been hastily thought out and carried out with 'reckless haste' and without any attempt to win the co-operation of the service. (3) The charge that Fisher surrounded himself with 'yes-men', officers who were said to be in the 'Fishpond'. This is related to the third charge below.

As regards the second category of criticisms, Fisher's methods, it was asserted: (1) the changes had been carried out with 'public advertisement' ('drum-beating, trumpet-blowing methods of heralding the introduction of every so-called naval reform,' Fitz-Gerald declared) and through an unblushing use of the press, which were at variance with naval tradition and custom, and offensive to naval sentiment. (2) Fisher was guilty of espionage in the Fleet. (3) Treating the Navy as his pocket preserve, he was promoting his 'favourites and sycophants', while harassing all independent officers who did not belong to the Fishpond.

Let us examine these serious charges. It is true that, as First Sea Lord, Fisher was the Royal Navy and the Royal Navy was Fisher. There were not many Board meetings; the First Sea Lord as a rule dealt with each member individually. (Note, however, that the First Lord and the First Sea Lord were under no legal obligation to consult the Board collectively or Board members individually.) The policies adopted were *his* policies, and everything had to be done at once, if not sooner; he did not stand procrastination of any sort. Even his good friend Esher complained that Fisher 'has things too much his own way' and 'wants to administer *solus*. That is his danger, and his pitfall.'[12] But the strong, resolute administrator will always carry his colleagues with him, and will always be denounced as an 'autocrat' by reactionary and timorous critics. Admiralty history abounds with examples of such 'autocrats'—men who through firmness of purpose and supreme driving

[12] Esher to Knollys, n.d. (ca. early Sept. 1906) and 21 Oct. 1906; Windsor MSS.

power carry their colleagues with them and attain their objectives.

At the same time it would be a serious mistake to believe that Fisher worked out all his changes and reforms personally or with a minimum of assistance, and that he overrode everyone else. The Sea Lords were not cyphers. They *were* consulted. Jellicoe, who knew the inner workings of the Admiralty, compared Fisher very favourably in this respect with his successors. 'I most fully agree as to the 1st Sea Lords', he wrote to the Second Sea Lord in 1915. '*None* of them have collaborated sufficiently with the other Sea Lords since Fisher left in 1910. He was all right when he was originally 1st S.L., but I daresay he altered this last time. A.K.W. [Sir Arthur Wilson, First Sea Lord, 1910–11] was quite hopeless in that way.'[13] Admiral Sir Reginald Bacon, who was one of Fisher's naval assistants in 1904–5 and remained in close touch with him for years after, has left this unimpeachable testimony as to the Admiral's methods:

No man of strong views was ever so open to argument as Lord Fisher. Open to be convinced on any matter of which he had not himself accurate and technical knowledge, but adamant where prevision led him to form his own conclusions. . . . We remember battles royal and conflicts of views in which immediate decision was not required, when two sides for and against a line of action were put before him, how one day the arguments inclined him in one direction and another the reverse—how he feigned to take a side in order to sharpen the antagonistic criticism of the other, and at the last when finally convinced came his decision and then no alteration. In particular, one memory arises. When bent on a certain immediate action, argument stopped his pen until a reasoned criticism could be put on paper. All that day, fuming internally, he waited impatiently for the paper, and when it was given him he seized and devoured it, then laid it down, and said, 'All right, I see it will not do.' He was bitterly disappointed, but his judgment stayed his impetuosity. It is details such as these that, for those who knew him, dispelled the idea that he was a hasty, self-willed autocrat in all matters affecting his opinion. . . .

Lord Fisher worked largely by appointing committees to thrash out his many schemes. He has been accused of packing these committees with men of his own views. How short-sighted the carping critic can be! Lord Fisher had no desire to introduce any scheme that would fail. This would spell discredit to the originator and disadvantage to the nation. He had all views represented on committees which dealt with

[13] Jellicoe to Vice-Admiral Sir Frederick Hamilton, 25 Nov. 1915; Hamilton MSS.

the examination of a scheme from the point of view of its feasibility. In fact, we have known him delay the convening of a committee to consider a subject of which he was greatly in favour for two months to enable one officer to be a member who had written and expressed himself strongly adverse to the proposals. When, however, a scheme was once decided on, then naturally the members of the committee who were to settle the details and methods of carrying out the proposals were chosen from those in sympathy with the scheme. To have diluted such a committee with objectors could only have resulted in discords and delays.[14]

Were the reforms hastily thought out? Nothing is further from the truth. They were the results of years of thinking, and of thinking tested by experience. But were they not carried out with 'reckless haste'? This brings us to a consideration of Fisher's treatment of the profession itself. He was in a great hurry and drastic in his methods, knowing that his term of office was limited to five years. He did not realize that the ultimate success of sweeping transformations in a conservative service could be achieved only by the hearty co-operation of all concerned and by appealing to the spirit of patriotism and sense of unity of the service. He made no attempt to convert his opponents or to get them to moderate their criticism. His unbounded confidence in himself and in his judgment were only matched by his complete contempt for the abilities and (supposedly malevolent) motivations of his opponents. Besides, conversion and compromise were utterly alien to his nature. 'Never explain' and 'it is only damn fools who argue' were favourite maxims. His closest friends remonstrated with him over the perfectly idiotic way in which he insulted and alienated many of the senior officers. Esher begged him to 'be Machiavellian and play upon the delicate instrument of public opinion with your fingers and not with your feet—however tempting the latter may be.'[15] 'I am going to kick other people's shins if they kick mine!' was his reply to those who urged tact and moderation. The results were most unfortunate. Fisher inevitably made enemies—he made them right and left. 'He took them all on, and there was something about him which goaded enmity to dementia.' Out of power, he repented nothing: 'Nelson was a fighter, not an administrator and

[14] Unsigned obituary notice on Fisher in the *Transactions of the Institution of Naval Architects* (1920).

[15] Maurice V. Brett and Oliver, Viscount Esher, *Journals and Letters of Reginald, Viscount Esher* (London, 1934–8, 4 vols.), ii. 199. (Hereafter cited as *Esher*.)

a snake charmer—that's what a First Sea Lord has to be.'[16] His idea of a fighting epitaph for himself was 'Death found him fighting'—the epitaph of one of Nelson's captains.

To convert lay opinion, Fisher made extensive use of newspaper publicity. Journalists who used to go away happy if allowed to see a junior captain at the Admiralty after waiting for two hours in a draughty corridor, were now privileged visitors to the First Sea Lord's august private sanctum. There, on his own responsibility, Fisher supplied friendly naval writers with what he termed 'ammunition' to support his policies. This consisted of confidential and secret Admiralty papers, intended for the general guidance of his journalistic allies. Or such materials would be posted to them. J. A. Spender has written how the Admiral 'cultivated the Press unblushingly . . . He gave with both hands to each in turn, and we rewarded him with such an advertisement of himself and his ideas as no seaman ever received from newspapers, and probably none ever will again.'[17] Fisher went further and used a few naval writers to review and revise, and occasionally even to write, his more important papers. Corbett, whose strategical views were highly valued, was particularly so favoured. It is small wonder that the heads of many journalists were turned and that they praised all, or nearly all, actions of the Board. To be sure, most of them—Corbett, for example (who was, of course, a good deal more than a journalist)—were sincere believers in Fisher and in what he was trying to do. The only defence that can be made of the Admiral's practices is that without press support he believed his reforms stood no chance. He acted, Spender says rightly, 'from the loftiest and most patriotic of motives.' In short, the ends were good, the means rather questionable. Fisher's intimate relations with the press, a matter of general knowledge, was wholly opposed to the service tradition of the 'silent service'. It was deeply resented by many officers and others, who contemptuously referred to Fisher's 'journalistic janissaries' and questioned whether independent thinking and candid criticism could exist in such an 'unwholesome atmosphere'.

[16] Fisher, *Memories* (London, 1919), p. 105.

[17] Spender, *Life, Journalism and Politics*, ii. 67. A. M. Gollin's *The Observer and J. L. Garvin, 1908–1914: a Study in a Great Editorship* (London, 1960) contains fascinating documentation of Fisher's exploitation of the press. See, for example, pp. 68–77, which reveal Fisher's intimate relations with Garvin at the time of the 1909 Navy Scare.

Concerning the espionage charge, the facts are these. Fisher used to get his information about the various fleets, not only from official sources, but from private correspondence with certain relatively junior officers, of whom Bacon, then a captain, was one. He was an ardent Fisherite and an exceptionally gifted officer in *matériel* matters. Fisher considered him 'the cleverest officer in the Navy'. He had pioneered the submarine branch of the Navy, served on Fisher's Committee on Designs, and was shortly to become the first captain of H.M.S. *Dreadnought*. In the spring of 1906, when he was serving in the Mediterranean under Beresford, he was asked by Fisher to keep him posted on what was going on. This resulted in six or seven forceful letters to the First Sea Lord, the later famous 'Bacon Letters'. Bacon has explained that 'it was an advantage to the Navy for me to point out to Sir John the weak points in the Admiralty proposals which were being discovered by the brains of those at sea . . . not one of these [letters] contained a word of criticism of any senior or junior officer on the Station; nor, with one exception . . . did I mention any of their names.'[18] There was historical precedent for this correspondence. Lord Barham, a century earlier, had gone much further, encouraging admirals and captains to send in secret reports upon the professional capacity of their superiors. But the system of encouraging confidential reports on one's superiors was regarded as no less detestable in the Navy of the twentieth century. Rumours of the Bacon letters—of 'espionage' in the Fleet—were circulating in naval circles as early as the autumn of 1907. The real explosion came later, when Fisher, searching for material to use against Beresford, had the letters printed (without Bacon's knowledge) for circulation among selected officers. This was in dubious taste, as the letters were intended by the writer to be private. They inevitably got out—in the spring of 1909.

The charge of 'favouritism' is less valid. Before Fisher became a power, naval appointments and promotion were largely a matter of interest (family, service, or political) and seniority, and not of merit. He altered all this against the fierce opposition of mediocre senior officers who got no further employment. If Fisher

---

[18] Bacon, *From 1900 Onward*, p. 126. The exception was Commander (ret.) Carlyon Bellairs, a Liberal M.P. and leading critic of Admiralty policy in Parliament. He had 'always [been] an incompetent officer and therefore not likely really to succeed at anything' (letter of 31 Mar. 1906).

had favourites, he chose them strictly for their brains. 'Favouritism is the secret of efficiency,' he wrote in the log of the *Vernon*, by which he meant selection on the basis of merit, ability, and efficiency. Fisher had owed his own chances as a young officer to the favouritism which puts seniority on one side when there is merit lower down the ladder, and he now gave other men the same chance over the heads of their seniors, so further raising up his enemies. But he did not suffer 'fools', 'asses', and 'congenital idiots'. 'If I haul a man up over the shoulders of his seniors, that man is going to take care to show I haven't made a mistake.'

Of course the men who were pushed ahead were men in sympathy with his policies. This was particularly true of the younger men who were given key appointments at the Admiralty. But what was more natural than for a person in authority to gather round him able officers who were in sympathy with his ideas and reforms and who would work as a team? These appointments were quite unaffected by personal relationships. Fisher might have replied to criticism as had St. Vincent, when there was bitter criticism by senior admirals against his choice of Nelson for the mission that ultimately led to the Nile : 'Those who are responsible for measures must have the choice of the men to execute them.' 'Fisher's jackals' they were called by the opposition, but they were on the whole among the most capable of the captains, men of brains and experience, who were not likely to acquiesce in unsound proposals. Scott, Jellicoe, Bacon, Madden, Oliver, Richmond, and Henry Jackson were among Fisher's assistants. Through this fillip to younger men, many of them were in very responsible positions in 1914.

But did he not penalize those who opposed him? He was credited with a vindictive nature, and it is a fact that the most brutal threats were heaved at those who actively opposed his reforms. He believed in the 'three R's'—'Ruthless, Relentless, Remorseless'. 'Their wives should be widows, their children fatherless, their homes a dunghill' was a common threat, by which he meant that he would, so far as he had the power, wreck the service career of the officer in question. However, his bark was generally more dangerous than his bite. It is true that some competent and efficient men were replaced by others better disposed towards his reforms, but this was really essential if the changes were to be whole-heartedly and thoroughly carried out. Moreover, during his long administration the more important commands, afloat and ashore, were often held by men out of sympathy with his views—men who in some cases carried their opposition to the verge of mutiny.

As an example, there is the case of Admiral Sir Gerard Noel, a fine officer, though stern and hard, with a high reputation as a seaman of the old type. When C.-in-C., China, he was notified by Admiralty telegram on 6 June 1905 that his five battleships were to 'return immediately to European waters where they will be most required if complications should arise out of peace negotiations' (between Japan and Russia). Noel boldly telegraphed the First Lord direct, challenging the wisdom of the order in view of the fact that the United States had three first-class battleships on the station. The Admiralty's brusque reply was for him to carry out his orders. Noel hollered some more. The removal of all his big ships was an 'indignity to the C.-in-C.', and he tried to retain one of his battleships. A sharp telegram from Cawdor rebuked the unruly Admiral: '. . . After my previous reply I consider that orders should have been carried out without further comment and all communications on this subject should have been addressed to Admiralty for consideration of Board and not to First Lord.'[19] Despite this insubordination and Noel's open hostility to Fisher thereafter, he served as C.-in-C. at the Nore, 1907–8, and was promoted to Admiral of the Fleet in December 1908 (though Hardinge circulated the canard that 'the secret of Noel's appointment to the Nore is that Noel is a difficult person to tackle and Fisher is afraid of him!').[20]

This is not to suggest that Fisher was an angel. Even the testimony of his friends would indicate that the spirit of vengeance was not entirely absent. Thus, Prince Louis of Battenberg could write: 'He is a truly great man, and almost all his schemes have benefited the Navy. But he has started this pernicious partisanship in the Navy . . . Anyone who in any way opposed J. F. went under.'[21] Winston Churchill asserts that Fisher 'acted up' to his 'ferocious declarations. . . . To be a "Fisherite", or, as the Navy called it, to be in "the Fish pond" was during his first tenure of power an indispensable requisite for preferment.'[22] J. L. Garvin had this to

---

[19] Cawdor to Noel, 19 June 1905; Admiralty MSS.

[20] Hardinge to Knollys, 30 Oct. 1906; Windsor MSS.

[21] Battenberg to Vice-Admiral George King-Hall, 24 Feb. 1909; Admiral Mark Kerr, *Prince Louis of Battenberg, Admiral of the Fleet* (London, 1934), p. 226.

[22] Churchill, *Great Contemporaries* (rev. ed., London, 1941), p. 299.

say: 'I do not think we should exactly define him if we said he was vindictive in the ordinary, narrow, personal way. But that the spirit of vengeance was not absent from his composition during the naval controversies I think we must admit.'[23]

That Fisher was not entirely innocent is also the impression of the present writer. It is fortified by the knowledge that Sir George Clarke, who opposed the dreadnought policy and several times interfered in naval matters which were, in Fisher's view, no concern of his, was booted upstairs—from the secretaryship of the Committee of Imperial Defence to an exalted post overseas (1907). And the impression is strengthened by this detailed and authentic case history. In 1906 Lieutenant (afterwards Admiral Sir) Barry Domvile wrote the Royal United Service Institution's prize essay on the 'ideal battleship', in which he urged a stronger secondary armament in dreadnoughts. Fisher was angry, and from this time on he was hostile to Domvile. In the summer of 1907, Domvile was in the *Dreadnought* as assistant to Bartolomé, the gunnery commander. Fisher, not enamoured of Domvile serving in his pet ship after disapproving of her armament, prepared to transfer him to a ship in Lord Charles Beresford's fleet. The wily Bartolomé, informed of the First Sea Lord's intention, pointed out to him that he was sending Domvile into the enemy camp, primed with the secrets of the new undermanned ships, of which Beresford did not approve. This argument appealed to Fisher, who cancelled the appointment upon Bartolomé standing responsible for Domvile's good behaviour. The next incident occurred in December 1909, when Domvile was ordered from his Sheerness office (Home Fleet) to the Admiralty to see the First Lord, McKenna. When he arrived, he was told that his name had come up before the Board of Admiralty for promotion, but that the First Sea Lord had said that he, Domvile, was too deaf, and had arranged to have him medically examined and invalided. Admiral Bridgeman, the Second Sea Lord, had questioned this opinion and pointed out that Domvile's deafness did not interfere with his duties. McKenna, surprised to see two senior officers quarrelling over a mere worm of a lieutenant-commander, told the Board he would examine Domvile himself. He addressed Domvile back and front in varying tones. Domvile was 'having a good day' and passed the 'ordeal by ear. Then this kind little man told me that he was

[23] Garvin to Bacon, 9 Jan. 1929; Kilverstone MSS.

surprised to find how well I could hear, and that I should be promoted at the end of the year, but must keep it secret.' Fisher had one more go at Domvile in 1912, when he tried vainly to stop Hankey, Secretary of the Committee of Imperial Defence, from taking him on as his assistant. At a later date Hankey sent Domvile over to the Admiralty to see Fisher. The past was forgotten; they had a friendly interview.[24]

Two things are beyond dispute. One is that the fear of reprisal haunted those who were not in the Fishpond. Admiral H. M. Edwards remembers how, 'not being in the "Fishpond", and averse to running the risk of incurring his displeasure—in case he didn't like the cut of my jib—I took the greatest care if I spotted him in one of the Admiralty corridors of slipping down another.'[25] Also, there can be no doubt that Fisher's vendettas and manœuvres were inspired by a burning patriotism and by a passionate devotion to the Navy, his one absorbing interest. The efficiency and strength of the Navy, one ready for war at a moment's notice, was his megalomania. Personal success was of little account. He was pleased with the many honours that came his way, including a mass of British and foreign decorations and orders (which at state functions made him look, as he said, 'like a blooming Christmas tree'). But he kept two feet on *terra firma*. He could have retired from the Navy and have made his fortune by accepting a post with one of the great armament firms. But he was never to know the pleasures of a healthy bank account. Country and Navy came first. 'I have voted consistently for both sides, whichever did most for the Navy!' he told Lord Knollys.

Moreover, it could be argued that the violence with which he disrupted the old order of things was to some extent a necessity. He realized that unscrupulous toughness alone would shake the Navy out of its sail and cannon-ball mentality, and that the road to enhanced fighting efficiency and readiness for war could only be made by a wholesale sweep of all that was redundant, ineffective, and useless—'a lifelong war against limpets, parasites, and jellyfish.' No one who was a 'perfect gentleman' could have done what he did—riding roughshod over all opposition and vested

---

[24] The facts in the Domvile affair are contained in a letter of 10 Oct. 1950 to the writer from Admiral Domvile. The Admiral's authority for the *Dreadnought* incident is Bartolomé; for the second tale, McKenna; for the third, Lord Hankey.

[25] Letter to the writer, 2 June 1948.

interests in pursuit of his aim and breaking many popular figures, and in the end himself, in the course of doing so. A personality like his was needed at the time, and the Royal Navy and the British nation owe much to him.

3. FISHER AND BERESFORD

The acknowledged leader of the 'Syndicate of Discontent', though hardly the brains, was Admiral Lord Charles (afterwards first Baron) Beresford. Here was one of the most engaging personalities of the time—frank, open, dashing, impulsive, fluent. 'The weak side of his character was his love of publicity, vanity, and a certain shallowness of moral feeling. On the other hand, so far as these defects allowed, he was sincerely attached to the service, and a patriot.'[26] The officers and men under his command loved and admired 'Charlie B.' because of his charm, geniality, high spirits, humour, and his unvarying kindness and thoughtfulness. He was also amazingly popular in the country. People remembered his exploit at the bombardment of Alexandria in 1882, when he ran the gunboat *Condor* in close under the Egyptian guns at Fort Marabout, and for ninety minutes maintained a vigorous battle with the fort, mounting thirty-two guns, sixteen of which were of large size. The audacity of this attack was superb. When the *Condor* was recalled, she was cheered by the flagship and honoured with the signal, 'Well done, Condor.' Her commander was specially promoted to captain. People also remembered Beresford's battle for the Navy in the House of Commons.

His intellectual and professional attainments unfortunately did not match the attractiveness of his personality. Though a forceful speaker, he was not strong in argument and his public speeches often left a mournful impression on his listeners. Churchill once said of Beresford, in reference to his later career in the House of Commons, that before he got up to speak he did not know what he was going to say, that when he was on his feet he did not know what he was saying, and that when he sat down he did not know what he had said! J. L. Garvin once called Beresford 'the great dirigible . . . the biggest of all recorded gasbags'. And this is the appraisal of the German Naval Attaché: 'As an Irishman he has

[26] Sir W. Graham Greene's appreciation of Beresford in a memorandum of 24 Mar. 1925; Graham Greene MSS.

a strong power of imagination, is of a lively temperament, has an original humour and a gift of gab. He talks a lot, exaggerates much, and does not always adhere to the truth.'[27] On another occasion Coerper described him as 'the indefatigable twaddler'. As a naval officer, Beresford was tireless; he had a singular gift for handling men and getting the best out of them; and he excelled in the art of pure seamanship. But very definitely he was not a tactician or strategist of note. His command of the Channel Fleet was, in some respects, old-fashioned. Reminisced one of his officers: 'Never have I known such a "flagshippy" flagship. . . . Everything centred round the person of the Admiral, and ceremonial had become almost an obsession with him. . . . My principal recollection of those days is endless pipings, callings to attention, and buglings.'[28] Nevertheless, whatever his professional failings, it is only bare justice to point out that Beresford and his supporters honestly believed he would make a better First Sea Lord than Fisher.

He had been Second-in-Command under Fisher in the Mediterranean (1900–2) and in those days they had seen eye to eye on many subjects. However, various incidents (of which I note but two) resulted in bad blood. The first occurred when, following a summer cruise of the Mediterranean Fleet, Beresford's flag-captain made such a mess out of mooring the battleship *Ramillies* in Malta harbour that the entrance of the second division into the harbour was delayed. Fisher, losing his temper, signalled to his Second-in-Command: 'Your flagship is to proceed to sea and come in again in a seamanlike manner.' Admiral Chatfield is of the opinion that this signal started the whole naval feud.[29]

Bacon, on the other hand, claims that the real trouble between the two began when Fisher was promoted by special order-in-council to be an additional admiral of the fleet (4 December 1905), which gave him four or five more years on the active list in order

[27] Coerper to Tirpitz, 25 Jan. 1905; German Ministry of Marine MSS.

[28] Captain Lionel Dawson, *Gone for a Sailor* (London, 1936), pp. 131–2. Elsewhere Dawson writes: 'His was, assuredly, the "grand manner"! To hear him make a speech to the ship's company with the solemnity with which he had addressed the House of Commons and many a public gathering was really an experience. In a sonorous voice he would begin: "Ship's company of *my* flagship, *your* ship, Captain Pelly . . ." As he progressed it was interesting to watch the rapt faces of the sailors, who would have listened to him just as cheerfully had he been delivering a lecture on the binomial theorem!' Dawson, *Flotillas: a Hard-Lying Story* (London, 1933), p. 65.

[29] Chatfield, *The Navy and Defence*, p. 41.

to carry out his reforms. Lord Walter Kerr and Sir Frederick Richards, the two previous First Sea Lords, had continued in office when promoted to Admiral of the Fleet, so Fisher was hardly breaking naval custom. Beresford, according to Bacon, was so set on becoming the next First Sea Lord that he was very upset when he realized that Fisher had no intention of retiring upon reaching the age limit in January 1906.[30] This interesting theory receives support from a letter written by Lord Cawdor at that time: 'In some way he has possibly done his work at the Admiralty—and I believe done invaluable service—but (1). What would be the effect just now if he went? Would it not be considered a victory on the part of Charlie B.? and might not that have a *very* bad effect? (2). Who would we put in J. F.'s place? . . .'[31]

The incidents stressed by Chatfield and Bacon strike the writer as being at most contributory causes. The fact is that Fisher and Beresford remained on reasonably good terms until the autumn of 1906, although gradually drifting apart because of Beresford's opposition to several of Fisher's reforms. In September 1905 Fisher could complain that 'that blatant, boastful ass Beresford has been writing the most utter bosh I ever read in my life. The outcome is that the Sea Lords of the Admiralty are imbeciles and Beresford is the *one* and *only man* who knows anything!'[32] The definite break began with the navy agitation of 1906, and, more particularly, with the fleet redistribution scheme. Thereafter Beresford, prodded by the malcontents, found more and more to criticize in Fisher's reforms. The role of being 'agin' those in power came naturally to Beresford, a real Irishman and a delightful rebel always spoiling for a fight. He came into a considerable fortune at the end of 1906 when a brother died. This windfall enabled him when ashore to keep open house in Grosvenor Street and to dine and wine those of like mind freely, and thus to serve as the centre of the agitators. Fisher observed: 'Beresford says he can do more with his chef than by talking.'

A word must be said about Beresford's Second-in-Command,

[30] *From 1900 Onward*, pp. 123, 131, probably on the authority of a letter from Captain T. E. Crease (Fisher's Naval Assistant at various times), 9 July 1928; Kilverstone MSS. Crease goes so far as to attribute the 'whole Beresford business' to Lady Charles's disappointment and spite over not becoming the wife of a First Sea Lord and so cutting a big figure in London society.

[31] Cawdor to Balfour, 5 Dec. 1905; Balfour MSS.

[32] Fisher to Balfour, 12 Sept. 1905; *Fear God and Dread Nought*, iii. 27.

who egged on his chief. Custance was a very able officer, well informed and well read in the naval literature of all countries. But he had a nasty temperament devoid of generosity, and he was a doctrinaire, holding strong and outspoken views on all service matters. There may have been a personal facet in Custance's animosity towards Fisher. At least Fisher thought so. Custance 'hates me like poison because I gave him [when D.N.I.] a bit of my mind when I was Second Sea Lord and capsized his apple cart.'[33] Fisher, with what he called 'low cunning', sent Custance out to the Home Fleet as Second-in-Command, because he knew that Beresford hated him. He never foresaw that Custance, who had the cleverness of a monkey, would twist 'Charlie B.' round his little finger in a very short time. And this is what happened; hence the cause of much of the trouble between Beresford and the Admiralty. Custance plotted and pushed Beresford forward, though Beresford was never one to be backward in a fight. Sturdee, Beresford's able Chief of Staff, should have kept Beresford's head straight. Unfortunately, he would not, for he hated Fisher. We have here further illustrations of how much personality affects history, yet how little the historian can assess the effect it has in shaping events.[34]

As Channel C.-in-C., from April 1907, Beresford adopted an attitude of marked antagonism. He criticized Admiralty policy, commented on Admiralty orders, and repeatedly addressed the Admiralty on many topics in a decidedly tactless and insubordinate manner quite without parallel in British naval history. His opinions of the Admiralty and of Fisher ('our dangerous lunatic') were known to every officer and man in his fleet. He was opposed to the introduction of the dreadnought ('we start at scratch with that type of ship'), to the scrapping policy, and to the economies. His most serious grievance, which was generally known to the public, was over the new Home Fleet. It was, he informed the Admiralty (13 May 1907), a 'fraud upon the public and a danger to the Empire.' He was strongly of the opinion that all ships intended for the defence of home waters should be under his supreme command in time of peace as well as in time of war, so that all the ships could be trained and exercised together. He

[33] Fisher to Arnold White, 16 May 1905; *ibid.*, ii. 68, n. 1.
[34] The information in this paragraph, following the preceding footnote, is based on a letter from Admiral Bacon to the writer, 12 Nov. 1941.

charged that a sudden German naval attack would have a good prospect of 'inflicting most crushing reverses at the initial stages of hostilities, in the present totally unprepared states of the Home and Channel Fleets in regard to their preparation and organization for war' (14 June 1907).

The Admiralty chastised the C.-in-C. (5 June 1907) for a similar outburst: 'It was not conceivable that at any time such a war would come upon us without any period of strained relations or any ostensible cause. If it were to be assumed that our plans for war were to be based on such a contingency being possible, it would mean the fleet being maintained on a permanent war footing. . . . Nevertheless, the highest degree of warlike preparation is desirable. . . . The fleet is more ready for war than it has ever been, especially in celerity of mobilizing and in fighting efficiency.'[35]

Throughout the spring of 1907 Beresford pressed Whitehall for an increase of strength to his own fleet, especially in the smaller craft. Another major criticism was that the Admiralty would not send him its war plans. This was true, but it was the traditional policy of the Admiralty to provide commanders-in-chief with brief 'War Orders', not war plans. War Orders contained only broad outlines ('the general intentions of the Admiralty') of the policy to be adopted and included the 'nature of reinforcements to be placed at the disposal of the Commander-in-Chief' in specified contingencies. On the basis of the War Orders the commander-in-chief was expected to draw up his own detailed war plans, which dealt with the actual disposition of the ships under his command, and to have them examined and approved, with or without amendments, by the Admiralty. In this particular case the Admiralty War Orders for the Channel Fleet were contained in a letter of 24 June 1905 to Sir Arthur Wilson, Beresford's predecessor. This letter was handed over to Beresford when he assumed command of the Channel Fleet. To assist him further in drawing up his own war plan, he was at the end of April handed a 188-page volume entitled 'War Plans', which had been drawn up by the Admiralty. A note on the cover made it clear that these plans were not an executive order: 'The opinions and plans herein (to which others will be added from time to time) are not in any way to be considered as those definitely adopted, but are valuable and

[35] Admiralty MSS.

instructive because illustrative of the variety of considerations governing the formation of War Schemes.' None of these plans appealed to Beresford, and he drew up his own war plan—a 'Sketch Plan of Campaign' against Germany—and gave it to Fisher on 13 May. It was an extraordinary war plan, involving the employment of many more cruisers and several more battle-ships than the Royal Navy possessed! The whole purpose of this sketch plan, which was based on the War Orders of 1905, was to criticize Admiralty policy. The Admiralty did not approve the plan and on 14 June issued revised War Orders, cancelling the 1905 War Orders and directing Beresford to submit detailed plans to give effect to the revised orders. Beresford found the new War Orders impracticable.

Another criticism was that the C.-in-C. should know in advance exactly what ships he could count upon as reinforcements in the event of war. 'It is manifestly impossible,' he wrote on 27 June, 'for me to submit "detailed plans for the carrying out of operations under the several contingencies of an outbreak of war with the Powers indicated" unless I know what ships are available to carry these plans out, and where such ships are to be found.' This reason offered by the C.-in-C. for his refusal to submit war plans was contrary to Admiralty policy.

. . . in every instance the Admiralty are careful not to embarrass themselves or the Commanders-in-Chief, or cloud the issue in a mass of detail by naming any specific vessels in the reinforcements to be sent out. By a wise generalization, they frustrate any tendency on the part of our Admirals at sea to lose themselves in unimportant minutiae. The preparation of 'touch and go' plans, based upon a too nice calculation that on a given day certain vessels could be counted on which were not available the day before, plainly has hitherto rightly found no favour with the Board.[36]

Beresford's letter of 27 June was regarded as the culmination of a series of 'improper' and 'provocative' letters from him. Relations between the Board and the C.-in-C. were strained to the near-breaking point. Tweedmouth suggested that Fisher have a talk with Beresford to see if matters could be arranged 'without further irritating correspondence'. On 5 July a conference was held at the Admiralty between Fisher, Beresford, and Tweedmouth. Four

[36] Admiralty 'Memorandum on the Relations of the Commander-in-Chief, Channel Fleet, and the Board of Admiralty', June 1907; Lennoxlove MSS.

questions were put to the C.-in-C. by the First Lord, of which the two important ones were:

(3) 'Why do you not try to cultivate good and cordial relations with the Admiralty?' and

(4) 'Will you explain to us your reasons for saying that "the Home Fleet is a fraud and a danger to the Empire"?' These are a few excerpts from the verbatim minutes of this extraordinary meeting:

Beresford: . . . Then this thing—Question No. 3—You will allow me to smile for at least ten minutes over Question No. 3. . . . Although my views are very drastic, there is not any question of want of cordial relations with the Admiralty. Not privately or publicly have I ever said anything against the Admiralty . . .

Tweedmouth: If you say, in a letter to me, as First Lord, that our Home Fleet 'is a fraud and a danger to the Empire', that is not very pleasant to the Admiralty, and you have repeated that again and again. . . . I must tell you that to tell the First Lord of the Admiralty that what is a very important part of his Board's policy is absolutely useless and is a fraud and a danger to the Empire, I do not think that is very friendly to the Admiralty.

Beresford: It is a private letter. We have all written much stronger things than that on important questions of that sort. . . . It was only a 'term'. If we went to war suddenly you would find it is true. If I had said officially that the Admiralty had created that, or if I had pitched into the Admiralty about it, it would be different. . . . That I had any notion of insubordination I absolutely deny. That letter of mine to the First Lord has no right to go before the Board, a private letter like that . . .

Tweedmouth: It is not marked private. Other letters have been marked private.

Beresford: . . . I ought to have put 'private' and 'confidential' on it.

Tweedmouth: I cannot look on that as simply a private communication to me. I think that is a very important letter.

Fisher: I am quite sure you understand we are all equally interested, as you are, in having friendly and cordial relations, but it is absolutely impossible if the Chief Executive Officer of the Admiralty afloat is going to be 'crabbing' the Admiralty in everything the Admiralty is doing, and writing such letters to the First Lord. . . .

Tweedmouth: I think so serious a charge against the Home Fleet ought to be substantiated; you ought to say how it is a fraud, and how it is a danger to the State.

Beresford: It is a 'term'. I can write it all out to you in detail. The

public think it is ready for instant action. What is your own term?—
Without an hour's delay: well, it is not.

. . . .

Beresford : I do not dictate to the Board of Admiralty. The Board has
the right—it is the constituted authority, and so long as it is the
constituted authority, it is responsible, and nobody else. It may do wrong
things, but it is the responsible authority—I have never written to you,
officially or privately, except in the most respectful manner.

So far as the Admiralty was concerned, the conference had been
a total failure. 'The answers to the questions put to the Commander-in-Chief are a series of clumsy fencings, evasions, and
dodgings, and are often contradictory.'[37] A concession was made
to Beresford's demand (27 June) for 'an adequate fleet, complete
in all details, with battleships, cruisers, scouts, and destroyers
ready for instant action.' Two armoured cruisers and two divisions of destroyers (twenty-four) with their attendant vessels
were attached to the Channel Fleet, though not the two extra
battleships Beresford wanted. Beresford expressed his satisfaction
(18 July), adding, 'I can now make out a plan of campaign on
definite lines.' But it was not until the following 6 June that he
submitted his revised plans to the Admiralty.

While relieved, the Admiralty ended this phase of the controversy by reminding Beresford (30 July) that they were 'always
ready to give consideration to representations made to them in the
usual manner by Officers in high command, but they cannot enter
into a controversy on matters of policy with an officer acting under
their authority. The disposition of the fighting units of the Fleet
and the strategic policy to be followed are matters solely for the
decision of the Board of Admiralty.' Actually, nothing had been
settled in July, and to the very end of his command Beresford
continued to raise the question of the composition and organization
for war of the fleets in home waters. He later used the whole
episode of war plans and war orders to support the charge that
the Admiralty never had any war plans during his Channel command, and that the greatest shortcoming of the Admiralty was the
lack of a strategical department—a naval war staff.

Incidents multiplied, each straining relations further. On

[37] Admiralty memorandum, 'Remarks on Interview with Commander-in-Chief,
Channel Fleet, Friday, July 5, 1907'; Admiralty MSS.

12 November 1907 Beresford complained to the Admiralty of the anticipated early removal of three important officers of his command—his Chief of Staff, Captain Sturdee, his Second-in-Command, Vice-Admiral Custance, and Rear-Admiral Montgomerie, in command of the Home Fleet destroyers.

14. It has come to my notice that a feeling has arisen in the Service that it is prejudicial to an officer's career to be personally connected with me on Service matters. This may not be a fact, but the impression I know exists. It is certainly borne out by the late procedure. . . .

17. The removal of three such important officers from my command at or about the same time will add enormously to my already exceptionally hard work. Their removal cannot help me to add to the efficiency of the Fleet. It may not have been intended, but it most certainly has the appearance of a wish to handicap and hamper me in carrying out the responsibilities connected with by far the most important appointment within the Empire . . .

18. The ordinary etiquette, civilities, and courteous dealings which officers of high and distinguished command have hitherto so markedly received from the Admiralty have been entirely absent in my case. . . .

Patiently, the Admiralty replied (21 November) that he was incorrect about Custance; that Sturdee had been offered and had accepted the command of a battleship in order that he might qualify for promotion, which was what Beresford himself had been urging; and that the reasons for the termination of Montgomerie's appointment had been set forth in Admiralty letters to Beresford of 7 and 21 August. Strong exception was taken to paragraph 14 of Beresford's letter. 'The allegation is of a very serious character', and he was asked for 'specific evidence'. (It was never submitted.) The Admiralty 'strongly demurred' to the tone of paragraph 17, and reminded him 'once more that the responsibility for the Naval defence of the Empire, whether in Home waters or elsewhere, rests with the Board of Admiralty.' Nor could they understand the basis of paragraph 18. 'They would, however, observe that it becomes increasingly difficult for them in their correspondence with you to avoid overstepping the usual limits of official reserve while you continue to employ language which has no parallel within their experience as coming from a subordinate addressed to the Board of Admiralty.'

On 9 December 1907 we find Beresford viewing 'with considerable apprehension' the 'dangerous shortage' of unarmoured

cruisers and destroyers in home waters and charging that, consequently, the safety of the battle fleet in North Sea waters was
jeopardized by the possibility of the German destroyers being able
to leave their bases without detection. The Admiralty dissented
'strongly' (16 December): the Fleet was, as in other respects,
incomparably stronger than the German Fleet; his language was
'unnecessarily alarmist'.

On 17 January 1908 the Admiralty censured Beresford for a
memorandum of 11 November 1907 which he had circulated
before Christmas among the officers of the Channel, Home, and
Atlantic Fleets on the joint exercises of October 1907. In it he had
asserted that the destroyers under Commodore Bayly had not
been properly trained, and that the idea underlying the armoured
cruiser was fundamentally unsound. The Admiralty requested
that he recall the memorandum and expunge the two offensive
paragraphs before reissuing it, because 'the former reflects on the
competence of the Commander-in-Chief of the Home Fleet
[Bridgeman], and the latter on the policy of the present and past
Boards of Admiralty.' And so it went, incident following incident
with scarcely a pause. Most serious was the paint-work affair, a
cause célèbre of the time.

On 4 November 1907 Beresford issued an order that exercises
would have to be curtailed, to enable the ships to be painted and
tidied up for the forthcoming fleet inspection at Spithead by the
German Emperor (11 November). Percy Scott, Rear-Admiral of
the 1st Cruiser Squadron, then engaged in carrying out a gunnery
programme, lost his temper. He was, remember, a gunnery crank.
He cancelled *all* the planned gunnery exercises, and when the
cruiser *Roxburgh* asked to continue her practice, he sent her captain
the signal: 'Paintwork appears to be more in demand than
gunnery, so you had better come in, in time to make yourself look
pretty by the 8th instant.'

When, on 8 November, Beresford heard of this interchange of
signals, he sent for Scott. White with suppressed anger, he told
him off in a tense scene on board the fleet flagship in the presence
of Admirals Custance and Foley. His signal, Beresford snapped,
was 'pitiably vulgar, contemptuous in tone, insubordinate in
character, and wanting in dignity.'[38] Scott was stunned. 'Silent

[38] All the correspondence quoted is from Admiralty sources. It is duplicated, with
supplementary tit-bits, in the Carson MSS. Beresford expected Sir Edward Carson,

and white-faced, he never said a word, and his gait was slow and dragging' as he left to return to his flagship, the *Good Hope*. The Commander-in-Chief now made a general signal to the Fleet recapitulating the circumstances and ordering Scott to have the offensive signal expunged from the logs of the *Good Hope* and the *Roxburgh*. There is no possible justification for Beresford's humiliation of Scott, any more than there was for Scott's signal. As it turned out, the Emperor, arriving two hours late owing to bad weather, was not able to inspect the fleet!

Beresford's report to the Admiralty (8 November) asserted that Scott had 'held up to ridicule' an order that he had given to the fleet. This 'public insult' to his authority called for 'severe punishment in the interests of discipline and loyalty to command', to wit, Scott's supersession from the command of the 1st Cruiser Squadron. He received no support from the Admiralty. Their Lordships did convey to Scott an expression of their 'grave disapprobation, it being a matter vital to discipline and good order that perfect loyalty to superiors should govern the conduct of all officers of the Fleet', and Beresford was so informed (13 November). But that was all. The 'grave public censure' already administered to Scott by Beresford was, with the Admiralty letter to Scott, considered sufficient punishment.

Beresford was enraged that the Admiralty should regard 'a private admonition sufficient for so gross an offence against discipline'. He took his feelings out on poor Scott, who was ordered in future to communicate with him only in writing. He did not invite Scott to any of his social functions and he kept his squadron away from the flag as much as possible.

The paint-work incident had quickly become public property. Such utterly different journals as the *Daily Mail*, *Naval and Military Record*, and *Manchester Guardian*, among others, thought it strange that a man who had been guilty of indiscipline against the Admiralty should be protesting so vociferously a breach of discipline by one of his subordinates. Some of the writings went much further, claiming that the Admiral had depreciated a junior officer before the whole fleet on an unfounded charge, that he had refused Scott the right to offer an explanation, and so on. On 5 January 1908 Beresford invited the Admiralty's attention to the many

M.P., the eminent lawyer, to champion his cause 'when the fracas begins in the House of Commons'.

articles and statements in the press 'derogatory' to his position as C.-in-C. He requested that they have the charges refuted, he being debarred by service regulations from replying. The Admiralty was neither prepared to reopen the subject nor to become involved in controversy with the press.

On 18 January the (then scurrilous) weekly *John Bull* published an article which accused Beresford of suffering from 'swelled head' and of aiming 'from first to last' to 'humiliate' Scott, and declared that he had 'proved himself unfit' to succeed Fisher. Every officer in the Channel Fleet received a copy under a sealed envelope. The enraged Beresford asked the Admiralty to prosecute the publishers of the periodical for the 'libellous' article and to make the details of the paint-work incident public. The best the Admiralty would do was to give him permission at the end of February to circulate to the captains of his ships, for their information only, copies of their letter to him of 13 November. Beresford's *amour propre* was satisfied and the incident was closed.

It had the effect, however, of solidifying the breach between the rival gladiators, since Beresford detected Fisher's hand in the entire episode. He attributed his inability to secure Scott's ouster to Fisher personally—Scott was in the Fishpond—and he was certain that the *John Bull* article 'emanated' from him. 'There is no doubt it is one of the most determined, audacious, treacherous and cowardly attacks on me, inspired by the gentleman from Ceylon.'[39]

The paint-work incident ushered in the most acute phase of the Beresford–Fisher vendetta and the quarrel in the Navy. It was no longer possible to conceal the existence of a feud that had split the upper ranks of the service into two camps of warring partisans, both of which were represented at Whitehall as well as in the Fleet. (A third group of officers adopted a neutralist position.) Gone was the 'band-of-brothers' tradition. Naval officers were reminded of the fierce quarrel between Admirals Keppel and Palliser in the eighteenth century, when, also, the Navy was divided into two camps, with the lamentable result that it was unsuccessful in war. Each side was making speeches, issuing pamphlets, and flooding those newspapers and journals predisposed in its favour with articles and letters (often under

[39] Beresford to Carson, 21 Jan. 1908; Carson MSS. For the Ceylon reference, see above, p. 14.

transparent pseudonyms). Beresford, on leave, was holding forth in London drawing-rooms, deploring the disappearance from the Navy of 'all the good comradeship' and preaching a holy war against the arch-infidel. 'The naval clubs rang with the outraged sentiments of half-pay officers, and ancient admirals grew purple at the unspeakable name, and fired broadsides at the iconoclast through the portholes of *The Times*.' Humorous incidents were not lacking, as when, in January 1908, Beresford shammed illness in order to coax Cabinet Ministers and other potential supporters to his bedside! It was 'worthy of the XVIIth Century and Mr. Pepys. Imagine interviewing Beresford in a night cap, with Lady Charles holding his hand on the far side of the bed. What a picture of Naval efficiency and domestic bliss.'[40]

How did Fisher react to the campaign against him and his policies? In January 1907 he already felt that he was 'standing on the edge of a precipice to which all great reformers are led, and over which they ultimately fall.' But a fighter like Fisher never hauled down his flag. His skin was 'like a rhinoceros,' he told the Prince of Wales, 'and all the envenomed darts don't pierce it!' At the same time, and despite the current opinion which represented him as a man without feeling, he was cut to the heart by the attacks made upon him. 'When I retire,' he said to a friend, 'I shall write my reminiscences. I shall call them "Hell. By One Who Has Been There."' ' Had it not been for the loyalty of his friends, and above all of the King, he would have gone under. Privately, they could be critical of his methods and, sometimes, his policies. But the loyalty of men like King Edward (who kept telling Fisher 'to keep his hair on'), Esher, Knollys, and a host of newspaper editors and naval journalists never wavered.

By the beginning of 1908 the schism in the Navy had become so subversive to the discipline of the service, so scandalous in the eyes of the public, and so dangerous to the security of the nation, that all shades of press opinion were calling for a halt to the dissension. The Beresfordians sought to accomplish this by the demand, first made at the end of 1906, but now pressed, for an independent inquiry into Admiralty policy. A case for an inquiry had been fairly established, it was maintained, by the impairment of the Fleet's fighting strength through the dreadnought policy,

[40] Esher to Knollys, 19 Jan. 1908; Windsor MSS.

the destroyer and small-cruiser shortage, the disposition of the Fleet, etc., etc., all of which had been 'disastrous'.

The inquiry proposal only added fuel to the flames. The cry of Fisher's partisans was that discipline must be restored in the Navy—that the only way to achieve harmony was for Beresford to give up his insubordination and disloyalty, and to co-operate loyally and heartily with the Admiralty, else haul down his flag and, if he wished, enter Parliament and argue his case there with the Admiralty spokesmen. The position of the Admiralty was explained in a memorandum for the Cabinet (25 January 1908): '... the Admiralty fear no inquiry; but it would be simply impossible for the Members of the Board to retain office if such a blow to discipline and to the authority of the Admiralty as the investigation of its fighting policy by its subordinates were to be sanctioned.' In February the Admiralty got a 'distinct promise' (elsewhere Fisher spoke of a 'written engagement') from the Prime Minister, Campbell-Bannerman, that no form of inquiry into Admiralty policy would be entertained. His successor, Asquith, confirmed this promise on 15 April.

The row got more intense, following various incidents in the spring and summer of 1908. At the Academy dinner on 1 May Fisher had insisted on shaking hands with Beresford, although the latter tried not to see him. But a few days later, at the Levée on 11 May, in full view of the King, ministers, and naval officers, Beresford had refused to take Fisher's offered hand and had turned his back. This disgraceful behaviour was all over the Fleet in no time.

There followed the second signalling incident on 1 July. Beresford signalled to the two columns of the 3rd Division of the Fleet, under Scott's command, to turn inwards together. This would have led to a collision between the cruisers *Good Hope* and *Argyll*, which were abeam of one another on a parallel course, 1,200 yards apart. The *Argyll* obeyed the signal to turn sixteen points to starboard; but with Scott's sanction the officers of the *Good Hope* disobeyed the signal to turn sixteen points to port, thus apparently avoiding another *Victoria* disaster (1893). A bitter controversy resulted. Beresford wanted to order a court-martial of Scott. The Admiralty felt that a preliminary court of inquiry would be necessary to obtain sufficient evidence to justify a court-martial, and this the First Lord, McKenna, believed would be against the best interests of the Navy. It would rake up much scandalous matter and, moreover, would give the appearance that Beresford was acting from vindictive motives. Beresford was upset. 'It is difficult to believe,' he wrote the Admiralty (27 August), 'that the Board can fully understand the injury to the discipline, not only of the Channel Fleet, but of the Navy as a whole, which must result if open and flagrant disloyalty is allowed to pass . . .' Of course the incident leaked out into the press (7 July).

At this time a sensation was created by Arthur Lee's letter in *The Times* (6 July): '. . . it can no longer be denied that the Commander-in-Chief of the Channel Fleet (who is presumably the Admiralissimo designate in the event of war) is not on speaking terms with the admiral commanding his cruiser squadron on the one hand, or with the First Sea Lord of the Admiralty on the other . . .' *The Times* insisted (8 July) that Beresford

must be confronted with the historic alternative *se soumettre ou se démettre*. It is not a question whether he or the Board of Admiralty is right in the opinions they may respectively hold concerning the acts of policy about which they are understood to differ. That is a question which may very properly be raised by Lord Charles Beresford as soon as he is in a position of greater freedom and less responsibility. But so long as he holds his present responsible position he is not free to let it be known, whether by his action or by his demeanour, either to his fleet or to the world at large, that his attitude towards the Board of Admiralty is one of scant respect for its authority and avowed dissent from its policy.

This was an excellent statement of the crux of the matter. Whether the Admiralty reforms were good or bad, it was the duty of the whole Navy to be obedient and loyal to all in authority over them. There could be no amateur Admiralties outside the Admiralty, nor, as Fisher put it, could 'the tail be wagging the head'.

By the summer of 1908 a number of partisans on both sides were indulging in a 'plague on both houses' line of talk. Even such well-wishers of Fisher as Austen Chamberlain were beginning to feel that all three principals should be dismissed, and that Fisher's 'usefulness has ceased and that his influence now is mischievous'. Some of Beresford's partisans, too, were urging that only such a drastic solution as the dismissal of Fisher, Scott, and Beresford would end the personal animosities in the Navy and restore the camaraderie of the service. Something of this sort did come about.

In August the Admiralty removed Scott to another command (this was part of an arrangement with Beresford, who had agreed) and allowed him to fly his flag until February 1909, when he hauled it down for the last time. It was now Beresford's turn.

Mrs. Asquith told Stead, the Editor of the *Review of Reviews*, that 'her husband thought Jackie had been woefully feeble about Beresford: that when they have in *their* household servants who could not "get on", they invariably got rid of one or both !'[41] Yet in the last analysis it was the weakness and shilly-shallying of the Cabinet that prevented a quick and efficacious solution to the whole problem. Haldane and other Cabinet Ministers who parleyed with Beresford did not realize that, in effect, they were, in Fisher's words, 'coquetting with mutiny and dealing an irreparable blow to naval discipline.' And the Cabinet did nothing about sacking Beresford.

As early as January 1908 the Admiralty was considering Beresford's supersession. A precedent was found in 1795. When Admiral Lord Hood failed as a C.-in-C. to carry out the Board's policy, he had been ordered to strike his flag and come on shore. By late May, McKenna had satisfied himself that in the interests of the service, and for the safety of the Empire, Beresford simply had to be relieved of his command. The most cordial personal relations between the C.-in-C. of the Channel Fleet and the whole of the Board were essential, and this was impossible with Beresford as C.-in-C. In July the First Lord tried to get Cabinet approval for the termination of Beresford's command on the absorption of the Channel Fleet into the Home Fleet early in 1909, which would result in the abolition of Beresford's billet. There was 'strong objection' by the Cabinet. Fisher himself had written earlier: 'They are all "blue funkers" about Beresford and over-rate his power of mischief and his influence.'[42] In December McKenna was at last successful, and on the 16th Beresford was ordered to strike his flag when the fleet reorganization in home waters took effect (March 1909). This would be a year before the expiration of the C.-in-C.'s normal term of three years.

All appeared to be serene in the Navy; but appearances were very deceptive. The King, who in August had called the Cabinet a pack of cowards for not getting rid of Beresford, was not sure

[41] As reported by Esher to Knollys, 20 Apr. 1908; Windsor MSS.
[42] Fisher to Esher, 24 Jan. 1908; *Fear God and Dread Nought*, ii. 43.

now that the Admiralty had acted wisely. It might have been better to have allowed Beresford a third year, 'as he [the King] is afraid he now will make a disturbance and give trouble and annoyance.'[43] The Prince of Wales had similar misgivings. 'Apparently,' he wrote on 2 January 1909, 'he has taken it lying down; what he will do afterwards remains to be seen. He will probably agitate for a Parliamentary enquiry into the Navy and God knows what.'[44] The royal pair were clairvoyant.

The prologue to the last phase was the great Navy Scare of 1909. The last nail in Fisher's coffin, from the Beresfordian point of view, was the Admiralty 'negligence' in dreadnought construction that made possible that scare, which was about to hit Britain with the force of a tornado as the new year opened. To the story of the German naval menace and the background of the 1909 scare we must now turn.

---

[43] Knollys to McKenna, 22 Dec. 1908; McKenna MSS.
[44] John Gore, *George V: a Personal Memoir* (London, 1941), p. 222.

VI

The German Naval Challenge, 1900–1908

It is not merely or even principally the question of naval armaments which is the cause of the existing estrangement. The building of the German fleet is but one of the symptoms of the disease. It is the political ambitions of the German Government and nation which are the source of the mischief.

Sir Eyre Crowe in a memorandum of 20 October 1910.

There is no doubt that during these [pre-war] years the naval question loomed like a heavy cloud over the relations between England and Germany. We had absolutely no question at issue with Germany except the minor controversy of participation in the Bagdad Railway, and had it not been for the strenuous naval competition initiated by Germany, there was no apparent cause for disturbance in Europe for the next ten years, and no need for the large naval programme that England was forced by Germany to adopt in order to maintain the security of our shores.

Lord Hardinge of Penshurst, *Old Diplomacy*.

I. GENESIS

THE YEARS 1900–5 witnessed a steady deterioration in the relations of the two peoples and the two governments. The German press and many speakers violently condemned the 'buccaneering adventure' in South Africa, insulted the British Army as a pack of 'mercenaries', and slandered the Queen in gross caricatures. It was in Germany that the British reverses in South Africa were hailed with the most joy. The attitude of the German Government during the war was technically correct, but the persistency with which it took advantage of Britain's preoccupation elsewhere to press its claims was deeply resented in England. There was a growing suspicion of German aims. In short, English opinion was becoming unpleasantly Teutophobe.

Feeling in both countries was running so high that the alliance negotiations of 1901 were doomed from the start. Oil was poured on the fire by Joseph Chamberlain's reference (he was then Colonial Secretary), on 25 October 1901, to the cruelty practised by the German troops in the Franco-Prussian War of 1870. It touched off an uproar in Germany. The two governments became involved in this unedifying affair which completed the estrangement of English opinion. *The Times* noted with regret (20 November 1901): 'These daily manifestations of German hatred, which at first caused surprise rather than indignation, are gradually sinking into the heart of the British people.' Cecil Spring-Rice, the rising young diplomat, wrote from London in April 1902 of the 'extraordinary' change in English opinion. 'Everyone in the [foreign] office and out talks as if we had but one enemy in the world and that Germany.'[1]

It was against this background of a serious deterioration in Anglo-German relations that the 'portentous' development of the German Fleet began to be viewed with apprehension. The Navy Law of 1898 had set the first-class battleship strength of the Fleet at nineteen, with eight armoured coast defence ships, twelve large and thirty small cruisers. The building programme to reach these figures extended to the financial year 1903–4. A much larger fleet was provided under the Navy Law of 1900. By 1920 (the last year of the programme would be 1917–18) there would be a Battle Fleet of two fleet flagships, four squadrons each of eight battleships, eight large cruisers and twenty-four small cruisers; a Foreign Fleet of three large and ten small cruisers; and a Reserve Fleet of four battleships, three large and four small cruisers. The 1900 programme was executed silently, rapidly, and systematically, without the shipbuilding delays which were occurring in England. Between 1900 and 1905 twelve battleships were laid down and proceeded with swiftly. Fourteen battleships were launched in these years, only two fewer than the British (omitting the two purchased by the Admiralty from Chile in 1903). The consensus of British expert opinion was that in 1906 Germany would be the second naval power in the world. What rendered the German Navy even more formidable was the excellence of its gunnery, training, and personnel. To thoughtful Englishmen the centre of continental naval power seemed to be shifting from Toulon and Brest to Kiel and Wilhelmshaven.

It was in 1901–2 that the Admiralty first became seriously concerned about the German Navy. On 15 November 1901

---

[1] Stephen Gwynn (ed.), *The Letters and Friendships of Sir Cecil Spring-Rice* (London, 1929, 2 vols.), i. 750.

Selborne circulated a memorandum to the Cabinet in which the crucial passage read:

The naval policy of Germany is definite and persistent. The Emperor seems determined that the power of Germany shall be used all the world over to push German commerce, possessions, and interests. Of necessity it follows that the German naval strength must be raised so as to compare more advantageously than at present with ours. The result of this policy will be to place Germany in a commanding position if ever we find ourselves at war with France and Russia, and at the same time to put the Triple Alliance in a different relative position to France and Russia in respect of naval strength to that which it has hitherto occupied. Naval officers who have seen much of the German navy lately are all agreed that it is as good as can be.[2]

An October 1902 Cabinet paper by Selborne went a step further. The Admiralty was now convinced that the German Fleet was being built with a view to a naval war with England.

The more the composition of the new German fleet is examined the clearer it becomes that it is designed for a possible conflict with the British fleet. It cannot be designed for the purpose of playing a leading part in a future war between Germany and France and Russia. The issue of such a war can only be decided by armies and on land, and the great naval expenditure on which Germany has embarked involves a deliberate diminution of the military strength which Germany might otherwise have attained in relation to France and Russia.[3]

In a statement to the writer (1938) Lord Selborne amplified the 'manifest design' consideration in this paper: 'The Admiralty had proof that the German Navy was being constructed with a view to being able to fight the British Navy; restricted cruising radius, cramped crew quarters, etc., meant that the German battleships were designed for a North Sea fleet and practically nothing else.'

By 1902 the Government, the Admiralty, and large segments of public opinion were as one in viewing the German Fleet as a potential menace far greater than that offered by the fleets of the Franco-Russian Alliance. It was in October 1902 that the Emperor signed a letter to the Tsar as 'Admiral of the Atlantic'. The news somehow reached London, where it was regarded as

[2] 'The Navy Estimates and the Chancellor of the Exchequer's Memorandum on the Growth of Expenditure'; Lansdowne MSS.

[3] Extract from Selborne's 1902 memorandum quoted in his Cabinet paper of 7 Dec. 1903, 'Naval Policy'; *ibid.*

a fresh and impressive proclamation of Germany's resolve to possess a navy which would be able to rival Britain's. During the winter of 1902–3 Great Britain co-operated with Germany in forcing a settlement of financial defaults on Venezuela through the use of naval pressure. When the German commander, acting independently, bombarded a Venezuelan fort, thereby bringing Germany to the verge of war with the United States, British public opinion was enraged and held up Germany's behaviour as still another instance of the aggressive purposes for which the German Fleet was being constructed.

Several events in the summer of 1904 pointed up the growing menace of the German Navy. In June King Edward made a state visit to Germany for the Kiel regatta. To impress his uncle with the efficiency of his Navy, the Emperor had almost the whole available strength of the German Navy collected in Kiel Bay. During the King's inspection of the German ships, Tirpitz recollects, 'he exchanged many meaning [sic] looks and words with Selborne . . . which impressed me unpleasantly.'[4] The reports from the commanding officers of some of the British warships which helped escort the royal party substantiated and strengthened the impressions gathered by it. That by H.M.S. Dido contained these observations: 'Although the officers met with spoke most cordially and made themselves very agreeable, it was obvious that the general tone and feeling, more especially on shore, was decidedly anti-English. . . . evident that the Germans are straining every nerve to perfect their Navy as a fighting machine. . . . Their ships are in excellent order.'[5]

The English newspaper correspondents at Kiel were equally impressed with the progress of the German Navy. The Times Berlin Correspondent described the German dockyards (25 June) as 'a scene of such busy preparation that it must present to every one the spectacle of a new naval Power arming in a hurry. . . . What struck one most . . . was the readiness of the fleet and the sleepless energy of the officers and men. The Kiel squadron is always mobilized.' The Times summed up its feelings (1 July): 'No phantom as to German aggression haunts us; but the consciousness we feel that it is our duty to watch the progress of German

---

[4] Tirpitz, *My Memoirs*, i. 200.

[5] N.I.D. Report No. 745, Jan. 1905; *Reports on Foreign Naval Affairs, 1904–5* (Admiralty Library).

GENESIS OF THE GERMAN CHALLENGE

naval power, and to consider the possible purposes for which it might be used, will certainly not be lessened by what we have seen at Kiel or by any such assurances as we have heard there.' Other newspapers were still more outspoken, as, for instance, the *St. James's Gazette* (25 June) : 'Forewarned is forearmed, and this growth of rival construction can have only one object—conclusions, some day, with ourselves.'

The Kiel festivities were followed in two weeks by the visit of a German squadron to Plymouth on the invitation of King Edward. It was accorded a frigid reception. The German Ambassador reported to Berlin (12 July): 'Most of the papers regard every step in the progress of our Fleet as a menace to England. Many voices also loudly declare that the curiously frequent visits of German ships in British waters can be with no other object than to obtain information as to the disposition of the British Navy and coast defences for the benefit of the German Admiralty. The sight of the German Fleet at Plymouth reminds Great Britain that she must be sufficiently armed to uphold absolutely her supremacy at sea.'[6] This is an excellent summary of British press opinion.

The simultaneous announcement of the signing of an arbitration treaty was received without comment or with cool approval. To the *Globe* (13 July) it was 'all "leather and prunella" beside the grim fact of the German Fleet', and even the well-disposed *Manchester Guardian*, which approved the treaty (14 July), feared that the Anglo-German hostility 'springs from forces too manifold and lying too deep to be radically affected by an agreement of this slight description.'

August Niemann's novel, *Der Weltkrieg : Deutsche Träume*, translated into English in July as *The Coming Conquest of England*, showed 'the ineradicable hostility of Germany to England'. Some 25,000 copies were quickly sold in Germany. The book has to do with a Franco-Russo-German coalition against England whose aim was a new division of the world. While the Russians penetrated into India and a German army landed in Scotland, conveniently unopposed by the British Fleet, a Franco-German squadron defeated the Royal Navy at Flushing. French and Russian troops landed in England, and the Emperor made a victorious entry into London

---

[6] Johannes Lepsius, Albrecht Mendelssohn-Bartholdy, and Friedrich Thimme (eds.), *Die Grosse Politik der Europäischen Kabinette, 1871–1914* (Berlin, 1922–7, 40 vols. in 54), xix, Pt. 1. 194–5, n. (Hereafter cited as *Die Grosse Politik*.)

to dictate terms of peace. These included the surrender of a large part of Britain's oversea possessions. 'The meaning and the moral,' said the English translator, 'should be obvious and invaluable.' It was in 1903–4, too, that English writers began to spin their own German invasion yarns. Most publicized was Erskine Childers's *Riddle of the Sands*, published in the summer of 1903. This imaginary war story involved a plan for a sudden descent from the Frisian coast while the Channel Fleet was decoyed away. It was the proto-type of many popular invasion stories in the following years that contributed to the awakening of the public to the threat of the German Navy.

The upshot was that already, in the summer and autumn of 1904, talk of the inevitability of an Anglo-German war was in the air. It was at this point that Fisher took over the helm.

2. THE MOROCCAN CRISIS

The Entente of April 1904 had removed the French naval incubus as the primary consideration in the plans of the Admiralty and tended to set its hands free to cope with the emergency that was arising in the North Sea. However, the strength and disposition of the French Fleet remained an important factor in Admiralty calculations for over a year following the Entente. One good reason was the Russo-Japanese War, which put Anglo-French relations under some strain. This was particularly true in April 1905. The French, to please their allies, stretched the laws of neutrality to permit the Russian Baltic Fleet, *en route* to the Far East, to use the French harbour of Kamranh Bay in Indo-China. It needed a further deterioration in Anglo-German relations to raise the German Navy to the undisputed role of the Royal Navy's ranking potential adversary. This came during Fisher's first year.

On 22 October 1904, before the new First Sea Lord had had a chance to warm his chair, there occurred a delightful *opèra-bouffe* performance. The Baltic Fleet, in the first stage of its ill-fated voyage, fired on the Hull fishing trawlers off the Dogger Bank in the belief that they were Japanese torpedo boats. For some days there was a real danger of war. The Admiralty had the Russians shadowed as they left English waters, and made other preparations for destroying this 'fleet of lunatics', as the *Naval and Military Record* had uncharitably called it. Beresford, commanding the Channel Fleet, fidgeted off Gibraltar, eager for a scrap. The crisis blew over by 3 November, although the danger of a clash remained in view of the Prime Minister's decision (at the C.I.D., 9 December) to oppose any attempt by the Russian Black Sea Fleet to pass the Dardanelles, in defiance of treaty obligations, and effect a junction with the Baltic Fleet. As late as 1 May 1905, Ottley, the D.N.I., felt there was 'a considerable chance that we may find ourselves at war with France, Germany, and Russia before next August'. The next day the Board, after meeting with the Prime Minister, decided to cancel the annual 'Grand Manœuvres' (due to begin on 13 June) in view of the unsettled state of naval affairs in the Far East and the possibility of a sharp collision of interest between Britain and Japan on the one hand and the three great Continental powers on the other. It was considered more prudent not to scatter the Fleet, as would have been necessary in the manœuvres. The situation eased after Tsushima and the Peace Conference at Portsmouth.

The Russo-Japanese War led to a sharpening of Anglo-German relations. The story was current in England that the Germans were behind all the trouble, trying to embroil England with the French and the Russians. Even the Admiralty gave credence to this hallucination, for such it was. 'Things look very serious. It's really the Germans behind it all . . .' 'Peace seems assured to-night, but one never knows, as that German Emperor is scheming all he knows to produce war between us and Russia.'[7]

Tension was increased by a war scare in Germany in the winter of 1904–5. The Government seriously feared an English attack. German war vessels stationed in the Far East were recalled to home waters and all Christmas leave was cancelled in the Navy. This apprehension was founded on the coincidence between certain articles in the English press, the concentration of British naval strength in home waters, which the Emperor regarded as directed solely against the Fatherland, and loose talk in English naval circles. The last-named included the tactless public declaration, 3 February 1905, by Arthur Lee, the Civil Lord, that, were war declared against Germany, the Royal Navy 'would get its blow in first, before the other side had time even to read in the papers that war had been declared.' The sense of imminent danger

[7] Fisher to Lady Fisher, 28, 30 (?) Oct. 1904; Kilverstone MSS.

in Germany was heightened by the rumours concerning the *Dreadnought* and flared into a fresh invasion scare in November 1905, when the Emperor partially mobilized his Fleet and summoned his Ambassador from London. The Emperor was angry. 'Here am I, who for twenty years have done my utmost in the cause of Peace, misrepresented in the most disgraceful way on all and every occasion. For ten years I had to face German music because I was too friendly to England, and now for the last ten years I have had to face English music because I'm a German.' He singled out the *National Review*, *The Times*, and especially the *Daily Mail* and 'scandalous articles' by 'Ignotus', 'Calchas' [J. L. Garvin], and their kind, in a blast against the iniquities of the British press.[8]

A word about Fisher's methods of making war is in order. Much has been made of the ferocity with which he always spoke on the subject of war. 'War should be terrible,' he said, and there is his oft-quoted statement at the Hague Peace Conference of 1899: 'The humanizing of war! You might as well talk of humanizing Hell . . . as if war could be civilized.' In reality, there was nothing bloodthirsty about Fisher. He was a man of peace and it was his conviction that war was the greatest idiocy of life. But once it happened, he urged, it must not be conducted weakly. 'My sole object is PEACE in doing all this [the 1904 fleet redistribution]! Because if you "rub it in" both at home and abroad that you are ready for instant war with every unit of your strength in the first line, and intend to be "first in" and hit your enemy in the belly and kick him when he's down and boil your prisoners in oil (*if you take any!*) and torture his women and children, then people will keep clear of you.'[9] In other words, as he often expressed the same thought, it was the duty of the British Fleet to 'hit first, to hit hard, and keep on hitting', so that by one colossal effort the enemy might be destroyed and the nation saved from all the horrors of a long-drawn-out series of indecisive contests.

Fisher's jingoism is supposed to be proved by his 'plans' for a preventive war. In private conversations with intimate friends he did put forward the idea that it would be a good thing to 'Copenhagen' the growing German Fleet before it became too strong, following the precedent of his hero Nelson in 1801 *vis-à-vis* the

[8] Report of farewell audience, 16 Jan. 1906, by Captain R. A. Allenby (the British Naval Attaché in Berlin); Admiralty MSS.
[9] Fisher to ?, 22 Feb. 1905; *Fear God and Dread Nought*, ii. 51.

Danish Fleet. (Actually, Fisher confused the Battle of Copenhagen of 1801, in which Nelson defeated the Danish Fleet, with the Battle of Copenhagen in 1807, when Admiral James Gambier forced the surrender of the neutral Danish Fleet in the midst of peace.) On at least two occasions, in moments of particularly high spirits—late in 1904 and early in 1908—he suggested this course to the King. The King's reaction the first time was 'My God, Fisher, you must be mad!' On the second occasion the King appears to have been receptive.[10] In May or June 1905 Fisher was reported to have said to Lord Cawdor: 'Sir, if you want to smash up the German Fleet, I am ready to do so now. If you wait five or six years, it will be a much more difficult job.' The First Lord is supposed to have hustled this proposition over to Balfour. The Prime Minister asked that Fisher be told 'we don't want to smash up the German navy—but to keep in readiness.' The Admiral's reaction was: 'Very well, remember I have warned you.'[11] Despite this evidence, the present writer is convinced that the idea was never advanced seriously by Fisher, even if he did lament, in his *Memories*, that 'we possessed neither a Pitt nor a Bismarck to give the order', for he realized that such action by a British government was impossible. It was never considered by the Board and it was never part of British naval policy in the Fisher administration.

Regrettably, as so often happens in history, the legend was far more important than the fact. Many Germans in responsible positions, the Emperor among them, really believed that Fisher planned to attack, a feeling reinforced by occasional preventive war speeches and articles in England.[12] This will explain at least some of the German jitteriness in 1904–5. The feeling persisted. The Emperor told Captain Dumas, the British Naval Attaché, in June 1906: 'You know that our Officers think that Sir John Fisher's great aim is to fight us.' Dumas also reported, on the basis of talks with many German naval officers and those in authority, that the fear of a war with Britain was 'very real' and that the Germans were sincerely anxious for an understanding. The Germans, stated a report sent to the Admiralty from a non-official source, 'fear Sir John Fisher particularly, who they look on

[10] *Ibid.*, pp. 20, 168, n. 1.
[11] An unsigned document among Lord Northcliffe's papers written by a correspondent who claimed to have got the story from Cawdor himself; Reginald Pound and Geoffrey Harmsworth, *Northcliffe* (London, 1959), p. 425. See below, pp. 116–17.
[12] But see below, pp. 172–3.

as the strongest man in England, and think he is bent on crushing Germany's Navy before it proves too strong. It was stated that the Emperor shares this opinion.'[13] The belief that 'Fisher was coming' actually caused a panic at Kiel at the beginning of 1907, and cautious parents kept their children from school for two days. There was a similar panic on the Berlin Bourse. Years later, Admiral Müller, the Chief of the Naval Cabinet, described Fisher to the British Ambassador as 'the arch-rascal who wanted to commemorate his leaving the Navy with a "Trafalgar" against Germany, so that his name would go down in history as Lord Fisher of Heligoland.'[14]

Russia's paralysis offered Germany an opportunity to break up the Anglo-French Entente before it had had time to harden. In assuming a diplomatic offensive against France, ostensibly because of France's failure to square the Germans in Morocco, the German Government was encouraged by the opinion of the generals that France was not prepared for a land war, and that any possible British military aid would be too slight to make any difference. The idea, then, was to disrupt the Entente by humiliating France and showing her the worthlessness of England's friendship, or, as expressed by the British Ambassador in Paris, 'to show to the French people that an understanding with England is of little value to them and that they had much better come to an agreement with Germany.'[15] The Emperor's flamboyant speech at Tangier, upholding the independence of Morocco (31 March 1905), touched off the Moroccan crisis. German pressure was applied to force the resignation of the French Foreign Minister, Delcassé, and was successful on 6 June. This did not end the crisis. Germany demanded an international conference on Morocco; the French were forced to accept, 1 July.

Instead of breaking the Entente, German tactics only succeeded in welding it into an effective quasi-alliance, since Germany's motive was understood by the British Government and public opinion. A factor in the situation was the Admiralty's apprehension

[13] 'German Feelings about War with England in December 1906'; Admiralty MSS. Fisher explained: 'These notes were made from repeated conversations with the highest official naval and mercantile personages in Germany.'

[14] Müller to the Emperor, 18 Oct. 1910; German Ministry of Marine MSS.

[15] Bertie to Lansdowne, 25 Apr. 1905; G. P. Gooch and Harold Temperley (eds.), *British Documents on the Origins of the War, 1898–1914* (London, 1926–38, 11 vols.), iii. 75. (Hereafter cited as *British Documents*.)

regarding German designs on the Moroccan coast. Fisher held that the German acquisition of coaling stations on the Moroccan Atlantic coast would be disastrous inasmuch as it would greatly increase the danger to British commerce going via the Cape in time of war. 'Without any question whatever the Germans would like a port on the coast of Morocco, and without [any] doubt whatever such a port possessed by them would be vitally detrimental to us from the naval point of view and ought to be made a *casus belli, unless we get Tangier*, which would perhaps (but only perhaps) be a *quid pro quo*.'[16] Balfour had his doubts that the consequences would be as disastrous as Fisher and the D.N.I. (Ottley) supposed. But Lansdowne, the Foreign Minister, felt the same way Fisher did. He was prepared to have Britain join France in offering 'strong opposition' to a German request for a port on the Moorish coast. However, his successor (December 1905–16), Sir Edward Grey, was unable to work up much steam over this possibility. Grey was even prepared to use the naval base issue as a bargaining point. As he confided to the Prime Minister:

In more than one part of the world I find that Germany is feeling after a coaling station or a port. Everywhere we block this. I am not an expert in naval strategy, but I doubt whether it is very important for us to prevent Germany getting ports at a distance from her base; and the moment may come when timely admission that it is not a cardinal object of British policy to prevent her having such a port, may have great pacific effect. It may for instance turn out that a port for Germany on the west Atlantic coast of Morocco may solve all the difficulties of the Morocco Conference . . . The concession of a port to Germany is a card which might any day take a valuable trick in diplomacy.[17]

The effect of the Moroccan crisis on Anglo-French relations was immediate and profound. Delcassé, before he was compelled to resign, believed, or professed to believe, that Great Britain had offered to sign a formal alliance and was ready to come to the aid of France in the event of a German attack. The extent to which the English committed themselves to the French on this occasion is a point which has baffled historians. Was an explicit offer of an alliance made? In all probability, no. Nor can the present writer find authority to support Delcassé's insistence that England had

[16] Fisher to Lansdowne, 22 Apr. 1905; Lennoxlove MSS.
[17] Grey to Campbell-Bannerman, 9 Jan. 1906; Campbell-Bannerman MSS.

promised to send 100,000 troops to Schleswig, or to blockade the Elbe, though the latter was part of British War Office strategy and the former was prominent in Fisher's strategic views.[18] But 'though the offer of an alliance by the British Government is a legend the situation had undoubtedly changed, and the contingency of joint resistance to a common foe had been envisaged for the first time.'[19]

The contingency was not only envisaged, but steps were taken to provide for it. After all, as Lansdowne warned the German Ambassador, there was no telling how far the Government would be forced by public opinion if Germany light-heartedly launched a war against France.[20] Light is thrown on the problem by a very interesting Admiralty document entitled 'British Intervention in the Event of an Attack on France by Germany'. It reveals that on 24 June 1905 Fisher asked the D.N.I. to prepare a statement regarding (1) 'the possibility of manning the existing War Fleet in the event of sudden action being necessary in support of France'; (2) fleet dispositions in the event of naval action against Germany. The fact is that in 1905–6 the Admiralty, the War Office, and the C.I.D. were considering the strategical implications of a possible Anglo-French war with Germany.[21]

Unofficial, non-binding military conversations were begun between the British and French general staffs in December 1905–January 1906. The evidence is that informal naval conversations were initiated earlier, in the time of the Balfour Government. We know that Fisher originally had favoured a close arrangement with the French Fleet. Indeed, one gets the impression that he would have relished a showdown with the Germans at this time. 'This seems a golden opportunity for fighting the Germans in alliance with the French, so I earnestly hope you may be able to bring this [alliance] about. . . . All I hope is that you will send a telegram to Paris that the English and French Fleets are *one*. We could have the German Fleet, the Kiel Canal, and Schleswig-

---

[18] A search of the Foreign Office, Admiralty, and War Office records for 1905 revealed no trace of an alliance offer or a promise to send troops to the Continent. Lansdowne at the time categorically denied the German allegation that an offensive-defensive alliance had been offered to the French. Lansdowne to Lascelles (the British Ambassador in Berlin), 16 June 1905; *British Documents*, iii. 82.

[19] G. P. Gooch, *Before the War* (London, 1936–8, 2 vols.), i. 59.

[20] Metternich to Foreign Ministry, 28 June 1905; *Die Grosse Politik*, xx. (Pt. 2) 635–7.

[21] See below, p. 386.

Holstein within a fortnight.'[22] Esher, who was in a position to know, felt there was 'far more risk of J. F. taking the initiative and precipitating war' than there was of the Emperor doing so, though he did not think he would be that rash.[23] Ottley, in replying, 26 June 1905, to Fisher's request of 24 June, remarked: 'It would also be advisable to exchange views with the French naval authorities in order that there should be no misunderstanding or confusion in applying the overwhelming superiority which the Alliance could bring to bear.' This would indicate that naval conversations had not begun yet. They may have started in July. All we know for certain is that under Lansdowne, in 1905, 'the French Naval Attaché had been unofficially and in a non-committal way in communication with Fisher, as to what help we could give in a war between Germany and France.'[24] This is confirmed by Grey's dispatch of 15 January 1906 to the British Ambassador in Paris: 'As to taking precautions beforehand in case war should come, it appears that Fisher has long ago taken the French Naval attaché in hand and no doubt has all naval plans prepared.'[25]

This gives the impression of amicable and close Anglo-French naval relations. The fact is that, whatever may have been the extent and nature of Fisher's contacts with the French naval authorities in 1905, he was completely unco-operative in the critical early months of 1906.[26] His attitude was the result of several considerations. For one thing, he was now convinced that there would be no war. Again, he was always secretive about war plans, preferring private arrangements in this case with the Channel C.-in-C., A. K. Wilson. Also, he believed the Navy could do the whole job—the French Fleet would be in the way. (Fisher ignored French susceptibilities throughout the crisis.) This was in the best British naval tradition. A distrust of coalitions and alliances can be traced back to the inaction of the allied French commander in the Battle of the Texel, August 1673, in the third Dutch War. A particular reason at this time for British distrust of

---

[22] Fisher to Lansdowne, 22 Apr. 1905; *Fear God and Dread Nought*, ii. 55.
[23] Esher to Clarke, 18 Feb. 1906; *Esher*, ii. 144.
[24] Grey to Tweedmouth, 16 Jan. 1906: *British Documents*, iii. 203; George M. Trevelyan, *Grey of Fallodon* (London (Longmans), 1937), p. 135.
[25] *British Documents*, iii. 178.
[26] Much of the material that follows is from the Clarke correspondence of Jan.–Mar. 1906 in the Esher MSS.

the French Navy was the startling decline in French sea power since 1902. By 1905 the French Fleet had sunk to the position of a poor third among European navies. Shipbuilding was carried on in a leisurely fashion. The pre-dreadnoughts, on which France relied for battleship superiority over Germany, were distinctly inferior to their German opposites. Many of them were too small, ranging from 6,000 to 8,950 tons, to be of much value in twentieth-century battle. The French admirals themselves spoke of these small battleships in terms of contempt. 'Deux hommes faibles ne vaudront jamais un homme fort,' a one-time French Chief of Naval Staff (equivalent to British First Sea Lord) sarcastically remarked. The new armoured cruisers were badly designed. They put their noses under water, used too much coal, and manœuvred badly. There were loud complaints of too many types of guns in the Fleet and about the quality of the powder, etc., etc. One reason for the parlous condition of the French Navy was the frequent changes of ministers of marine, which brought about frequent changes of naval policy. As late as 1908 the French naval situation remained depressing.

In any case, Fisher felt that the Royal Navy could do the job alone. As he had boasted to the French Naval Attaché on 2 January 1906, if England participated in a war against Germany, the Germans would soon find themselves without a ship or a colony. The only French naval help in which he was interested was the co-operation of French submarines based on Dunkirk with British submarines based on Dover. No plan of co-operation with the French Fleet was elaborated at the Admiralty, still less presented to the French for their consideration. Fisher would not even agree to prepare a code of identifying signals as an elementary precaution, or to arrangements for communication between the two fleets, should they find themselves fighting side by side. There was never any real exchange of views and no definite plan of co-operation in war. At the time of the Bosnian Crisis, late in 1908, and again at the time of the Agadir Crisis, in August–September 1911, there were exchanges of views between the two Admiralties designed to define the wartime roles of the two fleets. There is no record of their specific content. It was not until 1912, after Fisher and his equally uninterested successor, A. K. Wilson, had retired that the Anglo-French naval conversations truly began.

To return to the winter of 1905–6, as a last straw Fisher refused to be a party to military co-operation with France on French soil. The war plan adopted on 12 January 1906 by the C.I.D. and the War Office called for landing 100,000 troops at the French Channel ports within fourteen days, were Britain forced into war by German aggression against France. Fisher balked at working out the naval aspects of this ferrying operation. It would be a 'nuisance' to the Navy to have to guard the passage of the troops; the Navy wanted to 'get away to sea'. His mind was full of an amphibious operation, specifically, a landing on Schleswig-Holstein. The French were not enthusiastic. They preferred British military help in Belgium, if Germany violated its neutrality, otherwise, on the left of the French line of deployment. Fisher's general attitude during these months provoked Clarke to make this outburst (21 January 1906): 'The difficulties of getting anything to go right in this muddle-headed country are enormous.' The generals, too, were quite fed up with the Admiral. A pattern for Army–Navy relations had been set, which persisted down to the eve of the war.

The possibility of war with Germany faded by the spring of 1906. In April there was a *détente* of war preparations, after the Algeciras Conference (January–April 1906) had, after a fashion, settled the Moroccan question. But in the same month Ottley wrote: 'The European storm-centre has shifted from the Mediterranean to the North Sea.'

3. MOTIVATIONS

Two new factors of incalculable significance had emerged by the winter of 1905–6: first, 'The Entente had been tried in the furnace without melting away. . . . Though bound neither by formal alliance nor secret guarantee England, it was generally understood, would support France if she were attacked by Germany. At last, after decades of isolation, we had transformed a dangerous rival into a powerful friend.'[27] The close Anglo-French co-operation at the Algeciras Conference further strengthened the Entente. In the second place, the German Navy menace had become an *idée fixe* in Britain and would undergo little change except for an intensification at the time of the Navy Scare of 1909. There were some journals (in particular the *Nation*, *Spectator*,

[27] Gooch, *Before the War*, i. 62.

and *Westminster Gazette*) and some politicians, mostly of the Liberal persuasion, who minimized the aggressive policies of Germany and deprecated the habit of regarding every increase in naval armament by another power as an act of aggression against Great Britain. So long as the two-power standard was maintained, it was altogether unnecessary to introduce invidious and irritating references to particular powers. The German Navy was intended essentially for defensive purposes and the English need not take offence.

The navalist press never tired of repeating that the German Navy had no legitimate defensive functions: it was not intended to keep open the ocean highways and to secure German food supplies from overseas, because if necessary Germany could be supplied overland; nor for coping with Russia, now a third-class naval power; nor with France, whom Germany could overwhelm with her Army; nor with the United States, because the limited radius of action of German battleships showed they were not meant for operations far from home waters. Much was made of the fact that the whole German battle fleet was concentrated in the North Sea, and that it was backed by an immense military power. Germany was developing her sea power simply and solely to challenge British sea power. The Foreign Office and Conservative and Liberal Imperialist politicians shared this point of view. Thus, the Liberal Prime Minister, Asquith, 'gave Grey a few suggestions for his talk, on the lines that nobody here can understand why Germany should need, or how she can use, twenty-one Dreadnoughts, unless for aggressive purposes, and primarily against ourselves. They are clearly not the least necessary for the defence of her coasts, nor for the protection of her own sea commerce, which latter is the function of cruisers.'[28]

The Royal Navy, on the other hand, was held up as a *defensive* navy, constituting a threat to no other power. This was proven by the absence of a large standing army which could be used for invading the territory of any of them. The crux of the British position was summed up by Grey: 'If the German Fleet ever becomes superior to ours, the German Army can conquer this country. There is no corresponding risk of this kind to Germany: for however superior our Fleet was, no Naval victory would bring us any nearer to Berlin.'[29]

[28] Asquith to McKenna, 1 Jan. 1909; McKenna MSS.
[29] Grey's memorandum for the King, 31 July 1908; *British Documents*, vi. 779.

The Germans had a simple explanation for their naval policy. The Emperor and his Chancellors repeated *ad nauseam*, publicly and privately, that the German Fleet was not intended for aggressive use, that Germany's colonies, shipping, and oversea commerce had developed so considerably that a strong navy was essential to the defence of these interests. There was a second motive for naval expansion that was not bruited so much in public—that a powerful battle fleet was a necessary adjunct to German foreign policy. It enhanced Germany's alliance value and it strengthened the hands of German diplomats. German sea power, added to her great land power, would give her a commanding influence in the world. But it was precisely *that*—the diplomatic, and, if need be, *military uses* to which Germany would put such overwhelming sea power —which disturbed the British Government, the Admiralty, and public opinion. Balfour's testimony is especially valuable, since he did not scare easily. (He was Leader of the Opposition, December 1905–November 1911.)

Personally, I was one of those who was most reluctant ever to believe in the German scare. But I cannot now resist the conclusion that every German thinks that 'the enemy is England'; that while the more sober Germans probably admit to themselves that they will never be able to deal single-handed with the English navy, the German Staff and, what is much worse, the German nation, have ever before them the vision of a time when this country will find itself obliged to put out its utmost strength in some struggle with which Germany is not at all connected, and that then the opportunity will come for displacing the only Power which stands between it and the universal domination of Europe, or hinders the establishment of a colonial Empire.[30]

The harrowing forebodings of alarmists apart (which imputed to the Emperor all the wild annexationist plans of the Pan-Germans), sober Englishmen feared that Germany had expansionist aims in the Near East, China, Africa, and especially *vis-à-vis* Denmark and the Low Countries. The mouth of the Rhine, together with the mouths of the Meuse and Scheldt, would be very valuable to Germany—for naval and military, as well as economic, purposes, since Germany did not have enough harbour room for her warships. Kiel was awkwardly situated and Wilhelmshaven was a narrow, artificial port. Such aims must be opposed by

[30] Speech before the C.I.D. Sub-Committee on Invasion, 29 May 1908; Lennoxlove MSS.

Britain, since their realization would completely upset that cardinal axiom of British foreign policy, the balance of power in Europe, and would confront England with a most formidable antagonist across the narrowest part of the Channel. 'If Germany should become the ruler of the Continent of Europe, Great Britain would become the outpost and the sentinel of Anglo-Saxondom. She would have to be in constant readiness for war, watching with sleepless vigilance a gigantic and aggressive military and naval Power, ruling the Continent of Europe, and she would have ever to be prepared to bear the brunt of a formidable and sudden German attack.'[31] Eyre Crowe, Senior Clerk at the Foreign Office, warned that 'the union of the greatest military with the greatest naval Power in one State would compel the world to combine for the riddance of such an incubus.'[32] In short, the English believed that the object of German sea power was less the security of Germany than it was the building up of a German world hegemony.

It was believed increasingly after 1904, in both official and non-official circles, that the ultimate object of the continual growth of the German Fleet could only be to try conclusions with the Royal Navy at the first favourable opportunity, if it had a reasonable hope of victory. Grey agreed with 'alarmist' public opinion that 'if the German fleet was strong enough to challenge ours we should have to choose between war and diplomatic humiliation. . . . I do not mean that it is what Bethmann-Hollweg [Bülow's successor as Chancellor in 1909] would intend or desire, but it would be forced upon him.'[33]

The Royal Navy, then, must prepare for that war, a conflict which more and more Englishmen came to regard as inevitable. '. . . that we have eventually to fight Germany is just as sure as anything human can be, solely because she can't expand commercially without it.'[34] Such views of Fisher's were unceasingly and vigorously pressed on the King, who 'admitted the force of his general argument'.[35] Lord Esher, confidant of Fisher and

---

[31] * * *, 'The Continental Camps and the British Fleet', *Fortnightly Review*, Apr. 1906.

[32] Crowe's 'Memorandum on the Present State of British Relations with France and Germany', 1 Jan. 1907; *British Documents*, viii. 416.

[33] Grey to Goschen, 31 Dec. 1909; *ibid.*, vi. 319.

[34] Fisher to King Edward, 14 Mar. 1908; *Fear God and Dread Nought*, ii. 169.

[35] Lee, *Edward VII*, ii. 604.

King Edward, and one of the most influential behind-the-scenes makers of policy during the King's reign, had no doubt as early as September 1906 that '*L'Allemagne c'est l'Ennemi*', and that 'within measurable distance there looms a titanic struggle between Germany and Europe for mastery. The years 1793–1815 will be repeated, only Germany, not France, will be trying for European domination.'[36] A year later: 'Germany is going to contest with us the Command of the Sea, and our commercial position. She wants sea-power, and the carrying trade of the world. . . . She must have an outlet for her teeming population, and vast acres where Germans can live, and remain Germans. These acres only exist within the confines of our Empire. Therefore, *l'Ennemi c'est l'Allemagne.*'[37] This was also the bed-rock of Foreign Office thinking.

Behind the naval rivalry lay the true cause of British Teutophobia and suspicion of the German Navy—what Crowe once called 'the generally restless, explosive, and disconcerting activity of Germany in relation to all other States.' In last analysis, the political factor was the true explanation of the British reaction to the expanding fleet across the North Sea, yet it is remarkable how this tended to be obscured and how the continual growth of the German Fleet had *per se* become as early as 1905–6 *the* great stumbling block and 'only obstacle' to satisfactory Anglo-German relations.

The new importance of the German Navy led to the drawing up, in 1904–5, of a revised standard of naval strength.

4. THE TWO-POWER STANDARD

The two-power standard of naval strength, which was as old as the time of the Earl of Chatham (1770), was rediscovered by Cobden and others after the Crimean War. It was officially accepted by Lord George Hamilton, the First Lord, on 7 March 1889 when he stated that the idea underlying the speeches of all first lords and prime ministers had been 'that our establishment should be on such a scale that it should at least be equal to the naval strength of any two other countries'. The standard was confirmed time and again by responsible statesmen of both parties in the next fifteen years.

[36] Esher to M. V. Brett, 4, 6 Sept. 1906; *Esher*, ii. 180.
[37] Journals, 3 Dec. 1907; *ibid.*, pp. 267.

By 1905 the two-power standard was rapidly becoming obsolete. It had been applied to the French and Russian Fleets at a time when they were the second and third strongest in the world, and when there was a likelihood of a clash with them. In 1904, according to Admiralty calculations, the German Fleet replaced that of Russia as one of the 'two next strongest fleets' after the British. This fact and the danger of Britain becoming involved in the Russo-Japanese War prompted Balfour to enunciate the germ of a new policy (1 March 1904)—namely, that after exhausting herself in a war with two great maritime powers, Britain must not find herself at the mercy of some *tertius gaudens* with an intact navy. Therefore, the two-power standard must be a two-power standard with a margin. The margin was not defined, nor was there any specific mention of the probable two-power combinations Britain might have to fight. But the Government clearly regarded a Franco-Russian coalition with possible German intervention as the most likely combination until the latter part of 1904.

Fisher's return to the Admiralty in October was signalized, among other things, by an elaboration of the revised two-power standard. A special Admiralty committee presided over by Prince Louis of Battenberg recommended, in November 1904, that England maintain a superiority in battleships of at least 10 per cent over each of these 'most likely combinations against us . . . in order of probability, 1. Germany and Russia; 2. France and Russia; the United States being regarded throughout as friendly.' The 10 per cent margin would be established by the end of 1907. On 20 February 1905 a committee headed by Ottley reaffirmed the findings of the Battenberg committee, although a Franco-German combination and a Franco-German-Russian combination were also taken into consideration. After Tsushima the Russian Fleet was no longer regarded as a factor in determining the standard of strength of the British Fleet. This eliminated all possible combinations but one, France and Germany, now the 'next two strongest' European naval powers after Great Britain. Since absolute equality of numbers could not give a 'reasonable prospect' of victory to either side, a preponderance of 10 per cent in battleships was held to be necessary against this hypothetical Franco-German coalition.

Fisher justified the policy of building against two powers after 1905, viz., France and Germany, on these grounds: the United

States and Germany were competing for second place, which the French had practically yielded. Of the four leading naval powers, Japan was Britain's ally, France her close friend, America 'a kindred state with whom we shall never have a parricidal war'. The other considerable naval powers were the friendly nations of Italy and Austria, 'whose treaty obligations are in the highest degree unlikely to force them into a rupture with us which could in no possible way serve their own interests'.

There remains Germany. Undoubtedly she is a possible enemy. . . . For the moment, it would be safe to build against Germany only. But we cannot build for the moment: the Board of Admiralty are the trustees of future generations of their countrymen, who may not enjoy the same comparatively serene sky as ourselves. The ships we lay down this year may have their influence on the international situation twenty-five years hence, when Germany—or whoever our most likely antagonist may then be—may have the opportunity of the co-operation (even if only temporarily) of another great naval power. Hence a two-power standard, rationally interpreted, is by no means out of date.[38]

As matters shaped up in the second half of 1905, the English were quite safe. The 1905 programme included the first representatives of the revolutionary types—one dreadnought and four battle cruisers ('Invincible' class), but well before the end of the year it was decided that one of the latter could safely be dropped. There was nothing in foreign building programmes, as known to N.I.D. at the end of 1905, to spoil the happy picture of relative naval strength, especially as regards the lead in all-big-gun ships. At the end of 1907 the British would have the equivalent of fifty-two 'A' class battleships, instead of the minimum of forty-eight needed (two-power standard plus 10 per cent) *vis-à-vis* the Franco-German forty-three and three-quarters.[39] The general public, while, naturally, not in possession of all the facts, viewed the naval situation through the same rosy glasses as did the Admiralty.

5. THE CAWDOR PROGRAMME

On 4 December 1905, shortly before it resigned, the Conservative

[38] Fisher's memorandum, 'Admiralty Policy: Replies to Criticisms', Oct. 1906; Fisher, *Records*, pp. 103–6.

[39] Admiralty memorandum, 'The Building Programme of the British Navy', 15 Feb. 1906; *Naval Necessities*, iii. 13–16. The numerical units of value used were 1, ½, and ¼, representing Class A, B, and C battleships, respectively.

Government laid down, in the 'Cawdor Memorandum', the shipbuilding policy which it would be necessary for England to follow in the future: four large armoured ships (that is, dreadnoughts and battle cruisers) a year. This programme was accepted 'without prejudice' by Campbell-Bannerman's Liberal Government. But after the 1906–7 estimates, which had been completely worked out by the Cawdor Board, had been approved by Parliament in March 1906, the Government had a change of heart. It was influenced by two considerations: the desire to cut down the estimates, in fulfilment of pledges given by so many Liberal candidates at the elections in January, and the desire to set an example for international armaments reduction. Underlying both was the Liberal conviction that the money needed for the amelioration of the living conditions of the masses, to which they were pledged, could never be secured unless the 'ruinous waste' of the national resources on armaments was checked. Time and circumstances were by 1909 to prove to the Liberal Imperialist or 'big-navy' wing of the party, led by Asquith, Grey, and Haldane, and, in the press, by the *Westminster Gazette* and *Daily Chronicle*, the impracticability of Liberal idealism in armament matters. There was not a simple choice between social reform and 'bloated armaments'. But the Radical wing of the party—pacifists, economists, and ardent social reformers—for the most part remained 'little navy' in its thinking until the outbreak of the war. This group was led by Campbell-Bannerman and, after his death in 1908, by Lloyd George and Winston Churchill, and was supported by the *Manchester Guardian*, *Daily News*, and *Nation*.

The Government now, in the spring of 1906, argued that Britain had got such a jump in dreadnought construction (one dreadnought and three battle cruisers were building under the 1905–6 programme) that it was safe to mark time. It was impossible for the Admiralty to defend the laying down of four dreadnoughts in 1906, since not a single dreadnought or battle cruiser had been laid down by any European power, and none were immediately in prospect. Fisher and his colleagues were therefore amenable (26 May) to dropping one big ship of the 1906–7 programme; if there were no evidence of unusual shipbuilding activity on the part of their potential enemies, another armoured vessel would be dropped from the 1907–8 programme. The Government proposed to go further, believing that the Hague

Conference of 1907 would be helped by Britain's moderation in her building programme. The Board was induced (12 July) to agree to insert only two armoured ships in the 1907–8 estimates, with a third to be laid down if the Conference were unsuccessful in reducing armaments.

These changes in the Cawdor Memorandum were announced in the House of Commons on 27 July 1906. Edmund Robertson, the Parliamentary Secretary, assured the House that the reductions were made on the Board's recommendation. He and the Prime Minister advanced the argument that the delay was a practical demonstration to the other powers of Britain's desire for disarmament and an earnest of her readiness to carry it out. Campbell-Bannerman added: 'The man who has had an ample dinner, as much as he can digest, does not make himself stronger by going on eating dinners in order to dazzle other people.'

The Parliamentary Opposition, the big-navy press, and the Navy League castigated the Sea Lords for permitting the Government to use them 'as a cloak for its cowardice' and allowing themselves to be made the 'tools of the Little Englanders'. Fear was expressed that the reductions were but the entering wedge and that the traditional two-power standard was threatened. These rumblings of discontent flared into a minor navy scare which reached its peak in October. The catalytic agents were the announcement from Berlin early in August that the first German dreadnought would be larger in size than the *Dreadnought* and much more heavily armed, and rumours of a German supplementary programme to be introduced late in the year (an amendment to the 1900 Navy Law added six armoured cruisers to the Foreign Fleet and the Reserve Fleet, for a total of twenty large cruisers in the projected German Fleet), and of an accelerated rate in construction. The navalists admitted the existing situation was satisfactory. The fears that were expressed were entirely founded upon gloomy and exaggerated forecasts of what the naval position would be in a few years, when the vessels projected by rivals were in commission. The *Standard* (22 October) set the tone of the scare: 'The advent of a Liberal Government has in ten months done more damage to the nation than we might anticipate from conflict with a first-class European Power.' The denials of Bülow, the Chancellor, in an interview published in the *Daily Mail* (4 September) and in a long Reichstag speech (14 November), that the Germans aimed to rival Britain at sea did not mollify the prophets of misfortune in England.

The agitation was received with stony indifference on the Front Benches and received little support from many navalists. The service press expressed confidence that the Admiralty would sing out if there was any danger. Fisher thought the scare was 'stupid'. The Board would not be frightened by paper programmes. Britain had seven capital ships: one dreadnought (1905-6 programme) practically completed, three more (1906-7 programme) on the point of being laid down, and three battle cruisers (1905-6 programme) half completed. So far as was known, no other European nation had laid the keel of a single all-big-gun ship. (Germany did not lay down her first dreadnought and first battle cruiser until 1907.) But Fisher was thereafter regarded by big-navy enthusiasts like the *National Review* as the obedient tool of the 'cheese-paring Cobdenite Cabinet' and responsible for the abandonment of the two-power standard.

The Admiralty derived considerable satisfaction during 1906 from the reports and enclosures of the Naval Attaché in Berlin, Captain Dumas. Thus, an article in the *Dresdener Nachrichten* (5 February), which had an enormous circulation in Germany, conceded that the Royal Navy was 'equal to the united forces of the three most powerful sea Powers of the second rank . . . What could Germany . . . do in comparison with this mighty Power?' The D.N.I. commented: 'This paper shows a very just appreciation on the part of the German writer of the true meaning of the recent reorganisation of the Navy, and of the danger Germany will incur if she ever ventures to dispute the command of the sea with us. It is a wholesome sign and tends to peace.' Dumas submitted (28 July) an article from the *Schlesische Volkszeitung* of 15 July entitled 'Shall the German Fleet in Case of War Take the Offensive or the Defensive?' The Attaché's covering note said that it embodied what he believed to be 'the views of the more thoughtful German Naval Officers'. The article took issue with the many books on the war of the future since 1903, all of which assigned an offensive role to the German Navy. 'These views can do much harm and cause untold mischief. The German does not like the defensive, but in a future war our fleet cannot do better than to confine itself to the defensive if it does not wish to experience another Tsushima and disappear.' Again, on 12 November, the

Naval Attaché reported what he had picked up at a dinner party given by a member of the Admiral Staff. (The study of foreign navies was one of the functions of this department.) '*They consider our Fleet stands towards theirs in the proportion of four to one.* . . . As is usual of late they all spoke with unfeigned admiration of our mobilisation last summer for the Grand Naval Manœuvres. It is curious how immensely this has impressed not only naval men but, I might add, the whole of Germany. I do not think a week ever passes without my seeing it alluded to in the papers.' Fisher scratched this marginal note: 'We sent every vessel of the British Navy to sea at 3 hours notice at 3 a.m. in the morning without a single hitch, defect, or breakdown!'[40]

The cumulative effect of these and other reports was to imbue the Admiralty with the feeling that all was going for the best in the best of all navies. The two dreadnoughts projected in the 1907–8 estimates would maintain Britain's relative battleship strength. Indeed, the country's 'present margin of superiority over Germany (*our only possible foe for years*) is so great as to render it absurd to talk of anything endangering our naval supremacy, *even if we stopped all shipbuilding altogether!!!*'[41]

Although the main features of the building programme of 1907–1908 had been made public in July 1906, the 1907–8 estimates, published on 28 February 1907, were greeted by the big-navy party as fresh evidence of the Liberal conspiracy against the national safety. They were critical of the 'abandonment' of the two-power standard and saw only futility in the Prime Minister's 'visionary' invitation (his article in the first number of the new Liberal weekly, the *Nation*, 2 March) to other nations to limit their armaments by international agreement. 'The time has come,' declared the *Daily Mail* (6 March), 'to remind the Admiralty and the Government that the nation gave no mandate to weaken its Navy for the sole purpose of providing funds for doles to the Socialists.'

The attitude of the House of Commons presented a contrast to the storms and alarums of the critics outside. Robertson's speech expounding the estimates, 5 March, was not seriously challenged in any quarter. 'I am here on the part of the Admiralty to say that, in their opinion, the Two-Power standard will be adequately

[40] Dumas's reports are all with the Admiralty MSS.
[41] Fisher to Tweedmouth, 26 Sept. 1906; *Fear God and Dread Nought*, ii. 91.

maintained with the programme of shipbuilding which we are bringing forward today.' In the spring of 1909, as regards completed ships of the dreadnought type, they would have completed four dreadnoughts and three 'Invincibles'; at that date France and Germany would have nothing at sea equal to those vessels. Balfour himself had to confess that the Navy was stronger than any reasonable definition of a two-power standard could require it to be.

On 17 April Tweedmouth declared with determination that the Government was going to the Hague Conference 'absolutely unpledged, or pledged only to this—that if foreign countries do extend their programme, we, in our turn, will also extend our programme in order to keep our relative position among Naval Powers'. Clearly, the next move in the naval competition was contingent on the results of the Conference.

6. THE HAGUE CONFERENCE

The first Hague Peace Conference (1899) had left much undone. On 13 September 1905 the Russian Government proposed a second conference. Its programme for the Conference (April 1906) was seen to contain proposals only for revising and adding to the international law of war and peace, without any suggestion of discussing armament limitation. Other countries were not inclined to accept this restriction. Campbell-Bannerman's Government had come into office committed to a policy of reduction or limitation of the British arms budget and of trying to get general European limitation of arms budgets. Germany was informed in June that Britain intended to bring the latter subject up at The Hague. The Italians supported the British proposal. The United States, while doubting the wisdom of attempting a limitation of armaments, at least wanted to have the matter discussed at The Hague. The Russians and French were lukewarm. They would not directly oppose Britain, but both favoured giving the proposal 'un enterrement de première classe' at The Hague.

It was only Germany, blindly followed by Austria-Hungary, which categorically opposed any discussion of arms limitation at the Conference and curtly refused to take part in the discussion should the matter be raised there. She made no secret of the fact that she felt the British limitation plans were directed solely at her—that it was a brazen attempt to freeze the naval *status quo*. The Germans had allies in King Edward and the Admiralty, who, however, deferred to the Government, which felt so strongly on the matter. At the Cronberg meeting of King Edward and the Emperor, 15–16 August 1906, the King was reported to have said that the Conference was a 'humbug' which he regarded as not only purposeless but even as dangerous, as being likely to lead to friction. The Emperor heartily agreed and expressly stated that if limitation of armaments were to be brought before the Conference, he would not send representatives there. 'Each State must decide for itself the amount of military force which it considered necessary for the protection of its interests and the maintenance of its position, and no State could brook the interference of another in this respect.'[42] Germany, he made it clear, would not recede from the naval programme of 1900.

The conflict between Campbell-Bannerman's wish to limit armaments and still keep British relative superiority constant and the German determination to increase their relative strength seemed irreconcilable. Moreover, the effect of the British gesture in July (see above, p. 127) was nullified on the Continent by the repeated assurances of Admiralty and Government spokesmen that Britain's superiority was in no way endangered by the reduction in the building programme, that the Navy had never had such a commanding position, and that England far surpassed the two-power standard. Some of the German newspapers in the summer of 1906 made very strong remarks about the honesty of Britain in bringing forward her proposal. When Dumas mentioned this to Tirpitz (9 January 1907) and said that Britain was sincere, the latter replied:

Yes, perhaps it is true; but our people do not and will never understand such a scheme. I myself realize the Puritan form of thought such as is possessed by Sir Henry Campbell-Bannerman, and that he is perfectly honest and feels it a religious duty; but look at the facts. Here is England, already more than four times as strong as Germany, in alliance with Japan, and probably so with France, and you, the colossus, come and ask Germany, the pigmy, to disarm. From the point of view of the public it is laughable and Machiavellian, and we shall never agree to anything of the sort. . . . I am prepared to acknowledge

[42] Lascelles to Grey, 16 Aug. 1906, giving the Emperor's position; *British Documents*, viii. 192.

that it is a correct religious aspiration, but not practical for people who live in the world. We have decided to possess a fleet, and that fleet I propose to build and keep strictly to my programme.[43]

The Admiralty position on the question of the limitation of naval armaments, no less realistic than Tirpitz's, was the prototype of the kind of argument that was to be heard again and again in succeeding decades, whenever statesmen attempted to check an arms race:

As regards the suggested agreement to limit new construction amongst the Great Powers to repairs and renewals so as to keep the total and relative strength of their respective navies as it is at present, the attitude of the Admiralty is as follows:

From the selfish standpoint of pure opportunism, it seems clear that our present relative naval position is so good that we might express our adhesion to the principle, on condition that other countries were willing to do likewise. [But] . . .

In the first place, who is to see that each country loyally carries out its pledge to limit its navy? Are penalties to be imposed for evasions or failures to do so, and, if so, who is to exact these penalties?

And next, what is to be done with old ships; are they to be destroyed or broken up? And if so, when is this to be done?—*before* the keel of the new ship is laid, or *at the date of her launch*, or on the day she hoists the pendant for the first time; or at what particular point?

A clear understanding on this matter is vital to the success of the scheme, for unless some practical means can be devised for keeping Europe informed that such obsolescent vessels have been effectually got rid of beyond possibility of resuscitation, there will be nothing to prevent an unscrupulous Government from building new ships on the plea that the new vessels are being constructed to *replace* older ones, without any real intention to get rid of the latter.

And again, will a country in Russia's present naval plight be likely to find the scheme palatable? Will not Russia insist that *her* relative maritime position must be that which she occupied three years ago?

The notorious hostility of Germany to any limitation of armaments is also a stumbling-block which bids fair to effectually frustrate the pious intentions of the advocates of 'limitation of armaments'. For how can this country or (still more) France agree to check the growth of her navy, while a potential enemy as enterprising and unscrupulous as Germany is adding ship to ship in this ruthless game of naval beggar my neighbour? . . .

And if, indeed, a majority of the Great Powers was so strongly in

[43] Dumas to Lascelles, 9 Jan. 1907; *ibid.*, vi. 2–3.

favour of the scheme as to incline them to endeavour to forcibly impose their will upon the minority, we can scarcely suppose that the latter would gracefully acquiesce or would consent to see their freedom of action fettered by diplomatic pressure.

In such an event, the peaceful objects of those in favour of a limitation might, so far from being fulfilled, result in precipitating war. . . .

A great range of *practical* difficulties are also involved.

For example, what is there to prevent a State (which has agreed to the Convention) from devoting its shipbuilding energies to the construction of numbers of large, swift steamers, ostensibly for mercantile purposes, but of a character which would fit them for employment as auxiliary cruisers and corsairs in war? The distinction between vessels of such a character and *ordinary* merchant steamers would be almost impossible to draw. And yet it is certainly undesirable to limit (by international convention) the expansion of the mercantile marine of any of the signatory Powers.[44]

The Government persisted as late as the spring of 1907 in its intention to bring up arms limitation at the Conference. The *coup de grâce* to the whole arms limitation idea was administered by Bülow in a memorable Reichstag speech, 30 April. 'The German Government cannot participate in a discussion which, according to their conviction, is unpractical even if it does not involve risk.' Grey regretted the German attitude, but something had been gained. 'Bülow has now come into the open, and we know where we are. If discussion is impossible or fruitless, we shall go on with the Naval expenditure which we now have in suspense.'[45]

The question of reducing expenditure on armaments was not discussed at the second Hague Conference, which opened on 15 June 1907. The funeral of arms limitation was held on 17 August and lasted twenty-five minutes. Sir Edward Fry, the senior British delegate, presented a pious *voeu*, adopted unanimously amid general applause, declaring it was 'highly desirable that the Governments should resume the serious study of this question'. At the same time Fry stated the willingness of His Majesty's Government to enter on an annual confidential exchange and discussion of naval programmes with any power that might so be disposed, 'with a view to facilitating a restriction of naval armaments

[44] 'Memorandum on Limitation of Naval Armaments . . .', 29 Jan. 1907 (prepared for Grey); Admiralty MSS.
[45] Grey to Nicolson, 1 May 1907; *British Documents*, viii. 228.

from year to year by mutual consent'. The Conference ended its labours on 18 October.

The Conservative press had been very sceptical or cynical about what could be expected of the Conference in the way of arms limitation. Arguments having to do with human nature, the existing distrust among the powers, and the practical difficulties involved, were advanced. The lesson drawn from the Conference was that preparation for war was the only way to prevent war. To check the tendency towards the increasing armaments competition, 'we must check human nature itself. It would be almost as easy to impede love and marriage, or to regulate hunger' (*Daily Express*, 19 August). The Liberal press had professed to believe that the Conference would achieve something. When these hopes were not realized, its disappointment was grievous, but it tried to get what crumbs of comfort it could from the *voeu* and from Fry's proposal. The *Manchester Guardian* (19 August) expressed Liberal disillusionment: 'A Conference which treated the limitation of armaments as though it were an Anarchist bomb, to be thrust as soon as possible into a pail of water, was not likely to take any important step forward to that Millennium of which statesmen often speak with their lips, though much less frequently with their hearts.'

The failure of the Hague Conference to check the naval armaments competition had disastrous consequences. Lord Reay, one of the British delegates, put it succinctly: The Conference 'has not given a greater sense of security, but rather the reverse'. This was reflected in the Anglo-German naval rivalry, which henceforth was the dominant factor in the European situation. The hopes of large reductions in the navy estimates were based on The Hague, or, failing a general international agreement there, upon arrangements with particular powers for an arrest of armaments. The Conference led in this respect to nothing. The third dreadnought of the 1907 programme, held up until after The Hague, was now laid down, and Germany enlarged her building programme at the end of the year. An important consequence of The Hague was that, for years after, English navalists found it difficult to hear with patience the reiteration of the argument that Britain should make advances to Germany with a view to reducing armaments. 'Campbell-Bannerman did, and, not only so, he checked the Cawdor programme in order that Germany might perceive how sincere British intentions were. And what was the result? Germany built ships faster than ever before.' This was the line of reasoning.

During the Hague Conference, in August 1907, there came the announcement of a settlement of Anglo-Russian differences in Asia. 'Calchas' (J. L. Garvin) caught the inner significance of the Entente: 'She [Germany] has challenged the naval supremacy which is the life of our race. That is precisely why we have been so urgently moved to settle our outstanding differences with the rest of the world. That is why we have been brought in the last seven years to view in a totally altered light our relations with the Third Republic and the Empire of the Tsars. That is why we have made the real but sensible sacrifice of minor interests to major interests.'[46]

7. THE DARKENING HORIZON

Tirpitz 'has privately stated in a secret paper that the English Navy is *now* four times stronger than the German Navy! *And we are going to keep the British Navy at that strength. Vide* 10 Dreadnoughts built and building and not one German Dreadnought last March! But we don't want to parade all this, because if so we shall have Parliamentary trouble.' So Fisher wrote to King Edward on 4 October 1907.[47] The Admiral's cockiness overflowed into a breezy and confident speech at the Lord Mayor's banquet on 9 November. He told his countrymen that they might 'sleep quiet in their beds', with every assurance of security, and not to be frightened by 'bogies'. The speech was generally well received, but it reminded the anti-Fisher wing of the big-navy party of 'advertisements which bear no relation to the quality of the goods advertised', and of 'the tragic swagger of inefficient War Ministers on the eve of historic disasters'.[48] (Shades of Le Boeuf, the French War Minister in 1870!)

The skies were already darkening when Fisher spoke. Dumas reported on 3 October the frequent statements in the German press about a new Navy Law or an amendment to the 1900 Navy Law to be introduced in the forthcoming session of the Reichstag. It took the form of the latter, was published on 18 November and passed by the Reichstag in February 1908. By the amended law,

[46] 'The Anglo-Russian Agreement', *Fortnightly Review*, Oct. 1907.
[47] *Fear God and Dread Nought*, ii. 141.
[48] *Spectator*, 16 Nov. 1907; L. J. Maxse's letter, *Daily Express*, 12 Nov. 1907.

ships of the dreadnought type would be replaced (that is, the substitute ship would be laid down) after twenty years instead of twenty-five years as in the original Navy Act of 1898. This fixed the rate of new and replacement capital ships at four a year (three dreadnoughts and one battle cruiser) in 1908–9, 1909–10, 1910–1911, and 1911–12 (instead of three as before the amended Law), with the number dropping to two annually thereafter until the programme ran out in 1917–18. The amended Navy Law also specified that the 'large cruisers' in the 1900 Law should be battle cruisers. This meant that instead of the thirty-eight battleships and twenty armoured cruisers provided for in the 1900 Law (as amended in 1906), the Fleet was to be increased to fifty-eight dreadnoughts and battle cruisers.

The new German programme sounded the tocsin across the Channel. 'The dominant idea is to build a fleet which shall fulfil the hopes and desires of the Pan-Germans, and be mightier than the mightiest Navy in the world,' cried the *Daily Mail* (25 November). Twice, on 19 December and 15 January, Grey sounded a public warning that the increase of the German Navy might compel Britain to add to her own Navy. For the Conservative press Germany's action demanded a practical and immediate response in the form of such a strengthening of the Navy as would put an end to doubts on both sides of the North Sea. It was now, in the winter of 1907–8, that the two-keels-to-one standard in dreadnoughts came to the fore. W. T. Stead, who for years had been preaching universal disarmament and the gospel of peace at almost any price, was generally credited with introducing the idea. He was echoed by the *Daily Mail*, *The Observer*, *Morning Post*, *Standard*, *Spectator*, *Saturday Review*, *Naval and Military Record*, *Army and Navy Gazette*, the Navy League, Lord Esher, H. W. Wilson, Hurd (as 'Excubitor' in the *Fortnightly Review*), and other writers. There was some scepticism about the scale of counter-preparations that could be expected from the Tweedmouth–Fisher Board.

The Liberal press, on the other hand, while unhappy over the revised German programme, did not find it alarming. The British margin of superiority was still overwhelming, therefore there was no need for a 'scare' programme of construction in 1908. The Government was reminded by the *Nation* (18 January) of its 'absolutely overwhelming' election pledges in favour of a substantial reduction of armaments. The *Manchester Guardian* (29 December) recognized that the naval rivalry was 'rapidly becoming the principal outstanding question of European politics', but thought that four dreadnoughts a year to Germany's three would keep the country safe for the immediate future.

The Admiralty's reaction to the German naval programme was anything but panicky. In December 1907 the Sea Lords presented the First Lord with their shipbuilding programme for 1908–9. Once again the Cawdor programme, which allowed for four capital ships annually, was reduced. It was impossible to justify building up to it in view of this hard fact: in 1910 Britain would have in commission seven dreadnoughts and four battle cruisers; Germany, three and one, respectively. The Sea Lords accordingly proposed a 'very modest' new construction programme of one dreadnought and one battle cruiser, six unarmoured cruisers, sixteen destroyers, and £500,000 for submarines. The cruisers and destroyers were urgently needed to replace old units. Even the single new dreadnought had to be fought for in view of the Cabinet hostility to any increase in the new estimates.

Although it is quite true that our preponderance in battleships at the present moment might justify the omission of the solitary battleship proposed, yet with the full knowledge and absolute certainty (now afforded by the German programme just issued) of having to commence a larger battleship programme in 1909–10, it would be most un-businesslike, and indeed disastrous, to close down the armour plate industry of this country by the entire cessation of battleship building. It would be similarly disastrous to abruptly stop the manufacture of heavy gun mountings, which the omission of the battleships would also involve. In fact it would really be the right course, to help the Estimates of 1909–10, to lay down two battleships next year (1908–9). If the Germans maintain their programme (and there is no reason to doubt it) we should be forced to a programme of five battleships a year in 1910, and perhaps in 1909—this will depend on the rapidity of their shipbuilding. Anyhow, it would be on all grounds quite inadmissible to omit the one battleship in next year's programme, and indeed severe criticism must be expected at our not commencing two battleships.[49]

The Sea Lords looked upon the increase of a million and a quarter-odd pounds over the 1907–8 estimates as 'most moderate', particularly since the originally proposed increase of £2,150,000 had been

[49] 'Report to the First Lord, on the Navy Estimates 1908–1909, by the Sea Lords', 3 Dec. 1907; Lennoxlove MSS.

trimmed in November to appease the shocked Chancellor of the Exchequer, Asquith.

A crisis ensued all the same. The Cabinet was mindful of its economy promises, anxious to carry out social reforms, and feared it would be defeated in the Commons on an amendment to the Address moved from the Radical benches and supported by the Conservatives. The Government was therefore adamant that the estimates should not exceed those of 1907, indeed that they be brought, through a £1,340,000 cut, *below* the 1907 figures. There were spirited Cabinet discussions on the estimates between 21 January and 12 February 1908. Ultimata and threats of resignation (including one by Tweedmouth) filled the air. On 4 February, when Fisher assured Lewis Harcourt (in the Cabinet as First Commissioner of Works) that the estimates were at their irreducible minimum, the latter, in an 'arrogant' tone, intimated that either five Cabinet ministers (apparently himself, McKenna, Lloyd George, Burns, and Crewe) or the Board would have to resign. When Fisher replied that the Government might, under such circumstances, find it difficult to replace the Board, Harcourt blurted out that Beresford was ready to relieve Fisher as First Sea Lord. At a dinner party that evening Lloyd George repeated the substance of Harcourt's remarks. Unless there was a reduction in the estimates, a change in the Ministry or the Admiralty was inevitable, and Beresford was ready to accept Fisher's post and cut the estimates by £2,000,000. Fisher retorted that Beresford would 'sell' the Government in three months, and he reasserted that the irreducible minimum had been reached. The next morning Lloyd George attended a meeting of the Board. The estimates were gone over microscopically; the Board decided to stand by its guns. Fisher then had the Parliamentary Secretary see Campbell-Bannerman and carefully explain each vote and the impossibility of further cuts. The Prime Minister was convinced and decided that the navy estimates were to stand, but that Haldane would slash £300,000 off the army estimates instead! In the end, however, the increase in the navy estimates was shaved to £900,000, but without affecting new construction. Fisher was satisfied.

Not for years had the estimates been anticipated with so much interest. Their publication on 24 February brought fresh imprecations on the Government. The new construction was termed scandalously inadequate by the Conservative press, the *Daily*

Mail (25 February) asking: 'Is Britain going to surrender her maritime supremacy to provide old-age pensions?' *The Times* was, as usual, more temperate. 'Not guilty,' it summed up its verdict (25 February), 'but don't do it again.' The service press and various naval writers, including Archibald Hurd and Sir William White, accepted the policy of 'marking time' in capital-ship construction: no heroic measures were necessary that year. The Liberal press divided on the issue. The *Manchester Guardian, Daily Chronicle,* and *Daily News* hailed the 'nominal' increase in the estimates as a signal victory over the alarmists. The country's naval position being unassailable, the modest building programme sufficed. But Radical organs like the *Nation* and *Morning Leader* raised the cry of 'bloated armaments'.

The high point of the navy debates came on 9 March. The existing rate of comparative building was giving rise to serious misgivings, and Opposition speakers had been pointing out that if Germany could build dreadnoughts in less than two years, it would upset the figures as to relative strength given by Robertson in the Commons on 2 March: that, in the autumn of 1910, not including 1908 programmes, there would be twelve British capital ships (two 'Nelsons', seven dreadnoughts, three battle cruisers) to Germany's six (four dreadnoughts, two battle cruisers). Robertson had admitted the possibility of German acceleration, which might give Germany ten capital ships at the end of 1910 (7–3). In that case the two ships of the 1908 British programme could be accelerated so as to produce a 14–10 lead at the end of 1910. Balfour now asked (9 March) if it was not true that the German Navy would have a 13–12 lead in capital ships in the autumn of 1911, given existing programmes and building rates.[50] Asquith, deputizing for the ailing Prime Minister, made an important statement in reply. He reiterated Grey's offer of 13 February in the Commons that the British proposal at The Hague for a regular exchange of information on building programmes was open (the Germans still showed no interest), reaffirmed the two-power standard, and explicitly stated that should a German 13–12 edge at the end of 1911 appear possible, the Government would, in the

---

[50] Germany: five already building plus four in the 1908 programme plus four in the 1909 programme; Britain's 12 : 10 building plus the two ships of the 1908 programme, but not including the two 'Nelsons', which were declared to be not of the dreadnought type.

spring of 1909, provide 'not only for a sufficient number of ships, but for such a date of laying down those ships that at the end of 1911 the superiority of Germany which the right honourable gentleman foreshadows would not be an actual fact'.

Asquith's statement was accepted by the Liberal press (only the *Nation* took umbrage) and was received with profound relief by all but the most extreme navalist organs. For the moment, then, navalist fears about the future were allayed. Lord Esher attributed Asquith's satisfactory declaration to the Emperor's letter to Tweedmouth. This, he believed, had put the Government at a disadvantage in resisting Opposition pressure on the naval issue. The famous episode of the Tweedmouth Letter also led to a fatal weakening in the First Lord's position.

The Times of 6 February had published a letter from Esher to the Imperial Maritime League. This organization had been founded at the end of 1907 by some Navy League dissidents with the removal of Fisher from office as one of its prime objectives. Esher's last paragraph contained an explosive sentence: 'There is not a man in Germany, from the Emperor downwards, who would not welcome the fall of Sir John Fisher.' To allay British fears, as reflected in this letter, the Emperor, on his own responsibility and in his own hand, wrote a personal and private nine-page letter to Tweedmouth (16 February). This 'astounding communication', as Tweedmouth described it, reached him on 18 February. The Emperor professed himself wholly unable to understand why any special apprehension should exist in England regarding the rise of the German Navy. German naval preparations were not aimed at England and did not challenge British naval supremacy. Esher's reference to the German opinion of Fisher was described as 'a piece of unmitigated balderdash'.

It was a most extraordinary thing for the German sovereign to write to a British Cabinet minister at all, and King Edward let his nephew know his displeasure over this 'new departure'. Tweedmouth, flattered at receiving a letter from such an exalted source, talked about it everywhere and showed the letter to everybody. It has been suggested that 'the first insidious assaults of the cerebral malady' that would prove fatal in 1909 might account for Tweedmouth's lack of discretion. He compounded his indiscretion by a reply to the Emperor (20 February) which included the new navy estimates a few days before they were due to be submitted to Parliament. This was done, to be sure, with Grey's approval.

The Times Military Correspondent, Repington, got wind of the Emperor's letter at the end of February. It appeared to him 'an insidious attempt to influence, in German interests, a British First Lord, and at a most critical moment, namely, just before the Estimates were coming on in Parliament'.[51] To prevent a recurrence of this action, Repington published an exposé in the form of a letter in *The Times*, 6 March. A strong leader by *The Times*, whose Editor had seen the Emperor's letter, supported Repington. 'If there was any doubt before about the meaning of German naval expansion, none can remain after an attempt of this kind to influence the Minister responsible for our Navy in a direction favourable to German interests; an attempt, in other words, to make it more easy for German preparations to overtake our own.' Few newspapers followed the lead of *The Times*, which was generally denounced for attempting to raise a scare. Rather did the press turn its attack on the hapless First Lord and his 'extraordinary indiscretion'. Tweedmouth's explanation in the Lords, 9 March, dealing mainly with the terms of his reply to the Emperor, was not regarded as satisfactory.

It is both surprising and amusing that Asquith was unaware of the correspondence that had taken place between his First Lord and the German Emperor until he read his *Times* on 6 March![52] The Prime Minister was, naturally, annoyed, but a special Cabinet meeting that day decided to gloss over the whole incident. Accordingly, the same day Asquith told the House that the Emperor's letter had no official character and had therefore been treated as a private communication. He did not reveal the fact that the estimates had been seen by the Emperor before they were submitted to Parliament. The Government's success in concealing the real facts and in preventing a Parliamentary eruption was largely due to its policy of taking Balfour and Lansdowne into its confidence, and so winning their neutrality. The Conservative leaders appreciated that the publication of Tweedmouth's reply would have resulted in an alarm in the Commons that would have injured Anglo-German relations. Nevertheless, the whole affair led to an

---

[51] Lieutenant-Colonel Charles à Court Repington, *Vestigia* (London, 1919), p. 284.
[52] Hardinge to Sir Arthur Davidson (Assistant Private Secretary to the King), 7 Mar. 1908; Windsor MSS.

intensification of bad blood, as many Englishmen were angered over what they considered to be an uncalled-for interference by the German Emperor in a purely British concern.

A second result was a fatal weakening of Tweedmouth's position. The country, and no doubt Tweedmouth himself, was relieved when he retired as part of the Cabinet reshuffle that followed Campbell-Bannerman's death in April. Asquith stepped into the premiership. Unlike Campbell-Bannerman, who had never shown any profound interest in naval policy and who, in any case, had been overtaken by what Esher called 'the indolence of senility', Asquith always took an interest in naval affairs. He had a singularly powerful mind, though one which rarely initiated ideas or schemes. The Admiralty would have to reckon with him, whereas it had been able to ignore his predecessor. The new First Lord was Reginald McKenna. The emotional and energetic Lloyd George moved from the Board of Trade to the Exchequer, and Winston Churchill entered the Cabinet as President of the Board of Trade. For the next three years and more these two led the social reform–arms reduction wing of the Cabinet. It was only a partial offset, from the navalist point of view, that Robertson, with his 'true Scottish tenacity for arithmetical calculations', was retired with a peerage and relieved by the big-navy-minded Macnamara.

The Lloyd George–Churchill team lost no time in going into action. At a meeting of the Board on 4 May McKenna agreed to four dreadnoughts and, if necessary, six, in 1909—'perhaps the greatest triumph ever known,' exulted Fisher, who had come out for the two-keels-to-one standard in dreadnoughts. Grey was ready to resign if the four-to-six dreadnought programme for 1909 were not accepted. But Lloyd George and Churchill insisted that four big ships would be ample, and they seemed to have Asquith on their side. Churchill's determined opposition to substantial increases in the defence estimates was strengthened by a visit to the German Army manœuvres, where he had been the Emperor's guest. He returned convinced of Germany's peaceful intentions and certain that no profound antagonism existed between the two countries. Harcourt chimed in with a speech to his constituents (2 October) strongly reprobating the naval scare-mongering of a section of the press. Nothing but the 'diseased imagination of inferior minds' could see in the German naval programme any overt menace to the peace of the world. Faced with the unpleasant prospect of soaring estimates, which would threaten the Government's programme of social security legislation, the Liberal press during 1908 harped on the theme that the key to armament reductions lay in a naval understanding with Germany—an agreement that would enable both sides to slow down their naval construction.

Anticipations of a naval understanding were raised in Britain as a result of the King's visit to Cronberg on 11 August. Grey himself was hopeful that it would pave the way for a mutual reduction of naval expenditure, which in turn would lead to a friendlier feeling and a sense of security in both countries. He would have been less hopeful had he seen the Emperor's comment on a report from Metternich, the German Ambassador, of 16 July: 'I have no desire for a good relationship with England at the price of the development of Germany's Navy. If England will hold out her hand in friendship only on condition that we limit our Navy, it is a boundless impertinence and a gross insult to the German people and their Emperor, and must be rejected *a limine* by the Ambassador! ... The [Navy] Law will be carried out to the last detail; whether the British like it or not does not matter! If they want war, they can begin it, we do not fear it!'[53]

At Cronberg the King's co-operation with the Foreign Office was something less than enthusiastic. He touched on the tender subject of naval expenditure, but quickly dropped it when the Emperor showed no interest. Later that day (11 August) Hardinge raised the question with the Emperor, stressing the fact that an extensive new construction programme would have to be introduced in 1909, failing an agreement to slacken or modify the building pace. The naval rivalry would embitter Anglo-German relations, 'and might in a few years' time lead to a very critical situation in the event of a serious, or even a trivial, dispute arising between the two countries.' The Emperor was annoyed with Hardinge for raising the naval problem. The German naval programme need disturb no one in England, nor should it lead to any increase in the British Fleet: the German Fleet was not intended for an attack against England, and the British Fleet was already at more than a two-power standard. As for the German programme, 'it had become a point of national honour that it should

[53] *Die Grosse Politik*, xxiv. 104.

be completed. No discussion with a foreign Government could be tolerated; such a proposal would be contrary to the national dignity, and would give rise to internal troubles if the Government were to accept it. He would rather go to war than submit to such dictation.'[54] The Emperor was by this time quite excited. The conversation of Lascelles, the British Ambassador, with the Emperor that evening was equally negative.

The reports from Lascelles and Hardinge convinced the Foreign Office that the German attitude on the naval question had hardened and that nothing more could be done for the present owing to the 'wearisome' repetition of the German refrain (by the Emperor, the German Government, and the press alike) that no foreign influence could be permitted to dictate the size of the German Navy. One result of the Emperor's intransigence was that the King became a convert to the two-keels-to-one standard, 'the only right and safe thing'. And never again did the British Government take the initiative in proposing a settlement of the naval rivalry.

During 1908 the country was often warned in the press that a German invasion attempt, a 'bolt from the blue', was in the offing. Journals as different as the *Army and Navy Gazette* and the Socialist *Clarion* indulged in this kind of talk. Evidence of aggressive intentions was seen in the fact that the High Seas Fleet cruised in the Atlantic in July for the first time. In October Alan H. Burgoyne, Editor of the *Navy League Annual*, published an imaginary invasion novel, *The War Inevitable*, which featured a treacherous German attack on the Fleet.

The situation was hardly improved by the Emperor's famous interview with an anonymous Englishman (actually, Major Stuart-Wortley) which was published in the *Daily Telegraph* of 28 October. The German ruler complained bitterly of the way his actions were misunderstood in England. 'You English are mad, mad as March hares.' He protested that he was a good friend of England, but plainly intimated that the great majority of his subjects were not. He repeated that his Navy was not a menace to England. It was being built, not in preparation for a war with Britain, but to protect the steadily increasing German trade and German interests in the Far East. Grey feared, and told Metternich so, that the British people 'would be shocked by hearing, on the

[54] Hardinge's memorandum, 16 Aug. 1908; *British Documents*, vi. 185-6.

authority of the Emperor, that the majority of the German people are very hostile to us'. He was a true prophet. 'Never since I have been in office,' he sadly declared some weeks later, 'has opinion here been so thoroughly wide awake with regard to Germany, and on its guard as it is now.'[55]

The immediate effect in England of William II's indiscretion was an almost unanimous demand in the navalist press for more battleships, heightened by the realization that the season for Cabinet decisions on the estimates was approaching. To ensure the British position in 1912, the laying down of six dreadnoughts in 1909, the two-keels-to-one-standard, was the 'irreducible minimum' demand. *The Times, The Observer, Daily Express,* and *Standard* preferred seven in 1909, to allow for a 10 per cent margin over the two-power standard; the Navy League asked for eight. The navalist press took the attitude that it was idle to be told that the Navy was invincible at the moment and that the Government intended to maintain the supremacy of the Navy. What they wanted to know was what the Government was doing and proposed to do to make good these protestations. As the *Pall Mall Gazette* put it (10 November): 'Instead of [ministers] paying their debt of information in hard cash they offer the nation their cheque; but the nation likes not the security; it wants to see the colour of their money.'

The Government attempted to remove some of the anxiety by clarifying the standard of strength. There was considerable confusion regarding its meaning. It had been suggested that the Admiralty must lay down one keel to every French and German keel, thus adopting a two-power standard based on the activity of the two most formidable navies in Europe. It had also been urged that there should be a 10 per cent margin over such a standard for contingencies. And it was claimed that, as American ambitions were outrunning those of France, safety lay in a two-power standard calculated by German and American building. Another suggestion was that the Admiralty abandon the two-power standard and adopt a two-German standard (two keels to one). The Prime Minister now, in the Commons on 12 November (again on 23 November), accepted this definition of the two-power standard: a predominance of 10 per cent over the combined

[55] Grey to Sir Edward Goschen (successor to Lascelles in Berlin), 7 Nov. 1908 *ibid.*, p. 206; Grey to Bertie, 1 Dec. 1908; *ibid.*, p. 226.

strengths, in capital ships, of the two next strongest powers. Asquith's declaration went much further than Campbell-Bannerman's declarations of 27 July and 2 August 1906, which had accepted the two-power standard only 'as a rough guide', and qualified it by considerations about 'who the two Powers are': they were to consider which powers were friendly to Britain and which were 'antagonistic to one another'. Asquith's statement was cheered on both sides of the House of Commons and in the navalist press. The Liberal press, excepting the *Daily Chronicle*, was unhappy over a definition that was 'unrealistic' and which threatened the country with financial ruin. There was one important navalist reservation. As stated by one daily, 'The only thing which now remains is to build the ships,' which was precisely what Asquith had not promised to do. Arthur Lee, Balfour's picturesque and able lieutenant in defence matters, expressed the matter with his gift of words (at the Royal United Service Institution, 9 December): 'The Government has, in short, given to the country an I.O.U. payable in three months, and I believe the country means to see that the I.O.U. is not only honoured but honoured in full.'

Since the Government steadfastly refused to disclose its building programme before the next session of Parliament, the navalist agitation continued during the winter, growing more intense as the time approached for the publication of the estimates. Public opinion was 'in a mood of intense suspense and even of painful anxiety' (*The Observer*, 7 February 1909). There was also near-panic on the other side. The Liberal press felt that the inevitable and unavoidable addition to the estimates should not exceed £3,000,000; three or four capital ships would be ample and would prove to Germany that Britain was not out to secure a 'provocative and crushing hegemony'. Liberals were appalled by a rumour at the end of January that the estimates would show a £6,000,000 increase and a programme of eight dreadnoughts. If this became an actuality, it would destroy the unity of the Liberal Party, warned the *Nation* and the *Daily News*.

The Admiralty throughout 1908 saw no sign of immediate danger. It shared Dumas's confidence that the Germans would keep the peace for the next three or four years. The Attaché's conclusion was based on various considerations, among them: (1) British forces in home waters were at least twice as strong as those of Germany. (2) The Germans had only two harbours of refuge in the North Sea for their ships, Wilhelmshaven and Brunsbüttel. The latter was open to attack by torpedo craft; the former could not accommodate more than ten or twelve ships until the works in progress were completed, which would be four years or more. (3) Until the widening of the Kiel Canal was completed, the new big ships must make the passage from the Baltic to the North Sea round the Skaw, which was a dangerous trip. (4) German experts viewed the present state of their coast defences 'with the greatest misgivings'. They were to be reconstructed.[56]

However, Dumas's long report a few months later, on giving up his post, was pessimistic as regards Germany's intentions a few years hence and gave the Admiralty cause for apprehension. He spoke of the 'widespread hatred' of England on the part of the German masses. He traced this to envy of Britain's colonies, exasperation over the hampering of her economic expansion in every direction by British vested interests, a feeling of fury that Britain would not recognize Germany as a great power, and anger that British diplomacy had worsted the Germans at the time of the South African War and the Moroccan Crisis. The very powerful German Navy League had done its work so well that 'I even doubt now whether the Emperor, much as he might desire it, could restrain his own people from attempting to wrest the command of the seas from Great Britain, if they saw a fairly good chance of doing so.' Germany would bide her time until the happy day of reckoning, which day 'is felt to be not so very far distant and wholly to depend on the rapid construction of their fleet and the coincident maintenance of their army—on account of France—at the highest level of efficiency'. The new Navy Law would give Germany thirty-seven 'sound' battleships by the spring of 1915, which, taking the British figure at, roughly, fifty-four, would give the German Navy two-thirds of British naval strength in 1914. All that would be lacking then for an irresistible cry for an attack on England would be 'some temporary trouble abroad' which, by forcing the withdrawal of, say, eight battleships from home waters (above those already in the Mediterranean, and bearing in mind that, according to many British critics, a considerable proportion of H.M. ships were never ready to fight), would give Germany a temporary battleship supremacy. The four

[56] Dumas to Lascelles, 12 Feb. 1908; *British Documents*, vi. 124–5.

occasions for possible action were, Dumas heard, an American-Japanese war, an Anglo-Turkish war for the possession of Egypt, the expiration of the Japanese alliance, and the time (about 1920) when, having colonized Korea, Japan would turn her attention to Australia. The upshot of Dumas's report was that Germany meant to fight England the moment she felt strong enough, for 'at the bottom of every German heart today is rising a faint and wildly exhilarating hope that a glorious day is approaching when by a brave breaking through of the lines which he feels are encircling him, he might even wrest the command of the seas from England and thus become a member of the greatest power by land or sea that the world has ever seen.'[57]

Graham Greene, the Assistant Secretary of the Admiralty, dryly observed that the paper would have been more interesting, had Dumas mentioned the sources from which he derived his impressions. It could not have been from German naval officers, because in one place he expressed his regret of lack of opportunities for social intercourse with them. Greene's assumption, doubtless correct, was that the Attaché had relied on current German literature.

A dispatch by Colonel Trench, the Military Attaché in Berlin, was similar in tone to Dumas's. He drew attention to the very general state of 'nervous irritation' in Germany. The responsibility for this he attributed mainly to the 'shocks' received by German foreign policy in the last few months, especially the meeting of King Edward and the Tsar at Reval in June, the Pan-Slavic Congress at Prague in July, and the Turkish constitutional movement, with its accompanying displays of Anglophilism. Trench's conclusion was that 'as far as mental preparation for war goes, the country is mobilized, so that, should it be determined to appeal to arms at any time before a relaxation of the tension takes place, all that will be necessary will be to give the word to start.'[58]

Trench's report made a deep impression at the Admiralty. Slade, the D.N.I., felt (9 September) that the causes of German irritability were two. There was a 'natural' cause: the necessity for territorial and trade expansion because of the annual population growth of a million. And there was an 'artificial' cause: the campaign of abuse of England—England held up as the source of

[57] Dumas to Lascelles, 30 July 1908; Admiralty MSS.
[58] Trench to Lascelles, 17 Aug. 1908; *ibid.*

all Germany's ills—engineered by the Government to enable it to pass the Navy Bill. 'The Emperor has . . . sown the wind and is now . . . reaping the whirlwind. The impetus given to uneducated opinion is such that he cannot now control [it] if he will.' Slade pointed to the 'loss of prestige in Turkey' as another ominous factor. 'The possible outlet for Germany in that direction is for the moment closed, and apparently closed in our favour, which adds another incentive to a possible irrational attempt to cut the Gordian Knot with the sword.' The D.N.I.'s conclusion was that the situation was 'most serious and any hope of a diminution of will to maintain our superiority would only encourage Germany to take some step which both Powers would ultimately bitterly regret'. Admiral May, the Second Sea Lord, was convinced (18 September) that 'an overwhelmingly strong and superior Navy to Germany is the best way to keep peace'.

Evidence piled up at the Admiralty during the year of the formidable nature of the German naval challenge. The new Attaché, Captain Herbert L. Heath (August 1908–August 1910), had the same impressions of the efficiency of the Emperor's Fleet as had his predecessors. One of his first reports stated flatly that 'in the course of a few years the German officer may equal ours in readiness of resource and capability of action. Under these circumstances it appears that the safety of the Empire will be entirely dependent on superiority of fighting units.'[59] Slade minuted this report: 'There is no doubt that the German Navy has made great advances lately and that they are straining every nerve to improve.' Disturbing reports towards the end of the year seemed to put in jeopardy Britain's all-important 'superiority of fighting units'. They put into the shade the principal event of the British naval year, the assemblage of over 300 warships for manœuvres in the North Sea during the summer. This armada, of unparalleled strength in the numbers and the fighting capacity of its ships, had been mobilized with ease and without a single mishap in the three weeks of war manœuvres. This magnificent demonstration of naval efficiency tended to be forgotten at the Admiralty as the reports of German naval progress poured in.

The backdrop against which the greatest navy scare in English history was to be played was the gloomy international scene. On 25 September 1908 the French had forcibly recaptured three

[59] Report of 26 Aug. 1908; *ibid.*

German deserters from the French Foreign Legion who were being assisted in their escape by the German consulate in Casablanca. The Germans demanded an apology. The French refused and proposed arbitration. The Germans insisted that an apology must come first. The resulting Franco-German crisis did not end until mid-November, when it was agreed to refer the question to arbitration. For a while France was within an inch of war, and with a good chance of British participation. Esher noted in his journals, 5 November: 'I have never known a more anxious day. I was at the Defence Committee for many hours,' and, on 12 November: 'On Saturday last it looked like war. . . . [the French] never asked or attempted to enquire whether we were going to their assistance. In point of fact, Asquith, Grey, and Haldane had decided to do so.'[60] The Bosnian Crisis during the winter of 1908–9, provoked by the Austrian annexation of the Turkish provinces of Bosnia and Herzegovina in October 1908, came hard on the heels of the Casablanca crisis.

Only one ingredient was needed as 1908 neared its end to convert public uneasiness as well as uneasiness at Whitehall into a first-class scare, and that was intelligence of German acceleration of their naval building programme.

[60] *Esher*, ii. 356, 359.

VII

The Navy Scare of 1909

> . . . other things being equal, the naval power of a nation can be easily and quickly assessed with a close approximation to accuracy by an examination of her strength in battleships . . . . to an Empire such as our own, which must maintain the command of the sea in war or perish, it will not be misleading . . . if we decide to assess our relative naval strength upon the basis of the numbers of battleships we possess, compared with the numbers of similar vessels in the hands of our potential enemies or rivals.
>
> *Admiralty memorandum*, 'The Balance of Naval Power, 1906',
> 30 April 1906.

> The nervous tension, not to say fear of the German Fleet, increased so much in England that in the spring of 1909 it presented a spectacle which was unworthy of the proud tradition of this first sea power.
>
> WIDENMANN to Tirpitz, 28 July 1912.

> I have looked up the word 'scare' in the dictionary and I find that it is an 'imaginary alarm'. Well, it was not an imaginary alarm. Another dictionary says, 'a purely imaginary or causeless alarm', and it was not a purely imaginary or causeless alarm.
>
> SIR MAURICE HANKEY before the Royal Commission on the Private Manufacture of and Trading in Arms, 1936.

> In the end a curious and characteristic solution was reached. The Admiralty had demanded six ships: the economists offered four: and we finally compromised on eight.
>
> CHURCHILL, *The World Crisis*.

I. PROLOGUE

THE QUESTION of possible German acceleration had come up in the House navy debates of March 1908. Now, in the late autumn and early winter of 1908–9, there was growing public anxiety over rumours of acceleration of German shipbuilding and in the production of armour-plate, guns, and gun-mountings, on which the shipbuilding rate itself depended. On 8 December 1908 McKenna recommended to the Cabinet a new shipbuilding programme of six dreadnoughts (Fisher would have preferred eight), instead of the planned four dreadnoughts for 1909–10. In spite of Churchill and Lloyd George, the Government intended to carry out the Admiralty recommendation unless it received a definite assurance from Berlin that there would be a slackening in the German programme. Metternich was so informed on 18 December.

The situation was as follows : the first two German dreadnoughts had been authorized in 1906, and three more in 1907 (of which one was a battle cruiser). Four of these five big ships had been laid down in August 1907, the fifth in March 1908. Under the supplementary German Navy Law of 1908, four more (including a battle cruiser) were scheduled for 1908 (laid down in November 1908), and four again in 1909. This made a grand total of thirteen German capital ships building and projected, and expected to be ready in 1912, although not one was actually in commission in March 1909. This was the British position early in 1909 : ten capital ships built or building, plus the two authorized in the 1908 estimates, plus the six the Admiralty wanted in the 1909 estimates, would give England eighteen big ships in 1912. Now, 18–13 would hardly allow for a two-power standard in dreadnought-type ships. But worse still—and this is the crucial factor, which explains the navy scare that developed and the Admiralty's insistence on a minimum programme of six—it was believed that for a certainty the Germans would have seventeen by the spring of 1912, and that they *might* have twenty-one. How? Through an acceleration of the German programme. What evidence was there at Whitehall of German acceleration?

From official and private sources, it was evident that (1) German shipbuilding capacity had been significantly increased, and with it went the possibility of quicker shipbuilding. (2) The time required to manufacture turret gun-mountings was the determining factor in the production of big ships. Jellicoe, the new Controller, learned through private sources that the productive capacity of Krupp's (principal contractors for guns and gun-mountings) in gun-mountings had been greatly increased, now 'considerably exceeded' that of British gun-mounting firms, and gave the Admiralty 'good reason' for believing that the Germans had the capacity to build eight big ships a year. Actually, the Admiralty had exaggerated (honestly) the increase in Krupp's productive facilities for gun-mountings. (3) Krupp's had been secretly accumulating nickel, and the main use of nickel was in the construction of guns, armour, and gun-mountings. The German Government had fairly recently purchased an 'unusually large amount' of nickel for the manufacture of armour. There was, then, every indication that the Germans meant to build up to the full extent of their capacity. The business firms, McKenna thought, would hardly be expending vast sums in plant expansion and accumulation of material if they did not expect a spurt in shipbuilding. For these reasons the Admiralty believed that the German *capacity to build capital ships* was at the moment equal to theirs, and that the British yards could no longer count on having a one-year advantage in shipbuilding speed (two years *v.* three). This was a 'most alarming conclusion'.

We know today that, mainly due to the improvised facilities at Krupp's for stepping up the manufacture of capital-ship armament, the German yards *could* build a dreadnought or battle cruiser in twenty-seven to thirty-three months, instead of the thirty-two to thirty-six months allowed in the contracts and always given by Tirpitz as the minimum time.[1]

The Admiralty deduced from the following facts that the Germans actually were using their increased engineering facilities to speed up dreadnought construction: (1) An analysis of the German estimates for 1909–10 (available to the British Government in December 1908) showed that the *first three* instalments for the 1906–7 and 1907–8 capital ships were little more than the *first two* instalments for the 1908–9 ships. This could be taken to mean that the later ships were, as Jellicoe believed, 'vastly more powerful than our later ships', or, as the Admiralty concluded, that the German building rate had been speeded up. In the event, Jellicoe was right. (2) The Admiralty had information that the materials for the capital ships building had been collected in advance of their laying down, and that, in similar fashion, the four big ships of the 1909 programme had been anticipated. They had been ordered in October 1908, and the firms were collecting the materials and making preparations for laying down the ships early in the financial year, which began on 1 April. The Admiralty hypothesis was based on reports in the German press in October 1908, confirmed by the Naval Attaché in Berlin and by the Consul in Danzig, that contracts had been given out in advance for three

[1] Ship Construction Office of the German Ministry of Marine, 'Memorandum on the Shortening of Construction Time . . .', 2 Dec. 1908; German Ministry of Marine MSS.

of the battleships belonging to the 1909–10 programme. This was at least six months before the usual time, and before the Reichstag had voted the necessary credits. 'Hence,' as McKenna summarized the matter, 'the terms of the law are no guide to the dates when the ships will be completed. We are bound therefore to look at the German capacity to build, and we can best judge what they can do by what they are doing.'[2] The German capacity to build dreadnoughts was, McKenna believed, equal to the British, which 'last conclusion is the most alarming, and if justified would give the public a rude awakening should it become known'.[3]

Although the placing of contracts for the 1909 ships was denied by the German Naval Attaché, Widenmann (15 December 1908), it was later admitted by Metternich (18 March 1909) that the contracts of two of the four ships of the 1909 programme had been placed in October 1908,[4] prior to the Reichstag grant of funds but conditional on it (tenders for the other two would be called for in the autumn of 1909), *and that only because of financial considerations.* As Grey explained, '. . . the German Government had found that the shipbuilders were forming a Trust to put up the prices against the Government, and in order to prevent the formation of this Trust contracts for these two ships were promised in advance to two shipbuilding firms, on the understanding that the Reichstag would be willing to vote the money subsequently.'[5] No evidence has ever been unearthed that would challenge the truthfulness of Metternich's statement; but it came a little late in the day and was, in any case, suspect.

Taking all factors into consideration, it was regarded by the Sea Lords in January as a 'practical certainty' that Germany would have seventeen dreadnoughts and battle cruisers by the spring of 1912, not thirteen, as in the official schedule. This was based on the assumption that the four dreadnoughts of the 1910

[2] McKenna to Grey, 30 Dec. 1908; Stephen McKenna, *Reginald McKenna, 1863–1943* (London, 1948), p. 72.
[3] McKenna to Asquith, 3 Jan. 1909; Asquith MSS.
[4] 'Six months ahead of the financial year, about eight months before the money is voted and about fourteen months before British ships of a corresponding year are allotted. If this practice is continued, there is no reason why Germany should not complete her ships in little more than two years from April of the Programme Year': Slade's minute (he had succeeded Ottley, now Secretary of the C.I.D., as D.N.I.), 21 Oct. 1908, on a dispatch from H.M. Consul in Danzig, confirming that two battleships of the next year's programme had already been given out; Admiralty MSS.
[5] Grey to Goschen, 18 Mar. 1909; *British Documents*, vi. 245.

programme would be ordered in the autumn of 1909 (just as the four capital ships of the 1909 programme had, supposedly, been ordered in the autumn of 1908) and laid down in April 1910. There was a 'possibility' that Germany would have twenty-one capital ships by 1912 if she used her full shipbuilding capacity without financial restriction. 'Owing to the fact that four slips will be vacant by next summer, and the workmen of the appropriate trades will then be idle, it is quite practicable for 4 more to be laid down during the latter part of 1909, and to be ready before the end of 1911: thus making the 21 ships ready by April 1912.'[6] This frightening possibility caused the Sea Lords to amend their recommendation on the 1909 building programme. According to them, including older battleships (but omitting the fifteen 'Majestics' and 'Canopuses' for England and the ten 'Kaisers' and 'Wittelsbachs' for Germany, whose total value was 'about equal') and assuming Britain laid down six ships, the comparison in April 1912 would be: Germany, seventeen dreadnoughts (for certain) and ten pre-dreadnoughts; Great Britain, eighteen dreadnoughts and twenty-five pre-dreadnoughts. Giving a comparative value to each type of ship (dreadnoughts, 100 points each; pre-dreadnoughts, between 40 and 80 points each), the figures worked out at 3,200 versus 2,300 in Britain's favour, or a ratio of 4 : 3. If Germany completed twenty-one ships and Great Britain twenty (based on an eight-ship programme in 1909–10), the figures became 3,400 to 2,700, or a 5 : 4 ratio.

The Two-Power Standard has not been mentioned in this memorandum for the simple reason that at the present moment the struggle is to maintain the One-Power Standard against Germany alone. . . .

Looking to the fact that our superiority of power over Germany will in 1912, even on the most favourable hypothesis, be dependent almost entirely on older ships, and that these older ships will gradually fall out, when only Dreadnoughts will count as line of battle ships, we consider the situation is serious, and we wish to emphasize the point that Great Britain's 18 to Germany's 17 Dreadnoughts in 1912 is not considered in any way adequate to maintain the command of the sea in a war with Germany without running undue risk.

We therefore consider it of the utmost importance that power should be taken to lay down two more armoured ships in 1909–10—making eight in all, as, unless there is an unexpected modification in Germany's

[6] Memorandum by the Sea Lords for the First Lord, 15 (?) Jan. 1909; Lennoxlove MSS. The material that follows is from the same document.

anticipated shipbuilding programme, resulting in her not completing 17 ships by the Spring of 1912, it will be necessary to provide for eight new British ships to be completed by this date, the last two being laid down at the end of March 1910.

As a matter of fact, eight capital ships was the very maximum construction possible in one year. There were slips for laying down many more than eight ships in a year, but there was not the plant for turning out the armament for more than eight.

The Admiralty position was strengthened by an acute depression in the shipbuilding and engineering industries during 1908. On the Clyde alone, warship building had fallen in two years from something over 50,000 tons to about 5,000 tons. By September more than a third of the engineers were out of work. The *Daily Mail* sounded a clarion call on 18 April 1908: 'If the Government is not composed of stoney-hearted pedants, the shipbuilding vote should be given out now . . . 80 per cent of the cost of a battleship goes in wages to the British worker. A large shipbuilding programme is the best preventive of distress.' The service press and the Navy League took up the cry in September–October. While there is no evidence that the grave situation in the shipbuilding industry was a factor in the formulation of the 1909 big-ship programme by the Admiralty, it did strengthen the Admiralty case. The Conservatives made political capital of the unemployment situation. Leaflets issued from party headquarters in April 1909 recommended the construction of battleships as a proper method of providing for the unemployed. 'Our Navy and our unemployed,' said one, 'may both be starved together; and soon will be if you don't turn this Government out!'

2. THE MULLINER AFFAIR

Enter H. H. Mulliner, the able Managing Director of the Coventry Ordnance Works. This was a new armament firm, established in 1904–5 and owned by three large shipbuilding firms, John Brown, Cammell Laird, and the Fairfield Shipbuilding Company. In May 1906 Mulliner had warned the Admiralty that Germany had the capacity to accelerate her naval construction in view of the 'enormous expenditure now going on at Krupp's for the purpose of manufacturing very large naval guns and mountings quickly'. But he made no statement that the German programme was in fact being accelerated, nor did he do so when, at various times, down to April 1908, he supplemented his information. The facts were substantially correct, but the Admiralty had not been moved by Mulliner's statements to enlarge its shipbuilding programme in 1906, 1907, or 1908. Intelligence received at the Admiralty in the autumn of 1908 from its own sources caused Mulliner's earlier disclosures to be treated seriously. He was able to add some 'new and important' information, 'if reliable' (Ottley), in a conversation with the Secretary of the C.I.D. on 24 February 1909. He drew Ottley's attention to the enormous development of Krupp's works during the past six years—45,000 workers in 1902, 100,000 in 1909—and to the fact that Krupp's had recently made arrangements for increasing their output of heavy guns and mountings at a moment's notice. Their maximum output of heavy guns and mountings was double that of the three British sources combined. Krupp's system of gun construction, together with the superior type of machinery they possessed for constructing gun-mountings, gave them a great advantage over the English and enabled them to turn out a gun in a third less time. Mulliner's deduction was that, if the Germans suddenly so decided, they could outbuild the English in battleships, since they would be in a position to arm the ships as soon as they were built.

That Mulliner was actuated by patriotic motives need not be doubted. But that is not the entire story. Coventry Ordnance and the three parent shipbuilding companies were operating in the red, largely because Coventry had received no orders for heavy guns and mountings since its organization, and the parent firms had had no big-ship orders. Mulliner certainly hoped for some gun-mounting orders as a result of a large new dreadnought programme. He 'pestered' the Government, as Hankey afterwards charged.

The pressure of armament firms was nothing new. It had been a factor in the big-navy movement and the great expansion of the Navy from the 1880's. The armament industry held various trump cards: (1) It was well equipped for the exercise of pressure on the Government through the large number of distinguished shareholders or directors, and through the employment of former high officials in the civil, naval, or military service: able men who 'knew the ropes'. It was certainly not exceptional when, in 1909, Rear-Admiral Bacon, D.N.O. since 1907, became Managing

Director of the Coventry Ordnance Works, and when, in 1912, two officials occupying highly confidential and influential positions on retirement from service joined the board of Armstrong's as directors: Sir Charles Ottley and Sir George Murray, until 1911 the Permanent Secretary of the Treasury. (2) The intimate interdependence of the industrial fabric and the manufacture of armaments, especially in time of economic stress: outlay on the Navy provided work for very large numbers of men. (3) The insistence of navalist opinion, publicly affirmed to some extent by the Government, that in an era of international strife it was imperative that the private armament firms be kept in efficient condition, able to expand production at a moment's notice. (4) The intimate and cordial co-operation among the armament firms, which were nominally rivals.

The reality of the first two trumps is confirmed by this excerpt from an Admiralty memorandum prepared for the Government prior to the Hague Conference of 1907, stating its views on the suggested limitation of naval armaments:

The vested interests concerned in war-ship construction are moreover, nowadays, very large, with ramifications in almost every branch of manufacture and trade.

The immediate effect of any proposal to limit naval armaments will be to deal a heavy blow at these interests, with the result that the latter would in all probability array themselves against the movement, and the consequent opposition thus created would be a formidable obstacle.

And, again, this country more than any other has a supreme interest in the maintenance of her shipbuilding trade in a flourishing and healthy condition. Will it be advisable for Britain to enrol herself under the banner of 'Limited Naval Armaments' if, as seems inevitable, such limitation will react seriously upon one of our premier national industries?[7]

Obviously, the armament firms had a direct interest in the inflation of the Army and Navy estimates, and their pressure could be very real and effective. Nevertheless, we should not exaggerate the role played by the armament interests in naval expansion and particularly in the great scare of 1909. The Mulliner affair was later blown up into the legend that he was responsible for the eight-dreadnought building programme in

[7] 'Memorandum on Limitation of Naval Armaments . . .', 29 Jan. 1907; Admiralty MSS.

1909–10, and his name became a symbol for the nefarious influence of the 'merchants of death'. The facts are that, so far as we know, Mulliner was the only representative of an armament firm who was in touch with the Government during the 1909 navy scare, and that his information had no part in the formulation of the Admiralty's building programme. Mulliner did, however, play an important role in the scare through his private disclosures to the Opposition of the facts he had given to the Government. (He did not make any statement publicly until an anonymous letter from him appeared in the *Standard* of 26 June, and a signed letter in *The Times* of 2 August.) Thereby he helped to stoke the fires of the agitation that eventually resulted in a larger building programme. Balfour and Lee, in the Commons debate of 29 March, revealed that it was from the private firms (meaning Mulliner) that they had obtained their information.

3. PEAK OF THE CRISIS

Inside the Cabinet during January and February the pot was simmering and on the verge of boiling over. The Ministers had been given all the Admiralty information as well as the revised recommendation of the Sea Lords. But the Radicals in the Cabinet, seeing the party's social reform programme menaced by the large navy estimates in the offing, were not impressed. Moreover, many of them believed that substantially increased estimates would topple the Government. Thus, Lloyd George to Asquith: 'I will not dwell upon the emphatic pledges given by all of us before and at the last general election to reduce the gigantic expenditure on armaments built up by the recklessness of our predecessors. Scores of your most loyal supporters in the House of Commons take these pledges seriously and even a £3,000,000 increase will chill their zeal for the Gov^t and an assured increase of 5 to £6,000,000 for next year will stagger them. . . . [and they] will hardly think it worth while to make any effort to keep in office a Liberal Ministry.'[8] The two musketeers, Lloyd George and Churchill (with the latter taking the lead), were unable to agree with McKenna and his professional advisers that a dangerous situation would exist in 1912. They did not believe that Germany was building dreadnoughts secretly in excess of the 1900 law. (Lloyd

[8] 2 Feb. 1909; Asquith MSS.

George thought that the German Government was only trying to relieve unemployment in the shipyards by starting ships a few months in advance of the statutory period of construction.) Four dreadnoughts in the new estimates would be enough to ensure adequate British superiority in 1912. (Custance and Sir William White were providing Churchill with technical arguments for a programme of four—because, said Fisher, they knew that he would resign if that programme were adopted.) But Lloyd George and Churchill were willing that it be intimated to the House of Commons that, if the progress of German construction during the year showed it to be necessary, Parliament would, later on, be asked to sanction two additional ships. Other Radical members of the Government who felt the same way included Morley, Loreburn, Burns, and Harcourt. The Radical argument stressed Britain's overwhelming superiority in pre-dreadnoughts. The big-navy group in the Cabinet, led by McKenna and Grey, and including Crewe (with reservations), Runciman, and Haldane, was equally adamant on six dreadnoughts, without reservations, as the minimum programme. (Fisher and McKenna were, during February, working behind the scenes for *eight*, although they believed six would be sufficient.) The Radical ministers would have resigned on anything above four. The Prime Minister favoured six.

The battle raged around the question of six or four. Personalities were involved and tempers were frayed. 'What are Winston's reasons for acting as he does in this matter?' asked Knollys. 'Of course it cannot be from conviction or principle. The very idea of his having either is enough to make anyone laugh . . .'[9] Esher, a Liberal in politics, was furious with the two leaders of the economist faction of the Cabinet. An interesting letter of his reveals how deeply distrusted they were even in their own party. Churchill's tactics, he thought, were dominated by his ambition to lead the Radical wing of the party. 'George, on the other hand, will some day drift over to the Tories. . . . George is a round man in a square hole. He *believes* in the Navy but is just now hampered by the fact that he is a representative radical. So he is dragging on the tail of Winston. . . . I never believe these people will fight to the death. Their case is too bad.'[10]

[9] Knollys to Esher, 10 Feb. 1909; Esher MSS.
[10] Esher to Knollys, 12 Feb. 1909; Windsor MSS.

McKenna violently disliked Lloyd George for his lack of moral principle. The latter now made certain that McKenna never would have any use for him. The occasion was a meeting in Grey's room at the Foreign Office, 24 January, during a general discussion of German facilities for the manufacture of gun-mountings, etc. The Sea Lords were present as well as McKenna and various other Cabinet members. Lloyd George, who was pacing the floor, suddenly threw out a remark to the following effect: 'I think it shows extraordinary neglect on the part of the Admiralty that all this should not have been found out before. I don't think much of any of you admirals, and I should like to see Lord Charles Beresford at the Admiralty, and the sooner the better.' McKenna fired back: 'You know perfectly well that these facts were communicated to the Cabinet at the time we knew of them, and your remark was, "It's all contractors' gossip," or words to that effect.'[11]

There was absolute deadlock in the Cabinet by the end of January. The Admiralty played a waiting game. On 23 February, Fisher, meeting Austen Chamberlain, one of the Conservative high command, in the middle of Palace Yard, in a loud voice assured him (while asking for secrecy!) that 'he was sitting tight, that the Government didn't want to go out, and that therefore he knew he had the whip hand.'[12] Asquith's patience was wearing thin. 'The economists are in a state of wild alarm, and Winston and Ll. G. by their combined machinations have got the bulk of the Liberal press into the same camp. . . . [They] go about darkly hinting at resignation (which is bluff) . . . but there are moments when I am disposed summarily to cashier them both.'[13]

All this time, from the turn of the year, the Conservative press and politicians had been demanding in the most strident tones that British naval supremacy in 1912 be put beyond any doubt with a programme of six capital ships. Conservative leaders like Austen Chamberlain urged the Sea Lords to 'stand firm' and they would win out, as they had over the Spencer programme in 1893–4. Feelings were running so high that when the *Daily Chronicle* on 26 February announced that the Government had reached agreement on a four-battleship programme, though with power

[11] Quoted in Jellicoe's memorandum for McKenna, 24 Jan. 1909; McKenna MSS.

[12] Austen Chamberlain, *Politics from Inside* (London, 1936), pp. 150–1.

[13] Asquith to Mrs. Asquith, 20 Feb. 1909; McKenna, *McKenna*, p. 79.

to increase the number later in the year if they thought it necessary, Chamberlain exploded. If the Sea Lords accepted that, 'they deserve to be shot, and unless the whole story is false . . . Asquith deserves to be hung.'[14]

Yet the newspaper story was, in substance, correct. With a disruption of the Cabinet a distinct possibility if either four or six were adopted, a compromise was inevitable. It was reached at a crucial Cabinet on 24 February. Asquith hit upon an ingenious solution that satisfied both sides. Four dreadnoughts would be laid down in the ensuing financial year, and four more no later than 1 April 1910 if the necessity for them was proven. The dangerous phase of the Cabinet crisis was over.

Considerable wrangling followed between McKenna, egged on by the Sea Lords, and Asquith as to the exact form in which the compromise should be worded in the estimates. The Sea Lords were afraid that the Government only intended to lay down four capital ships in 1909–10—that, in the words of Hardinge, 'the compromise is meant to throw dust in the eyes of the public by promising more than it is the intention of the Government to carry out.'[15] The First Lord, therefore, on the Sea Lords' insistence, wanted a definite statement to be introduced, as a note to the estimates, that the Government proposed, if they thought proper, to gather materials for the second four ships and so incur liability for them, although no liability was to be discharged during the coming year. The Admiralty felt this would commit the House of Commons, after it had passed the 1909–10 estimates, to voting the necessary money for the contingent four in a future session. The footnote, as finally approved on 5 March, appeared on page 226 of the estimates, and read:

His Majesty's Government may, in the course of the financial year 1909–10, find it necessary to make preparations for the rapid construction of further ships commencing on the first of April of the following financial year. They therefore ask Parliament to entrust them with powers to do this effectively. Such powers that would enable them to arrange in the financial year 1909–10 for the ordering, collection and supply of materials for guns, gun-mountings, armour, machinery and shipbuilding, thus making possible the laying down at the date above indicated of four more ships to be completed by March 1912.

[14] Chamberlain, *Politics from Inside*, p. 153.
[15] Hardinge to Knollys, 26 Feb. 1909; Windsor MSS.

Churchill and Lloyd George, smelling a rat, were now willing that there should be six dreadnoughts in the estimates. It was too late. The Admiralty would not hear of it.

The Sea Lords made it clear, in a memorandum to the First Lord (forwarded to the Prime Minister at their request), that the naval situation was 'far more grave than ever before' and that nothing less than eight ships would do. '. . . the orders for the four ships for April 1st, 1910, must be made absolute in July next, and tenders should be invited at once.'[16] Attached was Fisher's account of a highly significant interview on 2 March with members of an Argentinian naval mission that had just made a close inspection of all the German shipbuilding yards and Krupp's works. The Argentinians had been tremendously impressed by Krupp's enormous capabilities of output and the vastness of the manufacturing plant. They had counted a hundred 12-inch and 11-inch guns nearing completion at Krupp's. This indicated to Fisher the ease and rapidity with which the big German ships could be equipped. The Argentinians also reported that twelve capital ships were in progress (though some had only had their material collected), with a thirteenth begun or about to be. Fisher concluded that Germany would therefore have twelve or thirteen capital ships in April 1911. She would lay down four more in the next few months —there were vacant slips for them. 'They really might lay down *8 fresh ships, as 4 will be launched. We have now only 12 in hand* [built and building]! WE OUGHT TO BUILD AS FAST AS EVER WE CAN. The Germans could certainly have 21 dreadnoughts in April 1912 if they wished it.'

On 10 March, Metternich informed Grey, 'from the most authoritative source', that Germany would not have thirteen dreadnoughts until the end of 1912, and that she would not accelerate her building programme. If the materials for the ships to be laid down in 1909 were being collected in advance, it was at the risk of the contractors. Grey, who had revived his old plan for mutual inspection of shipbuilding in a conversation with Metternich early in March, now reiterated the desirability of the two Admiralties keeping themselves informed through their attachés as to the actual progress of shipbuilding. Otherwise, the Admiralty could never know for certain when ships ordered at any particular time would be completed. 'In default of any arrangement

[16] Undated, but very probably 4 Mar. 1909; McKenna MSS.

between our two countries, it was necessary that we should have some margin on our side.'[17] The Germans showed no interest. Under the circumstances the Government felt it had no choice but to proceed with the estimates. On 17 March, the day after the big navy debate in the House of Commons, Metternich expressed his surprise that the Government spokesmen had not accepted the official assurances of 10 March. But the Admiralty had definite information, Grey replied, that more than thirteen ships were already under construction, and that the discrepancy between this statement and Metternich's was due to the German figure not including battle cruisers. For the third time that month Grey repeated that the only way to prevent such misunderstanding was through the naval attachés being allowed to visit the yards and learn the facts as to the actual progress of shipbuilding. The Ambassador assured Grey (18 March) that the thirteen ships Germany would not complete before the end of 1912 did include battle cruisers.

The assurances given by Metternich in March had no effect on Admiralty calculations and plans. The Ambassador was lying, Fisher believed. 'We have got to have a margin against lying!' Accidentally meeting Metternich on 24 March, and after the two had glared at each other for a moment, Fisher blurted: 'How all this scare then would vanish, Ambassador, if you would let our Naval Attaché go and count them [the capital ships building]!' 'That is impossible!' was the reply. 'Other Governments would also want to—*besides, something would be seen which we wish to keep secret.*' Fisher's inference was that the Germans were building 'much bigger ships than they say they are'.[18]

The estimates (showing an increase of £2¾ million) and the First Lord's explanatory memorandum were issued on 12 March. Caught in a Radical-Tory crossfire, the Government had to tread warily in the navy debates that followed. Their programme had to be palatable to their Radical supporters; at the same time the Opposition had to be satisfied as to the sufficiency of the programme, otherwise the navy scare might well be intensified. The House of Commons was crowded for the first day's navy debate, 16 March. It had been many years since there had been so much eagerness to hear the opening statement on the navy estimates.

---

[17] Grey to Goschen, 10 Mar. 1909; *British Documents*, vi. 241–2.
[18] Fisher to King Edward, 24 Mar. 1909; *Fear God and Dread Nought*, ii. 235–6.

The members listened intently and, for the most part, silently. The tea hour came and went, and nobody left! In the Peers' Gallery sat the Prince of Wales, an eager listener, his head, resting on his hands, thrust forward to hear every word. Behind the Speaker's chair sat Fisher. McKenna, who opened the debate, had his place by the Prime Minister's side. Asquith occasionally prompted him with a word. Near the Prime Minister was Churchill, very much alive with emphatic 'Hear, hears' when McKenna emphasized the necessity for British strength at sea. McKenna rose amid Liberal cheers and proceeded to explain the estimates. His speech, lucid and frank, was entirely free from menace or false rhetoric. The Prime Minister, after a Balfourian interlude, followed in the same strain. When Asquith sat down, the Speaker looked at the House and the House looked at the Speaker, and for three or four minutes no one rose, so grave had been the disclosure of the essential facts.

There was no question of the two-power standard in the debate. All naval comparisons were made with Germany alone. Indeed, the question for the House, Balfour asserted, was whether even a one-power standard was being maintained by the Government with regard to Germany in the crucial question of capital ships. The vital difference between Balfour and Asquith was as to the date of completion of the German ships. According to their respective versions:

	Dreadnoughts and Battle Cruisers		
	Britain	*Germany*	
		Asquith's Version	*Balfour's Version*
April 1911	12	9	13
August 1911	14	11	17
November 1911	16	13	17
April 1912	20[19]	17	21[20]

At the best, therefore, in 1912 Britain would have twenty to the German seventeen; at the worst, sixteen to the German twenty-one. The Prime Minister said it was a physical impossibility for

[19] Included the four conditional dreadnoughts for which the Government took power to order essential parts in 1909-10 if it saw a prospect of Germany having 17 dreadnoughts and battle cruisers in April 1912.

[20] Founded on the assumption that Germany would again lay down eight battleships in 1909 by anticipating four future large armoured ships authorized under the 1908 amendment to the Navy Law.

the Germans to have the extra ships mentioned by Balfour; but Arthur Lee, the principal Opposition speaker in the continuation of the debate on the 17th, repeated Balfour's gloomy vaticinations, thereby deepening the profound impression made by the preceding day's debate.

Nothing further was heard of a Radical mutiny. The motion to reduce the estimates that had been made by the little-navy group in the Commons, 140 strong, was forgotten. Similarly, the Liberal press, chastened by the disclosures in the Commons, no longer questioned whether the dreadnought programme was too large. But it opposed allowing the four contingent ships to become part of the year's programme. Much was made of the 'brutal superiority' in pre-dreadnoughts. Extra ammunition was found in Tirpitz's statement in the Budget Committee of the Reichstag (17 March), an attempt by the Germans to reach the British public with a disclosure of the information Metternich had given Grey that day: Germany would have only thirteen, not seventeen, dreadnoughts (including three battle cruisers) in 1912, and not until the autumn; Germany was not proceeding faster than was prescribed by the law, nor faster than the grants were made. (These assurances were repeated by the Foreign Ministry and Ministry of Marine as late as August. Tirpitz nourished a personal grievance for a long time because his official statements were not officially accepted in England.) Liberal press opinion therefore opined that there was no need for panic regarding 1912 if four dreadnoughts were laid down in 1909. The contingent four were acceptable *only if regarded as an anticipation of the 1910–11 programme*, not as a supplement to the 1909–10 programme.

If Asquith and McKenna had brought the Radicals back into the fold, with a serious reservation, through their convincing disclosures, the same disclosures played into the hands of the Conservatives. The Government 'thought they had got to justify their estimates against a Radical attack on the size of their programme and they prepared their speeches from this point of view. But they were quite wrong. All they said in their defence against the Little Navy men only served to strengthen the real attack—the charge that they are not doing enough.' This was Austen Chamberlain's analysis,[21] and it was a correct one. Whereas Conservative politicians and press had until 16 March agreed that six dreadnoughts

[21] *Politics from Inside*, p. 160.

in 1909 would be ample, the speeches on the 16th touched off a fierce agitation in Parliament and press. The Government's naval policy must be explicit and free from all ambiguity. The conditional clause of the estimates must be made compulsory. The Government must lay down all eight big ships without delay, and the second four must not be looked upon as the ships of next year's building programme. Even with the eight, they would have only a three-ship superiority over a one-power standard. Pre-dreadnoughts no longer counted for much. This was the gist of the Conservative case.

'We want eight, and we won't wait,' coined by the Conservative M.P. George Wyndham, was the slogan of the hour. Battle was joined between the 'panicmongers', or patriots, as they preferred to be called, and the 'pacifists' or 'Little Englanders'. Declared the *Daily News* (23 March), 'Panic, always infectious, is spreading like the plague.' Around the four contingent ships the two sides fought like Greeks and Trojans over the body of Patroclus. The *National Review* (April) blamed the transfer of naval supremacy to Germany on Fisher, 'the re-incarnation of Marshal Leboeuf'—the French War Minister who had boasted, on the eve of Metz and Sedan, that the French Army was ready 'to the last gaiter button'. The *Saturday Review* (20 March) termed McKenna's speech of the 16th 'the most miserable, humiliating piece of news that the public have read since the time of Stormberg and Maggersfontein [South African War].' *The Observer* (21 March) advised Englishmen to 'insist on "the Eight, the whole Eight, and nothing but the Eight," with more to follow, and break any man or faction that now stands in the way.' The *Pall Mall Gazette* (18 March) passionately cried out that, 'as in the France of 1792—and of 1870—the cry is beginning to re-echo through the land—"Citoyens, la Patrie est en danger!" ' '. . . we are not yet prepared to turn the face of every portrait of Nelson to the wall,' declared the *Daily Telegraph* (18 March), 'and to make in time of peace the most shameful national surrender recorded in the whole pages of history.' The other Conservative journals, including *The Times*, expressed themselves with equal vigour, as did the Navy League, the Imperial Maritime League, the Defence Committee of the London Chamber of Commerce, and a new organization, the Society of Islanders. Esher was so aroused that he spoke of hanging the Board of Admiralty if they did not get the eight ships ordered at once.

The King was another outspoken eight-dreadnought supporter. Curiously, the service organs—the *Army and Navy Gazette, Naval and Military Record*, and Brassey's *Naval Annual*—were not victims of *hysteria navalis*. They minimized the elements of alarm in the situation and would have been satisfied with a programme of six dreadnoughts.

On 19 March Esher wrote: 'The Government are not yielding an inch—so they will have to be smitten hard.' And smitten hard they were that day when Balfour gave notice of a vote of censure, 'That, in the opinion of this House, the declared policy of His Majesty's Government respecting the immediate provision of battleships of the newest type does not sufficiently secure the safety of the Empire.' The motion was introduced because of the Prime Minister's persistent refusal to pledge himself to the certain building of the four contingent dreadnoughts. The motion was taken by the Liberals to mean that the Opposition had frankly decided upon an attempt to make party capital out of the Navy. The Prime Minister, in rather excited language, spoke in the Commons on 22 March of the 'unscrupulous, unpatriotic, and manipulated party agitation'. The Conservative responded in kind. 'Since Nero fiddled there has never been a spectacle more strange, more lamentable than the imperilling of the whole priceless heritage of centuries to balance a party Budget' (*Daily Telegraph*, 24 March).

The debate on the vote of censure was held before a packed House on 29 March. There was a combination of quietness and strength in Grey's speech, the principal one on the Government side. He did not deny the gravity of the situation. Nevertheless, the Government should not be pledged specifically in regard to the contingent four. To build these ships now, when they were not necessary, would deprive the Government of the power of adapting the British programme to any improved types the Germans might build. Again Grey suggested that the two Admiralties exchange information as to the progress of their expenditure and their building, each power to give the representatives of the other free access to its dockyards and arsenals. (The Emperor got very excited over the reiteration of this proposal, deeming Grey's advances an 'offence and comparable to the request of Benedetti's in 1870'!)[22] He accepted Tirpitz's statement of 17 March, but he pointed to the increase in German shipbuilding facilities as

[22] Addendum to Tirpitz's report of 3 Apr. 1909; German Ministry of Marine MSS.

making acceleration possible, should the German Government ever decide to speed up the execution of the Navy Law. Accordingly, H.M. Government declined to let Tirpitz's assurances alter its proposals for power to begin the four supplementary dreadnoughts in April 1910. These ships were not intended as a limitation on the next year's programme. In the speech was a solemn warning that if the armaments race among the powers continued to be stepped up, 'sooner or later I believe it will submerge civilisation'. Balfour concluded the debate with a strong statement about the scant margin of superiority on which the Government was relying. The resolution was lost by 353 to 135.

Few were converted by the debate. Each side insisted that its case had been proved by the debate, and each side continued to use Brassey's *Naval Annual*, Jane's *Fighting Ships*, and other reference books to work out its own comparative tables. A little juggling with ships completed, completing, or projected could bring out almost any desired result! The game could be, and was, played at the highest levels. Churchill, when First Lord, was to write that 'in the technical discussion of naval details there is such a wealth of facts that the point of the argument turns rather upon their selection than upon their substance'.[23] And so, in 1909, for example, in making naval comparisons much depended on whether one reckoned the two 'Lord Nelsons' as dreadnoughts (as the Radicals were prone to) or as pre-dreadnoughts (Admiralty, Conservatives).

The agitation for eight dreadnoughts at once continued into April and May, but its force had been largely spent. By the end of May the *Hysteria Germanica* had simmered down considerably. The publication of Lloyd George's revolutionary budget on 29 April was an important distraction. All this time the Admiralty was proceeding on the assumption that the contingent four were as good as definitely promised and would be ordered in the financial year 1909–10, though their keel plates would not be laid until 1 April 1910. It was by no means certain that the Admiralty and their Cabinet supporters would have their way in the face of the unyielding attitude of Lloyd George, Churchill & Co., who considered that no definite promise had been made about the second four dreadnoughts. (Fisher had facetiously suggested to Churchill that the four additional ships be named *Winston*,

[23] Cabinet paper, 'Naval Estimates, 1914–15', 10 Jan. 1914; Asquith MSS.

Churchill, Lloyd, and *George.* 'How they would fight! Uncircumventable!') If forced to accept an eight-ship programme, they would count the contingent four as the 1910–11 programme, so making the two years' programme one of eight, or at most ten, big armoured ships. The Admiralty envisaged twelve: the eight in 1909–10 plus four in 1910–11. As the Cabinet die-hards stubbornly held their positions, resignation rumours involving McKenna and Grey in particular filled the spring air. McKenna was reported as 'very sore with his colleagues about the way he has been treated in regard to the contingent Dreadnoughts'. His ire was directed against Lloyd George and Churchill, and to some extent against Asquith because of his 'weakness'.[24] Grey was apparently ready to leave the Cabinet if the four contingent ships, or at least two, were not ordered during the current financial year.[25] Asquith lent aid and comfort to the die-hard cause. In his Glasgow speech of 17 April the Prime Minister asserted that the large number of pre-dreadnoughts secured Britain's position for some years to come, and that it would be unwise to lay down eight battleships that year, because a better type might possibly be discovered thereafter.

Even as Asquith spoke, the naval situation was being revolutionized through intelligence of Austrian dreadnought plans. On 3 December 1908 Fisher had warned the Prime Minister that the new Austrian naval programme included dreadnoughts, but the whole matter was forgotten until early April 1909. Austria had nine effective pre-dreadnoughts in commission with three more building. Intelligence reports now revealed that, while no work had yet been started on an Austrian dreadnought, the intention to build three or four of them was serious. 'Strong if not convincing evidence' was the order given some months earlier for the construction of a large floating dock at Pola. There was the possibility of Germany building the ships for Austria. Asquith was so disturbed that he sent a special messenger to Fisher on a Sunday night (Easter Sunday, 11 April) at 11 p.m. to ask for immediate information on the Austrian dreadnoughts. Austrian construction plans caused even greater anxiety in Italy, where the British Naval Attaché reported that the Italians were 'suffering from an attack

[24] Knollys to King Edward, 27 Mar. 1909: Windsor MSS.; Journals, 20 Mar. 1909: *Esher,* ii. 378.
[25] Hardinge to King Edward, 31 Mar. 1909; Windsor MSS.

of nerves, and they look upon Austria as being able to produce first-class battleships as easily as a conjuror pulls eggs out of a hat'.[26] The upshot was an Italian dreadnought programme.

The Austrian and Italian plans had a decisive impact on British naval policy. The German Navy practically fell out of account in the Government's exposition in Commons on 26 July. The House was bidden to look at what Italy and Austria were doing. Each would probably build four dreadnoughts. One Italian ship had been laid down, the other three would follow later in the year. Consequently, McKenna announced, the Government would make the four contingent dreadnoughts part of the year's programme—'without prejudice' to the 1910–11 programme, as Asquith made clear. One of the four ships of the unconditioned programme had already been laid down, a second would follow in a few days, and the other two (one of them a battle cruiser) in November. Although the keels of the second foursome (again three dreadnoughts and a battle cruiser) would not be laid down until April 1910, the ships would be completed by March 1912, since plans were to be prepared and orders placed in advance. The announcement was in general received with signs of relief by the Conservatives; but, excepting the *Daily Chronicle*, the Liberal press did not believe a case had been made by the Government for the extra four ships. The pre-dreadnoughts, added to the dreadnoughts, would give England a decisive superiority over Germany in 1912; there was no trace of German acceleration; and the Austrian and Italian dreadnoughts would neutralize each other. But the navy scare was over. The restoration of calm and confidence was aided by three grand spectacles of naval strength, the fleet reviews at Spithead on 12 June for the Imperial Press delegates, on the Thames at Southend, 17 July, and, for the Tsar, at Cowes, 31 July.

4. FUTILE NEGOTIATIONS

Bülow, who was eager for good relations with England, was positive that the ill-feeling in England was caused by the fear that Germany was a threat to Britain's historical dominion of the seas. When Tirpitz emphasized that the excitement in England had been caused by the 'false statements' of English ministers regarding

[26] Captain A. H. Williamson to the D.N.I., 25 Apr. 1909; Admiralty MSS.

German shipbuilding, the Chancellor brushed this aside as 'only a side issue'. The important fact was that 'the Germans were building a large fleet and thus arose the danger of a conflict with England. . . . England will oppose us in the whole world and they will take the first opportunity, together with other European powers, to attack us. That could be in two years, as soon as the reorganization of the Russian Army was completed.' Tirpitz saw the root cause of the tension in Britain's economic jealousy, and he cited examples of British interference with German economic enterprise in China, Russia, the Middle East and elsewhere to prove that Germany was 'exposed to economic impoverishment through this ruthless behaviour of the English'. It was a question of whether one believed in a future for Germany or not. If the former were the case, they could ensure decent economic treatment only through a strong navy. Bülow disputed Tirpitz's major premise. It was the *naval* question that was the important consideration.[27] In conversations with Admiral Müller and the Emperor on 14–15 April Bülow 'expressed again and again great apprehension about the maintenance of peace'.

The naval scare [he informed Müller] has reached the point where it hits the money-bags of the English middle classes, otherwise peacefully inclined. They think of the enormous expense made necessary by new building (raising of taxes). They think of the subsequent crash of 'consols'. All of this causes the middle class to turn to that party which promises through a bold policy to do away with the bothersome rivalry for the domination of the seas. A Conservative government in England would represent a very real war danger for us. . . . we should do all in our power to keep the Liberal party, to which all peace-loving elements in England adhere, at the helm. Therefore we should meet the aims of this party for a mutual reduction of the armament burden half way.[28]

The Emperor and Tirpitz (to say nothing of Widenmann) refused to admit the possibility of a preventive war. Tirpitz's argument was that the British Navy, on the whole, was as much opposed to war as were the German armed forces, and that English business circles wanted war even less, as their business would suffer. 'The possibility of a preventive war is a scarecrow

[27] Tirpitz's report of a conversation with Bülow, 3 Apr. 1909; German Ministry of Marine MSS.
[28] Müller to Tirpitz, 17 Apr. 1909; *ibid.*

and a fiction of our diplomats [Metternich] to make people who resist them pliable.' They had to face the fact that there was in England a very general feeling of hostility towards Germany, and that their naval policy had greatly aggravated this situation. The question was whether they could improve the political situation by a modification in their naval policy. German diplomacy in the Bosnian Crisis and the 'quiet, unconcerned' naval expansion had greatly raised German prestige.

A retreat in the fleet question would again lose the ground we have gained. I cannot understand that others do not consider this in the same light. The best solution seems to be to stick it out . . . After two years the building tempo will be lowered to two large ships. So far as it is possible at all, the tension will be eased by that, but still more by our growing stronger in the coming years. . . . His Majesty is entirely right under the present conditions to advocate that we wait until the English advance new armament ideas. I do not think this very probable, but if it should happen, we cannot approach the negotiations with a definite formula. . . . Military concessions on our part against political promises on the English part are out of the question. As far as I can judge, the way indicated by you to Herr von Kiderlen [the Foreign Minister] is the correct one. First, 'détente' and then 'entente' in the political field, then an agreement for disarmament, but not in the reverse order, first, military weakening and then vague promises for better treatment.[29]

This was, in fact, the approach adopted by the German Government, and without waiting for the English to take the initiative. In the spring there were feelers for a political understanding, specifically, for a neutrality and non-aggression pact between the two countries. They were received with little interest by the Prime Minister and the Foreign Office. The proposed *entente* was regarded only as a medium for the establishment of German hegemony in Europe. The Government's decision to proceed with the contingent four capital ships stimulated the Germans to try again. Bethmann Hollweg had succeeded Bülow on 14 July, and he was, if anything, more anxious for an agreement with England. A more attractive package was prepared. On 21 August the new Chancellor stated his Government's readiness to discuss a naval arrangement, provided there was also a general political understanding.

[29] Tirpitz to Müller, 6 May 1909; Tirpitz, *Politische Dokumente* (Stuttgart and Berlin, 1924–6, 2 vols.), i. 150–2.

The Cabinet 'cordially welcomed' proposals regarding naval expenditure and promised to receive with the 'greatest sympathy' any political proposal 'not inconsistent with the maintenance of [Britain's] friendships' with other powers. Tirpitz's absence from Berlin delayed the next move. On 14–15 October the German proposals were presented to the British Ambassador. Their gist was that the German programme would have to be carried out —only a Reichstag vote could alter it—but, for two or three years, the Government was prepared to 'relax the tempo' of the programme without consulting the Reichstag. The four ships to be laid down each year could be reduced to three by spreading the expenditures for the year over a greater length of time. Goschen raised the obvious objection that in the end the whole number provided by the programme would be built, therefore no limitation of gross naval expenditure was possible, and hence no limitation of British expenditure was possible. Bethmann Hollweg could only reply that if the arrangement worked and if, together with the political understanding which must accompany a naval agreement, it calmed public opinion in both countries, it was 'highly probable' that in a few years the Reichstag would favour a reduction in the number of ships in the programme. As for the political agreement, something along the lines of the Baltic agreement of April 1908 was envisaged by the Germans. This agreement, signed by Germany, Russia, Sweden, and Denmark, guaranteed the territorial *status quo* in the Baltic states.

The German proposals were received coolly in London. The Foreign Office was not enthusiastic over either proposal, the naval or the political. The latter would involve a guarantee of the German possession of Alsace-Lorraine, and this might break up the *entente* with France. Grey explained to Metternich (28 October) how difficult it would be for Britain, in a political agreement, to go beyond a statement 'that we did not desire to direct our understandings with other countries against Germany, and that we had no hostile intentions whatever with regard to her'. Anything else would 'give the impression that we were entering into closer relations with Germany than we had previously entered into with any other Power'. But the crucial point was the naval problem.

I understand that it was felt in Germany that some general understanding was necessary, to cause the atmosphere to become more genial, and thus to make a naval arrangement possible. Here, however, there was an opposite feeling: a general understanding would have no beneficial effect whatever on public opinion, and would indeed be an object of criticism, so long as naval expenditure remained undiminished. In order to remove suspicion here, a naval arrangement was essential. . . . a frank exchange of information between the German and British Admiralties would be the most effective factor in making both countries believe that the naval expenditure of each was intended for general purposes, and had not in view the stealing of a march or the gaining of an advantage at the expense of the other country. The drawing up of satisfactory formulae would, however, be difficult, and would take time.[30]

The Germans countered on 4 November with the compromise proposal that the naval and political agreements be negotiated and announced at the same time. The suggested naval agreement now was that, for about three or four years, England and Germany should not build more capital ships than a number to be agreed upon by their naval experts. The experts would also decide what could be done about the difficult problem of exchanging information on naval construction. The political proposal was the exchange of assurances that (as reported by Goschen) 'neither of them entertained any idea of aggression the one against the other, that they would not attack each other, and further that in the case of an attack made on either Power by a third Power or group of Powers, the Power not attacked should stand aside'.[31]

The German offer was wholly unacceptable to the Foreign Office. To Crowe the bargain was 'a little one-sided'. The Royal Navy would be 'tied as to the amount of shipbuilding not only as against Germany, but as against the rest of the world', and Germany would have a free hand against any other state. Langley, the Assistant Under-Secretary, objected most to the provision of British neutrality in the event of a German war, which, however worded, 'must have a disastrous effect on our relations with France and Russia'. Hardinge saw no advantage in any naval agreement that did not modify, not merely slow down for a few years, the German naval programme. The proposals for a political agreement were even less acceptable, as they would upset the political equilibrium of Europe. 'It must be remembered that the one obstacle to German hegemony in Europe has been the strength

[30] Grey to Goschen, 28 Oct. 1909; *British Documents*, vi. 303.
[31] Goschen to Grey, 4 Nov. 1908; *ibid.*, p. 305.

175

and independence of the British navy . . . and for England to tie her own hands and to remain neutral while Germany established her supremacy on the Continent would be a derogation from the honourable role which Great Britain has played in Europe for more than three hundred years and which has greatly contributed to the peace of the world.'[32] To avoid a point-blank rejection of the German proposals, Grey informed Metternich on 17 November that the pending general election made it difficult and undesirable to reach a decision before January. This shelved the question for at least two months, and probably for much longer, since the two sides were worlds apart.

Summarized, the situation was that the Germans regarded the political agreement as the important thing, and it must be one that would ensure British neutrality come what might, for the Germans believed that the Franco-Russian alliance could become a menace to Germany only if the two allies could depend on British military backing in case of a showdown. The British were more interested in the naval agreement, not one that merely spread the completion of a few German capital ships over a longer period than contemplated in the Navy Law, but an agreement for an actual reduction of the German programme. This would make possible a substantial mutual reduction of naval expenditure. Financial relief was the great objective of the Liberal Government, bursting with unfulfilled plans for social reform. The Germans were willing to negotiate both agreements *pari passu*, but they would not sign the only kind of naval agreement that was meaningful to the British unless they got the kind of political agreement that was meaningful to them. That is, the Germans would not consider naval reduction unless it was quite clear that Britain would never be lined up with Germany's foes in any possible war. An indefinite promise that Britain would not be a member of any aggressive coalition against Germany was not enough. Not that the Germans contemplated a war of aggression. But as the Chancellor later declared (17 December 1910), tension would not slacken 'unless France knows that she cannot depend upon England's support for a restless policy'. A written assurance that England had no aggressive purposes was one thing, but a promise of neutrality was out of the question for the British Government, as it would estrange France and Russia and leave Britain at Germany's mercy. The gulf, or,

[32] Minutes of Crowe, Langley, and Hardinge, 8–10 Nov. 1909; *ibid.*, pp. 310–12.

really, chasm, between the British desire for German naval reduction and the German desire for a British pledge of neutrality in a European war was too wide to be bridged. Faced with a choice between a continued naval race, with its ever mounting financial outlay, and the acceptance of political conditions that would lead to German hegemony on the Continent, the British unhesitatingly chose the first course as the lesser of the two evils. The alternatives were to present themselves again, but the Government never wavered from the decision made in the autumn of 1909.

An American historian has wisely observed: 'No one can blame the British for desiring to equate naval predominance with low expenditure, neither can one blame the Germans for sticking to their naval law in the face of British cultivation of a system of ententes that deprived German diplomacy of all freedom of movement.'[33] The British never appreciated that the French *entente* was for Germany a potential threat to their safety, but no more did the Germans ever realize that in a world of armament races, *Realpolitik*, and imperialistic rivalries, naval supremacy was vital to Britain's safety.

5. EPILOGUE

Looking back, it is a fact that the Admiralty anticipations of early 1909 were not fulfilled in 1912. That there had been no German acceleration was apparent to the Government by the end of 1909. Had Tirpitz's explanations been truthful? Or was McKenna correct when, years afterwards, he asserted that 'the German acceleration, at first denied but subsequently admitted, was later discontinued after its exposure in the House of Commons'?[34] The German Ministry of Marine archives indicate the former, although the writer confesses he has not made an exhaustive study of them as they bear on the question.[35]

[33] Oron J. Hale, *Publicity and Diplomacy, with Special Reference to England and Germany, 1890–1914* (New York, 1940), p. 309.
[34] 'Mr. McKenna's Memorandum', 18 July 1935, enclosed in a letter from Sir Oswyn Murray (Secretary of the Admiralty) to Sir Maurice Hankey, 24 July 1935; Admiralty MSS.
[35] This impression is borne out by an exchange of interesting telegrams between the Emperor and Tirpitz. The two private yards had been promised one ship each (autumn of 1908) with the approval of the Emperor. But he was angry upon learning in August 1909 that one of the ships had been started on 1 March (the other had not yet been laid down). 'His Majesty the Kaiser sees in this a justification, though only a

In any case, the German ships of the 1908–9 and 1909–10 programmes were not completed in advance of the 'normal' time, and the four ships of the 1910 programme were delayed eight months to meet the surprise increase to 13·5-inch of the big-gun calibre on British ships. When the 'really critical date' of April 1912 arrived, the date which had figured so largely in the debates of 1909, instead of the seventeen German capital ships which had been stated as 'a possibility', or the thirteen which were said to be 'a certainty', nine only were completed and ready. It is a fact, too, that only fifteen British capital ships were in commission on 31 March 1912, since only three of the eight ships of the 1909–10 programme were ready in the 'danger' year, 1912. Churchill's conclusion was therefore historically sound: 'Looking back on the voluminous papers on this controversy in the light of what actually happened, there can be no doubt whatever that, as far as the facts and figures were concerned, we [Churchill and Lloyd George] were strictly right. The gloomy Admiralty anticipations were in no respect fulfilled in the year 1912. . . . There were no secret German Dreadnoughts, nor had Admiral Tirpitz made any untrue statement in respect of major construction.'[36]

We must enter an important caveat. As Churchill later noted, though he and Lloyd George 'were right in the narrow sense, we were absolutely wrong in relation to the deep tides of destiny. The greatest credit is due to the First Lord of the Admiralty, Mr. McKenna, for the resolute and courageous manner in which he fought his case and withstood his Party on this occasion.'[37] (He might well have included Fisher in this encomium!) Churchill no doubt had in mind the probability of a German war, and the necessity of a substantial naval margin to allow for the vicissitudes of war. Had the four contingent ships not been approved in 1909,

formal one, for the English claim that building is being accelerated. . . . His Majesty has always emphasized that no acceleration of building has taken place . . .' Tirpitz denied there was any acceleration. 'Start of building has nothing to do with delivery [April 1912, in the contracts signed on 8 April] and is solely a private business matter for the firms. In my opinion, therefore, there was no reason to notify His Majesty. Schichau [shipyard] began the ship in March at its own risk and with its own money, to avoid dismissing workers. So far as I remember, I became aware of this at the end of April.' Müller to Tirpitz and Tirpitz to Müller, 4 Aug. 1909; German Ministry of Marine MSS.

[36] Churchill, *The World Crisis* (London, 1923–9, 4 vols. in 5), i. 37. (Hereafter cited by title only, and note also that the pagination of the American edition is different.)

[37] *Ibid.*, pp. 37–8.

in January 1915 the Grand Fleet would have had only twenty-one capital ships available (allowing for one that had been sunk and five absent for repairs or refitting) to fight Germany's twenty. In a word, it was the contingent four capital ships of 1909 that gave the Navy its rather bare margin of security in the critical early months of the war.

There were several very important by-products of the 1909 scare: (1) the beginnings of an Imperial Fleet, originating in the offer of dreadnoughts by some of the Dominions; (2) a hardening of the feeling of the inevitability of a war with Germany; (3) the policy of naval limitation by agreement was henceforth regarded in all but the Radical section of the Liberal Party as chimerical; (4) the virtual, though undeclared, scrapping of the traditional two-power standard; (5) the intensification of the anti-Fisher campaign.

(1) With 'the weary Titan groaning under the weight of Empire' the Dominions lent a helping hand. On 22 March 1909 the Government of New Zealand telegraphed an offer to bear the cost of the immediate construction of one dreadnought and another if necessary. This example was followed in June by the Australian Government, which offered to contribute one dreadnought. These offers of assistance were gratefully accepted by the Imperial Government. It was decided that summer, at the Conference on Imperial Defence, that the two dreadnought offers should take the shape of a battle cruiser each. They were laid down in 1910 and completed in 1912.

(2) In Churchill's words, 'General alarm was excited throughout the country by what was for the first time widely recognised as a German menace. There was a deep and growing feeling, no longer confined to political and diplomatic circles, that the Prussians meant mischief, that they envied the splendour of the British Empire, and that if they saw a good chance at our expense, they would take full advantage of it.'[38] Warnings of the aggressive intentions of the German Navy and of the inevitability and even imminence of war multiplied. J. Ellis Barker, in the *Nineteenth Century* (April 1909), warned of the danger of a surprise attack. A more or less plausible *casus belli* could be produced overnight, as through a German fishing boat drawing fire from a British gunboat. Captain David Beatty, at a Guildhall luncheon, declared

[38] *Ibid.*, p. 38.

that 'the time must be drawing very close when the efficiency of the Navy may be put to the test'.[39] Lord Northcliffe, the press lord, told a Winnipeg luncheon gathering in September that Germany was going to fight Great Britain as soon as she saw any chance of a successful issue. The *National Review* repeatedly made the same point. Spenser Wilkinson's book, *Britain at Bay*, which attracted much attention, singled out as 'the dominant fact' that 'from now onwards Great Britain has to face the stern reality of war, immediately by way of preparation and possibly at any moment by way of actual collision'. Ten articles on 'England and Germany' in the *Daily Mail*, 13–23 December 1909, created quite a stir in both countries. The author was Robert Blatchford, Editor of the Socialist *Clarion* and a newly-elected member of the Navy League's Executive Committee. The object of this emotional, highly inflammatory series, full of exaggerated language and factual errors, was to prove that Germany aimed at world domination and conquest. As a first step she was cold-bloodedly preparing to attack and destroy the British Empire. One article singled out the German Navy as the strongest evidence of Germany's designs against Britain. King Edward 'lamented Blatchford's violence', and the author was denounced on Socialist and Radical platforms and in the Liberal press; but Cromer, Cawdor, Curzon, Beresford, and other influential men were impressed, to say nothing of the million readers of the *Daily Mail*, who eagerly accepted Blatchford's writings as the gospel truth.

Imaginary war novels, featuring a German invasion of England (Childers's *Riddle of the Sands* was still the most highly publicized), and spy stories, based on gossip and rumour, reflected the nervousness of the country, intensified the navy scare, and contributed importantly to the bad blood between England and Germany. Spies were supposed to be swarming along the East Coast, making maps and taking soundings. A Major A. J. Read and William Le Queux, author of imaginary war stories, reported there were 6,500 German spies in England and Scotland. Even the Government began to see rats everywhere. A C.I.D. sub-committee, appointed by the Prime Minister on 25 March, met three times in the next few months to consider the 'nature and extent of the foreign espionage' in the country. Although the records showed

---

[39] Chalmers, *Beatty*, p. 100 (similarly, in correspondence with his wife during 1909, pp. 91, 94, 102).

there were only 49,000 Germans in the Kingdom (1901 census), which meant there might be 10,000 among them with military training, estimates of the number of trained German reservists in the country ranged from a Colonel Driscoll's 350,000 to Lord Roberts's 80,000 and Sir John Barlow's 66,000. One newspaper 'discovered' that the Germans had stored many thousands of rifles in the cellars of a bank near Charing Cross. They were to be used to arm German reservists on *Der Tag*. (It turned out that these rifles were obsolete weapons which had been purchased by the Society of Miniature Rifle Clubs.)

The air danger to the Fleet was pointed out by many writers. In two years, it was said, Germany would have twenty airships able to travel thirty hours, that is, over 600 miles, and each would carry 1 to 3 tons of explosives. England had nothing with which to meet these airships. The possibility that the Germans might employ their 'aeroplane' fleet to attack the Navy with high-explosive grenades as a preliminary to an invasion of England was considered at the Admiralty in December 1908. It was not held to be feasible, but the matter was felt to deserve watching.

There was also the story about special German mines, first told by the Emperor as a joke. These mines were to be carried over in packing cases in cargo ships and dropped overboard in the Solent or the Thames estuary, when a large part of the Royal Navy was concentrated in either place. This fairy story was taken seriously by Balfour and others, but the War Office could find no confirmation, and Fisher, when it was called to his attention, scornfully replied: 'I am too busy to waste my time over this cock-and-bull story!' Then there was the ridiculous story in the *Standard* (September) that a powerful magnet had been patented in Germany which would be able to work the destruction of warships. Sunk at the entrance of ports, and connected with a power station by a cable, it would render British ships unmanageable and deliver them into the hands of the Germans.

The jitteriness of the country infected Whitehall. On 8 May the Home Fleet was suddenly alerted by urgent telegrams to a possible German attack. The Admiralty had received information from the Colonial Office that the German naval reservists in Canada had been ordered to return to Germany. Fisher himself thought the whole thing was moonshine, and he was right. The tempest ended five days later when the Admiralty learned that nothing unusual was under way in Canada. It was routine practice to notify members of the German naval reserve when they were due for training, which was all that had happened.

(3) Organs like the *Manchester Guardian, Daily News,* and *Westminster Gazette* still laboured to achieve a friendly understanding with Germany that would check the naval competition; but 'it began to be realized that it was no use trying to turn Germany from her course by abstaining from counter measures. Reluctance on our part to build ships was attributed in Germany to want of national spirit, and as another proof that the virile race should advance to replace the effete, over-civilized and pacifist society which was no longer capable of sustaining its great place in the world's affairs.'[40] The building of the four extra dreadnoughts was having a sobering effect in Germany, and it was possible that the Navy Law would not be expanded in spite of the efforts of the German Navy League. This, at least, was the opinion of British diplomatists in Germany. For example, Goschen submitted evidence that the determination of Britain to maintain her supremacy at sea had contributed not a little towards strengthening 'the [German] current of opinion in the direction of better relations with England. . . . while it is also certain that the enormous increase of the cost of battleships of the newest type . . . is beginning to be regarded with some uneasiness by the German tax-payer.' N.I.D. agreed with these estimates of the situation.[41]

There was, at the same time, a hardening of the demand for a naval standard specifically directed at Germany, and this brings us to another by-product of the scare:

(4) The virtual scrapping of the two-power standard. In November 1908 Asquith had stated unequivocally that this standard required 'a preponderance of 10 per cent. over the combined strengths in capital ships of the two next strongest Powers, whatever those Powers might be'. But on 26 May 1909 in the Commons the Prime Minister, in Balfour's words, 'befogged and beclouded the perfectly clear utterances which he had previously made to the House'. The two-power standard, said Asquith, 'is not

[40] *The World Crisis,* i. 38.
[41] Goschen to Grey, 25 Aug. 1909, with a minute by the D.N.I., 14 Sept., and, similarly, a D.N.I. minute, 25 Aug., on a report to the Foreign Office from the British Minister in Munich; Admiralty MSS.

to be understood as a transcendent dogma, but as a convenient rule-of-thumb, to be applied with reference to political and strategical conditions'. Behind the smokescreen of the Prime Minister's verbiage, it was apparent that the traditional standard was no longer valid. Although the question of the naval standard was subsequently discussed periodically in Parliament, the Government's statements were not very clear or precise down to 28 March 1912. It was then that Churchill, as First Lord, told the House of Commons that the official standard was one of 60 per cent superiority in dreadnoughts over Germany. Later, in March 1914, Churchill told the Commons that the Admiralty had adopted this standard 'in 1908 or 1909'. The date was April 1909, and the standard was originally suggested by Jellicoe, the Third Sea Lord and Controller.

What were the considerations that prompted the change in the standard of strength? The crux of the situation was the United States Navy, which ranked just after the German Fleet in numerical strength. British Governments and British public opinion in the pre-war decade simply refused to recognize the American Republic as a possible enemy, no matter what complications might arise out of the American-Japanese question and the Anglo-Japanese Alliance. The *Review of Reviews* (March 1908) expressed the mood of the country: 'We are not going to fight the United States for the sake of twenty Japans . . . we are not going to be dragged into a civil war with our kith and kin in the United States.' The C.I.D. held an Anglo-American war to be 'not merely the supreme limit of human folly, but also to be so unlikely as to be a contingency against which it is unnecessary to make provision'.[42] The same Admiralty memorandum saw no likelihood of a German-U.S. coalition against Britain, because of the numerous points of antagonism in their foreign policies. When the C.I.D. discussed the problem of Canadian defence on 14 May 1908, it was felt by all present that a state of war between Great Britain and America was an unthinkable proposition and that, anyway, the defence of Canada was beyond the capacity of Great Britain. The Government never swerved a hair from this position. One of the conclusions reached by the C.I.D. on 14 May 1914

[42] Quoted in an Admiralty memorandum, 'Comparative Strength in Battleships and Armoured Cruisers of Great Britain, France, United States, and Germany', June 1907; Lennoxlove MSS.

was: 'In considering the question of the defence of the British islands in the West Atlantic, there is no need to take into account the scales of attack that may be brought to bear against the islands by the United States . . .'[43] Fisher himself never accepted 'the possibility of our waging a war with the United States, and so deprecate any steps tending to encourage that idea'.[44] He was, indeed, a strong proponent of a federation of English-speaking peoples.

An important communication from Ottley dealt with the heart of the matter from the naval standpoint.

. . . my real anxiety is that, do what we will we *cannot* indefinitely maintain an equality with U.S.A. plus Germany as regards shipbuilding. The resources of this Country simply cannot compete with the resources of such a power as the American *plus* Germany. As some one said very forcibly to me a day or two ago, there are probably at least 100 millionaires in the U.S.A., each one of them could spare a million dollars to build ships with, and, if the patriotism of the American people were once engaged, money on this sort of lavish scale will be forthcoming to assert America's claims as a naval power. . . .

The conclusion . . . is that we must renounce (as unattainable) the Two Power Standard vis-à-vis the U.S.A.[45]

Jellicoe termed the old standard 'an unsafe and treacherous dependence'. It contemplated diplomatic and strategical conditions that no longer applied. 'Take the case of Germany and the United States. No one dreams of having to meet them in combination. But if we did so dream, the two-Power standard applied to that combination would not give us sufficient superiority in the near seas over Germany alone.' A two-keels-to-one standard over Germany was not necessary, since she had a very short coastline whose exits could be easily watched in the Straits of Dover and between the Shetlands and Norway. A standard of '60% above German strength in every class of vessel' would meet England's

[43] Minutes of the 126th meeting; Asquith MSS.

[44] Fisher to McKenna, 12 May 1908, McKenna MSS., enclosing proposals of the D.N.I. (Slade) for helping Canada in a war with the United States. The D.N.I. was disturbed about the United States maintaining more warships on the Great Lakes than had been contemplated by the Treaty of 1817. It was this problem that led to the C.I.D. discussion of 14 May 1914.

[45] Ottley to Vaughan Nash (Asquith's Secretary), 26 May 1909; Asquith MSS. The Prime Minister probably received it before his parliamentary statement that day on the two-power standard.

needs.[46] This became the new standard, though in practice applied to capital ships. Officially, then, from 1909 only the German Navy seriously counted in British naval calculations. (Austrian and Italian naval expansion, we shall see, complicated matters in the last year or two before the Great War.) Apparently, the new standard was not divulged to the Cabinet before 1912.

The last of the important by-products of the 1909 scare was the intensification of the anti-Fisher campaign, a topic deserving its own chapter.

[46] Undated memorandum of 1909 (April?) commenting on J. L. Garvin's article in the April *Fortnightly* which called for a navy 'at least twice the power of the German Fleet'; Jellicoe MSS.

VIII

Fisher's Retirement

Never before in the History of the Navy has any Admiral or officer been singled out for so much adverse opinion except it be poor old Admiral Byng . . .
BEATTY to his wife, 6 April 1909.

So really sorry that I cannot come to celebrate the great day [Fisher's retirement, 25 January 1910] at your dinner. Must go to Deptford to speak. Your toast should be—'To the death of Fraud, Espionage, Intimidation, Corruption, Tyranny, Self-Interest, which have been a nightmare over the finest Service in the world for four years.
BERESFORD to Capt. the Hon. H. H. Molyneux, R.N., 24 January 1910.

I may be wrong, but I shall always believe that he has been actuated for 27 years by the *unique desire* to make the British Navy the strongest in the world. I do not say that he has not made mistakes. Who has not? But he is a great public servant, and at the end of a long life, devoted to his profession and to the state he is the victim of Asquith's want of moral courage.
ESHER to J. S. Sandars [Balfour's Secretary], 9 September 1909.

No one, I think, has ever had such a five years. . . . It will mark an epoch as clearly and indisputably as Nelson did his.
CORBETT to Fisher, 25 January 1910.

I. THE NAVAL INQUIRY

THE TONE of the intensified drive to oust Fisher is indicated in a *Daily Express* leader of 20 March 1909:

The sole responsibility for the fact that in a few months [*sic*] Great Britain will be in a more vulnerable position than she has been since the battle of Trafalgar belongs to the First Sea Lord. . . . Above all, he is responsible for the starving of the Navy during the last three years. . . . If he had threatened resignation when an unsatisfactory programme was being prepared he would have forced the hands of the economaniacs. Moreover, his notorious 'sleep safely in your beds' speech [November 1907] was a direct justification of Radical policy. We arraign Sir John Fisher at the bar of public opinion, and with the imminent possibility of national disaster before the country we say again to him, 'Thou art the man!'

186

The First Sea Lord was also scolded for having been caught 'napping' by the German acceleration and for not pressing for the whole eight. The facts are: (1) There had been no 'starving' of the Navy. At no time during the scare was there any doubt, in Whitehall or in the country, about the existing British naval superiority. (2) The Sea Lords stood firm in the crucial months of January–February 1909. Fisher relied on the weight of public opinion to see them through. (3) Fisher and McKenna, in the spring of 1909, worked to convert the contingent four into a reality, while proceeding on the assumption that they were as good as definitely promised. Undoubtedly Fisher would have resigned had the Cabinet vetoed the contingent four during the financial year. (4) As regards the 'napping' charge, Fisher brushed it off as 'an awful lot of lies. . . . We knew within a week of the German acceleration in shipbuilding and of Krupp's extensions, also when they first began, and I have copy of memorandum given to Tweedmouth [3 December 1907] for the Cabinet.'[1] The memorandum in question reveals only the Sea Lords' anxiety over the new German building programme. It is a fact that Fisher was to some extent caught unawares by the reported acceleration in 1908 and had done nothing until, with more and more alarming information on German acceleration pouring in at the end of 1908, he and his colleagues had decided to make a determined stand. In the event, as already indicated, Fisher had exaggerated the extent and purposes of German building policy in 1908–9.

The Admiral's critics in both political camps attributed the increase in German naval activity since 1905 to one or more of these factors: his boastfulness, the introduction of the dreadnought type, and his large dreadnought programmes. These, they said, added fuel to the passions of the period, baulked the chances of peace, and practically made war certain. As Lord Riddell noted in his diary, 'He is a great man, but too prone to make the pace, so that other nations are urged to do more than they would otherwise.'[2] Fisher's later critics have made the same point. One must admit Fisher's 'boastfulness'. The justification of the dreadnought has been examined above. As regards the third charge, the Admiral was, of course, only following the maxim in vogue in all the admiralties (and other defence departments), then and since:

[1] Fisher to Davidson, 20 Mar. 1909; *Fear God and Dread Nought*, ii. 210.
[2] 25 Mar. 1909; Riddell, *More Pages from My Diary, 1908–1914* (London, 1934), p. 17.

'*Si vis pacem, para bellum.*' War was not averted by British naval superiority, but that superiority did win the war for Britain and the Allies.

But it was the inquiry into Admiralty policy that finally torpedoed Fisher, and this brings us back to Beresford. The hauling down of his flag at Portsmouth, 24 March 1909, was accompanied by extraordinary scenes. The unparalleled enthusiasm and emotion displayed by the crowds at Portsmouth and, later in the day, in London suggested that a national hero had returned home from a great naval victory. The platforms at Waterloo station were a seething mass of people, and the crowds, numbering several thousands, filled all the approaches to the station. When Beresford stepped on to the platform, there was a mighty roar of cheering, hats were thrown in the air, women wildly waved handkerchiefs, and all sang 'He's a Jolly Good Fellow'. Many enthusiasts scaled the massive pillars that supported the roof of the station, and from their insecure footholds led the crowd below in cheers and song. The remarkable demonstrations were a striking testimony to the popular esteem in which 'Charlie B.' was held.

Beresford's career of active service afloat was apparently brought to a close, though he had two years to go before reaching the age of compulsory retirement. The *Standard* (24 March) expressed the Beresfordian viewpoint perfectly: 'Because he has fearlessly told the truth, he has been dismissed by Mr. McKenna. There is the whole situation in a sentence.' The *Review of Reviews* (March) voiced the sentiments of the Fisherites: 'When two men ride on horseback, says the old proverb, one must ride behind. Lord Charles never could realise that he might be that one. Hence arose a state of friction which was at once a scandal and a danger to the Service.'

A month before he gave up his command Beresford had had a long interview with Balfour. The two men had been friends for many years. Their correspondence went back to 1887, and by the turn of the century they were writing to each other as 'My dear Arthur' (whose colleagues usually addressed him as 'Mr. Balfour') and 'My dear Charlie Beresford', the latter becoming 'My dear Charlie' by 1908. Beresford had many times sought aid and comfort from Balfour in his campaign against Fisher. On this occasion Beresford had the effrontery to ask Balfour what he meant to do when he became Prime Minister. (Apparently Beresford expected the navy scare to topple the Government.) If Balfour made him First Sea Lord, he would keep quiet about the state of the Navy; otherwise, he would 'stump the country and agitate'. Balfour told him the Government would probably remain in power another two years, therefore he had not thought about a new Cabinet or Board of Admiralty.[3]

A month later, now a free man who could, if he wished, speak his mind, and encouraged and stimulated by his reception ashore, Beresford planned an all-out attack on Fisher. Before launching the campaign he consulted Balfour on 26 March. His was a dreadful tale of woe. The naval situation, in spite of Britain's immense superiority in ships and guns, was full of peril: the strategic distribution of the Fleet was faulty, there was a great deficiency in cruisers and destroyers, and the Admiralty's war plans were practically non-existent. Did Balfour see any objection to his publicly raising these points in the near future? No, he did not; but he advised the Admiral to tell the Prime Minister what he proposed to do. Balfour added that he was confident that the Admiralty was well supplied with war plans; whether they were sound or not was another matter.[4] Incidentally, he was in the uncomfortable position of serving as father confessor to both Beresford and Fisher. He succeeded so well in his wire-balancing act that he retained the confidence of the two gladiators.

On 30 March Beresford saw the Prime Minister and explained his case against the Fisher administration in general terms. He followed this up with a letter on 2 April which contained details of his principal charges. He threatened to take his case to the country if the Government did not act. With McKenna's blessings Asquith decided (19 April) to appoint a sub-committee of the Committee of Imperial Defence to investigate the charges in private. He would be chairman, and four Cabinet ministers, Crewe, Morley, Grey, and Haldane, would be the other members. The procedure was quite different from that suggested by the advocates of a general inquiry by a royal commission (which itself would amount to a vote of censure) into the whole conduct of naval affairs by the Board of Admiralty. The C.I.D., in carrying out this inquiry, would be operating within the lines of its regular

[3] Esher to Knollys, 23 Feb. 1909; Windsor MSS. Esher had got all this from Balfour the day before.
[4] Balfour to Beresford, 27 Mar. 1909; Balfour MSS.

duties, and the scope of the inquiry was confined to specific charges.

But Fisher was maddened. 'Imagine what a state of affairs when a meeting of Naval Officers on the active list in a room in Grosvenor Street is able to coerce the Cabinet and force the strongest Board of Admiralty to totter to its fall! Why, the "Young Turks" are not in it! The country must indeed be in a bad way if so governed!'[5] Momentarily, he was so exasperated by the turn of events as to threaten resignation. He was persuaded by Esher (14 April) and the King (20 April) to retain office 'in spite of all'. Thereafter he was full of fight. *I am not going till I am kicked out!*

One of the 'humiliations' which he had to endure was that, for the first time in history, a Board of Admiralty was to be put on trial to defend itself against the charges of an undisciplined subordinate. Another humiliation was the public revelation of two of the Bacon Letters (21 March, 15 April 1906)[6] through Sir George Armstrong's speech at the Constitutional Club on 2 April and his letter in *The Times*, 23 April. The particular reason for Armstrong's venom—he was one of the principal Beresfordian leaders, sharp and quick-witted—was diagnosed as follows by the German Attaché: 'After Sir George Armstrong was discharged as a young naval officer [1892] on account of imprudent remarks about Sir John Fisher, for which he had to apologize publicly, he had vowed vengeance to him. To fulfil this vow he collected material for years and now makes use of some of it (the Bacon Letters, which had been slipped to him) to proceed against Fisher according to plan and with the knowledge of his fellow conspirators.'[7]

Armstrong's revelations created a sensation and brought into the open the charge by Beresford and his friends that a system of espionage had been worked from the Admiralty—specifically, that Bacon had been sent to the Mediterranean by Fisher to spy on Beresford. Many sharp questions were asked in Parliament and the press was full of the subject. Fisher's case was not particularly convincing. He asked Esher (13 April) to tell Balfour 'your unanswerable dictum that in the carrying out of a huge campaign

[5] Fisher to Esher, 13 Apr. 1909; *Fear God and Dread Nought*, ii. 211.
[6] See above, p. 83.
[7] Widenmann to Tirpitz, 22 July 1909; German Ministry of Marine MSS.

there was no alternative but to print every single thing as it came along, otherwise references impossible with such a mass of correspondence as there was.'[8] McKenna did somewhat better in Parliament. On 19 May he regretted this much: 'The only complaint is that before these letters were printed the reference to my hon. Friend [Bellairs] was not struck out. That is a matter for which he [Fisher] is extremely sorry, and for which I am also extremely sorry. As regards everything else in the letters it was entirely proper that they should be printed, because they were worth preserving.' He reversed himself on 27 May: 'Is the House seriously going to be asked to condemn a great man because, at a time of great labour, he has ordered to be printed a number of letters it would have been better, I would say, not to have been printed at all? . . . this sort of attack is doing a cruel injustice to the First Sea Lord, who has had the unreserved confidence of four successive First Lords of the Admiralty . . . and I appeal to the House not to be misled by any such trumpery matters as these into censuring in the slightest degree a man who has given the very best service to the public that any man could give.'

The *Westminster Gazette* (28 May) cut through to the heart of the matter: 'But when the worst has been said about these things, they are quite trivial compared to the interests of the Service, and to return again and again to them is to produce the impression that the object in view is not merely to vindicate the proprieties but to conduct a campaign against a particular individual.' That was precisely the case. The Beresfordian camp was, naturally, not going to let the First Sea Lord off the hook. The Bacon disclosures only intensified the virulence of the anti-Fisher campaign, which more and more featured scurrilous and scandalous personal attacks on the First Sea Lord. The Prince of Wales, hitherto reasonably neutral as between Fisher and Beresford (while violent on the general subject of the warfare in the service), now definitely cast in his lot with the Beresford camp. Fisher was never to forget this; it coloured his attitude towards the Prince when he became George V (he frequently likened him to Rehoboam), and towards the monarchy itself. Sir Harold Nicolson has written of the Prince: 'Although he was bombarded with pleas and counter-pleas from his former commanders and colleagues in the Navy, he managed to maintain an attitude of neutrality. He deeply regretted, and

[8] *Fear God and Dread Nought,* ii. 211–12.

remained aloof from, the internecine quarrel . . .'[9] That was certainly no longer the case by the spring of 1909. Convincing evidence is supplied by Knollys:

He takes up a far too violent and partizan tone both about 'Jackie' and the Admiralty. . . . and he really talks as if he had a personal grievance in the matter. The truth is that all the men he talks to on the subject are strong anti-Fisherites, and a naval friend of his [Captain H. H. Campbell, Assistant D.N.I.], who is constantly with him and who I think behaves in a very disloyal way to his chiefs, is the worst of the lot. The Prince of Wales never hears anything on the other side of the question except from you and me, and we are not in the profession![10]

Fifteen meetings of the sub-committee of the C.I.D. were held between 27 April and 13 July. They were devoted to the hearing and taking of oral and documentary evidence, offered by McKenna, ably representing the Admiralty, and Beresford, who was accompanied by his 'naval brains', Custance. (Custance offered evidence at two of the meetings.) Fisher was kept in the background on purpose, and spoke only in reply to questions addressed to him by the Committee. Sir Arthur Wilson, a member of the C.I.D., testified at the thirteenth meeting, 24 June, and was cross-examined. Beresford, on the first day, presented his case 'with ability and (on the whole) with moderation', thought Asquith. But as the inquiry continued, one fact became indelibly impressed on a number of those present: the absolute incompetence of the man and his inability even to comprehend, much less to substantiate, the charges. Beresford's cause was not helped by the questionable methods used to obtain a certain supporting document. It was discovered that the two Assistant Directors of Naval Intelligence, Captain Campbell (head of the Trade Division) and Captain Arthur R. Hulbert (head of the War Division), had been supplying Beresford with ammunition—an official paper which they had no right to communicate to him. Months later Campbell assured the Prince of Wales that he had never divulged the contents of any paper, confidential or otherwise,

[9] Nicolson, *King George the Fifth* (London, 1952), p. 178.

[10] Knollys to Esher, 13 Apr. 1909; Esher MSS. If further proof is needed, when Beresford saw the Prince at Newmarket (27 October), the latter was 'quite violent' against Fisher. 'I could have said nothing stronger. He said it must cease, and that he must go, or the Navy would be ruined'; Beresford to Sturdee, 28 Oct. 1909; Sturdee MSS.

to Beresford. All that he had done, he explained, was merely to suggest to Beresford that he ask by number for a certain letter that would support his case![11]

The Committee's report was issued as a Parliamentary paper on 12 August. The evidence that led up to the conclusions was not given, by reason, it was stated, of the confidential character of most of the data supplied. The full proceedings, which have never been published, fill two closely printed volumes: 328 pages of proceedings (i.) and 245 pages of appendices (ii.).[12] Upwards of 2,600 questions were put to Beresford, McKenna, and other witnesses. Beresford's general charge was to the effect that from 15 April 1907, when he assumed command of the Channel Fleet, down to 2 April 1909, when he wrote to the Prime Minister, the Admiralty's arrangements for war were inadequate to ensure the safety of the country. The principal defects alleged by Beresford were under three main headings: I. Organization and Distribution of the Fleet in Home Waters. II. Small Craft and Destroyers in Home Waters. III. War Plans and Intelligence.

The principal charges under the first head were (1) that the fleets for the defence of home waters were dispersed under separate commands, a dangerous arrangement; (2) that the Channel Fleet had rarely been maintained at its numerical establishment owing to the constant withdrawal of ships for repairs and refits, a situation that invited a sudden enemy attack. At the inquiry Beresford considered that the system of concentration the Germans had adopted could be met only by the adoption of a similar policy, specifically, that there be maintained in home waters an active homogeneous fleet in full commission and complete in every type of ship. The battleships and cruisers should be organized in three main divisions, two of which would always be with the C.-in-C., the third usually detached to cruise independently.

The numerical establishment of ships in each of these main divisions should in his opinion be such that, after allowing for a percentage absent for purposes of refit, any two combined would possess a superiority in capital ships over the largest hostile force which could be assembled against them at short notice. . . . Behind the active fleet there would

[11] Knollys to Esher, 18 Sept. 1909; Esher MSS.

[12] 'Report and Proceedings of a Sub-Committee of the Committee of Imperial Defence Appointed to Inquire into Certain Questions of Naval Policy Raised by Lord Charles Beresford', 12 Aug. 1909. The material that follows is from the unpublished report, mainly from the summary of evidence at the end of Volume i.

be a reserve fleet manned with nucleus crews. The effect of these proposals on the existing organization would be to abolish the Home and Atlantic Fleets and the cruiser squadrons in Home waters as separate commands, and to merge them in a single augmented fleet under the orders of one Commander-in-Chief.

The lengthy reply by the Admiralty is conveniently summarized in the unpublished report. A few excerpts will give its flavour.

Put briefly, the Admiralty case is that the organization of the fleet in Home waters during Lord Charles Beresford's term of command formed a necessary transitional stage in the gradual process of building up a great fleet in Home waters under a single command, and trained in its probable battle-ground in the North Sea. While their dispositions fully ensured the safety of the country, having regard to the strength and organization of our possible enemies at the time, they were necessarily subject to certain imperfections, which must be partly attributed to the sensitiveness of international relations and partly to the desire of the Admiralty to bring the nucleus-crew division to a state of complete efficiency before incorporating it as a separate division of the Home Fleet.

The Admiralty also explained that if the important principle of training the fleet on its probable battle-ground is to be adhered to, a certain amount of dispersion is inevitable. A good deal of training must be carried out in harbour, but there is no harbour in the North Sea capable of permanently and suitably accommodating two divisions of our Home Fleet. In the opinion of the Admiralty, this dispersion did not constitute a danger, since there would always be time to concentrate the separate divisions before hostilities commenced, and even in the event of a 'bolt from the blue', which would probably take the form of a destroyer attack, the losses would be less if the divisions were separated than if they were all massed as a single target. In their future policy, therefore, the Admiralty contemplated concentration as a general rule when the German fleet is in the North Sea, but at other times they reserved their liberty to base the several divisions for training at Portland, Rosyth, or elsewhere.

The Admiralty admitted the truth of Lord Charles Beresford's statement that the replacement of ships withdrawn from the active fleet for refits by vessels with nucleus crews had not invariably been carried out, the principal reason being that, as already shown, the Channel Fleet was always more powerful than the German High Sea Fleet at full strength even after allowing for ships away refitting.

They resisted the suggestion that they had failed to carry out their declared policy in this respect, and explained that what the Board had contemplated and announced was the provision of ships in substitution for ships of the Channel Fleet when withdrawn for *extensive* refit, but not (as assumed by Lord Charles Beresford) the replacement of vessels undergoing their ordinary annual refits. . . .

The Admiralty traversed Lord Charles Beresford's statements regarding the inefficiency of the Home Fleet as a striking force. They stated that the nucleus-crew ships had been proved by frequent surprise tests to be capable of mobilization within five hours, and they produced figures to show that the gunnery efficiency of the Home Fleet was even greater than that of the Channel Fleet.

Admiral Sir F. Bridgeman, who had commanded the Home Fleet during almost the whole period criticized by Lord Charles Beresford, stated that he was entirely satisfied with the readiness and complete efficiency of that fleet. . .

Referring to the fleet organization propounded by Lord Charles Beresford, the Admiralty pointed out that it could be scarcely distinguished in principle from the existing organization of fleets in Home waters, the only important difference being that the Atlantic Fleet, for reasons already given, was retained as an independent command, instead of becoming a third fully-manned division of the Home Fleet. . . .

The gist of Sir Arthur Wilson's opinion regarding this heading of the inquiry was that there is a great deal of force in Lord Charles Beresford's criticism of the organization which existed in his time, but that his objections have been met by the organization recently introduced.

The principal charge under the second head was the grave deficiency in small craft and destroyers in home waters. As regards unarmoured cruisers, there were only twenty-seven immediately ready against Germany's thirty-eight. Beresford ascribed this to the policy of 'scrapping', which he considered had been carried out without regard to war requirements. To utilize large armoured cruisers to perform the duties of small craft was a mis-application of force and exposed valuable warships to unjustifiable risks. Beresford further contended that, owing to the cruiser shortage, the Admiralty was not able to provide effectively for the protection of seaborne commerce in time of war.

With regard to the number of cruisers, the Admiralty showed that Beresford's figures were of second- and third-class cruisers only. All ships capable of doing the work required of cruisers should be included, and this would show that Britain had eighty-eight (30 armoured cruisers, 42 unarmoured cruisers, 16 torpedo-gunboats) to Germany's forty-four (6 armoured, 38 unarmoured cruisers). Armoured cruisers would not be used for the inshore watch on the egresses of German harbours, but they were even more suitable than unarmoured cruisers for scouting in the open sea by day, and for watching passages at a distance from the German coast (the Skagerrak, for instance), since their offensive and defensive power enabled them to push home a reconnaissance. For present needs the number of cruisers was sufficient for both scouting and the protection of trade. To provide for the future the Admiralty were laying down six unarmoured cruisers annually, as compared with Germany's two. Concerning trade protection, the Admiralty pointed out that no danger could arise from German warships, since there were few abroad and these were no match for British naval forces in the same areas. Beresford's case depended on whether German merchant ships were in peacetime equipped with guns and ammunition. The Admiralty's information was that these ships did not carry guns or ammunition.

On the question of torpedo craft, Beresford gave these totals: 123 British destroyers versus 71 German; 75 British torpedo-boats versus 83 German. Considerable deductions, he maintained, should be made from the British figures because a large number were always undergoing refits. Moreover, out of the 123 British destroyers, he considered only thirty-eight suitable for work in the North Sea; the older destroyers and all the torpedo-boats had been built with a view to operations on the French coast, that is, at a short distance from their base. He also alleged that British destroyers were not as powerfully armed as the latest German destroyers. Finally, Beresford questioned the utility of submarines. 'The submarine is always in a fog.' They were merely a defensive weapon, and therefore unsuitable for use in an offensive fleet like the British.

This was the Admiralty reply. The fifty-five earlier destroyers (30-knot class) which Beresford considered could not be used were admittedly less suitable for offensive work in the North Sea than were the newer types. Nevertheless, they could be used there effectively. They were superior in radius of action and equal in sea-going qualities to the Japanese destroyers which had been used so successfully in the war with Russia. The Japanese boats had been employed continuously for eighteen months at a distance of 200 miles from their base in the China Sea, where the prevailing weather conditions were worse than in the North Sea. The

Admiralty was therefore satisfied that the number of destroyers suitable for offensive purposes (95) was sufficient. If the Germans took the offensive (Beresford's assumption throughout), the situation was even more favourable: they could include the old 27-knot destroyers, the ex-coastal destroyers (or modern torpedo-boats), and 50 torpedo-boats, or a total of 158 destroyers and 50 torpedo-boats to throw against the very small number of German destroyers capable of offensive action. The future had been provided for by the inclusion of sixteen destroyers in the 1908–9 estimates and twenty more in the 1909–10 estimates. As for destroyer armament, the older German craft, mostly with one 12-pounder and five 6-pounders, were entirely outclassed by the 12-pounder guns of the British destroyers. Recently the Germans had introduced a 23-pounder, and it had been decided to match this by arming the new British destroyers with a very successful 31-pounder (4-inch) gun. Finally, the Admiralty could not accept Beresford's evaluation of the potentialities of submarines, the later types of which could be used offensively.

Under the third heading, 'War Plans and Intelligence', Beresford charged that the Admiralty, in case of war, could not immediately put any war plan into execution, also that he had never been able to obtain any strategical scheme or plan for the disposal in war of the forces under his command. Concerning the first point, his case rested on the validity of his contentions under the first two headings. The second charge was 'very considerably modified under cross-examination'. The convincing Admiralty rebuttal of this charge featured a narrative of the transactions with him in 1907–8 on the subject of war plans and war orders. In addition Beresford objected that he had not been furnished with the material to enable him to form his own plans or to keep them up-to-date. He had lacked, in particular, the latest information on the state of the readiness of ships in the Home and Atlantic Fleets, which would in time of war come under his command. There were rights and wrongs on both sides here. The underlying difficulty seemingly lay in the absence of cordial relations between Beresford and the Admiralty.

The summary of Wilson's evidence on war plans is of special interest in view of his close association with Fisher in matters of strategy and because these ideas were to guide him as First Sea Lord when he succeeded Fisher.

Sir Arthur Wilson did not consider it either practicable or desirable to draw up definite plans in peace which would govern the action of the fleet on the outbreak of war. If such plans were forwarded to the Admiralty by a Commander-in-Chief they would pass through so many hands that secrecy could not be guaranteed. Moreover, the Admiralty would be apt to direct their preparations for war mainly towards the fulfilment of that particular plan, and if the conditions under which the war arose were different from those postulated therein—which was almost certain to be the case—it might be difficult to change the plan to suit the altered circumstances. *He was perfectly certain that any plan drawn up in peace would not be carried out in war.* He agreed with Lord Charles Beresford that the drawing out of a plan was very valuable for instructional purposes. . . He considered plans of the kind handed by the Admiralty to Lord Charles Beresford, which were adversely criticized by Lord Charles Beresford and Admiral Custance, to be extremely useful, provided it was made clear that they were not to be carried out without regard to the circumstances of the moment.

He regarded a plan, such as Lord Charles Beresford had required, in which every ship is told off by name for its duties, as practically *impossible*. If [concluded the Committee] Sir Arthur Wilson's view on this subject is correct, it would appear to minimize the importance of Lord Charles Beresford's demand for constant and exact information concerning the state of readiness of our own ships.

The Committee's report was issued as a Parliamentary paper on 12 August.[13] The essential issues and arguments were given, and these were the Committee's conclusions as regards the defects alleged by Beresford:

Part I.—*The Organization and Distribution of the Fleet in Home Waters.*

Since March 1909 the whole of the naval forces in Home waters, with the exception of the Atlantic Fleet, have been united in the Home Fleet under the command of a single flag officer. . . .

In the opinion of the Committee the above organization . . . satisfies in substance all of Lord Charles Beresford's requirements, the only important difference being that the Atlantic Fleet is retained for strategical reasons as an independent command. . . They concur with Sir Arthur Wilson in regarding the present organization as free from the objections which might, in their opinion, have been fairly urged against the arrangements which preceded it, upon any other view than that those arrangements were of a transitory and provisional character.

[13] Command Paper 256 (1909), 'Report of the Sub-Committee of the Committee of Imperial Defence appointed to inquire into certain questions of Naval Policy raised by Lord Charles Beresford.'

Part II.—*Small Craft and Destroyers.*

Lord Charles Beresford stated that during the period of his command there was such a deficiency in Home waters in small craft and destroyers as to constitute a grave weakness. . . They are satisfied . . . there is no such deficiency as to constitute a risk to the safety of the country.

One of the consequences of the alleged dangerous shortage of cruisers was that, in Lord Charles Beresford's opinion, the Admiralty were not in a position to make adequate provision for the protection of trade. . . . there is no sufficient foundation for Lord Charles Beresford's apprehensions.

Part III.—*War Plans.*

Lord Charles Beresford's original statement in his letter to the Prime Minister that 'upon assuming command of the Channel Fleet I was unable to obtain any strategical scheme or plan for the disposal in war of the forces under my command,' was modified under cross-examination, and the Committee are satisfied that he had no substantial grounds for complaint in this matter.

In connection with the question of War Plans it should be mentioned that Lord Charles Beresford attributed many of the Admiralty's alleged shortcomings to the absence of a proper strategical department.

The First Lord of the Admiralty furnished the Committee with a résumé of the steps which have recently been taken to develop a War Staff at the Admiralty, and indicated further advances in this direction which are in contemplation.

General Conclusion

In the opinion of the Committee, the investigation has shown that during the time in question no danger to the country resulted from the Admiralty's arrangements for war, whether considered from the standpoint of the organization and distribution of the fleets, the number of ships, or the preparation of War Plans.

They feel bound to add that arrangements quite defensible in themselves, though not ideally perfect, were in practice seriously hampered through the absence of cordial relations between the Board of Admiralty and the Commander-in-Chief of the Channel Fleet. The Board of Admiralty do not appear to have taken Lord Charles Beresford sufficiently into their confidence as to the reasons for dispositions to which he took exception; and Lord Charles Beresford, on the other hand, appears to have failed to appreciate and carry out the spirit of the instructions of the Board, and to recognize their paramount authority.

The Committee have been impressed with the differences of opinion amongst officers of high rank and professional attainments regarding important principles of naval strategy and tactics, and they look forward with much confidence to the further development of a Naval War Staff, from which the Naval members of the Board and Flag Officers and their staffs at sea may be expected to derive common benefit.

It is perfectly clear that the Committee had not sustained the general indictment and that its verdict was by and large in Fisher's favour. However, Beresford derived 'in the main a great satisfaction' with the report, as he announced in a circular letter to the press of 16 August. He claimed that his agitation and charges had been justified by the event, and his supporters followed this line. The report, in the opinion of the Beresfordians, showed that several reforms consistently advocated by Beresford and strenuously resisted in Whitehall were now being officially adopted and on precisely the lines he had indicated. Among them were stated to be these: a large homogeneous fleet in home waters had been formed; this fleet was under a single supreme control; the nucleus-crew ships were now regarded as a reserve; a naval war staff was in process of formation. Only the last-named may have been in some degree due to Beresford's complaints. Beresford's smug satisfaction was based on a false assumption, already exposed in the report. He assumed, with regard to the first of the three main counts, that arrangements which were essentially 'transitory and provisional' were meant to be permanent, and would in fact have been so but for his intervention. And as the *Manchester Guardian* cleverly pointed out (17 August): 'Only Beresford himself can explain how a scheme which in April was a danger to the country can now be cited as the fruits of his judgment and sagacity.' Beresford's cockiness and conceit were no mere show. His private correspondence shows that he sincerely believed he had emerged the victor. 'The Committee as a matter of fact could not have found more strongly in my favour without removing the heads of the Ad^{ty}, but by judicious legal verbiage it was inferred that I was insubordinate, which, as you would define it, is a "frigid lie".'[14]

Fisher's supporters, from the King down, hailed the report as a decisive vindication of the Admiralty. The Admiral himself was profoundly disappointed. He resented the shadow of censure on him in the second paragraph of the 'General Conclusion'. 'It was a dirty trick to say that the Admiralty had not given its confidence

[14] Beresford to Balfour, 29 Oct. 1909; Balfour MSS.

to Beresford, when Beresford abused that confidence within 24 hours of hoisting his flag!'[15] Underlying his bitterness and resentment was this thought: 'Had they *smashed* him, as they could have by the evidence, as a blatant liar, he would have been so utterly discredited that no newspaper would have noticed him ever again!'[16] He never ceased to believe that the Committee members had been afraid, and even terrified, of Beresford and his minions. Knollys thought so, too. 'I am not surprised myself at the colourless report, considering the composition of the Committee, which I always thought an absurd one, and that the members of it were terrified at C. Beresford, as shown by the way they all treated him when examined, especially Asquith.'[17] Asquith had great intellectual gifts and he was a very able parliamentarian; but he was never noted for his willingness to face facts. One gets the impression that he preferred in this case to find neither admiral entirely guilty. This would have the merit of avoiding a schism in the party. There is justice in Bacon's conclusion that 'the discipline of the Navy was badly injured by the condonation of insubordination by the cabinet.'

There was an unpleasant aftermath to the inquiry report, when Beresford published (*The Times*, 25 October) his correspondence with the Prime Minister since April concerning the 'intimidation on the one hand and favouritism on the other for which the Admiralty have of late years been notorious'. The justification for this action was explained by the Admiral in a private letter: 'I have not been able to show up Ad[ty] methods of blackmail before, as it would have looked personal, but now I have begun to fight for my brother officers, all disgusting intimidation must come out that has been practised for the last 5 years.'[18] In these bullying letters to Asquith (there were some ten, of which that of 23 October was the most important), Beresford stressed the cases of Sturdee, Hulbert, and Campbell, who, he charged, had been treated unfairly because of their connexion with him—Hulbert and Campbell, in breach of the Prime Minister's guarantee of 22 April that no officer's career would be prejudiced by his giving or not giving evidence before the inquiry committee. Hulbert had been ordered

[15] Fisher to Crease, 22 Aug. 1909; *Fear God and Dread Nought*, ii. 214.
[16] Fisher to Arnold White, 23 Sept. 1909; *ibid.*
[17] Knollys to Esher, 23 Aug. 1909; Esher MSS.
[18] Beresford to Balfour, 29 Oct. 1909; Balfour MSS.

by the First Lord to proceed upon leave (2 July–11 October), and on 12 October both he and Campbell had been put on half-pay. The 'immediate and sufficient reason' for this move, McKenna explained to Asquith, was a reorganization of N.I.D. This involved the abolition of the Trade Division (of which Campbell had been head), whose duties were transferred to the Board of Trade, and the transfer of the work of the War Division (of which Hulbert had been head), as well as of the Mobilization Division, to a new Naval Mobilization Department under its own director. (This left N.I.D. as a department solely for the collection and distribution of intelligence.) It was usual for officers to go on half-pay on the conclusion of one appointment until they received a new appointment. Both Hulbert and Campbell would 'receive early consideration for employment'. But McKenna frankly admitted that the retention of the two officers in N.I.D. was 'undesirable in any case' in view of their disclosure to Beresford at the inquiry of the confidential document. 'To reveal a confidential document to persons outside the office is obviously a gross breach of duty. . . . [and it] caused no small friction between the two officers concerned and their immediate superior, Admiral Bethell [D.N.I.]. The mutual confidence which should exist between the head of a Department and his subordinates was destroyed, and the removal of Captain Campbell and Captain Hulbert became inevitable.'[19] Beresford charged (23 October) that 'the real reason for carrying out the "reorganization" ' of N.I.D. was the removal of the two officers.

As regards Sturdee, who had been his Chief of Staff, May 1905 to February 1908, Beresford asserted that since his promotion to rear-admiral in September 1908, seven admirals junior to him had been given employment over his head. McKenna explained the Sturdee situation this way: 'Rear Admiral Sturdee is a most distinguished officer, whose talents and experience are more particularly connected with service at sea. Only 2 Admirals junior to Rear Admiral Sturdee have received sea appointments [Slade, ex-D.N.I., and Bradford, ex-C.O.S. to Wilson, both with special claims]. I believe that if Rear Admiral Sturdee were asked, he would himself say that he would prefer to wait for an appointment afloat rather than obtain immediate employment ashore.'[20]

[19] McKenna to Asquith, 19 Oct. 1909; Asquith MSS.
[20] See the following footnote.

PLATE V

2. ADMIRAL SIR PERCY SCOTT

1. ADMIRAL LORD CHARLES BERESFORD
C.-inC. Mediterranean, 1905–7, C.-in-C. Channel, 1907–9

PLATE VI

2. ADMIRAL SIR PERCY SCOTT
Cartoon by 'Spy'
[from Vanity Fair, 17 September 1903

1. ADMIRAL LORD CHARLES BERESFORD
Caricature by Max Beerbohm
[from Fifty Caricatures (Heinemann)

The general recklessness of Beresford's charges is exemplified best in this accusation (23 October): 'When Rear-Admiral, then Captain, Sturdee ceased to be my Chief of Staff, on being appointed to the command of H.M.S. *New Zealand,* I approached no less than 5 Captains asking them to succeed Captain Sturdee as Chief of my Staff. They all declined on the ground that their future careers would be prejudiced. I reported this fact officially to the Admiralty in November 1907.' This would have been a most serious charge indeed against the McKenna–Fisher administration—if it could have been substantiated. But had Beresford referred back to his November 1907 letter, he would have read: 'They [the five Captains] stated that they could not afford to lose the chance of being promoted to flag rank, citing the case of Captain Sturdee being compelled to leave my staff in order to qualify in sea time.' McKenna brought this fact to Asquith's attention.

In the same letter to the Prime Minister, McKenna effectively demolished another loose charge of Beresford, that (as he had put it in his letter to the Admiralty of 12 November 1907) 'a feeling has arisen in the Service that it is prejudicial to an officer's career to be personally connected with me on service matters'. The First Lord listed Beresford's staff and the senior officers of his flagship when C.-in-C., Mediterranean, January 1907, and again when he was C.-in-C., Channel, December 1908. He showed in each case their present employment. The actual records showed that officers serving with Beresford had not been penalized in any way. As a matter of fact, the records of the Channel in particular revealed 'an unprecedented number of promotions from one ship'.[21] Beresford fired a last broadside (*The Times,* 1 November): '. . . the validity of my case still remains unaffected. . . . I say again, as I said before, that a system of espionage, favouritism, and intimidation exists at the Admiralty.' Privately, he used even stronger language. 'I have proved by the correspondence that blackmail was going on in order to enable the mulatto to carry out his autocratic and dangerous administration.'[22]

[21] McKenna to Asquith, 27 (29?) Oct. 1909; Asquith MSS. Asquith had this letter published (*The Times,* 1 Nov.). The original letter included the Hulbert–Campbell affair, going over some of the essentials of the ground covered in McKenna's letter to Asquith of 19 October. The published version, however, eliminated the reference to the introduction of the confidential document at the inquiry and to the relations between the two captains and the D.N.I., though it mentioned, without amplification, that Hulbert had been asked to take his annual leave 'for disciplinary reasons'.

[22] Beresford to Sturdee, 28 Oct. 1909; Sturdee MSS.

Thereafter Beresford degenerated into a party hack, full of spitefulness towards the Government as well as the Admiralty. In his election speeches at the end of the year (he won a seat in the House of Commons in the January general election, which he held until raised to the peerage in 1916) he surpassed his former efforts. His theme was that for four years the Navy had been run in the interests of personal and party motives. After the election he faded from the naval scene, temporarily emerging from semi-obscurity in January 1912 with the publication of a book, *The Betrayal*. It was a vitriolic indictment against naval policy since 1902. Beresford alone had been right.

2. RESIGNATION AND RETROSPECT

The inquiry report had unloosed another barrage of invective against the First Sea Lord. New lows were reached. The *National Review* (September) could find 'no end to the catalogue of his high crimes and misdemeanours', and 'should it come to hanging, he will be entitled to the nearest lamp-post'. There was, in October, a revival of the periodic rumour that Fisher was about to relinquish his post and receive a peerage. This time the rumour-mongers were correct. The Admiral was profoundly hurt by the Cabinet's failure to back him 100 per cent against the attacks of the Beresford clique. Also, he wanted to ensure the succession of A. K. Wilson, who could be depended upon to continue his policies, while the latter was still of age. (Wilson was only a year younger and could therefore only serve for two years, even if Fisher went in January 1910.) The decisive consideration was that his position had been weakened by the inquiry. The arrangement worked out on 20 October between McKenna and Asquith was for the Admiral to resign early in November and to be created a peer. The plunge having been made, Fisher was 'in good spirits and quite contented about it all', Knollys reported. On the occasion of the King's birthday, 9 November, and to the great disgust of his enemies, the Admiral was elevated to the peerage as Baron Fisher. Very few naval officers had been raised to the peerage, except for actual war services. In modern times there had been only one exception to the rule. Admiral Sir Arthur Hood was made a baron in recognition of his work in strengthening the Fleet under the Naval Defence Act of 1889. Although Fisher was happy to accept a peerage, he had hoped it would be a viscountcy. The King withheld this higher honour after research had revealed that no First Sea Lord had ever been made a viscount straight off, and that even in wartime, Nelson, St. Vincent, Anson, *et al.* had been created barons, to begin with, at least. Fisher's resignation, effective on 25 January 1910, his sixty-ninth birthday (not in April, as had been originally decided upon), and Wilson's succession, were officially announced on 2 December.

It was just as well that Fisher left Whitehall when he did. In the Navy he had by now as many enemies as he had friends. More serious, the spirit of unity, which had long been one of the most marked characteristics of the service, had been shattered. This was not entirely Fisher's fault, yet because of his methods he must bear a portion of the blame for weakening the old band-of-brothers feeling, which had been Nelson's principal legacy to the Navy. The Navy needed a period of rest, a surcease from recrimination and bickering. Furthermore, new problems were coming to the fore, problems which could best be solved by a Naval General Staff, and here Fisher, as will be seen, was a major obstacle. For this reason, too, it was well that he retired in 1910. Again, relations between the two services were distinctly bad. Fisher was far from blameless. Thus, the General Staff's schemes for using the whole British Expeditionary Force as an extension of France's left wing made his hair stand on end. To dispatch English troops to the front in a Continental war would be an act of suicidal idiocy, and he fought it hard. Also the Admiral still had his running feud with the Army over the invasion and conscription issues. As if these were not enough, Fisher despised the War Office and all its ways, including alleged conceit, waste of money, and ignorance of war. Finally, he had developed an extreme dislike for the War Minister, Haldane ('a soapy Jesuit'), for his role in the row over the 1909 estimates, his advocacy of a naval staff and, more recently, a 'Ministry of Defence', and for his supposedly pro-Beresford role in the inquiry committee. For all these reasons Army-Navy co-operation and the working out of joint war plans were rendered all but impossible so long as Fisher remained at the Admiralty.

By 1910 Fisher's work had been done. A tornado of energy, enthusiasm, and persuasive power, a man of originality, vision, and courage, a sworn foe of all outworn traditions and customs, the greatest of British naval administrators since St. Vincent, 'Jacky' Fisher was what the lethargic Navy had been in dire need of. His five years' tenure of the post of First Sea Lord was the most memorable and the most profitable in the modern history of the Royal Navy. He fell on the old régime with a devastating fury. During these strenuous years there was no rest for anyone connected with the service. 'It was as though a thousand brooms were at work clearing away the cobwebs.' In the teeth of ultra-conservative traditions, he revolutionized the Navy, cramming in a few years the reforms of generations and laying foundations that can never be destroyed. He gave his countrymen a new Navy, stronger and better organized than he had found it, and purged as by fire of 'those obese and unchallenged old things that stifled and overlay' it in the past.

It is easy to criticize his methods; it is just as easy to argue that an exceptional situation could be dealt with only by an exceptional man of strong, commanding, and uncompromising personality. It would be foolish to claim infallibility for him. As we shall see, the Navy in 1914 had certain definite weaknesses, and Fisher must share the responsibility for some of them. No doubt he made mistakes, as in his opposition to the creation of a Naval War Staff and in his perhaps too ruthless scrapping policy. But, as Napoleon once said, the man who never made a mistake never achieved anything, and Fisher achieved much: the foundations of that victory at sea which determined the issue of the First World War were laid by him. One shudders to think what the Navy's chances might have been but for his work in the first decade of the century. Rear-Admiral Sir Robert Arbuthnot, who had never been in the Fishpond, could point to the fleet assembled for the grand naval review in July 1914 and say: 'All that is best and most modern here is the creation of Lord Fisher.' Winston Churchill, no uncritical admirer of Fisher, has contributed this fair estimate:

There is no doubt whatever that Fisher was right in nine-tenths of what he fought for. His great reforms sustained the power of the Royal Navy at the most critical period in its history. He gave the Navy the kind of shock which the British Army received at the time of the South African War. After a long period of serene and unchallenged complacency, the mutter of distant thunder could be heard. It was Fisher who hoisted the storm-signal and beat all hands to quarters. He forced every department of the Naval Service to review its position and question its own existence. He shook them and beat them and cajoled them out of slumber into intense activity. But the Navy was not a pleasant place while this was going on. The 'Band of Brothers' tradition which Nelson handed down was for the time, but only for the time, discarded.[23]

A man truly great despite his idiosyncrasies and truly good despite his violence.

[23] *The World Crisis*, i. 74–5.

PART II

Prelude to War, 1910–1914

IX

The McKenna–Wilson Régime, 1910–1911

I wonder what the German game is, and why they are so fearfully keen about a political understanding. I suppose it is something in this way: We know that the phrase 'Balance of Power' stinks in their nostrils. In fact they have told me so. They want the Hegemony of Europe and to neutralize the only thing which has prevented them from getting it, viz., England's naval strength. They want an understanding which would have that effect.

SIR EDWARD GOSCHEN to Sir Arthur Nicolson,
22 October 1910.

How wonderfully Providence guides England! Just when there is a quite natural tendency to ease down our naval endeavours comes AGADIR!

FISHER to Esher, 1 August 1911.

1. THE NEW ORDER AT WHITEHALL

WHEN Wilson hauled down his flag in March 1907, he was within a few days of the age of compulsory retirement for admirals. By a special order-in-council he was promoted to Admiral of the Fleet, which gave him a further five years on the active list. As there was then no command afloat for an officer of that very high rank, he spent the next two years at his home at Swaffham, in Norfolk. In April 1909 he became a member of the Committee of Imperial Defence. When the call came that autumn, he was extremely reluctant to succeed Fisher. His natural talents, he realized, were for executive command afloat rather than for administrative duties at the Admiralty. It took the pressure of King Edward to induce him to become First Sea Lord. The public announcement of the appointment (2 December) was received with profound satisfaction by the Navy and the public. For one thing, Wilson had never been tainted with the faintest suspicion of partisanship. From the controversies which had rent the Navy he had kept entirely aloof, and he had conspicuously ignored journalists and politicians. His selection therefore exercised a soothing influence upon the controversies. 'There is a little blue sky showing,' said Beresford. 'Wilson's appointment will have the cordial support of all of us in the Service.'[1]

In the second place, his record inspired admiration and confidence. Everybody knew the story of how he had earned his Victoria Cross. He won it at the battle of El Teb, in the Sudan in 1884, with what Sir Redvers Buller described as one of the most courageous acts he had ever witnessed. The enemy had made a gap in the British square, and, seeing a half-dozen of them making a dash for it, Captain Wilson threw himself into the breach. He cut down one or two with his sword. When it broke off at the hilt, he shifted to his fists, bowling over the attackers until a detachment of infantry came to his relief. He had been employed in the highest commands afloat, the Channel and Home commands, continuously between 1901 and 1907, during which time he had won the reputation in England and abroad of being the foremost living strategist and tactician. His skill in handling fleets in narrow waters and during fogs was almost legendary. He also had outstanding mechanical aptitudes and inventive skill. He had invented the double-barrelled torpedo tube and adapted the searchlight for distant daytime signalling.

What manner of man was Sir Arthur Knyvet Wilson? He was of medium height (5 feet, 9 inches) with a sturdily built, athletic figure. His 'spade beard' was grizzled, as was his hair. 'His blue eyes always gave one the impression of being a little screwed up, as though from looking in the spindrift whipped from the wavetops in a gale.' He was often careless in dress and appearance. He never married, and the Royal Navy was his only interest in life, apart from his love of shooting and outdoor games. He was extremely reserved and unbending, self-reliant, untroubled with nerves of any sort, and hard as nails, physically. He made no close friends. 'He was, without any exception,' Churchill has written, 'the most selfless man I have ever met or even read of.' He was also kindly and human, and not lacking in humour, a dry humour, in his infrequent moments of relaxation. He was known as 'Tug' among his brother officers 'because he was always working, i.e., pulling, hauling, tugging'. To the bluejackets he was 'old 'Ard 'Art', since he worked all under him as hard as he worked himself. Twice he carried the Channel Fleet into Spanish waters at the Christmas season. In response to protests and appeals from officers

---

[1] Beresford to Balfour, 12 Dec. 1909; Balfour MSS.

and men pining for leave, he snapped out the single word, 'Service!' And yet he was greatly loved in the Fleet because of his modesty, simplicity, selflessness, and unfailing courtesy.

With all his ability Wilson was not a successful First Sea Lord. As an administrator he suffered from the serious defect of inability to delegate work of any importance to others. This had been characteristic of him as a fleet commander, when he had rarely explained his plans and the reasons for them to his officers. Again, he was obstinate and full of *idées fixes*. The King, after a fruitless conversation with him about the education at Osborne and Dartmouth, told him that he was 'one of the most obstinate men I ever came across!!'[2] It did not help that Wilson was reserved to the point of secretiveness. Excepting possibly Fisher and Captain H. F. Oliver (afterwards Admiral of the Fleet Sir Henry Oliver), his most trusted friend in the Navy, he refused to confide to anyone his views, motives, or intentions. 'He never says much, *but he thinks a lot!*' was Fisher's view. Finally, he displayed little tact in dealing with men.

Trouble began even before Wilson took over from Fisher. (In effect, though officially not until 25 January 1910, he was running the Admiralty from December 1909.) The Sea Lords resented his obstinacy, high-handedness, and secretiveness. Vice-Admiral Sir Francis Bridgeman, the Second Sea Lord (1909–11), had early forebodings. 'Wilson is the best solution, but I know from experience with him that there is no joy to be found in serving either with him or under him! Deadly dull! and uncompromising, as you know. He will never consult any one and is impatient in argument, even to being impossible!'[3] Six weeks later, Esher reported after dining with Fisher and McKenna: 'McKenna finds Sir Arthur Wilson "very difficult". He is high-handed and treats Admiral Bridgeman as if he were a second Lieutenant on board a ship—and he is very obstinate.'[4]

A new reform era could not be expected of Wilson. He did maintain the main lines of Fisher's policies; but he was not receptive to new ideas. His absorption in *matériel* policy, his neglect of personnel matters and the development of strategic thought, and his lack of vision made for a quiet though hardly progressive

[2] Knollys to Esher, 30 Dec. 1909; Esher MSS.
[3] Bridgeman to Fisher, 21 Nov. 1909; *Fear God and Dread Nought*, ii. 282.
[4] Esher to M. V. Brett, 4 Jan. 1910; *Esher*, ii. 433.

administration. Haldane lamented (September 1910) 'the change that has come over the Board of Admiralty . . . the doors of the Admiralty are closed to all new ideas and new developments.'[5] In the end, even Fisher had to confess, 'Wilson is no good ashore!'[6]

2. DREADNOUGHTS AND POLITICS

The first task of the reorganized Board was to see the 1910–11 estimates through the Cabinet and Parliament. The Board had decided in November 1909 that four capital ships would suffice for the ensuing year, but that six would be required in 1911–12. The new programme was increased to six upon the news, around 1 December, obtained from Trevor Dawson, Managing Director of Vickers, that Austria had laid down two dreadnoughts. A Cabinet crisis resulted when McKenna submitted the revised programme to his colleagues towards the end of January 1910. The First Lord, Grey, and others were prepared to resign if Asquith threw his lot in with Lloyd George and his followers. The storm blew over quickly when the Admiralty proposed a 5–5 programme for the two years: four dreadnoughts and one battle cruiser each year. (The new estimates showed an increase of five-and-a-half millions. They were now over £40,000,000.) The 1910–1911 programme, McKenna informed the Prime Minister, would give Britain twenty-five dreadnoughts (apart from the two battle cruisers promised by Australia and New Zealand) in March 1913 against seventeen German and two Austrian nearing completion. 'The only troublesome point of the Austrian development is that we shall have to send Dreadnoughts into the Mediterranean and thus reduce our advantage over Germany in this type of ship.'[7] This foreboding was the germ of the radical redistribution of naval force in 1912.

The Foreign Office was not very happy with the five big ships, since Germany would be laying down four in the new year. The programme should have been six at least. 'It will encourage the Germans in their idea that we are growing very weary in the competition and that the occasion will soon arise when they will be able to snatch our superiority from us. . . . the proportion of

---

[5] As reported by Esher to Balfour, 30 Sept. 1910; *ibid.*, iii. 25.
[6] Fisher to J. A. Spender, 25 Oct. 1911; *Fear God and Dread Nought*, ii. 398.
[7] McKenna to Asquith, 30 Jan. 1910; McKenna MSS.

5 to 4 new ships can hardly be called a two-Power standard.'[8] This anticipated the line taken by the navalist critics when the new estimates were presented on 9 March and debated a week later. The *Daily Mail*, however, took the view that 'the Estimates are as much as we can expect from a Radical Government, though far from ideal', and this was the official position taken by the Opposition.

The Liberal press accepted the 'unparalleled demands' with extreme reluctance. The *Daily News* (10 March) lamented that 'the appetite of this monster of armaments grows by what it feeds on. Give it four Dreadnoughts and it asks for eight, eight and it asks for sixteen, sixteen and it would still be unsatisfied. It is an appetite without relation to needs or facts. It is the creation of irrational hates and craven fears. It can only be stopped by the determination of the democracies of the two countries that this wild rivalry shall end.' Churchill represented this point of view in the Cabinet. The programme of the year was 'unexampled', he wrote to the King. Fifteen capital ships would have been undertaken in scarcely a year (the eight of 1909–10, the two Colonial ships, and the five of the new programme). The German acceleration in dreadnoughts had ended, and the biggest dreadnought fleet they could have ready in April 1912 would be thirteen only, perhaps only eleven, certainly not the seventeen they were led to expect or the twenty-one they were told might be built. Against these eleven or thirteen, the Admiralty would have at least twenty. 'In ordinary circumstances these Estimates would have led to vehement debates in the House of Commons, [but] . . . no difficulty will arise. The political issues between the two Houses [the bill for the reform of the House of Lords] dominate the situation. The resistance to expenditure of all kinds was never at a more feeble ebb.'[9]

Churchill was right. In 1909, when the First Lord made his annual statement, the House was packed. A year later (14 March), the chamber was only half-filled and the debates that day and on 16, 17 March were uneventful and, indeed, dull. There was no trace in the House of Commons of the alarm which had agitated public opinion a year earlier.

The lull in agitation was only temporary. Navalist attention

<hr />

[8] Hardinge to Knollys, 20 Feb. 1910; Windsor MSS.
[9] Churchill to King Edward, 11 Mar. 1910; *ibid.*

was directed in the spring to the transfer of the base of the 1st Division of the High Seas Fleet (that is, of half of the Fleet) from Kiel to Wilhelmshaven in the North Sea and the construction of a harbour at Brunsbüttel, where the Kiel Canal enters the estuary of the Elbe. At Wilhelmshaven two docks capable of containing the largest warships were complete, a third nearly complete. These moves pointed to the removal before long of the entire High Seas Fleet, and of the centre of gravity of the German Navy, from the Baltic to the North Sea. This was cited in England as evidence of Germany's sinister design to make ready her Navy for a war with England. There was a press agitation for the development of British bases in the north to counter the German shift. The East Coast was practically undefended. The only naval base that faced or touched the North Sea was at Chatham, although there was to be a base at Rosyth at some indefinite future date. The positions of existing British bases at Milford Haven, Plymouth, Portsmouth—and Chatham, too—were not favourable for a rapid concentration of ships in the North Sea or for maintaining a large fleet during operations in that sea.

Agitation also mounted for a national defence loan to finance a naval programme like the Naval Defence Act of 1889—a steady, regular programme that would provide a two-keels-to-one or other unchallengeable standard of strength. With a fixed programme there would be no hand-to-mouth proposals and no violent oscillations between over-confidence and panic. The Imperial Maritime League issued an appeal to the Prime Minister in June to obtain Parliamentary sanction for a defence loan of £100,000,000. The memorial was signed by over a hundred admirals and fifty generals. Sir Edmund Cox had a brighter idea. England should pick a quarrel with Germany, then destroy her Fleet, as the only alternative to 'this endless yet futile competition in shipbuilding.'[10]

In September–October there was what Liberal journals called 'a recrudescence of scare', or what navalists called 'a patriotic outcry', over the country's naval position. The drums were beaten for a capital-ship programme of at least six in 1911–12, to ensure a margin of superiority over the Triple Alliance, and talk of a naval loan was revived. A stirring speech by Balfour (Glasgow, 19 October) heartened the big-navy party. The Leader of the

[10] Cox, 'The English and German Navies', *Nineteenth Century and After*, Apr. 1910.

Opposition brought a tremendous indictment against the Government's conduct of naval affairs. He termed the narrow dreadnought margin over Germany (25 to 21 in 1913) 'most lamentable and dangerous', and he strongly hinted that the expedient of a £100,000,000 naval loan might have to be adopted. McKenna replied in the House (20 October) that, with rare exceptions and for brief periods only, the British margin of superiority had never been so high in time of peace. The peril was at worst a peril of the future, and it constantly moved on in the calendar of the scaremongers. In 1908, the First Lord pointed out, Balfour dated the danger-point in 1911. In 1909 it was to come in 1912; and now, in 1910, it was to come in 1913. McKenna corrected Balfour's estimate: the British margin in 1913 would be *eight* dreadnoughts, not four, because Balfour had included the four German ships to be laid down in 1911, but not the 1911–12 British programme of five ships. The margin would be twelve if one reckoned the two 'Nelsons' and the two colonial ships.

The Government was far more concerned with the growing uneasiness in 1910 among its Radical supporters, abetted by the Labourites, over the 'senseless bloating of armaments'. Pressure began to mount within the party, with the encouragement of some Cabinet members, rumour had it, for ousting McKenna as the first step towards arresting the huge naval construction programmes. Although McKenna, a fighter, was not upset by the plotting and the sniping, his admissions in the House on 8 February 1911 stoked the ire of the economists and the pacifists. In reply to a question, the First Lord frankly declared that his predictions of March 1909 had been inaccurate. His statement amounted to this: Germany now had but five dreadnoughts, not the nine he had said she would have in the autumn of 1910, since the four ships of the 1908 programme were not finished; she would have no more than nine in 1911, not the thirteen predicted, since none of the four 1909 ships would be finished in the course of 1911; she would have seventeen in 1913, not in 1912, as had been predicted; and, finally, Germany would have twenty-one completed in 1914, not in 1913, as he had expected. In view of McKenna's confession of 'overbuilding', he must, said the Radicals, atone for his 'blunders' by a corresponding economy, that is, by reducing the new estimates. This could be achieved through a reduction in the number of new ships to be laid down (four would be ample; rumour had it that the Admiralty wanted six, the Cabinet, five) and through slackening the shipbuilding pace. £40,000,000 navy estimates was the Radical goal.

Their programme was championed in the Cabinet by Lloyd George. On 16 February 1911 he had agreed to the 1911–12 naval estimates of £44,392,500 and the programme of five new capital ships on the understanding that McKenna would bring expenditure on the Navy down to some £40,000,000 by 1913–14. McKenna made his pledge conditional upon Germany making no amendment in her Navy Law prior to March 1914 which would add materially to her shipbuilding programme. He understood that a reduction in army estimates in the next two years was a part of the bargain, so that the £4,400,000 reduction would be a joint-service effort. When Haldane proved 'unyielding' at a Cabinet on 1 March (he had considerable support), McKenna would promise no more than a £3,000,000 reduction. Lloyd George sympathized with his colleague in the double attack he had to contend against 'from economists behind you and scaremongers in front of you', but he insisted on holding McKenna to his agreement. A reduction in army estimates was no part of the bargain. McKenna had undertaken to 'deliver the goods'. The Chancellor of the Exchequer advanced five considerations to support his thesis that it was not too much to expect a return to estimates of £40,000,000 in two years' time:

1. Even with the Navy at £40,000,000, it would represent an increase of £8,000,000 per annum on the Estimates as they stood three years ago.

2. The last two years we have laid down (without counting Colonials) at least three more dreadnoughts than you thought necessary when you submitted your shipbuilding plans to the Cabinet in November 1908.

3. You were then under the impression that German preparations were much more advanced than they have turned out to be.

4. There is a much better feeling with Germany now. Grey feels very sanguine that we may be able to secure an understanding as to slowing down. This would save enormously in 1913–14.

5. Grey seems hopeful as to [a reduction in Britain's] fleets in foreign waters.[11]

McKenna held firm (3 March). 'When I undertook to "deliver the goods", I am sure you will agree that they were to be both

[11] Lloyd George to McKenna, 3 Mar. 1911; McKenna MSS.

PLATE VII

2. ADMIRAL SIR FRANCIS BRIDGEMAN
First Sea Lord, December 1911–December 1912

[portrait by Ernest Moore

1. ADMIRAL OF THE FLEET SIR A. K. WILSON
First Sea Lord, January 1910–December 1911

[photograph at the Admiralty

PLATE VIII

2. ADMIRAL SIR GEORGE CALLAGHAN
C.-in-C. Home Fleets, 1912–14

[photograph by Russell, London

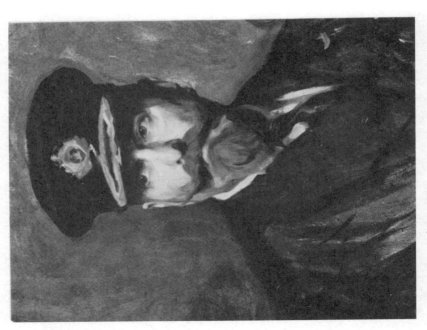

1. ADMIRAL PRINCE LOUIS OF BATTENBERG
First Sea Lord, December 1912–October 1914

[from the portrait-sketch by Philip de Laszlo

Army and Navy goods.' He would pledge himself to no more than three millions, but added that if Lloyd George's anticipations, under the fourth and fifth heads above, were realized, he could find the whole £4,400,000 from the Navy alone. And there the matter was allowed to rest. The ambiguous situation was to make for serious dissension in the Cabinet over subsequent navy estimates.

As was to be expected, the 1911–12 estimates, published on 9 March, were condemned by elements of the little-navy party (*Daily News, Manchester Guardian, Nation*) as 'enormous', 'exaggerated', on an 'alarmist scale', 'provocative', and incapable of justification in view of the 'overbuilding' since the 1909 scare. The *Daily Chronicle* and, surprisingly, the *Westminster Gazette* believed that the estimates were high, but that it could not be helped. McKenna's figure (Commons, 13 March) of a thirty to twenty-one dreadnought superiority in European waters in 1914 (the two Colonial ships would be stationed in Australasian waters) was not considered excessive for security.

Some of the organs of Toryism, *The Times* among them, gave the estimates a more or less qualified approval. Others accused the Government of betraying the nation with so small a new dreadnought programme, one that continued the policy of keeping only a little ahead of a single power, Germany, which was due to build four ships in 1911. Balfour and Lee, in the House (16 March), took the position that the provision of capital ships for 1914 (the spring of 1914 was the new critical period) was altogether inadequate. The Navy would have only twenty-nine dreadnoughts in European waters (since one was destined for the Far East) to oppose an equal number of Triple Alliance dreadnoughts.

McKenna had his usual difficult task (Commons, 13, 16 March) of defending the naval programme as adequate to maintain an absolute supremacy at sea, while at the same time making things as agreeable as he could to the little-navy section of his own party. He spoke with his customary earnestness and lucidity; but it was easy to observe that he was a good deal more uneasy over the opposition of his nominal friends than over the regular Opposition. He held out to his party (13 March) the hope that the country had reached the 'high tide' in its navy estimates. He made it conditional on the absence of any change in the German Navy Law—it fell automatically at the end of 1911 from four to two capital ships a year—adding that the Government had reason to believe that there would be no alteration. Grey, in an eloquent passage (13 March), hoped that the nations would yet discover that law was a better remedy than force, and would recognize that, in all the time they had been in bondage to the tremendous expenditure for armaments, the prison door had been locked on the inside. All were feeling the burden of taxation, all were faced with grave internal difficulties in the effort to raise the money for defences. Grey saw light breaking. If there were no change in the German Navy Law, he, like McKenna, anticipated a substantial reduction in British naval expenditure.

The Germans regarded Grey's speech as a vindication of their naval policy. The British seemed to be having financial difficulties. 'Grey's surrender is due to the Naval Law alone and the unshakable resolution of the German nation not to allow any diminution of this important instrument.' The Emperor echoed the sentiments of the Naval Attaché. 'If we had followed the advice of Metternich and Bülow for the last four or five years and ceased to build we should now have had the "Copenhagen" war upon us. As it is, they respect our firm resolution and surrender to the facts. So we must go on building undisturbed.'[12]

The little-navy wing of the Liberal Party was not impressed with the Government spokesmen. On 13 March a Radical motion that the House 'views with alarm' the 'enormous increase' in recent service estimates, and opining that they should be reduced, was defeated, 276–56. On 16 March a Labour amendment, declaring the increased naval expenditure was 'not justified by foreign events, and is a menace to peace and to national security', was beaten down, 216–54. The Government had won handsomely on both occasions, but the restiveness of Radicals and Labourites might sweep the boards if the naval competition continued unchecked.

McKenna and Grey had no reason for optimism about Germany's intentions, and their statements in the House were probably made as much for German as for home consumption. For some months there had been rumours of an amendment to the German Navy Law, with the object of increasing the number of ships to be commenced in 1912 and succeeding years. Now, on

[12] Widenmann to Tirpitz, 14 Mar. 1911, and the Emperor's minute; *Die Grosse Politik*, xxviii. 397–8.

17 February 1911, the Naval Attaché in Berlin (Captain Hugh Watson, August 1910–October 1913) submitted the probability that the German Navy Law would be amended so that the navy estimates for 1912 and after would provide for the construction of three capital ships a year, instead of the two called for in the Navy Law. However, despite the mounting agitation for such a change, it was not a fact yet. Everything depended on the outcome of the naval conversations which had been renewed in the summer of 1910. These, if successful, would have greatly reduced the likelihood of an amendment to the German Navy Law in 1912. This, in turn, would have led to a reduction in the British navy estimates, as promised by the Government. Were that stage ever reached, a larger naval agreement would have become a distinct possibility.

3. THE NAVAL CONVERSATIONS

The Government felt obliged by the pressure of Liberal public and Parliamentary opinion, to say nothing of pressure within the Government itself, to make another attempt to reach some kind of naval agreement with Germany. When, in July 1910, the German Chancellor offered hope that something might be done about retarding the rate of construction, without altering the Navy Law, the Asquith Government felt it was impossible to leave this overture unanswered. There was no optimism about the result at the Foreign Office. Crowe, still the Senior Clerk, was suspicious of every German proposal. They were 'traps', and the German Emperor and statesmen 'are none of them to be believed on their word'. There was the fear that all the Germans were after was a political agreement, without any naval understanding at all, by which England would abandon her understandings with France and Russia, thereby upsetting the balance of power entirely in Germany's favour. Sir Arthur Nicolson, who had succeeded Hardinge as Permanent Under-Secretary of State for Foreign Affairs in 1910, was nearly as suspicious of German sincerity and designs as was Crowe. During the coronation festivities of June 1911, Nicolson's neighbour at a dinner party remarked what a pity it would be not to take advantage of the friendly reception in London of the Crown Prince and Princess of Germany, and of the German naval officers forming part of the German deputations, to try and put Anglo-German negotiations on a better footing. '. . . upon which, jumping up as if he had been stung, Sir Arthur had emphatically declared that as long as *he* was at the head of the Foreign Office, England should never, never be friends with Germany!'[13] Sir Edward Goschen, at Berlin, and Grey, while not quite so Teutophobe, were not exactly bubbling over with optimism as to what could be achieved in the naval conversations.

A memorandum summarizing the new British position was handed to the Chancellor by Goschen on·14 August 1910. There were, it pointed out, two ways of arresting naval expenditure. One was through an alteration in the German Navy Law. Since the Germans had made it perfectly clear that this was impossible, H.M. Government was willing to abandon its previous contention that this was a *sine qua non* for any agreement. The other way was through a 'reduction of the tempo' (Bethmann Hollweg's expression) in German shipbuilding without any alteration in the Navy Law. This the British Government was prepared to discuss. As regards the political understanding, which the Germans insisted must precede or accompany a naval agreement, Britain could not accept an understanding 'different in kind' from that which existed between her and other European powers, but was 'always ready to give assurances that there is nothing in any agreement between themselves and any other Power which is directed against Germany, and that they themselves have no hostile intentions respecting her'.

Grey, at the behest of the Cabinet, who 'thought it would be better than nothing', put forward another suggestion in the same memorandum—an agreement that the Germans should not increase their naval programme, accompanied by periodic exchanges of naval information on shipbuilding progress. Such an agreement would at least 'remove the apprehension of indefinite future increase; and it would have a moral effect considerable and very favourable'. There was an equally important hidden motive. In England the details of new ships—dimensions, protection, armament, speed, horse-power—were available to the Germans either through the navy estimates, or from the press generally at the time when vessels were completed or nearly so. But in Germany the details were kept secret, and became known only when they gradually

---

[13] Lady Wester Wemyss, *The Life and Letters of Lord Wester Wemyss* (London, 1935), pp. 127–8.

leaked out. Also the security precautions taken in Germany to prevent ships building from being seen far exceeded those taken in England. The Admiralty was, therefore, all in favour of an exchange agreement, while not thinking it likely that the Government would succeed in persuading the Germans.

A year and a half of intermittent, fruitless negotiation followed.[14] As regards the reduction of tempo, which the English strove to keep separated from the exchange-of-information proposal, the Germans were hazy on exactly what they meant. In any case, this never reached the serious stage. Concerning the other naval proposal, on 12 October Bethmann Hollweg formally accepted in principle the idea of the exchange of naval information, but, as regards its complementary feature, he asked what 'equivalent' was offered in return for a pledge not to increase the building programme in the Navy Law. However, a political understanding was 'an indispensable preliminary condition for any naval agreement'. Without it German public opinion would feel that German naval interests were being sacrificed. As Admiral Müller explained to Goschen (17 October), 'the Russian-French Entente which England had joined is a connection absolutely hostile to Germany; it is a very intimate one, and is based on mobilization measures and war plans. England's joining had to be interpreted as an act unfriendly to us.' Other unfriendly acts of England which he cited were England's Moroccan and Baghdad Railway policies. Müller went on to restate Germany's naval policy in plain terms.

We acknowledge English supremacy on the sea. England has to claim it on account of her colonies and her commerce. However, we cannot accept a supremacy so overwhelming that England can attack us at any time without a real risk. We want a navy strong enough to knock about the English Navy sufficiently in case of attack so that other nations do not have to fear it any more. That is the present status of the fleets. ['Intentionally,' Müller added, for the Emperor's information, 'I avoided mentioning the ratio 2:3, which is the ratio now.'] If you keep it that way by building annually 5–6 new dreadnoughts, we will not object. But if you go beyond that and build 8, 10, 12 new dreadnoughts each year, then we will answer with a strong amendment,

[14] There is a convenient summary of the 1910–11 negotiations (to May 1911) in *British Documents*, vi. 633–6 (pp. 631–3 summarize the 1909 discussions). The full correspondence is in *ibid.*, pp. 496–665. The quoted material that follows is from *British Documents*, except when otherwise indicated.

for we have not forgotten what history teaches, and we are not willing to share the fate of the Netherlands and Denmark.[15]

The Cabinet deferred a reply to the Chancellor on account of the general elections in December. Meanwhile, a report by the Naval Attaché, of 29 November 1910, underscored the importance of a regular mutual exchange of naval information between the two Admiralties. It was decided by the Foreign Office early in December to attempt to pursue this 'minor question' independently of the 'larger questions' of the limitation of armaments and a political agreement, which weighty matters were being discussed by a Cabinet Committee. When Metternich assured Grey (16 December) that his Government was willing to proceed on this basis, the decks were cleared for action. The Foreign Office already had the Admiralty's recommendations (3 December) as to the kind of information that should be exchanged: dimensions of ships to be laid down, protection, armament, speed, and horse-power, and the laying down and completion dates of the ships. To supplement the exchange, the Admiralty wanted to allow the naval attachés to visit the shipbuilding yards periodically to check the progress of ships building.

With the British elections out of the way, Goschen was instructed on 24 January 1911 to go ahead. On 7 February he laid his Government's views before Bethmann Hollweg, who said he was ready to proceed with the details once he had consulted Tirpitz. The Emperor nearly upset the applecart in his peculiarly impulsive way when he informed the British Military Attaché (3 March) that an exchange of naval information would be of no use, that the important thing was a political understanding. 'England and Germany together would ensure the peace of the world.' This bit of Imperial spontaneity did not augur well for the success of the negotiations for the exchange of naval information.

The British chose this very time to reopen the larger questions of naval limitation and a political agreement. A Cabinet memorandum of 8 March for the Chancellor began with a kind word for an exchange of naval information. It would have a 'considerable effect in convincing public opinion in both countries and elsewhere that the two Governments do not cherish any hostile designs against each other'. As regards the larger questions (and

[15] Müller's report to the Emperor, 18 Oct. 1910; German Ministry of Marine MSS.

here the memorandum was replying to Bethmann Hollweg's statement and memorandum of the preceding 12 October), Great Britain was no party to any understanding 'aimed directly or indirectly against Germany; no such understandings exist, and they are ready to give their sympathetic attention to any formula which the Imperial Government may suggest'. The memorandum made it clear that the political formula must not be such as would impair Britain's friendly relations with France and Russia. The Baghdad Railway and Persian questions were touched on as specific questions which should form part of a political agreement. The significance of the memorandum lay elsewhere. The Government had at last accepted the German thesis that a political agreement was essential to any agreement on the mutual reduction of naval expenditure; it only insisted that the discussions go on *pari passu* and that the two agreements be reached at the same time. The memorandum was without doubt strongly influenced by the Lloyd George faction in the Cabinet Committee.

The German reply was embodied in a memorandum handed to Goschen by Bethmann Hollweg on 24 March. The Chancellor had shaken his head over the last paragraph of the British memorandum. 'He said,' Goschen reported to Grey, 'that your idea of a political understanding seemed to be a settlement of the Bagdad Railway and Persian Railway questions and that, in return for that, you wanted an agreement for the mutual reduction of naval expenses. Such an agreement was, he thought, a good deal to ask for such a limited political understanding. Warming to his subject he reminded me that he had always said that the atmosphere must be thoroughly cleared and a good understanding secured before any reduction of naval armaments could be made.'

The views of the Admiralty on the exchange-of-information agreement were on the whole acceptable to the Germans, though with two stipulations which represented Tirpitz's thinking. One was that the information should be exchanged simultaneously and at a particular date (between 10 October and 15 November) every year; the details of the shipyard visits by the attachés could be arranged by the naval authorities of the two countries. The other stipulation was a far more serious matter. The Germans wanted the information exchanged to include a statement of the number of ships to be laid down by the two Governments in each year, *which statement should be of a binding nature for that year*. This went considerably beyond the exchange of details of ships suggested by the Admiralty, though, to be sure, the number of ships to be laid down would be incidentally known through the information exchanged as well as through the naval estimates of the two countries. Tirpitz's reasoning was that otherwise the English would have a considerable technical advantage. 'For example, the English must not subsequently change their own construction for 1912 after having received in October 1911 our reports of the types of ships to be asked for in the budget of 1912; otherwise, they would surpass us, technically. For the following fiscal year, 1913, *each* nation would have a free hand.'[16] Kiderlen, the Foreign Minister, employed a different tack. He told Goschen (25 March) that it was his Government's opinion that 'in order to ensure strict reciprocity, the exchange of such [technical] information should be so arranged that neither Power could use the information obtained for the purpose of amending their own ship-building programme. For instance if Germany announced that she was going to build say three ships in a certain year and Great Britain had made up her mind to build five, the latter should not on the strength of the German information bring up her programme for that year to six or seven or *vice versa*. In order to avoid any proceeding of that nature they had proposed that the exchange of information should be made simultaneously,' between 1 October and 15 November, which was the time the German estimates were submitted to the Ministry of Finance. But the exact date was unimportant.

Watson's views were fully endorsed at the Foreign Office. The Attaché advised that the agreement be restricted to an exchange of naval information, thinking that it was 'all to the advantage of England not to enter at all into such a binding agreement, but still more not to do so until the German Fleet Law has shown by its provisions for 1912 whether it is going to be adhered to or not'. The Foreign Office saw various objections, such as that Germany's allies, not bound by the agreement, might step up their building, while Britain's hands would be tied. Also, there was the fear that once they knew the British programme, the Germans might reduce the official age of their ships, before they were regarded as obsolete, so enabling Germany to lay down more ships. For such reasons it was the Foreign Office opinion that the two questions, the ex-

[16] Tirpitz to Bethmann Hollweg, 17 Mar. 1911; *Die Grosse Politik*, xxviii. 401.

change of information and the limitation of armaments, must be kept distinct.

This, too, was the opinion of the Admiralty. A sharp minute by Sir Arthur Wilson termed the German proposal that neither power should use the information exchanged for the purpose of amending its building programme as

manifestly absurd, as in the first place the information is of no use unless it can be acted on, and, in the second place, it would act as a direct incentive to each Government to exaggerate its estimates, for fear of being called to account by public opinion worked up by their respective Navy Leagues, if, when both programmes were declared, their own might be found to be inadequate.

Again, to communicate our programme to a Foreign Government before it has even been submitted to Parliament, especially under conditions which prevent its being altered afterwards, would be to deprive Parliament of all voice in the matter. . . .

If we wait till the programme has received the approval of Parliament, it will already have been made public, and its communication to the German Government can only be a matter of form.

Further, our shipbuilding policy is not determined by that of Germany alone, and an aggressive policy on the part of some other Power might require an immediate increase of our programme without any reference to Germany.

If navies are to be built with a view to possible war and not only for show, formal agreements as to the exchange of information are manifestly absurd. As long as the present friendly relations between the two countries remain, they may be comparatively harmless, but as soon as the conditions for which the navies are maintained arise, namely the possibility of war, they must immediately be broken and thereby emphasise the state of international relations.[17]

The official Admiralty reaction to the German views (16 May) recommended that the problem of a limitation of armaments be kept separate from an agreement for the exchange of naval information, and that the exchange should be made between 15 November and 15 March, but that even then it could cover no more than the bare number of ships of each type in the new programme. The technical details were subject to change until the keel of each ship was laid, and that was the proper date for the exchange of detailed data. Regarding the question of visits to

[17] Minute of 28 Apr. 1911; Admiralty MSS.

shipyards, 'any arrangement involving strict reciprocity might well be agreed to'.

Bethmann Hollweg, it seems, was ready to propose a stabilization of the naval competition by a building tempo of 2 : 3 per year for the next six years. Tirpitz had strongly demurred. 'An obligation of such a long period is not practical with the progress in engineering.' 'By far the larger part' of the Fleet consisted of pre-dreadnoughts and of early dreadnoughts whose armament was so out-of-date that 'their replacement by units of higher quality will become necessary, possibly earlier than would have been anticipated at the time the present building programme was formulated'. Also, in Tirpitz's opinion, the Navy Law after 1917 would be endangered if they tied themselves down as the Chancellor proposed, 'for, if we consider it possible for six years to build *2* ships annually to England's *3*, the transition from 2 to 3 for us will be difficult in the year 1918, and nobody will accept our motive for it.' For these and other reasons the Admiral refused 'to oblige the English'. The Chancellor had to agree that a naval limitation agreement was not possible.[18]

Accordingly, in his full reply to the British memorandum of 8 March on the subject of a general naval and political understanding, Bethmann Hollweg reminded the English that he had, in 1909, expressed willingness to slow down the rate of shipbuilding within the limits of the Navy Law. The British Government having shown no particular interest in this proposal, it had been dropped. 'Now, in view of the fact that next year the rate of German Naval construction would reach its lowest limit, it was of course impossible that this offer would be renewed.' Germany had nothing further to propose and left it to the British Government to make any further suggestions for the mutual reduction of naval expenditure. He would not suggest a political formula until a 'negotiable basis' had been found for a naval agreement, since the British Government had said public opinion in England would attach little value to a political understanding unless preceded by or made simultaneously with a naval agreement. However, the memorandum Bethmann Hollweg handed to Goschen contained this stipulation, that a general understanding should 'exclude all possibility of an attack by one party on the other'.

[18] Tirpitz's notes of a conference with Bethmann Hollweg, 4 May 1911; German Ministry of Marine MSS.

Crowe seized on the vital point (14 May): 'The German gov[ernmen]t continue, without committing itself to tangible proposals, to lay stress upon the necessity of obtaining binding guarantees that Germany will not, whatever happens, be attacked!' The Germans would be delighted, he pointed out, to have France and Russia likewise committed. (Metternich reported, 18 May, the Chancellor as favouring the inclusion of France and Russia in the political agreement.) The arrangement would be one-sided, in favour of Germany, since only she was 'ardently bent on a policy of ascendancy'.

. . . Germany, if for a period definitely freed from any fear of attack by her three most formidable rivals, would use the opportunity to consolidate and strengthen her position in other countries, extending her political influence, creating fresh interests and rights, and above all acquiring positions of strategical value and importance in case of any future wars with the three other contracting States. . . .

It is quite conceivable that in this way . . . Germany might, simultaneously with a further rapid expansion of her navy, acquire coaling stations and naval bases abroad which could have no other object than to strengthen her hands in a naval conflict, and in the possession of which she could perhaps hope with a reasonable prospect of success to challenge British supremacy at sea, when necessary.

. . . if and when Germany shall thus have fortified her position, what chance will there be for Great Britain, for France, for Russia, or in fact for anything short of a general combination of all the world, to resist German dictation?

Prospects for a political–naval limitation agreement, never bright, were as good as dead, particularly after Watson, on 30 May, reported there was not 'the slightest doubt' that three armoured ships would be built annually from 1912 on, or 1913 at latest. But there was hope for an information-exchange and shipyard-visit agreement. On 1 June Grey sent a memorandum to the Chancellor embodying the Admiralty views of 16 May. On 1 July the Embassy in Berlin reported that the Germans were agreed in principle with the British conditions. The exchange, between 15 November and 15 March, was to be of the number of ships of the ensuing year's programme, but with the proviso that, once this information was communicated, there was to be no alteration of programme 'without previous and further information being given to the other party'. The technical data would be exchanged when the keels were laid down, but since this could not be done simultaneously, the Germans proposed a discussion between the two Admiralties to resolve the difficulty, also to work out the details of the shipyard visits. The German response was encouraging, and the way was now open for a speedy agreement.

Unhappily, on the very day that the German reply was forwarded to London the German gunboat *Panther* arrived at Agadir, on the Moroccan coast. This opened the acute phase of the Agadir, or 'Second Moroccan', Crisis, which brought the two countries to the brink of war. For all practical purposes, the discussions were over, since, said Crowe (5 July), 'this is not the moment for continuing the discussions, and we should not be in a hurry to answer'. Grey felt that more harm than good would be done by continuing the discussions with Germany. And the Admiralty concurred that in view of the political situation, it would be advisable to postpone replying to the German memorandum for the present, 'and the opportunity', said Wilson, 'might very well be taken of dropping the question altogether until the Germans raise it again.'[19] The Government took no further step, even after the Admiralty had, on 21 August, accepted the German proviso and proposed this solution for the strict reciprocity problem: the technical information would be communicated when information was exchanged on the number of ships in the *following* year's programme—'e.g. at the time when the two Governments communicate the number of ships to be laid down in the 1912–13 programme, the technical details of those belonging to the 1911–12 programme would be given.'

By the end of September the war scare was over, but the Government continued to defer any action. The reason now was the report from Watson (27 September) of the probability that the German navy estimates would in future be published in March, instead of in November. The change was

principally designed to further the advantage she has gained, in the hope that the English Government will not vote large naval estimates when the advantage of comparison with the formerly earlier-produced German estimates is no longer available. . . . the proposed change of date . . . arises out of the recent negotiations for interchange of information. The German naval authorities, having failed to secure an advantage by getting England's consent to her date, now propose to

[19] Minute of 27 July 1911; Admiralty MSS.

alter their own date for publication of estimates to the English date.
. . . The German admiralty authorities have only used the negotiations
to gain an advantage.

The last sentence was the nub of the matter. German intentions
and motives regarding the proposed agreement were suspect.
Bethmann Hollweg complained 'somewhat bitterly' to Goschen
(3 November) that his Government had suspended the negotiations.

The new Board of Admiralty, with Churchill as First Lord, and
Bridgeman, less obstructionist than Wilson, as First Sea Lord, was
more disposed than the old Board to reach an agreement. It
saw no

difficulties of an insuperable character [it informed the Foreign Office,
12 December] in the exchange of technical information, whether as
regards substance or time. The wider publicity given to details of new
construction in England renders this information probably less valuable
to Germany than to this country, and my Lords would not allow any
question of mere procedure to stand in the way of an agreement, the
object of which is to remove uncertainty and to disarm suspicion. . . .
What they [the Admiralty] desire is, indeed, an exchange of simple
and easily verifiable facts. It will be sufficient if at any dates convenient
to the two Governments when communicating the programme for the
ensuing year, the number of ships of each class . . . could be made
known to each other by the two Governments, if the dates of their
laying-down, launching, and completion, could be exchanged, and if
the first two conditions could be tested by the periodical and reciprocal
visits of the naval attachés [to the shipyards] . . .
So far as further information upon the character of the vessels in
each class is concerned, my Lords do not think there would be any
difficulty in arriving at an understanding. . . . My Lords agree with
the German Government that any contemplated variation in facts
which have once been communicated should be notified before it is
made.

Note that the Admiralty's latest position dropped protection out of
the data included in 'technical information'—also speed, although
this could be inferred from displacement and horse-power data.

These observations were well received at the Foreign Office, and
by the end of December the Government had decided to resume
negotiations on the basis of the Admiralty memorandum. The
German elections of January 1912 intervened, and it was not until

28 January that the British proposals (practically identical with the Admiralty memorandum) were given to Kiderlen. He promised 'to examine the matter closely'. This was the last that was heard of the scheme for an exchange of naval information. There was no mention of it during the Haldane Mission in February, at which time the Germans shifted the spotlight to a political agreement.

At bottom the naval-exchange proposal was only a subsidiary issue. The stumbling blocks to a naval limitation agreement, which is what the British were really after, were the same as in 1909: the German insistence on British neutrality as a condition for concessions in their building programme, and the British refusal to give the kind of guarantee that would have destroyed their *ententes* with France and Russia. So sensitive was the Foreign Office to the possible ruffling of French and Russian susceptibilities that it kept Britain's Entente friends *au courant* of the negotiations. For the same reason the Foreign Office reacted negatively to the idea advanced by such prominent German naval officers as the Chief of the Naval Cabinet (Admiral Müller) and the C.-in-C. of the High Seas Fleet (Admiral von Holtzendorff), in conversations with Watson, that frequent meetings be arranged between the two Fleets, or portions thereof. The Germans asserted this would enable the young officers and men to know and appreciate each other. Besides, they pointed to the undesirability of extreme methods of secrecy as to *matériel*; it was of little value and did considerable harm. Watson was censured by the Foreign Office for his 'injudicious action' in discussing such matters and endorsing the German suggestion. Such meetings as were proposed would have 'a serious political aspect'. The Admiralty concurred in this action.[20]

It is noteworthy that Grey never revealed to the British people that the Germans were ready to discuss naval limitation in return for a suitable political agreement. 'As a matter of fact, parliament, to say nothing of the nation, never had an opportunity, with all the facts before it, to express a choice between the Entente policy of the foreign office and the cabinet and its alternative, which was a political and naval agreement with Germany. . . . Grey doubtless felt that publicity for German terms, which were bound to

---

[20] Foreign Office to Goschen, Nov. 1910; Admiralty MSS. Watson had reported these conversations in a dispatch to Goschen of 17 Sept.; *ibid.*

meet with violent objections from Imperialists, Entente enthusiasts, and balance-of-power advocates, would react unfavorably on the general situation.'[21] One wonders why the German Government did not publicly reveal its complete position. To be sure, it was not *de rigueur* in the pre-war world to do such things. Or could it have been that the Government was afraid of the ire of the German Navy League, Anglophobes, imperialists, etc.?

The Agadir Crisis had so poisoned Anglo-German relations that an upward revision of the Navy Law was inevitable by the end of 1911. On 15 September Watson reported that he now had evidence 'from reliable high authority' that a further increase of the German Navy was certain as a result of the Moroccan crisis. Should this come about, any real prospect of any kind of naval, to say nothing of a political, agreement would be stone dead. Before examining the Agadir Crisis we must consider the Anglo-Japanese Alliance, whose termination would have had serious repercussions on Britain's ability to stay ahead in the competition with Germany.

4. RENEWAL OF THE JAPANESE ALLIANCE

The alliance would expire in 1915 if either party gave twelve months' notice of its intention not to renew. It was not going to be an easy matter to reconcile the Dominions to a renewal. Also there was very little public opinion behind the alliance. Finally, the naval aspects of the alliance had led to many difficulties, which prejudiced a renewal.

Since the arrangement under the original alliance on the strength and disposition of the allied forces in the Far East had not worked well in practice, a clearer understanding on the naval obligations of the two powers became desirable.[22] A conference between naval representatives of the two allies, held on 29–30 May 1907 at the Admiralty, drew up a list of principles that should guide allied naval relations. The more important follow.

2. It is considered improbable that the Allies would be attacked by any single Power, and it is the strength of some coalition therefore which should represent the standard of allied forces to be aimed at during the term of the Agreement.

[21] Hale, *Publicity and Diplomacy*, p. 379.
[22] The earlier history of the naval aspects of the alliance will be found in *The Anatomy of British Sea Power*, pp. 427–34, 450–5.

If the Anglo-Japanese Alliance is attacked, each of the Allies would naturally use its utmost endeavours to help the other, but neither side should count beforehand on any assistance from a material point of view from the other.

3. The Conference reiterates the principle that in order to secure sea communications—or in other words the command of the sea—the first objective in any war must be the destruction of the enemy's fleet; at the same time they recognise that in certain eventualities, it may become necessary for one of the Allies to transport large bodies of troops oversea prior to the accomplishment of the above-mentioned principle. [This had in view Japanese operations in Manchuria against the Russians.]

4. . . . It should be accepted in principle that the allied forces should never be unnecessarily strong in one place, if they become thereby undesirably weak in another.

Generally speaking, Great Britain could best guard the allied interests by destroying the ships of an enemy as they issued from their European bases, and thus prevent them from reaching any Eastern theatre of war at all.

The Conference, therefore, consider that no useful purpose can be served by making any detailed agreement either on strategical or technical questions. They confine their recommendations to those points that will tend to make the intimate relations already existing between the Allied Forces closer still, and to making provision for the fullest information to be furnished mutually by the Allies. . . .

9. The Transport Departments of the two Navies should exchange full information as to the suitable vessels on their respective lists, and keep this information always up to date. Any detailed arrangements which the military representatives of the Allies may mutually desire to make regarding the over-sea transport of troops are outside the scope of the purely Naval questions dealt with in this Memorandum. . . .

12. The fundamental principle would apply equally in peace and war, that any considerable transference of the naval strength of a foreign Power from one quarter of the globe to another should forthwith be met by a similar redistribution of the naval strength of the Allies, so as to ensure that wherever and whenever a war might break out the fleet of one or the other of the Allies would be present in adequate strength to cope with the situation.[23]

These principles were nearly all of Admiralty origin, since the Japanese really cared only about the question of transport. The principles also reflect to some extent Fisher's lack of enthusiasm

[23] 'Memorandum Regarding Naval Co-operation in War . . .', June 1906; Admiralty MSS.

for the alliance. He had always been opposed to it, 'the very worst thing that England ever did for herself!' The main object of the Japanese was to get British help in obtaining 142,000 tons of transport in three weeks' time to complete their arrangements for a campaign in Manchuria. The Admiralty had, at the conference, taken up a *non possumus* attitude (see paragraph 9, above), although the amount of tonnage asked for was reasonable and there was always a large amount available in Hong Kong, Singapore, India, and Australia. After pressure had been brought to bear on Tweedmouth by the generals and possibly by the Cabinet and C.I.D., the Admiralty completely changed its tune. It found (6 June) that there was any amount of transport in the East—nearly 1,500,000 tons! The Admiralty now undertook to charter the 142,000 tons the Japanese wanted, when the need arose.

Naval relations were still lacking in warmth and were not without friction. Under the alliance the two countries were bound to a mutual interchange of information as to intended building programmes each year, the disposition of naval forces, docking and repairing capabilities, foreign intelligence, and technical data. The exchange of technical data did not always go smoothly. When the Japanese Naval Attaché in London asked for particulars of certain warships, he was given what he wished on a strictly reciprocal basis. The Admiralty became wary as the termination date of the alliance approached. The possibility of non-renewal had to be kept in view. 'The nearer that date approaches, the more important it becomes to be increasingly careful in giving information to a country, which after that date may occupy only the position of a friendly foreign power.'[24] Rules were now adopted as a guide in dealing with Japanese requests for information.

No information should be given which in any way anticipates accomplished facts. For instance, details of ships which have not yet been laid down or improvements in guns, machinery, etc. which are still in the experimental stage.

Similarly as regards Fleet exercises, tactics, etc., information should not be given until changes are carried so far that they must be looked upon as definitely established and consequently as a part of the war organization with which it would be important that the two fleets, if allied in war, should be fully acquainted.

In determining the attitude of the Admiralty to the Japanese by such

[24] Memorandum by the D.N.C., Sir Philip Watts, Sept. 1909; *ibid.*

general principles it is to be expected that the Japanese will adopt a similar line, and therefore while avoiding the appearance of any marked tendency to increased reserve, both in giving and asking information, care should be taken to give and ask for no more than is really important and cannot be obtained in some other manner entailing no obligations.[25]

Rear-Admiral Bethell, the D.N.I., recommended that the best course was to ask for nothing themselves, except in exchange for what the Japanese asked. 'We had better I think in the future ask for nothing. They have not got much we want to know about and that cannot be found out by other means.' In practice, it was difficult to withhold information sought by the Japanese.

Some time before 1910 the Japanese proposed an arrangement for meetings of British and Japanese warships in Far Eastern waters. The request was refused by the Asquith Government, on the ground that such meetings, however natural, would only too probably cause embarrassment to the Government in its relations with third powers.[26] The 'third powers' were, of course, the United States and perhaps Russia and France.

It might well be wondered what British purpose the alliance was serving after 1907. Originally, it had in view hostilities with the Franco-Russian alliance; later, in 1904–5, with Germany as a probable member of the coalition. But the French threat was gone by 1906, the Russian, after the Entente of August 1907. The answer to the query lies in the enormous advance made by the Japanese Navy since the Russian war, when it had been an insignificant force. The British Naval Attaché in Tokyo reported on 1 January 1909 that

the Japanese Navy is at present in a high state of efficiency, and is of such strength as to render the position of Japan quite unassailable in the Pacific. The Navy has many weak points, as all navies have; but it has that paragon of advantages over any adversary that might come to attack it, 'fighting near its base.' The discipline and loyalty of the officers and men remain perfect; they seem to have few ideas outside their work; it absorbs their thoughts by day and affects their dreams at night. . . . but they just fail to reach that measure of brilliancy which distinguishes so many officers in our own Navy. They are too

[25] Admiralty MSS.
[26] Mentioned without dating in Foreign Office to Goschen, 1 Nov. 1910; *ibid.*

slow and too methodical, and require time to think where a smart officer should act instantly.[27]

The implications of Japan's naval progress were forcibly brought out in the discussions of the C.I.D., 29 June 1909, on the defence of Hong Kong in war. Its first conclusion was that 'So long as the Anglo-Japanese Alliance remains in force, the British possessions in the Far East are secure.' The second conclusion identified the potential aggressor: 'Care should be taken sufficiently to reinforce the fleet in the Far East before the termination of the Alliance, in order to neutralize the danger from a preponderant Japanese fleet in the China Seas.' The third conclusion had the same object—preparation for the day when the alliance was no more: 'The Admiralty and War Office should concert measures to ensure that the local navy and military defences at Hong Kong are on a sufficient scale to enable the fortress to hold out for a period of one month.' The idea here was that it would take a month before the fleet in the Far East could be reinforced. McKenna's view at this C.I.D. meeting was that the rupture of the treaty with Japan was not a 'reasonably probable contingency' against which they need take precautions.[28] The crucial point, however, was that the treaty was due to expire in 1915, and, if it did, British naval strength in the Pacific would have to be increased. This could only be done by sacrificing strength in home waters, where the Germans would be given an opportunity to grapple with the Royal Navy upon something like equal terms.

The C.I.D. discussed the standard of defences at Hong Kong again on 26 January 1911 in the light of a possible Japanese attack after the treaty had expired. Sir William Nicholson, the Chief of the Imperial General Staff, said that if the treaty were terminated, it would be necessary to keep a fleet in the Far East superior to that of Japan. 'Short of this, no additions [to the Hong Kong garrison] would be of any use, for the Japanese fleet would be able either to destroy our fleet, or to confine it to Hong Kong, as they did the Russian Fleet to Port Arthur.' A. K. Wilson disagreed. A naval force sufficient to deter the Japanese from sending troop transports to Hong Kong was all that was needed. Grey and Haldane observed that the whole question turned on the question

[27] N.I.D. Report No. 871, Apr. 1909; *Reports on Foreign Naval Affairs, 1908–9* (Admiralty Library).
[28] Minutes of the 102nd meeting of the C.I.D.; Asquith MSS.

of the alliance, which was due to terminate in August 1915 unless a year's warning was given of an intention to abrogate it. Grey thought that the year 1912 would be 'a favourable time to enter into a discussion with Japan on the subject'. Crewe stated that Australian public opinion was 'thoroughly hostile' to the alliance, and to a lesser degree New Zealand and Canadian public opinion. Harcourt suggested that a presentation of the strategic aspects of the alliance 'might perhaps have a useful educative effect on Colonial opinion'.[29]

The probability of an increase in the German Navy Law speeded up the time-table. Some time not long afterwards, Grey sounded out the Japanese about prolonging the alliance for ten years. They were favourable. During the Imperial Conference in London, at a C.I.D. meeting on 26 May 1911 attended by the Dominion Prime Ministers, Grey presented a cogent case for the renewal of the Japanese alliance on strategic grounds. The key passage follows:

If we, in 1914, were to give notice to Japan that we did not wish to continue the alliance . . . she certainly would infer that that meant some reversal of our policy, and she at once would look . . . at what other arrangement she could make with other Powers to secure her position . . . it cannot be doubted that not only would the strategical position be altered immediately by our having to count the Japanese fleet as it now exists as possible enemies, but Japan would at once set to work to build a fleet more powerful than she would have if the alliance did not exist. We, on the other hand, instead of keeping the modest squadron in Chinese waters which we do at the present time, would have to keep—if we are to secure the sea communications between the Far East and Europe, and also between the Far East and Australia and New Zealand—a separate fleet in Chinese waters which would be at least equal to a two-Power standard in those waters . . . in the interests of strategy, in the interests of naval expenditure, and in the interests of stability, it is essential that the Japanese Alliance should be extended.'[30]

Grey proposed an extension on two conditions: first, that it would not affect the question of the freedom of the Dominions to deal with the question of Japanese immigration; second, that (as already accepted by Japan) if an arbitration treaty were signed

[29] Minutes of the 108th meeting; *ibid.*

[30] Minutes of the 111th meeting of the C.I.D.; *ibid.* This passage is omitted in *British Documents*, vi. 789.

with the United States, or any other power, Great Britain would not have to support Japan in a war with that power unless (as stipulated by Japan) that power was assisted by another power or joined another power already at war with Japan. With these qualifications, the Dominions gave their consent to the renewal of the alliance for a period of ten years (that is, until 1921). The Admiralty was 'entirely in favour' of renewing the treaty (21 June). It was officially renewed on 13 July 1911, but without the Japanese stipulation. Article IV read: 'Should either of the High Contracting Parties conclude a treaty of general arbitration with a third Power, it is agreed that nothing in this Agreement shall impose on such contracting party an obligation to go to war with the Power with whom such an arbitration treaty is in force.' As it turned out, the Anglo-American arbitration treaty, signed on 3 August 1911, was never ratified by the United States.

The renewal of the alliance coincided with a serious deterioration in Anglo-German relations and a consequent stimulation of the naval competition. It was fortunate that there was no Japanese problem to divert naval strength from home waters.

5. THE AGADIR CRISIS

The background can be sketched quickly. Supposedly to protect European lives endangered by a revolt against the Sultan of Morocco, the French, in the spring of 1911, dispatched an expeditionary force to Fez. Germany, aware that the French move was the first step towards a speedy annexation of Morocco, did not propose to stand idly by. A first-class international crisis was touched off by the arrival of the German gunboat *Panther* on 1 July at Agadir, a port on the Atlantic coast of Morocco, ostensibly to protect German interests and nationals there. Actually, the aggressive German move had quite different objectives. 'Kiderlen aimed to impress upon the French the absolute determination of German statesmen to acquire a completely acceptable compensation at all costs, even war; second, to secure in Agadir both a hostage and position of advantage for the period of hard bargaining that was certain to follow; and third, to be in a strategic position if circumstances should open a way for a tripartite division of Morocco [among France, Spain, Germany].[31] The first

[31] Hale, *Publicity and Diplomacy*, p. 382.

objective was the most important one, the Germans being prepared to accept the French take-over in return for satisfactory colonial concessions.

But Germany did not make her intentions clear, despite an indirect invitation from Asquith, speaking in Parliament on 6 July. The Government was perplexed. Crowe confessed 'to being, for the moment, altogether nonplussed, and can find no answer to the question: "What is Germany really driving at?" Herr von Kiderlen's behaviour seems almost inexplicable.'[32] The Government did not believe the Germans were primarily interested in colonial compensation, else why would they have asked for anything so inadmissible as the most valuable part of the French Congo (news of which reached London on 18 July)? It seemed to the Cabinet that Germany's objective was to humiliate France through a colonial partition highly favourable to Germany, and so destroy the Entente.

There was also a widespread fear that Germany intended to secure a naval base at Agadir, something that Britain could not regard with indifference. We know that Kiderlen encouraged the Pan-Germans to believe that he would demand south-west Morocco, though as a colonial establishment rather than as a naval base. 'The plain truth of the matter,' trumpeted the *Standard* (5 July), 'is that no Government . . . could consent to allow a great foreign navy to station itself on the flank of our Atlantic trade and on the line of our route to the Cape . . .' Nicolson, at the Foreign Office, was impressed by the same danger. The Germans, in his opinion, intended to occupy a port on the Atlantic coast of Morocco and convert it into a second Heligoland. This would threaten British interests, as through the seizure of the Canaries by a *coup de main* or by negotiations with Spain. The Cabinet included among the British interests in Morocco that must be safeguarded in any possible arrangement 'no new fortified port anywhere on the Moroccan coast'.[33]

Sober journals like the *Manchester Guardian* (11 July) and *Army and Navy Gazette* (22 July) made light of the danger, pointing out what was obvious to both Admiralties, that a base at Agadir, 1,500 miles from home and needing support by a considerable

---

[32] Crowe's minute of 17 July 1911; *British Documents*, vii. 357.
[33] Asquith's report to the King of the Cabinet meeting of 4 July 1911; Asquith MSS.

detachment from the High Seas Fleet, would be a source of weakness to the German Navy. The Admiralty was perfectly calm over the possibility of Germany acquiring a port on the Atlantic coast of Morocco. Wilson assured Grey there was no site that could easily be converted into a naval base, and that if Germany were to undertake not to fortify any Moroccan port, the Admiralty would be satisfied. But the First Sea Lord added that under no circumstances must Germany be allowed to get a foothold on the Mediterranean coast of Morocco.[34]

Grey accepted the Admiralty point of view. In any case, the main danger of war, as he saw it, lay in the German resolve to establish their hegemony upon the Continent through humiliating France and smashing the Entente. Britain must show Germany in unequivocal terms that she was standing by France and would have to be considered. There followed Lloyd George's famous speech at a Mansion House banquet on 21 July. The text of the statement had been worked out by Lloyd George, Grey, and Asquith, but had not received Cabinet sanction. Lloyd George's well-known pacifism and desire for an Anglo-German understanding added to the significance of the warning: 'But if a situation were to be forced upon us in which peace could only be preserved by the surrender of the great and beneficent position Britain has won by centuries of heroism and achievement, by allowing Britain to be treated, where her interests were vitally affected, as if she were of no account in the Cabinet of Nations, then I say emphatically that peace at that price would be a humiliation intolerable for a great country like ours to endure. National honour is no party question.' The speech did not have unanimous Cabinet approval. It reminded Morley 'uncomfortably of Gramont's [Napoleon III's Foreign Minister] on July 6, 1870; received with tremendous applause, followed by bottomless mischief. . . . I utterly dislike and distrust the German methods. . . . But that is no reason why we should give them the excuse of this provocation.'[35] And it was so regarded—as an unnecessary provocation—in Germany.

Lloyd George's speech led to the tensest part of the crisis, which continued even after France and Germany, early in August, sat down to some hard bargaining. The bellicose press in both

<hr />

[34] Grey to Bertie, 12 July 1911; *British Documents*, vii. 358.
[35] Morley to Asquith, 27 July 1911; Asquith MSS.

countries complicated the negotiations and rendered a rupture in them imminent by mid-August. War seemed quite possible until well into September, a war in which England would be bound to take part if only because of her larger interests revolving about the balance of power. On 25 July Grey summoned Churchill and Lloyd George post-haste to his room in the House of Commons. He had just seen Metternich, who had expressed the anger of his Government over the Mansion House speech and asserted that if France refused an agreement, Germany would insist on the observance of the Treaty of Algeciras (1906) and the restoration of the *status quo ante*. Upset by this conversation, Grey's first words to his colleagues were: 'I have just received a communication from the German Ambassador so stiff that the Fleet might be attacked at any moment. I have sent for McKenna to warn him!'[36] McKenna arrived shortly after, and quickly left to arrange for warning orders to be sent to the Fleet. Lloyd George believed that Germany meant war. General Sir John French, the Inspector-General of the Forces, felt that the Emperor was not unwilling to go to war, and the King thought that he might be driven into war, whether he liked it or not.[37]

It was charged during the crisis and afterwards, notably in an alarmist speech of 18 November by Captain W. V. Faber, a Conservative M.P., that the Fleet had not been ready for war when the crisis was at its height. Beresford, who had warned the Prime Minister on 27 July about the unreadiness of the Fleet, told Sidney Low in November that 'if England had gone to war with Germany in July last we should have sustained a naval disaster'.[38] There was some truth in the charge. Hankey, Assistant Secretary of the C.I.D. and therefore in an excellent position to know the facts, pointed to the 'extraordinary apathy' with which the Admiralty regarded the crisis.[39] On 21 July, a Friday, when the crisis was at its height, *The Times* carried a story that the whole High Seas Fleet, sixteen battleships and four armoured cruisers strong, had put to sea and was somewhere in the North Sea. Ottley, Secretary of the C.I.D., twice (between 21 and 24 July) drew Nicolson's attention to the fact that the High Seas Fleet was

[36] *The World Crisis*, i. 47–8.
[37] Knollys to Esher, 24, 27 Aug. 1911; Esher MSS.
[38] Desmond Chapman-Huston, *The Lost Historian* (London, 1936), p. 245.
[39] Hankey to Esher, 9 Aug. 1911; Esher MSS. The account that follows is based on this letter.

concentrated off the coast of Norway and in a good position for a 'bolt from the blue'. He reminded Nicolson of the passage in the C.I.D. Invasion Report of 1908 which said the possibility of a surprise attack during *normal* diplomatic relations was not sufficiently remote to be ignored, and that in the existing strained relations there was even less ground for ignoring the possibility. While the High Seas Fleet had concentrated and 'vanished into the desolate wastes of the high seas', the British Fleet was in a very different condition. The Atlantic Fleet was at Cromarty, in the north of Scotland. The 1st Division of the Home Fleet was at Berehaven, in the south of Ireland. The 2nd Division was at Portland, in the south of England. The 3rd and 4th Divisions were at the three home ports paying off the complements and keeping only nucleus crews aboard. No precautions (for example, putting out the anti-torpedo nets) were taken by the Portland Division and the nucleus-crew divisions. Indeed, the men were given four days' leave! As a mitigating circumstance, the ships, just back from manœuvres, were short of coal, and the necessary colliers were delayed at Cardiff by a strike.

But what more could have been expected? Despite Grey's continual warnings to the Admiralty not to be caught napping, Wilson saw no possibility of danger. So certain was he that the crisis would not lead to war that he had gone off for the week-end to Scotland for some shooting! About this time Churchill was complaining that 'practically everybody of importance and authority is away on his holidays. . . . I cannot help feeling uncomfortable about the Admiralty. They are so cocksure, *insouciant* and apathetic, so far as one can judge from all that one sees and hears.'[40] The possibilities of that week-end of 21 July horrified Hankey. 'What a chance for our friends across the water! Supposing the High Sea Fleet, instead of going to Norway as announced, had gone straight for Portland, preceded by a division of destroyers, and after a surprise night torpedo attack had brought the main fleet into action at dawn against our ships without steam, without coal, and without crews! Simultaneously another division of destroyers might have gone for the Atlantic Fleet at Cromarty, leaving only the Berehaven Division and the scattered remnants of the 3rd and 4th Divisions to deal with.'

[40] Undated letter (to Lloyd George?); Frank Owen, *Tempestuous Journey: Lloyd George, His Life and Times* (London, 1954), p. 213.

It was not until 25 July, five days after the crisis had become acute, that any precautions were taken. 'Then ensued a mild panic,' including a scene out of Gilbert and Sullivan. It was suddenly discovered that the Navy's cordite reserves' at Chattenden and Lodge Hill were not well protected. Wilson disclaimed Admiralty responsibility: the police were responsible and should send out some extra men. The Home Office maintained the Admiralty was responsible and should send out some marines. In the end, on 28 July, Churchill, the Home Secretary, assumed responsibility and sent a hundred police. The Admiralty then sent marines, and, finally, the War Office sent soldiers. 'So the magazines were saved and all three Departments were responsible!' But no one in authority would listen to the entreaties of the C.I.D. that the precautionary telegram should be sent. This would have automatically provided for the necessary defensive measures. 'It was no use. No one would listen at all, and they continued their desultory, spasmodic, and inadequate precautions' (Hankey).

The Cabinet was shocked and amazed to find, during Wilson's absence, that the Admiralty could produce no war plan for the Navy. It was so secret that only the First Sea Lord knew what it was! It was locked up in his own brain, though one story has it that it was scratched out on a single sheet of paper locked up in a safe to which only he had the key! Whatever its precise contents, events showed that the military authorities had quite different ideas. The profound difference between the Admiralty and War Office points of view was brought out at a special all-day C.I.D. meeting summoned by the Prime Minister, 23 August, to examine the state of Britain's preparedness. The immediate impetus seems to have been reports of German mobilization activity along the Rhine. Sir Henry Wilson, the Director of Military Operations, stated the views of the General Staff in a brilliant, well-prepared exposition. Briefly, the soldiers wanted to send six divisions to France immediately Britain was drawn into a Franco-German war, to fight on the extreme French left. Were this done, there would be a good chance of checking the great German offensive. In the afternoon, Wilson propounded the Admiralty version of British war strategy. His war plans—he could only outline them— were based on a close blockade of the German ports, the capture of advanced bases, and possible landings on the enemy's coast. The Admiral felt that Britain's main efforts should be confined to the sea. An expeditionary force would be swallowed up in the conflict of immense land masses. Besides, the enemy's fleet must be disposed of and command of the sea established before the Expeditionary Force could be transported to France. It would be much better to keep the troops in ships, drawing off far more than their own numbers from the German fighting line, and ready for the counterstroke of landings on the German Baltic coast. Wilson's ideas were those of Fisher.

The Army and Navy representatives violently combated the other's views. Nothing was settled; but Sir Henry Wilson, far more voluble and lucid, had stated his case much more effectively than had Sir Arthur Wilson. Taciturn by disposition, the Admiral simply could not express himself with the force and clarity of the General. Most of the politicians present were consequently more impressed with the General Staff point of view and with the fact that it had worked out preparations for military co-operation with the French to the minutest detail.[41]

The Agadir Crisis blew over in October with an agreement (signed on 4 November) for the German recognition of the French protectorate in Morocco in return for a substantial slice of the French Congo. The results of the Crisis were profound. A fresh bout of naval competition between Germany and Britain was rendered inevitable. The German Navy League made the most of the charge that, but for England's unwarrantable interference, Germany would have secured a much more favourable settlement with France. The moral drawn was that the Fatherland must have a still bigger fleet in order to save her from diplomatic reverses at the hands of Great Britain. Tirpitz was ready to use the inflamed state of German public opinion to bring forward a supplementary navy bill, and he had the Emperor with him. William's speech at Hamburg, 27 August, foreshadowed another increase in the German naval programme, 'so that we can be sure that nobody will dispute our rightful place in the sun'. Aiding German naval propaganda was the fear, expressed to the British Naval Attaché by some of the highest German naval officers, that the British Fleet had been preparing to attack Germany in the summer of 1911. In Captain Watson's opinion, the German officers did not really believe this, but were using the argument to promote the

[41] See below, pp. 389–93, for a more detailed account of this historic C.I.D. meeting.

purposes of the big-navy party. The Attaché could not ascertain how far the responsible naval authorities had encouraged this campaign, although their silence implied their connexion.[42] Nevertheless, there was some sincerity, if not validity, in the German complaint. Thus, Widenmann reported that 'in August and September the Admiralty made a series of preparations which were to increase the preparedness of the English fleet to the utmost and were to get it ready for immediate action', and he proceeded to detail some of the preparations that had been made: special night guard duty at the Admiralty, denial of furlough to the Third and Fourth Sea Lords, a stay of the Atlantic Fleet in Portland instead of in Norwegian harbours as had been planned, concentration of the 1st and 2nd Divisions of the Home Fleet 'in the Firth of Forth or Firth of Moray', large orders of ammunition placed with different factories, etc., etc.[43]

The Cabinet and C.I.D. were shocked by the fundamental disagreement between the Admiralty and War Office on plans for a German war, by the Navy's unpreparedness at the end of July, and, above all, by the Admiralty's lack of war plans, in contrast to the War Office, which had all its plans ready. Decisive action followed.

6. THE RESHUFFLE AT WHITEHALL

The key person in the dramatic changes of October 1911 was Haldane, the brilliant Secretary of State for War since 1905, who had taken over the War Office at a time when practically everything was wrong with the Army. The reforms that followed, including the formation of the Territorial Army for home defence and the Expeditionary Force, and the institution of a General Staff as a thinking brain for the Army, had effectively prepared the Army for the contingency of war. Agadir had been the last straw for Haldane. After the C.I.D. meeting of 23 August 1911 had broken up, he made it clear to the Prime Minister that he could not remain at the War Office unless the Board of Admiralty was able to work in complete harmony with the plans of the General Staff, and this would not be possible until a proper Naval War Staff was organized. 'The Fisher method, which Wilson

[42] Especially Watson to Goschen, 19 Mar. 1912; Admiralty MSS.
[43] Widenmann to Tirpitz, 1 Nov. 1911; German Ministry of Marine MSS.

appears to follow, that war plans should be locked in the brain of the First Sea Lord, is out of date and impracticable. Our problems of defence are far too numerous and complex to be treated in that way. They can only be solved correctly by a properly organized and scientifically trained War Staff, working in the closest co-operation with the military General Staff under the general direc-tion of the War Office.' Unless the problem were tackled 'reso-lutely', he would resign.[44]

McKenna, on 23 August and afterwards, refused to see any analogy between the two services. He opposed a naval staff as an attempt to apply to the Navy a system primarily designed for an army. He shared to the full the Fisher–Wilson reluctance for a war staff. Both admirals preferred to hold full control over every-thing having to do with the administration and training of the Fleet. They believed that war plans must be prepared in the greatest secrecy by the First Sea Lord alone, kept to himself, lest there be a leak, and divulged to the Army only on the outbreak of a war. 'Only Sir Arthur Wilson and myself, when I was First Sea Lord of the Admiralty, knew the Naval plan of war.'[45]

The establishment and great development of the Naval War College at Portsmouth, with a section of it devoted to the study and elaboration of war plans, had done something to regenerate strategic thought in the Navy. This progress was not enough, since the supremely important department of naval strategy was still left to the First Sea Lord and the D.N.I., both of whom had other duties that taxed their strength and time. A true naval staff had not been established, as Corbett and others had hoped—the Navy's thinking department, whose purpose would be to work out in peacetime the main problems of war and to assist in the formu-lation of scientific war plans.

The Beresford inquiry report had strongly urged 'the further development of a Naval War Staff'. To appease its critics—the *Morning Post, Standard, The Times*, Spenser Wilkinson, Haldane, Beresford, *et al.* led a public agitation for a naval staff—the Admiralty had, before the Beresford hearings, projected, and, now, on 11 October 1909, announced the establishment of a Navy War Council at the Admiralty for the consideration of strategic

---

[44] Haldane to Asquith (undated, though no doubt soon after 23 August); Major-General Sir Frederick Maurice, *Haldane* (London, 1937–9, 2 vols.), i. 283.

[45] Fisher, *Memories*, p. 102.

problems and war plans. Its regular members were the First Sea Lord as President, the Assistant Secretary of the Admiralty, the Director of Naval Intelligence, and the Director of the newly-formed Naval Mobilization Department, which had taken over plans and mobilization from N.I.D. The head of the Naval War College would attend when the business made his presence desirable. This modest reform was not a true naval staff. The trouble was that the new department's function was merely advisory and that it met only on the initiative of the First Sea Lord. Herbert W. Richmond, then a rising captain, noted at the time of its foundation that the Navy War Council was 'the most absurd bit of humbug that has been perpetrated for a long time'.[46] Herbert King-Hall summed up its brief career under Fisher and Wilson very succinctly when he spoke of a seed sown on 'stony ground ... it withered and died, for, whereas Sir John suckled the infant on skim-milk, Sir Arthur denied it even that nourishment, and starved it to death.'[47] Wilson, even more than Fisher, resented any interference with the First Sea Lord's prerogatives. The Council met four times during Fisher's last three months at the Admiralty, and only seven times during Wilson's tenure of nearly two years. The Navy War Council therefore did not hush the agitation of those who were urging a 'thinking department', a genuine naval staff corresponding in function to the General Staff of the Army.

Agadir was the turning-point. Impressed by Haldane's cogent arguments, Asquith decided on a change at the Admiralty, with the new First Lord to be charged with the formation of a naval staff. It should be stressed that Asquith reached this decision without choosing between the naval strategy of a sea-war, with a mobile army poised for landings on the enemy coast, and the 'continental' strategy of the Army, with the Navy's main role that of transporting a continental army and keeping its lines of communication open. This, in Asquith's view, was not the primary issue at that moment. Haldane had proposed himself as the man best qualified to go to the Admiralty and fashion there a war staff on lines similar to the General Staff. At the end of September the

[46] Diary, 27 Oct. 1909; Arthur J. Marder, *Portrait of an Admiral : the Life and Papers of Sir Herbert Richmond* (London, 1952), p. 62.
[47] Admiral Sir Herbert King-Hall, *Naval Memories and Traditions* (London, 1926), pp. 217–18. He was Director of Naval Mobilization at the Admiralty, 1909–11.

Prime Minister invited Churchill and Haldane to discuss the situation with him at Archerfield House, East Lothian, where he was holidaying. He saw both men, who were equally importunate about going to the Admiralty. Asquith decided to move Churchill over from the Home Office with McKenna assuming Churchill's Cabinet post. One consideration was that Haldane as First Lord would look like a direct snub to the Admiralty in view of his sharp criticisms. Also, Lloyd George favoured Churchill over Haldane. The 'deciding factor' was the importance of having the First Lord in the Commons. The change was settled at Archerfield, after which the Prime Minister motored to Balmoral (2 October) to discuss the problem with King George. The decision had already been reached, but it was apparently necessary to appease the King, who did not relish the idea of Churchill at the Admiralty.

The bolt from the blue struck McKenna in mid-October. 'As we are on the eve of completing our sixth year of office, I am contemplating a certain amount of reconstruction both inside and outside the Cabinet. . . . I am going to ask you to undertake what is undoubtedly one of the most difficult and responsible places in the Government—the Home Office. Your legal training and your large and tried administrative experience and capacity give you special qualifications for its duties, and I am very confident in the wisdom of my selection.'[48] The Prime Minister's letter gave no reason for the sudden change. McKenna did not want to go, and was, privately, very angry at what he regarded as his 'ejection' from the Admiralty. Although he held Haldane responsible rather than Churchill, his relations with Churchill cooled rapidly.

McKenna accepted the situation. He asked only for the postponement of his transfer until the end of the year, on the ground that his health did not permit his undertaking a new office in the middle of a session and immediately before the meeting of Parliament. Asquith at first agreed, then went back on his word and insisted (15 October) on an immediate transfer. One of the reasons he gave was that the intended change would be bound to leak out, resulting in 'rumours and agitation'. Another reason was that the King refused to allow anybody but himself to give the seals to Churchill's successor at the Home Office, and if the transfer was not arranged before the King left for India, it could not take place before February 1912. Still another reason given was that this was

<hr />

[48] Asquith to McKenna, 10 Oct. 1911; McKenna MSS.

the time when the navy estimates were considered and settled, and it was essential to have it done under the new First Lord, who would have to present and defend them.

McKenna saw Asquith at Archerfield on 20 October.[49] He 'had come to tell him all that was in his mind.' He insisted that so long as he remained as First Lord, 'the Admiralty must get earliest notice of intention to use British troops [in France] and could then oppose it.' This was relevant to the question of the postponement of his resignation. 'Perhaps after Christmas foreign situation might give no ground for alarm. Hence when postponement was now refused and power to prevent scheme withdrawn, the existence of scheme was relevant to postponement.' Asquith pointed out that there was no ground for anxiety, since he was himself opposed to the scheme. McKenna countered that 'he might be rushed into it by situation being developed by W. O. and Admiralty': within the month the War Office had still been working out the scheme and pressing the Admiralty, and so long as conversations continued between the British and French General Staffs, the danger existed. Asquith, unimpressed, 'repeated no danger so long as he was P.M., as he was opposed to the scheme.'

I objected that he had missed my point. Particular scheme of no consequence. The fact that there were conversations at all encouraged the French in the belief that we should fight on their side and led them to provoke Germany. If we failed to join them we should be charged with bad faith. If we joined in fact we should be plunged into war on their quarrel.

He repeated the argument in his own words and agreed, but he could not say there were no circumstances in which details should not be worked out.

I replied that there certainly might be cases in which we ought to join in the war but that in no case should our troops be employed in the first instance and the French should never be encouraged by such a promise. If the communications between the General Staffs were continued, I should have to resign. . . . The only chance for the French was to resist inch by inch, retreating all the while and defending themselves in trenches. If after twelve or six or three months the task was too heavy for them an English Army coming to their assistance might be an incalculable benefit. But the 'à Berlin' temper ought never to be encouraged, and if it were, it would inevitably lead to their defeat.

[49] The material that follows is from McKenna's notes of the extraordinary conversation; *ibid.*

He replied no such encouragement would be given while he was there.

I replied that the claim might be jumped by the W.O. and the Admiralty.

He protested that the assumption of my argument was that he was a figurehead pushed along against his will and without his knowledge by some energetic colleagues.

I said it was not that, but a situation might be created in which no other course was open to him. . . . the situation could be created by turning to use the accidents of the moment and by inflammatory speeches and that it would then be too late for him and for the Cabinet to resist public opinion.

He answered, 'On the question of postponement which we are now discussing do you suggest anything of this sort could happen within the next six weeks?'

I instanced the possibility of Caillaux's Government riding for a fall and Clemenceau succeeding.

[Asquith] 'Could there be a worse foundation on which to build war feeling in this country than the rejection by the French Chamber of proposals for settlement submitted by the Ministers?'

I agreed that standing alone British public opinion could not be inflamed by such an event but those who wanted war would take good care that other incidents were brought into play.

He replied he did not believe in war and that if he had thought that war were probable he would not have made the change. . . .

In the course of conversation there were many kind expressions of good will and assurance that no considerations except suitability for the offices at the particular moment had guided him in making the change.

This document is interesting for the light it throws on strategic thinking at the Admiralty in the McKenna–Wilson period, and it is remarkable for its omission of any reference to the basic issue involved in the Cabinet reorganization, the institution of a naval staff at the Admiralty. One can only speculate on the reasons for Asquith's deviousness, and certainly one cannot blame McKenna for assuming that he was being replaced because of the disagreement on higher strategy between the two services.

McKenna and Churchill exchanged offices on 25 October. Letters and telegrams poured in on McKenna from the Navy, containing expressions of gratitude for the magnificent fight he had put up for the service during his three and a half years. There was a feeling that the Navy had lost its staunchest friend, and mingled with it was apprehensiveness about the new order at Whitehall.

X

The Churchill Period, 1911–1914: Preparation for War

Mr. Gladstone once defined Lord Randolph Churchill as 'a young man in a hurry'. Lord Randolph's son is also a young man in a very great hurry to do striking things, and to give the world the fullest opportunity for appreciating his remarkable talents. Absorbed in these preoccupations he cannot slacken the pace to consider other people's susceptibilities.

The Standard, 21 Dec. 1912.

1. CHURCHILL AS FIRST LORD

IN 1902 Churchill had pooh-poohed Austen Chamberlain's ambition to become First Lord as a 'poor ambition'. Now, nine years later, he took what was commonly regarded as an inferior Cabinet post, after holding the Home Office, which comes next in titular precedence to the dignities of the Prime Minister and the Chancellor of the Exchequer. He made the change because the Admiralty was a more exciting spot in that era of intense Anglo-German naval rivalry and final preparations for Armageddon.

One cannot say that he suffered from any surfeit of public approval. There were serious misgivings in big-navy quarters, and in the Navy itself, on the announcement of the appointment, because of his reputation as a determined, cheese-paring, niggardly economist. There were personal objections, too. Declared the *Spectator* (28 October 1911), 'He has not the loyalty, the dignity, the steadfastness, and the good sense which make an efficient head of a great office. He must always be living in the limelight, and there is no fault more damning in an administrator.' Many in 1911 would have agreed with this opinion. Naval extremists never made their peace with him. For example, Maxse's influential *National Review* constantly referred to Churchill in the pre-war years by such epithets as 'a wind-bag', 'a political gambler of the worst type', and 'a self-advertising mountebank'.

What sort of person was the 36-year-old First Lord? He was far more brilliant than McKenna, but without McKenna's solid qualities. All the traits that were to win him global renown in World War II were clearly discernible before World War I : self-confidence, vivacity, inexhaustible vitality and power of work, courage, eloquence, temperament, and a great brain. He had wonderful argumentative powers in the Commons or when putting a case before the C.I.D. or Cabinet. He was aggressive and truculent in his official capacity, showing a disregard for the opinions and sensibilities of his opponents; but he was full of charm and tolerance and amiability in social intercourse. 'His companionship was exciting,' Lord Beaverbrook once remarked.

This ex-lieutenant of Hussars, a widely-read student of military history, could hardly pose as a naval expert in 1911, though he had followed naval affairs closely from about 1906. Of course, First Lords, invariably civilians, are not supposed to know much about the Navy, but Churchill was not content to lean too hard on his professional advisers. Unlike his predecessors, the new First Lord took an active part in formulating all important measures and policies. From the start he set out to familiarize himself with all aspects of the Royal Navy—administration, personnel, and *matériel*—and to re-establish the former close relationship between the First Lord and the sea service. During his first eighteen months at the Admiralty, he spent 182 days at sea to keep in touch with the actual work of the Fleet. He visited practically every dockyard, shipyard, naval establishment and important ship in the British Isles and the Mediterranean. No First Lord in modern times has displayed equal zeal in this direction. In 1912 Asquith and Churchill went to sea to witness some gunnery practice. Churchill was soon 'dancing about behind the guns, elevating, depressing, and sighting'. Observing this, Asquith remarked: 'My young friend yonder thinks himself Othello, and blacks himself all over to play the part.'[1] In all, he spent eight months afloat in the nearly three years before World War I. Beatty, his Naval Secretary, observed that 'Winston talks about nothing but the Sea and the Navy and the wonderful things he is going to do'.[2]

I cannot resist the temptation to include an anecdote which has appeared in various contexts. This would seem to be the original version. The First Lord turned up at a pre-war French Embassy

---

[1] Paymaster Rear-Admiral W. E. R. Martin, *The Adventures of a Naval Paymaster* (London, 1924), pp. 218–19.
[2] Beatty to his wife, 27 May 1912; Beatty MSS.

reception in the brand-new uniform of an Elder Brother of Trinity House. Paul Cambon, the French Ambassador, asked what this new adornment might mean, and Churchill, 'in courageous French with the accent of John Bull', replied: 'Je sweeze oun frair ehnay de la Trinnitay.' Murmured Cambon with mock reverence: 'Toutes mes félicitations. Vous avez de bien hautes relations!'

Churchill's frequent visits to the fleet and the yards earned him little popularity. The German Naval Attaché reported, on excellent authority: 'The sea-officers of the British Navy are often enraged against Mr. Churchill in spite of their unlimited appreciation of his merits in Navy politics, for the youthful civilian Churchill, on his frequent visits to the fleet and dockyards, puts on the air of a military superior. Through his curt behaviour he offends the older officers in their feeling of rank and personal pride. And thus, according to many, through his lack of tact he injures discipline by his ambition for popularity with the lower ranks, especially the "Lower Deck".' The Emperor noted on this paragraph: 'Thus, even in England civilians and the military don't get along!' The Attaché cited this illustration of Churchill's methods. When the First Lord recently visited a battleship, he ordered the commander to assemble the crew on deck for inspection. The commander, swallowing his annoyance, complied. As soon as the men had formed up, Churchill began to examine the officers, to see whether they knew their men.

'Do you know your men by name?'
'I think I do, Sir; we have had many changes recently, but I think I know them all.'
'What is the name of this man?'
'Jones, Sir.'
'Are you quite sure that the man's name is Jones?'
'Yes, Sir.'
(Churchill addressing the man:) 'What is your name?'
'Jones, Sir.'
'Is your name really Jones or do you say so only to back your officer?'
'My name is Jones, Sir.'

After Churchill left the ship, the commander and the officers were in a state of 'choking wrath'.[3]

[3] Captain Erich von Müller to Tirpitz, 3 Dec. 1913; German Ministry of Marine MSS.

Churchill's first-hand study of and interest in every detail of the Navy, together with his confidence in Lord Fisher's advice, fortified his unlimited faith in himself and resulted in frequent interference in technical matters and overriding of professional opinion. He could not sit still while mediocrities dilly-dallied, and before he had been in office many months he was expressing strong opinions even on strategical and other technical matters and trying to force his opinions on the Board of Admiralty, although technical matters belonged to the sphere of the Sea Lords. 'His fatal error,' in Jellicoe's opinion, 'was his entire inability to realize his own limitations as a civilian . . . quite ignorant of naval affairs.'[4]

Churchill gave an exhibition of omniscience at the time of the 1912 naval manœuvres. According to press reports, he not only gave wireless instructions to the Commanders-in-Chief from Whitehall, but on the return of the ships to harbour he lectured to the flag officers on how the manœuvres should have been conducted, and this even before the Umpire had completed his report!

Part of the difficulty lay in the fact that the First Sea Lords, successively (after A. K. Wilson), Admirals Sir Francis Bridgeman and Prince Louis of Battenberg, were not especially forceful characters and allowed Churchill a good deal of rope. One must admit at the same time that, while he assessed his naval *expertise* too highly, his intervention in technical matters often represented pure gain. Keyes testified after the war that Churchill's 'quick brain and vivid imagination were invaluable and, in the majority of cases, his intervention was in the best interests of the Service'.[5]

Churchill got into the hair of his own Sea Lords as well as that of the admirals afloat. There was, for instance, the Bridgeman affair, which brings us back to Sir Arthur Wilson for a moment. Wilson was due to retire in March 1912, on attaining 70 years of age. Churchill could not wait until then, personally fond of Wilson though he was. 'He impressed me from the first as a man of the highest quality and stature, but, as I thought, dwelling too much in the past of naval science, not sufficiently receptive of new ideas when conditions were changing so rapidly, and, of course, tenacious and unyielding in the last degree.'[6] Wilson was excellent in

---

[4] Bacon, *Jellicoe*, pp. 181–2, quoting from Jellicoe's post-war autobiographical notes.
[5] *The Naval Memoirs of Admiral of the Fleet Sir Roger Keyes* (London, 1934–5, 2 vols.), i. 43.
[6] *The World Crisis*, i. 81–2.

many ways, but the country had forgotten there was a First Sea Lord and there was a general lethargy in the country about the Navy. Few would have taken exception to the verdict of a former Sea Lord: 'Under dear old "ard eart" we had slept quite long enough.'[7] More to the point, so far as the new First Lord was concerned, were Wilson's strategic views and attitude towards the creation of a war staff at the Admiralty. It was, in Churchill's view, bad enough that he had no love for the War Office strategy of sending the B.E.F. to France in the event of British participation in a war against Germany. It was far worse that Wilson would not budge on the issue of a staff. He considered it absolutely unnecessary and defined the agitation for a naval staff as an attempt to apply to the Navy a system primarily designed for an army.

The conduct of wars on land depends mainly on the means of transport, and the supply of food and ammunition to the Army. Before a General can work out a plan of campaign or select the best line of operations, the Staff must make a most careful study of the topographical features of the country, the adaptation of the available means of transport . . . and especially it must consider the means of defending its lines of communications, without which the Army cannot exist.

To determine all these matters, even for one campaign, requires a very large staff of highly trained officers . . .

Ships, on the other hand, contain in themselves all that they require for war, including accurate charts of every sea in which they are required to operate, so that they are ready to move anywhere at the speed ordered as soon as they can get steam ready, and up to the limit of their coal capacity; they have no line of communications to defend. . . .

In the aggregate probably more thinking has to be done to produce an efficient Navy than an efficient Army, but it is entirely on different lines. The thinking in the Navy is mainly occupied with producing the most perfect ships, guns, and machinery, with crews trained and organised to make the most perfect use of them, and constantly practised under conditions approaching as nearly as possible to those of war.

All this requires an enormous thinking department, but the Staff that does this thinking is not called by that name. It is comprised of the principal members of every department of the Admiralty, supplemented by the Admirals, Captains, Executive Officers, and heads of the different departments in every ship afloat, all organised for one end. . . .

The preparation of war plans is a matter that must be dealt with by

[7] Admiral Sir Charles Drury to Fisher, 9 Dec. 1911; Lennoxlove MSS.

the First Sea Lord himself, but he has to assist him, besides his Naval Assistant, the Director of Naval Intelligence and the Director of Naval Mobilisation, and in the latter's department there is a war division, consisting of a Captain and a Commander especially allocated to this work.[8]

Wilson apparently did not realize that transport and supply were the function of the Quartermaster General's department, not of the General Staff. Indeed, as Admiral Dewar has remarked, the whole memorandum was based on a complete misunderstanding of the object and duties of a war staff.

The study of strategy, tactics and the special requirements of war are shouldered out of the way by the demands of technical work and the daily current of administrative routine. Under the circumstances, there is nothing surprising in the fact that the best drilled armies and navies often prove themselves the least efficient. The main object of the staff system is to guard against this danger by placing the control of policy, operations and training in the hands of officers who are, to a large extent, freed from the routine of technical and administrative work. Hence, the guiding principle of the system lies in a clear-cut distinction between administration—that is, the production and maintenance of the instrument of war—and operations, that is, its use.[9]

Churchill's reaction to Wilson's memorandum was to propose his removal to the Prime Minister. The memorandum was 'decisive in its opposition, not only to any particular scheme, but against the whole principle of a War Staff for the Navy'. Wilson had to go, and Asquith was in perfect agreement. He was a strong supporter of a naval staff and had seen for some time that nothing could be done while Wilson was First Sea Lord. The choice of a successor was a sticky problem. The field of selection, Churchill and Asquith realized, was narrow, once the First Lord with extreme reluctance had given up the idea of bringing Fisher back. The King at first gave his support to his good friend Admiral Sir Hedworth Meux (he had changed his name from Lambton in September 1911), a very able sea-officer with no great administrative talent. He then appears to have favoured Sir John Durnford, late President of the Royal Naval College. Asquith's first choice was Prince Louis of Battenberg, but when he 'tried it on' with

[8] Wilson's memorandum for Churchill, 30 Oct. 1911; Admiral Sir Edward E. Bradford, *Life of Admiral of the Fleet Sir Arthur Knyvet Wilson* (London, 1923), pp. 231–5.
[9] Dewar, *The Navy from Within*, pp. 140–1.

Lloyd George, the latter 'was horrified at the idea of a German holding the supreme place. Asquith says L. G. is an excellent foolometer and that the public would take the same view.'[10]

Ultimately, Churchill recommended the phlegmatic and colourless Sir Francis Bridgeman as First Sea Lord, having satisfied himself that they were in agreement on fundamental principles. Moreover, thought Churchill, he was 'a fine sailor, with the full confidence of the Service afloat, and with the aptitude for working with and through a staff, well developed'. Bridgeman's appointment *vice* Wilson, with other Board changes, was announced on 28 November. Wilson and Churchill parted on 'friendly, civil, but at the same time cool terms' (Churchill). Wilson characteristically refused a peerage on giving up his post. He retired to Norfolk, there to rusticate until, three years later, his services were again in demand.

Like Wilson, Bridgeman was a strong supporter of Fisher's reforms, and, indeed, it had originally been intended that he should succeed Fisher. 'But he had not developed the particular qualities required in the office—especially, holding his own on the Committee [C.I.D.] against practised debaters and insistent soldiers.'[11] Although not a particularly forceful person, and more a follower than a leader, Bridgeman did possess sound judgment and he might have made a moderately successful First Sea Lord, had he served under anybody but Churchill. The two simply did not get along, the root trouble being Bridgeman's resentment against the First Lord's interference in everything. One year of a none-too-happy association was enough for Churchill. Bridgeman's uncertain health was the First Lord's opportunity. On 28 November 1912 he suggested to Bridgeman that he retire, for 'if by any misadventure, we were to be involved in war, I feel that the burden might be more than you could sustain'.[12] Bridgeman had no desire to leave office. His health was better—his doctor had found him in good shape—and he was prepared to carry on. Churchill insisted on his resignation (2 December). Bridgeman met the First Lord's wish—he was succeeded by the Second Sea Lord, Prince Louis of Battenberg—but suggested that differences

[10] Journals, 4 Oct. 1911; *Esher*, iii. 61.

[11] Memorandum of 18 Nov. 1909, author unknown, of a conversation that day with Fisher; Kilverstone MSS.

[12] The entire Churchill–Bridgeman correspondence of November–December 1912, some twenty letters, may be found, in printed form, in the Beatty MSS.

in policy may have motivated Churchill. 'No,' the First Lord replied (9 December), 'there is absolutely no truth in the idea that any difference in policy or procedure or any divergence or incident between us influenced me at all. Honestly, I only thought about your health and the European situation and what would happen if war began and you broke down.'

When stories began to circulate in the Conservative press that Bridgeman had been forced to resign (it was suspicious that a newspaper correspondent found the Admiral in Yorkshire, evidently in vigorous health, and riding to hounds three days a week), the resignation became a party question. One of the most sensational debates of the session was held in the House of Commons on 20 December regarding the circumstances that had led to Bridgeman's resignation. The First Lord held it was due solely to Bridgeman's poor health and the resultant frequent absences from his post, and that there had never been any difficulty or dispute between them. Beresford and Bonar Law, the Leader of the Opposition, fought Bridgeman's battle, making a scathing attack on the First Lord. Bonar Law asserted that Bridgeman had been 'brutally ill-used', and he forced Churchill to read from his correspondence with Bridgeman. But Churchill went further and read from private letters written by Bridgeman to Beatty and Battenberg. The one to Prince Louis, 25 November, mentioned that he had been 'very depressed lately about my health: two attacks of bronchitis within a few months, and coming on top of appendicitis, seems to have weakened my constitution, and I sometimes feel inclined to give up my post.' The letter to Beatty, 26 November, stated that he had actually started to write a letter of resignation, but, feeling better, had changed his mind.

The whole 'politico-naval storm' did the Navy no good. Rear-Admiral Wemyss summed it up well: 'Seriously, the whole matter is damnable, undignified and extremely bad for the Service in particular and the general good in general.'[13] Bridgeman never ceased to believe that he had been forced out. As he told Sir Francis Hopwood, the Additional Civil Lord, 'I often think of your warnings. You know, I suppose, that I was fired out *without* warning, but that it was not because I was too weak, but because I was too strong!'[14]

[13] Wester Wemyss, *Lord Wester Wemyss*, p. 141.
[14] Bridgeman to Hopwood, 8 Dec. 1912; Windsor MSS.

Jellicoe, as Second Sea Lord, December 1912–July 1914 (and then as Commander-in-Chief of the Grand Fleet), was at constant loggerheads over Churchill's 'meddling'. The term 'meddling' will explain the fierce quarrel that raged between Churchill and his Sea Lords in November 1913. The facts in the case were as follows.[15] Early in November 1913 the Admiralty yacht *Enchantress* put in at Sheerness. H.M.S. *Hermes*, the parent ship of the Naval Air Service, commanded by Captain Gerald W. Vivian, was at anchor off Sheerness. There had been a discussion as to the use to be made by the N.A.S. of some ground on the bank of the Medway, and Vivian had given his decision on the subject. But one of the young lieutenants held other views very strongly. These he very improperly expressed to the First Lord, who, impressed, sent for Vivian and told him the Lieutenant's proposals were to be carried out. Afterwards the young officer had lost his head in discussing the matter with Vivian. He informed him that (as reported by the Captain) 'if he did not get what he wanted he would write to the First Lord, and that he (the First Lord) had told him so'. Then the row began.

The Captain complained strongly to the Commander-in-Chief at the Nore, Admiral Sir Richard Poore. The Admiral in turn (5 November) complained strongly to Jellicoe about the First Lord's methods, which were bound to undermine discipline. (Naval discipline was a matter largely in the province of the Second Sea Lord, and, besides, Jellicoe was the superintending Sea Lord in regard to the Naval Air Service.) Churchill, who somehow got wind of the correspondence that had been initiated, asked Jellicoe to send him immediately any dispatch on the subject received from the C.-in-C. But Jellicoe, when Poore's letter reached him, found it couched in such strong terms that he returned it for some amendment. Enclosed was a private letter from Jellicoe with comments. When, a few hours later, Churchill learned what had happened, 'he went dancing mad' and telegraphed the General Post Office, asking that the letter should be found and returned at once *to him*! He got it back from the G.P.O. and, of course, read it, though he claimed not to have read Jellicoe's private letter. Churchill announced that he intended to

---

[15] The story is in Sir Francis Hopwood's letters to Lord Stamfordham (the King's Private Secretary) of 9, 10, and 13 November (*ibid.*), Admiralty documents on the affair, and Jellicoe's notes on the incident in Bacon, *Jellicoe*, pp. 182–3.

telegraph Admiral Poore, ordering him to haul down his flag. Jellicoe threatened to resign from the Board if Churchill went ahead, and to make his reasons public. He informed the Sea Lords of what had happened. The Third and Fourth Sea Lords, Admirals Sir Archibald Moore and Sir William Pakenham, respectively, were ready to resign with Jellicoe. Battenberg, the First Sea Lord, was talked out of joining his colleagues by the First Lord. At one point in the crisis it seems that all four Sea Lords had signed their resignations and that Poore was about to do so. Churchill poured oil on troubled waters by telling the Sea Lords (or so it was reported) that criticism of his methods by any one of them must lead to his, the Sea Lord's, resignation.

The crisis ended a few days after it had flared up. Poore was induced by the Board (Churchill was not involved) to withdraw his letter and to express his regret. 'Under vast pressure', he agreed not to resign. The Lieutenant was lectured by the First Sea Lord, who told him that he was not justified in his action, that the usual means of forwarding a complaint were open to him, and that he should not have referred to the First Lord as he had in speaking to the Captain. At the First Sea Lord's suggestion, the Lieutenant apologized to the Captain and to the First Lord, and the affair was over.

> Winston would not be flattered [wrote Hopwood] if he knew the arguments used by the Naval Lords to keep the Commander-in-Chief from going. They were in short that he (Churchill) was so much off his head over the whole business that Poore need take no notice of it! We thought Poore would ask for a Court Martial, in which case the whole business would have turned on the accusations of the Commander-in-Chief against the First Lord, and the latter would really have been on his defence.
>
> If Poore had gone, Jellicoe and Pakenham would have resigned. I doubt whether the other two would have stuck to their guns. But if Poore had been dismissed or superseded (as Winston wished) all 4 Naval Lords would have resigned.
>
> *Laus Deo!* It is over for the time, but we shall have it again in some form. Jellicoe will not put up with it for long.

As an aftermath, Jellicoe resigned his control over the Naval Air Service, the Fourth Sea Lord taking over.

The fact of the First Lord's flagrant interference with the discipline of the Fleet leaked out. But already the Bridgeman affair had convinced the Opposition that, in the words of the *Globe* (21 December 1912), 'the methods of Mr. Churchill are wholly unfitted for the great Service of which for the time being he is the responsible head.' His own party had little more love for him. He was regarded as a blusterer, an opportunist, and a showman, totally devoid of integrity. The Prime Minister once described a letter from Churchill as 'very characteristic: begotten by froth out of foam'. But he had risen in the party because, undeniably, he was an extraordinarily able person. And, without doubt, one reason for his going to the Admiralty was the belief of the Lloyd George wing in the Cabinet that he could be depended upon to trim the navy estimates, as had been foreshadowed by McKenna. When, as will be related, Churchill, like McKenna before him, found the pressure of circumstances too much and had to work for higher estimates, he lost the support of the Radical section of his party.

Nor was the King an admirer of Churchill's. He distrusted him and had accepted his appointment with reluctance. Churchill quickly made sure that the King would have no reason to change his mind. On 27 November 1911 the First Lord submitted to the King, as was the custom, names for the new super-dreadnoughts in the 1911–12 programme: *Africa, Oliver Cromwell, Liberty,* and *Assiduous.* The King approved of *Africa* only, and suggested in place of the others *Delhi, Wellington, Marlborough.* In October 1912 Churchill again suggested *Oliver Cromwell* for a battleship, and again had it turned down. This time he fought back. The Prime Minister and others of his colleagues

fully concur that such a name is not inappropriate for one of His Majesty's Ships, and is desirable on general grounds. . . . Oliver Cromwell was one of the founders of the Navy, and scarcely any man did so much for it. I am quite sure nothing in history will justify the view that the adoption of such a name would constitute any reflection, however vague, upon His Majesty's Royal House. On the contrary, the great movement in politics and in religion of which Cromwell was the instrument, was intimately connected with all those forces which, through a long succession of Princes, have brought His Majesty to the Throne of a Constitutional and a Protestant country. The bitterness of the rebellions and tyrannies of the past has long ceased to stir men's minds; but the achievements of the country and of its greatest men endure. His Majesty is the heir of all the glories of the nation, and there is no chapter of English history from which he should feel himself divided.

I am satisfied that the name would be extremely well received . . .[16]

The King would not change his views, and Stamfordham, for the King, reminded Churchill that when the Government had proposed in 1895 to erect a statue of Cromwell, they met with strong resistance from the Irish and the Opposition and were defeated by a majority of 137. 'If the idea of a statue aroused so much animosity it is reasonable to expect no less opposition to the association of Cromwell with a War-ship costing millions of public money.' Churchill's proposal would only 'revive similar feelings of antagonism and religious bitterness' at a time when the nationalism of the Irish was being intensified. Churchill did not press his advice further. He suggested an acceptable substitute, *Valiant*.

Nomenclature controversies were by no means over. In August 1913 the King vetoed the *Ark Royal* and the *Pitt* as the names of two of the new battleships. Regarding the latter, it might wound the susceptibilities of the French; also, monosyllabic names of battleships were as a rule a mistake, although they might well be used with smaller classes. Churchill stubbornly held out for his two names, saying that he alone was responsible for naming all the ships in the Navy. In the end he gave way, after a chat with the King at Balmoral in September, and agreed to name the ships after the pre-dreadnought 'Royal Sovereign' class, which were about to be sold out of the service. The King graciously agreed to change the name of the *Delhi*, which had not yet been christened, to *Emperor of India*.

By the outbreak of war Churchill was regarded much more favourably in the Service than during his first two years. The German Naval Attaché could now write:

On the whole the Navy is satisfied with Mr. Churchill, because it recognizes that he has done and accomplished more for them than the majority of his predecessors in office. There is no doubt that there has been friction between Mr. Churchill and the officers at the Admiralty as well as those at sea. That is not surprising with such a stubborn and tyrannical character as Mr. Churchill. The intensive co-operation of all forces for an increase in the power and tactical readiness of the English Navy has under Mr. Churchill's guidance not only not suffered

[16] Churchill to Stamfordham, 1 Nov. 1912; Windsor MSS. The entire story is from the Windsor MSS.

but has experienced rather energetic impulses and inspiration. The English Navy is very much aware of it.[17]

2. AN ERA OF REFORM

If Churchill's methods were not always popular, he did possess the invaluable attributes of foresight, courage, and unbounded energy. These assets, coupled with his reliance on Lord Fisher's advice, particularly in technical matters, were productive of tremendous naval progress in the years 1911–14. Churchill had not dared to call Fisher back as First Sea Lord in 1911. He was apprehensive of his age (70) and he feared the revival of the feuds. But finding Fisher 'a veritable volcano of knowledge and of inspiration', Churchill had quickly installed him as his unofficial adviser and uncrowned First Sea Lord. The old sea-dog operated from abroad during the first eight months, as he felt he would find it 'very awkward between McKenna and Winston Churchill—like balancing on a tight rope!' There would, therefore, be less embarrassment if he stayed away from England. Also, he did not want to hurt the susceptibilities of his good friends on the Board by giving any appearance of 'intriguing or wirepulling'. And finally, having been 'the First Violin', he refused to come back to 'play 2nd fiddle! . . . *Aut Caesar aut nullus!*' He gave Churchill his word, however, that he would come home at once in case of an emergency.

And so there began a long series of Fisher–Churchill letters, Fisher's closely-written eight-to-ten page effusions containing, as Churchill said, 'every sort of news and counsel, from blistering reproach to supreme inspiration.' The correspondence, especially voluminous in 1912, was supplemented by lengthy conversations on the Admiralty yacht. Fisher wrote of one of these sessions on the *Enchantress* (November 1911) that there were three days of 'continuous talking, and practically no sleep'. Many of the most significant achievements of the pre-war Churchill régime owed much to the ideas and stimulation of Fisher. It was rumoured at the time that Fisher was Churchill's 'dry nurse', although the extent of the Admiral's influence was not suspected by the service and the general public. Most of all, Fisher proved stimulating to Churchill in everything that related to ship design. Let us turn to

[17] Müller to Tirpitz, 4 June 1914; German Ministry of Marine MSS.

the accomplishments of the Churchill Board of Admiralty before the war, beginning with the first fundamental decision made.

'The dead weight of professional opinion was adverse [to a staff]. They had got on well enough without it before. They did not want a special class of officer professing to be more brainy than the rest.' So Churchill wrote years later. Under 'professional opinion' we must include nearly everyone in high position at the Admiralty. The Navy at large did not understand the staff system and dreaded any appearance of copying the example of the War Office. This did not deter Churchill. With the strong support of the C.I.D., the Cabinet, and his reorganized Board (especially the new Second Sea Lord, Battenberg), he converted the Navy War Council into an Admiralty War Staff on 8 January 1912. A 'Chief of the War Staff' responsible to the First Sea Lord was in charge of three divisions—Operations, Intelligence, and Mobilization. (A Trade Defence section of the Operations Division was formed in April 1914; expanded, it became the Trade Division of the War Staff soon after the war began.) Churchill had wanted the Chief of the War Staff directly under himself as First Lord, but Battenberg and Haldane in particular had put the quietus to that. The overall function of the Staff was to make a special study of the operational side of war in contradistinction to its technical and material side; but it was only an advisory body.

The announcement of the War Staff was hailed with satisfaction, even enthusiasm, in most quarters. It 'ensures to him a great reputation as First Lord,' declared the *Daily Express*. Lord Esher congratulated Churchill 'most warmly upon the most pregnant reform which has been carried out at the Admiralty since the days of Lord St. Vincent'. Even Fisher welcomed the Staff! Almost the only dissentients were the *Morning Post* and those whose views it expressed—Beresford, for example. While accepting the Staff as an improvement, they wanted to see it invested with authority in strategical matters, and imposing its views and its will upon the Board.

Though a Staff had been created, there were no officers trained in staff work. Accordingly, the next step was to set up a 'Staff Course' for junior officers (commanders, lieutenant-commanders, lieutenants)—the R.N. Staff College, started in 1912 at the Naval War College, Portsmouth. It ceased at the outbreak of war and was resumed, at Greenwich, as an entirely separate organization, in June 1919. There it still is, though closed during World War II. The Staff College was none too successful in its first years. The candidates chosen for training were sometimes below average ability, possibly a reflection of the opposition of some admirals to the idea of a Staff. Also there was not much study of tactics and strategy, the stress being on technical subjects. 'We had the opportunity but not the intellectual capital to float a staff,' Admiral Dewar has remarked. The other major flaw in the scheme was that the Chief of Staff had no executive authority. The First Sea Lord should have been Chief of Staff. The divorce of the two offices was unworkable, as Churchill had been warned by Wilson would be the case. This was to some degree the fault of the First Sea Lord, Battenberg. He 'won't listen to the idea that the First Sea Lord is really the C.O.S. He says he could not lower the position of his office by becoming the C.O.S. to a civilian First Lord. That, I think, was the principal objection in his mind. Then he said that theoretically it was wrong, as he was the Executive head of the Navy and he could not mix up Staff duties with executive work.'[18] The two offices were fused in the latter part of the war.

There was no serious effort made in Churchill's time to separate staff from administrative duties. The First Sea Lord, who was responsible for operations, continued to carry out a multitude of other duties. At any rate, war plans were no longer locked up in the brain of the First Sea Lord.

It was charged in 1924 by the editor of a certain professional journal that the plans provided by the Admiralty War Staff down to the start of the war 'were turned down on account of economy or because the Board considered them a departure from traditional policy and custom, and they were not taken seriously'. That was the case. This is not to say that the Staff had no concrete achievements to its credit. Among the important Staff plans that were officially adopted before the war were the 'distant blockade' policy (which replaced the policy of a 'close blockade' of the German coast); the establishment at the Admiralty of a department for the arming of merchant ships; the construction of fortifications in Cromarty Firth and their protection by certain armament and a garrison of marines; the creation of a trawler minesweeping

[18] Rear-Admiral Sir Edmond Slade to Captain H. W. Richmond, 26 Sept. 1913; Richmond MSS.

organization; the reorganization of the East Coast Command. Although a good beginning had been made, the war came too soon. There simply had not been enough time to mould an effective Staff by 1914 and to win for it the confidence of the Board and of Downing Street. The Staff was taken somewhat more seriously once the war began.

Churchill was anxious about Lower Deck dissatisfaction, which was once more acute in 1911–12. The main grievance was with regard to pay. It had remained almost stationary for sixty years, since in that interval only a penny a day had been added to the 1s. 7d. granted in 1852! The petty officers and men were also dissatisfied with the old-fashioned methods of maintaining discipline, with the restrictions upon their leave, and with the system of unofficial punishments. Churchill, with Fisher's advice, support, and occasional nagging, improved the conditions of the Lower Deck in a series of sweeping reforms during 1912 that removed much, though not all, of Lower Deck discontent. These included the abolition of certain humiliating forms of punishment, the curtailment of the powers of the ships' police, a new and more generous system of leave, the right of trial by court martial to petty officers, a modest rise in pay for the officers and men, and promotion from the ranks. Regarding the last item, the petty officers and seamen had long complained that there were no possibilities of promotion, that only rarely did one of them become an officer, and then as a reward for good service at the tail-end of a career. Churchill, through a scheme announced in August 1912, made it possible for a number of young and exceptionally promising warrant officers and petty officers qualified to be warrant officers to be directly admitted to commissioned rank after a year's period of probation. This was a revolutionary variant upon the existing policy of offering commissioned rank to certain ratings after a long and meritorious service. Churchill was applying the Napoleonic-Fisher maxim of 'careers open to talent'. It was the real beginning of a movement for democratizing the Navy, and the credit goes to Churchill the aristocrat. However, the workings of this reform were something less than perfect. In his later years Fisher was angry over the second-class treatment given to officers who had come up from the Lower Deck. 'Is there a single Post-Captain who has risen from the ranks? When they make a sailor a lieutenant, they stow him away in some small vessel so that he shan't mess with the blue bloods! King Edward said I was a Socialist! So I am! Because like the French Revolution riches now come before merit.'[19]

Merit, and *merit alone*, Churchill believed, must be the passport to advancement, with seniority minimized. Accordingly, on 16 November 1911, he passed over several important senior admirals and made Rear-Admiral David Beatty his Naval Secretary. Again, on 5 December 1911, with a little prompting from Fisher, Churchill moved Jellicoe, though twenty-first in seniority on the active list of twenty-two vice-admirals, into the choice appointment of Second-in-Command of the Home Fleet (renamed the Grand Fleet when the war came). This virtually designated him for the supreme command as Admiral Sir George Callaghan's successor.

In the realm of *matériel*, three fundamental decisions were made in the 1912 battleship programme. It was decided to build a fast division of battleships armed with 15-inch guns and driven by oil fuel. This was the famous 'Queen Elizabeth' class, which gave such a splendid account of itself in the war. In 1909 Fisher had made a revolutionary plunge by increasing the gun-power of the dreadnoughts from a 50-calibre, 12-inch to a 45-calibre, 13·5-inch primary armament, so raising the weight of the shell from 850 lbs. to 1,250 lbs. (1,400 lbs. in the 1910–11 and 1911–12 capital ships) a projectile 40 per cent (or more) heavier than the biggest fired by the German Fleet. The heavier blow appealed to Fisher, though the main technical reason for the change was that the 12-inch gun was erratic in its shooting owing to the high muzzle velocity. The last six of the eight capital ships of the 1909–10 programme received the new 13·5-inch gun. On coming to the Admiralty, Churchill at once planned to go one size better—to introduce 15-inch guns hurling a 1,920-lb. projectile 35,000 yards for the five dreadnoughts of the 1912 programme. Any doubts he may have had were dispelled by Fisher's enthusiastic support: 'What was it that enabled Jack Johnson to knock out his opponents? It was the big punch.' It took courage to enlarge the gun, since it meant enlarging the size of the ships and increasing the cost, which was bound to meet opposition in the Cabinet.

The next step was the decision to make the new dreadnoughts a fast division. The big argument was that such a division could

---

[19] Fisher to George Lambert, n.d. (Dec. 1917); Lennoxlove MSS.

'cross the T' and manœuvre around the German Fleet, whichever way the enemy might deploy, and bring him to bay. Bridgeman supported the fast division, but Fisher's influence was the decisive one here. He peppered the First Lord with such remarks as that Jellicoe's '*one, one, one* cry is SPEED! *Do lay that to heart!* Do remember the recipe for jugged hare in Mrs. Glasse's Cookery Book! *"First catch your hare!"* ' Again : 'Sea fighting is pure common sense. The first of all its necessities is SPEED, so as to be able to fight—*When* you like, *Where* you like, and *How* you like.'[20] Churchill did not need much coaxing.

Came the third step. To give the fast division 25 knots, an increase of four or five knots, as recommended by a War College study, fuel oil had to be used. (24 knots was the highest speed actually attained.)

In equal ships oil gave a large excess of speed over coal. It enabled that speed to be attained with far greater rapidity. It gave forty per cent. greater radius of action for the same weight of coal. It enabled a fleet to refuel at sea with great facility. An oil-burning fleet can, if need be and in calm weather, keep its station at sea, nourishing itself from tankers without having to send a quarter of its strength continually into harbour for coal, wasting fuel on the homeward and outward journey. The ordeal of coaling ship exhausted the whole ship's company. In wartime it robbed them of their brief period of rest; it subjected everyone to extreme discomfort. With oil, a few pipes were connected with the shore or with a tanker and the ship sucked in its fuel with hardly a man having to lift a finger. Less than half the number of stokers was needed to tend and clean the oil furnaces.[21]

The Navy had already adopted oil for submarines and destroyers (in 1911, the U.S. battleships *Oklahoma* and *Nevada* had been fitted for oil only), but to build any large additional number of oil-burning ships meant basing Britain's naval supremacy on oil. This had its dangers, since there was virtually no oil in Britain. It could only come from overseas, whereas the finest supply of the best steam coal in the world was right in Britain. There were also large problems connected with the accumulation of a large oil reserve and the installation of tanks. To change the foundation of the Navy from British coal to foreign oil was a formidable decision. As Churchill recognized, 'To commit the Navy irrevocably to oil was indeed "to take arms against a sea of troubles".' He thought

[20] 14, 16 Jan. 1912; *The World Crisis*, i. 140-1.
[21] *Ibid.*, p. 129.

the gains worth the difficulties and risks, and so did Fisher, who plumped for oil like mad. It was the most vital decision Churchill made, and, to use a Fisherism, 'The camel once swallowed, the gnats went down easily enough': oil was adopted for the smaller ships of war. However, there was what Churchill calls a 'lamentable exception': the five 'Royal Sovereigns', super-dreadnoughts of the 1913–14 programme, were coal-burning ships. The design was modified, oil replacing coal, as soon as Fisher was recalled to the Admiralty in 1914.

It was in April 1912 that the decision was reached to include the fast division of five oil-fired super-dreadnoughts in the estimates. To solve the many procurement and technical problems involved in the adoption of oil, Churchill proposed to appoint a Royal Commission on Fuel Oil. Fisher, the 'Oil Maniac', was its logical chairman, and he was persuaded to undertake the task. He returned to England in June and plunged into the work of the Royal Commission with characteristic energy and enthusiasm. The particular tasks of the Commission were indicated by the First Lord in this letter: 'You have got to find the oil: to show how it can be stored cheaply: how it can be purchased regularly and cheaply in peace; and with absolute certainty in war. Then by all means develop its application in the best possible way to existing and prospective ships.'[22] The latter included an investigation of the internal combustion engine and an exploration of the possibility of utilizing it on British ships. The Commission was also to find methods of protecting the oil from air attack.

The Commission had virtually finished its work by early 1913 (though it was not terminated until February 1914, after a final report had been issued), and on 17 July 1913 the First Lord was able definitely to announce in Parliament the opening of a new chapter in British naval history. Though coal might remain for some time the basis of the Navy's motive power, oil would gradually take its place. The new policy called for the acquisition of oilfields. Pursuant to this policy, in August 1914 the Government purchased for £2,200,000 a controlling share in the Anglo-Persian (later renamed the Anglo-Iranian) Oil Company, but not before Churchill had fought off a 'confusing variety of oppositions', including economists fighting increases in naval expenditure; M.P.s from coal-mining constituencies who sensed the danger to

[22] Churchill to Fisher, 11 June 1912; *ibid.*, pp. 132–3.

the economic welfare of their constituents; those who (like the *Manchester Guardian*) foresaw an increase in Britain's political dependence upon Russia, else payment of blackmail to her; and arm-chair strategists (like the *Daily Mail*) who asserted the Persian fields and the oil tankers were vulnerable to land and sea attack, respectively, in time of war.

There is one debit aspect in Churchill's oil policy. In 1913, Jellicoe (Second Sea Lord) 'vehemently' pressed for a large increase in the contemplated oil reserves from three months' war consumption to six months'. The Fisher Royal Commission favoured *four years*' war consumption in reserve. Churchill could not accept either of these 'extravagant' demands because of strong Treasury and Cabinet opposition to excessive expenditure. There was a compromise after Jellicoe threatened to resign: four and a half months' war consumption, to be effected gradually. Churchill is incorrect in saying that 'these conclusions stood the test of war',[23] because during several months of 1917 the shortage of oil fuel was most critical, due to successful submarine attacks on so many British oil-carrying vessels. Oil was down to a three weeks' supply as a whole, and to six days' supply at some of the fuelling bases. Jellicoe, as First Sea Lord in 1917, had to direct the Fleet to remain in harbour as much as possible, and destroyers were limited to 20 knots speed. The pre-war politicians had been responsible for that state of affairs.

[23] *Ibid.*, p. 171.

XI

The Churchill Period, 1911–1914:
On the Eve of Armageddon

If our Fleet was not superior to the German Fleet, our very independence would depend on Germany's good will; and even granting that people like Jagow [the German Foreign Minister] would not take advantage of such a situation, there must be others who would take advantage of it, or be compelled by public opinion in Germany to do so. The Prussian mentality is such that to be on really good terms with it one must be able to deal with it as an equal. Hence the persistent and inevitable comparison here of German and British Navies. These comparisons are resented in Germany as evidence of a gratuitous and unfriendly assumption on our part that Germany is hostile to us. But this is not their real motive. Germany has the biggest Army in the world as well as her Navy, but the Navy is our one and only means of defence and our life depends on it and upon it alone.

Sir Edward Grey to Sir Rennell Rodd,
13 January 1913.

Exceptional expenditure on armaments, carried to an excessive degree, must lead to catastrophe, and may even sink the ship of European prosperity and civilization. What then is to be done? I am bound to say, at the present moment I can see very little to be done except to keep our own expenditure within the limits of national safety and our obligations to other parts of the Empire.

Sir Edward Grey at Manchester, 3 February 1914.

I. THE HALDANE MISSION

THE EFFECT of the Agadir Crisis in Germany had been to exasperate feeling against England and to convince the press that Germany must have more ships. Tirpitz was not slow to take advantage of this situation. He felt that Germany had suffered her first diplomatic reverse since Bismarck's day and that the only way to restore the nation's prestige was by strengthening the Navy. Accordingly, in the autumn of 1911 he pressed for a *Novelle*, or supplementary navy bill, as a counterbalance to the diplomatic check. The objective of such a bill, as agreed to by Tirpitz, Müller, and the Emperor in September, was to achieve a 2 : 3 ratio in capital ships with the British Navy. The plan was now presented to the Chancellor for his approval. The *riskflotte* idea which had guided German naval policy since 1900 had 'fulfilled its purpose', declared the Emperor. They now needed a clear new goal which would be easily intelligible to the man in the street—one which could be expressed in a short slogan, like the two-power standard in England, which was used and understood 'from the King down to the beggar'. It was to be found in the ratio of 2 : 3.

It offers the advantage of limiting and rejecting the reproaches of the petty zealots and worrywarts about the 'unlimited character of the fleet plans', etc. On the other hand, it readily grants the English an important supremacy and cuts short the talk of 'competitive building', 'bidding for the sovereignty of the seas', etc. It is at the same time a certain commitment to them, such as they have always wished for, and surprises on our part are excluded since the ratio is determined once and for all. Since it is thereby a relation of strength of *whole fleet* to *whole fleet* which is determined clearly before the whole world, the *tempo* of annual *construction* does not have to be taken into account. This is a factor which has caused much excitement and misunderstanding up to now. In the future it will be of no importance . . . loyalty and a frank treatment of this matter render it necessary that England be informed of it [the new goal] *ahead of time*. Whether they accept the ratio or not is immaterial. We will have done our share in showing them that we have nothing frightful or underhanded up our sleeves, and the rest of the world will judge our self-limitation with respect. If in spite of it the English go ahead with excessive construction, they saddle themselves with the *odium of provocation* and hostile *intention* towards us before the world . . . Since according to all reports their finances are not so sound . . . I believe commerce and the stock exchange will rejoice over our proposal . . . We are undeniably at a decisive turning point in the history of our Fatherland. . . .

From the above Your Excellency will see that the way proposed by me releases you from the necessity of having to talk in a 'lofty manner' ['*hohen Töne*'] to England when the amendment is introduced, a fact which you feared so much because of the inherent danger of provocation. With our acknowledged limitation of the 2 : 3 ratio this is superfluous, since everybody knows that we are only 1 : 2, and in armoured cruisers only 1 : 4, thus we are self-evidently compelled to reach the limit first.[1]

The Chancellor balked. He had been willing to accept a 2 : 3

[1] William II to Bethmann Hollweg, 30 Sept. 1911 ; Tirpitz, *Politische Dokumente*, i. 216–18.

ratio in the Spring as regards new capital-ship construction, but the proposal of the Emperor and Tirpitz, of building up to, then maintaining, a 2 : 3 ratio, went far beyond that. The announcement of a 2 : 3 standard would be a provocation to England, since they had so far avoided a direct reference to the English Fleet and had always maintained that the building of the German Fleet was not directed against anybody. Tirpitz attempted to allay the Chancellor's serious misgivings. 'The purpose and aim of our naval policy is political independence from England—the greatest possible security against an English attack—and a promising chance of defence if war should come. To accomplish this purpose and this aim, we must *diminish* the military distance between England and ourselves, not increase it. If we do not succeed, then our whole naval policy of the last 14 years has been in vain. However, we relinquish the possibility of a diminishment in military distance *voluntarily* if we go down to a tempo of two.'[2] Bethmann Hollweg and Kiderlen, the Foreign Minister, continued to have their doubts, fearing the effect of a new naval bill upon Germany's relations with England. 'You are leading us to war,' Bethmann Hollweg warned Widenmann (4 September). The Chancellor adopted delaying tactics.

It was known in England that a supplementary Navy Law was probable. This would inevitably cause fresh alarm and increased naval expenditure in Great Britain. Churchill, making his first public appearance as First Lord, tried to head off the German bill in his Guildhall speech, 9 November, in which he intimated that a large reduction in the estimates was a certainty if no change were made in the German Navy Law. Two days earlier he had asked McKenna to indicate which votes he considered susceptible of the reductions he, McKenna, had promised the Treasury a year earlier. ('I expressed a hope,' McKenna corrected him.) Churchill was not optimistic, but, as he has testified, 'Apart from wider reasons, I felt I should be all the stronger in asking the Cabinet and the House of Commons for the necessary monies, if I could go hand in hand with the Chancellor of the Exchequer and testify that we had tried our best to secure a mitigation of the naval rivalry and failed.'[3]

[2] Tirpitz to Bethmann Hollweg, n.d. (ca. 5 Oct. 1911); German Ministry of Marine MSS.
[3] *The World Crisis*, i. 95.

Enter from the wings Cassel and Ballin. Sir Ernest Cassel, the great banker, was influential in British court circles, and Albert Ballin, the head of the Hamburg-Amerika Steamship Company, was a friend of William and Tirpitz. Ballin had for years feared that German naval expansion would lead to a clash with England, and he had often discussed the danger with his good friend, Cassel. The two now, in the winter of 1911–12, worked hard to bring about direct conversations between the statesmen of the two powers in a last-ditch effort to alleviate the tension. On 29 January 1912, Cassel, on the joint authority of Grey, Lloyd George, and Churchill, journeyed to Berlin and presented the Emperor with a concise memorandum which was to serve as the basis for the opening of official negotiations.[4] The first clause, described as 'fundamental', read: 'Naval supremacy recognized as essential to Great Britain. Present German naval programme and expenditure not to be increased but if possible retarded and reduced.' The second clause stated that England would offer no impediment to German colonial expansion, and would discuss and promote her colonial ambitions. (Churchill later explained that 'new oversea possessions are, to some extent, a hostage to the stronger naval Power, and might easily relieve the tension'.)[5] The third clause proposed an exchange of assurances that neither power would take part in 'aggressive designs or combinations directed against the other'. Cassel saw the Emperor, Bethmann Hollweg, and Ballin together. They all appeared deeply impressed by the overture, with the Emperor 'enchanted, almost childishly so'. Cassel returned to London on 31 January with a note expressing German approval of the memorandum, calling attention to the fact that the *Novelle* had already been drawn up, and suggesting that an English minister come to Berlin for a confidential interchange of ideas.

The Chancellor had also given Cassel a sketch of the new law. It called for the creation of a permanent third active squadron of eight battleships: five pre-dreadnoughts from the reserve and three new dreadnoughts to be laid down in 1912, 1914, and 1916. 'We devoured this invaluable document all night long in the Admiralty' (Churchill). The facts were promptly laid before the Cabinet. The proposed German increases were 'extremely serious'.

[4] The Foreign Office material on the Haldane Mission, which is not cited in footnotes, is in *British Documents*, vi. 666–761.

[5] At the 118th meeting of the C.I.D., 11 July 1912; H. H. Asquith, *The Genesis of the War* (London, 1923), p. 81.

If the old programme had not been changed, the Admiralty would have built 4–3–4–3–4–3 against the German six years' programme of 2–2–2–2–2–2. If the new bill were passed and the Germans built 3–2–3–2–3–2, the new British tempo must be 5–4–5–4–5–4, or two additional ships for every ship added to the existing German Navy Law. This would maintain the 60 per cent preponderance in dreadnoughts and battle cruisers. To counter the formation of a third active battle squadron, which would give Germany a striking force available throughout the year of twenty-five battleships, all dreadnoughts within four or five years, and eight battle cruisers, no fewer than forty or forty-one British capital ships must be kept in instant readiness. To effect this concentration the Admiralty was contemplating bringing home the six battleships in the Mediterranean. This would make it desirable from a naval point of view to seek French support in those waters. The German increase in personnel (15,000 officers and men were to be added in annual increments of about 1,600, raising the total from the old goal of 86,500 in 1920 to 100,500) must be met by doubling the additional 2,000 men the Admiralty had planned to ask for in 1912, and again in 1913. Altogether Churchill reckoned that at least £3,000,000 a year would have to be added to the estimates to meet the German challenge.[6]

After full discussion the Cabinet authorized Cassel on 3 February to inform the German Government through Ballin that England was prepared to proceed with the negotiations, 'on the understanding that the point of naval expenditure is open to discussion and that there is a fair prospect of settling it favourably'. The Germans were willing to continue the discussion in a friendly spirit, Bethmann Hollweg replied (about 4 February), and in the matter of the Navy Law to fall in with the wishes of the British Government if Germany, in return, received a political agreement 'that neither Power undertakes to join in any plans, combinations, or war-like entanglements directed against the other.' If England agreed with these sentiments, Germany would like an English minister to come to Berlin for a 'private, confidential exchange of opinions'.[7] After another exchange of communications, the way was clear.

---

[6] Undated Admiralty memorandum (early Feb. 1912) for the Cabinet: Asquith MSS; Churchill to Grey, 31 Jan. 1912: *The World Crisis*, i. 95–7.

[7] *Die Grosse Politik*, xxxi. 103–4.

On 5 February the Cabinet selected Lord Haldane for the mission to Berlin. He was to listen, explain, and explore with a view to determining the prospects for an agreement. The choice of Haldane was a happy one. He had the confidence of all the political parties in England, was a frequent visitor in Germany and on friendly terms with the Emperor, Chancellor, and other important personages, and had an insight into the German mind through his knowledge of the German language, philosophy, and culture.

There were, however, unfavourable auspices. Nicolson regarded the mission with anxiety and dismay. He clearly saw that Bethmann Hellweg would not be strong enough to impose any real reduction of the new bill on Tirpitz, and he was afraid that Haldane might be inveigled into making political concessions in return for some flimsy assurance of naval retardation. Haldane himself was 'far from sanguine of success'. And on 7 February, the day before he arrived in Berlin, the Emperor, in his speech from the throne at the opening of the new Reichstag, referred in general terms to bills for increased military and naval armaments which would be introduced. To this 'threat of continental domination' the impulsive Churchill replied in a defiant speech at Glasgow, 9 February, without troubling to secure the approval of the Prime Minister or Cabinet. He declared that England was absolutely obliged to maintain her superiority at sea, that 'as naval competition becomes more acute, we shall have not only to increase the number of ships we build, but the ratio which our naval strength will have to bear to other great naval Powers, so that our margin of superiority will become larger and not smaller as the strain grows greater.' He added that whereas the Fleet was a vital necessity to the British Empire, 'from some points of view the German Navy is to them more in the nature of a luxury'. Offence was taken at the speech in Germany, especially at its maladroit expression, a 'luxury' fleet. Tirpitz complained bitterly and repeatedly of Churchill's reference to the German Navy as a *Luxusflotte*. Widenmann considered the speech 'solely a bluff mixed with a threat' to get Germany to withdraw the *Novelle*. Morley, Lloyd George, and other ministers, men earnestly desirous of an understanding with Germany, were dismayed, as was a large part of the Liberal press. Lloyd George told Churchill that his speech was 'imprudent and calculated to mar Haldane's mission to Germany, which was on a fair way to success'. The Conservative press, however, chose to regard the speech as a friendly warning to Germany, not a threat.

The Emperor was sincerely anxious that something should come of the talks. 'There is no doubt,' he wrote on Haldane's second day in Berlin, 'that in large measure the fate of the Entente, and of Germany and the whole world, depends on today's conversation between Tirpitz and Haldane. It is imperative that Tirpitz realize this. He must work in an open and frank manner without any suspicion and mental reservations. . . . If he succeeds, and England and Germany come to an understanding, then I will announce it so that Germany and the whole world will be thankful to him as the man who made peace. Then he will hold a position in the world which no German Minister has held since Bismarck!'[8] There was little chance of Tirpitz becoming another Bismarck. 'England will stand by her obligations and promises to France. The German political demand is that England shall keep out of a war which starts between France and Germany. It does not matter who the aggressor will be. If we cannot get this guarantee from England, then we must continue with our armament, so that we will be as strong as the Entente Cordiale. This Entente has the character of an offensive combination. Our naval demand must be a 3 to 2 ratio.'[9] Tirpitz's attitude foredoomed the Mission.

Haldane's conversations with the Emperor, Bethmann Hollweg, and Tirpitz, 8–10 February, boiled down to this:

(1) *Regarding a political formula*, the Chancellor suggested one which amounted to a promise of unconditional neutrality by Great Britain in case Germany were involved in war. The crucial clause was the third: 'If either of the High Contracting Parties becomes involved in a war with one or more Powers, the other will at least observe a benevolent neutrality towards that Power, and shall use all its efforts for the localization of the conflict.' Haldane objected, since England would under this pledge be precluded from coming to the assistance of France should Germany attack her. He suggested modifications to make the pledge of neutrality applicable only to an 'unprovoked' attack in which the contracting party was not the aggressor. Bethmann Hollweg's formula was redrafted on this basis, but the Chancellor did not commit himself to the view that it would be sufficient.

[8] William II to Müller, 9 Feb. 1912; Tirpitz, *Politische Dokumente*, i. 285.
[9] Tirpitz to Müller, 8 Feb. 1912; *ibid.*, p. 282.

(2) *Regarding colonial questions*, understanding was easy on Persia, the Baghdad Railway, Zanzibar, Pemba, and the Portuguese colonies. Bargains on a give-and-take principle were discussed and left in general terms for further negotiation.

(3) *Regarding a naval agreement*, Haldane politely rejected Tirpitz's proposal for a fixed 3 : 2 ratio between the two fleets; England had to be equal with her Fleet to any possible combination. He bluntly pointed out that any agreement for settling differences and introducing a new spirit would be 'bones without flesh' if Germany began new shipbuilding and forced England to lay down two keels for every one which Germany added to her programme. Public opinion in England would attach very little importance to an agreement that did not modify the German naval programme. All that Haldane got from the Germans was the promise of a slackening of the rate of building : the three new battleships would be postponed until 1913, 1916, and 1919, and even this concession was contingent on a satisfactory political agreement.

When Haldane left for London on 12 February, he had with him a confidential copy of the text of the *Novelle* which the Emperor had given him. After his experts had sat up all night examining it, Churchill reported to the Cabinet (14 February) that the German Navy Law was much worse than they had thought. Its most serious feature was not so much the addition of the three dreadnoughts, which would give the German Fleet forty-one battleships (ultimately all dreadnoughts), nor even the creation of a third battle squadron, but 'the extraordinary increase in the striking force of ships of all classes immediately available throughout the year'. At this time the Admiralty maintained in the waters of the United Kingdom sixteen fully-commissioned battleships, with six more at Gibraltar and six more in the Mediterranean (respectively three to four days' and nine and a half days' distant from England with another day for coaling). Whereas formerly the Admiralty had reckoned against seventeen battleships, four battle cruisers, and twelve small cruisers in the German Active Battle Fleet, demobilized to a great extent during the winter months, they had in future to prepare against twenty-five, eight, and eighteen, which would be kept permanently in commission, that is, ready for war. Full permanent crews were to be provided for ninety-nine destroyers out of the total of 144, and there was to be a large increase in the provision for submarines: seventy-two were to be built, of which fifty-four would have full crews.

It was made clear to Metternich (22, 25 February) that the *Novelle* would inevitably lead to a substantial increase in the British naval budget—two keels would be laid down for every capital ship added to the German Navy above the existing law—and to a further concentration in home waters, and that, under these circumstances, a new era of better Anglo-German relations was out of the question. Grey went further and informed Metternich (24 February) that the cession of Pemba and Zanzibar depended on the settlement of the naval question, and (a few days later) that it would be impossible to conclude a political agreement at the very time when both countries were planning to increase their navies.

Tirpitz, firmly convinced that England was only engaged in wringing naval concessions without giving anything in return, redoubled his efforts to have the *Novelle* laid before the Reichstag. He found ready assistance in Admirals Müller and the C.-in-C. of the Fleet, Admiral von Holtzendorff, and in the Emperor. Against them were ranged Bethmann Hollweg and Kiderlen. The Chancellor tried to persuade the Emperor and Tirpitz to abandon the three supplementary ships and to postpone the publication of the Navy Law. Tirpitz would not budge. 'The quicker we publish the *Novelle*, the more we limit the possibility of the English making greater demands on us.'[10] The Emperor agreed; but, needing Bethmann Hollweg because he was trusted abroad, he persuaded him to remain in office by postponing publication of the *Novelle* and continuing negotiations with England.

A memorandum handed to Grey by Metternich on 6 March contained the dominant idea that no success in the negotiations was possible unless political and naval questions were treated *pari passu*. The Imperial Government was prepared to restrict its demand for the construction of new battleships to the years 1913 and 1916, and to postpone the construction of the third battleship indefinitely, if the British Government came forward with a satisfactory political formula. The postponement of the third ship appears to have been a concession that Bethmann Hollweg had wrung from the vacillating Emperor. On 14 March Grey gave

[10] Tirpitz to Müller, 26 Feb. 1912; Tirpitz, *Politische Dokumente*, i. 300.

Metternich a draft formula which had been approved by the Cabinet. It was short and to the point. 'England will make no unprovoked attack upon Germany and pursue no aggressive policy towards her. Aggression upon Germany is not the subject and forms no part of any Treaty, understanding or combination to which England is now a party, nor will she become a party to anything that has such an object.' Certain that this formula, which made no mention of neutrality, would be found unsatisfactory in Berlin, Metternich strongly urged this addition (15 March): 'England will therefore observe at least a benevolent neutrality should war be forced upon Germany,' or, as an alternative wording, that 'England will therefore as a matter of course remain neutral if a war is forced upon Germany.' In essence, this formula (essentially the one Bethmann Hollweg had proposed to Haldane) did not differ greatly from the British proposal. It was, however, counter to Grey's constant desire to avoid creating any alarm in Paris and St. Petersburg. He admitted to Metternich that as Germany was strengthening her Navy, England could not imperil her old friendships. 'A direct neutrality agreement would inevitably offend French susceptibilities.' Grey offered in its place (16 March) his formula of 14 March with these additional words at the beginning: 'The two Powers being mutually desirous of securing peace and friendship between them, England declares that she will . . .' He added that while he was convinced that no difficulties would arise while Bethmann Hollweg was Chancellor, England could have no security that he might not be overthrown a short time after, and she could not therefore risk making her relations with France 'more distant'.

Shortly before this the Chancellor had begged the Emperor to defer publication of the *Novelle* until he had received Metternich's report and it was evident how England would act in the question of the political agreement, so as not to put any obstacle unnecessarily in its way. He was evidently determined, if the addition to Grey's formula were accepted, to demand a reduction of the *Novelle*. On 18 March, after the arrival of Grey's amended formula, the Emperor found Bethmann Hollweg in a state of collapse and pressed a glass of port wine on him. The Chancellor saw that the British formula was so elastic as to be valueless in German eyes. He was also irritated at Grey's taking account of the possibility of a future change in German policy, for, as he remonstrated, were an agreement reached, German policy would be bound, no less than English policy, for a considerable period. Moreover, the person of the Emperor was a guarantee that German policy would be conducted on friendly lines. When Metternich's dispatch was submitted to the Emperor, he burst forth in fury at Grey's remark that Bethmann Hollweg's personality was regarded as the one surety for peace. 'I have never in my life heard of an agreement being concluded with reference to one definite statesman, and independently of the reigning sovereign. It is clear that Grey has no idea who is master here, namely myself. He prescribes to me who my ministers must be if I am to conclude an agreement with England.'[11] The Emperor's second reaction was to draft an extraordinary 'Willy' to 'Georgy' letter in English to his royal cousin (18 March):

I am most distressed that the negotiations which are taking place between our two Governments respecting the agreement seem to have come to a deadlock. . . . I think there is a solution possible, and that is why I address myself to you. Sir E. Grey—as I before said—told the German Ambassador that he was anxious not to give France offence by his negotiations with Germany as he wished to remain on friendly terms with that country. Besides he remarked that it was his fervent wish that Europe should cease to be split up into 2 camps—Triplice and Entente. This is my fervent wish too! I therefore propose this solution, that instead of the agreement your Government has itself annulled, we should make an offensive and defensive alliance—as you have with Japan—with France as a partner and open to the other Powers to enter *ad libitum*. This would unite all the Great Powers of Europe and consolidate peace. In this case I should be able to make reductions in the 'Novelle' meeting your Government's wishes, which my Government would be able to advocate before Parliament and Public, where this is impossible with the proposed agreement. . . .[12]

The letter was not sent. It is probable that the Emperor's draft was discussed with Bethmann Hollweg and possibly with Kiderlen, and that the Chancellor advised against any direct intervention by the Emperor, using the argument contained in this minute written by Müller (24 April): 'His Majesty gave up the idea of making a direct approach to the King of England, since the King

[11] Marginal note on Metternich to Foreign Ministry, 17 Mar. 1912; *Die Grosse Politik*, xxxi. 183.
[12] German Ministry of Marine MSS., Tirpitz, *Politische Dokumente*, i. 331–2. Müller's minute (see below) is in the former.

cannot be expected to influence British policy.' The Emperor, however, reproduced the substance of the letter the same day when he drafted instructions to Metternich. The Ambassador was to suggest a new formula, an offensive and defensive alliance, in which France should be included. His aim, he informed the Chancellor, was to put England in the wrong if she declined this proposal. Bethmann Hollweg, compelled to let the Emperor's letter go, forwarded an explanatory letter to London giving a very different impression. He told Metternich to say that only a settlement in the nature of a defensive alliance—'an agreement of far-reaching character, and leaving no doubt as to any interpretation' —would make it possible for him to advise the Emperor to give up the essential parts of the *Novelle* and justify his action to German public opinion. What the Chancellor now asked for amounted to an agreement of absolute neutrality, although he did not use the word 'absolute'. Failing a guarantee of absolute neutrality, the *Novelle* must proceed. Grey's reply, when Metternich saw him on 19 March, was that he would refer the Chancellor's proposal to the Cabinet, but, as he noted in a minute, 'It goes without saying that this must be declined but I must tell the Cabinet of it.' The Cabinet, absorbed by the crisis in the coal industry, was unable for the time being to pass judgment on the 'absolute neutrality' proposal. For all practical purposes a complete deadlock had been reached. Churchill's speech presenting the 1912–13 estimates to Parliament (18 March) made it certain that the stalemate would not be broken.

Unlike McKenna's speeches on the estimates, which were apologetic and sometimes confused, Churchill was almost brutally clear and frank. The sham of the two-power standard was now publicly abandoned. He brushed aside the last remnants of pretence and stated bluntly that they were building against one power, and one power only—Germany. The principles which should govern British naval strength were, he declared, with Cabinet approval: (1) 60 per cent superiority in dreadnoughts (a 16 : 10 ratio) over Germany so long as she adhered to the existing Navy Law, that is, without the *Novelle*. This would be maintained by a dreadnought programme, beginning in 1912–13, of 4–3–4–3–4–3 against uniform German programmes of two. (2) Two keels to one for every additional ship laid down by Germany above the Law. If Germany added three big ships to her programme for the next six years, Great Britain would lay down six more during the same period: 5-4-5-4-5-4. (Ultimately, as the Germans dropped for the time being one of the three extra ships, the British six-year programme was fixed at 4-5-4-4-4-4 against the German 2-3-2-2-3-2. This was announced in Parliament on 18 July. The gift of the battleship *Malaya* by the Federated Malay States later in the year raised the first year's figure from four to five.) (3) As the British pre-dreadnoughts declined in relative fighting value, the ratio would have to rise above 60 per cent. Underlying these principles was the thought expressed in a letter to Fisher: 'Nothing, in my opinion, would more surely dishearten Germany, than the certain proof that as the result of all her present and prospective efforts she will only be more hopelessly behindhand in 1920.'[13] Other important points in the First Lord's speech were that the two 'Nelsons', though not dreadnoughts, were counted as such by Churchill on the advice of the War Staff, because they were stronger in some ways, especially in armour and subdivision, than the original *Dreadnought*. On the other hand, any ships contributed by the Dominions were to be additional to anything built by Britain. Churchill also invited Germany to lessen the colossal load of armaments by joining Britain in a 'naval holiday'. If Germany did not build any capital ships in any single year, England would follow her example. This would spare both countries enormous expenditures, while leaving the ratio of their navies unchanged. Although the proposal was not made officially to Germany, the Emperor sent Churchill a courteous message through Cassel, expressing his great regret and adding that such arrangements would only be possible between allies.

One novelty about the navy debates was that the game of hunting for 'years of danger' was dropped. The Conservative press congratulated Churchill on his first navy estimates and on his candid, lucid, and vigorous presentation of the facts. *The Times* (19 March) hailed it as 'one of the best expositions, perhaps, indeed, the best exposition, of naval policy which has been made since Lord George Hamilton's famous statement in 1889.' Arthur Lee declared it was the first speech by a First Lord to which he had listened with pleasure since the Liberal Government had come into office. The only serious Conservative criticism was of the Government's declared intention to leave the Mediterranean

[13] 19 Feb. 1912; *The World Crisis*, i. 105.

(which will be discussed shortly). Liberal opinion regarded Churchill's programme as a sad necessity, and urged, as always, that the only solution to the naval problem was the establishment of friendly and cordial relations with Germany, of which disarmament would be the natural fruit. Labour party spokesmen entered protests against the expenditure on the Navy.

Churchill's 'arrogant' speech (so the Emperor termed it) offended the Berlin Government, which interpreted it as a challenge to Germany. Together with Grey's refusal to accommodate the Germans in the matter of a political formula, it caused a complete breakdown of the negotiations. Bethmann Hollweg wrote that 'Churchill's speech did not come up to my expectations. He really seems to be a firebrand past praying for . . . my opinion is that our labours will now have to be dropped altogether for some time.'[14] Realizing that further negotiations for a political agreement were useless, Bethmann Hollweg no longer obstructed the desires of the Emperor and Tirpitz regarding the *Novelle*. It was anti-climactic that Grey, on 29 March, informed Metternich that the Cabinet had decided against the Chancellor's absolute neutrality formula. The die had been cast on 22 March, the day the Supplementary Navy Law was published. Presented to the Reichstag on 14 April, it was voted a month later.

Immediately after the failure of the negotiations, Metternich, 'hopelessly incurable' in the Emperor's eyes, was removed (9 May). He had long been considered by the Emperor and Tirpitz as too friendly to England. He may have been 'dull and sleepy' (Bülow), but he understood England and her way of life far better than did Tirpitz, the Chancellors, and the Emperor. For him the crux of German relations with England lay in the growth of the German Fleet. He saw that only if England obtained a sense of full security, through a far-reaching naval agreement, would she be able to consider the kind of political agreement Germany wanted. The Ambassador, alas, did not have the confidence of the Emperor or Tirpitz, never more so than in 1912, when he had been tireless in his warnings and had repeatedly urged the necessity of abandoning the *Novelle*, if an agreement were desired. In England his departure was regretted, and Grey paid him the unusual distinction of publicly expressing his regret (Commons, 14 May). Metternich's

[14] Bethmann Hollweg to Ballin, 19 Mar. 1912; Bernhard Huldermann, *Albert Ballin* (London, 1922), p. 184.

leaving signified the complete victory of Tirpitz's naval policy. One consequence was that thereafter the naval attachés in London completely disregarded the policies and wishes of the Ambassador and the Foreign Office and followed the directions of the Ministry of Marine.

The Haldane Mission had failed for the same reasons that had doomed earlier negotiations. The English were unwilling to commit themselves to neutrality, partly for practical considerations —they could not, for example, stand by and see the Germans attack the French and aim to get possession of the Channel ports— and partly from fear that their French and Russian ties would thereby be weakened. Tirpitz appreciated that the difficulty of the situation for England was that, 'in her opinion, the Entente with France gives her the best security against a too powerful Germany. I no longer believe that we can get out of this vicious circle . . .'[15] The Germans, on their side, did not go far enough in their naval concessions. They refused to modify or even to discuss the main provisions of the *Novelle*. All they would offer was a slackening in the rate of construction of the new capital ships, and this the English considered insufficient. Throughout, Berlin contended that the basis for discussions, as set by the conversations with Haldane, was the political formula. The British Government disputed the German interpretation and at all times treated the formula as a secondary affair and the diminution of the new German naval programme as the primary matter. The Government recognized where the rub lay. 'Nothing, I believe,' Asquith told Grey (10 April), 'will meet her purpose which falls short of a promise on our part of neutrality; a promise we cannot give.' In colonial matters the Cabinet, denying that Haldane had made definite offers in Berlin, showed no interest in accommodating the Germans, and made a satisfactory settlement dependent on the extent of the modifications in the *Novelle*. In the face of this vicious circle it is small wonder that the Mission failed to accomplish its purposes.

The Haldane Mission was not, however, without beneficial results. Relations between the two Governments became somewhat more cordial. During the negotiations Grey had expressed the hope that even if no agreements were reached, the Mission and the free and open exchange of views that it had brought about

[15] Tirpitz to Müller, 26 Feb. 1912; Tirpitz, *Politische Dokumente*, i. 299.

might serve as a basis for a more candid and confidential relationship in future. This expectation was partially realized. Combined work became much easier than before, and much more fruitful, especially during the Balkan Wars (1912–13) in the Ambassadors' Conference in London. Also, the discussions on the Portuguese colonies in Africa were continued. Agreements were eventually reached on them and on the Baghdad Railway which required only the signatures when the war broke out.

The failure of England to head off the *Novelle* meant a continuation of the intensive naval rivalry. It also led to closer Anglo-French relations, the last thing Germany desired.

2. THE MEDITERRANEAN PROBLEM: FIRST PHASE

No time was lost in taking up the German challenge. In a circular letter of 29 March (outlined on 18 March by Churchill in the Commons) the Admiralty announced its reorganization of the various fleets and squadrons, effective 1 May. The principal change was the formation of a new command known as the Home Fleets, charged with the responsibility for home defence (Callaghan, C.-in-C.). It consisted of a First Fleet (fully-manned ships), Second Fleet (two battle squadrons with 50 per cent nucleus-crew ships), and a Third Fleet (two battle squadrons with care and maintenance parties only). The four battle squadrons of the First Fleet had the newest and most powerful battleships (nothing older than the 'King Edwards') and cruisers. The first two squadrons were composed of ships already in home waters; the Atlantic Fleet, until now based on Gibraltar, became the 3rd Battle Squadron; four of the six Mediterranean Fleet pre-dreadnoughts (the 'Duncans'), until then at Malta, were to constitute the 4th Battle Squadron and be stationed at Gibraltar, available either to reinforce the squadrons in home waters or to re-enter the Mediterranean as circumstances might dictate. (The two 'Swiftsures' were kept in home waters.) A cruiser squadron was to be left at Malta. The first three squadrons had eight battleships each; the 4th, four ships, to be increased to eight. In addition there was to be a fleet flagship. When the 4th Battle Squadron was at full strength, there would be thirty-three battleships in full commission in home waters, and eight more with nucleus crews, or forty-one to face the expected German total by 1913 of twenty-five battleships ready, without mobilization, for war.

It was not only the latest amendment of the German Navy Law that prompted this redistribution. The Mediterranean situation itself had entered a new phase requiring the most serious attention of the Admiralty. An Admiralty War Staff memorandum of June 1912 showed that France had fourteen pre-dreadnoughts and six 'semi-dreadnoughts' (Jane) in commission (the latter, the 'Dantons', with a mixed armament of four 12-inch and twelve 9·4-inch guns, but comparable in power to dreadnoughts), with seven dreadnoughts due to be completed in 1913–15; Italy had eight pre-dreadnoughts and would have six dreadnoughts by 1915 four had already been launched); and Austria, with nine pre-dreadnoughts, was expected to have four dreadnoughts by 1915 (two had been launched), and there were rumours that they were proposing to build another four. It was recognized that Italy and Austria were building against each other; and neither Fleet was held in high esteem. (One admiral remembers 'our incredulous surprise when we encountered the Austrian Fleet at Pola and found them living in a "Merry Widow" sort of atmosphere'.[16]) It was, nevertheless, deemed prudent at the Admiralty to take account of their navies in the computation of naval strength, since they were building dreadnoughts and since a turn of the wheel might, any time, bring them into co-operation against England and her Triple Entente partners. Under these circumstances, the Admiralty could not justify the retention of the Mediterranean Fleet battleships in the inland sea. These six obsolescent pre-dreadnoughts would be no match for the Austrian and Italian dreadnoughts that would shortly be joining their fleets.

The redistribution, even if absolutely essential to the safety of the British Isles, obviously involved a weakening of Britain's Mediterranean position. In case of war with the Triple Alliance, the communications of the Empire would be cut at a vital point—unless France came to England's assistance. The Admiralty confided to the Government that, in the event of a war with Germany and at least one of the Mediterranean powers, it could not guarantee the safety of British communications through the Mediterranean until the situation had cleared up in the North Sea, and that might take several months. The alternatives that faced the

[16] Vice-Admiral R. D. Oliver to the author, 14 Dec. 1959.

Government were simple. It could (1) enter into a definite and binding alliance or naval arrangement with France; (2) increase the Navy to the extent necessary to maintain the British position in the Mediterranean as well as in the North Sea; (3) do nothing, that is, accept the Admiralty's reorganization without supplementary naval or political measures, in the frank realization, to quote Fisher, that *we cannot have everything or be strong everywhere. It is futile to be strong in the subsidiary theatre of war and not overwhelmingly supreme in the decisive theatre.*[17]

A great debate raged in the spring and summer over these choices. The third solution was favoured by the Liberal press for a variety of reasons. There was no cause for anxiety, it was said, since France was Britain's friend and she had a clear superiority over the combined fleets of Italy and Austria-Hungary; the Gibraltar fleet would be stronger in capital ships than Italy and Austria together for the foreseeable future; Italy and Austria would never be ranged together against Britain, because they feared and hated each other more acutely than they could dread any third Power; the maintenance of a fleet in the Mediterranean was not required for defence of the United Kingdom or for the security of British food supplies (the food supplies and trade which came through the Mediterranean could in time of war be diverted to the Cape route, while that from Russia could come overland to the Baltic); the Mediterranean was not vital to the defence of India; the home seas were the vital point: victorious there, they would recover what might be lost elsewhere.

Most Liberal organs were horrified by the alliance talk. This 'perilous leap in the dark' would involve conscription and would destroy British liberty to determine peace or war for themselves. The *Manchester Guardian* (27 May) rejected a French alliance as 'an absurdly disproportionate remedy' for the situation. This was, in general, the position of the Cabinet, too, although the Foreign Office was recommending an understanding with France whereby she would, at least in the initial stages of a war, undertake to safeguard British interests in the Mediterranean. This offered, said Nicolson, 'the cheapest, simplest and safest solution'.

The 'abandonment' of the Mediterranean was savagely attacked by prominent people (Beresford and Roberts, for example), the

[17] Fisher's memorandum for Churchill, 24 June 1912; *Fear God and Dread Nought*, ii. 469.

Conservative press, and the Navy League. The Mediterranean was the centre of naval-strategic gravity in Europe, they pointed out, and a main route for the food supply of Great Britain. The policy of concentration in the North Sea was wise, but they must have enough ships for safety in the Mediterranean as well in view of the expansion of the Austrian and Italian navies. To depend on the French Navy in the Mediterranean would be repellent to British national pride and sense of duty. The *Standard* (29 May) drew an historical parallel: 'Because of that formidable and threatening Armada across the North Sea, we have almost abandoned the waters of the Outer Oceans. We are in the position of Imperial Rome when the barbarians were thundering at the frontiers. The ominous word has gone forth. We have called home the legions. . . . Because of our preoccupation with the North Sea we have lost our hold upon the Mediterranean, the carotid artery of Empire.' Most of those who argued against 'abandonment' preferred to meet the situation by building more ships; but a few Conservative journals (the *Morning Post*, *The Observer*, and *Spectator*) would have the best of two worlds. They proposed to convert Britain's understanding with France into a formal alliance and at the same time add to the strength of the Fleet in the Mediterranean! Balfour, too, urged a French alliance, seeing great advantages from the military and diplomatic points of view. It was admitted by most supporters of an alliance that if France were to discharge Britain's duties for her in the Mediterranean, they must be prepared to do something more for her on land than was possible with their small army. That is, they would have to raise a much larger army and definitely allot it to appointed tasks on the Continent.

Esher, who led the fight against abandonment in official circles, had no use for the French alternative. 'Rome had to call in the foreigner to help her when the time of her decadence approached.' He pointed out that Churchill had thrown 'dust in the eyes of the public' by his suggestion in the Commons (18 March) that the 4th Battle Squadron could act, as required, eastward or westward, since at the outset of war it would be required in the North Sea. In eloquent letters and memoranda, he warned that the concentration of the Fleet in the North Sea, in itself a perfectly sound policy, would, by denuding the Mediterranean of battleships, surrender the power to hold Egypt, Malta, and possibly Gibraltar against potential enemies. The abandonment meant the weakening of the value to Japan of the British alliance and the eventual subservience to Germany of Italy and Spain. British prestige would be lowered in India, the Crown Colonies, and, indeed, everywhere. 'The choice therefore lies between such increases of Naval Power as will ensure sea command in the Mediterranean, or the substitution of a conscript for a voluntary Army, or the abandonment of Egypt and Malta and a complete reversal of the traditional policy of Great Britain in regard to her trade routes and military highways to the East. There is no alternative. Any attempt to rely upon "Alliances", or the Naval Forces of friendly Powers, is bound to prove illusory.'[18]

The Admiralty War Staff also considered the second of the three alternatives—naval increases—to be more satisfactory 'from every point of view except that of expense. France is a country of unstable politics, with no particular sympathy towards British interests except in so far as they represent French interests as well. . . . [Naval increases] would provide the Empire with a much more stable foundation and leave the future relatively free from anxiety as to French political tendencies.' Britain possessed twenty-seven dreadnoughts, built and building, against thirty of the Triple Alliance. Offsetting this inferiority in part were the British preponderance in pre-dreadnoughts and the weaknesses of a coalition fleet. Ten more British dreadnoughts laid down in 1912–13 (or four, together with the purchase of the six battleships building or projected in British yards for foreign powers) would make the British position secure in both home waters and the Mediterranean from 1915 onwards without extraneous help.[19]

The General Staff and the Foreign Office were up in arms against the Admiralty, although for different reasons. Their contrasting positions and recommendations were stated in papers prepared for informal C.I.D. meetings at Malta at Whitsuntide.[20]

[18] A paper of late May, enclosed in a letter from Esher to King George, 30 May 1912; Windsor MSS.

[19] 'War Staff Memorandum on the Mediterranean Situation', Apr. 1912; Admiralty MSS.

[20] C.I.D. Papers 92–C, 149–B, 93–C, and 147–B, all of 9 May 1912: respectively, 'Papers Prepared by the General Staff—1. The Attack on Malta by Italy. 2. The Defence of Malta against Deliberate Invasion'; '1. The Attack on Egypt by Turkey. 2. The Defence of Egypt against External Aggression'; '1. The Attack on Cyprus by Austria. 2. The Defence of Cyprus'; 'The Situation in the Mediterranean, 1912.' The last was the Foreign Office memorandum.

The General Staff concerned itself solely with the military aspects of the problem. It assumed that the Mediterranean Fleet had been withdrawn to Gibraltar and would not operate in the Mediterranean for at least two months, during which time the Triple Alliance and Turkey would command the Mediterranean (it was understood that this was the Admiralty position), and that the French Fleet must be disregarded, since it would be busy for ten to fourteen days in protecting the transport of troops from North Africa to France. The General Staff's conclusions were that Italy, Turkey, and Austria could, within a few weeks, capture Malta, Egypt, and Cyprus, respectively. The alternatives were increasing the sea defence or the peace garrisons in the Mediterranean. A later memorandum eliminated the second alternative. It would 'put a strain upon our military resources which, at their present strength and under their existing organisation, they are quite unable to bear.'[21] The Foreign Office considered that British diplomatic interests throughout the world would suffer through the 'evacuation' of the Mediterranean. Italy would definitely be thrown into the arms of the Triple Alliance; Spain would be detached from her understanding with France and England and gravitate towards the Triple Alliance; Turkey would be encouraged to work with the Triple Alliance and to attempt the reconquest of Egypt.

These consequences could to a certain extent be averted if the place of the British Mediterranean squadron were effectively taken by a powerful French fleet. If Anglo-French co-operation were assured in the case of either country being at war with the Triple Alliance, and if the French fleet were in a position to beat those of Italy, Austria, and Turkey combined, and to win the command of the Mediterranean, Italy would probably continue to refuse allowing her partnership in the Triple Alliance to involve her in a war with the two western Powers, and Spain would have no sufficient inducement to change her present policy. Malta and Gibraltar would be as secure as they are now. It is less certain that the British position in Turkey would remain unaffected; our hold over Egypt might have to be materially strengthened.

At the end of May Asquith, Field-Marshal Lord Kitchener (*de facto* Viceroy of Egypt), Churchill, and various professional

---

[21] C.I.D. Paper 156–B, 'Memorandum by the General Staff on the Effect of the Loss of Sea Power in the Mediterranean on British Military Strategy', July 1912; Lennoxlove MSS.

advisers met at Malta for the discussion of the Mediterranean question. Kitchener was dead against the Churchill naval redistribution. He opposed any diversion of the Fleet from the Mediterranean: the protection of Egypt was an important consideration and might cause Egypt to look to India instead of to England for supplies and reinforcements. The Admiralty reached a 'draft arrangement' with Kitchener that reflected both Foreign Office and War Office views. (1) A definite agreement should be made with France providing for British defence of the French northern coast in return for France keeping a Mediterranean Fleet large enough, with the British ships stationed there, to ensure victory against Italy and Austria; (2) the Admiralty would maintain a permanent squadron in the Mediterranean of two, preferably three, battle cruisers, and a squadron of four armoured cruisers; (3) the 4th Battle Squadron (four 'Duncans', to be raised to eight battleships with the addition of the two 'Nelsons' and two dreadnoughts in 1913), based on Gibraltar, would cruise in the Mediterranean, though available elsewhere in case of war with Germany; (4) submarine defence was to be maintained at Malta and Alexandria. A final decision on the Admiralty distribution policy was postponed until the strategic position had been discussed by the C.I.D.

The crucial meeting, held on 4 July, lasted practically all day.[22] Churchill stated the Admiralty case in a temperate and clear speech. The main points he made were: (1) The utility of the six Mediterranean battleships having come to an end with the building of the Austrian and Italian dreadnoughts, 'they became merely a useless and expensive symbol of power. . . . The exposure of a weak detachment to defeat was unsound strategically and tactically.' (2) They must keep a definite supremacy over the Germans in the North Sea, and 'all other objects, however precious, must, if necessary, be sacrificed to secure this end.' (3) A Battle Cruiser Squadron in the Mediterranean of two ships, if possible three, would, with the French Mediterranean Fleet, secure a 'reasonable but sure preponderance' for the two powers over Austria and Italy. 'If we were unsupported these ships could look after themselves and get away. If we were alone we could not face the Triple Alliance in the Mediterranean.' (4) When convenient, they would

[22] What follows is from the minutes of the 117th meeting of the C.I.D.; Asquith MSS.

send the Gibraltar fleet (4th Battle Squadron) into the Mediterranean. 'There was no necessity to publish the fact that the
Gibraltar Fleet was maintained primarily for use in Home waters.'

The ultimate conclusion of the C.I.D. after heated debate was:
'There must always be provided a reasonable margin of superior
strength ready and available in Home waters. This is the first
requirement. Subject to this we ought to maintain, available for
Mediterranean purposes and based on a Malta port, a battle fleet
equal to a one-power Mediterranean standard, excluding France.'
The language was Asquith's. Churchill made a final protest, but
the recommendation was accepted, and was subsequently endorsed
by the Cabinet. Note that nothing was done about the first point
in the Malta agreement. Apparently the feeling was that it would
compromise the country too deeply. The new policy meant, in
essence, that a battle fleet would be maintained in the Mediterranean—something more than the two or three battle cruisers of
the Churchill–Kitchener compromise. It was obvious, as Esher
put it, that

the diplomatic reasons for keeping a *Fleet* in the Mediterranean based
upon *Malta* were considered to render it essential that this should be a
principle laid down by the Defence Committee. . . . Now the whole
matter: cost—amount of margin—etc.—is relegated to the Cabinet
and the Admiralty to work out. . . . It was a hard fight. . . . The
Cabinet were so strongly represented that it is not likely that there will
be any backsliding. McKenna, Harcourt and L. George were all very
staunch. [Fisher, who was present, reported that 'McKenna and
Winston were tearing each other's eyes out the whole time.'] Anyhow,
the Mediterranean is to have a Fleet of *Battle ships*![23]

And to Knollys the next day: 'We can hold up our heads in the
Mediterranean and—beyond! If the thing had gone on, King
George's plight would have been far worse than Queen Mary's
when she lost Calais!'[24]

The naval situation in the Mediterranean was exhaustively discussed in all its aspects by the Cabinet on 15–16 July after
Churchill had presented the Admiralty's proposals for implement-
ing the C.I.D. conclusion.[25] The all-important one was that the

[23] Esher to King George, 4 July 1912; Windsor MSS.
[24] *Ibid.*
[25] The one source appears to be Asquith's report to the King on these meetings;
Asquith MSS.

Malta-based Mediterranean Fleet would, in the near future, consist of four battle cruisers and four armoured cruisers.

The criticisms offered by the McKenna-led opposition amounted to this: (1) Should war break out with Germany, the battle cruisers at Malta would have to be withdrawn at once to home waters, leaving Britain's Mediterranean commerce and territory unprotected or inadequately defended for the time being; (2) in the event of a war in which the Mediterranean was one of the theatres, and Austria, for example, was a hostile belligerent, the battle cruisers could not hold their own against the Austrian battle squadron of three pre-dreadnought battleships and two or three dreadnoughts. The British squadron would have to run away, with the same result as under (1). It was no solution to have a Gibraltar-based battle squadron which might fight in the Mediterranean, if it was to be regarded as an essential component of the naval force in home waters in case of war with Germany. The only answer to the problem was to maintain a one-power standard battle squadron at Malta, a force 'equal to giving a good account of any battle squadron which, say, Austria can put into the fighting line'.

Churchill satisfied his colleagues (1) that there would be no need to withdraw the four battle cruisers from the Mediterranean, in the event of a war with Germany, unless to meet some unlikely and unforeseeable emergency, and (2) that, in the opinion of his best expert advisers, the proposed Cruiser Squadron would, during the next two years, be more than a match in the Mediterranean for any force that Austria could oppose to it. The Cabinet thereupon unanimously approved the proposals of the Admiralty.

Grey outlined the Government's revised Mediterranean policy in the House of Commons, 10 July. His assurance that the Mediterranean would not be abandoned was warmly welcomed by the public, as was his clear statement that, in the absence of a British fleet, they could not make their position in that sea secure by any feat of diplomacy. He clearly intimated that the Government intended to keep a fleet in the Mediterranean superior to the naval forces of either Austria or Italy, but not of both. He elaborated the position in a statement at the C.I.D., 11 July, with the object of giving full and confidential information to Borden, the Canadian Prime Minister, and three of his colleagues, who were in London and who had been invited to the meeting. Grey justified a one-power standard in the Mediterranean on the ground that it was pointless to keep a fleet there which was superior to Austria and Italy combined, since Britain was not on bad terms with either power, and their interests conflicted with each other more than they did with British interests in the Mediterranean. 'If we were to find ourselves opposed by those two Powers jointly, it could only be because the cause of the quarrel was some European conflict bringing in the whole of the Triple Alliance. This would certainly concern France as well as ourselves, and so France would be brought into the conflict as well as we.'[26]

Churchill then gave a masterly review of the entire naval position. 'The ultimate scale of the German fleet is of the most formidable character. . . . The whole character of the German fleet shows that it is designed for aggressive and offensive action of the largest possible character in the North Sea or the North Atlantic. . . The structure of the German battleships shows clearly that they are intended for attack and for fleet action. . . . the position of the guns, the .armament, the way the torpedo tubes are placed—all these things would enable naval experts to say that this idea of sudden and aggressive action on the greatest scale against a great modern naval Power is undoubtedly the guiding principle of German naval policy.' Churchill found the same offensive principle in the smaller German types: the emphasis on speed in the destroyers and radius of action in the submarines.

We are sometimes told that the Germans only think of fighting a battle which will leave that greater naval Power seriously weakened after the battle is over; they will have destroyed themselves and the greater naval Power will be weakened. . . . Anything more foolish than to spend all these millions year after year and to make all these efforts and sacrifices and exertions for no other purpose than certainly to come off second best on the day of trial cannot well be imagined. . . . [the German Navy] is intended for a great trial of strength with the navy of the greatest naval Power. . . .

I do not pretend to make any suggestion that the Germans would deliver any surprise or sudden attack upon us. It is not for us to assume that another great nation will fall markedly below the standard of civilisation which we ourselves should be bound by; but we at the Admiralty have got to see, not that they will not do it, but [that] they cannot do it.

[26] Minutes of the 118th meeting of the C.I.D.; Asquith MSS. Churchill's speech, which follows, is from the same source.

We have at present . . . two safety signals which we watch very carefully. . . . First of all, we see that in the winter the German fleet is largely demobilised, owing to the fact that they are full up with their recruits; consequently, in the winter the strain is relaxed . . . Another indication which we have of security is when we see some of their greatest vessels of the newer type . . . on the Baltic side of the Kiel Canal, because they cannot come through the canal at present, and we know that if any great enterprise were on foot it would be very unlikely that units of the greatest consequence would be left on the wrong side of the canal, whence they would have to make a great detour to come round. Unfortunately both these safety signals are going to be extinguished in the immediate future; the deepening of the Kiel Canal, which is to be accomplished in two years' time, will enable the great vessels to pass through it in the same way as other vessels can now pass through. In addition, as regards the immunity which so far we have enjoyed in the winter, that too will be destroyed by the development of the new German Navy Law . . . The effect of the law is to put rather less than four-fifths of their fleet permanently into full commission, that is to say, in the category of ships instantly ready for action . . .

Churchill then turned to the Mediterranean. The Admiralty planned to have a battle squadron there of eight dreadnoughts or battle cruisers, a force strong enough to deal with any navy except the French. It was not possible to do it then, as the ships were needed at home. But if they took steps now, they would have the required force in the Mediterranean in 1915, that is, by the time the Austrian programme was completed. In the interval, the Mediterranean would be held with a battle-cruiser force. When the eight ships went out in 1915, the Navy in home waters would be three or four ships short of the 3 : 2 dreadnought margin over Germany that the Admiralty regarded as necessary.

The First Lord concluded with an appeal for three ships above the series of programmes announced in March. Financially it was inconvenient to lay down three new ships then. A more serious obstacle was that they had made their building programme correspond to the German. 'If we come forward now all of a sudden and add three new ships, that may have the effect of stimulating the naval competition once more, and they would ask us what new factor had occurred which justified or which required this increase of building on our part. If we could say that the new fact was that Canada had decided to take part in the defence of the British

Empire, that would be an answer which would involve no invidious comparisons, and which would absolve us from going into detailed calculations as to the number of Austrian or German vessels available at any particular moment. . . . The need, I say, is a serious one, and it is an immediate need.'

Borden was impressed. The situation appeared to be 'sufficiently serious to demand very careful consideration' on the part of the Canadian Government. On 5 December 1912 he introduced into the Canadian Parliament an emergency naval bill authorizing the expenditure of some £7,000,000 to build three super-dread-noughts, to be placed at the disposal of the Imperial Government for the common defence of the Empire and to be maintained and controlled as part of the Royal Navy. The bill was hotly debated for weeks. Passed by the Canadian House of Commons in February 1913, it was rejected by the Senate the following May and was never revived. Sir Wilfrid Laurier, the Leader of the Opposition, demanded a nationally controlled and built Canadian Fleet, and, besides, he believed 'there is no emergency, there is no immediate danger, there is no prospective danger.' The uncertainty of the Canadian contribution immensely complicated Admiralty planning in the last two years before the war.

3. THE MEDITERRANEAN PROBLEM: SECOND PHASE

In the House of Commons on 22 July 1912 Churchill drew this picture of the situation in the North Sea: Germany would have, possibly at the end of 1913, twenty-five fully-manned battleships in the High Seas Fleet, and four fully manned in the Reserve of the High Seas Fleet which might conceivably be used in an emergency. Against these, Britain would provide thirty-three fully-manned battleships in the First Fleet of the Home Fleets, including the eight with the 4th Battle Squadron at Gibraltar. Churchill's 33–29 figure did not include in the British total the eight half-manned battleships in the Second Fleet, although they could proceed to sea as soon as steam was raised in their boilers. He also announced that he would withdraw within six months the four 'Invincibles' and four powerful armoured cruisers from the North Sea for service in the Mediterranean. They were to be based on Malta and were to replace the Mediterranean Fleet battleships.

Bonar Law and Balfour, in the Commons debates (22, 25 July), asked whether the First Lord was not 'running it rather fine'. This was the keynote of the Conservative press reaction, which singled out for special criticism (1) the restoration of the Mediterranean position simply at the expense of Britain's North Sea forces, which made a positive addition to British naval strength more imperatively requisite than ever. The *Globe* (23 July) likened the situation to 'the Irishman who could find no better way of lengthening the skirts of his coat than by cutting off the sleeves'. (2) The 33–29 proportion of battleships in full commission was grossly inadequate (Churchill's qualifications of this ratio were disregarded), and even the forty-one battleships planned by 1915 would not achieve the promised 60 per cent standard of superiority. 'His words are worthy of Pitt; his acts are less robust' was the judgment of the *Standard* (24 July). The *National Review* (August) was even less charitable: the First Lord was 'a treacherous windbag'.

The Liberal press was divided over the First Lord's statement. The *Daily Chronicle* and the *Westminster Gazette* were, on the whole, pleased: 33–29 was a sufficient margin of superiority when the enormous pre-dreadnought superiority was taken into account, and the plans for the Mediterranean reasonably met their local needs. The *Manchester Guardian* and the *Daily News* were critical of the First Lord's speech. The latter was appalled by the First Lord's foreshadowing of a naval competition that would go on indefinitely and impose ever-increasing burdens upon the nation. The *Manchester Guardian* found 'the most alarming single passage' in Churchill's speech in his reference to the British and French Fleets *together* as being more than equal to any possible combination in the Mediterranean. There was good reason for concern.

Changing circumstances in the Mediterranean were driving the English and French towards closer co-operation in that sea. The Italian occupation of Tripoli and seizure of some of the Aegean islands in the Italo-Turkish War of 1911–12 (peace was concluded in October 1912) struck British opinion as having seriously changed the British naval position for the worse. The Italians now had a potential first-class base at Tobruk, and the occupation of the Dodecanese Islands in May 1912 brought the Italians close to the Anatolian coast and established them athwart the routes from Malta and Constantinople to the Suez Canal. The British, as well as the French, were disturbed by the naval implications of the Italian victory. There was the fear that Italy might hand over to her German allies a naval base in Tripoli or in the Dodecanese, or that the Central Powers, inspired by Italy's success, might take steps to establish themselves in the eastern Mediterranean. There was also some concern that the victorious Italians, a little cocky, would, as the *Saturday Review* expressed it (8 June 1912), 'hardly be prepared any longer to consider our feelings owing to sentimental memories of the Risorgimento'.

The Admiralty recommended (29 June 1912) that the maintenance of the *status quo ante* in the Aegean be the goal of the Government, and that, in association with the powers which were co-signatories of the treaties governing the navigation of the Dardanelles, the Government protest against any permanent occupation of the Islands by Italy. The Admiralty position was outlined for the Foreign Office in a memorandum by the Chief of the War Staff:

Admiralty policy in the Mediterranean has for many years been based upon the condition that our interests in the eastern basin of that sea (viz., the Black Sea and Levant Trade at its source—Egypt—and the Suez Canal route to the East) could only be threatened by hostile fleets operating from countries a thousand miles distant from the vital area in which those interests lie, which fleets could be observed, and their hostile movements controlled, by our fleets based upon Malta. A cardinal factor of this condition has naturally been that no strong Naval Power should be in effective permanent occupation of any territory or harbour east of Malta, if such harbour be capable of transformation into a fortified Naval base. . . .

We are now confronted with the possibility of Italy retaining full possession of certain of the Aegean Islands in full sovereignty. . . . The geographical situation of these islands enables the Sovereign Power, if enjoying the possession of a Navy, to exercise a control over the Levant and Black Sea trade and to threaten our position in Egypt to an unprecedented degree. A permanent menace to Turkey by the Sovereign Power would also be established, or, alternatively, greater facility would be given to the transport of Turkish troops to Egypt in the event of Turkey joining our enemies. Also the fact that the Italian Tripoli frontier now marches with that of Egypt must not be left out of consideration.

Such a condition of affairs would have compelled an entire reconsideration of Naval policy in the Mediterranean at a time when we maintained there a full squadron of Battleships and a squadron of Cruisers. It would have been necessary to detach sufficient ships to mask any force that might be present in the Aegean Sea or to invest the established Naval base. But at the present day, when our whole fleet is insufficient to provide for a sure preponderance in the North Sea coincidentally with an effective protection of our Mediterranean interests, the situation would plainly be aggravated by the establishment of a hostile Naval Station in the Aegean.[27]

On 15 November 1912 Grey warned the Italian Ambassador that 'if any Great Power was to keep an Aegean Island for a naval base we should certainly want something of the kind for ourselves; other Powers would want something also: there would be a regular scramble and the whole apple-cart would be upset.'[28] This and other Foreign Office *démarches* had no effect. No more successful was the French suggestion that the Straits of the Bosphorus and Dardanelles be opened to the Russian Black Sea Fleet, so that it might be used to right the naval balance in the Mediterranean; nor did anything come of an Anglo-French scheme for a pact signed by the Triple Entente powers with Italy guaranteeing the *status quo*. The Italian price was one England would not pay, viz., that she be allowed to keep at least one or two of the captured Dodecanese Islands. The chief result of the friction between England–France and Italy over the Dodecanese was that Italy was driven closer to her Triple Alliance allies. Of more immediate consequence was the establishment by Germany in November 1912 of a Mediterranean squadron consisting of the new battle cruiser *Goeben* and smaller cruisers. With the balance of naval power in the Mediterranean so precarious, it was more important than ever for England to retain the friendship of Turkey and keep her out of the Triple Alliance.

One method was to help the Turks to reorganize their navy. The Turkish Navy, which at one time had been the terror of the Mediterranean and which as late as the Russian war of 1877–8 had been able to dominate the Black Sea, was, in 1903, rated by Selborne as 'non-existent, absolutely and without qualification'. Of all the vessels in the Golden Horn early in 1904 only one small torpedo gunboat was capable of getting up steam in an emergency, and her condenser tubes were out of order and she had neither coal nor provisions on board! The Turkish Fleet was assessed by the D.N.I. (Ottley) in November 1905 as being 'in a deplorable

---

[27] Troubridge's memorandum, 20 June 1912; *British Documents*, ix (Pt. i). 413–16.
[28] Grey to Bertie, 15 Nov. 1912; *ibid*. (Pt. ii), p. 158.

condition, and quite useless for fighting purposes'. In 1911 the Fleet possessed two practically obsolete battleships, purchased from the German Government (10,000 tons, six 11-inch guns), two modern protected cruisers, ten destroyers, and a few lesser vessels. In addition there were eight battleships of no real fighting value. The inevitable result of the long neglect of the Navy was the inglorious role it played in the Italian war. A better day was in prospect, however.

Taking advantage of improved Anglo-Turkish relations after the Young Turk Revolution of 1908, the British Government secured the appointment of Rear-Admiral Sir Douglas Gamble in December 1908 to undertake the reorganization of the Turkish Fleet. He was succeeded in April 1910 by Rear-Admiral H. P. Williams, who gave way in April 1912 to Rear-Admiral Arthur H. Limpus and a British naval mission of seventy-two. Officially, Limpus was Naval Adviser to the Ottoman Ministry of Marine. The British naval missions improved the efficiency and spirit of the Sultan's Fleet. It performed somewhat better, if still ineptly, in the two Balkan Wars (1912–13), twice engaging the enemy's squadron at sea and making an attempt to interfere with their opponent's maritime communications. However, the main purposes of the British naval missions—each, note, headed by a flag officer on the active list—were to exercise some political influence, counteract German activity, and obtain shipbuilding orders for English yards. The last-named goal met with success. In May 1911 contracts were placed with Armstrong and Vickers for two dreadnoughts, of 23,000 tons and ten 13·5-inch guns. One was to be delivered in September 1914, the other in December 1914. The Russians, aware that these, and smaller, warships building in England would upset the balance of naval power in the Black Sea, tried to get the British Government to delay deliveries. The Government turned a deaf ear to these suggestions. It was interested in helping Turkey build an efficient fleet as an aid to the maintenance of Turkish independence. Besides, it was realized that if the British refused aid, the Germans would undoubtedly have stepped into the breach. As it turned out, H.M. Government took over two Turkish dreadnoughts soon after the war broke out (see p. 440).

The growth of German influence in Constantinople was profoundly disturbing to the Admiralty. Limpus predicted a 'much more decided leaning towards Germany', including the employment of German instructors for the Navy and the consequent elimination of English influence in the Turkish Navy, unless the British Government did two things: (1) sold the Turks two pre-dreadnoughts (the *Triumph* and a 'Royal Sovereign' or two 'Royal Sovereigns') after the Balkan Wars, and at a price approaching the £120,000 to £160,000 for which the nineteen-year-old German pre-dreadnoughts *Worth* and *Brandenburg* had been offered to the Turks; and (2) consented to receive some thirty Turkish naval officers for training after the war. Battenberg's reaction—he was First Sea Lord—was cool. He opposed the sale of any pre-dreadnoughts and he even questioned the value of the naval mission itself, whose

officers have twice in a short time passed through the humiliating position of being associated in war with a fleet whose exploits have been beneath contempt. . . . From a Naval point of view it must be realized that the Turkish Navy is hopeless. They are welcome to buy worn-out German ships. They will never make any use of them. The rising Sea Power of Greece is much more worthy of our care and assistance, and I earnestly hope that the Naval Mission will be definitely withdrawn from Constantinople and that a Naval Mission of specially selected Active Service Officers will be offered to Greece in the place of the handful of retired Officers now in the pay of the Athens Admiralty and which carry little weight in their councils.

Churchill took the opposite position. 'Surely we cd. sell the "Royal Sovereigns" at £100,000 apiece, and buy airships with the money. There is no reason why the Turkish Naval Mission should not continue.'[29] The Board decision, communicated to Limpus on 3 April 1913, was that the Admiralty was prepared, once peace had been signed, to sell two 'Royal Sovereigns' to the Turks, probably for a price less than he had suggested, but that it would be impossible to spare any ship of a more recent class. That was the end of the matter, so far as Admiralty records show. Mahmoud Chevket Pasha, the Grand Vizier, with whom Limpus had '*just* got into really confidential relations', was removed early in June 1913, and that may explain something.

It is against this background of the improving naval position of the Triple Alliance in the Mediterranean that we must consider the development of tighter Anglo-French naval relations in this

---

[29] Limpus to Churchill, 12 Mar. 1913, and Battenberg and Churchill minutes, 27, 28 Mar.; Admiralty MSS.

period. Another factor in the picture was the renaissance of the French Navy since 1909. It had begun with the appointment of the vigorous Vice-Admiral Boué de Lapeyrère as Minister of Marine and virtual naval dictator (1909–11). By 1911–12 there was evidence in nearly every department that the period of stagnation, suspense, and unrest was at an end. The dockyards had been set in order, the period of construction much reduced, and a building programme put in hand which would make the French Navy again a formidable force.

During the spring of 1912 French naval authorities pressed for a renewal of the conversations, dormant since Agadir, regarding naval co-operation in the event of war. As matters stood, there was still no understanding on the respective roles of the two navies should they find themselves engaged against a common enemy. There was no definite British response until 17 July. Churchill then informed the French Naval Attaché, the Comte de Saint-Seine,

we were now prepared to bring the arrangement for joint action made last autumn up to date. He must clearly understand that no discussion between naval or military experts could be held to affect in any way the full freedom of action possessed by both countries; that the basis was purely hypothetical, and that nothing arising out of such conversations or arrangements could influence political decisions. On such matters the Foreign Office alone would express the views of H.M.G. The Comte de St. Seine said that he perfectly understood this, and entirely agreed with it. It was arranged that he should meet the 1st Sea Lord next week to deal with the various technical questions involved.

I then told him the arrangements we proposed for the Meditn. and explained that these were arrangements made in our own interests, and adequate in our opinion to the full protection of British possessions and trade in the Meditn. . . . I told him . . . I thought that France wd. be wise to aim at a standard of strength in the Meditn. equal to that of Austria and Italy combined . . . In reply he said that that was the standard they had set before themselves; that they had already decided [June] to move their six remaining [pre-dreadnought] battleships from Brest into the Meditn. to form a 3rd squadron there, leaving their Northern and Atlantic Coasts solely to the protection of their torpedo flotillas . . .[30]

In September the Brest squadron was moved to Toulon to join

[30] Churchill's memorandum for Asquith and Grey, 17 July 1912; *British Documents*, x (Pt. 2). 600–1.

the twelve pre-dreadnoughts and six armoured cruisers of the Mediterranean Fleet. The new French dreadnoughts would be sent to the Mediterranean as completed. The French, facing the possibility of dealing with the combined Austrian and Italian fleets, were, then, willing to concentrate their whole battle fleet in the Mediterranean, and, in conjunction with such naval forces as Britain could maintain in the Mediterranean, to safeguard British interests in those waters. This involved exposing their Atlantic and Channel coasts to attack, but it was anticipated that the British Fleet would fill the vacuum. The decision was sound from every point of view. It was clearly better for France to be unassailable in the Mediterranean than to be weak in both the Atlantic and the Mediterranean. The Brest squadron, no match for the High Seas Fleet, could give a good account of itself against the Austrian and Italian pre-dreadnoughts. The first and paramount naval interest of France in a Franco-Russian war against the Triple Alliance would be to guard her maritime communications with her North African possessions. Were Britain allied to France, the French naval concentration in the Mediterranean would make still more strategical sense, as the British Fleet would in that case automatically safeguard all French maritime interests in the Channel and Atlantic.

There was speculation in many quarters as to the bearings of the new French naval disposition on the Anglo-French relationship. Almost all press comment in France took the concentration of the French Fleet in the Mediterranean to be proof positive of a naval agreement between England, France, and Russia, with the three fleets having mapped out their mutual obligations. This line of thought, or wishful thinking, disturbed Liberal press opinion in England, which took the attitude that the agreement, were it a fact, could not be reconciled with the rights of Parliament —it had been entered into without the authority of Parliament— and it would leave little hope of the rivalry between Great Britain and Germany ever ending. Moreover, it was certain that England could not be engaged in a war with the Triple Alliance without France and Russia also becoming involved. Conservative press opinion was critical from a different point of view. The notion of relying on French naval aid in the Mediterranean was 'absolutely repugnant to the mass of Englishmen' (*Daily Express*) and 'marked the limits of what a self-respecting people should endure' (*Globe*).

We know that closer naval and political links were the thing most dreaded by Churchill and the Cabinet. They were not happy over the appearance of dependence upon the French Fleet until a British dreadnought battle squadron had been developed in the Mediterranean. Churchill was anxious about the 'moral claims which France could make upon Great Britain if attacked by Germany . . . Indeed my anxiety was aroused to try to prevent this necessary recall of our ships from tying us up too tightly with France and depriving us of that liberty of choice on which our power to stop a war might well depend.'[31] In August 1912, when the Cabinet approved naval conversations with the French (informal conversations between the First Sea Lord and the French Naval Attaché had already begun), Churchill raised the question of British freedom of choice:

The point I am anxious to safeguard is our freedom of choice if the occasion arises, and consequent power to influence French policy beforehand. That freedom will be sensibly impaired if the French can say that they have denuded their Atlantic seaboard, and concentrated in the Mediterranean on the faith of naval arrangements made with us. This will not be true. If we did not exist, the French could not make better dispositions than at present. They are not strong enough to face Germany alone, still less to maintain themselves in two theatres. They therefore rightly concentrate their Navy in the Mediterranean where it can be safe and superior and can assure their African communications. Neither is it true that we are relying on France to maintain our position in the Mediterranean. . . . If France did not exist, we should make no other disposition of our forces.[32]

As Churchill had anticipated, the French raised objections when they received from the Admiralty (24 July) a draft of a proposed naval convention.[33] The first clause stated that the agreement 'relates solely to a contingency in which Great Britain and France were to be allies in a war, and does not affect the political freedom of either Government as to embarking on such a war.' The second article made it plain that the English and French naval dispositions had been made 'independently because they are the best which the separate interest of each country suggests,

[31] *The World Crisis*, i. 112.
[32] Minute of 23 Aug. 1912 for Asquith and Grey; *ibid.*, pp. 112–13.
[33] The draft, signed by the Chief of the War Staff, Troubridge, and dated 23 July, is in *British Documents*, x (Pt. 2). 602.

having regard to all the circumstances and probabilities; and they do not arise from any naval agreement or convention.' Then followed the broad lines of naval co-operation in the event of the two powers being allies in war: 'British objective. Protection of Anglo-French interests in Eastern Basin of the Mediterranean, i.e. East of Malta', and the 'French objective' was declared to be the 'protection of Anglo-French interests in Western Basin of the Mediterranean i.e. West of Malta.' 'Combined action if possible for the purposes of general engagement.' The combined patrol of the Straits of Dover was outlined. Cambon at once raised the point that if England did not take part in the war, the French northern and western coasts would be completely exposed. 'In short the engagement to be taken was really unilateral—France was to move practically all her naval force to the Mediterranean and leave her other coasts unprotected, and England was free to aid France or not as she liked. . .'[34] Poincaré, the French Prime Minister, complained that 'to begin a Military or Naval Convention by saying that it means nothing so far as the Governments are concerned is superfluous and quite out of place in such a Convention. If the Entente does not mean that England will come to the aid of France in the event of Germany attacking the French ports its value is not great . . .'[35]

The Asquith Government recognized the difficulty, yet it adamantly refused to allow the naval arrangements to tie its hands in any political sense. It was eventually agreed, in a famous exchange of notes between Grey and Cambon, 22–23 November, that the discussions between the military and naval experts of the two nations did not constitute 'an engagement that commits either Government to action in a contingency that has not arisen and may never arise'. But it was added (this was Cambon's suggestion) that 'if either Government had grave reason to expect an unprovoked attack by a third Power, or something that threatened the general peace, it should immediately discuss with the other, whether both Governments should act together to prevent aggression and to preserve peace, and if so what measures they would be prepared to take in common. If these measures involved action, the plans of the General Staffs would at once be taken into

---

[34] Nicolson to Grey, 24 July 1912, reporting a conversation with Cambon that day; *ibid.*, p. 603.

[35] As reported by Bertie to Grey, 30 July 1912; *ibid.*, p. 607.

consideration, and the Governments would then decide what effect should be given to them.'[36] 'This,' said Churchill later, 'was the best we could do for ourselves and for them.'

The naval conversations led to an agreement on 10 February 1913. It consisted of three documents laying the foundations of naval co-operation in the Mediterranean, the western Channel, and the Straits of Dover. Concurrently a similar co-operation was provided for in the Far East. These were technical arrangements (including the preparation of a joint book of signals) which did not imply alliance in time of war. This was made clear in such phrases as 'in the event of a war in which Great Britain and France are allied against the Triple Alliance', and 'in the event of being allied with the French Government in a war with Germany'.[37] The sole purpose of the technical naval (and military) arrangements, at least from the British point of view, was to give immediate efficacy to a British intervention, *should* Britain decide to enter a war in which France was involved.

To the end the Admiralty tried to keep its hands free. It was, in the correct evaluation of the German Naval Attaché, 'averse to a *tight* agreement'. In January 1914 the First Sea Lord rejected a French proposal that the joint signal books which had been worked out by the two Admiralties in 1912–13 should be put into use, on the ground that 'our Government have not authorised the Admiralty to do more than prepare for an alliance between the two countries, and that it is considered the actual use or practice with our joint signal books would go beyond that stage of preparation, and is therefore inadmissible'.[38] However, Jackson confirmed (31 January) Churchill's verbal concurrence as to the exchange of intelligence about the Austrian and Italian Fleets which had been proposed by the French. The loose relations between the two Admiralties will help explain the initial phase of the *Goeben* fiasco in August 1914.

The unwillingness of the Government and Admiralty to incur any obligations to France did not have the hoped-for effect. The Grey–Cambon formulae (which, incidentally, became known to the German Government in March 1913) in theory left the British Government with its hands free. Asquith gave a specific pledge in

[36] *Ibid.*, pp. 614–15.
[37] *Ibid.*, pp. 671–3.
[38] Jackson (Chief of the War Staff) to Saint-Seine, 29 Jan. 1914; Admiralty MSS.

the Commons (10 March 1913) that there was no military engagement to France. But the General Staff had created a different impression with the French General Staff, and Cambon angrily remarked to J. A. Spender on the day after the Prime Minister gave his answer, 'La question était maladroite et la réponse était inexacte.'[39] Asquith later admitted: 'There were . . . neither naval nor military "compacts". But France undoubtedly felt that she could calculate in such a contingency upon our vetoing any attack by sea upon her northern and western coasts, which were practically denuded of naval protection by her concentration in the Mediterranean. And that is what, in the event, actually happened.'[40] Nicolson confessed that the Government had in fact committed itself to a guarantee which would involve England either in a breach of faith or a war with Germany. Esher, too, believed at the time that Britain was honour-bound by the commitments of the General Staff. 'Are you going to let Cherbourg and Brest be bombarded?' Cambon asked Grey on 1 August 1914, 'when it is by your advice and with your consent, and to serve your interests as well as our own, that we have concentrated all our ships far away?' Sir Eyre Crowe used the 'moral bond' implied by the distribution of the two navies as an argument for going to war (31 July 1914). Grey was only technically correct when, in informing the House of Commons for the first time of the military and naval arrangements with France, 31 July 1914, he explained that the notes did not bind England to enter the war.

The Russians had been less successful than their French allies in starting naval conversations. On 24 September 1912 the Russian Foreign Minister, Sazonov, on a visit to England, sounded Grey out on an Anglo-Russian naval convention. He received no encouragement. In 1914 the Russians tried again. On 3 April the Tsar suggested a defensive alliance between Russia and England, and when the British Ambassador said it was then impracticable, the Tsar proposed a naval arrangement, similar to the Anglo-French one, that would provide for the co-operation of the two fleets in war. The Russians pressed their case for naval conversations through the French. Grey could see 'little if any strategic necessity or value in the suggestion. To my lay mind it seemed that, in a war against Germany, the Russian Fleet would not get

---

[39] Spender to Fisher, 25 Jan. 1914; Lennoxlove MSS.
[40] Asquith, *The Genesis of the War*, p. 83.

out of the Baltic and the British Fleet would not get into it; but the difficulty of refusing was obvious. To refuse would offend Russia by giving her the impression that she was not treated on equal terms with France . . .'[41] The British lack of interest in naval conversations also makes sense in view of the condition of the Tsar's Fleet. Although a five-year programme of battleship construction had been voted by the Duma in June 1912, the British Naval Attaché noted the obvious weakness in the new naval order in Russia. The German Attaché, 'equally with myself, has recognised the fundamental mistake of the Russian Admiralty in devoting its energy and money principally to increase of purely material strength rather than to the far more urgent problem of building up a system of honest administration and the creation of a well-trained, capable, well-paid, and contented personnel. Germany's older type battleships, together, say, with her four earlier "Nassau" class Dreadnoughts, will amply suffice to mask any strength by sea that this country is likely to possess before the year 1918.'[42] It was, nevertheless, important 'to reassure Russia and keep her loyal', and in mid-May, on the understanding that Britain kept her hands free in a Continental war, the Cabinet consented to naval conversations.

In May and June there were persistent rumours of a naval arrangement with Russia. The Liberal press was uneasy, and there were sharp comments in the German press. In reply to questions in the House of Commons as to whether an Anglo-Russian naval agreement had been entered into recently, or whether any negotiations with a view to a naval agreement had taken place recently or were now pending, Grey was forced to state (11 June) that 'no such negotiations are in progress, and none are likely to be entered upon, as far as I can judge.' The statement was, strictly speaking, true, but evasive. It did not answer the pointed Parliamentary questions, as Grey admitted in his autobiography. 'It was the only occasion,' G. P. Gooch has commented, 'on which he deliberately misled his countrymen.' Grey's declaration came as 'a great relief' to Jagow, the German Foreign Minister.

[41] Viscount Grey of Fallodon, *Twenty-Five Years, 1892–1916* (London, 1925, 2 vols.), i. 284–5.
[42] Commander H. G. Grenfell to Sir George Buchanan (the Ambassador), 19 Mar. 1914; *British Documents*, x (Pt. 2). 772.

The facts are that, whereas the Russians were eager to push on with the conversations, the English were in no haste to proceed. Apart from the fear of arousing the Germans, neither Grey nor the Admiralty saw any great advantages as likely to accrue. Battenberg suggested on 6 June that the conversations be held up until he visited Russia in August. The Tsar told the British Ambassador (24 June) that preliminary conversations should begin at once, with Prince Louis giving them the finishing touches during his visit. Russian pressure had its effect on Grey, who was chiefly responsible for the delay. Realizing how badly Russia wanted the discussions to begin, and hoping that her attitude regarding Tibetan and Persian questions would be influenced favourably, he apparently was ready, early in July, to allow matters to proceed. Churchill reported on 7 July that one conversation had taken place (presumably with the Russian Naval Attaché) and that another would occur soon, but that substantial progress was not possible till conversations 'between equals' took place. There had been no further progress when the war broke out.

4. THE 1913 AND 1914 ESTIMATES

On 6, 7 February 1913 Tirpitz made statements before the Reichstag Budget Committee announcing his readiness to accept the 16–10 standard (that is, a British predominance of 60 per cent) in dreadnoughts referred to in Churchill's speech of 18 March 1912 as Britain's irreducible minimum. More exactly, Tirpitz proposed a ratio of eight battle squadrons to five battle squadrons. This intimation that Germany would be content not to press the naval competition beyond the relative standard arrived at in the year 1912 had a mixed reception in England. Complications were seen in precisely defining what the ratio meant, the extent to which the Dominion and Colonial ships should enter in, the method of reckoning the units, etc. Nevertheless, the Liberal press treated Tirpitz's statements as a friendly assurance that should be followed up by Great Britain. Conservative journals regarded as impracticable the idea that the strength of the Navy could be regulated by agreement with any other power, the more so as the German Navy was only one of the factors to be taken into account; the naval activity of Italy and Austria was a new fact requiring attention. There is no record of the Admiralty reaction to Tirpitz's proposal, but E. L. Woodward's analysis is probably about the way it was viewed at Whitehall:

> Tirpitz's proposal was neither a great concession nor a fair description of the standard which the British Admiralty were taking as the basis of their policy. Mr. Churchill made two important qualifications when he suggested a superiority of 60 per cent. in Dreadnoughts. He pointed out that a margin of 60 per cent. would be sufficient only during the lifetime of the most recent pre-Dreadnought battleships. He also said that the standard of 60 per cent. superiority was intended only to meet the German programme before the passing of the supplementary law of 1912. If the German programme were increased, Great Britain would build two ships for every one ship laid down in Germany under the terms of a supplementary law.
>
> The supplementary law had been passed; Germany was building more ships, and keeping a larger number of ships in full commission. Tirpitz's suggestion therefore, so far from being a friendly acceptance of a British proposal, was an attempt, very cleverly made, to persuade Great Britain to lower the margin which the Admiralty had announced as necessary for British security. Tirpitz himself has explained in his memoirs that he made his proposal in terms of squadrons, because he knew that Great Britain could not easily increase her programme of construction by a whole squadron. . . . The proposal was made at a time when the German Admiralty realized that the plans for increasing the army would block any naval increase for a year.[43]

Nothing came of the German advance, since Grey did not rise to the bait. It was his belief that 'what Tirpitz said does not amount to much, and the reason for his saying it is not the love of our beautiful eyes, but the extra fifty millions required for increasing the German Army'. That is, it was to Germany's advantage to mark time in the naval competition. Also, he had no desire to enter upon a discussion of a 16:10 ratio, 'because we never intended Colonial ships to be included in that, and we do not wish to enter into explanations'.[44]

The decks were cleared for the 1913–14 estimates, which were issued on 13 March. They provided for five dreadnoughts, eight light cruisers, sixteen destroyers, and an unspecified number of submarines. The total estimates were £46,309,000, as against the 1912–13 estimates (including the supplementary estimate) of £45,075,000, or an increase of £1,233,900. Their reception by the

[43] Woodward, *Great Britain and the German Navy* (London, 1935), p. 406.
[44] Grey to Goschen, 5 Mar. 1913; *British Documents*, x (Pt. 2). 687–8.

press was on familiar lines. The Liberal organs greeted the estimates with regret and resignation. The navalist press reaction ranged from the *Daily Express's* verdict of 'They are not so good that they might not be better, nor so bad that they might not be worse', to the *Pall Mall Gazette's* appraisal, ' "Jam yesterday; jam tomorrow; never jam today". The Red Queen's interpretation of her promise to Alice of "jam every other day" is exactly applicable to Mr. Churchill's Navy Estimates.' It was the general feeling that the estimates should have included six, not five, battleships, and that the sum taken for three of the five big ships was too small, signifying that they could not be begun that year.

Churchill's speech in the Commons explaining the estimates, 26 March, branded the race in armaments as sheer stupidity and futility, and renewed his offer of a 'naval holiday'. The proposal was that all the powers should delay the commencement of any fresh building, at least in capital ships, for twelve months. Millions would be saved by Britain and Germany, while their relative strength would be absolutely unchanged. Churchill's other paramount proposal was for a mobile 'Imperial Squadron' based on Gibraltar and ready to operate at any threatened point at home or abroad. It would consist of the battle cruiser *New Zealand*, the dreadnought *Malaya*, and the three Canadian dreadnoughts, if voted. Little more was heard of this project. In his Parliamentary speech of 31 March the First Lord claimed that he was maintaining the 60 per cent standard of capital ship superiority which he had announced in March 1912, with a sufficient margin to meet requirements in more distant waters: 38–21 in March 1915, or five above 60 per cent; 44–23 in March 1916, or eight above 60 per cent. But a 50 per cent superiority in dreadnoughts was an adequate strength to keep in home waters. This was the first public announcement of this standard.[45] That would leave sufficient ships available for 'the whole world service'. After the spring of 1916 the margin for the whole world service of the Empire would slip to a dangerous low without Canadian help.

The Conservative-navalist opposition inside and outside Parliament charged that, to get his 60 per cent superiority in capital ships, the First Lord had to draw on the three Dominion ships, which he had in the previous March promised to count as

---

[45] The Opposition, according to *The Times* (but not *Hansard*), cheered the standard.

additional, and the two 'Lord Nelsons', which no self-respecting naval expert would classify as dreadnoughts. The naval holiday proposal was condemned out of hand either as 'utopian', or because it did not comport with the dignity of the Empire to renew an offer which had been rebuffed. Churchill's offer was received with incredulity and scorn in Germany. A naval holiday would interfere with the steady development of the German Navy, would lead to unemployment in the German yards, etc. The Naval Attaché, Captain Müller, shared the common Conservative belief that the proposal had been advanced as a sop to the Radicals.

The Admiralty's reaction to the 'grave' situation created by the Canadian Senate's rejection of Borden's proposal was to announce on 5 June the acceleration of the three contract ships of the 1913–14 programme. They were to be begun at the earliest possible date instead of the following March, so that they would be ready as soon as the Canadian ships would have been, that is, by the third quarter of 1915. This step was required, the First Lord said, in order that the margin of naval strength necessary for the whole-world protection of the Empire could be adequately maintained in 1915–16. He explained that acceleration was adopted in place of laying down three new ships because the Admiralty had not lost hope that the Canadian Naval Bill would go through. The other disturbing event of the year was the new Italian programme of four super-dreadnoughts, which became an accomplished fact in September. This meant that the strength of the Triple Alliance in dreadnoughts stationed in the Mediterranean would rise to fourteen at the end of 1915. More than ever did the British position in that sea depend on the French.

The worsening position in the Mediterranean was probably among the factors prompting Churchill's speech at Manchester on 18 October. Failing some general agreement as to disarmament, he indicated that the 1914–15 estimates must make heavy demands on the taxpayer. In the hope of allaying the intense competition between the naval powers, he reiterated in the clearest and most explicit form his suggestion to Germany of a 'naval holiday'. The offer was that if Germany would delay for twelve months the commencement of the two dreadnoughts which she was to lay down in 1914, Britain would put off beginning her four projected dreadnoughts for exactly the same period.

The renewal of Churchill's proposal was 'received with almost universal disapproval' in Germany, Goschen reported. It was regarded as interference in Germany's internal affairs, it would be unfavourable to German naval power, etc., and it was argued that Churchill had been influenced by three considerations: English yards were overcrowded, there was a shortage of personnel for the new ships, and the First Lord was trying to appease the Radicals. The last point was also made by Goschen and by many of the First Lord's critics at home, Esher, for instance, assuming that 'Winston was playing to the radical gallery in his recent speech, as it is inconceivable that so clever a fellow should have been silly enough to imagine that he had any chance of obtaining a favourable reply.'[46] The *Morning Post* advised Churchill to follow the tart suggestion of one of his German critics, Count Reventlow, and 'take a holiday from speech-making for a year, at least so far as dealing with the reduction of armaments is concerned'. Only the Liberals would not admit that the naval holiday suggestion was so hopelessly impracticable as so many critics on both sides of the North Sea would have them believe.

No official German reference was made to Churchill's proposal until 4 February 1914, when Tirpitz, in a statement to the Reichstag Budget Committee, threw cold water on it, and Jagow, the Foreign Minister, told Goschen that they were opposed to a naval holiday 'both on the general principle that the idea is Utopian and unworkable', and because 'the interruption for a whole year of Naval construction would throw innumerable men on the pavement . . .'[47] It was 'impracticable', Tirpitz had declared. 'For either the constructions must be postponed for a year, in which case the omissions must be made good in the following year. This would upset our finances, dislocate work in the ship-building yards, and also our military arrangements, i.e. the regular placing of ships in commission on their completion. In addition . . . England's shipbuilding yards are congested with vessels under construction, while our business is slack. . . . We should therefore have to dismiss a large number of workmen and the whole organization of our shipbuilding yards would be upset. If on the other hand it was desired *permanently* to drop the construction of the ships for the holiday year in question, that

[46] Esher to Stamfordham, 26 Oct. 1913; *Esher*, iii. 142.
[47] Goschen to Nicolson, 6 Feb. 1914; *British Documents*, x (Pt. 2). 736.

would mean, since we only undertake the construction of replacing ships, a reduction in our organisation as established by law.'[48] Despite the difficulties, Tripitz and Jagow promised that Germany would carefully examine any concrete proposals from Great Britain based on an 8 : 5 ratio in battle squadrons, each squadron consisting of eight battleships. This brought the conversations to the same dead end that had been reached the preceding March, and for the same reasons.

Long before this futile exchange it was clear that nothing would arrest the naval competition. Churchill, at the Guildhall on 10 November 1913, announced that the next estimates would necessarily show a large increase in view of the prodigious efforts of foreign powers. He repeated with greatly added emphasis the warnings of his Manchester speech that only increased estimates were to be expected from him. Lloyd George called the speech 'a piece of madness. The public will not stand provocative speeches of that sort.' Asquith, too, was 'furious' about the speech, the contents of which he had not known beforehand.

A fresh campaign against 'bloated' navy estimates was now started in the Radical press. 'A more megalomaniac speech [than the Guildhall speech] was never, we think, delivered by any First Lord,' opined the *Nation*. The *Daily Chronicle* asked (12 November), 'When will First Lords and naval experts realize that a financial reserve is one of the most important of all the sinews of war?' Denunciations of Churchill and his 'bombastic' naval programme, and demands for retrenchment, poured out of the Radical press and Radical meetings, that is, from the 'Economaniacs', as they were derisively dubbed by the navalists. Mr. Huth Jackson, an ex-governor of the Bank of England, declared in a speech (10 December) that he was expressing the mind of all the financial interests of the City irrespective of party when he delivered one of the weightiest pronouncements against the madness of armaments made at this time. 'If other countries will not join us in the naval holiday, let us take a holiday ourselves.' A week later, forty Liberal M.P.s (the 'Suicide Club', they were called by the navalists) waited on the Prime Minister to lay before him their concern that an enlargement of the programme already sanctioned by the House of Commons was contemplated. An additional fifty-six M.P.s who sympathized with the objects of the deputation

[48] Enclosure in Goschen to Grey, 11 Feb. 1914; *ibid.*, p. 739.

could not be present. Asquith assured them that he sympathized fully with their anxiety at the growth of naval expenditure, and that the matter was 'receiving earnest and constant attention from the Government'. This was, we shall see, more than a platitude.

The navy estimates, under consideration by the Cabinet at the end of the year, were awaited in the country with unusual anxiety. The Radicals, and not a few navalists, were confused over the requirements of the Navy. It was charged that the Government's naval policy was based upon a system of percentages so bewildering, subject to so many qualifications, and bearing so little apparent relation to the actual requirements of Imperial defence as a whole, that the public had long ago given up trying to understand it. The Radical press could not understand the 'insanity' which reckoned Italy and Austria as Britain's enemies, ignored the jealousy between them, and omitted to balance that combination by counting France and Russia as Britain's friends.

Impressive meetings were held by the Liberal mutineers during January, sponsored by such groups as local Liberal Associations and the Committee for the Reduction of Armaments. Lord Courtney of Penwith, Ramsay MacDonald, and other Radicals and Labourites introduced a new note. They asserted that the secret of British naval expenditure was the pressure of the 'armaments gang' and the 'armour press', which fomented the rivalry in armaments and poisoned the minds of men. The economy drive was intensified in the Liberal press. The *Daily Chronicle* warned (22 January) that the growth of armed forces 'cannot be indefinite; if the burdens of peace continue increasing, a time must come when the risks of war will be preferred to them'. 'The Liberal party demands,' according to the *Daily News* (6 January), 'not that it [British naval expenditure] shall be diminished, but that there shall be no addition to the monstrous expenditure. It takes its stand on Mr. Churchill's formula of 60 per cent over Germany and it asks for the observance of that formula.' Two ships would be enough in the next estimates to maintain that formula, the *Daily News* and the *Nation* insisted.

There was a remarkable change in the navalist attitude towards Churchill (excepting always Maxse's *National Review*). He was now hailed as a sort of patriotic saint, engaged in a terrific fight with the powers of darkness, and as such entitled to the support of the children of the light. *Punch* (14 January) printed an amusing cartoon that described the situation perfectly. The First Lord was shown in a sailor's uniform, a Union Jack in one hand and, on his arm, like a sweetheart, a life-sized scroll labelled 'Navy Estimates', while, behind them, a Tory chorus in the form of ballet dancers sang the popular song, 'You made me love you; I didn't want to do it'!

What the navalists wanted was the retention of the four dreadnoughts as a *minimum* in face of the Little-Navy campaign for two. Six or seven in the new programme would be much more satisfactory, to compensate for the Canadian ships. The Navy League organized a great national campaign, scheduling fifty-six meetings of protest in January and February.

There were rumours in January that the Board had threatened to resign unless the Cabinet accepted the new estimates, and that the Cabinet was split into two opposing camps on the question of the provision to be made for the Fleet in the coming financial year. Despite protestations by members of the Government, including Churchill, that Cabinet unity was complete in the matter of the Navy, the harmony was of the kind described by the unmusical curate as 'all singing together in different keys'. And the country knew it.

Lloyd George had made his views public by an interview published in the *Daily Chronicle* on New Year's Day, 1914. It was a strong appeal to the nations to abate the ever-growing expenditure on armaments, and gave three reasons why the present was a favourable moment: Anglo-German relations were much friendlier than they had been for years, Continental nations were directing their energies more and more to strengthening their armies, and the common sense of the industrial classes was revolting against 'this organised insanity'. He began the interview with a reminder that Lord Randolph Churchill had resigned sooner than assent to 'bloated and profligate' expenditure upon armaments. This was a hint to Lord Randolph's son that he might be forced out of office for the opposite reason. In effect, Lloyd George administered a slap in the face to Winston Churchill and encouraged the Little-Navy Liberals to the point of enthusiasm.

Lloyd George's intervention was regarded by the navalists as a usurpation in public of the functions of the First Lord of the Admiralty and as an act of gross disloyalty to a colleague. A few days after the interview, an attempt was made to interview Churchill in Paris on the subject of Lloyd George's remarks. He was not to be drawn in, but he framed his refusal in terms which constituted a stinging rebuke of the Chancellor's lack of decorum. He made it a rule 'not to give interviews to newspapers on important subjects of this character while they were under the consideration of the Cabinet.' Grey (above all), Samuel, Seely, and other ministers, as well as Churchill, were 'full of maledictions' of Lloyd George on account of his 'heedless interview' (Asquith). Lloyd George's justification was that the interview contained nothing he had not said before. Balfour's private analysis is of interest.

I think this move on L. G.'s part is purely political. I do not mean to say that, as Chancellor of the Exchequer and a taxpayer, he is not seriously alarmed at the growth of expenditure. I have no doubt that he is . . . What I do suppose is that he wants an Election cry which will rally what remains of the old Radical Nonconformist Party, the new semi-Socialist-Radical, and the Labour Party. A campaign against armaments is admirably suited for the purpose. He also, of course, wants the public mind to be, as far as possible, distracted from the question of Ulster, and he perhaps doubts whether his Land Campaign will be sufficient to attain this end. . . . [Also] there may be, and probably are, private and personal ambitions [in the Cabinet] which would be served by pressing these divisions to [the] breaking point over a subject like military and naval retrenchment. . . [49]

The Lloyd George–Churchill public exchange of words was the steam from the boiling cauldron. There had been almost daily arguments in the autumn between the Admiralty and the Treasury, as they failed to reach agreement in preliminary discussions on the 1914–15 estimates. The Churchill–Lloyd George alliance, under a severe strain since the 1912–13 estimates, now collapsed when Churchill presented the 1914–15 estimates to the Cabinet on 15 December 1913. They amounted to £50,700,000, or, roughly, an increase of £3,000,000 over those voted for 1913–14 and an increase on 1911–12 (the last for which McKenna was responsible) of nearly £8,000,000. Churchill defended the large increase during his administration on these grounds: the rise in the cost of materials and in the pay and allowances to seamen; the maintenance of a larger fleet of more costly capital ships; new

[49] Balfour to Selborne, 7 Jan. 1914; Balfour MSS.

services, especially aircraft. These would account for a total increase since 1911–12 of nearly £7,000,000.

The Cabinets of 15, 16, and 17 December were almost exclusively occupied with a consideration of the estimates.[50] Not since 1909 had the estimates been scrutinized so carefully, almost item by item. In the background were the pressing claims upon the Exchequer of education and other social services and the deep concern (a 'scared' feeling, said Hopwood) over the growing unrest of the Radicals and the business world. Sanctioning Churchill's estimates, Lloyd George pointed out, involved a substantial deficit or a resort to an increase in taxation, and the latter was not advisable politically in view of the possible general election in 1914. He and his cohorts (Samuel, Hobhouse, Pease, Runciman, Beauchamp, Simon, McKenna, and Harcourt) accused Churchill of extravagance in his administration of the Navy—he was spending a lot of money on 'unessentials'. (This was also the opinion of J. A. Spender, Fisher, and others outside the Government.) The First Lord's cause was not helped by the fact that he was a great trial, personally, to most of his colleagues.

The Cabinet directed Churchill to reconsider his estimates and to try to make a sizeable reduction. After consultation with the Board, he submitted (17 December) a revised estimate of £49,970,000. He had reduced the provision for oil by £400,000, that for the air service by £200,000, and had made a number of smaller economies. The estimates were still £2½ millions over the 1913–14 expenditure. Attention was now concentrated on the new construction programme and especially the four new capital ships. Lloyd George and his allies (actually, Samuel, the Postmaster-General, took the lead on this issue) strongly urged that the 60 per cent margin during the last quarter of 1916 and the whole of 1917 would be fully maintained if only two of the ships were laid down. Churchill would have none of this nonsense. No decision could be reached and the discussion was adjourned until after the holidays.

The crucial point in January came to be the number of dreadnoughts in the new programme, this being the one place where appreciable savings were possible. Churchill and the Sea Lords were ready to resign on less than four (they had the King with

[50] I have drawn liberally on Asquith's reports (Asquith MSS.) to the King on the Cabinets of 15–17 Dec. 1913 and 27–29 Jan. and 9, 11 Feb. 1914.

them and Asquith was benevolently neutral). Lambert, the Civil Lord, and Macnamara, the Parliamentary and Financial Secretary, Radicals though they were, would probably have joined them. Only Hopwood for certain would not have gone along.

'We continued,' says Churchill, 'to pump out arguments from the Admiralty in a ceaseless stream, dealing with each new point as it was challenged.' These were the main points made by the Admiralty in the fact-filled papers for the Cabinet during December and January which attempted to answer the two crucial questions:[51]

(1) *Was the battleship programme for 1914–15 to be four ships or two?* They were only just maintaining the 60 per cent standard. At that, they had to count the *New Zealand*, against which the Government of New Zealand had protested, and the two 'Lord Nelsons' (until 1917). (The *Malaya* was not included, as a specific pledge had been given by the Colonial Secretary that she was to be additional, nor was the *Australia*, which was not at the Admiralty's disposal.) Only the declared British programmes of 4–5–4–4–4–4 would maintain the 60 per cent standard against the German programmes. To have a 60 per cent preponderance over Germany's thirty-five dreadnoughts in 1920, they required fifty-six, and this meant building sixteen ships in the next four programmes, or four a year. The 50 per cent dreadnought margin in home waters, which meant, in 1915, three squadrons of eight dreadnoughts to Germany's two squadrons, was a minimum. It included the Gibraltar squadron, three-and-a-half days away and another day to coal, and the two 'Nelsons', and allowed for any vessels that might be unavailable through refits or other circumstances such as disablement by a surprise attack. 'If at her selected moment Germany attacked us, the average available margin (including any ships at Gibraltar) might not exceed 5 or 6 Dreadnoughts.' Churchill asserted that the programmes had never been challenged as excessive by his colleagues until the recent Cabinet discussions. 'I claim that my colleagues are equally committed with me to the series . . . and that we are pledged to Parliament to carry them out. . . . The reduction of this programme from 4 to 2 would cause a shock and a scandal throughout this country and throughout the British Empire.'

(2) *Was the Cabinet decision to maintain a one-power standard in the*

[51] The series of papers is among the Asquith MSS.

Mediterranean to stand or be revoked? It was not possible to carry out the Cabinet decision of July 1912 until the Canadian ships or their equivalents were built at the end of 1916 or the beginning of 1917. Until then there could be no British line of battle in the Mediterranean, and even then 'mutually provoked' dreadnought construction by Italy and Austria might mean more delay in reaching the standard and require additional construction. Meanwhile, the force of four battle cruisers and four fast armoured cruisers (also four light cruisers and sixteen destroyers) in the Mediterranean was all that was possible. This was not a one-power standard, but would make Britain a formidable factor for diplomatic purposes, and a decisive reinforcement if joined to the French Navy. If the Germans continued to keep the battle cruiser *Goeben* in the Mediterranean, the *New Zealand* would reinforce the Mediterranean squadron as soon as the *Tiger* joined the 1st Battle Cruiser Squadron at the end of 1914. The arrival of the *Malaya* (autumn of 1915) and the three Canadian ships would enable them, assuming no further Austrian or Italian ships were completed, to form a line of battle in accordance with the Cabinet decision. 'So long as the understanding with France remains unimpaired the delay will not necessarily be injurious.' However, the seven months gained by the acceleration of three of the 1913–14 battleships having expired and the Canadian ships not being begun, it was advisable to accelerate two ships of the 1914–15 programme and, if necessary, one of the 1915–16 programme, in order to safeguard the Mediterranean position.

The closing passages of one of the Admiralty documents, that of 10 January 1914, by Churchill, attempted to move the debate to a higher plane. Three overriding considerations underlay naval policy. First, British diplomacy depended largely for its effectiveness on the strength of the Navy. Second, 'we are not a young people with *an innocent record and*[52] a scanty inheritance. We have engrossed to ourselves, in time when other powerful nations were paralysed by barbarism or internal war, an *altogether disproportionate*[53] share of the wealth and traffic of the world. We have got all we want in territory, and our claim to be left in the unmolested enjoyment of vast and splendid possessions, *mainly acquired by violence, largely maintained by force,* often seems less reasonable to

[52] Passages in my italics are omitted in *The World Crisis,* i. 175–7.
[53] 'Immense' in *ibid.*

others than to us.' In the third place, they were 'now deeply involved in the European situation. We have responsibilities in many quarters. . . . The causes which might lead to a general war have not been removed and often remind us of their presence. . . . The world is arming as it has never armed before . . . . unless our naval strength is solidly, amply and unswervingly maintained, with due and fair regard to the opinions of the professional advisers of the Government, I could not feel that I was doing my duty if I did not warn the country of its danger.'

A Cabinet break-up was a strong probability during January. Churchill had, he said, his 'back against the wall'. Lloyd George confided to a friend (17 January) that 'the Prime Minister must choose between Winston and me'. The Prime Minister 'held his temper and listened.' At one point, around 20 January, Asquith, doubting that 'the thing can be patched up', began to think of dissolving Parliament and running the risk of a general election rather than chance 'a smash-up and resignation'. A sharp exchange of letters between the two main protagonists was prefaced by 'My dear David' and 'My dear Winston'—the two men remained fond of each other personally—but the old co-operation in defence matters was gone and a note of bitterness had crept in. On the 26th, Churchill, having revised his figures *upwards*, bluntly informed Lloyd George that 'the Estimates of 14/15 have been prepared with the strictest economy; for all expenditure incurred or proposed there is full warrant and good reason. . . . I cannot buy a year of office by a bargain under duress about the Estimates of 1915–16. No forecasts beyond the year have ever been made by my predecessors. I have no power, even if I were willing, to bind the Board of Admiralty of 1915 to any exact decision. . . . I am now approaching the end of my resources, and I can only await the decision of my colleagues and of the Prime Minister.'[54] It was Lloyd George's turn to throw up his hands. He replied to Churchill (27 January):

. . . your letter has driven me to despair, and I must now decline further negotiations, leaving the issue to be decided by the Prime Minister and the Cabinet. Your letter warns me—in time—that you can no more be held bound by your latest figures than you were by your original figure of £49,966,000. This intimation completely alters the situation. I now thoroughly appreciate your idea of a bargain: it

[54] Asquith MSS.

is an arrangement which binds the Treasury not even to attempt any further economies in the interest of the taxpayer, whilst it does not in the least impose any obligation on the Admiralty not to incur fresh liabilities. . . . The only certainty about them [Churchill's last proposals] is that the Exchequer would this year have to find 56 millions —supplementaries included—for the Navy, whilst the reductions promised for 15/16 do not bind either the Board of Admiralty or the First Lord. Therein you and your critics agree. I have been repeatedly told that I was being made a fool of; I declined to believe it. Your candour forces me to acknowledge the justice of the taunt. You proposed before Christmas to take 50 millions. As a compromise on that you proposed Friday last to take 4 [3?] millions more this year on condition of coming down 1½ millions next year. Not a sumptuous offer at best. Now you qualify that![55]

Lloyd George reported absolute failure to the Prime Minister the same day. 'I have laboured in vain to effect an arrangement between Churchill and the critics of his Estimates which would save you and the Cabinet the necessity for entering upon an unpleasant and maybe a disastrous controversy. I have utterly failed.'[56] The Prime Minister, with unwearying patience, held on, appealing (28 January) to 'the whole pack not to split at such a time on such a point'. Cabinets of 27, 28, and 29 January led to a shaky agreement on a supplementary estimate for 1913–14 of £2½ millions and the acceptance of Churchill's revised figure for 1914–15 of £52,800,000, including the four capital ships, and £49,500,000 for 1915–16. There were strong protests from Lloyd George and his allies. Their criticism was now directed mainly at the growing cost of maintenance, which had risen 25 per cent in three years. Large economies should be made under that head. Lloyd George pressed especially for a *definite* pledge of a substantial reduction in 1915–16. He expected an adverse balance, on the basis of navy estimates of £52,800,000, of about £9,000,000, which would have to be met by new taxation. He had no hope of getting this from the Commons unless he could assure them that in the following year the bulk of the proceeds would be devoted to education and the relief of local rates. That day, the 29th, possibly during an interval in the discussion, five members of the Cabinet—Beauchamp, Hobhouse, McKenna, Runciman, and

[55] Owen, *Tempestuous Journey*, pp. 257–8.
[56] Asquith MSS.

Simon—expressed their 'deep concern and uneasiness' in a letter to Asquith.

The effect of so enormous an increase in our Naval expenditure upon the German programme and policy is a matter of surmise; but such excuses as may be suggested cannot obscure the main fact—that the total is unprecedented; the increase is unexampled at a time of international calm; and the impression powerfully created that we are leading the way in yet more rapid outlay. . . .

These proposals expose us to Parliamentary attack far more serious than the sporadic efforts of a few Liberal 'economists'. The Labour party will surely be driven to go to any lengths in dissociating itself from such increases; defection by a substantial group on our own benches is likely; Ulstermen who profess that our defeat is the only protection against 'civil war' will hardly resist the temptation offered. . . .

We are not satisfied that the economies suggested (but not guaranteed) for 1915–16 might not, if pursued forthwith with vigour, justify a lower figure for 1914–15. . . . If so welcome a relief may be counted on after twelve months have passed, should not the earnest of it be more prominent now?[57]

The estimates were again exhaustively reviewed, again the Prime Minister warned his colleagues of the disastrous consequences of a split over the estimates, and again the First Lord was asked to have a hard look at the estimates, this time concentrating on the chief heads of the charge for maintenance.

The crisis finally ended on 11 February. Under a compromise formula the estimates were fixed at £51,580,000, and the Government would make an announcement that the 1915–16 total would show a substantial reduction. Churchill thought he could 'practically guarantee' a saving of £2,000,000. The 1914–15 estimates represented an increase of £5¼ millions on the gross estimates for 1913–14, and an increase of £2¾ millions on the final estimates of 1913–14 (£48,809,300), that is, after the introduction of a supplementary estimate for £2½ millions on 25 February, most of which was for contract work in connexion with the acceleration of the three dreadnoughts in 1913. The new-construction programme consisted of four dreadnoughts (two of which were to be accelerated and, if necessary, one ship of the 1915–16 programme, to fill the Canadian gap), four light cruisers, and twelve destroyers. Three other light cruisers and twelve torpedo-boats for harbour

[57] *Ibid.*

defence were cut out of the programme. The Operations Division of the War Staff had calculated that twelve new light cruisers were required, but Churchill had declined to press for more than four.

Churchill felt that he had got the substance of the expansion he held to be necessary. 'Winston is in high spirits,' noted Riddell, 'and well he may be.' The victory was a bit on the Pyrrhic side, as the dearth of light cruisers to neutralize the raiding German cruisers was proven in the early months of the war. Nor was the provision for oil all that it might have been, as the reduction in oil reserves promised by the First Lord in December 1913 remained in the final estimates.[58]

Churchill's speech in the Commons introducing the estimates (17 March) was described by the *Daily Telegraph* as 'the longest [two-and-a-half hours], and perhaps also the most weighty and eloquent, speech to which the House of Commons has listened from a First Lord of the Admiralty during the present generation.' The speech, though marked by Churchill's usual qualities of brilliant lucidity and strong argument, had a note of apology. He occupied half his time in explaining to the malcontents of his own side that the estimates could not possibly be smaller, and the other half in explaining to the Opposition why they should not be made bigger. These were the most important points he made: he aimed to complete eight battle squadrons in home waters (not including battle cruisers) by the time Germany had five, or sixty-five battleships to her forty-one. He also counted, when the British organization was completed, on thirty-three battleships in full commission to Germany's twenty-five, with sixteen battleships in reserve for each power. A battle squadron of six dreadnoughts and the two 'Lord Nelsons' would be based on Malta by the end of 1915, a substitute for the four battle cruisers then in the Mediterranean.

The Opposition, in press and Parliament, found considerable cause for dissatisfaction. Typical was the estimate of *The Times* (18 March):

Mr. Churchill's statement . . . will be received with disappointment by all except politicians on his own side who desire a reduction of British naval strength. . . . These three ships [the Canadian dreadnoughts, which were to make possible a strong battle squadron in the Mediterranean by the end of 1915] have for the present failed us. The

[58] See above, p. 271.

gap is patent. How is it to be filled? Whence are the Mediterranean Dreadnoughts to be obtained? The acceleration of three ships last year has afforded temporary relief, but the benefit of the acceleration will have disappeared by next year. What does Mr. Churchill propose to do? He tells us the building is to be accelerated of two ships of the new programme, and, if necessary, of one ship of next year's programme. And then, by some light process of arithmetic which we do not profess to follow, together with a vague and passing reference to more hopeful indications from Canada, the subject is brushed aside.

While, on the other side, the *Daily Chronicle*, the *Westminster Gazette*, and the *Manchester Guardian* applauded Churchill (the last-named with reservations), the *Nation* and *Daily News* were bitter. The latter (19 March) accepted the Labourite Snowden's indictment, which 'went to the whole root of Mr. Churchill's policy—absence of a fixed standard; the folly of speculating heavily in Dreadnoughts at a time when the best opinion is coming round to the view that the Dreadnought cannot live with the submarine; the treason of Liberal Ministers to the Liberal maxim of retrenchment; the waste in nine years of 360 millions on the Navy, one-half of which sum would have swept away many of our social diseases; the power and profits of the armament firms.' The Irish crisis intervened to distract the country from naval affairs during the spring.

The Churchill period was noteworthy for more than naval reforms, big dreadnought programmes, and futile negotiations with Germany. There were important developments in naval strategy in these years.

XII

Evolution of Pre-war Strategy and Tactics

More thought should have been given to the future of submarines and aircraft, but the operational planner is always limited by the progress of the inventor and designer, and he at once becomes unpractical if he jumps too far ahead of them. The British, like many others, lack the imagination for really effective forethought, but this almost requires a gift of prophecy. The British make up for this lack by the possession of many other sterling qualities, and they learn very quickly in the hard school of experience.

ADMIRAL THE HON. SIR REGINALD PLUNKETT-ERNLE-ERLE-DRAX
to the author in 1959.

We had competent administrators, brilliant experts of every description, un-equalled navigators, good disciplinarians, fine sea-officers, brave and devoted hearts: but at the outset of the conflict we had more captains of ships than captains of war.

CHURCHILL, *The World Crisis.*

I. THE REVOLUTION IN *MATÉRIEL*

ALTHOUGH the submarine, aircraft, the torpedo, and the mine all antedated World War I, few students of naval warfare appreciated the immense possibilities for attack latent in these new unproved weapons.

Fisher was impressed with the use of mines in the Japanese war. They had sent eighteen warships, including one Russian and two Japanese battleships, to the bottom, and had damaged many warships. However, he seems to have believed that submarines allowed the mine to be dispensed with. Down to 1914 mines were not regarded in the Navy as formidable weapons whether for offence or defence. They were looked upon as rather expensive luxuries in an unimportant branch of naval warfare. When the War Staff in 1913 drew up a scheme for mining the Heligoland Bight and Straits of Dover, which was rather similar in its main features to the scheme adopted late in the war, Churchill alone was interested in the scheme—until he got the figure for the cost of

50,000 mines. When war came, Britain had no mining policy and consequently very few mines. In the appreciation and use of the mine Germany and Russia were far ahead of England at the beginning of the war.

The locomotive torpedo first appeared at sea in the 1870's, but down through the Russo-Japanese War they had not lived up to their early promise, whether carried in a torpedo-boat. torpedo gunboat, or destroyer. The experts had not been impressed with the results achieved in 1904–5. The Japanese fired about 370 torpedoes and scored only seventeen hits, or about 4 per cent. The successful torpedo-boat attack at the outset of hostilities, which had disabled one Russian battleship and two cruisers lying off Port Arthur, was discounted because the Russian Fleet was lying at anchor in exposed waters outside the base. The torpedo flotilla did nothing to decide the issue of any of the sea battles. Thus, its contribution to the decisive naval Battle of Tsushima consisted in the sinking of the already heavily damaged Russian flagship and, after the battle was virtually over, of three other Russian ships. The major engagements were essentially gunnery duels, and it was the heavy gun which emerged with greatly increased prestige from the war. From that time, however, the advance in the torpedo, in range, speed, accuracy, and power, was most striking, as was the simultaneous development of its principal carriers, the destroyer and the submarine. During the Russo-Japanese War the torpedo attained its principal efficacy at ranges of not more than 4,000 to 4,500 yards; by 1914 it had an extreme range of 11,000 yards. In 1905, torpedoes had a speed of 19 knots if set for 4,000 yards, or as much as 33 knots at 1,000 yards; in 1914, up to 45 knots if set for 7,000 yards. The weapon evolved from 14 inches to 21 inches in diameter in this period. The gyroscope, which was introduced in the 1890's, helped give the torpedo an uncanny accuracy by enabling it to maintain its pre-set course.

Whereas the flotilla in 1905 consisted of torpedo-boats and destroyers, whose restricted endurance and inferior speed sharply limited their usefulness to a fleet, the substantial increase thereafter in the size, sea-keeping capacity, and speed in the torpedo craft considerably enhanced their battle value. No more torpedo-boats were built for the Navy after 1909. The 'M' class of destroyers building in 1914 were of 1,200 tons, 34 knots, and armed with four 21-inch torpedo tubes and three 4-inch guns, as compared with the first British destroyers, in the 1890's, of 220 tons, steaming at 27 knots, and armed with one 12-pounder and three 6-pounders, and two torpedo tubes. In 1911 one expert did not see how a hostile destroyer, 6,000 yards away from the Home Fleet lying at anchor, could fail to bag half a dozen ships in a single 'bouquet' of torpedoes.[1] The reports from the flag officers in command of the destroyer flotillas, after the 1910 operations of the combined fleets in the North Sea, brought out that 'in misty weather an attack by destroyers in a fleet action is not only possible, but unless recognized and means are taken to defeat it, such an attack would probably succeed. Personally, I fully concur with this opinion . . .'[2]

The power of the torpedo spurred the evolution of the sea-going submarine. The submarine had two great advantages over the torpedo-boat and the destroyer. Owing to its power of submersion it could make its approach in daytime as well as after dark, and, because it could take shelter under water, it was less vulnerable. The submarine had come into being as a practical weapon of war between 1898 and 1905. The early ones were primitive, thoroughly unreliable craft, 60-odd feet long, with a beam of 11 or 12 feet, and capable of only 8 to 9 knots on the surface through a single 4-cylinder petrol engine. The fumes were dangerous to the crew, being highly explosive and toxic. In 1914 the latest British submarines (the 'E' class) were 178 feet long, with a surface speed of $15\frac{1}{2}$ knots and a submerged speed of $9\frac{1}{2}$ knots.

Down to 1914 the Fleet, generally speaking, regarded submarines as merely 'local defence vessels whose officers and men, dressed like North Sea fishermen, were almost a service apart.' Beresford and others wrote officially that submarines were 'playthings', and Fisher was vilified for spending a million sterling on them annually while he was First Sea Lord. No great enthusiasm for these tiny craft is to be discerned in the service journals of the period. They were 'the weapon of the weaker power'; they could not work with the battle fleet because they could not go to sea in rough weather; they were slower than surface ships, particularly when submerged; they had not accomplished much during manœuvres (but see below); they did not possess the immunity from attack that was claimed for them (they stood a good chance

---

[1] Ottley to Esher, 8 Oct. 1911; Esher MSS.
[2] 'Use of Destroyers in Fleet Actions', a report by the C.-in-C., Home Fleet (May), to the Admiralty, 17 May 1910; May MSS.

of being caught on the surface at night or in poor light and rammed or destroyed by gunfire before they could dive); their range was very limited—an underwater run of about a hundred miles was the limit of the best submarines in 1914, although the latest boats carried fuel enough to take them about 2,000 miles on the surface. Service opinion explains why the construction of submarines remained limited, especially of overseas boats. At the outbreak of war, Germany had more overseas submarines built, building, and projected than the Royal Navy.

A War Staff evaluation of the results of the 1912 manœuvres saw the great development of the submarine as the outstanding lesson, and submitted that they ought not to expect the German submarines to remain content with the role of coast defenders, and that in a war with England the enemy submarines might prove a serious menace to the movements of the Fleet in the North Sea. Churchill was impressed, but the Board was not. It was too novel an idea. With the exception of the First Sea Lord, who sat on the fence, they all scoffed at such heresy and claimed that the Staff was raising scares.

On the other hand, among the more junior officers there were a number who had a deep faith in the new craft as offensive weapons, a confidence shared by very few senior officers. Captain Roger Keyes, Inspecting Captain of Submarines, 1910–13, and then Commodore in charge of submarines, was one of those with an unbounded belief in submarines. The experience of the last pre-war manœuvres proved to the submarine enthusiasts that the British submarine had greater possibilities than harbour defence, and that in wartime nothing could stand against it. In the 1910 manœuvres the one submarine taking part (first of the 'D' class) was able, when over 500 miles from her base, to torpedo two cruisers as they left port. Captain S. S. Hall, Keyes's predecessor as Inspecting Captain, reported these impressions of the 1913 manœuvres based on information he gathered from submarine officers, including Keyes:

> The general feeling is without doubt one of general satisfaction with the vessels and of enthusiasm for the handling of the submarines particularly of the 'D' and 'E' classes. The submarine service seem to be satisfied that during the short time the manœuvres lasted they would have accounted for about 40% of the large vessels employed! I understand that the *claims* amounted to this, but they say that the rules were

a very great handicap, and that the 'overwhelming seniority' factor was always present when a submarine claimed a surface ship. . . . There was a rule which compelled a submarine to come to the surface and remain there for half an hour after making a claim, after which she could not attack any vessel within 3 miles. This was a source of much annoyance to submarines and was unreal. For example, if they dived at a lot of ships and found themselves close to a small one, they would have to let her go by, otherwise they could not attack the big ones. In this way there would have been many more casualties among fleet look outs in the real thing.[3]

Fisher was among the first to foresee the offensive possibilities of the submarine. He had written in 1904: 'I don't think it is even *faintly* realized—*the immense impending revolution which the submarines will effect as offensive weapons of war.*'[4] It was, he kept repeating, 'the battleship of the future'. That submarines could destroy dreadnoughts and were therefore a formidable danger to the battle fleet, especially when at sea, was a not uncommon belief by 1914, inside and outside the service. Balfour in 1910 was not at all sure how they were 'going to employ a battle fleet at all when the submarine movement is fully developed', and in 1913 he was 'more than ever convinced that the days of the dreadnought are numbered.'[5] Repington, in *Blackwood's* of June 1910, predicted there would be no place for any great ships in the North Sea when Germany's submarine flotilla was fairly complete. Esher thought that the power of the battleship was over-estimated. He likened it to 'the old knight in armour after the discovery of powder', the powder in this instance being represented by the submarine.[6] A. K. Wilson had in 1902 described the submarine as 'underhand, unfair, and damned unEnglish', and wanted the crews of captured enemy submarines in war to be hanged as pirates. In 1907 he held it would be suicidal to expose the armoured units of the Fleet to a treacherous torpedo attack (it was the general naval opinion that Germany would try to redress the balance of strength by endeavouring to reach the British battle fleets with their torpedo craft) by stationing them before the outbreak of war within striking distance of the destroyers and submarines of the enemy. 'One Fleet on West Coast of Scotland and the other at

[3] Hall to Fisher, n.d.; Lennoxlove MSS.
[4] 20 Apr. 1904; *Fear God and Dread Nought*, i. 309.
[5] Balfour to Fisher, 25 Oct. 1910, 12 Sept. 1913; Lennoxlove MSS.
[6] Esher to Knollys, 23 July 1912; Windsor MSS.

Portland is quite near enough for any practical purpose. Destroyers alone need be in the North Sea.'[7] Fisher endorsed this 'great principle'. On the outbreak of war the East Coast and the North Sea should swarm only with British destroyers and submarines backed by their supporting cruisers, and with the armoured ships well out of range of enemy destroyers and submarines.[8] The question of keeping the heavy ships out of the North Sea altogether, until 'the small-craft menace' (meaning essentially the submarines) had been reduced, was frequently discussed at the Admiralty in the last pre-war years, although for reasons already indicated no decision was reached.

The future of the submarine was thoroughly aired in the press on the eve of the war. On 5 June 1914 *The Times* published a long letter from Percy Scott in which he categorically declared, as his main thesis, that the day of the battleship was over. 'Submarines and aeroplanes have entirely revolutionized naval warfare; no fleet can hide itself from the aeroplane eye, and the submarine can deliver a deadly attack even in broad daylight.' He could see no use for battleships. '. . . as the motor-vehicle has driven the horse from the road, so has the submarine driven the battleship from the sea.' His fleet of the future would be based on large numbers of submarines and aircraft. The critics, and they were many, fell on Scott. They defended the battleship and charged that Scott had grossly exaggerated the value of the submarine. Among his critics were six distinguished admirals (Cleveland, Fremantle, Bridge, Bacon, Bridgeman, Beresford), Sir Philip Watts (the late D.N.C.), and Lord Sydenham of Combe (Sir George Clarke). The Conservative press was ruthless in its criticism: Scott's ideas 'approached the boundaries of midsummer madness,' they were 'a mare's-nest', etc. Only the Liberal press and a number of able younger officers like Lieutenant A. C. Dewar and Commander Carlyon Bellairs supported Scott's main thesis. The Liberal journals were less interested in the technical aspects of the argument. What the *Daily News* and *Daily Chronicle* saw in Scott was an ally against 'bloated armaments'.

Scott was partly right and partly wrong. The experience of the war fully demonstrated that 'submarines and aeroplanes had

[7] Wilson's memorandum, 'Remarks on War Plans', May 1907; Admiralty MSS.
[8] Fisher's memorandum, 'War Plans and the Distribution of the Fleet', 1907 (spring?); *ibid.*

entirely revolutionized warfare'. Although battleships did not suffer so severely as Scott had prophesied, it is a fact that the strategy and tactics of the battle fleet were fundamentally influenced by the submarine peril. However, in the pre-war decade, despite the enthusiasm of Fisher, Keyes, and others, the Admiralty saw in the new craft mainly a potent defensive weapon, a final insurance against invasion. Until the war, therefore, the principal duty of submarines in British war plans was to co-operate with the older destroyer flotillas for coast defence. Tirpitz, it should be mentioned, showed no signs before the war of a belief in the submarine. He saw in it only a defensive weapon for German harbours and their approaches. The early war successes of the U-boats surprised him, and it was not until January 1915, or nearly six months after the war began, that he conceived the plan of a submarine blockade of Great Britain. Even Mahan did not forecast a greater future for the submarine than that it would prove a serious factor in blockade.

The crucial thing about the submarine, as regards British offensive naval strategy, is that its development helped to make close blockade a thing of the past by making the capture and retention of a German base for the blockading flotillas much more difficult, if not impossible, and by threatening the safety of British cruisers and battleships without whose support the flotillas would be mopped up by the German cruisers. The object of the June 1911 exercises off Berehaven was to test the ability of submarines to get past investing destroyers in order to attack the supporting big ships in the offing. Although 'the exercise was rather unreal, the most ardent supporter of the close blockade could have been left in no doubt as to the menace of submarines to such a disposition.'[9] An Admiralty study of December 1912 flatly declared that

the enemy's submarine, in conjunction with the destroyer, has made an efficient blockade impossible. They have increased the difficulty of getting intelligence of the movements of the battle squadron of the enemy, since the light cruisers which would have to be employed to watch the enemy's harbours have now to be thrown out so far from the main body that their support becomes difficult, and they can be driven off from their watching station by superior force before they can be sufficiently supported. Under cover of such a movement, the sailing of such squadrons or fleets as the enemy may wish to put to sea

[9] Keyes, *Naval Memoirs*, i. 42.

can be effected before the main body of the British fleet can arrive. It would then rest with the British overseas submarines to endeavour to frustrate whatever object the enemy's main body might have in view.[10]

Counter-measures against submarine attack had to be found, since it was believed that the High Seas Fleet would attempt to compensate for capital ship inferiority by a vigorous use of its torpedo craft. An Admiralty Submarine Committee was set up in March 1910 to investigate this highly important subject. It carried out all sorts of experiments, including attempts to smash a periscope with machine-guns, firing torpedoes from destroyers at submerged submarines, using lyddite shell as a kind of depth charge, and testing the visibility of submerged submarines from planes. Notwithstanding this work, the Navy entered the war ignorant of any means of detecting the presence or position of a submerged enemy submarine and without any weapon effective against it. Vice-Admiral Sir Doveton Sturdee, in a lecture at the War College in April 1914, referring to experience in manœuvres, 'deplored the fact that we appeared to have no means to hand of preventing the destruction of "surface vessels", and he somewhat bombastically said, "*It is high time we put the fear of God into these young gentlemen who lie about the North Sea attacking all and sundry without let or hindrance*", but he had nothing to suggest, and the word "How?" was passed along the front benches of his listeners on a bit of paper!'[11] Sturdee's remarks take on extra significance against this background: he had in 1911 served as president of an Admiralty sub-committee charged with the consideration of defensive measures against attack by underwater craft.

By 1914 it was taken for granted that safety for the battleship lay in ensuring that no torpedo craft ever got within range. The big ship must either avoid the torpedo herself by keeping clear of enemy destroyers and submarines—by high speed when at sea and zigzagging—or she must be protected wherever she went by a destroyer screen, or rely upon a combination of these measures. The destroyer forces were mainly intended to screen the battleships by attacking the torpedo flotillas of the enemy. The Home Fleet manœuvres of September 1912 saw the first of a series of trials towards devising the best destroyer screen for a fleet and the

[10] Probably by the War Staff; Admiralty MSS.
[11] Captain S. S. Hall to Fisher, 26 Apr. 1914; Lennoxlove MSS.

best anti-submarine tactics for it to employ. That is, destroyers were assigned an essentially defensive role, in contrast with the Fisher period, when they had been conceived of as primarily offensive vessels. This explains why on the eve of the war the latest British destroyers had a heavier gun armament but a lighter torpedo armament than the modern German destroyers, which, incidentally, were officially known as torpedo-boats. In addition to these measures, there was a change in ship construction. The ordinary double bottom of the warship no longer being sufficient protection against the torpedo, in 1913 the Admiralty adopted the bulge method for the dreadnought *Ramillies*. This consisted in the fitting of a bulge or 'blister' to the side, which, on being hit by a torpedo exploding, would allow the liberated gas to expand to such an extent that what actually reached the side of the ship would not have sufficient strength to make a hole. The *Redoubtable* (late *Revenge*, of the pre-dreadnought 'Royal Sovereigns') was fitted with blisters early in the war, as were the 'Edgar' class cruisers and the large monitors during the war.

The development of aircraft added to the difficulties of a close blockade, while offering fresh hope of neutralizing the submarine. When the Admiralty was offered Wright's patents in 1907, Tweedmouth had replied for the Board that these proposals 'would be of no particular value to the Naval Service'.[12] Two years later, however, C.I.D. was examining the possibilities of airships. With Fisher as the moving spirit, a C.I.D. sub-committee, impressed with their 'scouting and possibly destructive purposes', recommended (28 January 1909) the inclusion of £35,000 in the navy estimates to build one airship of a rigid type (Zeppelin). This airship (the *Mayfly*) was begun that summer, but was wrecked after completion in September 1911 when a violent crosswind broke her in two. (Another version has it that the *Mayfly* was broken by the manœuvres in getting her turned away from the shed, from which she was withdrawn stern first.) The failure of the *Mayfly* called a halt to rigid airship construction. There was a change in the British attitude in 1912, after Jellicoe had gone to Germany and flown in a Zeppelin (November 1911), and after Captain Murray Sueter, Director of the Air Department, and Mervyn O'Gorman, head of the Royal Aircraft Factory at Farn-

[12] Air Marshal Sir John Slessor, 'Air Power and World Strategy', *Foreign Affairs*, Oct. 1954.

borough, had gone over to Germany disguised as Americans and returned with a glowing report on the Zeppelins (July 1912). Jellicoe, when he returned to the Admiralty as Second Sea Lord (December 1912), in charge of aerial matters, developed an interest in airships for naval scouting, the radius of action of airplanes (or 'aeroplanes', as they were called) being too small for the purpose. The other Sea Lords and the First Lord were less enthusiastic. Thus, Churchill did not rate the airship high—'this enormous bladder of combustible and explosive gas would prove to be easily destructible' by airplanes. He had strong backing in the C.I.D., where various experts declared, in 1912 (at the 119th and 120th meetings, 1 August, 6 December), that airships were useless.

There was more interest at the Admiralty in airplanes and especially seaplanes. To the outbreak of the war, the Navy was ahead of the Army in the realization of the potentialities of aircraft, even though by 1914 they were capable of only 60 miles per hour and had a mere 500- to 600-mile range. The Navy had fifty-two seaplanes (of which only twenty-six were in flying condition) and thirty-nine airplanes at the outbreak of war. Whereas the War Office saw chiefly the reconnaissance possibilities of airplanes, the Admiralty under the imaginative Churchill (with Fisher's enthusiasm behind him) saw wider uses for the planes of the Royal Naval Air Service (the naval counterpart of the Royal Flying Corps, which was under the War Office). They would (Churchill announced in the Commons, 17 March 1914) be valuable for coast defence, for scouting at sea, either from land or from a 'seaplane ship', and for defence of vulnerable points like oil tanks, magazines, and docks. Planes were seen to have an especially important role as scouts. There were various scouting functions. (1) Fog was usually so shallow that a plane could see two fleets below even when they were hidden from each other by a thick sea mist on the water, and so could assist the fire control by spotting. Planes could also locate the warships of an enemy in harbour or at sea. (2) Planes could warn merchantmen of the position of commerce destroyers. (3) Since it was held to be a comparatively easy matter to spot a submerged submarine or a minefield from the air, planes could give warning of the presence and movements of enemy submarines, other torpedo craft, and minelayers. In the view of Battenberg, the First Sea Lord, the scouting role of airplanes was their principal function, and one of the points made by

Scott in his submarine letter in *The Times* was that, so far as cruisers were concerned, it was no longer the seaman's business to find the enemy—it was the airman's business. Fisher predicted, in March 1913, that 'aviation will *surely* supplant cruisers'. In 1912 the Admiralty carried on experiments for the spotting of submarines by aircraft, and in the 1913 manœuvres seaplanes proved their great value for short-distance reconnaissance and for the detection of submarines. That submarines in the near future would be liable to destruction by aircraft was not an uncommon belief. It was felt that a good pilot, passing close above a submarine, should be able to drop a charge of gun-cotton, arranged to explode under water, within a few feet of the submarine. This would destroy her or bring her to the surface.

As regards the use of planes as attacking and bombing planes operating from parent ships, this was too radical a notion to win general support, even if a plane was able to take off from the deck of a cruiser at anchor (1911), and one was successfully flown from the deck of the pre-dreadnought battleship *Hibernia* while she was under way (1912). In 1913 the *Hermes* was commissioned as the world's first aircraft carrier, accommodating three seaplanes, which could not return to the ship, once launched. She was abandoned as a carrier on the eve of the war.

The fact is that flying machines of all kinds were regarded before the war as primarily scouts attendant on navies and armies, not as weapons of offence. It was generally believed that aircraft would not be able to do much damage to battle fleets at sea through the dropping of explosives on warships, whether at rest or in motion. Exceptional were Aston, Repington, and other bold thinkers, who had faith, an exaggerated faith as it developed, in aircraft as a weapon of offence against warships. They predicted that aircraft would be able to destroy vessels at anchor or in dock by dropping heavy bombs on them. Beatty, in command of the battle cruisers, was apprehensive about Germany's 'formidable Aerial Force' and was 'busy preparing a scheme for the defence of our ships, which at present are absolutely at their mercy. . .'[13] *The Army and Navy Gazette* (17 May 1913) audaciously asserted that the real danger of aircraft was in their potential use as torpedo carriers.

The belief was prevalent in the last years before the war that somehow the command of the air was or would before long be an

[13] Beatty to Lady Beatty, 4 Apr. 1913; Chalmers, *Beatty*, p. 121.

essential adjunct to the maintenance of the command of the sea, and from 1912 there was a chronic agitation for a substantial strengthening of British air power, spearheaded by the Aerial Defence Committee of the Navy League. A two-power standard in aircraft was freely mentioned, and this was stimulated by the report of a foreign airship over Sheerness (autumn of 1912), by a great number of reports at the end of February 1913 of airships having been seen at night, and by the considerable increase in German air power, especially airships. Germany already had some twenty large airships, Britain had none. The German airships were concentrated at Cuxhaven, immediately opposite the bases of British destroyer and submarine flotillas, and within practicable navigation distance of all the British East Coast bases and docks. Repington predicted the descent of fleets of these airships on British arsenals, dockyards, and industrial centres.

Churchill was very concerned about the German airship menace. It was, he informed the C.I.D. on 6 December 1912, 'a matter of great anxiety'. He stressed the importance and urgency of the problem of airships, 'both from the point of view of airships as auxiliaries to the Fleet ['for the purposes of observation', he made clear later] and from that of defence against their attacks. . . . Our dockyards, machine shops, magazines, and ships lying in the basins, were absolutely defenceless against this form of attack if an enemy airship were to succeed in reaching a position whence it could attack.'[14] The First Lord was obviously more interested in the latter aspect of the airship. The Admiralty, he stated, asked for the development of a suitable type; they must know the capabilities of airships in order to work out a defence against them. A. K. Wilson, at the same meeting, insisted the danger from German airships was exaggerated. They could not carry much explosives, and while land-based guns could not be used against them in urban areas, since 'the projectile would eventually fall among your own people', at sea there was no such difficulty. The target offered by an airship was larger than that offered by any battleship; the usual system of gunnery and fire control was applicable, and except for the lack of means of 'spotting', there would be no more difficulty in hitting than in ordinary circumstances. If it were argued, Wilson continued, that guns were no adequate defence, there was still defence by aeroplanes. Although the airship

[14] Minutes of the 120th meeting of the C.I.D.; Asquith MSS.

could rise quicker, the aeroplane could rise higher and, when once above her, could travel faster and turn in a smaller circle, and so easily close and destroy her. Wilson did admit there was danger at present, especially to a blockading fleet, since the problem had not been worked out. Asquith thought Wilson's criticisms of the airship were pertinent. There were other possible means of defence, including aeroplanes, guns, and passive protection. The matter, he felt, needed further consideration. Accordingly, the meeting adjourned consideration of the report on airships by the Technical Sub-Committee on Aerial Navigation, which had recommended that the best way of dealing with enemy airships would be by a superior force of airships.

By 6 February 1913, when the C.I.D. resumed discussion of the airship problem, the Technical Sub-Committee had amended its recommendation. It now asked merely for 'the evolution, with the least possible delay, of a type of airship in no wise inferior to the best airships available in foreign countries for naval purposes and the training of personnel to handle airships of this type. The numerical standard of the Airship Fleet to be maintained will require consideration as soon as a satisfactory type of vessel has been produced.' Colonel Seely, Secretary of State for War, made the position of the Army clear: they were leaving airships to the Navy, with the Army concentrating its efforts on aeroplanes. The meeting degenerated into an intra-service squabble. Wilson again charged that aeroplanes were more useful than airships and that hostile airships could most easily be dealt with by aeroplanes. Jellicoe disagreed with Wilson. Aeroplanes had serious limitations, he insisted. They were inefficient at night, their radius of action was only four hours, and landing at night was a risky business. He thought that the aeroplane would not find it easy to get above the airship. The former had an advantage of speed—70 miles an hour to 50—but the airship rose when stationary, and its buoyancy increased as its fuel was consumed. Churchill once more outlined the menace posed by the twenty-four German airships, most of which were able to reach England. 'The Admiralty and all the Government buildings were now exposed to an attack, which, if successful, might have very grave consequences. These craft must be kept away altogether and that would only be done by attacking them.' Wilson was not opposed to the experimental construction of airships, which was all the Admiralty and the Technical

Sub-Committee were asking for, and in the end the Committee's recommendation was approved.[15]

The Admiralty had a change of heart on airships early in 1914 and started a programme of eight. None was ready when war broke out. The Navy then had only seven (small, non-rigid) air-ships, four of which, utterly unreliable, had been transferred from the Army. A fifth was used as a training ship. The only two of operational value, the *Astra-Torres No. 3* and the *Parseval*, had been purchased in France and Germany, respectively (1913). 'We our-selves have not a single large airship, though we live in daily apprehension of Zeppelin attacks', moaned the Secretary of the C.I.D.[16] And as Bacon later pointed out, 'a very useful scouting adjunct was denied to the Grand Fleet, whereas the High Sea Fleet had the benefit of their Zeppelins'.

2. THE COMMITTEE OF IMPERIAL DEFENCE

The strategy with which the Royal Navy entered the war was formulated in the Churchill period. As a necessary preliminary we must touch lightly on the Committee of Imperial Defence. This was a permanent advisory committee on defence questions estab-lished in 1904, whose genesis was the Defence Committee of the Cabinet set up by the Salisbury Government in 1895. The Defence Committee held no regular meetings, and no records were kept of its deliberations or decisions. By a Treasury minute of 4 May 1904 the Committee was remodelled to include both the political and professional heads of the Army and Navy. The functions of this new Committee of Imperial Defence were defined as 'obtaining and collating for the use of the Cabinet all the information and expert advice required for shaping national policy in war, and for determining the necessary preparations in peace.' In the same year a permanent secretariat was established with the duties of preserving the minutes of C.I.D. meetings, collecting and co-ordinating for the use of the Committee information bearing on imperial defence, and preparing memoranda required for the C.I.D. Campbell-Bannerman initiated a plan of appointing sub-committees to inquire into and report on strategic and technical questions, with authority to call witnesses and to take shorthand

[15] Minutes of the 122nd meeting of the C.I.D.; Asquith MSS.
[16] C.I.D. Paper 81–A, 'Invasion. Notes by the Secretary' (Hankey), 15 Oct. 1914; *ibid.*

notes of evidence. The C.I.D. was, as laid down in 1904, 'merely a consultative or advisory body', putting its 'conclusions' and evidence in support of them at the disposal of the Prime Minister and the Cabinet. Since the Prime Minister was the chairman of the C.I.D., and the ministers responsible for the Treasury, Foreign, Colonial, India, and War Offices, and the Admiralty were always summoned (together with certain of their advisers), C.I.D. conclusions were, in practice, by the eve of the war, authoritative. The Secretary would officially notify the conclusions reached at a meeting to the departments responsible for taking action. Cabinet approval, still necessary for the conclusions, was largely a formality.

The C.I.D. remained in swaddling clothes for a long time. It was unpalatable to many Cabinet ministers, because it exalted the Prime Minister and increased the prestige of those ministers who were its permanent members. Many officers at the War Office and the Admiralty did not regard the C.I.D. with favour, fearing it might take over some of the functions of the War Office and the Admiralty. This was one reason for Fisher's formidable opposition. Other factors were his desire for secretiveness and his hostility to the War Office and the generals. General Sir John French thought he was 'inclined to resent any participation by the Army in the work of National Defence. He regards them as *Marines* pure and simple!'[17] Still another reason for Fisher's distrust of the C.I.D. was his antagonism to its first Secretary (1904–7), Sir George Clarke. Clarke was a retired army officer, very able but devoid of 'flair'. He considered the fleet scrapping as having gone too far, described the *Dreadnought* as a 'blunder of the first magnitude' and a policy of 'forcing the pace in the building of monsters', accused Fisher of running a one-man show, termed the 1906 redistribution a 'dangerous' policy, criticized the stress on submarine development, protested Fisher's choice of Ottley to represent the Admiralty at the Hague Conference (Ottley looked too much like a 'Portuguese Eurasian', was flighty and a 'flibbertigibbet', had not sufficient rank, and had never commanded a big ship), and, to top his misdeeds, he considered that the general direction of a great war must be the responsibility of the C.I.D. These sins incurred Fisher's wrath and damned Clarke and the C.I.D. in his

[17] Major the Hon. Gerald French, *The Life of Field-Marshal Sir John French, First Earl of Ypres* (London, 1931, 2 vols.), i. 172.

eyes. He fought to restrict the role of the C.I.D., for example by trying to keep the invasion question out of its province.

One measure of the C.I.D.'s early ineffectuality is that it was not consulted at all during the negotiations preceding the signing of the agreement with Russia in August 1907, although military considerations were important factors. Clarke's retirement as Secretary in August 1907 removed some of the Admiralty antagonism to the C.I.D. Captain Charles L. Ottley, his successor, was an ardent disciple of Fisher's. He was a very well-informed naval officer, noted for his tact, patience, and persuasiveness, and his knowledge of languages and ability to express himself as a writer and speaker. And whereas Clarke had 'broken the admirable conception of the Committee of Imperial Defence by trying to force it too fast in an executive direction, Ottley . . . made it merely a place where the Departments concerted their policy in common.'[18] This disarmed some of the suspicion of the Admiralty and the War Office. Nevertheless, even with Ottley as its Secretary, Fisher never quite reconciled himself to the C.I.D. A. K. Wilson obstructed its work as much as Fisher had, maintaining that it had no business meddling with the general planning of naval and military operations. In short, as late as 1911 the C.I.D. was lacking in prestige and real authority, thanks in large part to Admiralty obstruction and hostility. Esher, in December 1909, was 'annoyed at the stagnation of C.I.D.' It met infrequently and its decisions were 'treated as the amiable aberrations of a few well-meaning but harmless amateur strategists.'[19]

The C.I.D. only began to come into its own in the last two or three years before the war. An important factor was the 35-year-old Royal Marine Captain of Australian parentage, Maurice Hankey, who succeeded Ottley in 1912. He had served in N.I.D., 1902–7, and as Assistant Secretary of the C.I.D. under Ottley. Fisher's influence in his appointment was very strong. He had the highest opinion of Hankey, a little man but an indefatigable worker possessed of a fine brain and superlative tact. Thorough, objective, loyal, and discreet, Hankey came to be trusted and relied upon by all. Under his inspiration and driving power, the C.I.D. began to exercise a powerful influence on defence matters,

[18] Hankey to Esher, 19 Feb. 1919; Esher MSS.
[19] Esher to Balfour, 24 Dec. 1909, and to M. V. Brett, 29 Dec. 1909; *Esher*, ii. 428–9, 430.

without encroaching unduly upon the prerogatives and functions of the War Office and the Admiralty.

The weightiest strategic problems were discussed and guiding principles laid down in a series of important C.I.D. meetings during 1912–14. By 1914 the principle had been pretty well established that the C.I.D. (with its affiliated sub-committees), and not the Admiralty or War Office, or General Staff or Admiralty War Staff, drafted the important general principles of strategy.

3. DEFENSIVE STRATEGY: THE INVASION BOGEY

The purpose of British sea power was to maintain the command of the sea, in order to (1) be able to defeat the enemy fleet, should it seek battle; (2) deny the sea to enemy commerce; (3) support amphibious operations; (4) smash any attempted invasion; (5) ensure the uninterrupted maritime flow of food and supplies by keeping a *guerre de course* in check. The first three pertain to the offensive aspects of naval strategy; the other two, to the defensive facets.

Preparation against a surprise German attack on the Fleet without any formal declaration of war was the foundation of defensive strategy at the Admiralty in the pre-war decade. The D.N.I. prophesied, 'if history is any guide', that a 'sudden and dramatic outbreak would be distinctive of future wars, especially of warfare at sea. The advantages . . . are so enormous as to quite outweigh any lingering scruples of international comity.'[20] The 1908 C.I.D. Sub-Committee on Invasion warned: 'The possibility of a surprise attack being made upon this country during normal diplomatic relations is not sufficiently remote to be ignored. They agree with Mr. Balfour that if the German Government believed that the adoption of such a plan made the difference between failure and success, it is conceivable that they might resort to it.' This conclusion was reaffirmed by another sub-committee in 1914.[21]

Now, the Hague Conference had agreed that hostilities 'shall not be commenced without a preliminary and unequivocal notice,

[20] Ottley's memorandum, 'Suddenness in Naval Operations', 1 Mar. 1905; Balfour MSS.
[21] C.I.D. Paper 70–A, 'The Strategical Aspects of the Channel Tunnel . . .', 7 May 1914; Lennoxlove MSS.

which shall have the form either of a declaration of war stating its grounds [*motivé*], or of an ultimatum with a conditional declaration of war.' But this did not go beyond the most general practice of the preceding half century; and, so far from insisting on a substantial interval of notice between a declaration of war and the commencement of hostilities under it, the Conference did not even accept the moderate proposal of a twenty-four hours' interval made by the Netherlands delegation.

The Admiralty had, then, to bear in mind the possibility of a German 'Port Arthur'—a surprise torpedo attack on home ports before the declaration of war that might catch the Fleet unawares or unready and end the war before it was fairly started. All steps were taken to guard against this menace from Fisher's time on. Churchill, believing the danger was 'by no means fantastic', increased the precautions.

$$* \quad * \quad *$$

The problem of invasion remained a hardy perennial.[22] In the 1905–14 period it was debated, with far more heat than light, by the proponents of two schools of thought. The 'Blue-Water' School, which represented the thought of the Navy, believed that so long as the Fleet maintained the command of the sea, an invasion of the British Isles, other than trifling and sporadic raids of a few thousand men (for which mobile coast defences and a home defence army were adequate), was impossible. The competing 'Bolt-from-the-Blue' School reflected the point of view of the Army. (General Sir John French was one of the few high-ranking military officers who supported Blue-Water views.) It argued that surprise being the essence of success in war, a bolt from the blue was always possible. The Fleet might be decoyed away and a sudden invasion in force launched. (70,000 was the standard figure, first mentioned by Field-Marshal Lord Roberts, the acknowledged leader of the School, at the Defence Committee discussion of invasion in 1903.) Therefore, there was a need to reinforce the Navy with an adequate second line of military defence. This, in the view of Roberts, meant a compulsory service army for home defence. He led the fight for national service after he resigned from the C.I.D. in December 1905 to carry on the fight publicly. The National Service League, founded in 1909 to

[22] For the pre-Fisher era background of the invasion problem, see *The Anatomy of British Sea Power*, pp. 65–82.

press for universal training, had a membership of 35,000 by 1909, including many retired officers of both services. Far from all the bolt-from-the-bluers supported national service, and the War Office itself never officially came out for national service before the war. Strengthening the Regular Army and the Territorials was War Office policy, with the question of national service left for solution when war broke out.

The Admiralty dreaded compulsory service for fear it might divert money from, and lower the prestige of, the Navy. Even Haldane shared this fear of the Blue-Water School! As he told the French Prime Minister, Clemenceau, in 1908: 'If we maintained a large and costly army at home, down would go the resources and money which we could pour into the Navy and that I would not stand for. He was not impressed but then no Frenchman has ever understood what the Navy means to us.'[23] Most Liberals, and certainly the Liberal press, suspicious of large standing armies, tended to support the Blue-Water School. They claimed that Roberts & Co. wanted conscription, not for home defence, but for foreign aggression, that their aim was to involve the country in Continental wars. Not a huge Army, but a Territorial Force able to cope with raids was all that was required on the military side.

The 'manacled fleet' argument won the Bolt-from-the-Blue School the support of a number of retired admirals. If the Navy knew that the Army could deal effectively with a considerable force of invaders, as through compulsory service for home defence, it would be freer to prosecute offensive operations. It would not be tied to the British Isles, or be liable to recall in response to public sentiment which recognized and dreaded the deficiencies of British defence on land. As matters stood, declared the *National Review* (January 1909), 'The single result of this one-eyed strategy is to tether British squadrons like so many goats to British shores.' Much was made of the Spanish-American War of 1898, where the popular dread of a raid by Admiral Cervera's weak little squadron tied the hands of the U.S. Navy Department and compelled it to retain Commodore Schley's Flying Squadron on the coast of the United States.

To the Blue-Water School the Navy was an absolute bar to invasion, its slogan being those immortal words of Mahan: 'Those

[23] Maurice, *Haldane*, i. 228.

far-distant, storm-beaten ships, upon which the Grand Army never looked, stood between it and the dominion of the world.' They often quoted St. Vincent's words to a group of nervous fellow peers at the time of the French invasion danger: 'I do not say they cannot come, my Lords. I only say they cannot come by sea.' In short, it was believed that history had taught that invasion would never be attempted until the enemy had established control of the sea and his communications were secure. The whole bolt-from-the-blue hypothesis was regarded as absurd. How could 100,000-or-so men be massed on the German coast without exciting suspicion? And how could the necessary transport be collected without exciting any suspicion? And how was a large army to be landed in a few hours upon a strange beach? British warships would be on the scene within a few hours. And how could the invaders, even if successfully landed, be supplied in the face of British command of the sea? The conclusion was that no landing in force on the English coast could be effected—indeed, would not be attempted—except after a naval battle in which the Fleet would be crippled; but, given a superior Fleet, that was not a possibility that need seriously be considered. The Fleet was the first and only line of defence, the absolute bar to invasion. To assign to the Army a co-responsibility with the Navy for the defence of the United Kingdom was to misconceive the fundamental principles of the problem.

Fisher saw in submarines, then in their infancy, a final insurance against invasion. In a paper of October 1903 he wrote: 'It affects the Army, because imagine even one Submarine Boat with a flock of transports in sight loaded each with some two or three thousand troops! Imagine the effect of one such transport going to the bottom in a few seconds with its living freight! Even the bare thought makes invasion impossible! Fancy 100,000 helpless, huddled-up troops afloat in frightened transports with these invisible demons known to be near.'[24] At the least, as the Admiralty paper of December 1912[25] pointed out, 'the defensive submarine, by making a disembarkation upon the East Coast hazardous, has the power of forcing the enemy to select a more distant spot, which means a longer voyage and therefore more danger of being attacked at sea by surface vessels.'

[24] Lennoxlove MSS.
[25] See above, pp. 334–5.

The air was thick with historical arguments drawn from earlier wars. When the bolt-from-the-blue people emphasized the incident of Nelson being 'decoyed' on a wild-goose chase to the West Indies in the days of Napoleon, the opposition retorted that the incident could hardly be paralleled in the twentieth century, an age of steam and wireless, when ship movements were far more certain and touch far more easily maintained; and even were it possible, wireless stations rendered recall easy, should the dreaded 'invasion during the absence of the fleet' take place. (Incidentally, both sides argued from a false premise, since the common belief that Nelson was 'decoyed' by Villeneuve is erroneous.)

Balfour, a blue-water advocate, had stated in the House of Commons, 11 May 1905, in summarizing the findings of the Defence Committee invasion inquiry of 1903 (which had supposed the enemy to be France), that, provided the Navy was efficient, 'serious invasion of these islands is not an eventuality which we need seriously consider'. The speech created an enormous impression and encouraged Englishmen to dismiss even the thought of invasion, since there could be no question about the superiority of the Royal Navy. Balfour's statement was explicitly accepted by the Liberal Government after it came to power (Commons, 12 July 1906). The Blue-Water School was triumphant, and the whole question was for a time laid to rest as one which had been settled in the most authoritative and decisive way.

Lord Roberts, Repington, and their allies continued to agitate. They held that the problem had changed to a material extent with Germany's replacement of France as Britain's potential enemy, and with the changes in the conditions of modern warfare which facilitated the task of the invader. In 1907, Roberts collaborated with Repington, Lord Lovat, and Sir Samuel Scott in a thorough study of the facilities possessed by Germany for overseas invasion and the possible preparations which could be made secretly by Germany. They envisaged an act of treachery directed against the British Fleet—a surprise attack by torpedo craft, immediately followed by an invasion (150,000 men) in the region of the Firth of Forth or the northern ports of the United Kingdom, while the German Fleet held the Straits of Dover for the crucial forty-eight hours. Balfour, convinced by the Roberts group that a *prima-facie* case had been made out for a re-examination of the problem, forwarded their findings to the C.I.D. (20 July 1907), with the request that they be studied with a view to a possible re-examination of the invasion problem. The Admiralty objected strongly to any fresh investigation by the C.I.D., on the 'silly ground,' said Balfour, 'that the question is one for the Navy alone.' Campbell-Bannerman overruled the Admiralty, and Esher rapped Fisher's knuckles hard for maintaining that Balfour's paper was 'purely an Admiralty business' and for talking of an 'irresponsible sub-committee'. Fisher regarded the appointment of the C.I.D. Sub-Committee on Invasion (November) as a personal attack on the Navy and its traditional dominance in national defence. For him the 'mischievous agitation' or 'invasion bogey' was, at bottom, a scheme for putting through compulsory service when the Territorial Army was quite enough. His famous 'sleep quiet in your beds' speech at the Guildhall banquet in 1907 must be read in this context.

The C.I.D. Sub-Committee proceeded with a fresh and exhaustive investigation of the question of invasion, this time of the possibility of invasion of the United Kingdom by Germany. The members were Haldane, Grey, Tweedmouth (whose incapacity and ignorance were glaringly revealed), Rear-Admiral E. J. Slade (D.N.I.), Ottley (as secretary), Fisher, General Sir William Nicholson (Chief of the General Staff), and General Sir John French (Inspector General of the Forces). Asquith, who served as chairman, handled the evidence given before the committee in a masterly fashion. Sixteen meetings were held between 27 November 1907 and 28 July 1908. The committee's report was issued in October.[26] At the third meeting, 12 December 1907, Roberts and Repington were cross-examined in a session featured by many sharp clashes between the military and naval spokesmen. During this session the invasionists made three fundamental assumptions: (1) The Germans would arrange that the Fleet would be to the west of Portland, 'either by surprise or by false information'. The Navy spokesmen would not accept this. Slade pointed out that there were always ships at Devonport, Portland, Portsmouth, Chatham, Sheerness, and Harwich. (2) The German Fleet would be able to hold the Straits of Dover for forty-eight hours as a protection for convoys. The Admiralty denied this.

[26] C.I.D. Paper 44–A, 'Invasion. Report and Proceedings of a Sub-Committee of the Committee of Imperial Defence Appointed by the Prime Minister to Re-Consider the Question of Oversea Attack', Oct. 22, 1908; Lennoxlove MSS.

There was always enough force at the home ports to cope with anything the Germans could throw at them. (3) The preparations for the embarkation of the invading force would take place in secrecy. Fisher's comment was: 'The whole of this question rests upon a naval surprise. . . . We keep reiterating and reiterating that you cannot have this naval surprise; it is inconceivable.' 'The Russians [in 1904] thought so' was Repington's riposte.

The Sub-Committee's conclusions, accepted with some unimportant amendments by the full committee, found:

(1) That so long as our naval supremacy is assured against any reasonably probable combination of Powers, invasion is impracticable.

(2) That if we permanently lose command of the sea, whatever may be the strength and organization of the Home force, the subjection of the country to the enemy is inevitable.

(3) That our army for Home Defence ought to be sufficient in number and organization not only to repel small raids, but to compel an enemy who contemplates invasion to come with so substantial a force as will make it impossible for him to evade our fleet.

(4) That in order to ensure an ample margin of safety, such a force may, for purposes of calculation, be assumed to be 70,000 men.

(5) That in the event of our being engaged in a war on the frontier of India which required 100,000 regular troops to be sent from the United Kingdom during the first year, the new organization of the Army at Home will secure that there will be left in this country during the first six months a sufficient number of regular and other troops to deal with a force of 70,000 men.

(6) That on the assumption that the Territorial Force is embodied on the outbreak of war, there will also be, after the expiration of six months, a sufficient number of regulars and trained Territorials to make it practically certain that no enemy will attempt the operation with a smaller force than is assumed above.

The agitation continued until the Prime Minister, on 29 July 1909 in the Commons, publicly set forth the C.I.D. judgment on the problem. He did not go into the evidence, but he stated in his own language the main conclusions (the first four) reached by the C.I.D. Balfour endorsed these views. The acute stage of the controversy was over, although Roberts was not satisfied and invasionists and anti-invasionists continued their guerilla warfare in the press.

A fresh Admiralty opinion on invasion was given by A. K. Wilson in a short appendix, dated 19 November 1910, to the second edition of Lieutenant-General Sir Ian Hamilton's book on *Compulsory Service* (January 1911). His assurance of safety against invasion was contingent upon the maintenance of naval supremacy. He based his opinion on the difficulty the enemy would experience in attempting to evade a superior British Fleet in the epoch of wireless telegraph. Even if 'by some extraordinarily lucky chance' the transports reach English shores, they would be attacked and sunk by submarines, and if the submarines failed, there would still be destroyers to tackle them. Wilson admitted the possibility that the Fleet might be decoyed away, but he did not forget, as Roberts & Co. generally did, that the force detached in such an event would be exactly proportioned to whatever force the enemy chose to use as a decoy. 'Taking all these facts into consideration, he [the enemy] would probably decide as the Admiralty have done, that an invasion on even the modest scale of 70,000 men is practically impossible.' Wilson's remarks led to a grand-scale re-airing of the problem on the platform and in the press. Nobody was converted, of course.

Italy's experience in her invasion of Tripoli, in October 1911, proved to the satisfaction of the blue-water advocates the impracticability of the sudden invasion of an island kingdom. If ever a modern war was begun on the bolt-from-the-blue theory, it was this affair in the Mediterranean. The Italians transported only 35,000 men, enjoyed throughout absolute command of the sea, had no opposition whatever, the transports had to cover only 400 to 500 miles, and yet, so great was the difficulty of transporting an army by sea, three weeks elapsed between the issue of the mobilizing telegrams and the landing of the main body of the expedition on the enemy's shore. According to the calculations of those perpetually prophesying the invasion of England, it should have been about four days, for they estimated that three days would suffice for a German invading force to set foot on British soil, and in comparing that operation with the Italian invasion of Tripoli, it was fair to add one day for the extra distance to the hostile shore, which was about one day's easy steaming for ordinary vessels.

In this game of 'oneupmanship', the bolt-from-the-bluers had their innings. While the Admiralty kept the taxpayer in dark ignorance on the results of the 1912 and 1913 manœuvres, the invasionists said that both proved the possibility of invasion—that

British naval arrangements could not prevent the landing of anything between 30,000 and 60,000 men, and that without a national army the task of the British Navy might be impossible.

The purpose of the large-scale manœuvres in the summer of 1912 was to investigate the problem of intercepting the German Fleet before it could cover a landing of troops on the East Coast. Battenberg, in command of the 'enemy' fleet, succeeded, theoretically, in throwing a raiding force ashore, and escaped annihilation by the sacrifice of his weaker and slower ships. In Churchill's opinion, at least 12,000 men could have been landed from the fifteen transports during the four hours of calm weather that the Red Fleet was unmolested off Filey. The First Lord, however, appreciated that the 'artificial conditions of peace manœuvres' modified any conclusions that might be drawn from the facts. Among these was the money-saving convention that allowed the Red battleships to change to transports and back again to battleships by simply hoisting and hauling down a certain flag! 'Had 15 real vessels been available to represent the transports, it is certain that the landing would not have been accomplished without attack of some kind. According to the manœuvres rules, the Red battleships merely steamed in with the transport flag flying, hauled down their transport flag, steamed out again, and became the protecting battle squadrons, leaving nothing but water where the transports were supposed to be busily engaged in landing troops. The absence of real transports off the coast prevented the 3 Blue submarines in the neighbourhood from realising that any landing was in progress, and was the undoubted cause of their not attacking.' Churchill's conclusions were

That a German battle fleet seeking to maintain itself in the North Sea would be defeated; that German flotillas endeavouring to attack British battle fleets would be gradually worn down and broken up and their supporting cruisers brought to action or forced to fly; that landings would be interrupted; and that the forces landed would have their oversea communications immediately severed; all are conclusions which may be reasonably held. None of them, however, obviate the possibility of a determined enemy, not afraid of risking the loss of 15,000 or 20,000 men, making a series of simultaneous or successive descents upon different portions of the British coast, and landing men in bodies of from 5,000 to 10,000 strong. Such forces would not, of course, be formidable so long as we had on shore a compact force of regulars with good artillery which could strike swiftly and vigorously at the detached heads of invasion and destroy them before they could combine.[27]

In the 1913 manœuvres it was determined to repeat the experiment with real troops in real transports. The object of the Red Fleet (the German), under Jellicoe, was to effect a landing in Blue territory somewhere on the East Coast. This was considered to have been achieved if a transport were able to remain unmolested at the selected landing place for four hours after landing the thousand men carried, this being the time estimated to represent landing a further 5,000 troops. War was declared on 23 July, 5 p.m. Red succeeded in getting some 48,000 troops ashore in two landings on Blue territory (Blyth, Sunderland), although in an attempt to effect a third landing in the Humber the two slow transports were 'torpedoed'. No contact was made between the opposing battle fleets, but Callaghan, the Blue C.-in-C., lost a considerable part of his fleet by submarine attack. On 28 July, at 5 a.m., the Admiralty hastily signalled, 'Operations completed', Churchill being wary lest Germany learn too much. Active operations were resumed on 31 July, with Red failing to achieve its main objective of establishing a base in the Shetland Isles, and the manœuvres ended the next day with an action between the battle fleets.

The press made a great fuss over the vulnerability of the East Coast and the practicability of a surprise landing in force. This, too, was the opinion of the German Naval Attaché. Roberts, in a message to the National Service League at the end of 1913, reminded the British public that the 1913 manœuvres revealed 'the possibility of a raid which might entail a vital blow at the heart of the Empire.' Callaghan's report on the 1913 manœuvres—he was C.-in-C., Home Fleets—shocked the blue-water proponents at the Admiralty. The manœuvres revealed to him

the defencelessness of our East Coast harbours and, if the regular troops are out of the country, of our coast. . . . the only proper defence of the country against Invasion and Raid is by Military Forces, and to make the Navy responsible for this work is a grave strategic error, which hands the initiative wholly to the enemy. Given that the country is able to look after itself on shore, our fleet can *ensure* the complete destruction

[27] 'Notes on the Manœuvres: Prepared for the Prime Minister by the First Lord', 17 Oct. 1912; Admiralty MSS.

of German seaborne trade to the Westward as well as the seizure of her colonies, and stifle her as a force to be reckoned with overseas, whilst being ready at any moment for offensive operations against her fleet.[28]

The report of the Umpire-in-Chief, Admiral of the Fleet Sir William May, drew these as the main lessons of the 1913 manœuvres: that raids, 'provided the attack is a surprise, may be partially successful, especially in misty weather. The coastal patrol . . . is not sufficient. It therefore appears necessary to have fixed defences at the principal seaports in the United Kingdom and of sufficient strength to be able to check a determined raid for some hours until a battle fleet can be concentrated on the spot and at the same time give opportunity for the submarines to act.'[29] The C.I.D. report of 1914 (see below) saw in the 1912 and 1913 manœuvres a demonstration of 'the uncertainty of detecting a hostile fleet which has reached open water under the meteorological conditions prevailing in these latitudes. Instances have occurred when fleets of considerable size, sometimes favoured by fog which is prevalent in the North Sea, have penetrated through waters systematically patrolled and watched by large numbers of the opposing vessels, without being reported sufficiently soon to ensure their being brought to action . . . the Sub-Committee do not think it would be prudent to assume that an invading army could by no means possibly evade our fleets and arrive off the shores of the United Kingdom.'

Already, on 13 January 1913, a new C.I.D. Sub-Committee on Invasion had been appointed by the Prime Minister to consider whether any new factors had arisen which necessitated a reconsideration of the conclusions approved in 1908. The membership of the Committee was formidable: ten ministers, headed by the Prime Minister; Balfour, Esher, Battenberg, A. K. Wilson, Vice-Admiral Sir Henry Jackson (Chief of the War Staff), French (now Chief of the Imperial General Staff), two other generals, and Hankey, as secretary. The reason given by the Prime Minister for a fresh examination of the problem was that there had been 'developments and changes in many of the factors since 1908—in the strengthening of foreign navies in the North Sea, and in the

[28] 'Naval Manœuvres, 1913. Remarks on North Sea Strategy', 28 Aug. 1913; Admiralty MSS.
[29] N.d.; May MSS.

Mediterranean, in naval architecture, submarines, flying, wireless telegraphy, and other matters.'

The new factors brought out in the evidence[30] were:

(1) *The adoption of a new military scheme of Home Defence, based on the report of the 1908 Inquiry*—according to which local forces were provided to meet raids and to oppose as early as possible an attempted invasion, and a main army or Central Force to deal decisively with invasion.

(2) *The ratification of the International Convention relative to the Opening of Hostilities, signed at The Hague on 18 October 1907*, under which hostilities were not to commence without a previous and explicit warning, in the form of either a declaration of war, giving reasons, or an ultimatum with a conditional declaration of war. This Convention, however, did not preclude the possibility of sudden attack, since the interval of time elapsing between the declaration of war and the outbreak of hostilities might be so short as to forbid effective measures being taken to prepare for attack.

(3) *The compilation of the War Book*, which was reviewed annually, and which contained provisions to prevent Britain from being caught unawares.

(4) *The development of the Territorial Force*, which in 1908 was in embryo.

(5) *Developments in the military situation in Europe bearing on Germany's ability to spare troops for attacks on Britain.* Germany, if engaged in a war between the Triple Alliance and France, Russia, and Great Britain, would find it difficult to provide a force exceeding 10,000 men for an attack on Britain; but Germany could set free, by taking some risks, the moderate numbers required to attack Britain.

(6) *Revised figures for tonnage available in German ports for transport purposes*: 310,000 gross tons of suitable ships. General Wilson estimated that a fully equipped force of about 90,000–95,000 men could be embarked on that tonnage; 195,000 tons were ample for an invading army of 70,000 men lightly equipped.

(7) *Changes in the distribution of the Navy and in the relative strength of the British and German Fleets.* The redistribution had made Britain

[30] C.I.D. Paper 62–A, 'Report and Proceedings of a Standing Sub-Committee of the Committee of Imperial Defence Appointed by the Prime Minister to Reconsider the Question of Attack on the British Isles from Oversea', 15 Apr. 1914; Lennoxlove MSS.

more ready to meet attack at the outbreak of war, which readiness must be a strong deterrent against any attempt at invasion. But the British margin of superiority was not as great as in 1907.

(8) *Developments in the mine, torpedo, and submarine* made it impossible to establish a close watch on the exits from the Heligoland Bight with heavy ships.

(9) *The introduction of aircraft.* It was possible that the evasion of British warships might be facilitated by the employment of aircraft.

(10) *The Coastal Patrol Organization,* developed by the Navy since 1908, would in wartime be based upon the principal ports along the East Coast, and should considerably shorten the time during which a raiding force could remain unmolested.

(11) *The experience of the naval manœuvres of 1912 and 1913, and of recent wars,* more particularly of the *Italian expedition to Tripoli and of the Russo-Japanese War.* (More information regarding the latter was available than in 1908.)

The Report stated that these factors improved the British position in some respects and worsened it in others; but 'as to how far these changes in the position balance each other is not one that admits of mathematical solution.'

The first conclusion reached was the same as in 1908, only 'invasion' was now defined in a footnote as 'those [forms of attack] which are designed to strike at the heart of the Empire a blow that would either finish the war at once or so weaken our powers of resistance as seriously to imperil our chances of ultimate success.' The second conclusion was slightly changed from 1908. The words in italics were new. 'That if we permanently lose command of the sea, whatever may be the strength and organization of the Home force, the *position of the country would be desperate.*' The third conclusion was unchanged. The fourth conclusion underwent a small change. 'That, in order to ensure an ample margin of safety, such a force may, for purposes of calculation, be assumed to be *of a strength aggregating 70,000 men of all ranks and services lightly equipped with artillery and transport.*' In other words, the Admiralty continued to have every confidence that they could intercept any force other than a very small one, but in order to avoid cutting the margin too fine they considered that provision should be made to deal with 70,000 men. The Sub-Committee agreed with the Admiralty that no new factor had been brought forward which would justify any departure from the 70,000 figure, and so recommended that it continue to provide the basis of the arrangements for Home defence against invasion.

The fifth conclusion was brand-new, replacing both the fifth and sixth in the 1908 report: 'That the Territorial Force, which according to the existing mobilization scheme provides the bulk of the Home Defence army, was never intended to be, and is not sufficiently trained when first mobilized to secure conditions [conclusions] 3 and 4 and requires the support of regular troops until such time as it is fit to take the field. In the earlier stages of a war, if the interests of Home Defence only are considered, it is undesirable to leave less than the equivalent of two divisions of regular troops in this country.' The Sub-Committee felt that, at that time, in the absence of the whole of the Expeditionary Force, the army for Home Defence did not fulfil the requirements laid down in conclusions 3 and 4; and, therefore, that it was undesirable, at least in the earlier stages of a war, to leave less than the equivalent of two divisions of regular troops in the country. But the War Office continued to demand the immediate dispatch of the six divisions. The controversy was not settled until after the war began. Each side then gave up its position. Kitchener, Chief of the Imperial General Staff, decided to send only four divisions immediately, while Churchill on behalf of the Admiralty assumed the responsibility of guarding the United Kingdom in the absence of the whole six divisions.

The report, a unanimous one, was approved in principle by the C.I.D. on 14 May 1914. It was never published. The crucial conclusion, for the Admiralty, was the third. Churchill restated the Admiralty position in the House of Commons, 17 March 1914: 'We have said that in order that our naval defence shall be fully effective, there must be sufficient military force in this country to make it necessary for an invader to come in such large numbers that he will offer a target to the Navy, and certainly would be intercepted if he embarked. . . . It could not be better put than it was put to me by that brilliant naval commander, Sir Arthur Wilson, who said that for the Navy to have to guard this country without any military forces of any kind in this country would be like playing an international football match without a goalkeeper.'

357

It is a fact that the Germans never seriously considered an invasion of Great Britain. Tirpitz was not dissembling when he spoke his mind to Dumas, the Naval Attaché, in 1908. All the invasion talk in England was 'nonsense'. 'Out of the 30,000 military officers in Germany one might expect that one or two sheeps-headed Lieutenants might write such rubbish . . . it was impossible for them to even embark such numbers as say 100,000 men, . . . and in view of our sea forces, quite impossible that they should be disembarked on the other side.' Even if the troops could be landed, Tirpitz insisted, the Germans would not be able to keep open the lines of communication. ' . . . this foolish [invasion] panic was wholly stupid and impossible to understand.' For once the Admiralty was in agreement with Tirpitz! But not the Foreign Office, which regarded Tirpitz's disclaimer as 'absurd', since it was 'well known' that the German military authorities regarded invasion as practicable in certain circumstances and had made plans.[31] This was, of course, the position of the generals, too. We can see today that the Blue-Water School was far more realistic than the rival school of thought.

4. DEFENSIVE STRATEGY: THE *GUERRE DE COURSE* BOGEY

The invasion problem was always something of a 'bogey', an imaginary evil, so far as the Admiralty was concerned. The *guerre de course*, or strategy of commerce destruction, was regarded as a more real danger in time of war, albeit a manageable one.[32] As Balfour phrased the problem (13 January 1910, at York): 'If you drilled every man in this country to the picture of perfection now possessed by the German Army . . . what would it avail you if the sea was not free and open to bring to these shores raw material and the food upon which we depend?' Britain imported nearly two-thirds of the food supply required and did not, as a rule, keep more than a month's or six weeks' supply of food and of raw material for manufacturing industries in stock at any one time. It was therefore of the most vital importance that an uninterrupted supply of these necessities continue to reach British shores.

[31] Dumas to Lascelles, 3 Feb. 1908, and Foreign Office minutes; *British Documents,* vi. 116–17.
[32] For the pre-Fisher era background of the *guerre de course* problem, see *The Anatomy of British Sea Power,* pp. 84–98.

It was easy for one school of thought to prove from history, the French wars in particular, that the *guerre de course* was a weapon of the weaker power and could not win a war. Mahan was often quoted to the effect that the destruction of commerce, regarded as a primary and fundamental measure sufficient in itself to crush an enemy, was probably a delusion—that commerce-raiding in itself could do considerable damage but could never yield decisive results. His English disciples added that the changes which had occurred since the French wars, among them the introduction of wireless telegraphy and steam, were all in favour of the strong maritime power.

Fred T. Jane, the naval journalist, pointed out (*Heresies of Sea Power*, 1906) the logical fallacy in the reasoning of the Mahanites: the *guerre de course* had never been attempted against a power so vulnerable to it as England had become by the twentieth century. More and more it came to be realized that an unrestricted policy of commerce destruction could be exceedingly dangerous to Great Britain in the twentieth century. The Hague Conference of 1907 and the Declaration of London of 1909 were important turning points in this regard. The Hague Conference, while discussing the problem at length, had omitted to forbid conversion of merchant ships into warships upon the high seas. The British proposal that the right of conversion should be limited to ships previously specified in time of peace was rejected without qualification by the German and other delegates. The Declaration of London, a written code of international law to govern naval warfare drawn up in the winter of 1908–9 by the eight great naval nations, did not mention the question. But the intention to convert merchant shipping was frankly avowed, and the right claimed, by the delegates of the foreign states present. This appeared to create a new and gigantic peril for British shipping in the shape of a revival of privateering, which had been abolished by the Treaty of Paris in 1856. The converted liners of the enemy would enjoy at once the rights of neutral merchantmen and those of belligerent men-of-war. They would be able to change with equal facility from the one character to the other. For example, a German merchantman, with guns in her hold and a commission in her master's pocket, might set out from a neutral port while a British cruiser looked helplessly on. As soon as it seemed safe, up would come the guns, the war flag would be hoisted, and the peaceful merchantman would become a commerce-destroyer who might not even be treated as the privateer she really was. This threat was real, since Germany was reported to have fitted her fast merchant vessels for the reception of guns, so that in a very short space of time they could be transformed into commerce-destroyers or auxiliary cruisers. The establishment of the commerce-destroyer, through the inaction of the London Conference, was one aspect of the Declaration that was most vociferously criticized in England and one reason why it was never ratified by the Government.

A conference of N.I.D. chiefs and Fisher on 30 April 1905 considered the whole commerce-protection problem. Its conclusions were that in a future maritime war, 'the first duty of British fleets and squadrons will be to seek out the corresponding fleets and squadrons of the enemy with a view to bringing them to action and fighting for that which is the only really decisive factor—the command of the sea. It was considered that this policy also affords the most effective protection that can be given to our ocean trade against attack by the regular men-of-war of the enemy.'[33] However, the conference did recognize the necessity of providing an organization for the more direct protection of the floating trade in case a number of the enemy's cruisers or armed merchant vessels escaped from the surveillance of British squadrons and attacked merchant shipping. The point to be decided was which of the three systems of protection should be adopted as a general principle—convoy, patrolling trade routes, or stationing squadrons of cruisers at certain points.

Convoy was rejected as impracticable under modern conditions. All the hoary arguments were advanced against it, often in the teeth of history. (They came up again as late as 1938-9.) In sailing days, it was pointed out, ships travelled slowly and were often detained for considerable periods in dangerous localities by light or contrary winds. It was therefore necessary to have protection always at hand for these ships, and this was best done by convoys. Now, in the twentieth century, a steamer could pass quickly through dangerous waters, and could choose her own time for doing so as well as the safest route, and was therefore exposed to far less danger than a sailing ship, which was at the mercy of winds and currents, and whose escape was barred for twelve points

<hr>

[33] 'The Protection of Ocean Trade in War Time', report of an Admiralty meeting, 30 April 1905, to consider the question; Admiralty MSS.

out of the thirty-two of the compass. Moreover, since the assembly of a convoy could no longer be kept secret in these days of telegraph and full information, the convoy offered a splendid prize already prepared for the enemy. Then again, the mass of smoke would always by day, and often by night, mark the position of the convoy, and would attract the enemy from all sides 'like vultures to their prey'. For commercial reasons, the convoy system would be impracticable owing to the time lost by vessels while the convoy was assembling, and to its slow speed, restriction of route, and the delay in unloading because of the congestion at the ports of arrival. Finally, Great Britain's foreign trade was so gigantic that it would be quite impossible to convoy more than a fraction of all the vessels engaged in it; and that even were this attempted, the allocation of a number of cruisers to convoy duty would remove them from the more effective work of hunting down the enemy's commerce-destroyers.

Convoy had very few supporters at the Admiralty prior to the war, and indeed as late as 1917. Mahan had written that convoy, when properly organized, would have far more success as a defensive measure than hunting for individual commerce-destroyers, a process which resembled looking for a needle in a haystack. He was disregarded in this instance. Sir Arthur Wilson rejected convoy (1905) on the ground that the trade was 'too gigantic'. A War Staff study of 1913 on commerce protection considered convoy but did not recommend it, the grounds being quite similar to those of the Admiralty conference we are considering.[34] Churchill, in April 1914, envisaged the use of convoys only· 'in exceptional cases', but hoped that 'this cumbrous and inconvenient measure will not be required'.[35]

The Admiralty and service opinion were in full agreement. Thus, Commander K. G. B. Dewar's Gold Medal Prize Essay for the Royal United Service Institution in 1912, on 'The Influence of Overseas Commerce on the Operations of War', merely touched on convoy and emphasized a concentration of powerful forces in the focal zones as the answer to the problem. The second prize-winner, Commander E. V. F. R. Dugmore, considered convoy completely out-of-date.

[34] Captain Richard Webb, 'Proposed Scheme of Commerce Protection and Work of Trade Branch of the War Staff'; Richmond MSS.
[35] *The World Crisis*, i. 518.

To return to the Admiralty conference of 1905, there remained two other methods of protecting commerce: the system of patrolling vessels along the trade routes or of cruiser squadrons stationed at certain points on the trade routes in order that they might act, as necessity arose, on the information brought to them by passing merchant vessels or reaching them by wireless telegraphy. The conference decided on the latter. Merchant ships were in wartime to be directed to steer along certain clearly defined war routes, passing through focal points which would be guarded by cruisers. Wilson, C.-in-C., Channel Fleet, emphatically rejected the proposals for prescribed routes. His policy was to watch enemy forces and to bring them to action if they left harbour, and to destroy raiders that put to sea. It appears that his policy was the one that was put into effect. In 1913 the War Staff turned down the war routes plan in favour of these principles: (1) the immediate attack on an enemy's armed forces; (2) the dispersion of trade, except in isolated cases. Dispersion would render it very difficult for commerce raiders to locate any special route or to do any great damage while there, and at the same time would free most of the cruisers and mercantile cruisers for their primary duty of destroying the enemy's armed forces.

The fact is that the Admiralty, in this instance following Mahan, held that the *guerre de course* could not possibly be effective, and that nothing more serious than a temporary crisis need be feared. The defeat of the enemy's fleet was inevitable in the early stages of a war, therefore no extraordinary or carefully planned measures of trade defence were called for. A. K. Wilson was among those who underestimated the *guerre de course*. Such attacks 'might cause loss and annoyance, but with ordinary care they are not likely to do us any vital injury, and the enemy's vessels engaged in them will be sure to be gradually sunk, captured, or interned in neutral ports.'[36]

The 1906 naval manœuvres had appeared to prove the strategically fallacious nature of the *guerre de course*. They were designed, in part, to simulate the dangers to which British trade would be exposed in the north-eastern basin of the Atlantic in the earlier phase of a war with a great naval power, and to test the arrangements that might be made in order to minimize those dangers. The percentage of loss of merchant vessels was high

[36] Wilson's memorandum, 'Remarks on War Plans', May 1907; Admiralty MSS.

(fifty-two of the ninety-four ships), but, as the Chief Umpire pointed out, this enemy success was achieved only at the expense of the complete disorganization of his fighting forces. 'It is practically certain that the commencement of the third week of the war would have seen all commerce-destroying ships either captured or blocked in their defended ports.' The Admiralty's conclusion was that 'although a temporary commercial crisis might possibly be caused in London by this form of attack, the complete defeat of the aggressor could not be long delayed, with the result that public confidence would be quickly re-established and the security of British trade assured.'[37]

But what if the enemy fleet refused a general action? And what if the submarine assumed the role of a commerce-destroyer, as Fisher predicted with uncanny foresight in memoranda of 24 June 1912 and January 1914 to Churchill (the former was probably circulated in the Cabinet)? The latter memorandum included this passage: 'Those who lecture on International Law say the civilized world would hold up its hands in horror at such acts of barbarism as a submarine sinking its prey, but yet an enemy can lay mines without outraging propriety! After all, submarines can exercise discretion—mines can't!'[38] In his 1914 memorandum Fisher pointed out that the submarine 'cannot capture the merchant ship; she has no spare hands to put a prize crew on board; little or nothing would be gained by disabling her engines or propeller; she cannot convoy her into harbour; and, in fact, it is impossible for the submarine to deal with commerce in the light and provisions of accepted international law. . . . There is nothing else the submarine can do except sink her capture . . . this submarine menace is a terrible one for British commerce and Great Britain alike, for no means can be suggested at present of meeting it except by reprisals.'[39] This memorandum was sent to the Prime Minister for circulation at the 14 May meeting of the C.I.D. Asquith refused to circulate it, presumably because he, like so many others, thought it fantastic that any civilized people would resort to such savagely ruthless tactics. Jellicoe's revelation, in a speech at Hull in February 1918, that Fisher had predicted the

[37] Admiralty MSS.
[38] *Fear God and Dread Nought*, ii. 505.
[39] 'The Oil Engine and the Submarine', the first draft of which was written in June 1913. The text of the final draft is in Fisher's *Records*, pp. 183–5.

U-boat piracy of the war, and that the Admiralty and presumably the Government had known and ignored the warning, created something of a stir. The fact is that the possibility of the Germans sinking merchantmen without warning was discarded in the pre-war Navy as 'impossible and unthinkable', to quote Keyes. Churchill did not believe 'this would ever be done by a civilized Power' (1 January 1914).[40] He erred in the best of company.

Dr. Pearce Higgins, during his twelve lectures on international law at the War Course in 1914, 'insisted that no submarine would dare to touch a vessel without the proper visit and search being made. He said the civilised world would hold up its hands in horror at such acts of barbarism as a submarine sinking its prey !'[41] Richmond, surely one of the brainiest of British naval officers in the twentieth century, could write, when Assistant Director of Naval Operations, in a memorandum for his chief: 'The submarine has the smallest value of any vessel for the direct attack upon trade. She does not carry a crew which is capable of taking charge of a prize, she cannot remove passengers and other persons if she wishes to sink one.' Richmond's marginal addendum years later reads: 'I made a pretty bad guess there !'[42] The Admiralty memorandum of December 1912[43] flatly declared that the submarine had 'the smallest value of any vessel for the direct attack upon trade. She does not carry a crew which is capable of taking charge of a prize, she cannot remove passengers and other persons if she wishes to sink one. Therefore she will not affect the direct action in attack, which must be made by cruisers and other surface travelling vessels.' A paper read at the Naval War College on 11 June 1914 showed that not more than $5\frac{1}{2}$ per cent of the torpedoes fired during the Russo-Japanese War had taken effect, and anticipated no better results in the future. The difficulty in hitting, the slow rate of fire, and the small number carried made the torpedo a weapon inferior to the gun; the effect produced by a torpedo on a ship of modern construction seemed to be exaggerated and could be minimized.[44]

To the end the Admiralty, the Navy, and naval journalists

[40] Keyes, *Naval Memoirs*, i. 53; *The World Crisis*, ii. 280.
[41] Captain S. S. Hall to Fisher, 26 Apr. 1914; Lennoxlove MSS.
[42] 'Outline of a Memorandum re Submarines', 11–13 July 1914; Richmond MSS.
[43] See above, pp. 334–5.
[44] Cited by Admiral Sir Reginald Custance in a 'Memorandum on Strategy in the North Sea', 29 Oct. 1916, for the First Lord, Balfour; Balfour MSS.

tended to follow Mahan in assuming the indecisiveness of the *guerre de course*. Few appreciated the terrible possibilities inherent in an unrestricted policy of commerce destruction by German submarines. On the very eve of the war Churchill reiterated the traditional position of the Admiralty on trade protection in war:

> The first security for British merchant ships must be the superiority of the British Navy, which should enable us to cover in peace, and hunt down and bring to battle in war, every enemy's warship which attempts to keep the seas. A policy of vigorous offence against the enemy's warships wherever stationed, will give immediately far greater protection to British traders than large numbers of vessels scattered sparsely about in an attitude of weak and defensive expectancy. This should be enjoined as the first duty of all British warships. Enemy cruisers cannot live in the oceans for any length of time. They cannot coal at sea with any certainty. They cannot make many prizes without much steaming; and in these days of W/T their whereabouts will be constantly reported. If British cruisers of superior speed are hunting them, they cannot do much harm before they are brought to action.

But in addition to hunting down enemy warships and raiders, continued the First Lord's memorandum, protection would be afforded to wartime trade by these measures: (1) The provision of a sufficient number of armed merchantmen 'plying on the trade routes' to deal with the armed enemy merchantmen. (2) The best safeguard was the large number of merchant ships trading and of harbours in the United Kingdom. To induce the continuance of sailings, a war-risks insurance scheme was eminently desirable. (3) The dispersion of merchant ships about the ocean (advisory only); later, this might not be necessary or desirable and the ships could return to their regular trade routes. (4) Older cruisers should be stationed at focal points of trade.[45]

In July 1914 this policy was reaffirmed. Something had already been done about the menace of the converted merchant ship and was being done about war-risks insurance. It was not enough, in the opinion of the Admiralty, for the Government to hold out the threat of treating as pirates merchant vessels converted on the high seas, as proposed by Grey in the Commons, 7 December 1911.

The menace cannot possibly be met in the first phase of war operations by any practicable distribution of British warships. Further, the

[45] Churchill's memorandum on 'Trade Protection on and after the Outbreak of War', 23 Aug. 1913, revised in Apr. 1914; *The World Crisis*, i. 516–18.

number of German converted Mercantile Cruisers is such and their possible distribution, for example, in the North and South Atlantic, within two or three days after the Declaration of War, is so wide that it is impracticable for our warships to control them in the first phase. ... The solution of the problem ... is only to be found in an organised system of self-defence for individual merchant vessels, that is to say in a modified form of what was customary in the case of many of the larger Merchantmen during the old wars. In saying so we do not mean that it is necessary that every British merchant vessel should carry the means for self-defence, but we do advocate the adoption of this principle in so far as it may be found practicable.[46]

This report foreshadowed the defensive arming of merchantmen, which policy was announced by Churchill in introducing the 1913 estimates. The Admiralty offered to lend guns to British shipowners, to provide ammunition, and to train gun crews at the public expense, if the owners would pay for the necessary structural alterations. It meant that the Admiralty had gone back to seventeenth-century practice. By the outbreak of the war, thirty-nine ships had been armed with two 4·7-inch guns. It should be stressed that the original object of this defensive armament was to enable merchant ships to defend themselves against the attacks of improvised raiders, that is, lightly-armed enemy merchantmen. The possibility of the employment of the submarine against merchant shipping was not yet fully realized.

The Admiralty was also concerned about the probable panic that would ensue after the inevitable seizure of British merchant ships in the first week of a war, before the Navy could control the situation. It therefore advocated a national guarantee of merchant shipping during war—that is, for the war risks of shipping. It believed this 'indispensable to supplement their arrangements for the protection of overseas commerce in time of war, and there is every probability that prices in the United Kingdom may rise to prohibitive levels, that panic may occur, and that *great pressure may be exercised on the Government either to divert ships from the main theatre of war to the trade routes, thereby imperilling the success of the campaign, or even to submit to peace on unfavourable terms.*'[47] In other words, what the Admiralty feared, *au fond*, was that the public outcry over the rise in prices would have disastrous consequences

[46] Report of an Admiralty Committee on 'The Arming of British Merchant Vessels', 4 May 1912; Admiralty MSS.
[47] *Ibid.* Italics are mine.

upon British naval strategy. A C.I.D. sub-committee report of 1913[48] accepted the views of the Admiralty and the principle of a national guarantee. The full C.I.D. endorsed this conclusion (6 February 1913) and asked that a scheme be elaborated in detail. On 4 August 1914, as the war began, the Government promulgated a State War Risks Insurance Scheme.

* * *

In the war the threat of surface raiders turned out very much as the Admiralty had expected. Admiral Sir Herbert Richmond was, nevertheless, correct in judging that 'the harm done to our commerce at the beginning of the war by the enemy's cruisers, and the greater harm done later by submarines, are both traceable to an easy-going acceptance of the theory that a *guerre-de-course* must fail, without examining the reasons supporting the theory.'[49]

5. OFFENSIVE STRATEGY: FLEET ACTIONS AND BLOCKADE

That the primary duty of the Navy was battle at sea and the destruction of the enemy's battle fleet was the opinion of successive Boards of Admiralty as well as of naval opinion (barring a minority school of thought which became important only in the war and which believed that the 'control of communications' was more important than the destruction of the enemy's navy). 'The principal object,' stated the War Orders for the C.-in-C., Channel Fleet (1 July 1908), 'is to bring the main German Fleet to decisive action, and all other operations are subsidiary to this end.' Such a strategy, if successful, would secure the command of the North Sea and English Channel. This would prevent the enemy from making any serious attack upon British territory or trade, or from interfering with the transport of British troops to France or elsewhere. Trafalgar and the old Nelsonic tradition of attack inspired the Navy. They had won at Trafalgar, declaimed the *Spectator* (29 October 1910), 'because our Fleet, inspired by a great tradition and a great man, recognized that to win you must attack—go for, fall upon, fly at the throat of, hammer, pulverise, destroy, annihilate—your enemy.'

[48] 'Maintenance of Oversea Commerce in Time of War. Report and Proceedings of the Standing Committee of the Committee of Imperial Defence', 18 Feb. 1913; Lennoxlove MSS.
[49] Richmond, *National Policy and Naval Strength* (London, 1927), pp. 226–7.

It was expected that, in a war of the not distant future, the Germans, at their selected moment, would send out the High Seas Fleet to fight for the command of the sea. Churchill was certain, as he told the C.I.D. on 11 July 1912, that the German Navy was 'intended for a great trial of strength with the navy of the greatest Naval Power'. In 1913, the Naval Attaché in Berlin replied in these measured words to the query of the Chief of the Admiralty War Staff, as to whether the Germans in case of war would 'take a big risk': '. . . if war comes within the next two years they would not take a big risk, but that after that time they would do so if our Naval forces had been distracted elsewhere.' Among his reasons:

The Flag Officers suitable for such purpose, who have *not* served as Flag Officers in the days of the old more coastal defence policy, are not yet in the superior commands. But as a result of the Fleet increases and greater practice the junior Rear Admirals and Senior Captains show greater likelihood of taking a more forward policy. The results of the early enterprising training in the Destroyer Flotillas is now having wider effect in the senior ranks.

The serious practice of strategical operations in the North Sea, as opposed to the Baltic, and unhampered by military considerations, was only recently commenced from a wider offensive point of view than that of the mere defence of the River Mouths and Heligoland. It appears to me they require a couple more years of strategical practice in the North Sea. . . .

Until the 3rd Battle Squadron is a completely formed unit it seems unlikely that they will take any big risk. . . .

Further of course the completion of the Kiel Canal, the development of Cuxhaven, and the addition being made to the strength in submarines are all factors of a similar nature. . . .[50]

The ultimate aim in naval warfare is to exert such command at sea as will enable commercial or military traffic to flow unimpeded, and to deny the same command to the enemy. This can be attained either by destroying the enemy's sea forces in battle or, as the next best thing, by nullifying them through a close blockade of the enemy's ports. The latter time-honoured method of exercising command of the sea had been brought to near perfection during the Napoleonic wars. Fast-sailing frigates were stationed off the ports where the enemy ships were lying, and farther out at sea

---

[50] Watson to Sir Henry Jackson, 25 Apr. 1913; Admiralty MSS.

cruised the British ships-of-the-line. The blockaded ships could not proceed to sea without the grave risk of being brought to action. Blockade was then a comparatively simple matter, as a sailing fleet could lie off an enemy's harbour without much danger from attack and with no fuel problem. Steam increased the difficulties of close blockade, since the blockading ships had to be kept supplied with fuel, necessitating a certain number of ships always absent for refuelling. The hazards increased tremendously after 1900. Mines, torpedoes, submarines, and long-range coastal ordnance had by 1912 blown the idea of close blockade to bits. Battleships would never again lie off an enemy's port as the ships of St. Vincent, Nelson, and Cornwallis had lain off Brest and Toulon. The development of aircraft, particularly of airships, made a close blockade still more difficult. The airship, rising to a great height, could examine the sea and detect the location of the heavy ships of a blockading force, which could then be attacked with submarines or destroyers. The Russo-Japanese War was the last big one in which a successful close blockade of a fleet was carried on; at that, the Japanese Fleet off Port Arthur suffered severe losses from anchored mines.

The Royal Navy saw the handwriting on the wall by 1904. The Mediterranean Fleet exercises off Argostoli in October 1901, the joint manœuvres in September 1902 of the Mediterranean and Channel Fleets, and the torpedo-craft manœuvres off Milford Haven in August 1904, sounded the 'last post' of the close blockade. Recognizing that the submarine especially had given the traditional policy of close blockade its *coup de grâce*, Fisher had no great use for that strategy, but he did not entirely scrap it. The War Orders of 1 July 1908 to the C.-in-C., Channel Fleet, specified that the battle fleet would, on the outbreak of war, retire at night 'beyond the utmost limit which hostile destroyers could reach from their own ports if sent out at sunset with orders to return next morning'. This was reckoned at not less than 170 miles from the nearest German destroyer base. 'The main idea is that a force in the Heligoland Bight will be able to cut off any small force which may leave the Elbe or Jahde, or give notice of any movement of the main German Fleet. This service in the Heligoland Bight can be performed sufficiently effectively by a Division of six Destroyers and a scout or cruiser off each river mouth, the small cruisers or scouts out of sight of Heligoland and about thirty miles from the nearest part of the coast, and a squadron of armoured cruisers out of torpedo boat range beyond the small cruisers.'[51]

A. K. Wilson went further, In 1907–8 he wanted to see the close blockade given up entirely.

There are two policies open to us: (i) To endeavour to stop the enemy coming out of his harbours at all.·(ii) To tempt him out and to make the best arrangements we can to catch him at sea. The first course will no doubt be expected by Public opinion, but in the long run the second course, if skilfully conducted, will prove the most effective. A continuous close watch off all the German ports in sufficient strength to prevent anything coming out would be very difficult and costly to maintain, and if effective would bring us no nearer the end. [Fisher commented on this: 'It is interesting that this is the Japanese Minister of Marine's opinion also as secretly conveyed to us.'] The actual capture of their vessels at sea will do them much more harm than merely rendering them inactive in their ports, and if eventually they come to the conclusion that the risk is too great to venture out, we shall have arrived at the same result as if we blocked them in, with much less risk and loss to ourselves.[52]

Wilson had a change of heart when he became First Sea Lord, and the close blockade of the Heligoland Bight was resurrected and incorporated in the War Orders. The strategy was succinctly stated by the Home Fleet C.-in-C. in 1911: 'The present War Plans provide for a blockade of the Heligoland Bight by the 1st and 2nd Destroyer Flotillas, supported by the 1st, 2nd, and 3rd Cruiser Squadrons, with the principal object of (a) preventing raiding expeditions leaving German ports in the earlier stages of hostilities; (b) preventing the German Fleet putting to sea without the British Commander-in-Chief knowing it and, when it is known to be at sea, conveying him such information as to its movements as will enable it to be brought to action by the British Main Fleet.'[53] The Admiralty, or Wilson, anyway, had perfect faith in the strategy. 'There is very little doubt that the Military blockade will be also effective as a Commercial Blockade.'[54]

Close blockade was by this date too risky. No admiral would have undertaken to keep a squadron cruising constantly in the

[51] Admiralty MSS.
[52] Wilson's memorandum, 'Remarks on War Plans', May 1907; *ibid.*
[53] Vice-Admiral Sir Francis Bridgeman's memorandum, 'Blockade of North German Coast of German Empire', 31 Aug. 1911; *ibid.*
[54] Admiralty to Bridgeman, 26 Oct. 1911; *ibid.*

Bight thirty miles from Heligoland. In the middle of 1912 Wilson's close blockade was replaced by an 'observational blockade' of the Bight. This consisted of stretching a line of cruisers and destroyers from the south-west coast of Norway to a point about midway between England and Germany in the latitude of Newcastle-upon-Tyne, and then in a southerly direction towards the Texel and the Dutch coast. The Battle Fleet was supposed to cruise well to the westward of the cruiser-destroyer patrol line. Callaghan's fresh War Orders of 25 November 1912 incorporated the new strategy. 'The general idea of these Plans is to exercise pressure upon Germany by shutting off German shipping from oceanic trade through the action of patrolling cruisers on lines drawn across the approaches to the North Sea, and supporting these cruisers and covering the British coasts by two Battle Fleets stationed so as to be in a position to bring the enemy's fleet to action should it proceed to sea with the object of driving the cruisers off or undertaking other aggressive action.'[55]

The Admiralty explained its change in strategy to the C.I.D. sub-committee of 1913–14 which re-examined the question of invasion:

The continuous development of the mine and the torpedo make it impossible to establish a close watch on the exits from the Heligoland Bight with heavy ships. To do so for a long period of time would mean a steady and serious wastage of valuable units from the above causes, and, if prolonged, would effectually alter the balance of naval power. On the other hand, torpedo craft, which cannot keep at sea like great vessels, and must every three or four days return to port for rest and replacement, have no base nearer than Harwich, 280 miles away. The operation of controlling the debouches from the Heligoland Bight by means of flotillas would require twice the number of oversea torpedo craft than we now possess. The watch would have to be maintained in three reliefs: one on duty, one in transit, and one at rest, and therefore only a third of the existing vessels would be available at any given time. Such a force could be overwhelmed by a sudden attack of two or three times their numbers by a well-chosen blow, opportunities for which would frequently recur.

A supplementary factor was the difficulty and hazard of capturing one of the now fortified German islands. From about 1905 until the Agadir Crisis, Admiralty war plans included the capture

[55] 'General Instructions to the War Plans for the C.-in-C., Home Fleets'; *ibid.*

of one or more German islands, to be established as an oversea base for the blockading flotillas, where the ships could be replenished and the crews rested. Germany had greatly strengthened the fortifications of Heligoland and then fortified all the Frisian Islands that could be useful to the British.

The so-called observational blockade had serious weaknesses. Attrition of the British forces would probably have been more gradual than in the case of a close blockade, but naval manœuvres showed it was impracticable to watch effectively a line nearly 300 miles long by day and night, much less to support it effectively against concentrated German attacks. The attempt to do so would also have absorbed a large number of cruisers and destroyers and deprived the Battle Fleet of their support.

Fortune intervened on behalf of the Navy at the last moment. The last war plans, issued to the Grand Fleet a month before the outbreak of hostilities, abandoned the observational blockade.[56] In conformity with the main strategic idea,[57] the Grand Fleet, upon the warning telegram being issued, would be stationed 'in Northern waters, resting upon the Scottish coast and islands'; the Channel Fleet would be stationed in the English Channel. A few days later the Admiralty notified the C.in-C. that it was 'probable' that Scapa Flow would be his 'preliminary' station.[58] The new war plan of distant blockade, spelled out, amounted to this: the Fleet was to be so disposed in wartime as to block the exits from the North Sea. There would be a southerly line across the Channel from Dover, depending principally upon the Channel Fleet. A northerly line would extend from the Scottish coasts and islands to Norway, with the Grand Fleet based on Scapa Flow in the Orkneys and a line of unarmoured cruisers (the Northern Patrol, it came to be called) spread between the Shetland Islands and the coast of Norway. The last war plans defined the role of the Grand Fleet: 'As it is at present impracticable to maintain a perpetual close watch off the enemy's ports, the maritime domination of the North Sea, upon which our whole policy must be based, will be established as far as practicable by occasional driving or sweeping movements carried out by the Grand Fleet traversing in superior force the area between the 54th and 58th parallels. . . .

[56] 'War Plans (War with Germany)', 3 July 1914; Admiralty MSS.
[57] See below, p. 382.
[58] Admiralty to Callaghan, 11 July 1914; Admiralty MSS.

The movements should be sufficiently frequent and sufficiently advanced to impress upon the enemy that he cannot at any time venture far from his home ports without such serious risk of encountering an overwhelming force that no enterprise is likely to reach its destination.'

The German hopes of victory depended on a British blockade of the Bight, which would provide abundant opportunities to equalize naval strength. They were blissfully unaware of the changes in the war plans made in 1912 and 1914. They deduced from some evidence on recent British manœuvres and from their knowledge of how recent naval developments had outmoded close blockade that a distant blockade would be 'the principle on which the British Command will work'. So far so good; but they assumed that distant blockade and close blockade would 'alternate frequently or merge into one another as the situation changes. It is very probable that during the first days of the war, when attacks on our part may be expected, our waters will be closely blockaded . . . also when it is intended to transport the Expeditionary Force to the Continent.'[59]

Churchill, who was always on the side of the 'seek out, hunt down, and destroy' school, was never very happy over the scrapping of the close blockade strategy.[60] They awaited attack, and the war plans lacked the initiative: they were defensive and made no attempt to strike at the enemy's forces.

It is impossible by a purely passive defensive to guard against all the dangers which may be threatened by an enterprising enemy. When one menace has been provided against, another appears. Along the whole line from the Shetlands to the Straits of Dover we shall be dispersed, anxious, weak and waiting: the only question being where are we going to be hit. Whatever may be said in favour of distant blockade as the guiding policy of a long war, and I agree with what is said, such a policy can only be effectively maintained on a basis of moral superiority. Unless and until our enemy has felt and learned to fear our teeth, it is

[59] From a German Naval Staff paper, 'Information on the British Navy in May, 1914'; *Der Krieg in der Nordsee* (Berlin, 1920–37, 6 vols.), i. 56. This is one of the series in the official German history of naval operations in the war.

[60] The material that follows is from Churchill (writing from Cannes, where 'one gets more time to think on a holiday than in the hustle of daily administration') to Battenberg, 17 Feb. 1913, 'Remarks on War Plans and on the First Lord's Notes on the Subject', 11 Mar. 1913, by Jackson (C.O.S.), and remarks on Churchill's letter by the D.O.D. (Director of the Operations Division, Captain Ballard), n.d., and the Assistant D.O.D. (Captain Richmond), n.d.; Admiralty MSS.

impracticable. We must so conduct ourselves that the sea is full of nameless terrors for him—instead of for us. This means an offensive and at the outset, and recurrence to it from time to time throughout the war.

It is not clear that the passage of the army should be covered not by blocking the Straits of Dover but by blockading the Elbe. Nothing can give us the security we require during the first 10 days of the war except a strong offensive. All the arguments which oppose close blockade as a general and prolonged policy fall out when it is adopted as a vigorous interlude or prelude. The whole flotilla fleet can be used together for the duration of a week, and not merely one relief of a third at a time. With or without oversea bases we can *for a week* establish an overwhelming flotilla superiority in the Heligoland Bight. There lies the true protection for the transports in the Channel, as well as the first and best opportunity of meeting the enemy in conflict, and finding out boat for boat who was the better man. Once we know that unit for unit we are superior, war is easy. Until we do, it is a nightmare of insoluble problems.

The C.O.S. singled out a grave flaw in the plan proposed by the First Lord. On the principle that it was unwise to underrate one's opponent, the German flotillas should be credited with being as efficient as their own, especially when they were acting in their own waters. Moreover, the German North Sea coastline was only 150 miles in length, 120 miles across, and had but three important estuaries—Ems, Jade, Elbe—all very strongly fortified, and with Heligoland guarding the middle. 'Thus we may expect the German Patrol flotillas to deal with ours in their own waters in as efficient a manner as we hope ours will deal with theirs in our waters, and it would be unwise to despatch a weak force to blockade the Heligoland Bight. If we send a force, it must be a strong one, for the Germans can muster 200 torpedo craft besides submarines in the locality, to cover a coastline of 150 miles, or more than one per mile of their coast. They are thus more concentrated naturally than ours are.' Jackson then pointed out how impossible it would be to use all the British torpedo craft as the advanced force in a raid or watch on the Bight, as proposed by Churchill. Eliminating destroyers attached to the Battle Fleet, those guarding the Straits of Dover, and old vessels with a very limited radius of action, only four flotillas (fifty-six destroyers) of large, fast, modern destroyers were available for the operation, and they could remain out but three days, and even then they would require assistance and support from cruisers against the numerically superior enemy destroyers.

The conclusions of the D.O.D. in the main agreed with those of the C.O.S. The key sentence was: 'The First Lord bases this plan upon the assumption that we can establish an overwhelming flotilla superiority for a week in the Heligoland Bight. This is not the case if the enemy chooses to concentrate his own flotillas.' Richmond, the Assistant D.O.D., did not mince words.

I think the First Lord begs the question in his initial remarks. He presupposes that our forces are stretched awaiting the attack of the enemy at all parts of our coast, 'weak and waiting'. What would actually be happening is nothing of the sort. The main battle fleet of this country would be at some place in the North Sea or thereabouts, constituting a permanent barrier to the enemy, who, until he has driven the fleet away or beaten it so decisively that it cannot interfere with the sea-transport of his army, can do nothing which can effectively harm this country.

To say it is impracticable to adopt this attitude until we have made him 'feel our teeth' is not true. The sea will always be full of nameless terrors to him. He will never know either the strength or the where-abouts of our fleet, and until he does know this, and has acted upon it, it is he who is 'weak and waiting', not us. The First Lord speaks of taking an 'immediate offensive' at the outset and recurring to it from time to time. This presupposes that an offensive is possible. It is not. Merely to steam about at sea is not taking the offensive. To bombard the defences of Wilhelmshaven, to attack Wilhelmshaven with an army and attempt to destroy their fleet in the harbour, or to drive it out to destruction by a superior force, *would* be taking an offensive. But merely to do what the old seamen and others used to call having a Spithead Review is not an offensive.

I will agree that proper measures are necessary for safeguarding the passage of the army, and that blocking the Straits of Dover is a measure of doubtful success. But blockading the Elbe is absolutely impractic-able: one can appear off the Elbe, but one cannot blockade it. That is where the submarine and the torpedo craft and the mine come in.

It is just as difficult, from the point of view of the weapons of the enemy, for 10 days, as for a prolonged period. For this reason: that within 10 days the enemy can get all his torpedo craft to work in the area threatened and by the end of that time can materially have reduced our force. To reply that our destroyers would at the same time be on the enemy's coast as an inshore squadron does not get over the difficulty. Not more than $\frac{1}{2}$ of our Destroyers could be present, owing to the necessity of absence for reliefs, and our craft would be doing the most disastrous thing—viz., exposing themselves to defeat in detail. The whole flotilla *cannot* be kept out a week, as First Lord appears to imagine.

There is besides another highly important consideration. Our Fleet would have to be in that part, in full strength, every ship possible, so that the outcome of an action would have as little room for doubt as possible. The result of this would be that after the 10 days were over, our fleet would be exhausted and would have to retire to its own harbours to coal. The men and officers would be as exhausted as the fuel. And the enemy would then have the sea open to do as he chose. No sooner should he know that we had left the coast—and this with a well-organised service of scouting he could quickly know—and that we were back in the Humber or wherever it was, then he could put to sea with his whole undamaged fleet, and, if he chose, his transports, and make a passage across the North Sea. . . .

The whole idea has the basic fault of making war in the weakest manner, in the place best adapted to the enemy. You would allow him to use his whole strength, near his own harbours: if the fight is in-decisive, he can quickly return and be ready again, far more quickly than you [we] can.

The grand drive he suggests is the apotheosis of weakness: a long line of destroyers and cruisers, weak everywhere, strong nowhere, can do nothing. A well-handled, concentrated force can cut into it anywhere and capsize all our plans. As to driving everything before it in a jumble, it would do nothing of the sort, unless the enemy were ignorant of war. The First Lord supposes that after this drive we could 'picket' the Elbe with the full strength of our destroyers. We could not. We should not have 50% of them after this drive. Consider the fuel problem alone and you will see that it must be so. . . .

The question of taking steps to ensure the safe passage of our army certainly requires consideration. At present I do not feel that the torpedo craft in the Straits are a complete security. But there are many other measures for preventing the enemy from interfering besides sacrificing our fleet.

What the First Lord loses sight of is the real function of a fleet or squadron of battleships. It is because he fails to see where our real offensive powers lie that he propounds these fantastic measures,—for such I call them. Sweeps, hustling the enemy, getting him into a jumble —all these are words only. They mean *nothing*: they will not affect well-considered plans of a thinking enemy any more than beating drums or waving flags would do.

The whole incident has been presented in detail, because it was a sort of dress rehearsal for what was to happen in the early months of the war, when Churchill drove his professional advisers to the verge of mental breakdowns with his imaginative but often impracticable schemes for making war.

The First Lord was not put off by the harsh criticisms of the War Staff, and to the outbreak of war the possibility of reverting to some form of close blockade was under consideration. In June 1914 Callaghan was asked to prepare plans for 'a close blockade of the Heligoland Bight by strongly supported Flotillas for 4 or 5 days at the least, closing the Elbe absolutely during that period, without an oversea base.' He was also asked for plans 'with an oversea base'.[61]

One thing was never in dispute. The Admiralty expected that the High Seas Fleet would seek battle on the outbreak of war. The British Fleet would endeavour to oblige it.

6. OFFENSIVE STRATEGY: COMMERCE WARFARE

Britain's traditional conduct of war was based on the decisive economic pressure which sea power could bring to bear, supplemented by amphibious expeditions against the enemy's vulnerable points and the subsidization and supply of allied armies on the Continent. That was how the ambitions of Philip II, Louis XIV, and Napoleon had been frustrated—and, more recently, Hitler.

An American professor has shown that pre-war German economists and policy-makers, even when they had given it thought, were not too worried about the effects of an economic blockade. 'Most military men simply refused to consider the problem of blockade as pertinent to their conception of Continental war. German naval circles restricted their view of blockade, or were confined in it, to fleet problems.'[62] This attitude is extraordinary in the light of British naval thought, published as well as unpublished, on the subject, which accepted as gospel Mahan's celebrated passage telling how after the destruction of the French Navy, 'to the strife of arms with the great Sea Power succeeded the strife of endurance. Amid all the pomp and circumstance of

[61] The Chief of the War Staff (Jackson), at the direction of the Board, to C.-in-C., Home Fleets, 15 June 1914; Admiralty MSS.
[62] Henry Cord Meyer, 'German Economic Relations with Southeastern Europe, 1870–1914', *American Historical Review*, Oct. 1951.

the war which for ten years to come desolated the Continent, amid all the tramping to and fro over Europe of the French armies and their auxiliary legions, there went on unceasingly that noiseless pressure upon the vitals of France, that compulsion whose silence, when once noted, becomes to the observer the most striking and awful mark of the working of Sea Power.'[63] This was a theory of naval warfare which saw in economic pressure a consequence of command of the sea more pregnant of decisive influence than the power to move freely to some oversea objective the small army of an island state.

This is brought out clearly in the discussion of the right to capture private property at sea. By this was meant the existing right allowed to a belligerent state in time of war (1) to capture and confiscate enemy merchant ships and enemy cargoes on board such ships on all occasions when met with on the high seas or in the waters of a belligerent; and (2) to capture and confiscate, or otherwise penalize, neutral merchant ships if they offended against neutrality. The first point is of interest to us, as it poses the problem of the extent to which attack on German commerce in wartime figured in the offensive strategy of the Royal Navy. The second, the whole problem of neutral rights, concerned foreign policy mainly. The Declaration of Paris (1856) conferred protection upon belligerent property (other than contraband) if carried in neutral ships, but imposed no restriction upon the capture of belligerent ships and their cargoes, being belligerent property, except that privateering was abolished. While, therefore, since the Napoleonic wars a considerable advance had been made in the direction of mitigating the liability of neutrals, the privately-owned shipping and cargoes of a belligerent remained always at the mercy of an enemy. It was natural that the hardships which might thus be inflicted on innocent persons should have appealed to popular imagination, and for many years the principle of according immunity to private property at sea, under international agreement, had found powerful advocates. The government of the United States had urged immunity for private property at sea for over a hundred years; the British attitude had been consistently hostile.

The Admiralty was unanimous that the immunity of private

[63] *The Influence of Sea Power upon the French Revolution and Empire, 1793–1812* (Boston, 1892, 2 vols.), ii. 184.

property at sea could not be conceded. Its position never veered an iota from that laid down in 1906: '. . . the British threat upon German trade is a tremendous one, both by reason of Great Britain's overwhelming preponderance at sea and of her geographical position. The British Islands lie like a Breakwater 600 miles long athwart the German trade stream and *nothing* should elude our vigilance when once "War on German trade" is established. For the present therefore the Right of Capture of Private property at sea is of great value to this country and ought to be firmly maintained.'[64] This was the position of the C.I.D., too, Clarke, its Secretary, writing that the value of the right of capture to Great Britain would be at a maximum in the case of war with a power like Germany which possessed the largest foreign trade and shipping tonnage on the Continent. It followed from Britain's geographical and naval advantages that the German flag would quickly be driven from the high seas. 'It is impossible to estimate the degree of economic stress which would thus be imposed upon Germany; but clearly such stress would be severely felt throughout the whole commercial and industrial structure, and all the elements of the population depending thereon.'[65] Ottley, as D.N.I. and later as Secretary of the C.I.D., was another firm believer in the strategy of throttling Germany's sea-borne trade. This alone, he believed, could win the war by severing an artery essential to the existence of Germany. The problem was

constantly under investigation during the whole three years I was D.N.I., and Admiral Slade tells me he has given particular attention to it since he succeeded me. . . . throughout the whole period that I was D.N.I. the Admiralty claimed that the geographical position of this country and her preponderant sea-power combine to give us a certain and simple means of strangling Germany at sea. They held that (in a protracted war) the mills of our sea-power (though they would grind the German industrial population slowly perhaps) would grind them 'exceedingly small'—grass would sooner or later grow in the streets of Hamburg and widespread dearth and ruin would be inflicted.[66]

An elaborate set of war plans was prepared by a secret three-man committee at the War College (under the chairmanship of

[64] Admiralty to C.I.D., 12 May 1906; Admiralty MSS.
[65] Clarke's memorandum, 'The Capture of Private Property at Sea', 14 May 1906; Lennoxlove MSS.
[66] Ottley to McKenna, 5 Dec. 1908; McKenna MSS.

Captain G. A. Ballard) in 1906–7. It was made clear that they were 'not in any way to be considered as those definitely adopted, but are valuable and instructive because illustrative of the variety of considerations governing the formation of War Plans.' Of the eight plans of action in a war with Germany considered by the authors the two which were developed in some detail aimed at bringing pressure to bear on the enemy by 'the destruction or enforced idleness of shipping under the German flag.'[67]

Mahan and Corbett showed that the interests of Britain, as the chief maritime power of the world, would be most seriously jeopardized by abandonment of the right of capture. 'As a matter of European politics,' Mahan adumbrated, 'the right of maritime capture is the principal, if not the only, strong weapon of offence possessed by Great Britain against the nations in arms of the Continent.'[68] Corbett believed that although 'intrinsically the capture of property on the high seas has an almost negligible value, as a deterrent its value is beyond measure. . . . It is the feeling that a ship and her cargo are never safe from capture from port to port that is the real deterrent, which breaks the heart of merchants and kills their enterprise.'[69] The deterrent effect of the right of capture was emphasized by Clarke, too.

Despite the weight of opinion against abandonment of the right of capture of private property at sea, there were segments of British opinion, especially the Liberal press and the Lord Chancellor, Loreburn, which urged the abolition of the right. The principal argument was that abolition would destroy the German incentive to compete with the British Navy, since the most plausible justification of the increase of the German Fleet was the necessity of protecting Germany's maritime commerce. That is, naval disarmament and the exemption of private property from capture hung together. It was also argued that the exercise of the right of capture would not lead to decisive results because the enemy would be supplied by neutrals.

With neutrals demanding, as always, the abolition of the right of capture, under the attractive slogan of 'The Freedom of the Seas', there was a chance that the Hague Conference would act.

[67] 'War Plans', Apr. 1907; Admiralty MSS.
[68] Mahan's letter in *The Times*, 4 Nov. 1910.
[69] Corbett, 'The Capture of Private Property at Sea', *Nineteenth Century*, June 1907. Fisher congratulated Corbett on the article, and Mahan reprinted it as a chapter in his *Some Neglected Aspects of War* (1907).

Hardinge was aroused. 'The principal objection of a practical nature which I foresee in the adoption of such a principle is that once that merchant shipping is immune from capture by the enemy the chief danger to Germany from a war with England will have been removed.'[70] The fears of Hardinge, the King, and the Admiralty that the Hague Conference would blunt the offensive capacity of British sea power were not realized. Germany was the only naval power which gave the United States even nominal support in the attempts of the latter at The Hague to restrict the right of capture. Although twenty-one countries favoured, and only eleven opposed, the American resolution, the minority was so powerful as to make the vote of little practical weight.

A. K. Wilson was rather exceptional in placing a low value on commerce warfare *per se*. 'The stoppage of German trade or the capture of their ships would have little or no effect on the result.' But he was among the first to see in the pressure exerted by an economic blockade a good prospect of forcing the High Seas Fleet to come out and offer battle in the open sea.[71] Admiral of the Fleet Sir William May agreed.

In the event of war with Germany alone, it is considered that the British Navy cannot with any reasonable chance of success make an offensive movement, such as bombarding Heligoland or other fortified position, and, therefore, until their fleet proceed to sea, we are limited to capture Germany's over-sea trade: This, if done methodically, will cause Germany a vast amount of inconvenience. . . . In all probability, the capture of German merchant ships will exasperate the nation, and the public feeling will be so strong that the German war fleet will be forced to come out and give battle to the British fleet.[72]

The war plans pointed up the reliance on delivering a grave blow through the strangulation of German commerce. 'An effective commercial blockade of all German Ports' was part of the general orders furnished the C.-in-C., Channel Fleet, in June 1905. Later war plans stressed, in addition, the advantage seen by Wilson and May. The C.O.S., Jackson, pointed out the central feature of the war plans. They were 'directed against Germany's mercantile marine, with the hopes that sufficient pressure can be

[70] Hardinge to King Edward, 26 Aug. 1906; Windsor MSS.
[71] Wilson's memorandum, 'Remarks on War Plans', May 1907; Admiralty MSS.
[72] May's memorandum, 'Proposed Disposition of the British Fleet in the Event of War with Germany Alone', Dec. 1912; *ibid.*

brought, through dislocating her trade, for the German Fleet to seek action with ours, and so end the struggle.'[73] As stated in the 'General Instructions' to the war plans issued on 25 November 1912;

> Their general idea is to use our geographical advantage of position to cut off all German shipping from oceanic trade and to secure the British coasts from any serious military enterprise and incidentally but effectually to cover the transport across the Channel of an Expeditionary Force to France should the Government decide upon such an operation. . . . It is believed that the prolongation of a distant blockade will inflict injury upon German interests, credit, and prestige sufficient to cause serious economic consequences to Germany. . . .
>
> To relieve such a situation, Germany would be tempted to send into the North Sea a force sufficient not only to break up the lines of lighter vessels actually employed upon the blockade but to offer a general action. Such an action or actions would take place far from the German coast and close to our own.[74]

The last war plans to be issued before the war enunciate the same policy:

> The general idea is primarily to ensure the destruction of the enemy's naval forces and obtain command of the North Sea and Channel with the object of preventing the enemy from making any serious attack upon British territory or trade or interfering with the transport of British troops to France should the situation necessitate their despatch. Until the primary object is attained, the continual movement in the North Sea of a fleet superior in all classes of vessels to that of the enemy will cut off German shipping from direct oceanic trade, and will as time passes inflict a steadily increasing degree of injury on German interests and credit sufficient to cause serious economic and social consequences. To prevent or counter this Germany may send a force into the North Sea sufficient not only to break up the Squadrons actually employed in watching the entrances, but also to offer a general action. Germany may also in combination with the above attempt raids upon our coasts by military disembarkations.[75]

To sum up, there was full appreciation, certainly at the Admiralty, of the commerce-warfare method of applying force at sea, although the idea of 'commerce prevention' had by 1914,

---

[73] 'Remarks on War Plans and on the First Lord's Notes on the Subject', 11 Mar. 1913; Admiralty MSS.

[74] Admiralty MSS.

[75] 'War Plans (War with Germany)', 3 July 1914; *ibid.*

with the institution of the distant blockade policy, superseded the idea of 'commerce destruction'. British cruiser warfare on German trade was relegated to a secondary position, as it was foreseen that the closing of the exits from the North Sea into the Atlantic would cut German trade off from the world. As stated in Churchill's 'Trade Protection' paper of April 1914, 'British attacks on the German trade are a comparatively unimportant feature in our operations, and British cruisers should not engage in them to the prejudice of other duties. Economic pressure will be put on Germany by the distant blockade of her shores, which will cut off her trade, both export and import, as a whole.'[76]

British naval thinking in the pre-war decade did not anticipate the extraordinary degree to which blockade would throttle the German war economy in 1914–18. This was natural. In the past no nation, except England, was dependent upon oversea trade as were Continental nations in the early twentieth century. Europe had not yet seen a war in which a highly industrialized nation was confronted, soon after the outbreak of war, with unemployment on a large scale and an arrest of industry, consequent on successful prevention of oversea commerce. Nevertheless, it was considered at the Admiralty that a blockade would not only seriously weaken Germany, economically, but would very likely bring on an event devoutly desired by the whole Navy—a general fleet action.

7. OFFENSIVE STRATEGY: COMBINED OPERATIONS

Alice summed up the inter-service wrangle on the subject of combined operations when she said to the Cheshire Cat, 'They all quarrel so dreadfully, and they don't seem to have any rules in particular, and you've no idea how confusing it all is.'

In 1905 a sub-committee of the C.I.D. had been instituted, at Balfour's instance, to decide upon the practicability of various plans for combined naval and military action, and for working out these plans in detail. The sub-committee fell into abeyance after a few years and was re-established only on the very eve of the war, 21 July 1914, at the suggestion of the Admiralty War Staff. Esher complained in 1910 that 'in spite of all that has happened since 1904, Ministers and Sea Lords, etc., cannot get the idea out of their heads that you can fight a great war in water-tight

[76] *The World Crisis*, i. 517.

compartments—the Navy to manage the sea part of the business, the Foreign Office and the War Office to do their share, etc.'[77] The lack of a joint strategic planning staff headed by the Chief of the Imperial General Staff and the First Sea Lord was a grave defect. An American scholar has observed that 'While the Committee of Imperial Defense brought the professional leaders into organized relation with the statesmen, the experts appeared as *individual* advisers on problems connected with their services, and not as members of a *collective* military advisory organ encompassing *both* services. This left strategic plans somewhat compartmented . . .'[78] But a joint planning body was not possible at the time and, indeed, did not come until 1923.

Part of the difficulty lay in the snobbishness of the Executive branch of the Navy, which was the only branch that mattered then. This came out most clearly in the Executive N.O.'s relations with naval officers who were not executive.[79] He had the same kind of superiority complex *vis-à-vis* all his contemporaries. He was a finer fellow, say, than the lawyer or the doctor—or his Army opposite number. Typical, if rather extreme, was Fisher's opinion of the War Office and the generals—for example, that 'any silly ass could be a general'. This attitude made any kind of effective inter-service co-operation very difficult. Nor did the extreme reticence of Fisher and Wilson about the Navy's war plans help matters. The former told Knollys that 'if the War Office knew of them, they would be in the newspapers before a week was over, and it was on this account, principally, as I understood him, that the Admiralty were reluctant to divulge their war plans to anybody or to the War Department.' This struck Knollys as absurd, as well it might, since, obviously, the two services had to work together in the event of war.[80] More deadly still to the preparation in peacetime for Army–Navy co-operation in war was the clash between the 'amphibious' strategy of the Navy and the 'Continental' strategy of the Army.

The Fisher–Wilson school of thought believed in amphibious

---

[77] Esher to Balfour, 16 Aug. 1910; *Esher*, iii. 14.

[78] Franklyn A. Johnson, *Defense by Committee: the Origins and Early Development of the British Committee of Imperial Defense, 1885–1916* (unpublished doctoral dissertation, Harvard University, 1952), p. 306; published in revised and expanded form as *Defence by Committee: the British Committee of Imperial Defence, 1885–1959* (London, 1960). The passage quoted does not appear in the published book, but compare p. 110.

[79] See above, pp. 29, 48.

[80] Knollys to Esher, 29 Dec. 1909; Esher MSS.

warfare, that is, in joint naval and military operations designed to create a major diversion by throwing all or part of the B.E.F. ashore at some point on the German coast, near the heart of the enemy's power, or on the flank and rear of the main body of the enemy. Fisher's choice spot was fourteen miles of sandy beach on the Pomeranian coast, ninety miles from Berlin, 'impossible of defence' against the devastating fire-power of the British Fleet. He also envisaged joint operations for the seizure of a base for British torpedo and submarine craft on the enemy's coast—on Schleswig-Holstein, for example. A favourite quotation of his was Sir Edward Grey's statement, 'The British Army is a projectile to be fired by the Navy.' He was mindful that this had been the traditional task of the Navy, exploiting the advantages of speed and surprise against a numerically superior Continental army. Corbett's thinking had unquestionably influenced him. Corbett, then a lecturer in history at the Royal Naval War College, had written, in *The Successors of Drake* (1900): 'We speak glibly of "sea power", and forget that its true value lies in its influence on the operation of armies.' The same principle was brought out in his later works. Always he wished to elucidate the intimate relation between military and naval strategy and the fact that strategic thought had too long regarded these elements separately.

Fisher could never accept the strategic soundness of the General Staff's schemes for using the whole of the B.E.F. as an extension of the left flank of the French Army. These ideas of England engaging her small army in a great Continental war were 'grotesque' and 'made his hair stand on end'. Esher, Clarke, and King Edward were in sympathy with him. But was his own idea of diversionary attacks in the form of joint operations practicable? His critics have said that it ignored the fact that the real strength of such an operation could only be exercised against enemy territory overseas, cut off from reinforcements and far distant from his dockyards and industrial centres. Captain A. C. Dewar has observed: 'Any attempt to land and maintain a large force in the Baltic or Bight must have involved the blocking or blockade of Kiel and Wilhelmshaven. How on earth or sea this was to be effected, neither Lord Fisher nor anyone else has ever ventured to explain.' Another line of criticism stresses the narrow entrances to the Baltic, which could easily be mined. Are these strictures sound?

Yes and no is the answer. The subject will receive a fuller treatment when we consider Fisher's strategic ideas in the first year of the war.

More germane to the present discussion is that the generals saw nothing in Fisher's Baltic Scheme that recommended itself from a military point of view. Here, briefly, are a few case histories to illustrate the profound divergence in strategy between the sister services. In September 1905, at the time of the Moroccan Crisis, Fisher urgently proposed that the War Office and Admiralty work out (by the beginning of October!) plans for joint operations in the Baltic. The French were assumed to be allies. Privately, the General Staff officers were almost derisive. Officially, the scheme received a cold douche.

It seems doubtful if 120,000 troops, if they made a successful descent on the Baltic coast, would contain so many as 400,000 German regular troops and Landwehr, and relieve the French of that amount of pressure. The Germans have about 850,000 organised Landsturm for home defence, and although these troops would not be of the highest class or possess much manœuvring power they should be able to offer a stolid resistance to the advance of an army of inferior numerical strength. The railways lend themselves to rapid concentration. . . .

An efficient army of 120,000 British troops might just have the effect of preventing any important German successes on the Franco-German frontier, and of leading up to the situation that Germany, crushed at sea, also felt herself impotent on land. That would almost certainly bring about a speedy, and from the British and French point of view satisfactory, peace.

A covering note to the Admiralty added: 'This must not be taken to be in any way authoritative but I think the C.G.S. [Chief of the General Staff, Lyttelton] and D.M.O. [Director of Military Operations, Grierson], who are away, would probably concur in it.'[81]

The generals continued to think that the idea of a Baltic diversion had nothing to commend it from a military point of view. No important objective was vulnerable to a joint attack, and the British Army was too small to be able to occupy a large portion

[81] Memorandum by Colonel Charles E. Callwell (Assistant D.M.O.), 'British Military Action in Case of War with Germany', and covering note to Ballard, Assistant D.N.I., 3 Oct. 1905; Admiralty MSS. The interesting discussions of the General Staff leading up to the memorandum are in a folder marked 'E2/10' in the War Office MSS.

of the German army detailed for the defence of the German Baltic coast. Such an operation 'could produce no decisive military effect; while in the meantime the decisive battles of the land campaign might have been lost for lack of our support and assistance. Direct support to the French army affords a better prospect of useful result.'[82] Fisher, just as unyielding, never retreated an inch from his belief in a 'maritime' strategy for the Army. Although he co-operated with the soldiers to the extent of permitting the General Staff in 1909 to work out the details of the sea transport of the B.E.F. with N.I.D. and the Director of Transport, whenever he had an official opportunity of expressing his views on the larger question, he did not hesitate to do so and with his customary vehemence. One such occasion was at a joint meeting of the C.I.D. and the Cabinet on 3 December 1908. The French Government, at one point within an inch of war with Germany, had insisted on 120,000 British troops being sent to France. The Cabinet agreed. Fisher remained silent. The only question put to him was whether the Navy could guarantee transport, to which he answered 'yes'. Asquith then asked if he had anything to say, and the Admiral replied 'that he had nothing to say that anyone present would care to hear.' When Asquith pressed him, a scene took place. Fisher stated forcibly that if 120,000 English troops were sent to France, the Germans would put everything else aside and make any sacrifice to surround and destroy them, and they would succeed. Continental armies being what they were, Fisher's view was that the British Army should be absolutely restricted to operations consisting of sudden descents on the German coast, the recovery of Heligoland, and the garrisoning of Antwerp (from Belgium a British force would be in a position to threaten the flank or even the rear of a German army advancing into France). He reminded the meeting of the stretch of smooth, sandy Pomeranian coast only ninety miles from Berlin. Were the British Army to seize and entrench that strip, a million Germans would find occupation (a gross exaggeration, or was it wishful thinking?); 'but to dispatch British troops to the front in a Continental war would be an act of suicidal idiocy arising from the distorted view of war produced by Haldane's speeches and childish arrangements for training Territorials after war broke out. Fisher followed this up with an impassioned diatribe against the War

[82] Memorandum E2/17 by the General Staff, Nov. 1908; War Office MSS.

Office and all its ways, including conceit, waste of money, and ignorance of war.' At this point Asquith said, 'I think we had better adjourn'![83] For the balance of Fisher's term at the Admiralty and until the summer of 1911 the C.I.D. did not consider, nor did the soldiers propose, any plan for helping France by means of an expeditionary force to take part in the main fighting inland.

August 1911 brought a showdown. With the arrival of General Sir Henry Wilson at the War Office as Director of Military Operations, in August 1910, the military conversations with the French and the question of the employment of the British Army took a new turn. Wilson, an ardent Francophile and under the influence of General Foch, was an out-and-out advocate of unlimited participation in a Continental war and of alignment with the French Army against the common foe. He believed that the largest possible British army should go across in the shortest possible time after the outbreak of war to join up with the French Field Army. He had no high opinion of the value of the Navy in a great war (no more than did the French statesmen and generals— Generals Castelnau and Joffre did not value it at one bayonet, except from the moral point of view). Apparently Wilson conceived the role of the Navy as primarily defensive. Its principal function was to guard home waters against invasion and to help make British military assistance to France as prompt and powerful as possible by keeping open communications across the Channel, so that British troops, the B.E.F., could be hurried across to join the French Army as an extension of its left flank. Wilson had the support of both Haldane and Grey. A Wilson–Dubail (French Chief of Staff) agreement of July 1911 called for the dispatch of six divisions of British troops to France on certain specified days after mobilization, and enumerated the French ports where they were to disembark and the zone of concentration in France to which they were to proceed. But the naval arrangements for the transport of the B.E.F. had not been worked out and could not be worked out so long as the Admiralty remained hostile.

A head-on clash between the opposing viewpoints was inevitable,

[83] Memorandum of 18 Nov. 1909, author unknown, of a conversation that day with Fisher; Kilverstone MSS., quoted in Bacon, *Fisher*, ii. 182–3. The memorandum appears to be the only source extant on this meeting. The date, 3 December 1908, is suspect. International tensions had eased after the Casablanca Crisis, and the Bosnian Crisis had not yet reached its critical stage.

and it came at the historic C.I.D. meeting of 23 August 1911, called to consider what should be done if war resulted from the Agadir Crisis.[84] General Wilson stated the case for a Continental strategy with his customary lucidity and skill. Against the approximately forty divisions of the German main attack, the French could probably place thirty-seven to thirty-nine divisions. It was, he asserted, quite likely that the six British divisions, the whole of the available regular army, might prove the deciding factor in a Franco-German war, although their material value was far less than their moral value. The Germans would not hesitate to march through southern Belgium. Haldane asked if the War Office might assume the Admiralty could arrange for the safe transport of the B.E.F. across the Channel within the thirteen to fourteen days contemplated in the General Staff scheme. A. K. Wilson thought the Admiralty could perform this task without serious difficulty.

The Prime Minister now asked for the strategic views of the Admiralty. A. K. Wilson made three critical observations on the General Staff strategy: (1) There was considerable risk of panic in the country on the outbreak of war if the entire regular army were sent to the Continent, and this might result in circumscribing the movements of the Fleet. That is, there would be great pressure brought upon the Government to tie the Fleet to the defence of the coast. (2) Small enemy raids might cause serious damage unless promptly met by regular troops. (He made it clear later in his testimony that untrained Territorial troops would not do, since the speed with which raids were met was all-important; the Army proposed to denude the country of regular troops.) Also there were many undefended points on the East Coast which might be important to the Navy in time of war and for which, therefore, the Army would be called upon to furnish protection. (3) The Navy would need regular troops for co-operation in naval operations. Wilson then outlined naval strategy on the outbreak of war:

. . . to blockade the whole of the German North Sea coast. The important portions of this were the estuaries of the Elbe, Weser, and Jade. . . . Owing to the Kiel Canal we should also be compelled to watch the entrance to the Baltic. We had no wish to prevent the German Fleet from coming out, but unfortunately, if we left them free

[84] The account which follows is from the official minutes of this, the 114th, meeting of the C.I.D.; Asquith MSS.

to do so, their destroyers and submarines could get out also, and their exit it was anxious to prevent. If possible we should maintain our watch upon the German coast-line with destroyers. They would, however, be 300 miles away from any British base, so that none of them could remain very long at a time on the station, and consequently the number present at any moment would be reduced. . . . Outside the destroyers would be the scouts and cruisers, and on these the destroyers would retire when driven off by the enemy's larger ships.

It would facilitate a close blockade, continued Wilson, to capture: Wangeroog Island, at the entrance to the Jade, as it would be very useful to Germany as a signal station; Schillighorn, to prevent Germany laying mines in the Jade estuary at night, and it could be used as an advanced British destroyer base; the new fort at the entrance to the Weser; Büsum, from which the Kiel Canal could be threatened.

In this way, apart from the direct advantage to the Navy which would result from the capture of these signal stations and forts, etc., the German North Sea coast would be kept in a state of constant alarm. Our force, having its transports close at hand, would be highly mobile, and could be landed and embarked again before superior forces could be assembled to destroy it. If in this way we could retain 10 German divisions of which General Wilson has spoken on the North Sea coast, we should make a material contribution to the Allied cause by keeping these men not only from the theatre of war elsewhere, but from normal productive labour, possibly in dockyards or kindred industries. That meant that we should intensify the economic strain upon Germany.

One division of regular troops, perhaps more, was essential for these operations. They might even, later on, try to destroy or drive out the German Fleet at Wilhelmshaven, although this would involve regular siege operations. And it would be necessary to take Heligoland as soon as possible after the outbreak of war, which Wilson proposed to do with marines. He did not anticipate any difficulty.

The Admiral was subjected to a sharp cross-examination by Churchill and the generals. Field-Marshal Sir William Nicholson, the Chief of the Imperial General Staff, made the point that if the transports, in the Admiralty's operations, were kept close at hand, they would be exposed to attack by German submarines and destroyers (upon which Wilson had laid so much stress in his invasion memorandum of 1910); but if they were not, the mobility of the forces landed from them or re-embarked in them would be no greater than, if as great as, that of the enemy's land forces, served as they would be by excellent rail communications. The Admiral's rejoinder was that command of the sea enabled them to hold two or three places as bridgeheads and reinforce whichever they wished. General French claimed that the Germans would have equal facilities for concentrating overwhelming force secretly against any of these points. Wilson countered that all the places he had mentioned were exposed to fire from seaward, which would enable the ships to support the troops. This would involve keeping the Fleet very close to the shore, Churchill pointed out, exposing the ships to the fire of shore guns and torpedo attack. Nicholson added that at night, when the ships could not lie close in, there was nothing to prevent the Germans from overwhelming the detachments landed, regardless of how well entrenched or defended they might be. As to the economic pressure alleged by Wilson, the Germans, according to Nicholson, would mobilize these ten divisions in any case. 'The truth was that this class of operation possibly had some value a century ago, when land communications were indifferent, but now, when they were excellent, they were doomed to failure. Wherever we threatened to land, the Germans could concentrate superior force. . . . As to the fire of the guns of the Fleet, he thought its effect was overrated.' Both Nicholson and Churchill felt that the idea of taking Wilhelmshaven was out of the question. Nicholson cited the Japanese General Nogi, who lost 70,000 men before Port Arthur was captured (1905), although he had 200,000 men for the siege and was entirely protected from any interference with his operations by a large field army.

Undaunted, Wilson plodded on. It might be necessary for the Fleet to enter the Baltic—it was probable they could get through, as the Germans would not outrage the Danes by laying mines in their waters—and blockade the Prussian coast. For this purpose they would have to capture naval bases in those waters like Fehmarn Island, and Swinemünde and Danzig might be attacked. This was too much for Nicholson, who bluntly asked if the Admiralty would continue to press that view even if the General Staff expressed its considered opinion that the military operations in which it was proposed to use a regular army division were madness. No reply is recorded. Grey at this point threw in his lot with the Generals. He did not see that the combined operations mentioned by Wilson were essential to naval success; besides, the struggle on land would be the decisive one. Churchill raised a similar point. Were very close blockade and the landing of troops, involving the risking of ships against forts and in narrow waters, essential to British strategy? Yes, replied Wilson. 'All the experience of recent manœuvres showed that close blockade was necessary. Any other policy would require a greatly increased number of destroyers. The safety of our Fleet depended upon preventing the German destroyers from getting out . . . the intention of the Admiralty to order this close blockade was one which it was absolutely essential to keep secret. It was not even known to the Fleet. The occupation of the places he had indicated would enable our destroyers to lie near to the shore.' Churchill asked if it was of vital importance to keep the German destroyers shut in, and whether the Fleet would be able to beat off an attack by torpedo craft at night. Wilson replied that if the enemy destroyers knew the position of a fleet accurately, they would almost certainly meet with success at night. If a destroyer got within 3,000 yards of a battleship at night, she could sink her. Nicholson asserted that the creeks and islands along this coast were so numerous that nothing short of the occupation of the whole coastline by British troops would be of much service. Churchill asked why the Admiralty thought there was so much danger from raids in view of the proposed close blockade. The blockading ships might be driven off temporarily, said Wilson, and then the whole German Fleet might come out. But that was what the Navy most desired, Churchill retorted!

And so it went on. The many acrimonious exchanges had revealed how far apart were the Army and Navy positions. The following letter written by Hankey at the time suggests the spirit of the meeting better than the official minutes.

A tremendous battle was fought at yesterday's packed meeting. Crewe and Harcourt and Morley, who might be expected to take the naval view, were excluded. Winston and Lloyd George, who are more or less converts to the military view, were present. . . . After a battle which raged from 11:30 a.m. to 5:30 p.m. no decision was arrived at. No further meeting will be held at the C.I.D., and, if discussed again, it will be in the Cabinet, where the forces will be more properly balanced. A. K. W. put up a rare fight—considering that the thing had been sprung on him almost at a moment's notice, with his D.N.I. on leave—but, as you know, he is no dialectician and I don't think he made a good impression. He allowed himself to be drawn too much about his naval intentions, a subject on which you always declined to be drawn. McKenna was altogether admirable and redressed the balance of argument. Old Nick [Nicholson] lost his temper hopelessly, of course. . . . [Haldane] had many sharp passages with McKenna . . . Grey was entirely judicial.

The great point is that no decision was arrived at. This means, in my opinion, defeat of our opponents.[85]

Hankey was wrong. It was the War Office point of view that was to carry the day.

The immediate aftermath of the C.I.D. meeting was an Admiralty proposal to the War Office, 29 August, that it keep available a force of 6,000 infantry, a field company of Royal Engineers, three batteries of artillery, a cyclist company (for scouting), a small telegraph company, and a few airmen—this force to be ready, at the shortest possible notice, to assist the C.-in-C. in the North Sea

in such undertakings as seizure of an island or point of land, the destruction of a signal station, molesting the enemy in any attempt to erect new advanced works by surprise attacks, taking possession of works whose guns have been silenced by the fleet, and generally for the attack of any positions which are found by reconnaissance from the shore or inshore flotillas to be unprepared or inadequately defended. . . . The force should be embarked in transports as soon as possible after the outbreak of war and kept in the Thames or any convenient place on the east coast from which they can be ordered, when required by the Naval C.-in-C., to proceed to any desired rendezvous where they will receive their orders.

This was a rather cheeky proposal in view of the attitude of the Generals as expressed at the C.I.D., and the War Office reply (8 September) could have been predicted.

. . . in view of the precautions which in war the enemy may reasonably be expected to take for the purposes of coast defence, the fortifications which have already been constructed and armed, the large and efficient military force which is available to repel attempted landings, and existing facilities for the rapid concentration of the enemy's troops by rail and road at any threatened point, the [Army] Council are of

[85] Hankey to Fisher, 24 Aug. 1911; Lennoxlove MSS.

opinion that operations of the nature and on the scale proposed could only end in disaster. Even if a small force succeeded in landing, it would in all probability be forced hurriedly to re-embark after suffering heavy loss, or be destroyed or captured by the enemy.

Wilson minuted this letter (9 September): 'This places the responsibility for inaction very clearly on the War Office. I do not propose to take any further action at present, as assistance from the Army would be worse than useless if not cordially given.' McKenna, on the other hand, admitted (19 September) the 'undeniable force' of the argument of the Army Council 'in the absence of a proposal to land at defined places, at which both the present defences and the practicability of rapid concentration in war could be examined in detail.'[86]

Churchill was sent to the Admiralty charged with two tasks: the introduction of a naval staff system and exorcizing from the minds of the Sea Lords their heretical views on military operations, thus insuring that no further opposition would be raised by the Navy to the Army's Continental strategy. His paper for the C.I.D. on 13 August[87] proved he was the right man for the latter job. It recommended that in a war in which Germany and Austria attacked the Triple Entente, Britain could play 'an effective part in the decisive theatre of the war' by sending, on the outbreak of war, the four divisions of the B.E.F. with their auxiliary troops (about 107,000 men) to France, with another 183,000 men, almost entirely professional soldiers (including the two remaining regular army divisions), to follow, once the naval blockade had been effectively established, by the fortieth day.

With Churchill at the Admiralty and Wilson gone, things went much better, especially after Battenberg took over as First Sea Lord. Although Hankey, when he became Secretary of the C.I.D., tried valiantly to 'bust up the plots and intrigues' of the soldiers for a Continental army with the Navy playing second fiddle (he had the support of Fisher among others), the new Admiralty régime made no difficulty about working out with the War Office the rapid and immediate transport of the B.E.F. The details had been completed when the war came. Amphibious projects were as good as dead. It was left for Fisher's return in 1914 to breathe life into them.

[86] Admiralty MSS.
[87] 'Military Aspects of the Continental Problem'; *The World Crisis*, i. 60–4.

To keep our perspective, we should bear in mind that Army–Navy co-operation in Germany was, if anything, even below the British standard. In Germany, the generals decided upon the strategic plan to be followed, and the admirals had to fit in as best they could. The reasons for this state of affairs need not concern us here.

8. THE DEVELOPMENT OF TACTICAL THOUGHT

The genius of most of the Navy's leaders in the Fisher era did not shine in the field of tactics. Especially was this Fisher's blind spot. Often, when commanding the Mediterranean Fleet, he had to be taken to task by the Sea Lords for his faulty tactical dispositions in fleet exercises and manœuvres. As First Sea Lord he never seems to have taken much interest in tactics. In any case, the twin fetishes of naval tactics, the rigid line and centralized command, went unchallenged.

At this distance the disadvantages of rigid adherence to a single line would appear obvious. It was limited in speed to that of the slowest ship; it made no use of the skill of divisional leaders; above all, it invariably inhibited initiative and ruled out flexibility in tactics. The line-of-battle had been introduced in the middle of the seventeenth century to impose order and maintain cohesion in a fleet during battle. It formed part of the official Fighting Instructions and became by the middle of the eighteenth century an end in itself and almost sacrosanct. Hawke's victories at Finisterre (1747) and Quiberon Bay (1759) were a revolt against this system, as were Boscawen's tactics at Lagos (1759), Rodney's in the Battle of the Saints (1782), Howe's at the 'Glorious First of June' (1794), and Nelson's at Trafalgar (1805). These sweeping victories had been won not by discarding the battle-line concept, but by a judicious combination of the line and 'general chase' tactics. But once the men of genius were out of the way, the pedants got busy and reimposed rigidity in a new set of Instructions issued in 1816, after the Napoleonic wars. The document was, in Corbett's words, 'a consecration of the fetters which had been forged in the worst days of the seventeenth century'. The dogma of the line-of-battle persisted into the twentieth century, partly because the nineteenth century offered no suitable occasion for testing it. Richmond has written:

... though the record of battles fought in the line is one long, practically unbroken story of indecisive results, it retained its pride of place as a tactical formation. . . . The tactics of Togo [in the Russo-Japanese War] left it unchanged. . . . The war found it as strongly entrenched in the minds of men as it had been in the days of King Charles II. . . . Why was this? The line ministers to two common frailties. It obviates the unpleasant necessity for serious and sustained thinking in advance and for rapid alterations in an emergency; and, by placing no responsibility upon subordinates, prevents giving them an opportunity to make mistakes.[88]

Before the war the single-line formation was championed by Fisher, Wilson, Jellicoe, Bridgeman, and many other admirals of the time. Other officers, mainly junior, including Captain Herbert W. Richmond, Commander K. G. B. Dewar, and Rear-Admirals Beatty and Sturdee, powerfully advocated the utilization in a general action of a part of the battle fleet, acting in a semi-independent role. In the Battle Cruiser Squadron under Beatty, in 1913, much thought was given to divisional attack and divided tactics. Towards the end of his Home Fleet command, in 1910–11, Admiral May carried out a long series of exercises featuring divisional attacks and with divisional commanders given a free hand. That is, the purpose was to investigate the possibilities of breaking away from the main body and concentrating a superior force on part of the enemy's line. May's successor, Bridgeman, made little or no attempt to carry on what he had begun, perhaps because of the great difficulty experienced, even in good visibility, in co-ordinating such attacks. Neither short-range wireless telegraphy nor aircraft had been fully developed for tactical use by the time the war broke out. It was generally accepted, on the eve of the war, that the Fleet was to fight on a long single line.

The only problem that needed solution was how best to deploy the Fleet for battle. Should the Fleet approach the enemy in single line or should it cruise in columns, from which it would deploy into a single line as rapidly as possible? The second tactical method won the day, following A. K. Wilson's success in the 1901 manœuvres as C.-in-C., Channel Squadron. Down to the war, then,

the general conception of battle in the British Navy was that of an artillery duel in one long line on parallel courses. Hence, the Home Fleet

[88] H. W. Richmond, 'The Service Mind', *Nineteenth Century and After*, Jan. 1933.

always cruised in column so that it could deploy rapidly into line at right angles to the enemy's bearing. We must have expended hundreds of thousands of tons of coal in practising this highly artificial conception of two fleets meeting in massed formation, rapidly deploying into line and solemnly engaging in a methodical artillery duel at long range. . . . Was it likely that the weak and less heavily gunned German Fleet would expose itself to destruction in order to conform to our conception of how a battle should be fought?[89]

Of course a huge fleet *had* to cruise at sea in a disciplined formation such as columns in line-ahead, and deployment in a single line is the only way that a large fleet can get into line of battle without having the guns masked in some, or perhaps many, of the ships. Where the Navy went wrong was in a too rigid adherence to the line. This is closely related to an over-centralized command, which, like the rigid single line, was enshrined in the old Fighting Instructions and had not broken down before 'the solid rocks of tradition and torpidity of mind'. It was urged by a few of the younger officers that the doctrine be replaced by decentralization, that is, by the delegation of responsibility and initiative to subordinate commanders, who could adopt the formation and tactics suited to the immediate situation. 'The drama of battle is not a marionette show with one man pulling the strings.' The underlying consideration was that, in the stress and strain of battle, the C.-in-C. would hardly be able to visualize the rapidly changing situations which confronted his subordinates in the various sectors of a vast battlefield. The heretics were mindful of what that arch-heretic Nelson had accomplished with the principle of divisional control. Each of Nelson's divisional leaders had to work his division in such a manner as would best give effect to the known intentions of the Commander-in-Chief. The principle of divisional control was, indeed, one of the secrets of Nelson's victories; but after the French wars the fetish of centralized command had been re-established.

By 1914 fleet commanders were trying to write orders that would cover every conceivable situation. As expressed in the formula 'follow senior officer's motions', this excessive centralization produced a plethora of 'request instructions' from officers. Writing of pre-war Home Fleet tactical exercises under Admiral May (in the earlier period of his command, 1909–10), Admiral

[89] Dewar, *The Navy from Within*, p. 122.

Dewar recalls how they atrophied individual initiative and judgment:

> The system of signalling every movement from the fleet flagship tended to develop an acute kind of tactical arthritis. Captains and Divisional Admirals had only to follow discreetly in the wake of the next ahead. I frequently noticed cases in which divisions might with advantage have been manœuvred independently in order to bring their guns to bear more effectively, but I never saw it done after the line of battle was formed. Thus valuable opportunities were frequently missed because no one would act without an order. On one occasion, I noticed that the destroyers ahead of the fleet failed to attack at all because the Commander-in-Chief's signal was obscured by smoke.[90]

There were important exceptions. May himself, in the last months of his command (he hauled down his flag in March 1911), experimented with less centralized methods. Beatty's pre-war Battle Cruiser Orders indicated the importance he attached to initiative in captains and subordinate commanders, as for example: 'From a study of the Great Naval Wars it is impressed upon one that Cruiser Captains and Battle Cruiser Captains, to be successful, must possess, in a marked degree, initiative . . .' 'Orders should be complied with in spirit, but it is not desirable to be tied by the letter of a standing order in circumstances where perhaps it was never intended to apply.' 'Much must be left to the initiative and judgement of Captains. They are relied upon to act promptly in battle on their own initiative for dealing with all cases such as the following. . . .'[91] Callaghan, who relieved Bridgeman as C.-in-C., Home Fleets, in December 1912, tried to introduce a measure of decentralization, which would have given divisional leaders an opportunity to act on their own initiative in battle, subject to certain general principles being carried out. Jellicoe's Grand Fleet Battle Orders of September 1914 and December 1915 (the latter were in force when the Battle of Jutland was fought) provided for a large degree of decentralization of command. Unfortunately, it did not work out that way in action (*vide* Jutland), for reasons which will be examined in the next volume.

There can be no argument about the Fleet's backwardness in one tactical respect. Night-firing practice was unknown until 1907,

[90] Dewar, *The Navy from Within*, pp. 122–3.
[91] Admiral Drax kindly provided a set of Beatty's B.C.O.s.

mainly on the theory that the big ship could not defend herself against torpedo attack in darkness. A scheme of night firing was introduced in the summer of 1907, a fantastic scheme by which a ship would fire away at night with a half crew, the other half theoretically sound asleep! The Atlantic Fleet exercises with the Mediterranean and Home Fleets early in 1911 included a night action between the two fleets in close contact with each other. Of this experience Jellicoe wrote years later: 'The difficulty of distinguishing friend from foe, and the exceeding uncertainty of the result, confirmed the opinion I had long held that a night action between fleets was a pure lottery, more particularly if destroyers took part in it.'[92] The few night firings before the war were a pretty perfunctory business. With a certain amount of wishful thinking, the Navy pinned its hopes on achieving a formal artillery duel in broad daylight between two lines of capital ships. As a matter of fact, there was no real progress in night firing by heavy ships until the 1930's. Admiral Sir William James says that 'it was lack of instruments that hindered progress in night firing'. This is true enough, but how could these instruments ever have been developed in face of the standing pre-war rule that 'the British Fleet does not fight at night'?

The Germans, on the other hand, had made themselves very efficient at night fighting as well as at day fighting. Jutland was a rude awakening for the British in this as in other respects. The British destroyers did get practice in night fighting, but it was hardly enough, to judge from the results at Jutland.

More serious than the unprogressive tactics was the lamentable deficiency in tactical instruction. It was a chronic complaint of the abler young officers that there was not enough tactical training, the Home Fleet during May's command being an exception. Witness Beatty, then commanding the battleship *Queen*, Atlantic Fleet: 'The two days have been most productive, principally in demonstrating how unpractised our Admirals are in the manner and methods of handling large fleets. It is not their fault. We don't do enough of it, either sufficiently frequent or for sufficiently long periods to enable them to correct mistakes and put into full use the experience that is gained even by two days' continual manœuvring . . .'[93]

[92] Bacon, *The Life of John Rushworth, Earl Jellicoe* (London, 1936), p. 168.
[93] Beatty to his wife, 17 July 1909; Chalmers, *Beatty*, p. 99.

The lack of uniformity of thought on the fundamental principles of war, whether of tactics or strategy, was another weakness. Up to 1900 the word tactics was attached to the performance of certain quadrille-like movements, formal movements of trifling value which bore small direct relationship to the realities of battle. No real effort was made to work out battle problems, and there was no continuity. Each admiral was a law unto himself. Something, but not nearly enough, was done in the Fisher period to improve matters, with the War College in the van; but the Navy lacked original thinkers to sift its work and embody it in clear and simple principles. Moreover, the doctrines in which the War College believed, such as the rigid line and centralization in command, were not always the most progressive. The C.I.D. subcommittee on Beresford's charges (1909) stated that it had been impressed 'with the differences of opinion amongst officers of high rank and professional attainments regarding important principles of naval strategy and tactics'.

This remained the situation. At the beginning of the war no very comprehensive or authoritative tactical doctrine was in general acceptance. Indeed, very conflicting views were held. On one fundamental tactical objective only was there general agreement—from whatever formation, to cross the 'T', that is, to steam across the head of the enemy's line. This allowed all the guns and torpedoes of the fleet to concentrate on the enemy's van. The enemy's gun response would be, comparatively, almost negligible, and the torpedo reply, nil.

Admiral Dewar has also written critically of the strategical and tactical instruction at the War College:

Most of the [strategical] games were permeated by the fallacy that naval war is nothing more than a gladiatorial contest between two opposing fleets. The part which the control of communications plays in the disposition of ships and fleets was not generally realised . . . The close blockade of an enemy's coastline was often practised in these exercises and it never seems to have occurred to the President to question such a dubious plan. The most conflicting and divergent ideas were apparent in every type of operation. Some officers, for example, despatched large armies overseas in the face of powerful fleets, whilst others, like the United States Navy Department in the Spanish-American War, hesitated to do so even under the most favourable conditions. . . .

Tactical instruction took the form of games with small model ships on a scale of about one foot to the mile. The officers commanding squadrons, etc., sat at each end of the tactical table communicating their orders to the movers by written signals. The effect of gunfire was assessed by scoring rulers graduated in numbers corresponding to the range, muzzle velocity, armour protection, etc., but no attempt was made to investigate tactical principles. It was all very ingenious, but no amount of ingenuity can reproduce the conditions of a fleet action on a tactical board. . . .

The system of instruction at the War College did little to prepare the Navy for the realities of the coming war, but the hours were short and the leave generous, which gave one opportunities for thought and study.[94]

No effort was made to co-ordinate tactics and gunnery, since, as Admiral of the Fleet Lord Chatfield has pointed out,

tactics were the realm of the Flag officer and gunnery was still largely the realm of the Admiralty, the I.T.P. [Inspector of Target Practice] and the [gunnery school] *Excellent*. The task of harmonising the tactical lessons learnt, with their gunnery equivalents, had not been pursued. If it had been we should have had, before the Great War, some plans for long-range firing; for concentrating our fire on a smaller number of enemy ships, and for dealing with rate and deflection at full speed. The Flag Officer, wrapped up in his fascinating tactical movements, assumed too readily that the gunnery would be all right and would be able to respond to his tactical mind. The gunnery world, intent on its difficult material problems and on carrying out Admiralty-designed competitions, was not thinking enough of the tactical problems its Flag officers were going to set it in war.[95]

At the root of the whole difficulty was the ascendancy of the '*matériel*' school (Fisher, Jellicoe, Wilson, Jackson, *et al.*) before the war. This is not to suggest that its leaders were not interested in tactics and strategy and were devoid of ideas in these realms. For instance, Fisher's absorption in the material side did not blur his strategic vision. Yet the fact remains that the 'historical' school (Corbett, Custance, Richmond, K. G. B. Dewar, *et al.*) correctly saw that the 'sublime' aspects of the profession, strategy and tactics, went undernourished in comparison with the energies focused upon the ship, the gun, and the torpedo.

[94] Dewar, *The Navy from Within*, pp. 131–3.
[95] Chatfield, *The Navy and Defence*, p. 114.

Why should senior officers have had so little understanding of or interest in the higher aspects of war? For one thing, the revolutionary changes in *matériel* since the latter part of the nineteenth century captured the imagination of most officers. The less tangible aspects of the study of war suffered in consequence. This general outlook, in turn, resulted in a faulty educational system. Strategy, tactics, the principles of war, played a secondary role in the education of the young officer; the stress was upon the technical and mechanical aspects of the profession: gunnery, torpedoes, ship-handling, and so on. It was natural under these circumstances that naval history was not held in high repute at the Admiralty, and this in turn worked against any serious study of strategy and tactics. Listen to Fisher. 'Whatever service the past may be to other professions, it can be categorically stated in regard to the Navy that history is a record of exploded ideas. Every condition of the past is altered . . .'[96] Of one session of the C.I.D. inquiry of 1909 Fisher wrote, 'Custance went back to Cornwallis and Keith, etc. That damned him! Why not Noah!'[97] The whole situation is admirably summarized in the words of a British naval officer (1951):

The admirals of the decade before Jutland did not lack foresight. They honestly believed that the only place where 'the art of the Admiral' could be learnt and practised was in the fleet at sea. Although they were steeped in the traditions of Nelson, the close study of history did not appeal to them because in their youth they had never been taught how to extract its lessons, and in any case they felt that steam and science had so revolutionized naval warfare there was nothing much to be learnt from a dead past. . . . The Fleet was expanding so rapidly and there was so much to learn about new weapons and 'instrumentalisms' that every officer and rating was required to man the ships. Any surplus that existed was employed doing technical courses. In consequence naval thought was tending to become immersed in the intricacies of materiel, and the academic study of strategy and tactics suffered accordingly. In an attempt to remedy this state of affairs a war course for senior officers was started in 1910. But in the words of Mr. Churchill [*The World Crisis*]: 'At least fifteen years of consistent policy were required to give the Royal Navy that widely extended outlook upon war problems and of war situations without

[96] Fisher's memorandum, 'Navy Reforms', Feb. 1907; Lennoxlove MSS.
[97] Fisher to Esher, 12 June 1909; *Fear God and Dread Nought*, ii. 251. But see above, p. 16.

which seamanship, gunnery, instrumentalisms of every kind, devotion of the highest order, could not achieve their due reward.'

Indeed, officers solidly grounded in naval history or who showed any signs of an analytical critical faculty were often looked at askance. '. . . officers who made any real study of war from the point of view of Staff work were regarded as cranks or lunatics, hunters of soft jobs; and the gin-and-bitters school were quite content to be left to the guidance of their splendid but not always highly trained instincts.'[98] There were exceptions, of course— Custance, Drax, Bellairs, De B. Brock, and other students of war rose to the rank of admiral and held important appointments. The other side of the coin can be illustrated by the careers of Jellicoe and Richmond. The former had never read Mahan until he was C.-in-C. of the Grand Fleet![99]

Richmond is a splendid case history. He was among the lecturers at the first Staff Course in the War College, in 1912, giving a series of lectures on the War of the Spanish Succession. His knowledge of history was immense, and coupled with it was a very capacious memory. Some of the officers wondered at first what value this ancient history could be to them in the twentieth century, but they soon found that Richmond had the happy knack of painting a clear picture of every scene, and extracting from most of them the lessons and principles which would apply undeniably to that day as well as to 200 years earlier. In consequence of his inexhaustible storehouse of information and constant reflection thereon, his judgment on matters of policy or strategy was rarely unsound and was usually well ahead of his contemporaries. It was largely on his initiative that a small group of younger officers courageously founded, in 1913, the *Naval Review*, a privately circulated journal which still flourishes. Its object was defined as 'the encouragement of thought and discussion [by naval officers] on strategy, tactics, organisation, command, discipline, education, naval history and any other subject affecting the fighting efficiency of the Navy but excluding all technical and material subjects such as gunnery, engineering, etc.' Richmond was that rare character, a highly efficient blend between the practical sea officer, the teacher, and the historian—his books, packed with wisdom and

[98] Filson Young, *With the Battle Cruisers* (London, 1921), p. 10.
[99] Richmond's diary entry, 15 May 1917, quoting from a conversation with Beatty; Marder, *Portrait of an Admiral*, p. 251.

wide experience, will probably be read and referred to for as long as, if not longer than, those of Mahan. 'What a pity that we cannot find more men like him,' Admiral Drax has sighed. But Richmond's strategic recommendations when Assistant Director of Operations (1913–15) received scant recognition, and he rarely, during the war, and for that matter afterwards, received appointments commensurate with his rank and talents. Defects of character are one explanation. Although he could be quite charming, his strong views and frank criticisms, at times verging on arrogant intolerance, irritated and antagonized many of his superiors. Under these circumstances the Admiralty showed great forbearance indeed in continuing his employment. Nearly as damaging to his professional prospects, however, was his reputation as a bookish person. The 'practical' men who were in positions of authority simply could not believe that anyone as well-read as Richmond could possibly be the first-rate seaman that he was.

Lord Esher deplored what appeared to be the contempt with which historical studies were treated by the so-called 'practical man'—statesman, seaman, and man on the street. 'Why, my dear Hankey, do we worry about history? Julian Corbett writes one of the best books in our language upon political and military strategy [*Some Principles of Maritime Strategy*, 1911]. All sorts of lessons, some of inestimable value, may be gleaned from it. No one, except perhaps Winston, who matters just now, has ever read it. . . . Obviously history is written for schoolmasters and arm-chair strategists. Statesmen and warriors pick their way through the dusk.'[100] It was natural, therefore, that the Royal Navy contributed little, for the largest navy in the world, to the literature of naval history, tactics, and strategy.

[100] Esher to Hankey, 15 Mar. 1915; *Esher*, iii. 221. Churchill's appreciation of history is one of his most endearing traits. In describing the functions of the War Staff he wrote that it was to be 'the means of sifting, developing, and applying the results of history and experience and of preserving them as a general stock of reasoned opinion available as an aid and as a guide for all who are called upon to determine, in peace or war, the naval policy of the country'; 'Statement of the First Lord of the Admiralty Explanatory of the Navy Estimates, 1912–1913. Appendix: Naval War Staff', 1 Jan. 1912: Command Paper 6106 (1912). Few officers of that time could have taken the First Lord seriously.

XIII

The British and German Fleets in 1914

Where the Navy is concerned there is every reason for confidence. . . . the men are good; the machine is very good; the margins of superiority are very large; the detail has been most carefully attended to; the strategic advantages of our position are formidable.

CHURCHILL to Lord Roberts, 23 January 1912.

The fact is that in 1914 the Royal Navy was almost totally unprepared for war and remained in that condition for most of the period 1914–18.

COMMANDER STEPHEN KING-HALL, *My Naval Life, 1906–1929.*

The man who contemplates all the things that may be somewhat at fault and adds up his own war deficiencies with that curious failure to realise that his enemy has got as many if not more, has neither the Napoleonic nor the Nelsonic gift of Imagination and Audacity.

FISHER, *Memories.*

I. THE PERSONNEL

THERE were few really top-notch admirals in 1914—men who were exceptional tacticians and fleet commanders in the Hawke–Nelson tradition or war thinkers in the Anson–Barham tradition. One reason was that the pre-1914 generation of admirals had not had the opportunity to be trained in the hard school of war. Another reason was that, as already mentioned, the '*matériel*' school was in the ascendant. A third reason was that all senior officers had been brought up in sail and many of them never shook off the sailing-ship mentality.[1]

The opinions of a politician, a junior officer, and a senior officer are representative of contemporary opinion on the subject. 'There is,' Churchill complained, 'a frightful dearth of first-class men in

---

[1] There is nothing apocryphal about this story, which illustrates the sailing-ship mentality, or unprogressive outlook, to perfection. In about the year 1913 two elderly retired admirals were discussing, in a London club, the speeds of modern ships. One of them gave it as his opinion that 'no ship should proceed down the [English] Channel at more than 12 knots; it isn't safe!'

the Vice Admirals' and Rear Admirals' lists.' He could have added full admirals. 'We had competent administrators, brilliant experts of every description, unequalled navigators, good disciplinarians, fine sea-officers, brave and devoted hearts: but at the outset of the conflict we had more captains of ships than captains of war.'[2] Commander Stephen King-Hall has bluntly stated: 'There were a number of shockingly bad admirals afloat in 1914. They were pleasant, bluff old sea-dogs, with no scientific training; endowed with a certain amount of common sense, they had no conception of the practice and theory of strategy or tactics'.[3] Beatty could write in 1909, after Atlantic Fleet manœuvres (he was then commanding a pre-dreadnought), that 'we have eight Admirals, and there is not one among them, unless it is Prince Louis, who impresses me that he is capable of a great effort. . .'[4]

Fisher, whatever his defects, was a genius. He, A. K. Wilson, and Battenberg, were the best of the senior officers, and only Battenberg was on the active list in 1914. It was said of Prince Louis that he was born a Serene Highness, but had lived it down. Born in Austria in 1854, the eldest son of Prince Alexander of Hesse, he had been brought up in England, had married his cousin, Princess Victoria (a granddaughter of Queen Victoria), and become a naturalized British subject. Entering the Royal Navy as a cadet in 1868, he had got ahead on his own abilities. 'I hate the idea of getting anything, as regards naval work, at the hands of the King, my uncle. I want to get it on my own merits, *if* I have any.'[5] But he was also inordinately ambitious and made no bones of it when Fisher was at the Admiralty. His appointment as First Sea Lord commanded full approval both inside and outside the Navy. He was, reported a friend, 'in the seventh heaven of delight. It is a billet he always wanted.' Prince Louis was by 1914 generally considered to be the outstanding flag officer on the active list. Churchill thought him a second St. Vincent. Though handicapped by his German ancestry and by his gout, he was a first-rate, all-round seaman, a born leader, an efficient, even brilliant, tactician and strategist (he was never defeated in manœuvres until 1912). He was also a man of high intellectual attainments, a student and

[2] Churchill to Fisher, 12 Apr. 1912: Lennoxlove MSS.; *The World Crisis*, i. 93.
[3] King-Hall, *My Naval Life, 1906–1929* (London, 1952), pp. 97–8.
[4] Beatty to his wife, 17 July 1909; Chalmers, *Beatty*, p. 99.
[5] Battenberg to Fisher, 15 May 1904; Lennoxlove MSS.

a scholar, an accomplished linguist and a lover of the arts. His high-mindedness, cheerful personality, considerateness, and commanding presence—he looked the beau-ideal of the British naval officer—commended themselves to the profession. He was popular with all ranks and possessed the confidence of the service in a greater degree than any other active flag officer. 'There are literally hundreds of naval officers who would be quite ready to believe black was white if he issued a memo. to that effect.'[6]

The better senior admirals on the active list in 1914 included Callaghan, the even-tempered C.-in-C. of the Home Fleets. He did not excel in any field, but was 'full of sound common sense', in Beatty's opinion, and had shown a comprehensive grasp of fleet work. He probably would have given a good account of himself in war. Bradford was a highly competent seaman, and Slade was a keen student of war. Henry Jackson, Chief of the Admiralty War Staff in 1913–14, was modest, fearless, and very able, more particularly in the technical sphere. A pioneer of wireless telegraphy, he stood for the application of science to the practical work of the Navy. He never served as a C.-in-C. afloat, which is perhaps just as well, as his personality was hardly of the inspirational type.

There were few other admirals or vice-admirals of above-average ability. The dearth of outstanding talent at the top was illustrated by Bridgeman's appointment as First Sea Lord. He was the best man available at the time. Burney was 'a good example of a naval officer rather of the old school and of ordinary capacity'.[7] Egerton was a man of no ideas; Milne was not much good; the dashing and handsome Meux, a favourite at Court and with the ladies of high society, was a very able officer, but lazy and rather spoiled—'the Navy was an interest rather than a profession' for him; Warrender was average. Vice-Admiral Sir Douglas Gamble, who commanded the 4th Battle Squadron of the Grand Fleet early in the war, is a good example of the unprogressive senior officer.

---

[6] Ottley to Esher, 25 Oct. 1911; Esher MSS. Battenberg must have established some sort of record in his eating habits! 'Prince Louis was a big man and had a big appetite. At breakfast he began on porridge, then fish, then eggs and bacon or a meat dish, then a large plate of cold ham, then hot muffins or crumpets; and then a lot of toast and butter and jam, and finished on fruit. His meal would have fed an officers' mess'; Oliver MSS.

[7] Sir W. Graham Greene's appreciation of Burney in a memorandum of 23 Jan. 1935; Graham Greene MSS.

His Flag Lieutenant (afterwards Admiral Sir Bertram Ramsay of World War II fame) commented on a 'set-to' with his Admiral: 'He won't admit that a knowledge of war is the least necessary for any officers until they come to flag rank, but how they are to learn it then I don't know. . . . the old school will not admit that any one junior to them can have any ideas at all.'[8]

The situation was much better as regards the younger admirals and the captains. Among the outstanding rear-admirals at the outbreak of war were the very gifted Duff; Oliver, a hard worker and full of common sense; De Robeck, 'an exceptionally strong-minded, talented, and popular officer of great dignity and charm'; Arbuthnot, very able, though a harsh disciplinarian, a stickler, for example, for correct uniform as laid down in the regulations; the fastidious, witty, and immensely popular Pakenham, generally considered the best commander in the Home Fleet (1910–11); the energetic Bayly (acting vice-admiral), an able tactician with a mania almost for discipline and efficiency; Browning, a good all-round sea officer; Madden, a very composed man of few words whose record as a brilliant torpedo officer and a fine executive officer inspired confidence. Incidentally, he was Jellicoe's brother-in-law, the two having married sisters.

There was a brilliant galaxy of captains, already marked men in the service: Goodenough (commodore second-class), a superb tactician; W. W. Fisher, of keen intellect and exuberant vitality; Richmond, who was judged by Fisher (1906) as 'quite one of our very best and most accomplished officers'; Keyes (commodore second-class), who may not have been the greatest intellect of the service but who was a born leader and fighter who commanded the devotion of all under him; Chatfield, in the appraisal of the U.S. Naval Attaché (1921), 'one of the best men in the service—virile, energetic, capable, and forceful'; Hall, who was to become the greatest of all D.N.I.s; Dreyer, a gunnery genius; Osmond de B. Brock, possessed of a first-class analytical mind, a profound student and practical master of tactics, whose cabin 'had always the refreshing peculiarity of being like a branch of Mudie's Library'. Howard Kelly and Tyrwhitt (commodore second-class) were other officers of the highest quality, both grand fighters. That most of these talented younger officers made their mark during the

---

[8] Ramsay's diary entry, Sept. 1914; Rear-Admiral W. S. Chalmers, *Full Cycle: the Biography of Admiral Sir Bertram Home Ramsay* (London, 1959), p. 21.

war was due in part to Fisher. He recalled with pride after the war 'those glorious reforming years in which we reduced the age of our Admirals and produced men like Commodore Tyrwhitt.'

Beatty and Jellicoe deserve separate and more detailed treatment. Beatty had, at 25 in 1896, shown in the Nile campaign all the qualities of a born leader. He was awarded the D.S.O. for taking the gunboat *Fateh* up the Nile and close in to support the 21st Lancers with her fire. He was promoted to commander at 27 (1898) over the heads of four hundred of his seniors, after having served as a lieutenant for only six years. (The average time spent in that rank was $12\frac{1}{2}$ years.) After distinguished and gallant service in the Boxer campaign in 1900, he was promoted, at 29, to captain. (The average age of captains was then 42, and Beatty was 218th on the list of commanders!) In the following years he commanded three cruisers and a battleship and served at the War Office as Naval Adviser to the Army Council, a liaison post. At the end of 1909 Beatty was at the top of the captains' list; but since his total sea-time in the rank was a year-and-a-half short of the six years required for promotion to flag rank, it took a special order-in-council to promote him. The date was 1 January 1910, and he was not quite 39, the youngest flag officer in the history of the Royal Navy since the later eighteenth century, when Rodney and Keppel became flag officers at 31 and 37, respectively. Beatty jeopardized his chances for important appointments and further promotion by refusing an appointment in the Atlantic Fleet suited to his rank. (He could take the chance, being independent financially.) He had been unemployed for eighteen months when Churchill became First Lord. Impressed with Beatty after a personal interview, Churchill made him his Naval Secretary. (Beatty seems to have been put forward by Battenberg, whose flag captain he had been for a short time.) This made Beatty 'the power behind the throne', especially as regards appointments. In the spring of 1913 he was appointed to the command of the newly-formed Battle Cruiser Squadron, again over the heads of all. On 3 August 1914 he was promoted to acting vice-admiral.

Beatty's rapid promotions did not endear him to the service at large. It was even said that his heart was not in the service—that he had too many interests ashore, polo and horses among others. His energy and physical courage were acknowledged, but prior to the war few suspected that he had larger talents. Post-war writers often passed him off as a mere dashing officer in the Prince Rupert tradition. In fact, Beatty was a good deal more than an impetuous man of action. Although he lacked, at the outbreak of the war, the professional experience requisite in a commander of a large squadron, he did possess various supreme assets. Most important, he was a natural born leader at sea. This was rooted in his effectiveness as a speaker ('he knew what he intended to say and said it, tersely and crisply in a commanding voice'), his high spirit, and his passion for victory. He was distinctively offensive-minded and always willing to take a chance. The Archbishop of Canterbury, at Beatty's funeral service in St. Paul's, in March 1936, spoke the mind of the Navy when he described the Admiral as 'the very embodiment of the fighting spirit of the Navy. In him something of the spirit of Nelson seemed to have come back.' Another important leadership trait was his possession of that indefinable something called 'colour', two constituents of which were his love for doing everything with speed and dash, and his appearance. He was perhaps the handsomest officer of his day, always spick and span, and with his cap worn at a jaunty angle, suggesting a devil-may-care attitude to life. No theorist, he did have a solid grasp of strategy and tactics. He had, moreover, the tremendous asset of receptiveness to advice and criticism and the intelligence to surround himself with first-rate men.

Jellicoe, 55 and a vice-admiral when war broke out, had distinguished himself in a number of key appointments: D.N.O., 1905–7; Rear-Admiral, Atlantic Fleet, 1907–8; Controller, 1908–1910; C.-in-C., Atlantic Fleet, 1910–11; commanding 2nd Division, Home Fleet, 1911–12; Second Sea Lord, 1912–14, interrupted by his command of the Red Fleet in the 1913 manœuvres, the idea being to give him some experience in large-scale manœuvres. Widenmann gave him the highest marks. 'If one asks English naval officers which admiral would have the best chances for a brilliant career on the basis of his capability, it is immaterial to which group they belong (Fisher or Beresford), one almost always receives the same answer—besides Prince Louis of Battenberg, unquestionably Sir John Jellicoe. Sir John possesses the absolute confidence of his superiors as well as of his subordinates.'[9] Jellicoe was like Beatty in some respects. He was of a charming and happy disposition, whether at work or at play, and he lived a full life.

[9] Widenmann to Tirpitz, 11 Jan. 1912; German Navy Ministry MSS.

His many outside interests included tennis, golf, cricket, and racquets, in all of which he was above the average as a player. In many respects, though, he was the opposite of Beatty. For one thing, there was nothing heroic about his appearance. He was rather short in stature (5 ft. 6 in.), and he had none of the dash public opinion associated with the naval officer. He was an ineffective speaker, and he hated publicity. His strong points included great self-control (it was impossible to rattle him), a retentive memory, an anxiety to have the opinions of others (like Drake, he 'took counsel of many and then did what he thought was right'), and an alert and precise mind. 'No unsound however attractive proposal has a rabbit's chance when he turns his searchlight brain on it—it's riddled by a dry fact or two that he knows but that no one else seems to.'[10] His officers had absolute faith in him and were utterly devoted to him. He captured the affection of all who served under him. Even Churchill, despite a number of disagreements with the Admiral, developed a great admiration for his ability.

Jellicoe had his flaws. His critics say that his mind was rather too crowded with materialistic detail and that he lacked the burning offensive spirit of a Nelson or a Beatty. Others make much of his 'pessimism'. These criticisms, founded on Jellicoe's performance during the war, will be examined elsewhere. Without doubt his most serious weakness, clearly apparent by 1914, was his inability to delegate authority, since the power to decentralize is of the utmost importance in war. He looked after the petty details of administering a fleet or a shore appointment himself. Bridgeman's comment is very much to the point. 'He has had no experience of fleet work on a big scale, and is so extremely anxious about the work in it, that he really does too much. He must learn to work his captains and staff more, and himself less! At present he puts himself in the position of, say, a glorified gunnery lieutenant. This will not do when he gets with a big fleet. He must trust his staff and captains, and if they don't fit, he must kick them out!'[11]

Despite the paucity of real talent at the top of the officer class in 1914, the officers of the Royal Navy had one decisive advantage

[10] Admiral Sir William James, *Admiral Sir William Fisher* (London, 1943), p. 64, quoting Fisher, who had served in the Grand Fleet as Captain of the *St. Vincent*.
[11] Bridgeman to Fisher, 4 Dec. 1911; *Fear God and Dread Nought*, ii. 418–19.

over their German opposites : *confidence*. They 'still retained intact that tradition of success which had buoyed them for the last century. They faced a power which had been an empire for only fifty years. They knew the odds they could safely take on. They had the confidence born of absolute technical efficiency and the knowledge that every man in the womb of the steel mountain knew his job.'[12] By way of absolute contrast, note this valid appraisal by the Naval Attaché in Berlin of the German naval officer class : 'The German Officer, especially when married, has a strong hankering for shore billets, his heart is not really on the sea. They infinitely prefer sitting at a desk, pondering over official papers, to the more active sea life. . .'[13] Ottley could be excused for boasting that the British naval officer was 'on the whole immeasurably superior to any foreign sailor, and if I growl at the lack of Staff training, I am not blind to the splendid qualities and professional attainments of my old topmates!'[14]

The officers of the German Navy were, in many respects, the equal of the British. Watson, the Naval Attaché, even rated the flag officers and senior captains as 'in no way inferior' to their opposite numbers in the Royal Navy. They were on the whole 'hard-working, keen and zealous . . . on the whole . . . they appear to come from a better class and are better educated than our own. . . . On the other hand, it is indisputable that they lack a certain "go", possessed by our men and, somehow, impress one rather as being soldiers at sea than seamen.'[15] This lack of 'go' was reflected in a deficiency of the offensive spirit and in the 'peculiar psychological failing' displayed during the war of hating to lose ships. Admiral Bacon has attributed the origin of the latter failing to 'the military form of training' given to the German naval officers. 'In the army it is looked on almost as a disgrace to lose guns.'[16]

Whatever the deficiencies in the tactical doctrine and training of the Royal Navy, the Fleet had the tremendous advantage of

[12] E. S. Turner, *Gallant Gentlemen : a Portrait of the British Officer, 1600–1956* (London, 1956), p. 293.

[13] Heath to Goschen, 6 Aug. 1910; *British Documents*, vi. 507.

[14] Ottley to Esher, 8 Oct. 1911; Esher MSS.

[15] Admiralty War Staff, Intelligence Division, 'Foreign Naval Administration and Personnel: Germany. 1912'; Admiralty MSS.

[16] Sir Reginald Bacon and Francis E. McMurtrie, *Modern Naval Strategy* (London, 1940), p. 187.

being at sea considerably more than the German Fleet. This helps explain the magnificent seamanship and navigation of the officers in the war. The High Seas Fleet, in contrast, spent an immense amount of time in harbour, and a large part of its training was done not in the open sea, but in sheltered waters. Another indisputable advantage was the voluntary principle, which gave the British Navy an enormous nucleus of thoroughly trained long-service men. They entered the service young, at 18, for a twelve-year enlistment, with re-enlistment for ten years (to complete time for a pension) not uncommon. A great defect of the German Navy was its system of short service, although the men were hard-working and well-drilled and trained. The German naval officers complained a great deal about the three years' service, 'under which they are every year called upon to make trained men out of a fresh lot of conscripts totally strange to sea life.'[17]

To sum up, so far as the personnel went, the Royal Navy entered the war manned by a body of officers and men of high morale and superb technical training. In last analysis, the life-blood of the Navy was then, as always, the officers and men, a picked company with the sea in their blood.

The one grave shortcoming was in the quality of many of the senior officers on the flag list, although it is difficult to see that the High Seas Fleet was better endowed. Thus, the first two C.-in-C.s were nothing remarkable. Von Ingenohl was as much courtier as naval officer, and his successor, von Pohl, was a clever man who lacked imagination and the power of command. It was not until Scheer succeeded Pohl in 1916 that the Germans had a truly able fleet commander.

2. THE *MATÉRIEL*

The dominant idea in the service was that the gun, especially the big gun, was the naval weapon *par excellence*. It illustrates what Captain S. W. Roskill calls 'the fallacy of the dominant weapon', which in exalting one weapon tends to undervalue others far too much—in this case, underwater weapons. It also explains why the gunnery branch of the service was regarded as the surest road to promotion.

British capital ships nearly always carried guns of greater

---

[17] Watson to Goschen, 13 Oct. 1913; *British Documents*, x (Pt. 2). 716.

calibre than contemporary German ships. By way of example, the *Superb*, laid down in February 1907, carried ten 12-inch guns, with a broadside fire of 6,800 lbs.; the *Nassau*, laid down in August 1907, had twelve 11-inch, with a broadside of 5,280 lbs., or a British superiority of 1,520 lbs. The *Orion* and the *Kaiser*, both laid down in November 1909, had ten 13·5-inch and ten 12-inch, respectively, with broadsides of 12,500 lbs. and 8,600 lbs., respectively, or a British advantage of 3,900 lbs. As a final comparison: the *Queen Elizabeth*, laid down in October 1912, versus the *Kronprinz Wilhelm*, May 1912. The former's eight 15-inch had a broadside of 15,600 lbs., the latter's ten 12-inch, 8,600 lbs., or a British superiority of 7,000 lbs. Although the Germans could claim with justice that projectiles from their guns were equal or superior in penetration to those from British guns of the next higher calibre owing to their much higher muzzle velocity, there was no need for British apologetics. At long ranges heavier shells are more accurate than lighter ones, as, for example, the British 1,250-lb. shell fired by the 13·5-inch gun, as against the 860-lb. shell ordinarily used by the German 12-inch guns. This is because all guns achieved the greatest accuracy and the smallest spread of salvo at a little less than their extreme firing range. The bigger the gun, therefore, the greater its best fighting range. An even more decisive British advantage was that the 13·5-inch shell, say, had a heavier bursting charge and consequently greater shattering and pulverizing effect than the German 12-inch shell.

Guns, big guns, long ranges (battle practice was held at 14,000–15,000 yards in 1913, and the battle cruisers fired at 16,000 yards in the spring of 1914), good shooting—these were the articles of faith of the naval officer, and to the proper development of this method of attack all systems of tactics were directed and subordinated. A corollary of the creed was the importance of high speed, so as to be able to choose the range best suited to the guns.

Between 1904 and 1911 the Navy emerged from what Admiral Usborne calls 'stone age gunnery' to a high degree of proficiency at ranges up to 10,000 yards. There was, however, one potentially disastrous shortcoming. Scott argued that in action, funnel smoke, cordite smoke, and shell splashes, to say nothing of haze and mist, would practically blind the gunlayers, make accurate aim impossible, and nullify the whole intricate system for hitting at long ranges. Scott also appreciated the importance of ensuring that the guns were all concentrated on the same target, instead of the gun-layers often selecting wrong targets, thus rendering fire control impossible. After his retirement in 1909, he worked on a system of director firing, that is, of aiming and firing all the guns of the main armament simultaneously from a control position high up in the foremast, a position which, being above low-lying smoke and shell splashes, gave the best possible view. One man used a master-sight, a single telescopic sight electrically connected to the sights of each gun. He aimed the ship's broadside on the enemy's ship and fired it by pressing a single key. This method resulted in a remarkable increase in accuracy.

However, Scott's director sight was not adopted at once. He and Jellicoe, and their allies, fought a war of words with the Inspector of Target Practice, Rear-Admiral M. E. Browning, and his allies, who wanted independent gunlaying continued. Scott attributed the opposition to 'simply professional jealousy'. Browning and his cohorts objected that it was difficult to ensure precisely correct simultaneous alignment of guns and director, and emphasized the chance of the electrical communication from aloft being damaged by shell-fire. A dramatic test off Berehaven, 13 November 1912, conclusively proved the superiority of Scott's system. In a com-petitive battle practice the fire of the dreadnought *Thunderer*, equipped with the new system, was more accurate and faster than that of her sister ship, the *Orion*, using the old individual system, that is, the system of gunlayers' firing. The *Thunderer* scored six times as many hits as the *Orion* in three minutes of firing at a range of 9,000 yards, with the ships steaming at 12 knots.

Ships were now fitted with director firing, but there was still resistance. When the war broke out, only eight battleships had been fitted, and it was not until the time of Jutland that all the capital ships (except *Erin* and *Agincourt*) had the system for their main armament. The work of fitting the secondary armament as well as the main armament had not been finished when the war ended. Scott, after a visit to Kiel in 1911 or 1912, believed the Germans already had director firing. The fact is that the German system had features resembling Scott's system. Although it was not the same thing, the German 'Richtungsweiser', or Director Pointer, which had been generally introduced by 1914, gave the

German Navy brilliant gunnery results in battle, particularly in the earlier phases of the war, before Scott's system had been extended through the Fleet.

The excellence of German gunnery was also based on a very efficient and sophisticated stereoscopic rangefinder. It was never easy to find enough 'stereo' range-takers, since the instrument required a man with special qualities of eyesight: excellent and identical vision in both eyes. But the German rangefinder had a great advantage over the British rangefinder. The latter, working on the 'coincidence' principle, had a greater light absorption, which meant that little could be seen through it in bad light, whereas the stereo rangefinder, with less light absorption, was superior in low visibility. This was a telling factor at Jutland. (The Navy did exhaustive trials with both types after the war and decided to stick with the simpler and more rugged coincidence rangefinders.) Another German advantage was that their guns, calibre for calibre, were more accurate than the British guns, as Dreyer admitted.[18]

The efficiency of German gunnery was known at the Admiralty long before the war. For example, in 1909 German naval gunnery results were judged 'extraordinarily good' by the D.N.O. The German superiority in night fighting was, unfortunately, not suspected.

The German capital ships were, as a whole, better armoured than the British ships of like classes, having far greater protection above and below water.[19] This was made possible by the greater displacement of German dreadnoughts in particular as compared with their British contemporaries. The main armour belt was only 10-11 inches thick (maximum) in the first British dreadnoughts (and carried up to the main deck only). This was increased to 12 in later classes ('Orion', 'George V', and 'Iron Duke'). Not until the 'Queen Elizabeths' was the belt armour increased to 13 inches. German belt armour was considerably thicker—11¾

[18] Undated Dreyer memorandum, written in 1918 or just after the war; Jellicoe MSS. He was D.N.O. in 1917 and Director of Naval Artillery and Torpedo, Naval Staff, 1918.

[19] See Jellicoe's *The Grand Fleet, 1914-16* (London, 1919), pp. 312–13, where the weight of armour carried by British and German ships of the same date is given, showing, for example, an advantage for the Germans of 33 per cent in the case of the 'Orion' and 'Kaiser' classes, and of about 25 per cent in the case of the battle cruisers *Queen Mary* and *Seydlitz*.

inches in the first dreadnoughts, 13¾ inches in the 'Kaiser' and later classes. British battle cruisers were also thinly armoured, with a 9-inch maximum thickness compared to the maximum of 11·81 inches in the later German battle cruisers. Moreover, the Germans carried thick belt protection to the ends of their capital ships to a far greater extent than did the British, and their armour was carried up much higher on the side in ships of the same date of construction. The British ships did not have enough horizontal armour to protect properly their turrets and magazines. This may have been due, Admiral Drax thinks, to the ship designers 'basing their calculations on the assumption that an enemy projectile when it struck would be travelling horizontally! This of course was rubbish: perhaps they were not told early enough that the probable battle ranges were continually increasing, and by 1915 hits might well be obtained at a range of 20,000 yards.'[20] On the other hand, the German capital ships had an Achilles heel in the inadequate protection of their bows. One battle cruiser (*Lützow*) was sunk in the war, and two others were nearly lost (*Derfflinger, Seydlitz*) because of this vulnerable spot.

Before becoming too critical of the Royal Navy, one should bear in mind these two points: (1) the Navy lost capital ships during the war in various ways, but except for the three battle cruisers at Jutland (and this is a moot point), it was not due to the penetration of the armour plating which was their main protection. (2) German protection was made greater than that on British ships because of the heavier guns carried on the latter. Relative to the armament of the ships they were designed to meet, German capital ships were no more heavily protected than were their opposites. The comparatively thin armour on British capital ships was the price paid for a superior heavy armament, and was done as a calculated risk. The gun, the supreme offensive weapon, was everything. The tragedy of the situation is that the vast preponderance in armament was partly neutralized by ineffective shell.

As a result of extensive experiments in 1910, Jellicoe, the Controller, asked the Ordnance Board (18 October 1910) to produce an armour-piercing shell that would perforate armour at oblique impact and go on in a fit state for bursting. When he went to sea two months later, there was nobody around to press the matter,

[20] Admiral Drax to the writer, 11 Nov. 1959.

and when he returned as Second Sea Lord he was no longer associated with questions of *matériel*. His successors were anything but strong Controllers. Admiral Sir Charles Briggs, his immediate successor, was pretty impossible—'the old sheep farmer', he was contemptuously called by Battenberg and Fisher. It is a mystery how this incompetent officer could have been appointed to so exacting a post. On the authority of the late Admiral Sir Frederick Dreyer,[21] it seems that the person mainly responsible for the shell deficiency was an officer in the Department of the D.N.O., Lieutenant-Commander John A. Duncan. He was, in 1910–13, one of the naval officers employed on inspection and experimental duties under the War Office. In 1914 he served as Chief Inspector of Naval Ordnance, with the acting rank of Commander. Whoever and whatever were actually responsible, the result of the shell deficiency was that in the war British shell achieved poor results when they struck the heavily armoured big German ships at oblique angle. The shell either broke up on impact, or succeeded only in smashing a hole in the enemy's armour, instead of going on and bursting in the vitals of their target. 'We thus lost the advantage we ought to have enjoyed in *offensive* power due to the greater weight of our projectiles, while suffering the accepted disadvantage in the protection of our ships due to the heavy weights of our guns and ammunition which reduced the total weight available for armour plating.'[22] Dreyer has claimed that, had the Grand Fleet possessed efficient armour-piercing shell at Jutland, it would have sunk at least three of the German battle cruisers between 7 p.m. and 7.30 p.m., and also four or five of their battleships.[23]

The critics, clever after the event, have said that the Navy was stupid in connexion with anti-flash arrangements for the magazines. This brand of stupidity was no British monopoly. The Germans fortunately learned the necessity for anti-flash arrangements when the battle cruiser *Seydlitz* nearly blew up in the Battle of the Dogger Bank (January 1915). The British, not so lucky, had to pay expensive tuition to learn the lesson. After Jutland, when three battle cruisers and an armoured cruiser blew up, the

[21] In a conversation with the writer in 1946.
[22] Bacon, *Jellicoe*, p. 163, quoting Jellicoe's autobiographical notes.
[23] Dreyer's memorandum, 'The Study of War and Exercises and Training for War', prepared for Admiral Bacon, 15 Aug. 1928; Kilverstone MSS.

British took exactly the same precautions the Germans had a year before.

The German designers and builders made their capital ships more nearly unsinkable than the British ships were. Thus, the German capital ships had better protection against torpedo or mine attack in their more complete watertight subdivision below water, made possible by the great beam of the ships. It was an eye-opening experience for the British officers when they inspected the German ships salvaged from Scapa Flow in 1919 and saw their superb underwater protection.[24] One explanation is that it was not possible to get sufficient money to build large new docks in Great Britain, and therefore capital ships had to be built to fit existing docks. This involved keeping the extreme beam of British ships within 90 feet, whereas the Germans were able to go to nearly 100 feet. Lamented the Director of Naval Construction, in the light of war experience: 'Had wider docks been available, and had it been possible to go to a greater beam, the designs on the same length and draught could have embodied more fighting qualities, such as armour, armament, greater stability in case of damage, and improved underwater protection.'[25] The German capital ships were not handicapped in this way. As the Emperor William told Jellicoe, when the latter visited Kiel in 1910, he built docks to take the ships and not ships to fit the docks. Another factor militating against watertight subdivision to the same extent as in the German ships was the Royal Navy's much greater sea-keeping needs compared with the German Navy's. The British had to keep their ships reasonably habitable during long periods at sea, whereas the German never envisaged long war cruises by heavy ships and so could accept a lesser degree of habitability. Indeed, they designed their capital ships for operations within the confines of the North and Baltic Seas. The dreadnoughts of the 'Bayern' class, for instance, had a radius of only 1,200 miles at 21 knots, or 1,900 miles at 18 knots, and the battle cruisers could not exceed 2,000 miles at 14 knots.

British torpedoes were not entirely satisfactory—they often ran to the bottom—but the mines were out-and-out inefficient. The

[24] Let it be noted here, nevertheless—the point will be elaborated in Volume ii—that the efficiency of the German watertight subdivision as compared to the British has been somewhat exaggerated by post-war writers.

[25] Sir Eustace Tennyson-d'Eyncourt, 'Records of Warship Construction during the War, 1914–1918, Capital Ships,' Jan. 1918; Admiralty MSS.

offensive power and real place of mines in naval strategy were not appreciated at the Admiralty before the war. One consequence was that the only satisfactory mines at the start of the war were a batch acquired from the Russian Navy. Very early in the war it was realized that British mines were inefficient.

In ships, guns, gunnery, and signalling systems, the German Navy reached a level fully equal to the British Navy. In armour, mines, torpedoes, and shell they were definitely ahead. These things were not appreciated at Whitehall before the war and Churchill could speak with perfect sincerity of 'the undoubted superiority of our ships unit for unit'. Jellicoe was the exception. A memorandum of 14 July 1914 for the First Lord expressed apprehension over the 'very striking' inferiority in the protection of British battleships against guns and torpedoes, as compared with the German dreadnoughts, and over the 'far more complete [German] inner armour protection against torpedoes'. He concluded that it was 'highly dangerous to consider that our ships as a whole are superior or even equal fighting machines.' He also noted that the German battle cruisers had far more protection.[26]

There could never be any argument on where the numerical superiority in capital ships lay. At the outbreak of war, Britain had thirty-one modern capital ships : twenty dreadnoughts, nine battle cruisers, and the two 'Nelsons', with twelve dreadnoughts and one battle cruiser building. In addition, two nearly completed Turkish dreadnoughts building in England were taken over by the Admiralty in August, and one building for Chile was requisitioned in September. Thirty-nine pre-dreadnoughts rounded out the strength in large armoured ships. The German Fleet numbered thirteen dreadnoughts, with seven more building, five battle cruisers (if we include the *Blücher*, with twelve 8·2-inch guns) with three more building, and twenty-two pre-dreadnoughts.

3. NAVAL BASES

The redeployment of naval force against Germany that began in 1904 was accompanied of necessity by the evolution of a new policy on naval bases. The two first-class southern bases, Plymouth and Portsmouth, were too far from the new naval centre of gravity, the North Sea, to provide immediate support for a fleet

[26] Jellicoe MSS.

in a war with Germany, and Chatham, though on the East Coast, was too far to the south. (First-class bases were officially defined as ports where the naval dockyards were capable of building or repairing warships in all respects, and where permanent depots of men, and ammunition of all kinds, were maintained. Their scale of defence was designed to deter battleship attack.) Nor were there any second-class bases, like Pembroke and Queenstown, in the North Sea. (A second-class naval base was a port with dockyards capable of carrying out repairs on a lesser scale, and where permanent depots of certain kinds of stores only were maintained.) Of the third category, war anchorages (ports situated in important strategical localities which did not possess the qualifications of naval bases, but which afforded facilities for the replenishment of warships with men, ammunition, or stores) like Berehaven, Portland, and Dover, there was only one in the North Sea, Harwich.

A system of naval bases on the East Coast was an obvious need. This had been appreciated as early as 1903, in which year the Admiralty decided, with Cabinet approval, to establish a first-class base at Rosyth, on the northern side of the Firth of Forth, as the main operational base for the Fleet in a war with Germany. The Firth was a fine and spacious anchorage and was particularly well located as a base for the main fleet in a war with Germany, since the Forth was about the same distance, 375 miles, from Heligoland and from the Skagerrak. And the navigation from the Forth to these two places was perfectly clear and simple. The perennial postponement of serious work at Rosyth drew the ire of the navalists, especially the Beresfordians. Jellicoe, when Controller, was unsuccessful in getting the work pushed on with, despite pleas that the problem of dock accommodations on the East Coast was a matter of 'the utmost gravity and open to much criticism.'[27] Rosyth's two docks were being built so slowly that, as Churchill told the Commons on 18 March 1912, they would not be ready until 1916. Motives of economy were one factor. There were also technical snags about the Forth: the vulnerability of the long approaches to minelaying; the area of deep water above the only possible line of defence was quite insufficient to berth a Grand Fleet; and there was tidal stream in the anchorage above the bridge. The main obstacle at first was Fisher's belief that Rosyth

[27] Jellicoe to Fisher, 18 Apr. 1909; Lennoxlove MSS.

BRITISH & GERMAN NORTH
SEA BASES — 1914

SHETLAND
ISLANDS

10°   8°   6°   4°   2°   0°

ORKNEY ISLANDS

Pentland   SCAPA FLOW
Firth

58°

CROMARTY

56°   S C O T L A N D

ROSYTH
Firth of Forth
EDINBURGH

N O R T H

Newcastle-
upon-Tyne

54°   I R E L A N D   Hull
Humber

E N G L A N D

Berehaven
QUEENSTOWN

W A L E S

Milford
Haven
PEMBROKE

HARW

LONDON
Sheerness
CHATHAM
Dover
PORTSMOUTH

Straits of
Dover

50°   FR

PLYMOUTH &   Portland
DEVONPORT

E N G L I S H   C H A N N E L

8°   6°   4°   2°   0°

was an unsafe anchorage and badly located—inland—because the demolition of the massive Forth Bridge ('that beastly bridge', Fisher called it) would cut Rosyth off from the sea. He strongly preferred building up Cromarty as a fleet anchorage. A later reason for the delays at Rosyth was that when work began there, the war plan had called for a close blockading fleet with all manner of supplies and repairing facilities. When 'observational blockade' replaced this strategy in 1912, the battle fleet had to be based farther north to control the northern passage between Scotland and Iceland.

Owing to recent improvements in submarine mines, submarine boats, torpedo-craft, and torpedoes, the passage of the Straits of Dover and the English Channel by the ships of a Power at war with the United Kingdom would be attended with such risks that for practical purposes the North Sea may be regarded as having only one entrance, the northern one. From Germany this northern entrance is accessible either from her North Sea ports, which are about the latitude of Hull, or from the Skager Rak, which is about the latitude of Cromarty. It is only necessary to glance at a map to recognise that any attempt on the part of the German Navy to open the way to the Atlantic, whether for the passage of cruisers intended to prey upon British commerce, or for merchant ships, or for returning vessels, must be made in the northern half of the North Sea. This renders an action in those waters extremely probable.[28]

Scapa Flow and Cromarty now came into the centre of the picture as possible sites for a base in the north. The former was a vast natural harbour (a four-and-a-half-mile radius) formed by the Orkneys. It could easily accommodate the largest fleet, it had various entrances, and the strong tides, the depth of water, and frequent bad weather conditions would render operations of hostile submarines, destroyers, and minelayers difficult. Scapa had a serious disadvantage from the strategic point of view. The Fleet, if based there, would not be able to prevent tip-and-run raids by German battle cruisers on the East Coast, and this is what happened in 1914. In passing, let it be said that Fisher's account (*Records*, pp. 225–6) of how he 'discovered' Scapa Flow in

[28] C.I.D. Paper 54–A, 'Report and Proceedings of the Standing Sub-Committee of the Committee of Imperial Defence on the North-East Coast Defences', 29 Nov. 1912; Lennoxlove MSS. All its recommendations were approved by the C.I.D. on 6 Dec. 1912.

1904 is somewhat fanciful. It had been surveyed as far back as 1750.

The Board wavered between Scapa Flow and Cromarty Firth. In the end it decided for Cromarty, Churchill and Fisher being primarily responsible. Scapa Flow had advantages besides those mentioned above. It was just as near as Cromarty to the more important strategical points in the North Sea (Cuxhaven, Wilhelmshaven, Kiel via the Belts, Rosyth, Sheerness, though Cromarty was closer to the Skaw); it was situated on the Pentland Firth, the shortest route for ships proceeding between the south and west coasts of England and the North Sea; it was a more convenient base than Cromarty for ships engaged in the area lying between the Orkneys, Shetlands, and the coast of Norway; and it had much more anchorage space than Cromarty.

However, the C.I.D. Sub-Committee on the North-East Coast Defences accepted the Admiralty preference for Cromarty over Scapa Flow as a second-class naval base, finding a conclusive reason in the fact provided by the Admiralty that the sea could run so high inside Scapa Flow that at times the employment of a floating dock and repairing facilities there would be out of the question. Cromarty also, in the opinion of the sub-committee, had the advantage over Scapa Flow of being connected with the railway system of Great Britain. 'Apart from its primary value as a second-class naval base Cromarty has a secondary and slightly less important value as a War Anchorage. Under the protection of the defences provided for the security of the floating repairing facilities, vessels containing fuel and stores of all kinds may be accumulated for the use of the fleet, forming a source of supply alternative and supplementary to Rosyth. Owing to the vast size of modern fleets, which makes their accommodation at a single anchorage almost impossible, the provision of supplementary war anchorages is a matter of great importance.'[29] The sub-committee recommended that 'Cromarty, as a floating second-class naval base and war anchorage in a position of great strategic importance, should be fortified on a scale sufficient to deter armoured vessels, torpedo-craft, and submarines from attack.' It was also recommended that Scapa Flow, which was intended to serve only as a war anchorage for light forces (it was never described before the war as a base), 'should not be provided with

[29] *Ibid.*

fixed defences'. The Admiralty had first asked that permanent defences be provided for the protection of Scapa Flow. After learning that the cost of a modest defence would be at least £379,000, with an annual upkeep of £55,000, it decided that the advantage to be derived was not commensurate with the expenditure, and the C.I.D. Sub-Committee accepted this position.

The Admiralty had experimented during the 1912 manœuvres with an extemporized defence which would offer some deterrent to an enemy attempting an attack, in the absence of warships, on fuel and storeships, or attempting to lay mines in the anchorage. The results were judged sufficiently satisfactory to justify the provision of a special force for extemporizing defences at Scapa Flow when required. The consequence of this misplaced economy was that Scapa Flow, which became the operational fleet base of the Grand Fleet immediately the war began, was undefended in any way except for the local territorial artillery and the defences provided by nature. There were no nets or booms to guard the various entrances against the submarine, and there were no searchlights.

To sum up, the base situation was shocking. The only fully equipped first-class base on the East Coast at the outbreak of the war was Chatham. Harwich was the main base for the torpedo craft. Rosyth, officially described as the principal base of the Fleet, and Cromarty had some artillery defence against surface ships but were quite open to submarine attack. The construction of the dockyard at Rosyth had only just begun. Scapa Flow was an unprotected war anchorage with no provision for fleet repair and maintenance work.

By comparison the defences of the German North Sea ports and coastline, also of Heligoland, were simply terrific. The principal German bases were Kiel, in the Baltic, and Wilhelmshaven and Cuxhaven, in the North Sea where the German coast forms a right-angled corner, with Heligoland Bight (Bay) at the bottom. The Bay was of the greatest strategic importance, since it connected with Wilhelmshaven, the principal German base, through the River Jade, with Kiel through the Kaiser Wilhelm Canal (completed in 1914, and navigable by dreadnoughts), and with Hamburg and Bremen through the Elbe and Weser. The principal protection for the Bay was the powerful coast defences and the strongly fortified off-lying island of Heligoland. Cuxhaven, near

the mouth of the Elbe, was a strongly fortified point of refuge for
the Fleet. Just beyond the Bight, about fifty miles west of the Jade,
was the fortified island of Borkum, protecting the entrance to the
Ems. The Ems was connected with Wilhelmshaven by the Ems–
Jade Canal, which was navigable for destroyers. From the great
naval port of Kiel warships could reach the North Sea and the
oceans of the world by the Kaiser Wilhelm Canal or by way of
Danish waters: through the three international channels, the
Sound, the Great Belt, and the Little Belt (large ships had to use
the Great Belt), and on through the Kattegat and Skagerrak. The
strength of the German position was the shoals off the coast, the
first-class fortress of Heligoland, which partly covered the entrance
to the Elbe and Jade, and the torpedo bases, forts, and guns
placed at all suitable positions along the coast. These were among
the conditions that made the German coast difficult to approach.
A serious weakness was the impossibility of a quick sortie of the
High Seas Fleet from its North Sea bases, since the capital ships
needed high water to pass over the bars of the Elbe and the Weser,
and two high waters were necessary to pass the entire Fleet. Also,
the German naval bases did not receive anti-submarine net
protection until early in 1915.

*   *   *

Before proceeding with our story, a general observation must be
made on the catalogue of deficiencies mentioned in this chapter
and the preceding one. The pre-war Royal Navy had behind it
centuries of honoured traditions, and traditions tend to breed a
suspicion of change. The 'Young Turks' were distinctly in a
minority. At the same time, the failings of senior officers, the lack of
strategical and tactical preparedness, and the various weaknesses
in *matériel* were to a degree the natural outcome of an age of transition. Overwhelming changes were pressing on the Navy from
all sides with very little experience of modern war to guide it.
Trial and error were inevitable, and were, indeed, not peculiar
to the Royal Navy. The United States Battle Squadron, when it
joined the Grand Fleet in November 1917, was utterly unprepared for war, as its commander, Admiral Rodman, frankly admitted. Nor was the grass always as green in the German garden
as it appeared to post-war critics of the British Navy, who slurred
over or did not notice at all the serious deficiencies of the German

Navy. These included the short-service system and other weaknesses in the training of the personnel, an inferior intelligence organization (British naval intelligence ran rings around it during the war), and a chaotic naval administration, one facet of which, control of naval policy by the Army General Staff, was a partial cause of the disastrous strategic conception that limited the Fleet to a purely defensive strategy in the North Sea.

XIV

The Coming of the War

This sea service in the years prior to the outbreak of hostilities was one long preparation for war. We expected war, we were ready for it, and almost wished for it.

LIEUTENANT-COMMANDER J. M. KENWORTHY (Lord Strabolgi), Sailors, Statesmen—and Others: an Autobiography.

. . . if a European conflict, not of our making, arose, in which it was quite clear that the struggle was one for supremacy in Europe, in fact, that you got back to a situation something like that in the old Napoleonic days, then . . . our concern in seeing that there did not arise a supremacy in Europe which entailed a combination that would deprive us of the command of the sea would be such that we might have to take part in that European war. That is why the naval position underlies our European policy . . .

SIR EDWARD GREY at the Committee of Imperial Defence, 11 July 1912.

ON 23 July 1914, Lloyd George, in the House of Commons, forecast 'substantial economy' in naval expenditure, claimed to see distinct signs of a reaction against armaments throughout the world, and could not 'help thinking that civilisation, which is able to deal with disputes amongst individuals and small communities at home, and is able to regulate these by means of some sane and well-ordered arbitrament, should be able to extend its operations to the larger sphere of disputes amongst States.' Alas, the Chancellor of the Exchequer's crystal ball was cloudy!

The spring and early summer of 1914 was a relatively quiet period in Anglo-German naval relations. The British press, wrapped up in the Irish crisis, scarcely referred to the naval rivalry. No progress was made towards arresting the competition. Churchill proposed to Grey on 20 May that he, the First Lord, meet with Tirpitz if a good opportunity arose for a 'non-committal, friendly conversation' on four topics: the naval holiday proposal, Tirpitz's recent suggestion of a limitation in the size of capital ships, the possibility of 'reducing the unwholesome concentration of fleets in Home Waters' by sending more ships to foreign stations, and the reduction of espionage on both sides through granting the naval attachés 'equal and reciprocal facilities to visit the dockyards and see what was going on'.[1] Grey quashed this imaginative idea—more harm than good might result.

Although the British Government could not possibly have known it, the Germans were pulling in their horns in the spring of 1914. The Emperor was working for a fresh naval increase that would permit a strengthening of the German squadron in the Mediterranean with two smaller cruisers, and for the construction in 1915 of the third dreadnought in the supplementary law of 1912. It was, surprisingly, Tirpitz who said 'no'. He was afraid that any increase would give Churchill the opportunity to augment the British programme under cover of a scare. Tirpitz also appreciated (as did Bethmann Hollweg) that it would be a 'great political blunder', since the German taxpayer could not bear much greater burdens. 'The bow is overstrung here as much as in England,' he wrote the Naval Attaché in London. E. L. Woodward makes this acute observation on Tirpitz's *volte-face*:

> Tirpitz's acknowledgment that any further increase in the German navy would be 'a great political blunder' is a curious 'last word' in the history of the naval competition between Great Britain and Germany. Fourteen years had gone by since the Navy Law of 1900. The dangerzone was not yet passed. The 'risk' theory had lost any political meaning. Great Britain might hesitate for a score of valid reasons from entering upon a naval war with Germany. These reasons did not include the calculation that even a victorious war with Germany would leave a weak British fleet open to attack from France or Russia, the United States or Japan. The 'alliance' value of the German fleet had been one of the main arguments of the advocates of a strong navy. The effect of the fleet had been to draw Great Britain more closely to France and Russia. The fleet was one of the causes of the isolation of Germany, and yet it was not strong enough in time of war to protect German commerce or the German colonies, or to meet its main rival in battle on the open sea.[2]

Tirpitz was, like Fisher, a brilliant organizer and a great leader, indefatigable, resourceful, and utterly unscrupulous in methods. But he was neither a strategist nor a statesman. Thus, he was convinced of the superior utility of a battle fleet, though the construc-

[1] *The World Crisis*, i. 179–81, *British Documents*, x (Pt. 2). 746–8.
[2] Woodward, *Great Britain and the German Navy*, p. 431.

tion of battleships was bound to arouse English suspicions, and though Germany's defensive needs would have been better served by light cruisers, submarines, and coast defences. Tirpitz argued that cruisers would not be very effective, since Germany lacked good naval bases, and that submarines would not be effective because incapable of long journeys. But a battle fleet, he believed, could be effectively used despite a numerical inferiority. He took it for granted that the Royal Navy would attempt a close blockade of the High Seas Fleet in the initial stages of a war. This would give the latter opportunities for continuous guerilla attacks on the British Fleet in the vicinity of the Bight. When the 'brutal superiority' of the Grand Fleet had been whittled down to a *Kräfteausgleich*, an approximate equalization of forces, as well as through such tactics as the use of minefields, massed flotilla attacks, and other devices, the High Seas Fleet could risk a major battle in open waters. The whole strategy was negated by the secret change in British blockade strategy made in 1912, and the German Fleet found itself, when war came, hopelessly bottled up in the North Sea. Therein lay Britain's number one naval asset—her geographic position athwart Germany's oversea communications with the world. As Mahan had written in 1902, 'The dilemma of Great Britain is that she cannot help commanding the approaches to Germany by the mere possession of the very means essential to her own existence as a state of the first order.'

*　　*　　*

What was the role of the naval rivalry in Anglo-German relations? Despite Metternich's stream of letters making it clear that German naval expansion, that and that alone, was at the root of British hostility, Tirpitz became more and more obsessed with the idea that the Anglo-German trade rivalry was behind British apprehensions and that no naval concessions by Germany would remove this anxiety. The fact is that economic competition was by the pre-war decade no longer the decisive factor in the rivalries of nations. Metternich and even the Naval Attachés, Coerper and Widenmann, were certain that no one in business and industry in England wanted a war. Competition was highly preferable; it ensured the uninterrupted importation of food supplies for the people and of raw materials for industry, and of trade with Britain's best customer, Germany. But the arguments

431

of his own official advisers 'bounded off Tirpitz's neo-Marxist armour without effect'. That the economic competition was the cause of the hostile British feeling towards Germany was also rejected by Grey categorically, and by most British and German statesmen and writers. No, what poisoned Anglo-German relations was, basically, the security problem—the British belief that Germany aimed at Continental, then world, hegemony. How else could one account for the creation of a great fleet in addition to a formidable army? The rapid expansion of the German Navy was proof of what Grey called Germany's 'itch to dominate', and was giving her the weapon, combined with the massive German Army, for achieving this ambition. This was the inflexible belief both of British statesmen and of the general public. The German Naval Attaché recognized this as clearly as did Metternich when he wrote in 1907: 'The steadily increasing sea-power of Germany constitutes the greatest *obstacle to England's freedom of political action.* This is the central point of the unsatisfactory relations of the two nations to one another. All other frequently advanced grounds— competition in commerce, industry, and shipping, partisanship during the Boer War, etc.—are side issues.'[3] If the words in italics (those of the present writer) were changed to read 'danger to England's security', the statement would exactly represent the British position. Now, the naval rivalry did not cause the war; but it ensured that when war did break out, Great Britain would be on the side of Germany's enemies.

* * *

On 22 October 1913 Churchill had suggested to Battenberg that, as an economy measure, a test mobilization of the Third Fleet (normally with very small maintenance crews) be substituted for the usual summer naval manœuvres in 1914. The First Sea Lord had agreed, and the scheme was announced in Parliament on 18 March 1914. Orders were issued for the test mobilization on 10 July, and the mobilization began on 15 July. On 17–18 July a grand review of the whole fleet was held at Spithead.[4] 'It consti-

---

[3] Coerper's memorandum of 14 Mar. 1907; *Die Grosse Politik*, xxiii. 48.

[4] Admiral Drax well remembers that review, and the 'high German official—it might have been the Ambassador or the Naval Attaché (I forget which)—coming to pay a visit to Beatty. On his leaving, Beatty ordered our band to play "Rule Britannia" as he went over the side. Not perhaps completely tactful, but it made us smile and it delighted the sailors'; letter to the author, 11 Nov. 1959.

tuted incomparably the greatest assemblage of naval power ever witnessed in the history of the world' (Churchill). It was a wonderful stroke of luck, then, that the whole fleet in home waters was practically on a war footing in the middle of July. On the 19th the fleet put to sea for tactical exercises in the Channel. On the 23rd the ships of the Third Fleet dispersed to their home ports under orders to pay off. Only minor vessels had gone, when, on 26 July, on news that the Serbian reply to the Austrian ultimatum over the Sarajevo affair had been rejected, Battenberg, on his own initiative (Churchill was in the country owing to his wife's serious illness), stopped the demobilization. (Churchill, who promptly approved, has often incorrectly been given the credit for this master stroke.) By 28 July the Navy had been placed upon a 'preparatory and precautionary basis', as Churchill informed the King. The next day the First Fleet left Portland, and on the night of the 29th–30th it passed, lights out, swiftly and silently, through the Straits of Dover and then up the North Sea to Scapa Flow, its preliminary war station. On the 31st the Grand Fleet, as the First Fleet was to be officially designated in September, was at its battle stations: the battleships at Scapa Flow and Cromarty, the battle cruisers at Rosyth. The Second Fleet was at the same time assembling at Portland. With the Fleet concentrated and ready for anything Churchill could breathe freely. The 'nightmare' of a surprise torpedo attack was gone.

It was felt at the Admiralty that the occasion demanded a younger man in command of the Grand Fleet. Callaghan, on the eve of his 62nd birthday, was apparently in excellent health and had shown great powers of physical endurance. Moreover, he possessed the full confidence of the Fleet. But he was considered too old and not equal to the strains which war would entail upon the C.-in-C. His appointment was due to expire on 1 October. The decision to replace him was reached on 30 July—that, should war come, the fifty-two-year-old Jellicoe would become Commander-in-Chief. This was intimated to Jellicoe the next day as he was about to leave for his post as Second-in-Command of the Grand Fleet. On 1 August the decision to replace Callaghan was definitely made, and on the 2nd he was superseded by Jellicoe.

The appointment meant offending a string of admirals senior to Jellicoe. More serious was the resentment of many flag officers over the rough way in which the change was supposed to have taken place. There was a general feeling that Callaghan was being treated unfairly, and a protest to the First Lord was mooted. The King himself thought he had been 'very badly treated'. Beatty telegraphed to Churchill (and in similar terms to Battenberg) that the rumoured change 'would cause unprecedented disaster. . . . Moral effect upon Fleet at such a moment would be worse than a defeat at sea. It creates impossible position for successor. . .'[5] Jellicoe wired the Admiralty *six* times between 1 and 3 August, the gist of the telegrams being that Callaghan should be retained as C.-in-C. because he had the experience; he, Jellicoe, would need more time to be ready to take over; the morale of the Fleet would suffer, since the Fleet was 'imbued with feelings of extreme admiration and loyalty' for the C.-in-C. Behind these reasons were two not stated: Callaghan and Jellicoe were personal friends, and there was Jellicoe's fear that the Fleet would feel that he had been to some extent responsible for the change. Churchill was adamant, and Jellicoe took over the command from Callaghan on the morning of 4 August—a painful episode for both men. Jellicoe's anguish is reflected in a note to the Second Sea Lord: 'I hope never to live again through such a time as I had from Friday to Tuesday. My position was horrible. I did my best but could not stop what I feel is a grave error. . . . the tragedy of the news to the C.-in-C. was past belief, and it was almost worse for me.'[6] Churchill's decision was right and wise. It took 'guts'. As Fisher once said, 'You may not like Winston, but he has the heart of a lion.' Incidentally, Fisher's advice was the determining factor in both the original appointment in 1911 that had marked Jellicoe out as heir-apparent to Callaghan, as well as in overcoming Churchill's hesitation in 1914 before making the appointment.

At 11 p.m. on 4 August (midnight by German time) the Admiralty flashed the signal to all H.M. ships and naval establishments, 'Commence hostilities against Germany'. The deed was done, the First Lord reported to the Cabinet. Tears streamed down Churchill's face as the Prime Minister made the solemn announcement in the House of Commons the next day that Great Britain was at war. It was due, no doubt, to relief at the end of the wear and tear on the nerves involved in three years of intensive preparation. He was confident that every preparation had been

[5] Beatty MSS.
[6] Jellicoe to Hamilton, 7 Aug. 1914; Hamilton MSS.

made. From the beginning he had 'intended to prepare for an attack by Germany as if it might come next day'. 'Obviously the first thing was to be ready; not to be taken unawares; to be concentrated; not to be caught divided: to have the strongest Fleet possible in the best station under the best conditions in good time, and then if the battle came one could await its result with a steady heart.'[7] The Fleet had been kept in a very efficient state of readiness for war, constantly busy at target practices, manœuvres, working out tactical problems, or carrying out individual squadron or ship exercises. Every detail of the wartime disposition of the Navy had been so completely worked out that, within twelve hours of the issue of the mobilization instructions on 1 August, every one of H.M. ships, including the ships in reserve, was already at her war station or had her war orders, ready for all contingencies: the sallying forth of the High Seas Fleet, the attempted invasion of the United Kingdom, or an attempt to interfere with the transport of the B.E.F. or with Britain's oceanic trade. The war also came as something of a relief to the officers of the Navy. Beatty, for example, is said to have 'longed for it. We had not fought for a century; it was time we repeated the deeds of our forefathers.'[8]

The Fleet was ready, or, what was almost as valuable, *believed* itself to be ready. Percy Scott summarized the state of the Navy as it entered the war: 'In addition, we had no up-to-date mine layers, nor an efficient mine; no properly fitted mine sweepers; no arrangements for guarding our ships against mines; no efficient method of using our guns at night; no anti-Zeppelin guns; no anti-submarine precautions; no safe harbour for our Fleet, and only a few ships (eight) were partly fitted with a proper method of firing their guns [director firing]. Our torpedoes were so badly fitted that in the early days of the war they went under the German ships instead of hitting them.'[9] The indictment (which is really of the *matériel* school, of which, remember, Scott himself was a leading figure) is essentially accurate. But the many *matériel* weaknesses and inadequacies in the Fleet were not generally known or appreciated. The natural geographical advantages, the voluntary principle, the extra sea time, the British naval tradition,

[7] *The World Crisis*, i. 77, 166-7.
[8] Chatfield, *The Navy and Defence*, p. 120.
[9] Admiral Sir Percy Scott, *Fifty Years in the Royal Navy* (London, 1919), p. 201.

the marked edge in numbers of warships, and a great confidence in their ships, seamanship, and gunnery—these assets had inculcated in the officers and men a supreme faith in the ultimate superiority of British personnel and *matériel* which was itself to be the most important advantage held by the Navy.

Contrast this confidence with the sense of inferiority *vis-à-vis* the British Navy with which the German Navy was imbued, a feeling kept alive on the game board, where the side with the greater number of capital ships invariably won. The British sense of superiority on the eve of war, and the contrasting German inferiority complex, are both reflected in Admiral Scheer's study of the war. 'The English Fleet had the advantage of looking back on a hundred years of proud tradition which must have given every man a sense of superiority based on the great deeds of the past. This could only be strengthened by the sight of their huge fleet, each unit of which in every class was supposed to represent the last word in the art of marine construction. The feeling was also supported by the British sailor's perfect familiarity with the sea and with conditions of life on board ship . . .'[10]

And so the great war had come at last—the war which Fisher had in 1910 predicted would break out in the autumn of 1914. Armageddon was about to put the Fleet to the severest test in its proud and ancient history. On the performance of those 'far-distant, storm-beaten ships' depended the destinies of free men.

---

[10] Admiral Reinhard Scheer, *Germany's High Sea Fleet in the World War* (London, 1920), p. 11. Tirpitz, too, writes of 'the naval prestige of England, which had its effect on our navy, or at any rate on many of our senior officers, who were too modest in their judgments of themselves and of our young navy'; *My Memoirs*, ii. 371.

British and German Dreadnoughts and Battle Cruisers in August 1914

APPENDIX

BRITISH AND GERMAN DREADNOUGHTS AND BATTLE CRUISERS IN AUGUST 1914*

BRITISH DREADNOUGHTS

Name of Ship and Class	Programme Year	Completion date	Displacement tons	Speed (designed) knots	Belt armour (maximum) inches	Turret armour (maximum) inches	Main Armament
LORD NELSON CLASS (pre-dreadnoughts)							
Lord Nelson	1904–5	10–08	16,500	18·5	12	12	} 4–12 in., 10–9·2 in.
Agamemnon	1904–5	6–08	16,500	18·5	12	12	
Dreadnought	1905–6	12–06	17,900	20·9	11	11	10–12 in.
BELLEROPHON CLASS							
Bellerophon	1906–7	2–09	18,600	20·75	10	11	} 10–12 in.
Superb	1906–7	5–09	18,600	20·75	10	11	
Téméraire	1906–7	5–09	18,600	20·75	10	11	
ST. VINCENT CLASS							
St. Vincent	1907–8	5–09	19,250	21	10	11	} 10–12 in.
Vanguard	1907–8	2–10	19,250	21	10	11	
Collingwood	1907–8	4–10	19,250	21	10	11	
Neptune	1908–9	1–11	19,900	21	10	11	10–12 in.
COLOSSUS CLASS							
Colossus	1909–10	7–11	20,000	21	11	11	} 10–12 in.
Hercules	1909–10	8–11	20,000	21	11	11	
ORION CLASS							
Orion	1909–10	1–12	22,500	21	12	11	} 10–13·5 in.
Conqueror	1909–10	11–12	22,500	21	12	11	
Monarch	1909–10	3–12	22,500	21	12	11	
Thunderer	1909–10	6–12	22,500	21	12	11	

*British data from Admiralty sources; German, from the quite reliable Erich Gröner, *Die Deutschen Kriegsschiffe, 1815–1936.*

BRITISH DREADNOUGHTS (continued)

Name of Ship and Class	Programme Year	Completion date	Displacement tons	Speed (designed) knots	Belt armour (maximum) inches	Turret armour (maximum) inches	Main Armament
KING GEORGE V CLASS							
King George V	1910–11	11–12	23,000	21	12	11	
Ajax	1910–11	3–13	23,000	21	12	11	10–13·5 in.
Centurion	1910–11	5–13	23,000	21	12	11	
Audacious	1910–11	10–13	23,000	21	12	11	
IRON DUKE CLASS							
Benbow	1911–12	11–14	25,000	21	12	11	
Emperor of India	1911–12	11–14	25,000	21	12	11	10–13·5 in., 12–6 in.
Iron Duke	1911–12	3–14	25,000	21	12	11	
Marlborough	1911–12	6–14	25,000	21	12	11	
QUEEN ELIZABETH CLASS							
Queen Elizabeth	1912–13	1–15	27,500	25	13	13	
Warspite	1912–13	3–15	27,500	25	13	13	8–15 in.,
Barham	1912–13	10–15	27,500	25	13	13	14–6 in. (16–6 in.
Valiant	1912–13	2–16	27,500	25	13	13	in Queen Elizabeth)
Malaya	1912–13	2–16	27,500	25	13	13	
ROYAL SOVEREIGN CLASS							
Royal Sovereign	1913–14	5–16	25,750	21	13	13	
Royal Oak	1913–14	5–16	25,750	21	13	13	
Revenge	1913–14	3–16	25,750	21	13	13	8–15 in., 14–6 in.
Resolution	1913–14	12–16	25,750	21	13	13	
Ramillies	1913–14	9–17	25,750	21	13	13	
Canada*		9–15	28,000	22·75	9	10	10–14 in., 16–6 in.
Agincourt†		8–14	27,500	22	9	12	14–12 in., 20–6 in.
Erin‡		8–14	23,000	21	12	11	10–13·5 in., 16–6 in.

*Ex-Almirante Latorre, building for Chile; requisitioned in September 1914.
†Ex-Osman I, building for Turkey; requisitioned in August 1914.
‡Ex-Rashadieh, building for Turkey; requisitioned in August 1914.

BRITISH BATTLE CRUISERS

Name of Ship and Class	Programme Year	Completion date	Displacement tons	Speed (designed) knots	Belt armour (maximum) inches	Turret armour (maximum) inches	Main Armament
INVINCIBLE CLASS							
Invincible	1905-6	3-09	17,250	25·5	6	7	⎫
Inflexible	1905-6	10-08	17,250	25·5	6	7	⎬ 8-12 in.
Indomitable	1905-6	6-08	17,250	25·5	6	7	⎭
INDEFATIGABLE CLASS							
Indefatigable	1908-9	4-11	18,750	25·8	6	7	⎫
New Zealand	1909-10	11-12	18,800	25·8	6	7	⎬ 8-12 in.
Australia*	1909-10	6-13	18,800	25·8	6	7	⎭
LION CLASS							
Lion	1909-10	5-12	26,350	27	9	9	⎫
Princess Royal	1909-10	11-12	26,350	27	9	9	⎬ 8-13·5 in.
Queen Mary	1910-11	8-13	27,000	28	9	9	⎭
Tiger	1911-12	10-14	28,500	28	9	9	8-13·5 in., 12-6 in.

GERMAN DREADNOUGHTS

NASSAU CLASS							
Nassau	1906-7	10-09	18,873	19	11¾	11	⎫
Westfalen	1906-7	11-09	18,873	19	11¾	11	⎬ 12-11 in., 12-5·9 in.
Rheinland	1907-8	4-10	18,873	19	11¾	11	⎬
Posen	1907-8	5-10	18,873	19	11¾	11	⎭
HELGOLAND CLASS							
Helgoland	1908-9	8-11	22,808	20·5	11¾	11¾	⎫
Ostfriesland	1908-9	8-11	22,808	20·5	11¾	11¾	⎬ 12-12 in., 14-5·9 in.
Thuringen	1908-9	7-11	22,808	20·5	11¾	11¾	⎬
Oldenburg	1909-10	5-12	22,808	20·5	11¾	11¾	⎭

*In naval service of Australian Government.

GERMAN DREADNOUGHTS (continued)

Name of Ship and Class	Programme Year	Completion date	Displacement tons	Speed (designed) knots	Belt armour (maximum) inches	Turret armour (maximum) inches	Main Armament
KAISER CLASS							
Kaiser	1909–10	8–12	24,724	21	13¾	11¾	
Friedrich der Grosse	1909–10	10–12	24,724	21	13¾	11¾	
Kaiserin	1910–11	5–13	24,724	21	13¾	11¾	10–12 in., 14–5·9 in.
Prinzregent Luitpold	1910–11	8–13	24,724	21	13¾	11¾	
König Albert	1910–11	7–13	24,724	21	13¾	11¾	
KÖNIG CLASS							
König	1911–12	8–14	25,796	21	13¾	11¾	
Grosser Kürfurst	1911–12	8–14	25,796	21	13¾	11¾	10–12 in., 14–5·9 in.
Markgraf	1911–12	10–14	25,796	21	13¾	11¾	
Kronprinz Wilhelm	1912–13	11–14	25,796	21	13¾	11¾	
BAYERN CLASS							
Baden	1913–14	10–16	28,600	22	13¾	13¾	
Bayern	1913–14	3–16	28,600	22	13¾	13¾	8–15 in., 16–5·9 in.
Sachsen	1914–15	*	28,800	22	13¾	13¾	
Württemberg	1914–15	†	28,800	22	13¾	13¾	

GERMAN BATTLE CRUISERS

Name of Ship and Class	Programme Year	Completion date	Displacement tons	Speed (designed) knots	Belt armour (maximum) inches	Turret armour (maximum) inches	Main Armament
Blücher	1906–7	10–09	15,842	24·8	7·01	7·09	12–8·2 in., 8–5·9 in.
Von der Tann	1907–8	9–10	19,370	24·8	9·84	9·05	8–11 in., 10–5·9 in.
Moltke	1908–9	9–11	22,979	25·5	10·63	9·05	10–11 in., 12–5·9 in.
Goeben	1909–10	7–12	22,979	25·5	10·63	9·05	10–11 in., 12–5·9 in.
Seydlitz	1910–11	5–13	24,988	27	11·81	9·84	10–11 in., 12–5·9 in.
Lützow	1911–12	8–15	26,741	26·4	11·81	10·63	8–12 in., 14–5·9 in.
Derfflinger	1911–12	9–14	26,600	25·8	11·81	10·63	8–12 in., 12–5·9 in.
Hindenburg	1913–14	10–17	26,947	27·5	11·81	10·63	8–12 in., 14–5·9 in.

*Launched 21 November 1916, but never completed.
†Launched 20 June 1917, but never completed.

442

Index

All officers and titled people are indexed under the highest rank and title attained.

INDEX

Fisher, Beatty, 17; and Fisher's vindictiveness, 87; on Navy Scare of 1909, 151, Mulliner's pressure, 157; and Agadir Crisis, 242-3, 244; on airships, 341, C.I.D., 343; as C.I.D. Secretary, 343-4; and invasion problem, 354; on 23 Aug. 1911 C.I.D. meeting, 392-3; fights Continental strategy, 394

Harcourt, 1st Viscount (Lewis Harcourt, 1863-1922): and Cabinet crisis over 1908-9 estimates, 138; criticizes navalist agitation, 142-3; and Navy Scare of 1909, 160; on strategic aspects of Japanese Alliance, 238; and Mediterranean problem, 294, 1914-15 estimates, 320; at 23 Aug. 1911 C.I.D. meeting, 392

Hardinge of Penshurst, 1st Baron (Charles Hardinge, 1858-1944): 221; and 'policing of the seas', 53, new Home Fleet, 73; on Fisher–Noel relations, 85, Anglo-German naval rivalry, 105; at Cronberg meeting (1908), 143, 144; and Navy Scare of 1909, 162, 1909 German negotiations, 175-6; on 1910-11 building programme, 214-15, right of capture, 381

Hawke, Adm. of the Fleet, 1st Baron (Edward Hawke, 1705-1781): 19, 395, 405

Heath, Adm. Sir Herbert Leopold (1861-1954): on efficiency of German Navy, 149, German naval officers, 412

Henderson, Adm. Sir William Hannam (1845-1931): criticizes Selborne Scheme, 48

Higgins, Alexander Pearce (1865-1935): on submarines as commerce-destroyers, 364

Hobhouse, Sir Charles Edward Henry, 4th Bt. (1862-1941): and 1914-15 estimates, 320, 324-5

Holtzendorff, Adm. of the Fleet (Grossadm.) Henning von (1853-1919): proposes meetings between fleets, 232; and Haldane Mission, 280

Hopkins, Adm. Sir John Ommanney (1834-1916): on Fisher, 46; in Fisher's camp, 78

Hopwood, Sir Francis: see Southborough

Howe, Adm. of the Fleet, 1st Earl (Richard Howe, 1726-1799): 395

Hulbert, Capt. Arthur Russell (1871-1913): helps Beresford in C.I.D. inquiry, 192, 203n.; championed by Beresford, 201-2

Hurd, Sir Archibald S. (1869-1959): in Fisher's camp, 78; supports two-keels-to-one standard, 136; and 1908-9 estimates, 139

Imperial Maritime League: and Tweedmouth Letter, 140, Navy Scare of 1909, 167; agitates for defence loan, 216

Ingenohl, Adm. Friedrich von (1857-1933): ability, 413

Invincible, H.M.S.: genesis, 13, 44-5, 65; features, 44; criticisms, evaluation, 69-70

Italian Navy: 125, 185, 219, 311; dreadnought programme, 170-1, 288; battleship strength, 288; and Britain's Mediterranean position, 288-301 passim, 305, 308, 314, 322; in Italo-Turkish War, 351, 356

Jackson, Frederick Huth (1863-1921): on a 'naval holiday', 316

Jackson, Adm. of the Fleet Sir Henry Bradwardine (1855-1929): as First Sea Lord, 21; Fisher's assistant, 84; and naval relations with France, 308, invasion problem, 354, German naval strategy, 368; criticizes Churchill's naval strategy, 374-5; and commerce warfare against Germany, 381-2, 'matériel' school, 401; ability, 407

Jagow, Gottlieb von (1863-1935): 272, 310; reaction to Churchill's 'naval holiday' proposal, 315, 316

James, Adm. Sir William Milburne (1881-): on dreadnought, 69, night firing, 399

Jane, Fred. T. (1870-1916): on Reserve Squadron, 10, guerre de course, 359

Japanese Navy: 11, 45, 63, 125; in the Russian War: 16, 59, 60, 61, 64, 65, 328, 329, 369; and dreadnought type, 57; efficiency, 236-7; and see Anglo-Japanese Alliance

Jellicoe, Adm. of the Fleet, 1st Earl (John Rushworth Jellicoe, 1859-1935): 84, 408, 419; and gunnery renaissance, 34, 35; on battle-practice results, 66, Fisher–Sea Lord relations, 80; and German 'acceleration', 152, 153; suggests 60 per cent German standard, 183, 184-5; on Churchill's interference in technical matters, 255; clashes with Churchill, 260-1; appointed Second-in-Command, Home Fleet, 268; criticizes Churchill's oil policy, 271; and airship policy, 336-7, 340, 1913 manœuvres, 353; reveals Fisher's submarine prediction, 363-4; and naval tactics, 396, centralization of command, 398; on night firing, 399; and 'matériel' school, 401, naval history, 403; career, personality, abilities, 410-11; and introduction of director firing, 415; on capital-ship armour, 416n.; and armour-piercing shell, 417-18;

451

INDEX

Loreburn, 1st Earl (Robert Threshie Reid, 1846–1923): and Navy Scare of 1909, 160; opposes right of capture, 380
Lovat, Maj.-Gen., 14th Baron (Simon Joseph Fraser, 1871–1933): and invasion problem, 348
Lyttelton, Gen. Sir Neville Gerald (1845–1931): 386

MacDonald, James Ramsay (1866–1937): on armament firms, 317
McKenna, Reginald (1863–1943): 66; as First Lord, 21, 22–3, 253, 283; on Fisher's critics, 77; and Fisher's vindictiveness, 86–7, second signalling incident, 101–2, Beresford's supersession, 103, 188, Cabinet crisis over 1908–9 estimates, 138; becomes First Lord, 142; and early decision on 1909–10 building programme, 142, Navy Scare of 1909, 151, 159–71 passim, 177, 178, 187, C.I.D. inquiry into Admiralty policy, 189, 192, 193, 199; defends Fisher on Bacon Letters, 191; replies to Beresford's criticisms of Admiralty, 202–203; and Fisher's resignation, 204; relations with A. K. Wilson as First Sea Lord, 213; and 1910–11 estimates, 214, 215; confidence in British margin of superiority, 217; movement to oust him, 217; confesses his 1909 predictions inaccurate, 217; and 1911–12 estimates, 218–20, 262; on Japanese Alliance renewal, 237; and Agadir Crisis, 242; opposes a naval staff, 247; leaves Admiralty, 249–51; relations with Churchill, 249, 264, 294; discusses strategy with Asquith, 250–1; and 1912–13 estimates, 274, Mediterranean problem, 294, 295, 1914–15 estimates, 320, 324–5; at 23 Aug. 1911 C.I.D. meeting, 393; on amphibious strategy, 394
Macnamara, Thomas James (1861–1931): becomes Parliamentary Secretary of Admiralty, 142; and 1914–15 estimates, 321
Madden, Adm. of the Fleet Sir Charles Edward, 1st Bt. (1862–1935): Fisher's assistant, 84; ability, 408
Mahan, R.-Adm. Alfred Thayer (1840–1914): The Influence of Sea Power volumes, 4, 403, 404; on concentration of strength, 9; and criticism of dreadnought, 60, 61; on a fleet reserve, 74, submarines, 334, invasion problem, 346–7, commerce warfare, 359, 362, 365, 377–8, 380, convoy, 361, Britain's geographical advantage, 431
Maxse, Leopold James (1864–1932): on Fisher's Guildhall speech, 135, Churchill, 252, 317

May, Adm. of the Fleet Sir William Henry (1849–1930): 149; on destroyer attacks, 330, 1913 manœuvres, 354, commerce warfare against Germany, 381; and naval tactics, 396, 397, 398, 399
Mediterranean: and redistribution of naval force in 1912, 214, 276, 284–5, 287–8, 304–6, 326, 327; naval position in, 288–9, 314; debate over 'abandonment' of, 289–93; C.I.D. decision on, 293–4; Cabinet discussion of, 294–5, 321–2; announcement of revised policy in, 295–6, 297, 298–9; strategic results in, of Italo-Turkish War, 299–301; Anglo-Turkish naval relations, 301–3; Anglo-French relations and, 303–9, 314, 322
Metternich, Count Paul von Wolff- (1853–1934): 143, 144, 152, 173, 174, 176; on German 'acceleration', 154, 163, 164, 166, Anglo-German naval rivalry, 220, 285, 431, 432; and 1910–11 Anglo-German negotiations, 224, 229, Agadir Crisis, 242, Haldane Mission, 280–285 passim; is removed, 285–6; on role of economic competition, 431
Meux, Adm. of the Fleet the Hon. Sir Hedworth (Hedworth Lambton) (1856–1929): on Tsushima, 64; in anti-Fisher camp, 77; a possible First Sea Lord, 257; ability, 407
Milford Haven, Adm. of the Fleet, 1st Marquess of (Louis Alexander Mountbatten, Prince Louis of Battenberg, 1854–1921): 432; on Fisher's reforms, 85, and spirit of vengeance, 85; his committee revises two-power standard, 124; relations with Churchill when First Sea Lord, 255; as possible successor to A. K. Wilson, 257–8; becomes First Sea Lord, 258, 406; and Bridgeman affair, 259, Sea Lords' row with Churchill, 261, organization of Admiralty War Staff, 265, 266, Turkish Navy, 303, naval relations with France, 308, naval conversations with Russia, 311; on airplanes, 337; and 1912 manœuvres, 352, invasion problem, 354; co-operates with Army, 394; career, personality, abilities, 406–7, 410; backs Beatty, 409; on Admiral Briggs, 418; and test mobilization of 1914, 432–3
Milne, Adm. Sir (Archibald) Berkeley, 2nd Bt. (1855–1938): ability, 407
Mines: development, 328–9; effect on close blockade, 356, 369, 375; inefficiency of British, 419–20, 435
Montagu-Stuart-Wortley: see Stuart-Wortley

453